Excellence in Advancement

Applications for Higher Education and Nonprofit Organizations

William W. Tromble, PhD
Vice Chancellor for External Affairs
Indiana University Southeast
New Albany, Indiana

AN ASPEN PUBLICATION®
Aspen Publishers, Inc.
Gaithersburg, Maryland
1998

Library of Congress Cataloging-in-Publication Data

Tromble, William W.
Excellence in advancement: applications for higher education and nonprofit organizations / William W. Tromble.
p. cm.
Includes bibliographical references and index.
ISBN 0-8342-1062-2
1. Public relations—Universities and colleges—United States.   2. Educational fund raising—United States.   3. Universities and colleges—Alumni and alumnae—United States.   4. College publicity—United States. I. Title.
LB2342.8.T76 1998
659.2′937873—dc21
97–43539
CIP

Orders: (800) 638-8437
Customer Service: (800) 234-1660

About Aspen Publishers • For more than 35 years, Aspen has been a leading professional publisher in a variety of disciplines. Aspen's vast information resources are available in both print and electronic formats. We are committed to providing the highest quality information available in the most appropriate format for our customers. Visit Aspen's Internet site for more information resources, directories, articles, and a searchable version of Aspen's full catalog, including the most recent publications: **http://www.aspenpub.com**
Aspen Publishers, Inc. • The hallmark of quality in publishing
Member of the worldwide Wolters Kluwer group.

Editorial Services: Kathryn M. Lynch
Library of Congress Catalog Card Number: 97-43539
ISBN: 0-8342-1062-2

Printed in the United States of America

1 2 3 4 5

TABLE OF CONTENTS

CONTRIBUTORS

Janine Dlutowski, JD
Planned Giving Officer
The Pennsylvania State University
University Park, Pennsylvania

Jerry L. Gill, PhD
Executive Director, OSU Alumni
  Association
Oklahoma State University
Stillwater, Oklahoma

Leonard R. Raley, MBA
Vice President for Alumni Relations
  and Development and Executive
  Director of the Ohio University
  Foundation, Inc.
Ohio University
Athens, Ohio

Deborah Ann Weekley Read, BA
Vice President for Advancement
Lebanon Valley College
Annville, Pennsylvania

Jerry P. Rohrbach, MA, CFRE
Director of Planned Giving
Temple University
Philadelphia, Pennsylvania

Ronald J. Stephany, BA
Vice President for University
  Relations
University of Redlands
Redlands, California

Judith Tuch, MA
Executive Director of Information
  Management
University of California—
  Los Angeles
Los Angeles, California

M. Fredric Volkmann
Vice Chancellor for Public Affairs
Washington University in St. Louis
St. Louis, Missouri

Charles H. Webb, PhD
Vice President for University
  Development and President, MSU
  Foundation
Michigan State University
East Lansing, Michigan

FOREWORD

If you are responsible for facilitating philanthropic support for a not-for-profit organization, this book is for you. Your organization may call this activity *advancement, development,* or *fund raising;* but what you are really about is building relationships and developing donors.

To do so, you must understand the integration of philanthropic philosophy and ethics, various fund raising techniques, technology, marketing, public relations, and constituent relationships. Don't be fooled by the authors' terminology of advancement, used most often in higher education, for the activities are applicable to all not-for-profits, whether called *advancement, development,* or *fund raising.*

In reading *Excellence in Advancement,* you experience a rare thoroughness of principles and practice. Moreover, the exercise of applying these to your particular circumstance will, in most instances, prove to be a beneficial learning experience, especially for what professionals in the philanthropic process are all about.

To achieve excellence, we are challenged to observe how others reach their benchmarks for success, to apply the learning to ourselves, and to continue our own quest for achievements. *Excellence in Advancement,* written by professionals who strive for their own excellence, will contribute to yours.

Patricia F. Lewis, ACFRE
President and Chief Executive Officer
National Society of Fund Raising Executives
Alexandria, Virginia

PREFACE

Institutional advancement is about money, the people who give it, the people who get it, and the institutions and organizations that receive it. It is about alumni relations—the programs, publications, and activities that strengthen bonds of friendship between the institutions and former students, clients, or patients. It is about public relations and communications. *Excellence in Advancement* is about the theory and practice of institutional advancement. It is a sourcebook and a textbook. It is intended for all advancement professionals in colleges and universities, hospitals, and nonprofits. It represents the thinking of a select group of authors whose experience and expertise in certain highly specialized areas of advancement provide a broad exposure to what might generally be called "external affairs." Furthermore, they come from widely divergent parts of the country, north, south, east, and west. None of the authors are newcomers to the profession. What they bring to the following pages is a manner of looking at fund raising, public relations, and alumni affairs that may shed new light on topics that have been discussed and written about for many years. It was Peter Buchanan, former president of the Council for Advancement and Support of Education (CASE), in a conversation with the editor, who said "Books on fund raising are a dime a dozen, some good, some not so good," and he is right. Each, of course, has something to say. This book attempts a long hard look at the big picture, a review of the fundamental functions of institutional advancement.

The authors hope to inspire college and university presidents to be more supportive of the advancement professionals. They seek to encourage hospital administrators and executive officers of nonprofits to learn more about advancement and how it affects their institutions and organizations. Executive officers have the authority and the resources to effect change. Advancement professionals have the skills to bring financial and political resources to the table to assist presidents and chief executive officers (CEOs) in making it happen. For every development officer hired, gift revenue increases at least three times his or her salary. From a purely business point of view, it makes sense to hire advancement professionals, but presidents and CEOs over the years have not felt this to be a priority. "We are not a business," they say. "We are an institution with a long-standing heritage of teaching and ministry that is not tied to the bottom line." It is true: universities, hospitals, and other nonprofit agencies live and have their being in service and human welfare, but without strong business acumen they would cease to exist.

This book is an advocate for the profession. It builds a rationale for the several advancement specialties. It confirms what hundreds of experienced fund raisers and public relations people have known for years and it enlightens those who may wish to choose a career in institutional advancement. After more than a century, advancement has become a legitimate profession with its own standards, its own code of ethics, and its own certification. Salaries and fringe benefits are competitive. Employment opportunities are out there for those who aggressively seek them and are willing to relocate.

Finally, a word of appreciation for the support and encouragement received from members of CASE, the National Society of Fund Raising Executives, and the Association for Healthcare Philanthropy. Not only have these organizations provided a forum for discussion and development of principles and practice in advancement, but they also have established fund raising, alumni affairs, and public relations as career opportunities for thousands of adults across America and in foreign lands. Special thanks is appropriate to all the contributing authors, colleagues, and friends who helped make this book possible. Personal gratitude is extended to my wife, Joella J. Tromble, who proofread copy and offered helpful suggestions on content and style.

Introduction

Advancement in fund raising, alumni affairs, and public relations, like fine wine, continues to improve with age, and it continues to evolve as changes occur and trends develop in education and the nonprofit milieu. Policies and procedures change. Methods and materials change, as the political climate shifts increasingly toward restructuring, shared governance, and building consensus. College and university presidents are showing a renewed interest in marketing their institutions as they deal with concerns about enrollment management, admissions, retention, and balanced budgets. Increasingly, public institutions are seeking more support from the private sector as costs rise and government funds diminish. Private organizations are unhappy over the prospect of a perceived encroachment by the public institutions onto their heretofore relatively unchallenged hunting grounds for private gifts and grants. There is a greater emphasis on strategic long-range planning, corporate partnerships, and community relations, often referred to as "town-and-gown" relations.

In the face of all these concerns, challenges, and new directions, institutional advancement plays an increasingly important role. It is key to achieving more political and financial support. Its potential is great for shaping the public image, for securing necessary resources, and for bonding with alumni. As a profession, institutional advancement is still emerging as a respected and valued unit worthy of better salaries, better facilities, and more realistic budgets. The marketing piece alone is becoming enormously expensive, but necessary. A single full page advertisement in the *News Journal* of Wilmington, Delaware, is $6,700, and it is not uncommon for magazine and television ads, even with gift-in-kind discounts, to run in the thousands of dollars.

As the advancement unit matures, it will change to better serve its many publics just as it has in past years. For a long time the term "public relations" was commonly used to include media usage, informational service, publications, and promotion. Now the term "communications" is increasing in popularity. Twenty years ago "deferred giving" was the term widely used to indicate gifts of life insurance, bequests, wills, trusts, and annuities, because benefits to the charitable institution were expected, generally speaking, to accrue and be realized over time. The term most commonly used now is "planned giving." This reflects the idea that something is happening now through good preparation and planning. "Development" is the term most frequently used to mean fund raising, but over the last two decades the term "advancement" has been widely used, especially in higher education, to include fund raising as well as other necessary functions in gaining support.

Advancement is more than development, just as development is more than fund raising. It is fund raising and friend raising. It is public relations, alumni affairs, external affairs, marketing, promotion, legislative initiative, and certainly communications. It has a rather subtle connotation of forward motion or of movement to a better position or a new beginning. It implies a mindset, a global view, a comprehensive approach to change and betterment.

We are a part of all that we have experienced, all that we have seen or heard, or that which we have read about or heard about. Much of what has been written in recent books on advancement is secondary source material. This book gratefully acknowledges the work of previous authors and their research. It makes reference to some in selective quotations, but does not parrot their findings. Original sources, for the most part, are available in libraries and bookstores for those who desire further inquiry. What this book hopes to accomplish is a direct train of original thought that is tempered by the wisdom and writings of others, because the opinions we hold and the comments we make today are also a part of yesterday. After all, history is always of current interest. Nevertheless, the writings included here, while including a look back, are directed toward the present and the future.

Advancement professionals are interested in details of other years, the failures and the successes, but they have a present mission to fulfill in a different world than once existed. The future is as bright as the past is memorable, but the door to the past is shut. Our hope lies in the days and the decades just ahead. Men and women of the profession want to know current philosophy, strategy, and practice as these relate to their particular area of institutional advancement. Alumni professionals want to know what works best in today's world of constituent loyalties and changing views about reunions, for example, as they strive to achieve greater alumni participation and support for their alma mater. Development people are interested in refining the time-honored principles and procedures that produce greater financial support. Public relations personnel are just as pragmatic as the others. What are the best techniques? What seems to work best across the country in marketing, media relations, and image building, and how can we make it work for us? What are colleagues saying and doing?

All three groups, alumni, development, and public relations, have been represented in councils and associations, working together for many years. The Public Relations Society of America was founded in 1947. The American Alumni Council and the American College Public Relations Association merged in 1974 to form the Council for Advancement and Support of Education (CASE). The National Society of Fund Raising Executives (NSFRE) began in 1963. The National Association of Hospital Development, now known as the Association for Healthcare Philanthropy (AHP), began in 1967. The North American Young Men's Christian Association (YMCA) Development Officers formed a group in 1981. The American Prospect Research Association was organized in 1988. The largest and earliest fund raising organizations in America continue to serve humanity. They include the United Way, the Salvation Army, the American Red Cross, and the YMCA. Both the Salvation Army and the United Way raise nearly $1 billion a year.[1]

Americans continue to be generous people. *Giving USA 1997* reported total charitable giving from all sources for all causes to be $150.7 billion in 1996. When people are touched, and hearts are moved, generosity prevails. There really is no shortage of charitable giving in the United States. In fact, philanthropy has been increasing over the years. Tracking this financial largesse is the American Association of Fund Raising Counsel (AAFRC) through its Trust for Philanthropy. The AAFRC was founded in 1935. The venerable and often quoted Harold J. (Si) Seymour was the first president. The firm that handled the 1919 Harvard endowment campaign, John Price Jones Company, was one of the first members of the AAFRC and the leading consulting group of the early 1900s. Since then many others have joined hands to promote philanthropy in general and the business of consulting in particular. The first issue of *Giving USA* was published in 1955[2] by the AAFRC Trust for Philanthropy. The Trust is aided in its research by 66 organizations, including the CASE, the NSFRE, the Foundation Center, the Council for Aid to Education, the United Way, the National Federation of Non-Profits, the National Council of Churches, and the AHP, to name a few.[3]

Fund raising has always been a big part of the advancement function, and it has been practiced in early America and other parts of the world for centuries. Asking for money to support community projects, to help the poor, and for other causes dates back to early civilizations in the Middle East. For lack of space, however, that lesson in history will not be covered here. A recent and reliable source is Fisher and Quehl's *The President and Fund Raising*.[4]

In the seventeenth century in England and America, George Whitefield, Cotton Mather, John Wesley, and others wrote "begging" letters and asked friends for financial assistance, mainly for churches and schools. Wesley, on one occasion according to his *Journal*, felt so moved by the poverty and pain of French prisoners to whom he ministered that he quickly raised 24 pounds to buy clothes and food for them and persuaded others through his preaching to make contributions. Those contributions came from London and various other parts of the kingdom.[5] Later at the age of 81, Wesley was still walking the streets begging for money to feed and clothe the poor, and it was hard work he admits in his *Journal*, but he held out and raised 200 pounds that winter.[6]

Whatever the cause, fund raising always affects people in one way or another. As Si Seymour, the often quoted Harvard fund raiser, was known to say, fund raising is about people, not about money. It is about human needs and interests. Money is merely a means of exchange, a coin or currency of little value in itself, but an agent of extreme importance in meeting human need. Jerold Panas, widely known and respected in the advancement community as an individual of great experience and sensitivity, whom the author knows personally, concludes that donors respond to heroic causes to improve the human condition, not to needy institutions, and he is right. This is why the United Way is so successful in its fund drives, and colleges are often successful with student scholarship appeals. Donors make contributions for a number of reasons, but high on the list are people-related causes.

Supporting this centerpiece of advancement are service and communications. At the right is alumni affairs with its service orientation, and on the left is public relations and all it entails. Together they form a triad of harmony that works beautifully for the institutions and organizations they serve.

All things considered, *Excellence in Advancement* seemed to work best as the title for this book, because it is about more than fund raising or development. The book is about the latest and best theory and practice in fund raising and friend raising, in alumni and client relations, and in publicity and communication. Broadly speaking, the goal of advancement is to reach for greater excellence. The book is a treatise on how to make friends and win support and how to better understand and use current technology, but it is not a manual of procedure. It is not a handbook. It is a reference book with a point of view based on experience. It is designed for the professional staff member whose job it may be to make friends and raise money, to give information and facilitate intra- and extramural communication, and to build strong ties and loyalty with alumni. It is a book by experienced professionals for senior-level professionals as well as entry-level professionals in the college and university environment, the health care industry, and the nonprofit sector.

The book includes a prologue having to do with technology in advancement; three major sections, one concerning fund raising, one on alumni relations, and one dealing with public relations; and an epilogue. In addition to the discussion on technology, which is important to all who find themselves in the advancement arena, there is a relevant discussion of institutional foundations and their role in advancement.

Within the last two decades, advancement professionals have come a long way in their knowledge of technology and their skills in using it. Word processing, spreadsheets, desktop publishing, e-mail/voice mail, facsimilies, and the Internet are all a part of it. The telephone and the yellow legal pad, the dictaphone, the microcassette, the typewriter, and the mimeograph, which were once fairly standard tools of the trade, are anachronistic. Almost every advancement office now has a fax machine, a pentium computer with laser printers, and a fast and versatile copy machine. WordPerfect, Microsoft Word, Lotus 1.2.3, and QuatroPro are commonly used software applications that provide quick and easy ways of writing documents, reports, spreadsheets, and proposals.

University and hospital foundations emerged as a means of stewardship in the early years of this century. As a rule, they are fairly independent and serve the basic function of holding gift monies and distributing them according to the donor's wishes. Over time, foundations have increased in number and broadened their scope to include fund raising and investment. They are lauded by some university and hospital presidents and criticized by others. Most of the recent books on institutional advancement devote little or no space to foundations, yet they are a controlling factor in institutional advancement. For this reason a chapter on foundations is included in this book.

As Steven Muller noted 20 years ago in Westley Rowland's *Handbook of Institutional Advancement*, the advancement function in higher education is uniquely American.[7] Education in foreign countries has been the responsibility of the government. Funds for current and capital needs were appropriated by the government. Ownership and management were also in the hands of government. Likewise, control of who gets to attend institutions of higher learning is with the government.[8] There has been little need for fund raising in many foreign countries because the schooling was paid for and managed by the state. In America, fund raising, alumni cultivation, marketing, and promotion, even among state colleges and universities, is a necessary function. First and foremost, the Constitution of the United States assigns no responsibility for education to the federal government, leaving it to the states and the private sector. In recent years, however, with the establishment of a cabinet post for education, the federal government has gotten into the picture more substantially despite calls for the abolishment of the Department of Education.

Federal and state dollars presently appropriated, however, do not and will not cover educational expenses. Operational costs, not to mention capital needs, in private and state institutions are in the millions. In the past, state colleges and universities have had the good fortune to receive substantial funding from government sources while private institutions have had to look elsewhere for funding,

Excellence in Advancement

namely, to tuition and fees, auxiliary enterprises, and private contributions. The current trend, however, is toward less and less government funding, resulting in the need for more and more private funding. At Delaware State University, for example, state funding in the late 1980s for operational costs amounted to 60 percent of the total operating budget. Years later in the closing years of the century, state funding for operational costs decreased to 40 percent of the total operating budget. The story is the same for many public institutions across the nation.

Capital needs grow larger with the passing years. Inflation is one factor, but the awesome spector of aggressively deferred maintenance looms high on the horizon. Many colleges and universities are assessing costs of electrical upgrades, plant repair, and facilities renovation in the tens of millions, and there are no quick and easy answers.

Clearly, there is greater need than ever before for the advancement function in American colleges and universities. One source of new money is higher tuition and fees, but there comes a time in the marketplace when cost makes the product prohibitive, so raising tuition and fees can only go so far. It will vary with each institution, but tuition and fees cannot be raised high enough to balance the budget. Another source is profit-making auxiliary enterprises, and it may be in future years that manufacturing, sales, and service enterprises owned by colleges and universities could pick up the slack and balance the budget, but foresight through the telescope of time into the beginning years of the twenty-first century does not reveal any giant steps in this direction.

Philanthropy, one thinks, might be the answer. If through improved public relations, promotion, and communication, through better customer relations and enhanced ability to cultivate and solicit major gifts, and through better relationships with alumni and prospective alumni, advancement staff could increase contributions from all sources 50 percent or 25 percent, or even 10 percent, it would ease the financial load considerably, and it is possible, but the advancement function will need to be treated as a financial priority. From a business point of view, if one professional fund raiser could bring in an additional quarter of a million gift dollars, and it would cost the institution only $50,000 in salary, $6,000 in fringe benefits, and $15,000 in printing, travel, telephone, and other business-related expenses, the college or university would receive an awesome benefit of $179,000, which is a positive margin of 72 percent. Where else could such an investment return be realized so quickly?

The investment return on grantsmanship, also an advancement function, is much more dramatic than the major gift example cited above. Government relations, sponsored programs, and corporate and foundation relations have been by far the largest growth item in institutional advancement. The paperwork is difficult. Often there are complex forms to be filled out, detailed research that is necessary, faculty–staff cooperation, and time-consuming proposal preparation, but the outcome is abundantly rewarding.

More difficult to evaluate is the alumni piece of the advancement plan, and the same is true of individuals who are friends and not alumni. How does one put a value on a chance meeting at a reception, a thank-you letter to a classmate, or an alumni chapter meeting in some distant town? Yet it pays off. Sometimes it takes years, sometimes it happens immediately. There is something about that human touch, that personal contact that melts the heart and brings results, and that is the payback for generous investment in alumni relations programs and activities. It has been said many times, and it is a fund raising axiom, that people give to people. Alumni are the avant garde of the institution. They are the product of the college or university. They are the reflection of the institution. Alumni are the foundation of annual support and the first source of major and planned gifts.

The advancement function and the advancement team are vital to the good health of any institution of higher learning, of nonprofit organizations, and of hospitals and health care institutions. This book attempts to explore the folks and the function of the advancement operation. The following pages paint the picture as it is today and will be tomorrow as professional staff reach for greater productivity, greater participation, and greater excellence in the advancement of education, health care, and other nonprofit organizations.

Institutional advancement as a profession with several career tracks has come of age in the last half of the twentieth century, although the fund raising business was very much alive in the 1920s as was the alumni movement and public relations efforts. Fund raising for churches and schools was rather fundamental even in the formative years of our nation as Scott M. Cutlip points out in his well-researched book, *Fund Raising in the United States*.[9] As a source of information about fund raising history in America, Cutlip is without peer. His years of research culminated in the 1965 edition of his book, published by Rutgers University Press. A new edition was released by Transaction Publishers in 1990. There were fund raising efforts by John Eliot (1604–1691), John Wesley (1703–1791), George Whitefield (1714–1770), and other clergymen; statesman Benjamin Franklin (1706–1790); and by college alumni since the early 1800s. Nonprofit organizations like the YMCA, the Salvation Army, and the American Red Cross were out on the streets winning friends, influencing people, and raising money in the early 1900s. There were news releases, publications, and personal visits. Several multimillion–dollar fund drives were launched in the early 1920s, including ones for the University of Chicago, Harvard, Tuskegee, Johns Hopkins, and the YMCA. There were advocates, like the John Price Jones Corporation, and philanthropists like the Mellons and Rockefellers, and marketing campaigns, and alumni fund drives, but the logical linking of these functions by the concept of institutional advancement—with its plethora of specialists in public affairs, external relations, prospect research, prospect management, annual fund, major gifts, planned giving, communications, donor relations, alumni affairs, special events, reunions, publications, etc.—has come about during the last 50 years. Advancement people have become an association of professionals having their own standards of conduct, code of ethics, and most recently their own criteria and procedure for certification, including certified fund raising executive, advanced certified fund raising executive, fellow of the association for healthcare philanthropy, and accredited in public relations.

Four years after the merger of the American Alumni Council and the American College Public Relations Association in 1974, A. Westley Roland was commissioned by CASE to edit and compile a comprehensive book on advancement, which he called the *Handbook for Institutional Advancement*. It is the first comprehensive book on institutional advancement and was later revised in 1986.

The single most influential element of the last two decades, however, has been the emergence of technology. In the late 1970s and early 1980s institutions were scrambling to bring themselves up to speed in the knowledge and usage of computer technology. At Ball State University, for example, Vice President Bob Linson, the alumni and development people, and the foundation staff were converting hard copy records to electronic files. In prior years the source of information about alumni, donors, and prospects was the huge collection of file cards kept up to date by competent support staff. Then within a few months, the computer became the driver that led to better recordkeeping and reports, better publications, and better management of all advancement programs and activities. Shortly afterward, every office had to have a facsimile machine. Distance learning, interactive television, teleconferencing, high-speed processors, e-mail, voice mail, and the Internet with its plethora of Web pages have since become the order of the day.

The impact of distance learning and cybereducation is being felt across the nation. It must be addressed. Writers of books on the subject of institutional advancement are now collecting data and dealing with the issue of new technology and how it affects the profession. This book takes the matter seriously. Cybereducation and cyberfundraising are realities. A recent issue of *Forbes* magazine documents the existence of 762 cyberschools, a gigantic leap upward from the 93 cyberschools reported four years ago.[10] Peter Drucker is credited with saying that universities will not survive. The future is outside the traditional halls of ivy. Distance learning is coming on fast, and advancement professionals better be able and ready to move with the technological tide.

It is appropriate then to begin this volume with a treatise on technology in advancement. The contributing authors, Ronald J. Stephany of the University of Redlands and Judith Tuch of the University of California—Los Angeles, provide a current view of the state of the art as it relates to fund raising, alumni affairs, and public relations.

NOTES

1. J. Panas, *Official Fund Raising Almanac* (Chicago: Pluribus Press, 1989), 321.
2. Panas, 8.
3. A.E. Kaplan, ed., *Giving USA 1997* (New York: American Association of Fund Raising Council, 1997), 10.
4. J.L. Fisher and G.H. Quehl, *The President and Fund Raising* (New York: American Council on Education and Macmillan, 1989).
5. P.L. Parker, ed., *The Journal of John Wesley* (Chicago: Moody Press, 1952), 152.
6. Parker, 394.
7. S. Muller, "The Definition and Philosophy of Institutional Advancement," prologue to *Handbook of Institutional Advancement,* ed. A. Westley Rowland (San Francisco: Jossey-Bass, 1978), 2.
8. Muller, 2.
9. S.M. Cutlip, *Fund Raising in the United States* (New Brunswick, NJ: Transaction Publishers, 1990).
10. L. Guberick and A. Ebeling, "I Got My Degree Through E-mail," *Forbes*, June 16, 1997, 84.

Technology in Advancement

Ronald J. Stephany and Judith Tuch

THE STATE OF THE ART

Ask any old-timer to identify the most significant change that has taken place in an advancement office during the past 30 years, and the reply will likely be "the pace." It is, of course, a perspective that might be used to characterize the recent evolution of nearly any profession. For advancement officers, pace has been driven largely by pressure: government reductions in financial aid for students, the financial implications of the so-called knowledge explosion, public attitudes, and the increasing philosophical diversity of external constituencies. The list seems endless.

An argument might also be made that the degree to which pace has accelerated over the last three decades is proportional to the growth and development of technology. Let there be no mistake. Technology has not made it possible for any advancement officer to enjoy shorter days and longer vacations. Rather, it has simply allowed more work and, yes, more worry to be crammed into the same amount of available time.

Much of the responsibility for these additional pressures lies squarely on the shoulders of individual advancement officers. Technology can be mesmerizing. It is not difficult to understand that for many, the day begins with a review of phone-mail messages, responses to phone-mail messages, a review of e-mail messages, responses to e-mail messages, a review of inquiries on all appropriate list-servers, responses to each of those inquiries, a little surfing on the Web, and perhaps a few home pages from other institutions.

This is not to suggest that the benefits that have accrued to advancement as a result of technology are minimal. Indeed, enormous gains have been made. Yet to put the role of technology in the proper perspective, one must have some understanding of its development and how it can and should be used to help carry out the mission assigned to a particular institution's advancement operation.

It was during the 1960s that many advancement offices first gained access to a mainframe. Those computers, however, tended to be used primarily as electronic addressograph machines. Over time, gift and pledge data were added, although accessing the data was difficult. After all, "on-line" still referred to something those who fished did with a fly.

The first real technological leap of the typical advancement office occurred in 1969 when IBM introduced its Selectric typewriter with a magnetic card. While the company had added memory to the Selectric five years earlier, the new mag card gave offices the opportunity for much more extensive mail-merge functions. Supervisors watched in amazement as these machines spewed forth letters while the secretary in charge answered the phone and opened the mail. When the ink jet printer, a high-speed machine that prepared so-called personal letters and envelopes, was developed by IBM several years later, the use of direct mail for cultivation and solicitation was forever changed.

The advent of the personal computer and the explosive growth of the Internet have put to rest the last vestiges of how life in the advancement office was conducted during the good old days. Carbon paper, once synonymous with copies, has been replaced by the hard drive and CD-ROM.

Gone are the days when one could mail a letter in a stamped envelope and not have to be concerned about the follow-up for at least two weeks. Today, the very nature of e-mail demands an immediate response. The Web has moved research from the library to the office and has also imposed upon institutions new ways to compete. We cannot begin to imagine the impact on advancement that technology will have as it continues to evolve. Still, we must be prepared for whatever comes, and that preparation will require planning, management, and an understanding of the financial commitment required to produce the desired results.

PLANNING FOR TECHNOLOGY

Assessing Needs

Twenty years ago, one could conduct a day-to-day search of any advancement officer's calendar and never find the words, "Computer-Needs Assessment Meeting." A similar search conducted 10 or 15 years later might indicate such a gathering, but seldom more than annually. Projected technology needs were submitted to the director of the information management office, assuming such an office even existed. A list of needs was then compiled and reviewed by some group charged with that responsibility. For larger institutions, it was a fairly sizable and cumbersome committee. Very small organizations delegated the task to two or three people in the business office. Much debate would ensue as those responsible for making the final decision struggled to prioritize the list of technological needs requested. Often, those decisions became quite political. Yet agreement was eventually reached, and those charged with the implementation left the room, marching orders securely in hand. For the few institutions in which technology tracking was a priority, periodic meetings continued to be held in order to review progress and reassess the priorities.

Today, given the accelerated speed and fluidity with which the computing environment is changing, an annual assessment does not meet the requirements of most organizations. Due to the complexities of technology and the variety of requests being received, the number of participants involved in assessment has also been broadened to include most managers and key support staff. These professionals require, and sometimes demand, individual attention as they struggle to match their needs with technology's offerings.

In many organizations, needs assessment stretches over a period of several months. In others, no process exists. For some, there may be a defined process in place, but no opportunity for a collective gathering of all units. As a result, managers often lack the benefit of understanding what their peers in other areas of the organization are proposing. The result is the absence of a global vision for technology.

At a minimum, what comes out of the needs assessment process should be published and made available to the entire community of users. This kind of needs assessment does more than simply prioritize a list of software and hardware needs, thereby making it possible for an institution to remain focused. It also reflects the organization's short-term commitment.

Perhaps the greatest weakness found in the current needs assessment practices of most institutions lies in the failure to tie technology initiatives to a larger plan. Charlotte McGhee, senior counsel at Grenzebach, Glier and Associates, Inc., notes that this is more difficult than was once the case, simply because every organization is in the process of becoming something different than it was. Within that environment, technology, she suggests, must always be viewed as "an enabler." McGhee points out that "to be strategic, technology decisions have to be tied to strategic business decisions. The definition of the business objective and the business process to reach that objective must come first."

This understanding of needs assessment helps set the stage for several additional concepts related to the management of technology. Attention to these issues will help ensure the successful integration of new technology into the workplace creating an environment in which technology can become the enabler it is meant to be.

Establishing Partnerships

It is critical that advancement be represented at the table when key technology decisions are being made. It is equally important for technology to be represented during the development of major initiatives by the advancement staff. Without such a partnership, it is next to impossible for the information officer to ensure that technology is integrated into the day-to-day business environment.

It falls to the chief advancement officer and the chief information officer to make certain that the relationship between their two staffs is not an adversarial one. This is not always an easy task, for the two tend to come from different backgrounds. One can almost see glassy-eyed stares develop in the eyes of advancement officers as their technological counterparts break into "computer speak," using terms such as "mapping," "bits," and "nanoseconds." Nor do information services professionals look particularly alert as advancement officers reference "LYBUNTS," "column inches," and "events management."

In short, the skills that make for a good advancement officer traditionally have not been the same skills required of a competent technology or information management professional. Advancement professionals are committed to creating and building relationships, primarily with those outside of the organization. Their job descriptions include phrases such as "maintain close working relationships with donors, volunteers, and various governing boards," "organize events that promote the goals of the institution," and "maintain and enhance an aggressive stewardship program." The job card of the communications professional boasts phrases such as "ensure that all publications reflect the mission and quality of the institution," "maintain an up-to-date experts list," and "develop an aggressive media relations program."

The technology professional's job description includes phrases like "demonstrate proficiency in Windows, NetWare, Word, Access, and Excel," "gather, organize, and analyze data," and "maintain a system for managing information." Seldom, if ever, does one see any reference to building either internal or external relationships.

Too often the skill sets of these two professional groups collide. During the final implementation phase of a rather complex database system, an information officer at one research institution suggested that the technology staff held "all the power." At yet another meeting on the same topic, a senior development officer advised that "the information management staff should be subservient."

Such competing perspectives follow the road to nowhere. In today's world, advancement officers must take the time to acquire new technical competencies.

Those responsible for technology must hone their customer relations skills. No longer is there any logic to an approach that implies "separate but equal." The overlap between the two professions is simply too great. Equal, yes. Separate, no.

Setting Short- and Long-Term Business Objectives

A clear definition of your short- and long-term business objectives must be in place before any discussion regarding technology. A business plan ensures that both the organization and its management remain focused. One must never lose sight of the fact that the role of technology impacts only the delivery system. As has already been noted, technology remains first and foremost an enabler, not an end in itself.

As an institution's objectives and the series of activities needed to achieve those objectives are developed, the business plan takes form. It is during this evolution that technology becomes integrated into the plan. A knowledge of technology can often alert those involved to the need for additional definition that may be required.

For example, a new alumni donor database being considered presents a variety of challenges and opportunities. Research was never a high priority, and constituent information is limited. Data integrity is also an issue. The data reside in an old system with a limited number of data fields in which to store information. The inquiry screens are far from "user friendly." The new system, on the other hand, offers a wealth of data fields and screens that require several critical decisions regarding the collection and organization of data. One staff member responsible for major gifts requests screening and rating information, along with relationship data. Another, whose task it is to seek foundation and corporate support, asks for detailed profile information. The annual giving and alumni relations person makes known a wish for additional biographic information.

How does one craft a plan for systematically collecting timely and accurate information given the resources available? By tying its collection to the business plan. Rather than attempting to identify and capture information on all organizations that may have an interest in the institution, they are prioritized, with attention given to those at the top of the list. Initially, detailed biographical information is compiled for donors, volunteers, and major prospects, rather than for the entire constituency. A concrete business reason for gathering each piece of information ensures integrity, timeliness, and accuracy.

COPING WITH CULTURAL CHANGES

The advent of sophisticated prospect management and tracking tools provides an excellent example of how a change in culture may be required to accommodate a business plan. Information once maintained on index cards and in the heads of advancement officers is now maintained in systems that are easily accessible, and that access is instantaneous.

The prospect management system at the University of California at Los Angeles involves the on-line entry of contact reports by development officers after completion of a telephone call, letter, or visit with a major prospect. Before March 1996, these reports were entered by a central office into a stand-alone system. Development officers wre not given on-line access to these reports. Because the recap reports were produced and distributed on a monthly basis, the fund raisers tended to wait and submit their contact reports immediately before the generation of this monthly listing.

The current prospect management system at the University of California at Los Angeles (UCLA) was part of the alumni donor database implementation. During phase one, contact reports were again entered by the central office, but development officers were now able to view the reports on-line immediately. Later, the fund raisers were given update access and trained to enter their own contact reports. This, of course, meant that access to the information was dependent upon the timeliness with which the contact reports were entered into the system.

For UCLA, the move from central control of data entry to direct input by a development officer required a culture change, a different way of doing business. It was made possible by two major incentives:

1. the ability for any development officer to track contacts with all major prospects
2. management's ability to identify progress and set goals for the cultivation process

The pace at which the culture of an organization adapts depends entirely on the perceived benefit and the extent to which management uses the available tools. Top-down support is mandatory. Not only must the chief advancement officer communicate a vision for new technology. He or she must also model its use.

EXPECTATIONS AND PREPARATION

One must set realistic expectations for adapting and using technology and be prepared to manage these expectations. Change can be inherently frightening. It is therefore important that everyone in an organization have a basic understanding of how and why technology is being integrated into the day-to-day operation. If the decision either to embrace a new technology or alter an already existing one is not clearly articulated, the chances are good that the proposed change will be viewed with suspicion and as an end in itself.

It makes sense, then, to set realistic goals for the use of technology. It is always better to err on the side of caution than to promise every need will be met immediately by some wondrous technological widget. Senior management must also understand that learning curves can vary tremendously from individual to individual. It is easy to underestimate those curves when implementing a new system.

Developing Measurements

Good measurements determine the success of every key decision: Ask yourself the question, "How will we know when we succeed?" It is a question that cannot be answered in the absence of clearly defined criteria designed to measure progress. A lack of benchmarks will also impede the implementation process. Whether one is in the midst of a new software application or simply upgrading to the most recent version of an off-the-shelf software package, this principle applies. Management cannot possibly determine success if there is no way for it to know when goals have been met.

One must not be too rigid when developing the criteria used to determine progress. The development, design, and implementation of a new computer system can be a lengthy process, which begins with a detailed needs analysis and concludes with final implementation. It is often impossible to predict at the beginning of the project the organizational or market-driven changes that might occur during the cycle itself. Adjusting the originally established criteria in order to accommodate these changes can be time-consuming, yet it is time worth spending. Again, a lack of measurements prevents management from assessing performance. For lack of performance assessment, management is unable to refine the technology initiatives. For lack of an ability to refine the technology initiatives, management is unable to remain flexible. For lack of flexibility, management is ultimately unhappy once full implementation has been achieved, and when management is unhappy, everyone is unhappy.

When formulating a valid set of measurement criteria, turn once again to the business plan shaping the technology initiative, and focus on the small incremental points defined throughout that plan.

Developing an Implementation Strategy

A well-designed implementation strategy is key to ensuring the success of strategic technology decisions. Linda Worcel, director of operations and services at Stanford University, has observed that "a tight technical project plan and budget are obvious for the development and implementation of a fund raising information system. What has not been equally recognized is that similar planning and budgeting are imperative on the fund raising shop's side. Large new systems probably involve new hardware and desktop software. Users must be trained extensively and provided hotline support for maximum utilization of the technology and for minimum frustration."

Worcel's words apply to all areas of advancement. Unless training and help-line staff are provided for, either in departmental or project budgets, implementation will be slowed or impaired. The remainder of this section discusses the components of a solid implementation strategy.

Published software support guidelines and a service-level agreement. Developing software support guidelines for the organization goes directly to the heart of the matter. It is inevitable that some users will always want the latest and greatest software package to come down the pike. It is equally inevitable that others will use only a minimum of the technology available. The majority will fall somewhere between these two extremes.

Several factors affect the number of software packages that the information services group should support at any given time. That selection must be made in the context of personnel resources that can be allocated to training and problem resolution and the ability of the users to assimilate new technology. An additional consideration relates to the timing for the roll out of any new technology. Together the chief advancement officer and the chief information officer should agree upon the optimal number of applications that best support the needs of the organization.

A comprehensive software support policy constitutes the first part of a service level agreement (SLA) between the advancement officers and the internal service providers. Regardless of whether they are written or simply implied, SLAs define the roles and responsibilities of all involved and allow a framework for establishing realistic expectations. It is through the SLA that the information support staff inform their customers of the time frame within which support is provided. The SLA also sets the stage for ongoing improvement and superior "customer" support.

A comprehensive product introduction plan. The planning and introduction of either a new product or an upgrade to an existing system require understanding and corroboration at the highest levels within the organization. The primary ingredient in a successful plan considers the timing of the product "roll out" itself. Competing priorities can bring any implementation to a halt. Because access to the new equipment or application should be closely related to the timing of the training itself, the technical support staff must work closely with the training staff to ensure that every detail has been accounted for in the product "roll out" plan.

An effective testing plan, which includes the end user's perspective. It is virtually impossible to analyze each and every aspect of an application prior to implementation. However, with careful testing many problems can be avoided. This requires that different levels of users be involved as part of the evaluation group. The technical and support staff will not test products in the same manner as the "customers" simply because they will not recognize the issues that users encounter during the normal workday. Involving the users in testing has the added value of fostering a partnership with the technical group.

An effective communications strategy. A well-developed communications plan achieves three valuable goals. First, it provides a blueprint for communicating the goals of a technology initiative to all levels within the organization. Second, it helps keep the user focused on these goals. And finally, it helps manage expectations for what the new technology will and will not do. When designing a communications plan, consider a wide variety of delivery mechanisms, both verbal and written. In order to ensure coordination, generate a communications checklist and assign responsibility for maintaining it to an individual within the organization.

An effective training strategy. The road to new technology is littered with the bodies of those who were never able to adapt to that technology. There are two reasons for this. First, new technology is expensive. When something is expensive, managers tend to look for ways to cut costs, and training often becomes the target. Too many managers seem to believe that in order to understand new software, one need only turn on the machine and find the "HELP" key.

While management may underestimate both the time and budget required to ensure the successful integration of technology into the workplace, the users themselves are often resistant to training. Common complaints heard during a session include: "This training is taking too long," or "It takes me away from my real job." At some institutions, only 40 percent of the end users actually receive formal training.

Just-in-time training will help improve retention. It makes no sense to provide training for an application that will not be immediately available for use. Always remember the old advertising adage: people forget 60 percent of what they see or hear in a day. Retention of the material in a formal training situation can be as low as 10 percent after 30 days.

Also important is shaping classes to include processes that are relevant to the user's day-to-day work. Most people will use only a fraction of the features provided by software programs. Of course, making training relevant requires that it be tailored for varying levels of personnel, ranging from the technical support staff to the end users.

Preferred learning methods vary from user to user. Students do not always learn well in the traditional "schoolroom" setting. Today, elements of successful training for technology include the following: a facilitator; tutorials, which often are included with the software product; self-paced training using CD-ROM, multimedia, or manuals; on-line help features provided by the software vendor or customized by the organization's technical staff; documentation in the form of manuals, "how-to" sheets and cue cards; a structured environment in which information is shared by coworkers; laboratories in which the user works on specific processes with a facilitator available to answer questions; newsletters; and user-group meetings.

Involving the users in the development of a training plan is extremely important. Their commitment to participate in the training must be secured at the outset of the planning process. Include a formal review to determine the effectiveness of the training methods used. During training itself, be flexible enough to make changes based upon the users' recommendations.

An effective mechanism for trouble-shooting and problem resolution. Sophisticated software programs and applications require additional support. As users become more experienced, they ask more complex questions. Windows trouble-shooting, for example, has become increasingly time-consuming. No wonder the "help desk" industry is burgeoning. As the sun sets on implementation and training, all organizations must make certain that they have in place a mechanism for problem resolution. They must first determine whether or not that mechanism should be centralized. Other options, such as outsourcing, do exist. Although such alternatives may be appropriate for issues relating to hardware, they tend to be less suitable for those pertaining to software. The obvious drawback is the response time from a vendor who may not have formed relationships with the institution's users nor be familiar with management's policies.

Centralized support within the organization has several other advantages. It maximizes the resources of the technical staff. The relationship with users is maintained. Areas where additional training is required are more easily identified. One additional advantage of centralization is the reduction in the degree of peer involvement that occurs outside the official support framework. For example, a user may experience problems while trying to print a document. He or she first turns to the closest coworker. That person has no quick answer but spends time trying to resolve the problem anyway. The two then find themselves enlisting assistance from a third colleague. In the end, a problem that could easily have been resolved by a brief conversation with a technical support person within the organization has now consumed between 15 and 30 minutes of peer support time.

The term "centralized" is, of course, applicable either to the entire organization or to specific divisions. Each institution will have to make that decision based on its size and complexity. Regardless, it is important to remember that industry standards call for one full-time help desk staff person per 50 to 75 users.

A plan for vendor liaison and ongoing product review. Periodic contact with vendors to review contracts, technical support needs, yearly maintenance agreements, product quality, and product enhancements is a must. Witness the "roll out" of Windows 95. This operating system has had an extraordinary impact on the technical environment, forcing organizations to consider the manner in which they proceed with upgrades.

Any decision to enhance a product restarts the implementation strategy cycle. Someone within the organization must have responsibility for vendor liaison and product review. At the same time, users must be involved as decisions regarding timing and content are made. Ultimately, it is the users who must drive this process. Otherwise, technology will once again be perceived as an end in itself.

An effective plan to combat obsolescence. The rapid pace of change in technology requires that managers plan for obsolescence. An annual hardware plan should include replacement of between 20 percent and 33 percent of the equipment on hand. Yet as Kenneth Green, director of the Campus Computing Survey, has noted, "most campuses do not have a financial plan for their technology needs. The 1995 Campus Computing Survey reveals that almost three-fourths of all colleges and universities nationwide do not have a plan to acquire and retire technology resources. Rather, the Survey reports, most technology purchasing is opportunistic and episodic, often done with 'budget dust' at the end of the fiscal year."[1]

Equipment replacement does not necessarily have to translate into new equipment. In his article, "Mission: Ubiquity," Richard A. Detweiler, president of Hartwick College, describes the procedure that institution employs to control equipment costs. "We use a 'rebirth' strategy for faculty and staff personal computers," he wrote. "Those with the greatest needs may receive new equipment every year or two; their equipment is cleaned, enhanced, and reissued to those with lesser technology needs. Those with the lesser technology needs receive the oldest equipment. This approach can prolong the useful life of equipment to as long as five or six years."[2]

Of course, it is inevitable that during the implementation of a major technology initiative an organization will be faced with a requirement for new hardware. That need is, of course, driven by software development. During the implementation of the alumni donor database at UCLA, hardware requirements changed dramatically, necessitating a large number of upgrades to personal computers (PCs) distributed throughout the institution.

Planning for technology and managing technology in the context of institutional advancement are, in many ways, generic topics. Each discipline within advancement also operates in a unique technological environment that deserves special attention.

TECHNOLOGY AND COMMUNICATIONS

The director of communications at a large research institution was once asked by the new chancellor, "Where is our internal newsletter?" Replied the director, tipping her head toward the chancellor's computer, "In there." "I don't think so," responded the chancellor.

There are those who will remember a culture that many years ago called for keeping data up-to-date on hundreds of index cards while, at the same time, maintaining the identical data on those new storage sheds called "computers." Today, that same culture resists the change from paper to electronic communication. Reasons for supporting the former while inching slowly toward the latter abound. The chancellor has plenty of company.

Although the use of paper to carry words and pictures may never entirely disappear, electronic communication is becoming the dominant mode. This has tremendous implications for communications offices. Increasingly, for example, the Internet is being used by journalists for research and leads, with ProfNet the current and most popular method. When Linda Granell, director of public relations and publications at the University of Redlands in Southern California, noticed a ProfNet inquiry regarding men's issues, she immediately linked the reporter seeking the information with a professor of psychology who had written extensively on the topic. Several weeks after the reporter's column appeared, the professor found himself the guest on a two-hour St. Louis talk show.

Perhaps no technology is challenging communications offices more than the Internet's Web. What an appropriate name. While there is certainly structure, it is nonetheless tangled. Some know how to navigate it. Others get caught in it. In the October 1995 issue of the Council for Advancement and Support of Education *Currents*, Michael Stoner, vice president of the consulting firm, College Connections, wrote that "just about anyone with a little time and technical prowess can create a Web page."[3]

Frightening, isn't it? The result mirrors that which developed several years earlier with the introduction of graphics design software. Never before had so many people who had no professional training or any idea as to what they were doing had access to such sophisticated equipment. And they used it. And they smiled, and said, "That's good." But really, it wasn't.

Stoner went on to observe that of the 700 or so sites that at that time were on-line, many were "badly designed, difficult to navigate, and a poor reflection on the host institution." Unfortunately, in all too many organizations those words continue to ring true today.

In general, technical professionals were the first to develop home pages for most institutions. Why? Because they could. In many cases, communications offices, and certainly those in upper management, were not even aware the pages existed and, in fact, wouldn't know how to access them anyway. Indeed, even today there are those who associate "Yahoo" with rodeos.

All of this comes as no surprise to those who have chronicled the advent of technology. Philip Glotzbach, dean of the College of Arts and Sciences at the University of Redlands, has observed that historically the only people who knew how to use a new technology were the ones who initially built it, the airplane being a perfect example.[4] Still, in retrospect, it is all quite astounding. Colleges and universities spend tens of thousands of dollars on admissions brochures. Museums and symphony orchestras spend similar amounts on annual reports and brochures for membership drives. Never would they think of going to their computer people and saying, "Here. Write, design, and manage the printing for these publications." Still, consciously or unconsciously, explicitly or implied, that is exactly what has been said in regard to a presence on the Web, yet a home page IS a publication (soon to become a video).

Having said this, we must give credit where credit is due. It was the technical world that brought the Web to the attention of public relations and publications professionals and management. It was the technical world that recognized the potential the Web held for institutions. It was the technical folks who were determined that their institutions must not fall behind this advancing eight ball, and they did so when no one else either cared or was paying attention.

It is now time to pay attention. Step one calls for a partnership between the technical experts and public relations and publications specialists. For some institutions this partnership is alive and well. Others have miles to go. Both must address the following issues:

- Who sets policy? Where does final authority rest? With the director of communications? With a Web Committee? Which constituencies should be represented on that committee?
- What do you want to achieve? More important, what is achievable? For an educational institution, is admissions the first priority? If so, what in the admissions publications must be reflected in the home page? Is there a visual link between those publications and the home page? After all, one would never think of sending mixed written messages. Why send mixed visual messages?
- Define the "official" home page and stay focused on that home page, regardless of how the rest of the world links to it.
- Who is going to maintain this creature? Is the institution fortunate enough to have a full-time "Web Master?" If not, shouldn't the home page be designed and written with that in mind?
- Remember, the moment the institution's home page appears, it is in competition with all the home pages of similar institutions. What is done should be done well.

Today it seems as if everything is going on-line, including faculty experts, directories, and press releases. If the Internet were not enough to occupy one's mind, enter the Intranet: daily bulletins, calendars, reports from the president, minutes of faculty meetings, and so on.

Today it is the Web. What it will be tomorrow is anyone's guess. Regardless, the question as to what is achievable within the limits of budget and staffing is one that all areas of advancement must continue to raise. We must live within our means. We must establish priorities and stick to those priorities.

TECHNOLOGY AND CONSTITUENT RELATIONS

The alumni relations director of a well-known school, upon learning that any graduate could design his or her own home page and then link it to the institution's home page, was heard to exclaim, "They can't do that! It can't possibly be legal."

Oh, but it is. Alumni, alumni special interest groups, and even official alumni clubs have been swept into the Web. They have been caught, and they are having the time of their lives.

What's an institution to do? Very little, actually, other than to offer assistance or advice. And, of course, the extent to which that can be given is dependent upon staffing and resources. As noted earlier, total control is impossible, so keep the institutional eye on the organization's official pages. Again, it's a matter of priorities.

Technology is allowing institutions to provide new services for their constituencies and to enhance old ones. Nearly all computer packages for advancement now offer events management modules that enable both constituent relations and development offices to closely monitor the interest and involvement of individuals. Thanks to the Internet, alumni have unprecedented access to the services of college and university career planning and placement offices. Institutions use electronic communication to promote their events and to provide on-line registration as well. These kinds of offerings are now considered basic.

How those responsible for constituent relations use technology in the future will be largely dependent on the percentage of their constituents who have access to the Internet. The numbers are, of course, growing daily. Already many organizations are turning to the Web for some publications activity. The time will come when e-mail, not "snail mail," will be used almost exclusively to merchandise, advertise, and promote.

This transfer from paper to electronic communication will, of course, be gradual. The budget savings accompanying the process have the potential to be significant. Of course, there are those who claim that while the use of electronic communication in constituent relations will grow, it will always coexist with, rather than replace, the way business is now conducted. Electronic communication, they suggest, will never be available to everyone.

If such words sound familiar, it is because they were once used to predict the future of television.

TECHNOLOGY AND DEVELOPMENT

To the advancement professional, development's components are well-known: identification, cultivation, solicitation, and stewardship. No technology has been developed to replace any one of those elements, nor is such development likely.

Technology has, however, enhanced the development process. As has already been noted, it will continue to transform those areas upon which development depends for cultivation: constituent relations and communications.

Development is a process. It is not an event. The process starts with "suspect identification" and then narrows to prospect identification and prospect research. It is here that technology has had its greatest impact. Twenty-five years ago, prospect research consisted of development officers talking to members of a constituency about their friends or classmates. Today, it has its own professional association.

The growth of modern prospect research techniques has produced increasingly skeptical and concerned constituents. It is not because what is and what is not public information has changed dramatically. Rather, the discomfort results from the ease with which information can be recovered. People never seemed to mind when everything was on paper. If some administrative assistant wanted to sit in libraries, courthouses, and basements day after day, sifting through a host of unrelated publications and taking notes, more power to them. It becomes a different issue when a professional researcher can gather more information than one can imagine possible with just a few keystrokes. And now, the Internet has been added as a research tool, along with increasingly sophisticated programs for the electronic screening of entire constituencies.

Technology has also impacted the manner in which prospects are moved from research into and through the cultivation phase. Often referred to as "tracking," the procedure assigns to development officers a series of steps intended to culminate in the prospect making a major gift. Tracking provides a tremendous benefit to the development process because it forces an action.

That benefit, however, can quickly become a disadvantage if the system and the people who manage it try to impose an action step when none is warranted. It is the development officer who must always drive the strategy. Whatever the system used for tracking, it has to be flexible and responsive enough to accommodate that strategy.

TECHNOLOGY, ADVANCEMENT, AND THE FUTURE

Any 25-year veteran of advancement on the verge of retirement has probably rubbed elbows with at least six different computer systems during his or her career. In the next 25 years that number is likely to double or even triple. Think of how quickly technology has moved from those thin cards full of holes to CD-ROM, from mainframes to PCs, from DOS to Windows, from the 286 to the 586. An article in the January 1995 issue of CASE *Currents* provided advancement officers with some very helpful advice related to the Gopher. The Gopher?

Clearly, what is here today undoubtedly will be gone tomorrow. That does not mean that what technology comes up with next cannot be controlled. Some basic "rules of the road" will remain regardless of advancements in technology: Don't take on more than staff and resources permit. Mountain climbers climb Mt. Everest because it's there. That is not a good reason to purchase hardware and software. Don't build a business plan around technology. Prepare the business plan first, then fit technology into it. Communicate. Train, train, train. Be methodical. Be careful! Budget!

NOTES

1. K.C. Green, "Building a Campus Infostructure," *Trusteeship*, Special Issue, 1996, 4.
2. R.A. Detweiler, "Mission: Ubiquity," *Trusteeship,* Special Issue, 1966, 20.
3. M. Stoner, "Web Policies That Work," *Currents*, October 1995, 36.
4. P.A. Glotzbach, Presentation to the board of trustees of the University of Redlands, Redlands, California, February 8, 1997.

PART I

Development

CHAPTER 1

Overview of Development Practice

William W. Tromble

First, it seems desirable to take a broad look at advancement through the wide lens of personal experience, then a more focused look at the slightly more narrow concept of development.

Most of what is written in books about what is commonly called advancement or development is about fund raising, for example, Seymour's *Designs for Fund Raising* (1966, rev. 1988),[1] Panas' *Mega Gifts* (1984),[2] Fisher and Quehl's *The President and Fund Raising* (1989),[3] Rosso's *Achieving Excellence in Fund Raising* (1991),[4] Worth's *Educational Fund Raising* (1993),[5] Mixer's *Principles of Professional Fund Raising* (1993),[6] and Shaw and Taylor's *Reinventing Fundraising* (1995).[7] This book too is concerned with fund raising, but it also covers the two other related areas of advancement, namely, alumni affairs and public relations.

Twenty years ago A. Westley Rowland, who was then at the State University of New York at Buffalo, with the help of 36 other writers, edited a major publication on advancement. Under the watchful eye of the late Virginia Carter Smith of the Council for Advancement and Support of Education (CASE), he put together a volume titled *Handbook of Institutional Advancement*, a practical guide (1978, rev. 1986)[8] that has served the profession well. It was written for college and university personnel in development, alumni relations, public relations, and executive management. This book follows in that tradition with one significant addition. It includes a section on technology in advancement, and because technology is such a compelling factor in all areas of advancement, we have chosen to put it first in the succession of writings.

Si Seymour (Harold J.), 1894–1968, is often cited as the one to whom contemporary advancement people owe a debt of pride for his pioneering efforts in fund raising and friend raising. His earlier book, *Design for Giving* (1947),[9] is a valued treatise on American generosity in the war years and his 1966 volume,

Designs for Fund Raising,[10] is a benchmark work on the importance of personal relationships in fund raising activity. During his very active career at Harvard, he held to the idea that prospective donors respond best to heroic causes, causes that improve humanity and make a better world for all. Panas includes information about Seymour's writings in his *Official Fund Raising Almanac* (1989).[11]

Development is largely a product of the twentieth century, but it was going on much before then. In the formative years of our country, institutions depended on the generosity of wealthy individuals and churches. Many did not survive. Three hundred years later the business of encouraging generosity continues and the skills of solicitation have been refined and professionalized. In 1997, nearly 18,000 salaried fundraisers have joined the National Society of Fund Raising Executives (NSFRE). Early campaigns, like the often cited Harvard campaign in the late nineteenth century and the Yale fund drive by alumni for their alma mater, were launched for much the same reason campaigns are begun in modern times, for capital expansion and for student financial assistance. Fund raising efforts were largely volunteer driven, but guided by staff of the institution.

For nearly three-fourths of a century, two organizations worked side by side to accomplish financial and political goals. Each had its own agenda, but more frequently than not they both had the same function, SERVICE AND COMMUNICATION. They were the American Alumni Council and the American College Public Relations Association, and they merged in 1974 to become CASE. Now, for the past 25 years, CASE has provided leadership in all areas of college and university advancement.

The NSFRE, founded in 1963, meets the need for advancement officers in a wide variety of organizations, including youth groups, religious groups, and social service groups. NSFRE pioneered the certification of development officers.

The Association for Healthcare Philanthropy (AHP) is celebrating its thirtieth anniversary, 1967–1997. It too, like CASE and NSFRE, offers professional development. It is the leading professional association for the advancement of health care philanthropy in America. AHP is the only organization dedicated entirely to the support of hospitals.

The Public Relations Society of America (PRSA) is an important and valuable professional organization for public relations people, no matter what group they are affiliated with. It began 50 years ago in 1947 and continues to provide professional help and direction for those who chose public relations, publications, media relations, information and communications, or marketing as a career.

All of these organizations exist for the support of the advancement professionals they represent. This book would not be possible without the thinking and research reflected in many worthy publications produced by these organizations such as CASE *Currents,*[12] NSFRE's *Advancing Philanthropy,*[13] AHP's *Journal,*[14] and other periodicals like *The Non-Profit Times*,[15] *The Chronicle of Philanthropy*,[16] *Contributions,*[17] and *Fund Raising Management.*[18]

This book is not about philanthropy, although it is related to it. Philanthropy is giving. This book is about getting, but it is far more than that. It is about building those relationships that must be in place before a gift can be given or received.

In the original meaning of the term, and in the purest sense, philanthropy is the act of giving simply out of love for humankind. Fisher and Quehl draw a rather sharp line between philanthropy and charity when they say the former springs from a deeper and far-reaching desire to improve human existence. The latter is local, immediate, and need-based.[19] Be that as it may, this book is an attempt to review the other side of the question, namely, all those principles, ideas, activities, and programs that assist in securing financial, social, and political support for the institution or organization.

The state of advancement in American institutions is dynamic, changing, growing, and becoming more and more important to their economic stability. The cost of living is steadily increasing, and that includes consumer goods, real estate, and certainly health care and education. Colleges and universities have increased tuition and fees to a point where students are routinely paying on average $10,000 to $20,000 a year for education. For those institutions whose budgets are primarily tuition driven, fund raising and its related units are a vital piece of the revenue picture.

The annual fund, which for decades has been the continuing line of contingency for enhancing academic programs, a fund to be used by the president wherever the need is greatest, is now being invaded to help fund administrative needs. Lucky indeed are those schools that have large endowments, but unlucky are those forced to restructure or downsize to balance shortfalls in operating budgets. A progressive, healthy, and growing annual fund over the long-term remains the economic life blood of the organization.

Capital campaigns are still big business, and without doubt have contributed to the 7.3 percent increase in giving to charitable institutions in the United States in 1996 over 1995. Americans gave $150.7 billion in 1996.[20]

Marketing is becoming more important, especially to colleges and universities, but also to other nonprofits. Competition for students is fierce because of rising costs of tuition and fees, board and room. As schools become more and more tuition driven, the marketing piece takes on a new dimension, and in that connection media relations, printed materials, admissions, public relations, and the Internet Web page are crucial to enrollment management.

Planned giving is getting more attention by development officers. It is no longer a nice thing to have if you have the time and expertise to manage it. It is imperative to have a planned giving program. The great potential it holds for future revenue is awesome. Planned giving and major gifts are often merged into one position and experts, such as attorneys and financial planners, are hired to manage the program.

Management is becoming more important as the profession matures, according to James L. Fisher, former president of CASE.[21] Much has been written about ideas, activities, programs, principles, and practice, but little about management and leadership. Advancement professionals see themselves as successful and knowledgeable, not realizing, perhaps, that others may perceive them differently. Each through his or her own eyes sees things in a different light. We should take a deep breath, step back, and try to look at ourselves through a systematic and factual set of evaluative criteria designed by representative members of the profession across the nation. We should do our own internal audit before the official auditor arrives.

External audits are good but are limited by the life experiences and associations of the parties who conduct the audit. Their views may not take into account the unique attributes and characteristics of the particular institution. The danger, of course, of internal audit is the tendency to overlook shortcomings, or be so used to them we do not recognize them. Nevertheless, it is a healthy thing to do periodic internal audits based on predetermined guidelines and criteria.

In the early 1980s the Council for Advancement and Support of Education compiled a set of evaluative criteria for measuring the performance of advancement personnel.[22] Warren Heeman served as editor. The criteria were endorsed by CASE in 1984 and published in the following year. Although there are slightly different criteria for each functional area of advancement, the essence of it all is still valid today. Evaluation criteria for measuring advancement performance are as follows:

1. There should be written goals, objectives, plans of action, assessment methods, and persons responsible.
2. Directors should have the respect of those who work for them.
3. There should be a formal procedure for staff evaluation.
4. Advancement programs must be effective.
5. Progress should be measurable.
6. The work of the departments should relate positively to the institution's goals and mission.
7. There should be written policies and procedures, and they should be adhered to.
8. Job descriptions should be clear.
9. The budget should be well thought out and drive the action.
10. Gift transactions should be audited yearly.
11. Advancement priorities should be established and follow institutional priorities.

12. Realistic timelines should be established and adhered to by directors.
13. Staff should have adequate preparation for tasks required.

As has been mentioned, technology is playing a major role in performance. It is changing the way we do business, in fact, and we have seen only the tip of the iceberg. The virtual university and cyber solicitation are a reality, even as this writing is being completed. E-mail is a preferred means of communication for many. The Internet is expanding its linkage to thousands of new sites. Access is taken for granted, and yet we lose sight of the fact that many people do not have computers, and some claim not to want them. Delaware and other states are making computer literacy and Internet access a priority for elementary and secondary classrooms.

Institutional foundations deserve more attention than they have received in past writings. This book includes a full chapter dedicated to the subject. They play an important stewardship role as well as a fund raising role in many colleges and universities, and in a number of hospitals. Some presidents still are opposed to them largely on the grounds that foundation boards are too independent, but this is a selfish thing. Presidents want to control the foundations, and foundations are committed to being objective, detached, and independent stewards of charitable gift monies. In some states university foundations can do some things universities cannot, such as hold property.

The situation is somewhat similar to the relationship that exists between some alumni associations and the alma mater. Quite a number of situations exist in which the alumni associations are incorporated and independent with their own checkbook, as it were, collecting alumni dues and giving back to the college or university as they see fit. In some cases there has been a falling out between the university administration and the alumni leadership and it has been difficult for both the association and the university, but for the most part the relationship has been cordial and the generosity to the university has been outstanding. "Presidents are hired guns," as Bob Forman, former executive director of the University of Michigan Alumni Association, has said many times. Bob is always tongue-in-cheek when he talks about university presidents, and they highly respect him, but there is a "byte" of truth, to use computer terminology, in the notion that presidents sometimes want to control associations or foundations. The reverse is also true.

Alumni associations and institutional foundations sometimes want to hold the university hostage, which may not be in the best interest of the institution. In every case, it comes back to personality. People react to people. If the principal players enjoy a cordial relationship, the organizations are likely to reflect it. Associations, boards, and institutions are made up of people, people with ideas, people with egos, and people with big hearts.

Technology is becoming a dominant force in institutional advancement. Prospect research and management are made easier by the use of computer software. Gift processing is now done almost entirely by electronic means. The days of the index card file are gone. Less and less hard copy is being kept. Information and statistical data are entered into computers and retrieved as needed. Advancement officers are linked to the mainframe. Their computers are being upgraded to an enormous capacity. Hundreds of colleges, universities, hospitals, and other nonprofits now have a Web page on the Internet, and almost all advancement personnel are computer literate. It just comes with the territory. It is part of the necessary job skills.

This book is one of the first of its kind to include a section on technology in advancement. In the beginning years of the next century and beyond, technology is going to play a giant role in the way fund raisers, public relations people, and alumni personnel manage their programs.

Two major functions of institutional advancement are SERVICE and COMMUNICATION, especially in alumni relations, and especially as college presidents follow the current trend to seek greater funding from alumni. Like it or not, with downsizing and restructuring, colleges and universities are at the end of their ropes, so to speak. With rising fees for tuition, board and room, laboratory usage, airway science flight training, nursing, and a host of other programs, they are looking toward alumni for help. The national average for alumni giving is 14 percent. Some of the private schools enjoy a much higher percentage of participation, and in some of the state schools less than 5 percent of alumni make financial contributions to their alma mater. Word is coming from college presidents that greater efforts be made to build connections of loyalty and appreciation with alumni and link that to annual giving as well as capital campaign participation. The theory is that when people put their money into something, they value it and support it. "For where your treasure is there will your heart be also."[23]

The term "advancement" as it is currently used in connection with colleges and universities as well as other nonprofit organizations means all the programs, activities, and relationships that generate support from the several publics served by the institution. Advancement programs and activities are largely external in nature, e.g., public information, promotion, publications, marketing, alumni events, and fund raising appeals. There is, of course, a part of advancement that is internal—the contacts, communication, and contributions of faculty, staff, and students, for example, but 80 percent of the activity in the advancement division is external.

Advancement staff are concerned with everything that happens at the college or university, hospital, or other organization, because public relations, alumni affairs, and development support and assist the macroorganization. In the university setting, advancement is concerned with enrollment, management, academics, financial aid, graduate studies, student housing, and counseling. Nothing that happens at the institution is beyond the interest and influence of the advancement division. Strategic planning, institutional research, plant and facilities management, intercollegiate sports, and intramural sports benefit from fund raising efforts, alumni support, and good media relations. In the greater circle of institutional mission and vision, goals, and objectives, the several departments of institutional advancement serve to support and strengthen the institution as a whole and make it more competitive, which is precisely why public relations, development, and alumni affairs are highly valued by chief executive officers (CEOs), chancellors, and presidents alike. Their value and importance become greater in state institutions as federal and state support declines or becomes more regulatory. Often, in fact, government relations and legislative action are a part of the advancement division.

Advancement symbolizes a forward motion. The image it leaves in the minds of constituents and publics is one of action, progress, and productivity. Advancement is never static, always dynamic.

For years the term most commonly used was "development," and it serves well as a politically correct euphemism for fund raising, but for those who want the title to reflect the inclusion of other external functions such as alumni affairs and public relations, "advancement" is preferred.

The several functions within the advancement division include

- Fund raising and Friend raising
- Cultivation and Solicitation
- Prospect research and Donor relations
- Gift processing and Acknowledgment
- Donor relations
- Recordkeeping and Gift reporting
- Stewardship
- Alumni relations
- Public relations
- Publications
- Media relations
- External affairs/Community relations
- Information
- Communication

As the world brings closure to the twentieth century and prepares to cross the line into the new millennium, advancement professionals look back with pride on the accomplishments of the last 50 years and before; take a long hard look at present practice, threats, and opportunities; and begin to help position the institutions they serve for the competitive changes of the future.

This book is intended to address some of the issues and options advancement people are facing. Fund raising principles remain the same, but methods and techniques are changing as the book goes to press. If there is one fact of life everyone realizes, sooner or later, it is that revision and change are continuous. Nothing in the world remains unchanged for long. So, for those in the profession who raise money, for those who serve alumni, and those who deal with the media and handle publications and provide information to the public, the book will be an addition to the many fine volumes previously written on the subject. It is not intended to be a "how-to" manual. It is a statement of philosophy and current practice, a review of trends and professional thinking with respect to institutional advancement.

This book is intended to reach beyond colleges and universities to include hospitals, and a plethora of nonprofit agencies and organizations that regularly seek funding, serve alumni or previous clients, and are sensitive to public perceptions and opinions. In 1995 there were 1,136,564 nonprofit organizations in the United States, according to *Giving USA 1996*,[24] 599,745 of which were charitable gift-receiving 501(c)(3) organizations. Total giving in 1995 was $143.85 billion, 10.78 percent above 1994, and 7.75 percent above inflation.

The book reaches beyond fund raising to include the other essential parts of advancement. It might well have been a review and an exposition of fund raising philosophy and practice. Aside from Rowland's book, *Handbook of Institutional Advancement*, 2nd ed., most of the books on the subject focus on educational or nonprofit fund raising, but fund raising itself is only one part of institutional advancement. It could have been a collection of monographs on topics related to advancement, but the editor, in communication with others of the profession, felt the time is right for the publication of a book that links and integrates the three main functions of institutional advancement and presents them as vital units of institutional advancement.

Institutional advancement as a profession with several career tracks has come of age in the last half of the twentieth century. Granted there were fund raising efforts by Wesley and Whitefield, the men and women of Harvard, and the alumni of Yale and Princeton. There were news releases and publications. There were advocates and philanthropists and marketing campaigns, but the logical linking of these functions by one concept, institutional advancement, came to fruition during the last 50 years. One of the pioneers of the profession, Si Seymour, mentioned above, was on staff at Harvard in 1919 assisting in Harvard's endowment fund campaign. His book *Designs for Fund Raising* (1966) was revised in 1988, and his *Elements of Fund Raising* was revised in 1989. Exhibit 1–1 lists a few milestones in institutional advancement.

In his first book (1978), Rowland said, "Our colleges and universities must rebuild the public confidence in higher education and its value in the life of an individual and society."[25] Today, nearly 20 years later, the same is true. If not

Exhibit 1–1 Chronology of Events in Institutional Advancement

- American Association of Fund Raising Council, formed 1935
- National War Fund, 1947
- Public Relations Society of America, 1947
- National Society of Fund Raising Executives, 1963
- The United Fund became The United Way, 1964
- National Association of Hospital Development, 1967 (Now The Association of Hospital Philanthropy, c. 1993)
- The Fund Raising School, 1973
- American Alumni Council (1913) and the American College Public Relations Association (1917) merged to become The Council for the Advancement and Support of Education, 1974
- North American YMCA Development Officers, 1981
- Center for the Study of Philanthropy, 1986
- First National Philanthropy Day, 1986
- Indiana University Center on Philanthropy, 1987
- Chronicle of Philanthropy, 1988
- American Prospect Research Association, 1988

addressed, this lack of confidence will have a significant effect on the nation, elementary and secondary schools, citizens who compete on the world market with other scientists, business managers, teachers, lawyers, and other professionals. In the end, the survival of America, as we know it, depends on our educational system. Knowledge is power. Wisdom is the way it is used.

Computer technology began to develop in the early 1960s. "Harvard and M.I.T. each claim credit for having originated computers," according to Christopher Rand.[26] "Mechanical brains" they were called by some. Now in Harvard's 2.1 billion dollar campaign, the largest in the history of higher education, and America's first-ever mega campaign of that size, technology plays a major role.[27] Technology in most of its many applications, however, is frightening to many people. When Garry Kasparov, world champion chess player, was defeated by IBM's computer, Deep Blue, May 11, 1997, he was humiliated. The *Los Angeles Times* quoted him as saying, "I'm a human being. When I see something that is well beyond my understanding, I'm afraid." It did provide an opportunity for man to acknowledge one of the unspoken "terrors of life at the dawn of the 21st century: technology."[28]

Philanthropy seems to be changing faces. The question arises, is it philanthropy or investment? Many of the gifts and grants are not classical philanthropic gestures. When a donor makes a contribution to an organization or institution, is it philanthropy or quid pro quo? One gets the feeling that philanthropy in the style of the Rockefellers and Vanderbilts has given way to a less noble, more selfish motivation.

Philanthropy is giving for the love of mankind. It is voluntary, without strings attached. It embodies the universal qualities of truth and beauty, the benevolence and trust, the honor and respect people around the world are seeking. Investment, on the other hand, is a provisional preparation for use that is presumed to generate proscribed returns for the benefit of the donor. "Philanthropy" is a noble term with lofty connotation, and fund raising plays a significant role in it, but too often governing boards, CEOs, and presidents regard fund raising and the development officer as a mundane necessity to get more money for this or that project. Development officers are somewhat to blame with their incessant appeals to donors to "make an investment" in the project of the moment. Intelligent people know that investors who make investments expect investment returns. The underlying appeal of the pitch is the dividends the donor will receive. Under many circumstances this strategy is appropriate and effective. Donors in the 1990s and beyond tend to be motivated by what they get back, rather than by what they can give for mankind. Modern development staff persons will be inclined to use this strategy more and more in the future than in the past. With corporations in particular, charity begins at home, but the same can be said of individual donors who give to causes and organizations that directly or indirectly benefit the donor.[29]

Philanthropy, according to Jon Van Til, stands at the confluence of four major institutional sets in society:

- business, from which it draws money
- government, which permits it to exempt its donations from taxation
- nonprofit organizations, which draw support from its donations
- families, who forgo the chance to spend the gifts on their own individual needs

The true test of responsible philanthropy, put by Charles E. Gilbert and cited by Van Til, is reflected in these terms:[30]

- responsive to need
- flexible
- consistent
- stable
- leading
- candid
- competitive
- efficient
- prudent
- accountable
- follows due process
- compassionate

Some donors prefer to remain anonymous, and for various reasons. Their wish to give anonymously is respected and is appropriate, but only when the contribution is to a recognized charity for disbursement. Secret foundations may not be right for democracy. They frequently are self-serving, unethical operations, laundering money from questionable sources. As for shy millionaires, let them put their charitable dollars into a community foundation and ask the foundation to screen requests and disperse the fund according to their wishes, openly, fairly, and responsibly.

Among development professionals it is no secret that donors who wish to remain anonymous are seeking to hide something. It may be self-serving or, worse yet, unethical. It frequently turns out to be a way of shielding them from bothersome solicitors who might hound them for contributions.

Philanthropy, however, is still a wonderful part of human nature, and development staff need to continually sharpen their skills to promote it. Professional staff development is not only encouraged, but in some cases mandated by employers. With so many new people coming into the field of institutional advancement, there is a real need for professional growth. Colleges and universities in the United States and Canada employ approximately 9,000 full-time development officers. There are over 7,500 public relations people and 4,500 alumni staff persons listed in the 1996 CASE directory. Add to that approximately 9,000 members of NSFRE who are not in colleges or universities, plus the more than 3,000 development people in hospitals not counted in the above numbers and the number of professional staff engaged in advancement activities is 33,000—and that number is a conservative estimate. There are many turnovers, newcomers, burnouts, and simply good people who enter the profession and leave it for personal and other reasons. The influx of new advancement people is driven, no doubt, by money, namely, good salaries, but also because the demand for those who raise money is increasing. Since the late 1940s a whole new line of jobs has opened up. In the larger institutions there are now positions for prospect research, donor relations, prospect management, annual fund, major gifts, planned giving, alumni programs, special events, class reunions, staff writers, grants writers, computer technicians, advancement communications, publications, and media relations to name a few. Almost every organization or institution has at least one development officer.

In the future there will be more advancement people, and for one main reason. Advancement staff are the strategists and the practitioners, the fund raisers, the publicists, the image builders, and the connectors. Competition for services and support is the American way. Customers are turning up the heat, as it were. If they are treated poorly or unfairly, if they are treated with apathy or neglect, or if they are unsatisfied and unfulfilled, customers will back away and go elsewhere. Prospective students are customers, and they will back off quickly if someone treats them rudely or is insensitive to their needs. Their young lives are going by fast. They do not have time for a bad experience; education is becoming too costly. They are particularly good at shopping around to find what they want, and the same is true of clients of nonprofit organizations and of hospital patients. So, customer relations will be a big item in the first part of the twenty-first century.

When one looks into the crystal ball for the future of institutional advancement, several things stand out: (1) the need for competency in all areas of technology, (2) the need for increased private sector funding, (3) the need for better education across the spectrum of human intelligence, from preschool and kindergarten to old age, and (4) the need for better client/customer relations. Strategic long-range planning, facilities management, time management, and money management are rising in importance.

Institutional advancement, even as this writing goes to press, is playing an increasingly important role in the survival and progress of thousands of institutions and organizations across the country and around the world. The support groups, many having been around for decades, are becoming potent advocates for advancement, including CASE, which is soon to enjoy its silver anniversary, NSFRE and AHP, over 30 years old, and PRSA, now celebrating its fiftieth year. Institutional advancement as we know it today is approximately 50 years old, still fairly new, and it has great potential for future growth and expansion.

HISTORY AND BACKGROUND OF DEVELOPMENT

The history of development in American nonprofit institutions, including schools, colleges, universities, hospitals, and a host of other charitable organizations such as Girl Scouts, United Way, museums, and orchestras, is the history of fund raising. Other terms are sometimes used euphemistically to describe systematic efforts to attract financial support. "Advancement," "external affairs," and "public affairs" are often used, but "development" is by far the most common term for fund raising. There are subtle differences. Advancement implies gaining ground, "forward movement" on all fronts, and is used to reflect activity in media relations, marketing, and promotion as well as alumni programs and activities and fund raising. External relations places the emphasis on building goodwill and friendly relationships with outside organizations, friends, and alumni. Development is more than fund raising, but fund raising is certainly a large part of it.

Although philanthropy has existed for centuries, fund raising is a fairly recent activity. In the Middle East around the time of Christ, giving alms to the poor was thought to be noble and kind. Some would call it charity, and it still exists today in that same form. True philanthropy, others would argue, is giving of one's self and one's means for the benefit of society, and they would cite the generosity of many well-known philanthropists of the nineteenth century, Cornelius Vanderbilt, John D. Rockefeller, James Smithson, and others whose substantial gifts established museums, schools, and benevolent foundations to improve the quality of life for humankind. Fund raising, on the other hand, is the act of persuading others to make financial contributions for a cause or to an institution. Fund raisers are third parties in the transaction. They are not the beneficiary of the generosity they seek. They ask not for themselves but for the cause of the organization. Interestingly, fund raising as we know it today is largely a product of American entrepreneurship, and in modern times, the twentieth century to be exact, fund raising and fund raising management have grown to gargantuan proportions. Billion-dollar capital campaigns are not uncommon. Many colleges, universities, and nonprofit organizations are currently engaged in major fund raising campaigns. Following the recent national elections, multimillion dollar fund raising efforts have come to light, which is nothing new. Politicians have been doing it for as long as we can remember. Religious groups and health-related groups are also well experienced in asking for donations.

What is rather unusual, however, is the lack of degree programs in fund raising management. There are over 30 institutions that offer coursework in fund raising or non-profit management. Until recently, degree programs were nonexistent in colleges and universities. Today there are over 16,000 members of CASE, all of whom are involved one way or another in fund raising, 18,000 members of NSFRE, most of whom are development directors, and 2,500 members of AHP, many of whom are foundation directors, annual fund, major and planned giving specialists. The truth be known, most of the development vice-presidents and directors became fund raisers by default. They were, perhaps, education or English or business majors in college. Some have master's degrees in public administration or some other discipline, and some have PhDs (see Table 1–1).[31]

Thanks to organizations such as CASE and NSFRE, thousands of newcomers to development have acquired the knowledge and learned the skills of fund raising through conferences, seminars, workshops, clinics, and best of all through networking with more experienced colleagues. The national office of CASE in Washington, D.C., offers a number of conferences and seminars designed to prepare newcomers and update seasoned professionals in the practice of fund raising. NSFRE, headquartered in Alexandria, Virginia, in addition to conferences and seminars, offers its members professional certification upon completion of a rigorous four-hour examination. The Center on Philanthropy at Indiana University offers a fund raising curriculum leading to a master's degree in philanthropic studies, and Indiana University-Purdue University's Fund Raising School offers a certificate in fund raising management.

The current state of the profession is vigorous and healthy. More and more individuals are choosing fund raising as a career, and the time-honored principles

Table 1–1 Some Advancement Programs in Colleges and Universities

College or University	Degree	Program
Case Western Reserve University	Certificate and Masters	Nonprofit Management
George Washington University	Certificate	Fund Raising Specialist
Indiana University Center on Philanthropy	Masters	Philanthropic Studies
Indiana University and Purdue University at Indianapolis	Certificate	Fund Raising Management
New York University	Certificate	Book and Magazine Publishing
St. Mary's University	Masters	Philanthropy/Development
UCLA	Certificate	Fund Raising and Public Relations
Union Institute	PhD	Philanthropy/Leadership
University of Chicago	Certificate	Management/Institutional Advancement
University of San Francisco	Certificate	Development and Nonprofit Management
University of Texas—Austin	Certificate	Fund Raising Management
University of Washington	Certificate	Fund Raising Management
Vanderbilt University	Masters	Higher Education/Advancement
York University	Certificate	Nonprofit Management

Source: Reprinted with permission from *Currents*, pp. 20–21, © 1996, Council for Advancement and Support of Education.

that have guided fund raising practice for well over a century are still in place today:

- Identify the potential donor.
- Get to know the prospect.
- Get the prospect interested in your institution or cause.
- Involve the prospect in your cause.
- Ask for the gift.
- Follow up, bring closure.

It all seems so simple, and it is, although there are many steps along the way and many considerations, such as the amount of the ask, the person to make the ask, the time to make the ask, and best strategic means of closure. All things considered, it all comes down to people interacting with people, and it is often a matter of how you treat people, and how well you gain their respect. The modern fund raising professional would do well to study the psychology of adult personality.

In summary, the history of philanthropy goes back 4,000 years and more, but professional fund raising is fairly recent. Development offices staffed with professional solicitors are a product of the twentieth century. Present-day cause and institution-related fund raising is an outgrowth of the alumni movement at Harvard, Yale, and other colleges in the nineteenth century, when alumni rallied for the purpose of saving the institution, and thousands of dollars were raised for alma mater. In the 1920s college presidents and their assistants sought funding openly and aggressively. Development officers were employed by a number of colleges in the 1950s and 1960s, but it was not until the 1970s and 1980s that professional fund raisers became a necessity almost and were much in demand in colleges, universities, and other nonprofit institutions. Today the field is growing even larger. Approximately 61,000 fund raising professionals are employed, and over 300,000 fund raising volunteers are assisting.

It is a noble profession, not right for everyone, but rewarding for those who make it their career. If there is a downside, it is the high rate of turnover among development professionals. An average of 3 years is the length of tenure for one job. Interestingly, college presidents are moving on to other positions after an average of 5 years, which is a change from what it was a decade ago when presidents were frequently in one place for 15 or 20 years or more.

The upside for development people is salary. A decade or so ago, development directors were paid salaries in the $30,000–$40,000 range. Now it is rare for a development director to be paid less than $50,000 and more. The geographical location, of course, is a factor, as well as the size of the institution and gift-dollar potential. Interestingly, in the advancement arena, when development people are compared with public relations staff and alumni personnel, development professionals, generally speaking, are paid more than their colleagues. How true it is. Money seems to drive everything in life, even what we do and who we are.

The situational analysis of the profession today is reflected in a recent survey completed by Michael F. Piovane of Kutztown University in Pennsylvania.[32] He surveyed 77 colleges and universities to determine the state of major gifts programs in those institutions. Major gift activity is a potent measure of the strength of the development program in any institution. A total of 49 responded with relevant data. All but one had a formally structured fund raising program. Thirty-one of the respondents have had active development programs for only 6 to 15 years. Two of the schools reported development programs in existence 30 years, the longest in existence for any of the respondents. These were two research institutions. The remaining 16 colleges and universities said their development programs were from 1 to 5 years old.

Seventy-five percent of the institutions had major gifts programs. The rest did not. Most of the schools (17) were raising between $500,000 and $1 million in total annual voluntary support. Fourteen were raising $2 to $4 million per year. Five raised over $17 million annually, and seven raised less than $500,000 each year. Those raising the larger amounts had major gifts programs. Those with major gifts programs were more likely to have strategic fund raising plans. They employed more fund raising professionals. They made larger commitments of budget dollars to development. They were more likely to be sensitive to the mission, goals, and priorities of the institution. They had written development plans. They had assessment and evaluation activities.

A 1996 survey by NSFRE reveals the following statistical data with regard to salaries, gender, ethnic group, and age (Exhibit 1–2).[33]

George J. Mongon Jr., compiled the data and wrote the report for NSFRE. The survey was mailed to 2,000 members. Eight hundred sixty responded representing a 43 percent return, which is a good sample, though one might hope for more respondents. Based on all the data, Mongon concludes that the average development professional is 45 years of age and began his or her career at the age of 32, has held at least two jobs, and makes an annual salary of $46,100. Mongon sees a trend toward more women in the profession, and toward both men and women entering the profession at an earlier age. The data show clearly that the highest salaries are in the health care industry and the next highest in colleges and universities. Finally, he believes that professional fund raisers are, on the whole, highly satisfied with their careers in institutional advancement.

An honest look at the profession in the close-out years of the twentieth century leads to the understanding that the several functions of institutional advancement are performing well. In matters of personal relationships we have not moved far. The principles of conduct in the way advancement people treat clients and prospects are the same as they were when Jesus walked the earth. The Golden Rule, treating others as you would have them treat you, is still a sound principle of fund raising and public relations. The methods and procedures admittedly have changed since the days of Ben Franklin and, even more recently, Si Seymour. The changes in transportation from ground to air, the emergence of technology as a dominant controlling factor in prospect research, solicitation, and public relations—all of these and others too have changed the way we do business. The advancement professional today sees things through the eyes of contemporary experience, much the same as our forefathers did, but it is a different and more rapidly changing world. Everyone knows that. The question is, how can we best serve the present age?

The late Si Seymour, often quoted development professional of former years (d.1968), maintained that fund raising is not about money; it is about people and their needs and interests. Donors respond to causes that improve humanity, causes that move them emotionally. They will respond to a need or a problem, but not because the institution is needy or in trouble. When the opportunity to give comes

Exhibit 1–2 Salaries of Advancement Professionals

	Below $25,000	$40,000–75,000	Above $75,000
Universities	7.5%	54.4%	17.3%
Hospitals	4.2%	64.2%	29.5%
Youth Organizations	7.0%	42.1%	7.1%
Social Service	9.1%	54.5%	12.2%
Religious Organizations	11.3%	42.0%	8.0%

GENDER

Male	38.7%
Female	57.1%
No response	4.2%

ETHNIC GROUPING

Caucasian	79.1%
African American	9.2%
Native American	3.9%
Hispanic	3.4%
Asian	1.7%
Other	2.7%

Source: Reprinted with permission from G.J. Mongon Jr., *Membership Survey,* pp. 2, 13 © 1996, National Society of Fund Raising Executives.

to their attention, it is the heart that says yes, but the head that says how much. Donors make contributions for a number of reasons, but high on the list are people-related causes. For that reason, scholarships and fellowships have a strong appeal for donors, and likewise social and cultural programs.

Also high on the list is the desire to be associated with something good, something heroic, something successful. People give to winners, not losers. The poor and the needy may get a few pennies thrown into their tin cups, but the doers and the achievers are the ones who get the millions. All the world loves a winner. Our sports heroes, for example, and our screen idols get the big money. Hospitals and universities that are perceived to be in the vanguard of progress in health care and education get the mega gifts, and the more they succeed, the more political and financial support they receive.

In conclusion, the history of development—or systematic, purposeful, and planned third-party fund raising for a cause higher than one's self, as opposed to begging—is fairly recent. It is largely an American enterprise and it has grown to giant proportions as evidenced by recent billion-dollar capital campaigns. Educational programs in colleges and universities leading to a career in development have, up until now, been almost nonexistent, with the exception of The Fund Raising School, established by Henry ("Hank") A. Rosso. The school is now affiliated with the Indiana University Center on Philanthropy in Indianapolis, Indiana. Other programs are developing, and in the next decade we will see more and more academic curricula leading to certificates and diplomas in fund raising. Careers in institutional advancement are sound options for those who like people, those who are outgoing, well-organized, intelligent, and goal-oriented. The profession is vigorous and healthy, and the jobs are very rewarding. Much like nursing and the medical profession, those in advancement will always be in demand. Just as people will always need assistance as they strive for good health, people and institutions will always need assistance in maintaining good fiscal health. Money talks. It speaks to those who give and to those who get, and what it says to the prospective development officer is "Go for it. You can be successful. You can make a difference. You will be rewarded."

DEFINITION AND FUNCTION

Fund Raising and Friend Raising

Development is most often defined as fund raising by college presidents and board members, but as advancement professionals know, development is more than raising money. It is building relationships and securing political, moral, and financial support. It is growth and expansion of programs, the unfolding of plans, the building of the organization. In a very real sense, development is all of that because it facilitates the progress and evolution of the institution. Advancement people often refer to the development function as both fund raising and friend raising. Friend raising comes first, then fund raising. All things considered, however, the central and immediate purpose of the development office is fund raising.

Fund raising is asking for money. It matters not whether it be for educational purposes, welfare, recreation, social programs, political campaigns, health care, religious causes, or athletics, developing fund raising skills involves building relationships, being friendly, making friends, creating an interest, inspiring trust, and being honest. That is the friend raising part of it. Experienced development officers are often heard to say, "people give to people," and it is true. Human beings are, by and large, social animals. They interact and react naturally to other human beings. True, individuals have varying interests, likes and dislikes, and they keep those feelings and nurture them in relationships they form with other individuals. Sometimes these relationships are negative, causing them to repel and alienate other individuals. Sometimes they draw individuals together like a magnet.

On first impression, when two people meet, there is often an instantaneous attraction, neutral feeling, or repulsion, however slight it may be, and it is much easier to persuade someone to make a contribution if there is a personal dynamic that attracts, and a lot of it has to do with attitude. There are many attributes of personality that cause people to like and trust each other. Space will not permit a diversion into that realm of thinking. The point is, however, that when a fund raiser asks for the gift, there must be a degree of liking for him as a person. That is the beginning of friend raising. Without it, despite the pretty brochures and dynamite causes, the would-be fund raiser will not get far in asking for support.

Cultivation and Solicitation

The ageless principle of fund raising, stated in different ways by hundreds of fund raising experts, is IDENTIFY the prospect, CULTIVATE interest, INVOLVE the prospect in the affairs of the institution, then ASK for the gift. Friend raising comes first, of course, and when it comes time to ask, the manner of solicitation is crucial. The form it takes, the way in which it is done, the time it is done, and certainly the person who does it—all of these have a bearing on the success of the ask. The fund raiser's arc of progress moves from discovery to closure.

Prospect Identification   Cultivation   Solicitation $$$ Closure

Personal solicitation is the absolute best and most effective method of solicitation. There is something compelling about looking someone in the eye during a firm handshake and asking for the gift. The aura of sincerity and friendship leading up to the ask as the need is explained or the project is laid out creates a certain readiness. Assuming the solicitor has done his or her homework well and has learned everything possible about the prospect, built a compelling case for support, and taken into account the prospect's interests, desires, and present financial circumstance, this moment of the ask has all the potential of being a moment of favorable decision; and if it is, the follow-up is just as important. As every experienced fund raiser knows, positive closure is a most gratifying moment, but it is not over yet. After a simple thank you, a brief moment or two to get the prospect's signature on the card, or at least the promise of a letter of intent, it is wise to say a friendly goodbye and leave. Many an agreement has turned sour or lost because of "oversell," lingering on, going more into detail about the greatness of the institution or the cause, taking the prospect's time when the time is up. Fund raising is selling, and when the sale is made one should bring closure and leave, at least for that day. Later, but not too much later, the following day perhaps, a cordial thank-you note or letter is appropriate. Weeks later an invitation to a special event is sent, and the friendship continues. Donor cultivation and solicitation is a continuous cycle. The process is the same as it is in the course of human existence. First there is preparation—development people call it cultivation—then there is solicitation, which is the act of asking for the gift, and then there is follow-up, which is the acknowledgment of the gift, the expression of gratitude, and the report to the donor about how the gift was used. It is the *arsis*, *ictus*, *thesis* of early Greek poetry, the ascending unaccented syllable (*arsis*) of a metrical foot, the beat (*ictus*) or accented syllable, followed by the descending unaccented syllable (*thesis*).

Prospect Research and Management

One solicitation follows another, and each is preceded by donor research. In many development offices there are one or more persons who look for and record as much information about a prospective donor as possible. The more the fund raiser knows about the prospect, the better the chance to make the sale. The research officer wants to know what the prospect's interests are, what his or her financial condition is, what the prospect likes and dislikes. No bit of information is ignored. Finally, a confidential profile is developed and made available to the professional fund raiser. If some donors knew the depth of information institutions have about them, they would be amazed, but they need not be concerned. Development people are highly ethical and, as is the case with counselors and their clients or doctors and their patients, development officers will not disclose confidential information. They live by a strict code of ethics, and those who violate it are not welcome in the profession.

The Case for Support

Whether for a large capital campaign or a small project, the "case for support" is the most important piece in fund raising strategy. It establishes institutional needs and merit. It brings out the facts and makes the point. It draws the prospect's interest. It is persuasive and compelling. When presented correctly, the case for support leaves no doubt in the prospect's mind about what the organization is, who the executives are, what the campaign or project is all about, or what it will cost to complete the campaign or project. All of this can be verbalized and frequently is verbalized in the course of the fund raising cycle.

In most cases, however, it should be a written document, a brochure, booklet, pamphlet, even a letter. There is something about the printed word that is authoritative and believable, but more than that the message remains consistent. Each time it is read, the content and use of language are the same. In addition, the written document often includes pictures and graphs that spring to life much more realistically for the prospect as they are visualized. Seeing is believing. Words are so ethereal and passing, here for a moment as the sound waves play upon the ear, then gone quickly, leaving only the silence of one's thoughts in their wake.

The case statement is the logical compelling rationale for the campaign. It very well could be 25 or more pages long with four-color separation, onion skin overlays, and gilt-edged pages. It could also be a single-page, typed statement. Experience and observation have shown that the length of the case statement is in proportion to the size and complexity of the fund raising effort. As a general rule, advancement professionals would argue for brevity. The prospect's time is limited. Initially, there may be little or no interest in what is being proposed, and a lengthy dissertation about the institution's philosophy, mission, and vision, and long drawn out details about the campaign will not capture the donor's attention. The rule of thumb is to make it as long as it needs to be to send the desired message. It should be concise, accurate, on target, and above all easily read. Institutional jargon, the pompous claims for greatness, and endless back patting should be left for some other marketing piece. The document should be clear, written to inform in a style that is calculated to persuade. The case statement is not the place to be cerebral, entertaining, or provocative.

Ideally, the case statement should be directed toward a particular market segment, for example, alumni, parents, civic and business leaders, friends of the library, or sports fans. Each of them would need to be approached in a way that speaks to their interests, their needs, their hopes and dreams, because much of the persuasive power of the case statement is in promising to meet the needs and address the interests of the prospective donors.

Realistically, with capital campaigns, especially the comprehensive multimillion dollar campaigns "for excellence," the case statement has to be a rather broad, one-size-fits-all kind of document. Many institutions have been successful with this style of case statement. There are nearly 3,000 colleges and universities in the United States that belong to the CASE, not to mention the thousands of hospitals and other nonprofit institutions, and many of them at one time or another have launched large comprehensive campaigns.

The case for support used in these larger campaigns usually contains information about the organization's mission and vision, information about its history and background, about its recent achievements, its financial stability and strength. People go with winners, but quickly back away from losers. Prospective donors are not motivated to give because organizations are poor and needy. They will give to meet a need if the cause is of interest to them, so there is a world of difference between being needy and having a need.

Usually there is a problem that should be addressed, such as inadequate space, for example, that gives rise to the need for a new or expanded facility. In reading about the problem—some would prefer to call it a challenge—the donor wants to know quickly and clearly what the problem is, and furthermore what will fix it. A good case statement, of course, will enlarge on that to include circumstances that affect the problem, such as enrollment factors or client/customer relationships. There should be an explanation of how the problem came to be, but more important how the institution plans to cope with the problem, which leads to finding a solution to the problem. Here is where the voice of persuasion can embellish the cause, speak to the opportunity, and draw the donor's interest toward the campaign. Here is where the institution can show how the donor will benefit from a successful completion of the project.

Prospective donors must perceive benefits to themselves before they will part with a single dollar, and benefits are related to donor interests, desires, and dreams. Although purse strings are loosened when heart strings are pulled, twenty-first century donors will be less likely to contribute for philanthropic reasons than for the benefit they perceive will come to them. Some case statements boldly list the "named gift opportunities." A gift of $6.2 million, for example, may get the donor's name on the building. For a gift of $25,000, the organization may put a small brass plate engraved with the donor's name on the wall of a lounge area. Recently at a large sports arena in Philadelphia, a donor could contribute a nominal amount and have a brick installed with his or her name inscribed on it. A gift of $500 is an average amount for a brick. Organizations often make the mistake of giving a brick for too small an amount. A manufacturer in New Jersey guarantees its bricks will last 80 years, and for the privilege of having one's name before the public for 80 years, $500 is a small investment.

Some case statements suggest other benefits, such as cause-related satisfaction. How wonderful it is to be able to give to a cause in which one believes, such as education, health care, or wellness. Whatever the reward or benefit may be, the prospect of today is looking for it in the case statement, and it may be as simple as knowing that the contribution will make a difference.

Case statements miss the mark if they do not clearly point out to the donor what the contribution will accomplish. Donors apparently are united on this one thing, that their gifts will do something positive, will have an impact, will accomplish a desired goal. Frequently, long after gifts are received and acknowledged, donors will ask how their gifts were used, or how their money was spent. All donors, including corporations and foundations, are keen on knowing their gifts made something good happen.

In a seminar on "Building a Case Statement" for the National Society of Fund Raising Executives, the writer summarized the content of a good case statement as follows:

1. It introduces the organization to the prospect, tells who you are, where you have been, and where you are going; it reveals your corporate personality, your mission, and your vision.
2. It introduces the prospect to the problem, or the challenge if you wish, and tells why the campaign or fund raising appeal is necessary.
3. It proposes a solution to the problem, tells about a plan of action, the goal (or cost), the strategy for reaching a solution to the problem, ways the prospect can help and benefit, expected outcomes, and achievements.

Before moving to another topic, it may be helpful to explain what a case statement is not. First and foremost it is not a wish list. University presidents are big on wish lists. They do not call them by that name, using such terms as "needs assessments" or fund raising "objectives," but in fact they are "we need" lists. Hospital presidents and nonprofit CEOs will say "we want to get the story out," let the community know we need this and we need that. To identify these perceived needs a committee is sometimes formed, consisting of department heads and interested employees, to explore what is needed. The results are often a litany of things personnel want for their departments. Granted these "gathering" sessions are helpful. They do bring to the surface a number of unmet needs from which a consensus of priority can be drawn.

Experience tells us, however, that donors do not base their giving on institutional needs. They are inclined to see all these needs as self-serving and unproductive. Their generosity is awakened by things that pique their own interests. Therefore to be effective, case statements must focus on the needs, interests, and desires of the donor. A good case is not "our story" but rather a persuasive argument for a single cause or closely related objectives.

A good case is also built around a good marketing strategy that focuses on how the organization can meet and satisfy the donor's wants and needs. The successful institution is one that has the capacity to meet the needs of its patronizing constituencies.

In conclusion, regarding case statements, know who you are and where you are going, but write your case from the donors' perspectives, and base the case on institutional strengths, not needs.

An organization must take a long hard look at its character, its mission, what it has done, what it is trying to do, and what it is planning to do in the future. No organization or institution can be all things to all people. Inevitably there will be a special niche to fill, and until that niche is found, no real progress can be made in building a case for support.

Gift Processing, Acknowledgment, Stewardship, and Donor Recognition

Another function of the development office is gift processing, acknowledgment, stewardship, and donor recognition. When a donor makes a contribution, it is only common courtesy to acknowledge the gift and express gratitude for it. This is the first step in gift processing. Then there is recording, depositing, and allocating the gift. The process varies with each institution or organization. Figure 1–1 shows a typical gift receiving and processing flowchart.

The policy and procedure in Exhibit 1–3 is taken directly from the *Professional Manual of Policy and Procedure in Institutional Advancement* of Delaware State University.[34] Other institutions have similar fund raising policy statements.

In addition to the policy in Exhibit 1–3, there are 25 specific statements of policy and procedure. Policy No. 1, for example, deals with gift cultivation. Policy No. 5 deals with pledges. Policy No. 11 deals with gift accounts and stewardship, and Policy No. 15 deals with donor recognition. The format is usually brief and straightforward as in Exhibit 1–4. Appendixes to the *Manual* include such things as scholarship guidelines, sample forms, gift account information, and summary statements of policy concerning fund raising gift processing and donor recognition.

Donor recognition is a top priority for all advancement professionals. There is donor recognition in publications, special events, or quietly in conversation. Stewardship is the other side of gift receiving. It concerns how the gift is used or invested. Donors are very much interested in how their gifts are used and invested. Institutions of every type bring honor to themselves and build goodwill with the donor when they keep the donor informed about how the gift is being used. Donors want to know their gifts are being used for the purposes they were given. They become unhappy and cynical when they think the institution is misappropriating the funds they have contributed. Even the lack of periodic reassurance, though the gift is being used as it was intended, is cause for alarm with some donors. Many institutions have adopted a policy of writing the donor once or twice a year to express appreciation for the gifts and report how the gifts are being used. This is especially true of larger gifts, gifts in the $1,000 and above range. So, gift receiving, processing, and stewardship are an import function of institutional advancement that involves all advancement staff. Alumni need to know, especially if the donor is an alumnus(a), but even if the donor is not a graduate, alumni are always interested in knowing something about the gifts and good fortunes of their alma mater. Public relations/communications people need to be kept informed to get the news releases out and do the feature stories when desirable. Some donors wish to remain anonymous, and that is fine. Their gifts are processed just like other gifts, but their names are not disclosed. The advancement staff is bound by its code of ethics to maintain confidentiality.

The details of gift processing vary with the institution, but the days of the handwritten journal or the 3 × 5 cards in a file box are long past. As early as the late 1960s records were being computerized. Universities, YMCAs, and other institutions over the past three decades have gone through extensive and intensive

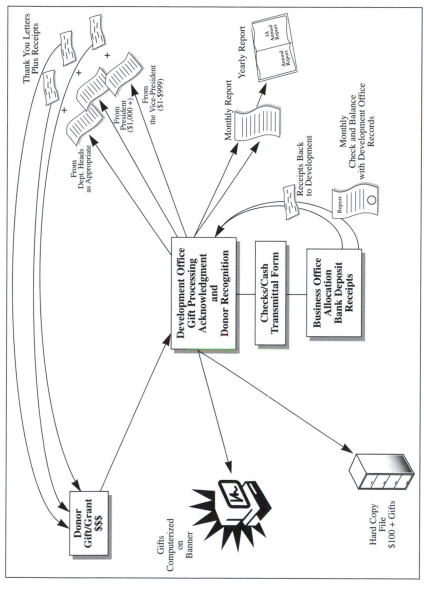

Figure 1–1 Gift Receiving and Processing Flowchart

Exhibit 1–3 Delaware State University General Policy and Procedure

---

The President of Delaware State University, as the Chief Executive Officer, is responsible for establishing policy and procedure necessary to meet the development needs of the University and for implementing action to fulfill those needs through private and public support.

By authority of the President, the Vice President for Institutional Advancement serves as the executive officer responsible for planning and coordinating all programs and activities designed to secure private-sector financial support for the University, its schools, departments, units, and programs. The Vice President works in consultation with the President and in cooperation with the other University Officers to achieve the goals of the University, but the responsibility for coordinating all fund raising activities is vested in him; and his authority in fund raising is by extension vested in the professional staff of the Division of Institutional Advancement.

Accordingly all efforts within the University to raise funds from non-governmental private sources, such as alumni, friends, parents, faculty/staff, corporations and other businesses, foundations, and other groups are approved by the Office of Development. This includes efforts for current and capital programs, research, and planned giving, whether restricted or unrestricted.

Failure to coordinate fund raising activity results in confusion, embarrassment, and duplicity of effort. Donors expect the University to determine its own priorities and make a single coordinated approach. Having several departments or individuals approach a potential donor at the same time is unacceptably non-productive. Consequently, Delaware State University has a centralized authority looking after the priorities of the University and coordinating all fund raising efforts.

In general, it is University policy that all fund raising efforts on behalf of Delaware State University or any of its units be approved and coordinated by the Office of Development. Standard procedure is that individuals connected with the University and desiring to raise funds for whatever reason will consult with the Vice President for Institutional Advancement or designated professional staff in the Office of Development to determine the appropriateness, timing, institutional priority, and potential donor interest before making the approach to a funding source.

Courtesy of Delaware State University, Dover, Delaware.

---

efforts to convert hard copy files to electronic computer files. Technology is making the whole process of recording and retrieving data and information quicker and easier. Communication via e-mail and voice-mail is fairly standard practice.

Good stewardship is taking care of gifts and grants received, making sure they are allocated as the donor has directed. Stewardship is being accountable for the

Exhibit 1–4 Policy No. 9, Memorial Gifts

Policy:

Gifts in memory of or honoring a friend or loved one are encouraged. What better way to demonstrate feelings of friendship and love than to make a gift in the name of that person so fondly remembered.

Procedure:

Memorial gifts and gifts honoring a living person are received and acknowledged by the Office of Development as follows:

1) A letter of thanks is sent to the donor.

2) A pre-printed card acknowledging the gift and naming the donor is sent to the family of the person being memorialized or to the family or agent of the person being honored.

Courtesy of Delaware State University, Dover, Delaware.

---

monies entrusted to the organization. It is looking after the details of investment and expenditures. It is important to the institution. What is more, donors expect it. In its basic form, good stewardship is keeping good books, following accepted accounting practices, being careful about investments and the use of investment returns. In a deeper sense, however, stewardship requires timely and accurate reporting. Administrative officials want to know, and have a right to know, what gifts have been received and for what purpose. Likewise, donors want to be informed. They want to know how the organization is doing, and furthermore, they really want to know how the institution is spending their gift dollars. If there is a percentage taken off the top of all gifts for administrative costs, donors and prospective donors want to know it. Ideally, nothing is taken off the top. Every dollar is allocated as the donor has directed, and operating costs are funded by the institution through its regular budget process. Most educational institutions handle it that way, and they proudly proclaim, as they approach alumni and friends for donations, that "every dime you is give is spent as you have designated." Many social service organizations have to fund operating expenses with gift dollars. They have no students from whom to collect tuition and fees. They have no financial support from the state, nor any other source of revenue, but even these organizations are expected to set prudent limits on the percentage of charitable gift dollars they use for salaries and overhead. Occasionally, a charity finds itself in difficulty because of perceived, or real, operational expenses that are out of line.

James Bennett and Thomas DiLorenzo made us all aware of certain "Unhealthy Charities" in a 1994 publication: "Americans donate money to health-related charities, like the American Lung Association, because of what they think they do, not what they really do."[35] The truth is, many of these charities, they say, are misguided and mismanaged, and he cites the 1992 United Way scandal, pointing out that top administrator, William Aramony, was accused of using funds raised for United Way to support his own lavish lifestyle.

If there would be one piece of advice concerning stewardship we could give to every development officer, it would be communicate. Keep donors and prospective donors, and the public, informed. It is just common courtesy. It is just plain good public relations (see Exhibit 1–5).

CURRENT THINKING REGARDING DEVELOPMENT

Technology

Much of the excitement now in development offices across the nation centers around advances in technology, changing attitudes and interests with respect to philanthropy, and changing means and methods of fund raising. Technology in fund raising is covered well in the Prologue of this book by Ron Stephany and Judith Tuch. It is perhaps the single most talked about element of change in development. One company in particular located in Malvern, Pennsylvania, Systems Computer Technology, is helping to reshape computer operations in hundreds of colleges, universities, nonprofits, and governmental agencies across the country. The software developed for educational institutions is called BANNER. It has several modules that work cohesively and are driven by the mainframe computer of the institution. There is a module for human relations, one for business and finance, and one for development and alumni operations, among others. The module for alumni and development includes programs for inputting and retrieving information concerning gift processing, prospect research, pledges, and campaigns. Increasingly, technology is driving the fund raising process. In the next two decades undoubtedly there will be an excess of new software programs similar to Black Baud™, Fundmaster™, and the Raiser's Edge™. Hardware will have the capability of processing many more data in a shorter length of time, and new hardware will be developed. Fund raising on the Internet and its successors will be a reality. I am reminded of a statement made to my grandfather by a neighbor one afternoon on his farm in Kansas after a long day harvesting wheat. "Abe," the neighbor said, "with this new tractor and other inventions, we have seen more changes in our short lifetime than our children will ever see." How wrong he was. Yesterday's telephone, tractor, television, or computer quickly is replaced by the products of tomorrow's technology.

Exhibit 1–5 A Donor Bill of Rights

Philanthropy is based on voluntary action for the common good. It is a tradition of giving and sharing that is primary to the quality of life. To assure that philanthropy merits the respect and trust of the general public, and that donors and prospective donors can have full confidence in the not-for-profit organizations and causes they are asked to support, we declare that all donors have these rights.

1. To be informed of the organization's mission, of the way the organization intends to use donated resources, and of its capacity to use donations effectively for their intended purposes.
2. To be informed of the identity of those serving on the organization's governing board, and to expect the board to exercise prudent judgment in its stewardship responsibilities.
3. To have access to the organization's most recent financial statements.
4. To be assured their gifts will be used for the purposes for which they were given.
5. To receive appropriate acknowledgment and recognition.
6. To be assured that information about their donations is handled with respect and with confidentiality to the extent provided by law.
7. To expect that all relationships with individuals representing organizations of interest to the donor will be professional in nature.
8. To be informed whether those seeking donations are volunteers, employees of the organization, or hired solicitors.
9. To have the opportunity for their names to be deleted from mailing lists that an organization may intend to share.
10. To feel free to ask questions when making a donation and to receive prompt, truthful, and forthright answers.

Courtesy of National Society of Fund Raising Executives, Alexandria, Virginia.

Philanthropy

Philanthropy per se for the love of man and the common good is much less a factor in development than it once was. Individual donors, corporations, and foundations of the late 1990s are giving to get something back. They are giving for a variety of reasons—recognition, personal interests, the urge to give back—but giving for the love of mankind seems not to be their first intent. More and more donors are dedicating their gifts to a particular project or cause in which they have great interest, and they are quick to ask how their gifts are being used. With all their downsizing and reengineering, corporations are asking "What's in it for us?" Accordingly, fund raisers must be increasingly sensitive to the interests of their prospects. Organizations that are pushing their needs and their wants will come up short when the donor makes a decision. What the organization needs and what the donor wants may not be the same.

With foundations, the trend is toward a more conservative posture. Foundations are reviewing priorities and changing priorities as contemporary board members find it in the foundation's best interests to do so. One foundation in Philadelphia has shifted focus from arts to health care in recent years. Several Chicago foundations have become even more localized than they were. Again, the truth is, development directors must continually research and review donor interests and approach each donor with that in mind. Development professionals must continue to do what they have always done: find out who the donor is and what the donor's interests are and attempt to match them with something the institution values as well.

Fund Raising Methods

In annual giving, the big emphasis on telefund or phonathon has reached its peak. In the 1970s and 1980s telephone solicitation was a large part of annual fund programs. At Ball State University, when I served as development director, we were raising $800,000 each year through the telefund effort, which was only a part of the $3.2 million annual giving program. Telemarketing is still widely used, but with less impact than formerly. People are getting so many phone calls asking for money that they are simply saying no and hanging up. Full-press, hard-sell, boiler-room fund raising by telephone, some of which has been misleading, has left a bad taste with the public in general. Nonprofits and educational institutions have had to be more careful in establishing a tie between the prospect and the institution immediately after the prospect picks up the receiver and says "Hello." Telemarketers often use tape-recorded messages and automatic dialing programs to get to as many prospects as possible as they try to sell credit card enrollment, home improvement products, insurance, and in some cases outright fraudulent securities. Many people are not pleased with these recorded messages. With all this increased telemarketing, the good ones get squeezed out by the bad ones. The conclusion is that fund raising by telephone is not as productive as it once was, and this has inspired renewed vigor in the use of direct mail appeals.

Direct mail, however, is also changing. With the advent of computer-generated addresses on envelopes, people are less inclined to toss the piece just because it has a printed address on front of the envelope, even if it appears on a label. Fund raisers, however, are stuffing less material in the envelopes. Prospects and donors are annoyed by direct mail appeals that have too many items enclosed, and this has come about because of the reaction to sweepstakes appeals from magazine publishers and department stores that are filled with flyers and little slips of paper. When one of these fat envelopes arrives in the mail and the prospect opens it, and 20 pieces fall out, the reaction is often to gather up the whole packet and throw it in the trash.

Development includes a number of organization-building activities, such as special events, participation in business and civic functions, and politics, but it remains essentially fund raising. It is more sophisticated and more comprehensive. It includes annual giving, major gifts, capital campaigns, matching gifts, memorial gifts, gifts-in-kind, and planned giving. It is concerned with every possible funding source, such as friends, alumni, corporations, foundations, religious groups, clubs, agencies, and other organizations. It frequently includes soliciting trustees, advisory boards, top administration, faculty, staff, parents, and students. Development staff members are often highly specialized as they pursue different career tracks in prospect research, development services, major gifts, corporate and foundation relations, annual fund, and planned giving. In larger institutions it is not uncommon to have one person responsible for donor relations, another for communications, and another for prospect management.

There is a continuing need for a long-term development strategy for annual giving, and with declining federal and state assistance, there is greater competition for gifts from the private sector. Generally speaking, gifts from individuals still make up the largest share of the statistical pie chart. Corporations give less than 5 percent of their net profits, and foundations typically have a 5 percent spend out rate on their investment returns.

Of the thousands of colleges, universities, and other nonprofits, nearly half of them are presently engaged in, or planning to conduct, short-term capital campaigns. In 1994–95 CASE made a survey of capital campaigns in progress. One hundred eighty-seven institutions responded. They reported fund raising goals ranging from $225,000 to $2.1 billion.[36] So, major gifts are a priority, and that means fund raising personnel must devote more time and energy to major gifts. Capital campaigns are just as popular with presidents and CEOs as ever, if not more so. This is true largely because these large campaigns, most of which are multimillion dollar campaigns, some at the billion-dollar level, provide the incentive and the means to revisit mission and vision, to set goals, and to make long-range strategic plans. They provide the opportunity to construct new buildings or renovate old ones. They increase endowments, acquire new equipment, enhance academic programs, and increase student financial assistance. Harvard, for example, is currently in the largest comprehensive capital campaign in the history of higher education, $2.1 billion.

Prospects are changing focus, however. Corporate donors are becoming more interested in strategic giving, that is to say giving in ways that make the most impact. They are also rather eager to show their community support. They want to be perceived as being civic-minded. It is just good business to form partnerships with educational institutions and social organizations. Much of corporate America functions in a climate of intense domestic and global competition, and the demographics of the work force and the customer are changing. Social problems are invading the workplace—divorce, child abuse, drugs, and illiteracy. Companies are concerned their business will suffer if somehow they cannot help to solve America's social problems.

Aside from the desire to be good corporate citizens, companies are, on the other hand, still very much concerned about making money, not giving it away. The current trend is toward building partnerships and encouraging cooperative efforts to solve problems. Universities, for example, are organizing corporate partners programs, enlisting the help of company employees and university faculty, in a sort of quid pro quo arrangement to share expertise and human resources to find a better way. The old axiom, two heads are better than one, is the basis of successful research and development.

During the past five years the nation has seen wholesale downsizing in many of the larger corporations, but we are also seeing a "second look" toward "right-sizing," a euphemism for hiring new and younger people to take the place of many who were let go. The irony of it is that the ones caught in the downsizing often were men and women of reasonably high salaries. Hiring new people, often more up-to-speed on technology, at lower salaries helps the cash flow and makes the company more competitive.

Actually, there are as many or more prospects as ever. They are just harder to find and cultivate. They are apprehensive and evasive. In Wilmington, Delaware, May 1997, there were a dozen or more campaigns going on, and there are 107 professional fund raisers in the local NSFRE chapter, not to mention those in the nonprofit organizations. The bottom line is, there is a lot of fund raising going on.

There is a renewed emphasis on ethics (see Exhibit 1–6), according to Dr. Steve Batson, vice president for planning and advancement at West Virginia State College. In light of the recent round of scandal in Washington, including Senator Packwood's alleged misconduct, Clinton campaign strategist Dick Morris's sexual indiscretions, the perceived inappropriate use of the Lincoln bedroom of the White House to raise money, and the United Way fiasco, Dr. Batson suggested that fund raisers and their organizations revisit ethical correctness of what we do to get the money and what we do with the money after we get it. The whole ethical question has to do with the correctness of what development officers do and the righteousness of what is done.[37]

Advancement professionals adhere to a code of ethics that places the donor's interests on a par with the organization's interests. It is imperative that fund raisers serve the interests and needs of the "stakeholders." If the institution does not agree with the donor's interests, it should not take his money. And what about the

Exhibit 1–6 Statement of Ethics

Institutional advancement professionals, by virtue of their responsibilities within the academic community, represent their colleges, universities, and schools to the larger society. They have, therefore, a special duty to exemplify the best qualities of their institutions, and to observe the highest standards of personal and professional conduct.

In so doing, they promote the merits of their institutions, and of education generally, without disparaging other institutions;

Their words and actions embody respect for truth, fairness, free inquiry, and the opinions of others;

They respect all individuals without regard to race, color, marital status, sex, sexual orientation, creed, ethnic or national identity, handicap, or age;

They uphold the professional reputation of other advancement officers, and give credit for ideas, words, or images originated by others;

They safeguard privacy rights and confidential information;

They do not grant or accept favors for personal gain, nor do they solicit or accept favors for their institutions where a higher public interest would be violated;

They avoid actual or apparent conflicts of interest and, if in doubt, seek guidance from appropriate authorities;

They follow the letter and spirit of laws and regulations affecting institutional advancement;

They observe these standards and others that apply to their professions, and actively encourage colleagues to join them in supporting the highest standards of conduct.

Courtesy of Council for Advancement and Support of Education, Washington, DC.

public interest? The public has a special interest in institutions and organizations that purport to serve the public good. State colleges and universities, for example, are frequently held up to the bright light of public scrutiny over unfair personnel and money problems.

The first order of business for all fund raisers is to be open and honest, to be clear with their employers and with prospective donors ahead of time. Mark Pastin, president of the Council of Ethical Organizations, warns against deceit and dishonesty.[38] Big donors often have big ideas about what will become of their gifts, and organizations often cover up their interests when telling the donor his interests are paramount. A large midwestern university the author once served did the right thing in the late 1980s when a big influential donor, responding to a proposal to endow a chair in a certain department, agreed to the gift but suggested that a friend of his be named to the chair. The university had someone else in mind for the chair and felt that to appoint the person suggested by the donor would compromise the position. Rather than accept the gift, with its unacceptable strings attached, the university kindly and tactfully refused a seven-figure gift.

To be ethical in situations where there is a conflict of interest, development officers must be willing to force the issue or resign. The choice is not easy. The fact is, the organization has an agenda, and the donor has an agenda. How wonderful it is when the two coincide. The primary concern of most donors is (1) where the money goes and (2) how it is spent. Organizational heads and fund raising executives should draw fine bright lines. They should have written ethical standards and adhere to them. They should be careful about those grey areas that have potential for alarm, such as commissioned fund raising, questionable appropriation of funds, and uncertainties over what is personal and what is business expense. If it smells like a skunk, it probably is a skunk. Finally, a bit of advice we can all take to heart is this. In all things be faithful to donors. Don't take the money and run! Be faithful to those that employ you, and never be uncertain or tentative about the institutions and organizations you serve.

Another item of current thinking is the need for capital, not only for new buildings and operational facilities and equipment, but also for deferred maintenance. The infrastructure of electrical distribution and water distribution in many institutions has been in place for 40 or 50 years. Underground iron pipes are rusting out, and plumbing in older buildings is hopelessly corroded and deteriorating. Buildings that were adequately wired for use in the 1960s are now inadequate for the demands of more inhabitants and new technology. The cost is high. Minor capital infusions of money in the range of $200,000 will put on a new roof or give the building a face-lift, but some real capital dollars in the range of $1 million to $10 million and more are needed to address the problem. Funders and fund raisers of the twenty-first century will need to explore new ways of securing capital funding. The old tried and true capital campaign may not be enough. Financial advisors are looking more toward such things as bond issues, higher fees, restructuring of the work force, and other means of revenue. For the construction of new buildings, financial consultants are suggesting the possibility of lease/buy agreements. Instead of a bond issue, for example, an outside firm would secure the financing, manage the construction, and build the facility, then lease it back to the institution with a payout agreement of 20 or 30 years, more or less, after which the ownership of the building would be turned over to the organization. The benefit of this arrangement is minimal upfront financial outlay with manageable yearly lease payments over time.

Competition for gift dollars is increasing. There are over a million nonprofit organizations now, which is double the number of nonprofits some years ago. There are over 3,000 colleges and universities, and 5,000 hospitals. There are 18,000 professional development people in NSFRE, 2,500 in AHP, and 16,000 in CASE. In addition, there are thousands of independent fund raisers not affiliated with any of the above. It would be safe to say there are close to one million voices out there on the streets asking for contributions, and the number is growing. It is the American way. Americans are generous people. They grow up putting money in the Salvation Army kettles at Christmas and giving to their churches and to politicians. Americans are also big credit card users. When the food is gone and the cupboard is bare, we don't eat. When the clothes wear out, we have none to wear. When the car is out of gas, we can't drive it. Oddly though, when the money runs out, we pull out our trusty credit card and get more. Americans give generously to worthy causes, institutions, and organizations, but the credit card debt we carry is staggering. There is a limit, quite honestly, to what we give and what we spend, and the competition for gift dollars will increase in the coming decades. We cannot overlook the current trend toward less government help and a shift to put more responsibility on the private sector. Charities that rely solely on gift money will have to explore alternate means of revenue to balance the budget.

In colleges and universities, alumni officers are facing greater fragmentation of loyalty. Graduates in larger schools are more loyal to their departments than to their alma mater. Class reunions are less important, and class gifts are less frequent. Young alumni are more focused on getting a job than giving money back to the university. Many are treating their brief tenure at the college or university like a revolving door. They come in, get what they want, and go back out, never having experienced the extracurricular activities, and never having developed social contacts and lasting friendships much less a deep loyalty to their alma mater.

Professional certification will be more important to advancement people in the coming years. Now that CASE, NSFRE, and AHP have joint certification agreements, members of those organizations will be urged to achieve certification. Individuals without certification will find it difficult to obtain and keep positions in fund raising and public relations.

The current buzzwords in higher education are "marketing" and "customer satisfaction," at least with college administrators. Faculty dislike the term "customer" very much. With tighter budgets and greater competition for students, however, colleges and universities are revisiting their marketing efforts. A number of institutions are writing new marketing plans. They are concerned about image-building, about enrollment management, about retention, and about recent trends in athletics for greater gender equity.

There is more emphasis on electronic media, including television and Internet than in prior years, but print media is still important. The written word is the more lasting form of communication, and it is appearing in new settings, design, and layout. Some of the college and university magazines are very attractive. Nonprofits too are producing excellent printed materials.

The big thing for the next century will be new, greater, and better use of technology. E-mail and voice mail are common forms of instant communication. Facsimile machines are in every office. Pentium™ computers and advanced Windows™ software are standard in most advancement offices. New software programs are coming on the market, especially in fund raising management, and in such variety that it is often difficult to choose. Mainframes are becoming more powerful, and the demands on personnel in computer centers is greater than ever before. The genius of Harvard and M.I.T. in the 1960s looks rather small compared to the advances in technology now on the market, particularly in hardware and software. In all of this technological explosion, as we settle into the new age of information and communication, people are still just as important as ever. Kasparov's defeat by IBM's "Deep Blue" computer is only a temporary setback for the human brain. Artificial intelligence will never displace human intelligence, and we look forward with confidence to a progressive and productive twenty-first century with better qualified and more competent advancement professionals in the institutions and organizations of our nation.

NOTES

1. H.J. Seymour, *Designs for Fund Raising*, 2nd ed. (Rockville, MD: Fund Raising Institute, 1988).
2. J. Panas, *Mega Gifts* (Chicago: Pluribus Press, 1984).
3. J.L. Fisher and G. Quehl, *The President and Fund Raising* (New York: American Council on Education, Macmillan, 1989).
4. H.A. Rosso and Associates, *Achieving Excellence in Fund Raising* (San Francisco: Jossey-Bass, 1991).
5. M.J. Worth, ed., *Educational Fund Raising* (Phoenix: American Council on Education, Oryx Press, 1993).
6. J.R. Mixer, *Principles of Professional Fund Raising* (San Francisco: Jossey-Bass, 1993).
7. S.C. Shaw and M.A. Taylor, *Reinventing Fundraising* (San Francisco: Jossey-Bass, 1995).
8. A.W. Rowland, ed., *Handbook of Institutional Advancement* (Washington, DC: Jossey-Bass, 1978).
9. H.J. Seymour, *Designs for Giving* (New York: Harper, 1947).
10. H.J. Seymour, *Designs for Fund Raising* (New York: McGraw-Hill, 1966).
11. J. Panas, *Official Fund Raising Almanac* (Chicago: Pluribus, 1989).
12. *Currents*, Council for Advancement and Support of Education, Washington, DC.
13. *Advancing Philanthropy*, National Society of Fund Raising Executives, Alexandria, VA.
14. *Journal*, Association for Healthcare Philanthropy, Falls Church, VA.
15. *The Non-Profit Times*, Cedar Knolls, NJ.

16. *The Chronicle of Philanthropy*, Washington, DC.
17. *Contributions*, Cambridge Fund Raising Associates, Medfield, MA.
18. *Fund Raising Management*, Hoke Communications, Garden City, NY.
19. Fisher and Quehl, *The President and Fund Raising*, p. 20.
20. A.E. Kaplan, ed. *Giving USA 1996*, 41st annual issue (New York: American Association of Fund Raising Counsel, Trust for Philanthropy, 1966), 28.
21. J.L. Fisher, "Forward," in *Criteria for Evaluating Advancement Programs*, ed. W. Heeman (Washington, DC: Council for Advancement and Support for Education, 1985).
22. W. Heeman, ed., *Criteria for Evaluating Advancement Programs* (Washington, DC: Council for Advancement and Support of Education, 1985).
23. *Holy Bible*, Matthew 6:21.
24. Kaplan, *Giving USA 1966*, 44.
25. Rowland, *Handbook of Institutional Advancement*, 528.
26. C. Rand, *Cambridge USA* (New York: Oxford University Press, 1964), 130.
27. M. Currie, "Inside Harvard Campus," *Advancing Philanthropy*, Winter 1995, 41–42.
28. S. Roan, "Technophobes Rejoice! Kasparov's Defeat by IBM Validates Fears," *The News Journal*, Wilmington, DE, Gannett, May 20, 1997, p. D-1.
29. J. Van Til, "Unmasking Generosity," *Non-Profit Times*, March 1997, 16–18.
30. Van Til, "Unmasking Generosity," 16–18.
31. *Currents*, Washington DC: Council for Advancement and Support of Education, June 1996, 20, 21.
32. M.F. Piovane, "Advancement Survey" (Kutztown, PA: Kutztown University, 1995).
33. *Membership Survey*, National Society of Fund Raising Executives, 1996, 2, 13.
34. W.W. Tromble, *Manual of Policy and Procedure*, unpublished document of Delaware State University, revised July 1993.
35. J. Bennett and T. DiLorenzo, *Unhealthy Charities* (New York: Basic Books, 1994), 4.
36. *CASE Report of Educational Fund Raising Campaigns, 1994–95* (Washington DC: CASE 1996), 7.
37. S.W. Batson, in his remarks to the NSFRE International Conference on Fund Raising, Dallas, TX, April 9, 1997.
38. M.J. Pastin, in his lecture on philanthropy at NSFRE International Conference on Fund Raising, Dallas, TX, April 9, 1997.

CHAPTER 2

Annual Giving

William W. Tromble

> An Annual Fund may not generate the most money.
> It may not be the most cost efficient form of fund raising.
> It will probably not provide the resources needed to
> build the newest campus cathedral. But it is the
> foundation on which the development program is built.
>
> Gary A. Evans, *Annual Giving Strategies*

Annual giving is an ancient concept. In earlier times and yet today, it is realized in tax revenues. Giving Caesar what is Caesar's has built kingdoms and burdened taxpayers for centuries. Annual giving, however, as is commonly related to institutions and organizations, means voluntary support from alumni, clients, former patients, friends, and other gift sources, year after year after year, to sustain the organization in the exercise of meeting current operational expenses and to enhance certain programs over and above operational expenses. The annual fund is not a "one-shot" drive occurring once a year. If it is, it falls short of its potential.

DEFINITION

It is a program of ongoing support that brings in gifts throughout the year, every year. It is not a major gifts program, although large gifts occasionally come through the annual fund program. It reaches out to all funding sources in an organized and timely manner. It utilizes the three main methods of solicitation: direct response mail, telemarketing, and personal visitation. The scope of its activity is determined by the budget, staff, and volunteers. It requires proper planning and implementation, as well as accurate assessment and evaluation. It requires a good system of gift receiving, acknowledgment, stewardship, and donor recognition.

The one most valuable component of the annual giving program, however, is intelligent and informed planning. Without it the program will not succeed.

What the annual fund campaign does for the institution is provide additional operating support. Pomona College calls it "funds to live by." It motivates donors to give again and again, year after year, and as they become more and more involved with the institution, they form a lifelong habit of making an "annual fund" contribution every year in addition to other contributions as opportunities arise. Often annual fund givers, at the $100 level, turn into major campaign donors later on, and it is not uncommon to find annual fund donors making substantial estate planning gifts to the institution after years of supporting at the much lower annual fund level.

For the individual donor, in an ideal annual fund campaign, the opportunity to contribute may come several times during the year, making possible a continuing benevolence for the organization throughout the year. Other funding sources are corporations, foundations, clubs, agencies, and other organizations. Special appeals are targeted to various constituent groups, such as physicians, patients, alumni, friends, parents, business, and industry.

ESSENTIAL ELEMENTS

Annual giving programs vary from institution to institution, but there are certain essential elements all have in common, such as fund raising methods like direct response mail, telemarketing, personal solicitation, and special events. The latter includes such things as concerts, dinners, car washes, dances, marches, roasts, auctions (real and silent), and just about any activity one can think of that will raise money for a cause. Methods, however, are not self-generating, and they are not run by computers. It takes people to do that, people who are dedicated to the cause, and people who know what they are doing, because it is abundantly easy to alienate donors and prospective donors by a wrong or misplaced set of words or actions.

Experienced advancement professionals have learned certain winning ways to raise funds for different purposes through years of trial and error, seminars, conferences, courses, and conversations. Newcomers will do themselves a favor by associating freely and working closely with experienced professionals, because the best way to learn fund raising techniques and methods is from hands-on experience with other fund raising mentors. Volunteers are somewhat like newcomers, though they do not get paid for their fund raising efforts. Well, actually, they do get paid, but not in silver or gold. Their pay is the joy of knowing they are making a difference for a higher cause they value. Volunteers are the drivers in many annual giving campaigns. What would advancement people do without them? It would be virtually impossible to match the depth and scope of the fund raising force of volunteers. What a joy it is to work with most of them, but what a pain in the neck some of them can be. Another book should be devoted to volunteerism.

Annual giving programs then need sound methods of fund raising, good people to raise the funds, both professionals and volunteers, and they need money, because it takes money to raise money. How often have we heard that! Any business that is undercapitalized is bound for failure, and the "Annual Fund," as it is often called, is just as much a business as health care or banking. It needs equipment and materials to process the letters and the telephone calls, the prospect research and management, the gift receiving, receipting, and acknowledgment. Printing costs alone can run into the thousands of dollars. Marketing is also costly, and there is travel and entertainment, plus all the cost-related items incurred in the so-called fund raising luncheons and dinners.

Recently at an eastern university, the income and expense sheet for the Annual Presidential Scholarship Ball revealed the event cost the university $12,500. From ticket sales and advertisements in the souvenir booklet, it took in $21,500. Had it not been for the additional corporate contributions amounting to $32,000, the event would have had only modest success. A county hospital in Delaware staged a fund raiser much like the scholarship ball, called "An Evening with the Stars," featuring the performance of a big name entertainer. The event took in $90,000, but cost the hospital $60,000, leaving $30,000 for the annual community campaign. It is even worse for the donor, because the Internal Revenue Service disallows any charitable deduction for goods or services received as a result of the gift. So, the cost of the tickets, less the food and entertainment, leaves the donor a smaller charitable gift deduction than might be desired.

The lesson often learned is that fund raisers are fun and involve many volunteers and lots of labor but they do not raise huge amounts of money. It is much easier to raise the money through outright asking for the gift. This is not to say that fund raisers are wrong or inappropriate. They do serve a social need, and they do help to create a bonding with the institution, which is valuable and important, but they are not an abundant source of gift revenue.

In past years it was fairly common to give premiums and incentives to donors, things like plaques, glassware, T-shirts, and other items of clothing, free tickets, parking, and food. Now gifts generating premiums and other incentives must be discounted by the cost of those items. It is generally understood that small items costing under $10 are exempt, but if, for example, an institution offers a $25 meal for a $100 gift, the donor's charitable contribution to the cause is only $75.

ALUMNI AND THE ANNUAL FUND

In colleges and universities a large component of annual giving is the alumni segment of the constituent population. Alumni are the first vanguard of support for college and university development. Since the eighteenth century, when alumni giving was first organized in a more or less formal structure in schools across the nation, alumni giving has increased remarkably, as is noted in Chapters 8 and 9. Fund raising as an organized, systematic, regularly recurring activity in schools of higher learning is an outgrowth of the alumni movement that began when Yale alumni organized to help alma mater around 1792. Development programs of the twentieth century are an outgrowth of the alumni movement that spread across the country. Colleges soon discovered that alumni are the best of all supporters. They have a vested interest in the schools that gave them a start. In terms of time, energy, and financial support, alumni often carry the load in annual giving programs.

Constituent Targets

In the early 1980s a trend developed to target alumni appeals to constituent groups as opposed to appeals to support the alma mater. Graduates of larger institutions were less inclined to contribute to the university and more inclined to contribute to the school or department within the university that claimed their attention while on campus. Alumni of the school of business, for example, were more loyal to that school than they were to the university. So, these segments of alumni became known as "constituent groups" and the term still holds today. In many universities degrees are given at commencement time by the colleges or schools in separate ceremonies after a short central mass university convocation.

At a Council for Advancement and Support of Education (CASE) conference in Cincinnati, November 19–21, 1980, Bob Forman, who was then executive director of the University of Michigan alumni association, and considered by some to be the "Dean of Alumni Directors" in America, stressed the importance of appealing to varying alumni interests, of showing alumni their university really cares about them, and impressing them with the idea that they are responsible for what the university is today. The best way to do that is to appeal to them through the departments in which they earned their degree.[1] Now in the closing years of the twentieth century as we face the dawn of the new millennium, alumni are still our greatest hope for support, both financially and politically—not other friends, or faculty, or even trustees, for that matter.

Trustees, Forman once said, "usually don't know the slightest thing about running the university. They come in for a meeting a couple times a year. They are chosen for their affluency or position and they serve out of some ego thrust that makes them feel important. Few of them have gone through the system as a student or served as a faculty member." And the presidents of many of our colleges and universities, according to Forman, "are hired guns." Most of them do good work, but they are not infallible. We tend to put them on a pedestal, but we shouldn't. They are just men and women who have no clearer understanding of how to run a university than many other capable individuals. Their employment tenure is based on their being well-liked.

Future Challenges

Forman predicted that by 1990, if the national debt were not curtailed, American educational institutions would face a shortfall in current funds for operational expenses. The colleges, he went on to say, that depend heavily on federal and state assistance will be forced into a survival mode, and for those who do not have a successful master plan for an annual fund campaign, the future is not bright.

His prediction has come true. The mood of the present is for less government control, less government spending on welfare and education, and greater attempts to shift the load to the private sector. Higher education is facing a radical change in the way it does business. There are challenges in enrollment management, diversity, marketing, tenure, regulatory agencies, and managing change. The current buzzwords in administrative circles are "restructuring," "reengineering," and "reinventing," and they all mean the same thing—changing the way we manage higher education. Something profound is happening here, something that has been coming slowly for a long time. Universities claim they are not a business. They are institutions rooted in tradition and longevity. They deal in matters of truth and scientific fact. Their greatest academic award and highest degree is in philosophy, the PhD. Education that is the product of higher education is highly prized by most Americans. Students pay dearly for it, so much so that the competitive market has soared. Tuition and fees in many colleges have risen one-hundredfold. This fall in 1997 at Ohio Northern University, students will pay $18,870, an increase of 161 percent from the $7,230 they paid a decade ago in 1987.[2] The same is true in other schools.

Yet in the face of rising costs, alumni and development professionals are rising to the challenge, trying to stay one step ahead of the anticipated revolution in higher education. In most cases they are called upon by their presidents to do more with less. By and large, however, they are meeting the challenge and being successful. Private giving to colleges and universities last year in 1995–96 increased 11.8 percent over the prior year, reaching $14.2 billion in support for education, according to the Council for Aid to Education.[3]

Alumni contributed more than any one single source, $3.51 billion or 29 percent. Next were friends (nonalumni), 24 percent; followed by foundations, 20 percent; and corporations, 19 percent. Religious groups contributed 2 percent and other organizations, 7 percent. The increase in gifts may have been made possible by the steady growth in the stock market, which by 1996 had not registered a major correction since the crash of October 1987. Oberlin College, a school that considers a major gift to be $50,000 or more, raised $14.2 million in Fiscal Year 1996 (FY1996), but in the first nine months of FY97 has raised $17 million. Young P. Dawkins, vice president for development and alumni relations, feels the increase is the result of paying close attention to alumni and friends who consistently make ordinary gifts, namely, annual fund gifts, not major gifts.[4]

The annual fund is basic to any development program. For that reason, advancement staff in alumni and development must place increasingly more importance on good planning, on goals and strategy, and on people, including both professional staff and lay volunteers. Too often annual fund programs tend to go off in all directions, raising money from all possible sources for all conceivable reasons, and they overextend financial and human resources. Seymour makes the point that "the function should always be defined clearly and sharply. . . . A tent that tries to cover too much ground is apt to fall down when the wind starts to blow."[5]

THEORY OF ANNUAL GIVING

The theory of annual giving is that people need to give to satisfy basic natural instincts to share with others, and furthermore, human beings are creatures of habit. Once in the habit of giving, donors tend to continue giving. We are taught to share our toys, our food, our money with others from the time we are little children. Parents often give their small children coins to drop in the Salvation Army kettles at Christmas time. As a member of the local rotary club and past president of the Fillmore New York Rotary Club, the author has volunteered to ring the bell for the past several Christmases, and it has been interesting to watch hundreds of people and their children as they approach the Salvation Army kettles with big smiles on their faces to drop their offerings in the kettle. Those who have a religious background have been taught it is better to give than to receive.

The habitual part of giving is the heart of the matter. Getting donors to give regularly year after year is the central goal of the annual fund operation. There is a strange and personal attraction that develops when an individual or an organization, but especially an individual, begins giving to a cause or an institution. The first gift is largely the result of friendly persuasion. The second is easier because the donor has already gone through the rejection analysis, ruling out why he should not give and becoming convinced a gift would be in his own interests. With the third gift, the donor begins to take on a small sense of ownership in the institution or organization, and from then on almost feels a void if a gift is not made. This is the process of habit, and that is not to say the donor would never change his mind. Actions or attitudes on the part of the institution, whether real or perceived, can quickly turn the donor around. Also, there could be a change in the donor's financial condition, such as going into retirement, losing a job, illness, or going through a divorce. All things working smoothly, however, with the continued communication and an appropriate amount of recognition, a donor once in the habit of giving annually will continue to give each year.

TWELVE COMMON TENETS IN FUND DEVELOPMENT

Whether for annual or capital campaigns, fund raisers across the nation and abroad hold these fundamental beliefs:

1. To be successful, there must be a strong commitment to the cause and an energetic pursuit of the goal by top leadership.
2. The organization of fund raising personnel must consist of like-minded people unified by a compelling interest in the cause.
3. Peer solicitation is the most effective solicitation. Prospects of wealth and social status should be approached by friends at the same level.
4. Goals stimulate action. There should be goals for every aspect of the fund raising effort, including an overall goal, a goal for each constituent part, a time line goal, a dollar goal, individual goals for each professional staff member, and a goal for each volunteer and group of volunteers.
5. Always have a backup, or "Plan B." Things may go wrong and often do. If the dollar goal proves to be unattainable, be prepared to make a midcourse correction. (1) Close the campaign and call it Phase I. Then regroup and launch Phase II. Or (2) simply extend the time line for the funding effort, perhaps another six months or a year.
6. All participants must benefit, not in financial gain, but in personal satisfaction. There has to be something in it for everyone. Every volunteer and every administrator must have a sense of ownership in the effort.
7. The effectiveness of any fund raising effort depends on a single-minded winning attitude, and the more people who catch the spirit, the greater will be the reward. It's the "get on the bandwagon" theme.
8. The more comprehensive the campaign, the more likely some aspects of it will not be fully funded. All good plans for raising big dollars for this and that are never realized, although the overall goal is achieved.
9. Fund raising efforts, like every other thing in life, must have a beginnning and an end. People become weary, even in well doing, if it drags on too long.
10. It takes money to make money. You can't go out with a Cadillac campaign if all you have to carry you is a motor scooter. The cost of fund raising is substantial, but the money raised is often far in excess of the cost.
11. The more the public perceives the rightness and goodness of the cause, the more it will respond with financial support.

12. Campaigns usually do not suffer from lack of prospective donors but rather from failure to interest and involve prospective donors in the effort.

PROSPECTS

Prospects are everywhere. Unlike looking for a four-leaf clover, they are not hard to find. Workshop leaders and seminar presenters often use the analogy of a bulls-eye, with its rings of circles, each representing target groups to shoot for. In the center is the eye of the chart representing the family, including the board of directors, top administrators, department heads, and other staff. These are the publics closest to the institution, and these are the prospective donors who should receive the first invitation to contribute. Charity begins at home, as they say. "If we don't care enough about our own institutions, how on earth can we convince others to give their support?" a wise mentor once said. The next circle might well be for alumni, or former patients, or clients. These are the first vanguard of external support for the organization. Although they are not the closest to home, they are usually the most likely to contribute. The next circle would likely be friends. They could be civic or business leaders, community citizens, volunteers, or frequent visitors to the organization for special events. These are the individuals who know the institution, either from first-hand experience or second-hand exposure. They are pretty much aware of the organization's programs and activities, successes and failures. They need more cultivation, but many of them will respond to annual fund appeals. The next circle is the community at large, which includes individuals, merchants, corporations, clubs, agencies, churches, youth groups, and other organizations. The last circle represents the masses or the universe surrounding the institution. These are the individuals and organizations who happen to be in the institution's geographical sphere of influence and outreach but have never contributed and possibly are unaware of programs and activities available.

Henry Rosso talks about the center being the core of energy that radiates out to the farthest circle like the ripple effect of a rock thrown into a pond. The big splash is the center core, and the ripple waves get weaker and weaker as the circles get larger and larger. That central core of constituents, usually comprising the governing board, the top administration, and family, also acts as a magnet, drawing support to lesser and lesser degrees from the outlying circles.[6]

Emily Pfizenmaier Henderson looks for prospects in two basic categories, internal and external sources of funding.[7] She looks first at all individuals and organizations on the inside, then those on the outside, and makes a list of names. Development officers call them "suspects," meaning we suspect they might have an interest in giving to the institution but have nothing to confirm that feeling. The suspect list goes through "triage" screening by staff and volunteers willing to assist. "Triage" is a term used in hospitals meaning a three-part approach to emergency room screening that separates the patients who are critical and need immediate attention from those who are serious, and those who are injured but are not in any life-threatening situation. Henderson likens this triage screening of suspects to separating the best prosects from the good and the good from the poor. In the world of fund raising, every individual or organization is a suspect, but only a limited number of suspects are prospects. Ed Collins, a consultant with Ketchum, Inc., for many years, and a former college president, always told his clients that suspects are those who have the ability to give, that is to say, they could give if they wanted to; and prospects are those who not only have the capability but who would give if properly cultivated and brought to closure.

In prospect research and management, once prospects are identified, there is much work involved in gathering information about them and evaluating them, or rating them, as some would say, for their ability to make a gift to the institution. Staff are eager to know everything possible about the prospect (much more is said about this in Chapter 3, Major Gifts). While that is going on, fund raising staff are busily engaged in doing things to pique the donors' interest in the organization. After gaining their interest, attempts are made to involve them in the organization by inviting them to receptions and other institutional events, and bringing them onto committees and into focus groups and other activities that will move them closer to the inner circle, thereby creating a desire to support the institution with their financial and human resources. Then plans and strategies are developed for approaching the prospect. Once that is accomplished, they are ready for final cultivation and solicitation.

In the annual fund campaign, this often lengthy process of cultivation is shortened considerably. Of course the stakes are not as high. The anticipated gifts are smaller, but there are thousands of mini-asks in the form of mail appeals, telephone solicitation, and personal visits.

With respect to annual fund prospects, the central questions are who are they and how do we get to them in the most efficient and productive way. First, they are any individuals or organizations that are felt to have an interest in the institution or cause. Some of these prospects are far more capable and willing to give than others. In the pyramid of donors so often touted by development people, these prospects make up the top 15 or 20 percent at the apex of the pyramid. These are the prospects who will give 80 to 85 percent of the annual fund goal.

The remaining prospects in lesser and lesser degrees will give less than a fifth of the goal. With that in mind, and it is rather constant in annual fund campaigns, it makes a lot of sense to spend most of the available time and resources on those with greater potential. Staff and volunteers should focus on the 15 to 20 percent, making prospects aware of the program through the media, the campaign literature, and personal visitation and telephone calls. They should make it easy for prospects to contribute by going to their places of business or their homes and picking up the checks, or putting response cards and self-addressed gift return envelopes in their hands. The rest of the prospects can and should be handled by direct response mail and telemarketing.

Annual fund prospects are employees, governing boards, management, alumni, former patients, clients, customers, friends, corporations, foundations, agencies, religious groups, parents, civic organizations, clubs, vendors, and funding consortia. All sources of funding should be catalogued, researched, evaluated, cultivated, and solicited. In the annual fund campaign, solicitation of the family, larger donors, and immediate past donors should get first consideration and the best of staff and volunteer time and energy possible, because prospects, however much potential they may have, are not donors until they respond with a pledge or contribution, and that is the number one goal of the campaign—to convert prospects into donors.

PROFESSIONAL STAFF

In annual campaigns as in capital campaigns, professional staff play an important role. They are the planners, the facilitators, the implementors, the managers, and the directors of the programs and strategies that produce the annual fund campaigns. They are to fund raising as faculty are to education, and since they are so important to this vital operation of the organization or institution, it is appropriate to consider who they are, their characteristics, their qualifications, and their personalities.

As the profession continues to grow and mature, there is a need for training, education, and certification. Most of the 1.1 million nonprofits in the United States have or would like to have fund development officers, and that includes colleges, universities, hospitals, youth groups, social services, arts, and cultural organizations, nature conservancies, and health-related causes. Among this large group of development people, some can rightly say they are professional, but there are many who are incompetent, many who are coming into development for the first time, and many who are changing development positions. In fact, there are more turnovers in the profession than one might imagine. Happily, there are more and more opportunities for development education and training. CASE, the National Society of Fund Raising Executives (NSFRE), the Association of Healthcare Philanthropy (AHP), and the Public Relations Society of America (PRSA) are publishing more and more professional materials, offering a wide variety of conferences, seminars, and workshops, and demanding a rigorous program of experience and education leading to professional certification. Also, as has been mentioned, college and university courses in philanthropy and fund raising, programs leading to certificates and degrees, are now available at several institutions.

What It Takes To Be a Development Professional

In a "Memo from the Chief," Jerold Panas puts it on the line unequivocally demanding the best from development staff.*

1. First, I want you to place high value on morals, ethics, standards, and integrity, on deeds not words.

2. I want the highest quality of work from you. Be the best you can be.

3. I want you to set goals, to be the best, to do the most, to get there first, to make a difference. Think big! Reach high!

4. Remember, those who serve come first. Team players make it happen.

5. Forget about the "good old days." Celebrate the past, but look to the future. Tomorrow will be more exciting than yesterday could ever be, more fulfilling, more productive, more rewarding.

6. I abhor shoddy work. Superior quality must be the norm, preeminence in planning and work. I want the highest level of work you can expect from me, and I expect it from you.

7. I want you to value innovation and creativity, avoid the dull, boring, and backward-looking, motionless zombies. Strive for the new, the attractive, the dynamic.

8. Ask, if you don't understand. Don't take anything for granted. It's your responsibility to know.

9. Develop measurable objectives! It's all right to hope and dream, but set concrete objectives in front of you and strive to reach them.

10. Do what you say you will do. Keep your promises.

11. It is better to do something well, though it is wrong, than not to act at all.

12. Be enthusiastic. En (within) theos (God), to have God within us. The Greeks used the term to mean in a state of being inspired by God. Donors will always respond better to enthusiastic people.

13. Be optimistic. Keep a positive attitude. It's easy to be negative, but look for the positive. It's infectious.

---

*Copyright © 1997, Jerold Panas.

14. Always have the will to win and a can-do attitude.

15. Have fun. Enjoy what you are doing.

16. Don't put it off; do it now.

17. Believe in your mission. Seize the day. Hold fast to the promise of tomorrow.[8]

Membership Survey

George J. Mongon Jr. completed and analyzed a membership survey for NSFRE in 1995. He surveyed 2,000 advancement professionals to compile a realistic profile of today's development officer.[9]

Today's Average Development Officer

. . . could be male or female, but more
likely to be female
45 years old
Began this career at age 32
Has 17 years of education
Has held two jobs
Has a current salary of $46,100

From the data gathered by Mongon, salaries ranged from under $12,000 to over $75,000, but the greater percentages of individuals were in the upper end of the range, 54 percent above $40,000, 17 percent above $75,000.

Regarding ethnicity and gender, 79 percent were Caucasian, 9 percent African American, 3 percent Hispanic, and the remaining 9 percent of other ethnic groups. There were more women than men who have chosen to be development officers. Fifty-seven percent were women.

Age statistics revealed that 67 percent of the individuals responding were between the ages of 35 and 55, only 19 percent below the age of 35, and 14 percent above the age of 55. At the upper-age levels development officers seem to feel "burned out" by the constant pressure to make the goal, get the big gift, and recruit more volunteers, and this is not one of Mongon's survey findings but comes as a matter of personal observation. One highly respected vice president in a large university spent his last four years in office accomplishing little if anything. Had it not been that he had a competent and productive staff of professional and support people, and that the university was not in a capital campaign mode, this wonderful and personable veteran of the advancement field would have been given the retirement option long before it did occur. In contrast to that situation, however, there are others who are brilliant and energetic advancement professionals who remain productive and are highly valued well into their later years.

Observations

The trend is toward hiring more women and minorities, at younger ages in entry-level advancement positions, but women are still earning less than men in similar positions. Generally speaking, advancement professionals are satisfied and happy with their work and choose to remain with the profession, though often change institutions or move to different functional areas, such as from annual giving to major gifts, or from corporate gifts director to the director of development position. Also, it would appear that development officers in hospitals and medical centers earn the highest salaries, followed by those in universities. Development people in other nonprofit agencies and groups tend to get the least compensation and change jobs frequently. Albeit, chief executive officers (CEOs) at the top of agencies like the United Way receive substantial compensation and benefits.

Certification

The certification programs for development and public relations professionals are gaining in popularity and respect, so much so that institutions are beginning to view it as a mark of professional legitimacy. The NSFRE was the first of its kind to develop a certification program. Then CASE joined in the effort after some years of delay, because for CASE people it was felt that a college or university degree was, in fact, the best membership card for personnel in higher education. The AHP had its own certification program but joined the NSFRE in 1996 in an agreement to establish a single program for certifying fund raising professionals. The new certification board is called the Certified Fund Raising Executive (CFRE) Professional Certification Board. It is comprised of 11 members, 6 from NSFRE, 3 from AHP, and 2 at large representatives. Ted Bayley, former chair of the NSFRE Certification Board, is the new board chairman. The credential offered is the CFRE. The price for the application and the examination is $300 for members and $400 for nonmembers.

The importance of this certification program is based on the fact that society places great value on certification by one's own professional group, whether it be the medical profession, teaching, law, nursing, accounting, insurance, or real estate. Certification gives authenticity and is perceived to guarantee competency and expertise. It increases public confidence and trust. To date, AHP, CASE, or NSFRE do not require it for membership but strongly encourage it. Increasingly, employers are seeking candidates who have it. Certification is a milestone in one's professional career.[10]

The PRSA also has a certification program. The credential is the Accredited in Public Relations (APR). It was approved by the PRSA Assembly in 1964. Much like those in fund raising, there are many public relations people who do not hold the credential. Those who do are in demand.

Staff Organization

In a small shop, staffing usually consists of a development director, who not only manages the shop but handles what major gift activity there is, an annual fund person, and a gift-processing individual who handles the recordkeeping and acknowledgment. The latter is frequently an administrative secretary. These three, give or take one or two more if operational funds permit, constitute the development office. All three should be crosstrained as soon as possible to assist each other in their respective jobs. All three are routinely engaged in prospect research, public awareness of their programs, cultivation, and solicitation.

In a medium-sized shop, usually found in colleges, universities, or hospitals, there would be a vice president for advancement, a director of development, a director of annual giving, a director of corporate and foundation relations, a gift-processing administrative assistant or senior secretary, and one other clerical person. Again, this would vary, depending on budget and priorities, with each institution. In a university setting, with student enrollment between 2,000 and 5,000, this staffing arrangement would allow coverage of the primary development functions. The small- and medium-sized shops are best suited to centralized development operations.

The larger shops include more specialized staffing. In addition to the vice president or vice chancellor for advancement, if the shop is a centralized shop, there would be an executive director of development, a number of development officers and support staff, including records, gift-processing, and acknowledgment personnel. Sometimes the development officers have titles like director of prospect research, director of prospect management, director of advancement communications, director of donor relations, director of major gifts, director of corporate and foundation relations, director of advancement technology, director of annual giving, director of planned giving, and director of special campaigns. If the program is decentralized, there would be development directors and assistants in the various schools and colleges in addition to those located in the central offices.

Assessment

In charting the progress and productivity of the annual fund campaign, and as a measure of staff involvement, a comprehensive plan of action is needed. Also, a chart of prior, present, and anticipated gifts is needed, and it could take the form shown in Table 2–1.

Given all the attention to techniques, methods, assessment, analysis, and preparation, one would think the annual fund campaign would be a great success, and it should be, but with every charitable cause imaginable out there on the streets chasing the dollar, the competition favors the institution that builds and maintains good relationships, irrespective of the bottom line. The dollar goal is important, of course it is. We all know that, but this dollar-signs-in-the-eyes approach will not increase charitable contributions to the annual fund and keep them coming and increasing year after year. When the fund raiser has used every trick in the book with the help of high speed modems and servers, fax machines, and laser printers, when he or she has mastered all the tactical moves and utilized all the strategies, his or her line of success will be only as long as the relationships that are built with internal and external communities remain strong.

Table 2–1 Annual Fund Campaign Planning/Assessment Chart

Item	Prior Yr	Current Yr	Next Yr
Annual Fund Goal	$800,000	$900,000	$990,000
Percentage of Increase	10%	13%	10%
AFC Receipts	742,343	903,648	—
AFC Donors	57,000	59,144	—
Theme	Making a Difference	Building for Tomorrow	A New Beginning
National Chair	H. Jeffreys	M. Jones	S. Bennett
Donor Base	110,000	115,000	120,000
Donor Amounts Rec'd			Goals
Trustees	231,141	243,758	263,000
Top Administration	62,054	64,182	70,000
Grateful Patients	284,227	289,325	309,000
Physicians	71,039	90,112	99,000
Employees	6,276	6,343	7,000
Friends	17,455	17,520	18,900
Corporations	26,273	57,103	62,000
Foundations	34,760	113,880	123,000
Other Groups	9,118	21,425	38,100

The Personal Touch

It has been mentioned that people give to people. In many instances the cause is secondary to the person doing the asking. People seem to have a biological urge to share, but they have an even greater urge to be liked, and the philanthropic urge is only one side of the coin. Seeking feedback of approval, friendship, and belonging is the other side, and it may be that feedback of commendation they get from personal solicitation is the strongest motivator of all. The most important thing to remember is, people give because they are asked to give. Again, the personal element is present. People respond to being asked by peers, friends, even strangers with whom they perceive common bonds of interest. A program of annual giving will be effective to the extent that it

- makes donors aware of the organization or cause represented
- makes donors aware of the purpose and need for the gift
- creates a feeling of partnership between the donor and the institution, a feeling of mutually invested interest
- creates a sympathetic understanding of the goals and purposes of the annual fund campaign
- establishes a strong base of regular contributors to the various appeals for the arts, the library, the Campus Campaign, the President's Club, student scholarships, faculty support, and academic programs

An effective annual fund campaign requires *think time.* In the solitude of the office, with no one else around, development professionals must take time to think about the institution, its past, its present, its potential. They need to take unhurried time to think about the people who make it what it is, the alumni, the friends, faculty, staff, and community leaders. They need to spend time thinking about the annual fund campaign, its goals, purposes, and strategies. They need to spend hours in careful planning of what is to be done, by whom, when, and how, in order to draft a viable annual fund campaign master blueprint. Also, they need to think about stewardship and ethical behavior. That means being honest with the donor, and not making promises or commitments that cannot be kept, or that might be perceived as a conflict of interest. It means spending gift monies as the donor has directed and keeping the donor informed. If a percentage of unrestricted monies is going to be used for overhead, the institution needs to be up front about it.

Then staff and volunteers can come to donors with clean hands, a good case for support, and informative progress reports, as well as financial reports. They can sow with pride the seeds of planned giving. They can conduct prospect research and learn to identify potential major donors, keeping in mind that it is wealth, not income that determines ability to give large gifts; and it is needs-comprehension, along with the friendly hand, that determines the desire to donate to the cause.

THE MASTER PLAN

A master plan for the annual fund campaign is vital to its success. It is necessary. The development officer cannot run the campaign out of his hip pocket or from memory. Well, it could be done that way, BUT a master plan serves as a checklist, a reminder, and a time schedule to assist both staff and volunteers. The annual fund plan of action enhances staff and volunteer morale. It gives all concerned a feeling that "We have thought this thing out carefully, and we know where we are going and how we are going to get there." The logic, the sequence, and the strategy is down on paper for all to see, and although it is never "cast in concrete," it serves as a guide through the campaign. Professional staff persons have been down the campaign trail many times and could easily travel the distance without it, but it sure helps to have a campaign road map available for reference.

Important Considerations

There are several things to consider in developing a master plan of action. Gary Evans puts it in the form of questions: "What do we want to accomplish with our annual fund program?" The answer is more dollars and more donors. "What is the best method of solicitation?" The answer is well-known to advancement professionals. Personal solicitation is the best method, telephone calls are next, and then there is direct mail.[11] Ann Gee Louden of Texas Christian University lists the four essential components of the annual fund plan as "the dollars to be raised, the overall objectives of the program, the strategy for soliciting each source group, and the timetable for each solicitation."[12] Years ago, Stanley R. McAnally of the University of Tennessee said, the whole concept of "annual giving can be summarized in four words, Attention, Interest, Involvement, and Commitment."[13] First you have to get their attention before anything can be accomplished. Only then can advancement staff begin to build interest through reunions, newsletters, and special events. Once you have their interest, you have to find ways to get them involved, because that is what builds relationships. Finally, you have to get the commitment. Without it, the annual fund is just an academic exercise.

Other Factors

Timing

When things are done is crucial. One must think ahead. Things should fall into logical sequence. Too much overlapping of campaign efforts can result in double solicitation. Also, experience teaches it is best to do personal solicitation first, then telephone solicitation, and follow with direct mail solicitation.

Best Window of Opportunity

March and April, October and November are the best months of the year for fund raising, but every campaign effort cannot be accomplished in these four months alone.

Campaign Length

The length of time spent in an annual fund campaign is important. Continuous solicitation for 12 months gets tedious. It wears out the staff and volunteers. There is no reprieve from pressure. Life cycles in general reflect the principle of stress and release. The ideal campaign is organized around 2 months of review, planning, and preparation, December and January, and 10 months of solicitation; but each institution or organization should develop its own fund raising tension-release formula.

"Case" Piece, the Annual Fund Brochure

The keystone of the annual fund campaign is the brochure. In pictures, graphics, and interesting copy, it builds the "Case for Support." No annual fund campaign can succeed without a strong case statement, a rationale for giving.

Other Campaign Materials

Pledge cards, response cards, flyers, #10 envelopes, #9 easy reply envelopes, campaign stationery with names of the chairman and the annual fund committee, letterheads and envelopes for President's Club and other high-level annual gift clubs, letterheads and envelopes for the varsity club (Panthers, Hornets, Eagles, Cardinals, whatever the club may be called), other brochures for Parent's Club, memorial gifts, gifts-in-kind, Friends of the Library, Art Gallery, or other special interest constituencies, booklets, newsletters, update sheets, invitations, and inserts—these and more are part of the annual fund gift solicitation process. Then there are all sorts of files and forms, receipts, decals, bookmarks, membership cards, T-shirts, baseball caps, paperweights, plaques, key chains, letters, memos, and computer software used in the gift receiving, acknowledgment, and donor recognition process. All these things and more make up the annual fund campaign.

Format and Style

Content, format, size, style, graphic design, layout, color, choice of pictures, font size, and style—all these create a psychological impact on past and future donors. This is all a part of the planning stage to which advancement professionals give a lot of time and thought. It is really a marketing function, because the objective is to persuade the donor to contribute.

Budget

Materials and services cost money, and the money comes from budget allocations or the contributions. For most institutions, the cost of the annual fund campaign is a budgeted item. It works best if it can be done that way so that the university can be ethically clear in saying to the donor, "Every cent you contribute will go to the programs or departments you designate." One hundred percent of every gift is used as the donor directs. Even the unrestricted monies are put back into academic programs, student scholarships, or student financial aid.

There is, however, a trend of late in schools that are feeling a tight budget squeeze to allocate a portion of unrestricted funds to help pay for the development office. The rationale is that this is money the donor has freely given the institution to be used "where the need is greatest," and the President or CEO may well decide that it is best used to help balance the development office budget. The ethical dilemma is that in so doing it creates a conflict of interest. Fund raisers do not talk about the glories of fund raising. They don't market themselves and raise money for themselves any more than the business office raises money for accounting operations, or the registrar's office raises funds for keeping records, and for a very good reason. Aside from the fact that it has little or no appeal to the donor, it is politically and ethically wrong to raise charitable gift money for yourself. When the institution uses unrestricted money to pay the people and programs that raise it, "you've got trouble right here in River City," to use a line from a popular Broadway musical. It is clearly a conflict of interest and leads to deceit.

Realizing that budget shortfall can be solved by raising more unrestricted dollars causes fund raisers to go after unrestricted dollars at the neglect of raising money for academic programs, faculty development, and student aid, and as fund raising professionals know, the best way to raise unrestricted money is to talk to donors about student need and academic support. It would be fund raising suicide even to imply that the school needs the money to support development operations, and not to enhance academic programs and deserving students. In fact, many corporations and foundations, as well as individuals, usually will not give money to support any operational budget. As Richard Evans, formerly of Delmarva Power and Light Company, said to the author on one occasion, "We do not fund operational expense period. If an organization is not strong enough to fund its own basic operational costs, it is not financially sound and Delmarva Power is not interested." Again, it is the same old story, whatever the organization.

All the world loves a winner. We tend to look with question on the losers and the weak. It is the same with investments. If a person buys stock, he expects a return. He expects growth, and increased value. If that investment is in education, the donor expects to see more graduates, better prepared to take their responsible places in society and better prepared to shoulder the load in the work force of our nation.

Funding the annual giving program begins then with budget building, and it is best to approach the budget committee, not with a long wish list, but with a well thought out list, line item by line item, with honest, realistic cost for each element of the operation. Knowledgeable administrators know it takes money to make money and will be responsive to the request. It is also not uncommon to have to go back to the drawing board and return to the committee with a revised request for fewer dollars. Every budget manager has had to face that possibility, and when it happens, prudent and careful decisions about cuts and readjustments must be made. The point is that planning for the annual fund campaign has to include budget appropriations.

SOLICITATION

Planning for the annual fund campaign has to include "personal solicitation," the most effective means of fund raising. Thought must be given to how it will be done and who will do it. Obviously, paid development staff will do it. That is expected, but also that wonderful group of individuals we call volunteers will do it. Personal solicitation is face-to-face, eyeball-to-eyeball, solicitation. It happens when two or more people face each other in person and talk to each other, and one of them asks the other for a gift to the organization.

Ball State University in Muncie, Indiana, where the writer served as an advancement professional for several years, uses personal solicitation very effectively. The method and procedure was well in place in the early 1980s when Bob Linson was vice president. The winning formula for the $3.2 million annual fund campaign is still effective today. First, volunteers from the community are recruited early, usually in November and December preceding the new calendar year. The fund raising year is the calendar year, not the fiscal year. Each volunteer accepts the responsibility to attend an orientation and card selection meeting at a date and time announced well in advance. The volunteer will select five prospect cards from a large number of cards displayed in alpha order on a table in the room at the time of orientation. The cards are in fact pledge cards with the prospect's name, address, and telephone number printed on them; the prospect's giving history (if any) for the past three years; a place for the amount of the current pledge being received; and a place for the donor's signature and date. Each volunteer bears responsibility for cultivating and soliciting the prospects whose names appear on the cards chosen, and for returning the cards to the development office. There are team captains for various categories of individuals, such as alumni, friends, corporations, merchants, and other groups. There are five or more volunteers assigned to each team captain, and it is the team captain's responsibility to make a pledge up front, and to make sure the volunteers make their contacts, solicit their prospects, and turn in their cards. All the follow-up work is done by the development office, including the thank-you notes, the gift and pledge processing, and the reminders.

Personal Solicitation

Personal solicitation at Ball State is done for two constituent groups only, though it could be done for almost any constituent group. The two groups are the President's Club and the Cardinal Varsity Club. The President's Club consists of all the many people, mostly alumni and friends of the university who have given at the President's Club level in past years, or who are prospects for the President's Club. The Cardinal Varsity Club is made up of alumni and friends who are fans of the sports teams and who support the various athletic programs, or who are prospects for the Cardinal Varsity Club.

Personal solicitation for each of the two groups is conducted in exactly the same manner as described above. The orientation meetings are held on separate occasions, usually the one for the President's Club on a Tuesday night of one week in February and the other on a Tuesday night of the following week.

The so-called orientation meetings have become quite a tradition. They consist of an introduction of the team leaders and volunteers. Public relations people are on hand to take pictures and write the story for news media the following day. Food service prepares light hors d'oeuvres and drinks, usually soft drinks, beer, and wine. The formal program begins with an introduction to the program by the development director, a full explanation of expectations and benefits, and a period for questions and answers. Following that, volunteers are invited to step up to the tables and choose cards representing the five prospects they will solicit. Each volunteer is given a packet of materials at the beginning of the meeting, and in that packet is a slip of paper with the volunteer's name on it. Following the card selection, the volunteer is instructed to write the names of the five prospects on that slip of paper and hand it to one of the office staff present.

After the card selection, volunteers are offered food, drinks, and fellowship. Sometimes the fellowship lasts until 11 PM or later, as volunteers exchange pleasantries and tell jokes and stories about past encounters with prospective donors. Eventually they leave, and the lights are turned out, leaving the development professionals a mountain of follow-up work to do the next day.

Volunteers are great to have! They help to broaden the donor base, because they know prospects the institution has not yet thought about. They need to be recruited early, as mentioned above, but more than that, it is necessary to spend some time deciding who approaches whom. There is a right match. Personalities sometimes do not match, and there will be some volunteers who are best used in some clerical capacity. The wrong volunteer to make the ask is one who has a negative outlook, one who puts off making the contact, or one who is afraid of the telephone, or who is extremely shy around other people. Even a nice and sincere person, even a V.I.P., may not be able to persuasively ask for the gift, and is therefore dead weight in the campaign. Volunteers, it has been said, are worth their weight in gold, more or less. We cannot do without them. It is physically impossible for the professional staff to make all the personal solicitation contacts necessary to the success of the campaign. So, they need to begin early to select and cultivate the individuals they seek as volunteers.

One further word about personal solicitation may be helpful. In the annual fund drive, just as in a capital fund drive, the largest gifts will come as a result of personal face-to-face solicitation. Some annual fund campaigns do not incorporate it in the plan, relying heavily on direct mail, telemarketing, and special event fund raisers, but in the author's years of experience in directing and managing annual campaigns, face-to-face solicitation has been a valuable and productive method of raising money. The best application of personal solicitation in the annual fund drive is with such groups as the President's Club.

Direct Mail

The term often given to solicitation by mail that expects a direct response, gives information, or expresses gratitude is "direct mail." It is the preferred method for targeted preparation, solicitation, and follow-up. It is used to prepare the way for personal solicitation or telephone solicitation.

Early in the campaign, fairly close to the annual kickoff breakfast or luncheon, a general mass mailing with the annual fund campaign brochure, a cover letter from the national chairperson or the university president, and a gift return envelope should go to every potential donor in the university's database, and to hundreds of prospects who are not yet in the database, such as parents, faculty, staff, and friends in the community.

The return on mass mailings, even though targeted to special markets, is relatively small, usually 10 percent or less, so it cannot be a basket into which all solicitation eggs are placed. Many other target appeals (rifle-shot appeals in contradistinction to shotgun appeals) should go at various times to special interest groups throughout the year. Certainly the various "friends of" groups and alumni constituent groups should direct at least one appeal to their members each year.

Direct mail appeals for annual giving should bear the unifying stamp of the campaign logo on all materials sent out for whatever reason. The unified image approach is always preferred and includes color, theme, logo, and campaign chairperson. These should appear on all direct mail pieces. Each envelope, each cover letter, each pledge card, each thank-you card, and each reminder carries the coordinated design and theme of the campaign to keep the campaign alive and before the public continually throughout the year.

There are only two kinds of direct mail, that which is effective and that which is not. A "bad" piece is illogical, unintelligent, unclear, boring, or sterile even if it is printed in four colors on gilt-edged parchment. Direct mail is good only if it has good content, if it is above all interesting (so the donor will at least read it), positive, friendly, and persuasive. Bad mail is a stupid, boring, unimaginative piece of promotion. Good mail is interesting and worthy of the time spent to read it. It is clear, informative, friendly, straightforward, and concise. A classic passage lifted from the Ludgin letters and included in Rowland's *Handbook* shows the tactful, sincere approach that gets the reader's attention and results in a gift.

> Instead of looking to the past with pride, let us look to the future with hope. We who have cause to be proud of the University have the means to implement and increase that pride by giving to the alumni fund, giving as generously as our means permit. May I say this is not an obligation? But if we asked you in time, would you have sent a thousand dollars to Newton, Galileo, or Madam Curie?

> We say a thousand dollars only wishfully. We are really very grateful for the checks of five, ten, or twenty-five dollars.[14]

A letter of today, using the three-part formula of design—the hook, the case, and the closure—might read as follows:

> Dear Mr. Chandler,

> Greetings from the beautiful university campus. The students are back from summer vacations, all eager and excited, faculty are getting ready for fall convocation, and there is an air of excitement about the opening of a new school year.

> You will be pleased to know enrollment has increased and the much-needed computer equipment has arrived for the new CD-ROM laboratory you helped to fund last year. Please feel free to stop by the library to see it in operation when you come back for Homecoming. Your gifts and those of many others are making a difference in the lives of deserving students preparing to take their places in the work force of our great nation.

> This letter seeks your support for the new School of Business facility much needed by our faculty and students. The building now being used was built for another time to accommodate 90 students in 1946. Enrollment in the Business School now is 655.

> Furthermore, technical advances in distance learning, computer science, and business management require state-of-the-art accommoda-

tions. The cost of the facility is $20 million. 165 alumni and friends have already made a financial commitment totalling $3.2 million. I know you will want to participate.

As you consider what your gift might be, I hope you will think largely. A gift in the range of $5,000–$10,000 would make a significant impact on the project. Please know, however, that no gift is too large or too small. Whatever you can see your way clear to contribute will be gratefully received. The future is as bright as the past is memorable, and we are proud to have you a part of it. A gift return envelope is enclosed for your convenience.

Sincerely,

Greg Johnson
Director of Development

Direct mail should not be a puzzle to anyone who receives it. The simpler it is, the better. That does not mean just a plain piece of paper with black printing stuffed into a plain unmarked envelope. Simplicity means the message should be articulated with clarity, so that there is no doubt in the donor's mind what you are "pitching," what the conditions are, and what specific action is expected. The cover letter should explain it all. Appropriate inserts are fine, but the cover letter should clearly tell the story, and it should be interesting to read, assuming it has caught the donor's eye and has been, in fact, opened.

In most cases, the organization has only five seconds to get attention and persuade the prospect to open the mail. Junk mail is bombarding our households these days, mail from insurance carriers, from sweepstakes operators, from politicians, supermarkets, department stores, and health-related causes. Of course, one person's junk mail may be another person's treasure, but generally speaking the donor will decide in only a few seconds whether to open or toss a piece of mail.

After opening it, the donor will take only four or five seconds to decide to read it. What is said in the very first sentence has to be the hook that catches interest. The sender has to get the reader's attention immediately. Sometimes it is done by a catchy phrase like "Put your best foot forward and help stamp out illiteracy," or a startling bit of news like "Are you ready for the coming revolution in college education?" Neither is particularly good but both do make you think. The first is a bit too cute, and the second is too controversial, but the point is made that what is said at the top of the letter is as important to hook the reader as anything else in the letter.

Once the reader is hooked, the writer must build the "case for support." In the second part of the letter, the reader needs quickly to find out what is going on, what the problem is, and how it can be solved. The reader still can toss it aside at any moment. The text has to be interesting, but to the point. A solicitation letter is not the time to chit-chat and ramble on about this and that. When we try to convey too much information, we often confuse the reader and bury the intent and purpose of the letter in a pile of unrelated words and phrases, however cute or fascinating they may be. The prospect is not often willing to piece the information together, like a puzzle, to find out what the sender expects.

As far as length is concerned, the rule used to be keep it short, only one page. Current wisdom is that it can be two or three pages long if it is written well and interesting to read, with lots of white space around the copy, but not front and back typing. Separate pages are easier to handle and read. The paper stock should be of reasonable quality, certainly not cheap copy paper or, perish the thought, onion skin paper, and it should be beige or white. Color highlights, graphics, underlining, and handwritten notes on the margin are fine if they tastefully focus the prospect's attention on the message. Extraneous markings only serve to confuse.

Too many inserts are also confusing. The prospect has to figure out what this piece is for, and how that piece fits in. Putting it all together soon becomes, like these dreaded sweepstakes offers, a nightmare quickly made to disappear with the help of a wastebasket. When the reader opens one of these direct mail envelopes and 25 pieces fall out, it becomes a problem to know what is important and what is not. In fund raising by direct mail, it is best to include only three and possibly four pieces: (1) the cover letter, which is the most important piece in the package; (2) a #9 gift return envelope, because always in every piece of mail a return envelope is appreciated, and often will bring in checks that otherwise would never have come; (3) a donor response card, because donors appreciate having some mechanism to give you their response (Rarely will they write a note or a separate letter. In our fast-paced world, people are just too busy to write); and (4) if you must, include a brochure. If it is attractive, colorful, and includes clear uncluttered pictures, it will support the appeal and may bring closure.

Telephone Solicitation

The second-best fund raising method, marketing experts agree, is that telephone call from a friend asking for a contribution to a worthy cause. It is hard to turn a friend, student, or alumnus(a) down. Some schools use the telephone campaign as a "mop-up" operation at the end of the campaign. Some universities, like Syracuse, Tennessee, and Purdue, run them as the main event of the campaign. At Ball State University a very effective and unique Telefund is conducted early in the campaign and raises $800,000 over a period of six weeks, beginning in February. A telefund specialist directs and coordinates a large number of regional sites as well as an on-campus student telefund. Alumni form the base of the prospect list, but many friends are called too.

The Ball State University Telefund was perfected by Ed Shipley, long-time alumni director. For years it was held over a period of approximately six weeks in the spring and consisted of the main telefund effort on the campus run with professional staff supervision and student callers. Alumni residing in Kokomo, Fort Wayne, South Bend, Indianapolis, and other outlying areas were served by regional telefund efforts run by staff and alumni volunteers at local business sites such as a bank in South Bend or a manufacturing plant in Kokomo. Student callers on campus reached alumni in Florida, California, Michigan, Illinois, and all other localities not served by the regional telefunds. The trend now at larger universities is to conduct telemarketing all year long, using computerized calling networks. Fewer volunteers are required. Calls are much more structured, and more quickly executed by automatic dialing. After a solicitation is completed, the caller presses "Enter" and the next call rings through. On the monitor in front of the caller, all pertinent data are shown for that particular prospect. The telephone headset frees the hands to make keystrokes as the conversation progresses. The pledge amount is entered, the caller says "Thank you," presses "Enter," and the data are saved while at the same time dialing the next prospect's number. It takes two seconds to dial the new number. If the prospect is at home and answers the phone, the new conversation begins. The caller uses a scripted conversation to ensure all bases are covered in the proper sequence. Calls continue every day for as long as there are calls to make. With alumni groups now totaling 350,000 or more, it takes a while to get through all of them, and what is more challenging is the fact that alumni are moving more often, and frequently do not give the alumni office their new addresses or telephone numbers. Some alumni, for personal reasons, prefer to remain "lost." Some are deceased, and some simply neglect to inform the university of their whereabouts.

GIFT CLUBS

Using major gift club categories to report contributions to attract additional gifts and to "bump" donors up to the next level of giving can be quite effective. Gift clubs are opportunities for giving at a particular level. Sometimes the clubs function as other societal clubs with a club president, dinners, luncheons, or other special events, and with membership cards and club stationery. Often, however, these clubs are paper clubs, used for recognition only. Even so they serve a good purpose. Birds of a feather, as they say, enjoy flocking together. There is a certain feeling of pride, for example, in being a President's Club member, or a Founder's Club member.

Also, donors have limitations. There are those who are able to give at the $500 level, but would be hard pressed to give at the $1,000 level. They need a special incentive to give $500, not $100, or even $250. Gift clubs are best treated as incentives for giving. They can be handled as a sort of mini-campaign within the annual fund, just as the campus campaign, or the varsity club campaign is run, having their own prospect list, their own campaign chair, and their own appeals. Some organizations use special stationery and envelopes for each club.

Gift clubs are called by many names, such as "Pacesetters," "Partners," the "1891 Society," the "Chancellor's Circle," the "Benjamin Franklin Society Associates," or some other name that has historical significance to the institution, or that carries the name of some distinguished person connected to the organization. Century Club is very common for the $100 givers.

Permanent gift clubs are not a part of the annual fund, but they are a part of fund raising strategy. They are sometimes called "lifetime" clubs, because once a donor's contributions have reached a certain high level, membership in that club continues in perpetuity. Such clubs usually start at $10,000 and are found at several upper levels, $50,000, $100,000, and $1,000,000. Names for these clubs are usually something like "Founders Club," "Trustees Club," or "Benefactors." Perks for members of these clubs might be a weekend retreat with the president, an annual banquet, a special plaque, or silver plate.

Whatever they are called, gift clubs are most important to the annual fund campaign. Their chief purpose is to upgrade individual gifts from lower to higher levels of giving. They often generate more than 80 percent of the campaign goal. Consequently, gift solicitation of major donors must be first class in every way, with the best personal solicitation, attractive materials, some association with the president or other top officials, and most of all first class in content.

SPECIAL EVENTS

Special events are great for socializing and bringing people together. They are often dramatic, exciting, and well attended. A dinner, a dance, a concert, all these can generate a great deal of excitement for the organization. The downside, as mentioned above, is that many fund raising events produce little profit and have little residual benefit.[15] Hard costs for room, food service, and entertainment usually eat up 50 percent of gross receipts, and soft costs for time, travel, energy, and arrangements take another 20 percent, leaving only 30 percent at best.

Then too, people forget very quickly. What was a gala event last week is lost in the mundane happenings of this week. On average, the general public will put it out of mind in two or three days. Considering the weeks and months of planning, the money, time, and energy consumed in getting ready for the event, and in executing the event, all the invitations and guest management, the recordkeeping, the decorations, the phone calls, the prizes, and the printing, the few moments in the limelight and the small profit cannot compare to a single "ask" for gift or grant support. In a business situation, most of us would not tolerate the time and expense needed to do an event unless the profit line looked very good from the start. Every advancement professional can tell a special event horror story or two. One that comes to mind from in the mid-1990s is a spectacular sports event that took place in a convention hall in a certain city. It was to be a big fund raiser featuring a football game, receptions, a parade, and other side attractions. Thousands of people were expected to fill the hall for the four-game tournament. There was much publicity. The mayor of the city got involved in promoting it. Alumni sold tickets, and preparations were made. Several thousands of dollars were spent to truck in sod from a nearby farm to form the playing field on the floor of the large indoor arena. Then came the day of the event. Sponsors had given verbal agreement, and it looked like it would be a highly successful fund raiser. Unfortunately it lost money for the athletic department and "proved to be a disaster" in the words of one university official. Ticket sales did not reach the goal. Fewer people attended than anticipated. Hotel and food service expenses were high. Worst of all, some of the anticipated sponsorships did not come through. A great time was had by all who attended, but the fund raising part of it was sadly disappointing. The lesson to be learned is, special events require a high level of expertise. Sponsorships must be confirmed in writing. A carefully crafted plan based on a reliable feasibility study is important. Management and implementation are crucial. Above all, nothing can be left to chance. The higher the stakes and the bigger the prize, the higher the risk and the harder the fall.

There are, of course, many wonderful special events success stories. These occasions are valuable opportunities for the organization or institution to get the public excited about a cause, or to celebrate a happening. An exciting personal dynamic comes into play when individuals meet to share an experience or an event. We are a gathering-influenced people. That is why people of all ages love to party, enjoy a concert together, watch a rocket launching, or be seen at a political rally or patriotic celebration. Special events are great for the development function in its larger sense, because development and progress result from relationships, from mutual interests, and a close match of needs and desires, as well as interests, with those of the organization. Fund development arises from that inbred human need to help each other while achieving personal satisfaction from the endeavor.

Fund raising is the act of soliciting money, and it is often very direct. In colonial days and earlier, it was called begging, often quick and dirty, often driven by basic human need. It is no coincidence that fund raisers are perceived by some to be in a class with used car salesmen. They have that quick smile, that ready handshake. They make you feel good, get your signature on the card, and move on to the next customer. Fund development is far more than that scenario. It is the building of institutions, the molding of relationships between individuals and organizations. It is personal and it is societal; and special events help to bring that about, but they are not the best or most efficient means of raising money for a cause or an institution, for the following reasons:

- The cost per dollar raised is high.
- There is little lasting goodwill benefit.
- People think the ticket they bought is the end of it.
- Special events seldom motivate donors to make additional gifts.
- Unless the event can net $30,000 or more, it is hardly worth it.
- A single major donor, properly cultivated, will produce far more.
- Staff time spent with guests is minimal at best, and the conversation is mainly small talk, unless a staff member is purposefully seated with particular guests at the table.
- Special events are the major cause of volunteer burnout.*

CAMPUS CAMPAIGNS

Soliciting employees is common in annual fund drives. Development professionals spend much time thinking and talking about raising money from alumni, friends, corporations, and foundations, but tend to overlook the wealth of support that exists within the campus community itself.

For some reason, university fund raisers are willing to spend hundreds of dollars preparing first-class fund raising materials for alumni and friends but only nickles and dimes on appeals to faculty, staff, and other employees of the institution. The argument is that faculty and staff already know what is going on. Of all people, they know the financial needs of the university and what progress is being made. A simple memo or letter once a year will suffice to let them know they may contribute as they see fit.

The fact is that individual faculty and staff members know very little about institutional needs or about needs, goals, and dreams of departments outside their limited scope of activity. In truth, every employee of the university could benefit from a campaign that brings an awareness of the needs and deeds of the macro university. It makes them informed partners, during the campaign and beyond.

This highly focused appeal to faculty and staff can be appropriately called "Campus Campaign," and it should be done with a change of leadership, goal, and campaign materials every year as a part of the annual fund campaign. First, it is a campus campaign because it is limited to the campus community, more specifically to the employees of the university, and second, because it is a true campaign by classical definition. It is managed by professional staff. It is goal-oriented. It follows a time sequence. It involves lay leadership and a corps of vol-

---

*Reprinted with permission from G. Jindra, Fund Raising Mistakes to Avoid at All Costs, *Contributions*, pp. 29–30, © 1997.

unteers. It reaches every trustee, administrator, faculty, and staff member. It is not a hard-sell campaign. The message is simply that gifts in support of the university are, in fact, gifts that benefit all employees.

After several years, employees come to expect it and support it. Each year brings a new slogan, a new chairman from the ranks of the faculty or staff, new posters to generate new interest, and new campaign letterhead. The pledge portion of the campaign typically would extend four weeks, but the campaign runs quietly throughout the year, with an appeal to new faculty and staff in September and special reminders at year's end. Growth in terms of dollars is minimal, but the aura of support from the family is significant.

Features of the campus campaign are (1) volunteer leadership; (2) committee involvement; (3) heightened awareness; (4) varied options for giving, i.e., payroll deduction, outright cash contributions, pledges, donations by credit card, appreciated securities, gifts-in-kind; and (5) varied options for gift designation. The two biggest motivators are the option to give by payroll deduction and the option to give to one's own department. These family campaigns in colleges and universities across the United States are not unusual, and they are effective in building morale as well as raising money for the institution. Many employees will contribute amounts in excess of $500 annually, and more than half of those who participate do so through payroll deduction, which is perhaps the easiest way to give. As one faculty member was heard to remark, "With payroll deduction, I never miss it." Generally speaking, universities make it as easy as possible for faculty and staff to give by payroll deduction. The employee fills out a card authorizing payroll deduction in a particular amount. The information is entered into the donor's gift record by the foundation or the development office. The card is sent to payroll for processing, and the gift is received by the organization, automatically, in a timely manner according to the wishes of the employee.

What keeps the campus campaign alive and fresh is the new leadership each year. No faculty or staff member should chair the campaign two years in a row. The current chairperson steps down at the end of the year and the vice chair becomes the new chairperson, who in turn recruits a new vice chair from a long list of loyal supporters. In addition, each new chair has a new campus campaign committee, which comprises approximately 15 to 20 persons, who represent a cross section of the campus. Some of them will have served on the committee before, but that is considered a strength, not a weakness, because it gives continuity in leadership and stability for campus campaign, year after year. The new faces, however, bring an air of newness and excitement to the campaign that is most valuable.

When new committee members are recruited by the new chairperson, they are expected to make their own gift commitment and lend their influence and support to the campaign throughout the year. Their names are printed on the campaign letterhead, and they must attend the Campus Campaign Kickoff for the new year.

The kickoff takes the form of a breakfast held by the new chairperson. At this breakfast, each committee member is given information about the campaign and is encouraged to ask questions or make comments in the interest of improving the campaign. Through the years, many excellent suggestions have been made and subsequently incorporated into the plan of action for the campaign. At one university where this program is in operation, it was suggested that greater publicity be given the fact that this family campaign is a part of the annual fund campaign to ensure greater awareness of the annual fund effort. It was done and proved to be a boost to the annual fund.

Public awareness is vital to the success of this campus fund raising effort. Posters displayed around campus help to accomplish this awareness, but other media are used as well, including news releases, announcements in departmental staff meetings, and campuswide word of mouth support. It is important that every employee knows about the effort and how to participate. Beyond that, however, the campaign is low key. No arms are twisted, no one is coerced to give or made to feel guilty.

The direct mail package consists of three mailings, in addition to selective correspondence with deans and department chairs. The first is an awareness letter from the new chairperson to each of the university's employees. What it says is the new campaign is under way, with new goals to be achieved, and it describes how the individual employee may participate. It closes with a message that a letter of solicitation will follow in a few days, and expresses the hope that the employee will participate when asked. Enclosed in this first letter is an annual fund brochure, nothing more.

The second letter should be mailed a week later. It should speak with pride to the amount raised last year. It calls attention to the ways in which one can contribute. It offers the clear option of unrestricted giving to "wherever the need is greatest," or designating the gift for any department or program of the university. Enclosed in this second letter are a pledge/payroll deduction card and a gift return envelope, self-addressed for easy campus mailing.

With a fund raising effort like the campus campaign just described, the solicitation is always a soft sell. It is largely accomplished by direct mail and word of mouth. Personal solicitation on campus should be reserved for special campaigns, such as a multimillion dollar capital campaign. Gift recognition is limited on most campuses to the publishing of an honor roll of donors. Some donors prefer not to have their names published, and their wish is always honored, but most faculty and staff are pleased to be included in the Honor Roll of Campus Campaign Donors.

These family campaigns targeted to the internal community have been successful for a number of years. The philosophy, methods, and procedures are no secret. Any college or university can do it, and most institutions and organizations are happy to share with others what works for them and what does not. All it takes is a phone call. If there is any secret to the long-term success of this program in many colleges and universities, it is widespread awareness, high quality materials, and the options to give by payroll deduction and to designate the gift to any department or program of the donor's choosing. Institutions that are not using some version of campus campaign, or in the case of hospitals and other nonprofits, some type of employee solicitation may be overlooking a gold mine right in their own backyards.

TARGET APPEALS

In addition to campus campaign, there are numerous potential appeals that come within the scope of the annual fund campaign, such as Friends of the Library, Friends of the Art Gallery, Friends of the "Y," Parents Club, Varsity Club, Dollars for Scholars, Retirees Association, Graduating Seniors ("A Class Act"), alumni reunion gifts, and many others. In the schedule of annual fund activities throughout the year, something should be happening every month. Some organizations make a number of different appeals in the 12 months of the calendar year. The argument for such activity is that donors and prospects will give as they choose. Once in the habit of receiving multiple appeals during the year from the institution, they understand it is just a part of the system and benefits the organization. They are not put off by it but give to those appeals that interest them. As John D. Rockefeller once said, "You can ask as often as you wish, but understand that I alone will determine whether or not I will give and the amount I will give."

Most of these appeals are direct response mail appeals to certain target groups. Some are mass mailings to large constituencies. The return is not great, but taken as a whole they do enhance the annual fund campaign. Asking the same donor more frequently than once a month, even if the appeals are for different causes, is "overkill." Donors will tolerate persistence and applaude aggressiveness up to a point. After that their smiles turn to frowns and could have a lasting negative effect on their giving to the institution. One should simply exercise good manners and common courtesy. The alert professional is usually quite painfully aware of the line that separates healthy assertiveness and destructive aggression. Annual fund campaigns can make any number of different appeals during the year, so long as they are going to different groups of individuals. Caution should be used, however, in appealing to the same group more than once a month, and something less than that is probably desirable. To get the best return, one should choose prospects wisely and let the appeal match their interests. If it is known that a donor has no interest in athletics, it is foolish to waste time and money sending a varsity club appeal. All things said and done, the central purpose of the annual fund is to raise money, and that means more dollars and more donors every year.

To achieve those goals, the annual fund staff have to concentrate on viable ways and means of doing it.

CONCLUSION

The annual fund campaign for any institution or organization is a continuing source of revenue for meeting current needs. It is conducted each year as a bona fide campaign with its own goal, leadership, strategies, volunteers, and budget. It is the long-range plan of gift revenue, as opposed to the short-range capital campaign for special projects.

The annual fund campaign operates as a unique fund raising entity, set apart from other fund raising drives, legislative appeals, grantsmanship, and federal and state assistance, including loans. It does not oppose other fund raising efforts but complements them. A proven formula for success in annual giving is that a good cause, plus a large base of potential donors, and a good "Case," will bring success in fund raising, and there are 10 criteria that play a role:

1. a good plan of action
2. first rate leadership
3. willing and competent volunteers
4. adequate budget and professional staff
5. up-front challenge gifts
6. compelling case for support
7. sufficient donor potential
8. strong organization and experienced management
9. full support of the governing board and administration
10. satisfactory time frame

Throughout the campaign, "friend raising" is just as important as fund raising. In fact, building friendly relationships with individual decision makers and bringing them into the loop comes first. It has been said, but bears repeating, the basic fund raising cycle is a simple three-point process before landing the gift. Find the prospect. Get the prospect interested. Bring the prospect into the loop. Then, ask for the gift.

The Cycle of Fund Raising
reduced to its essence

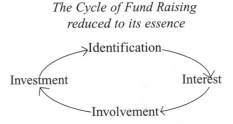

There are not too many different ways one can explain cultivation and solicitation. Donors have to be in the right frame of mind before they will make a gift.

They have to be interested in the institution and the cause, but it is more than that. They need to become involved in some way with the organization before they will invest their money in it. Once they have put some money into it, if the customer relations are right and they continue to feel good about the institution, they will give again and again, and that is the principle of annual giving. The objective of the annual fund director is to get people in the habit of giving, year after year, and once they have made a gift it becomes easier to make a second, and a third. Many college alumni, former hospital patients, and friends of nonprofit organizations have given over and over again for years. What the annual fund director wants to do is get them to increase the size of the gift.

As advancement professionals know, there are only two ways to increase annual giving—horizontal and vertical expansion, that is, more contributors, higher amounts:

1. Broaden the donor base, i.e., get more donors.
2. Keep current donors and get them to increase the size of their gifts.

A clear idea of where gifts come from and where they go is necessary to make intelligent fund raising appeals and meaningful progress reports. Development people sometimes get their apples confused with their oranges, statistically speaking, when they talk about gift income. Essentially there are only two major sources of gift income: (1) individuals and (2) groups of individuals. There are, however, many destinations for their gifts. On the one hand are the people and the organizations that make the gifts, such as alumni, patients, clients, vendors, parents, friends, corporations, foundations, agencies, clubs, religious groups, consortia, and other groups. On the other hand are the destinations, such as student financial aid, hospital program support, faculty development, internships, departmental support, special projects, memorials, and on and on. So, to report accurately the activity of the annual fund campaign, and to understand the role of the campaign in the affairs of the organization, it may be helpful to show a general breakdown of both source and destination of these gifts. (See Exhibit 2–1.)

Recordkeeping is a fundamental act of good stewardship in particular and fund raising in general. It almost goes without saying that a record of every gift transaction should be kept. There is a lot more to it than that, however. There are acknowledgments to be made, usually in the form of a thank-you letter. There are receipts to be sent to the donor. These are legal documents certifying the amount of the gift and the date, the names of the donor and the recipient. There are reports to be made, including reports from the business office verifying gift and pledge transactions, reports to the President or CEO and governing board, reports to advancement officers, and reports to the public. Often there are transmittal forms and deposit slips. In short, there is a lot of clerical work to be done in the processing of gifts and pledges. Advances in technology are making that process eas-

Exhibit 2–1 Gift Sources and Destinations

Sources	*Destinations*
INDIVIDUALS	Unrestricted
Alumni	Academic departments
Friends	Centers
Physicians	Scholarships
Patients	Fellowships
Clients	Faculty research
Trustees	Graduate assistantships
Administrators	Employee relations
	Endowed accounts
	Patient care
ORGANIZATIONS	Internships
Corporations	Professional development
Foundations	Rehabilitation
Religious groups	Women in social work
Agencies	Athletics
Clubs	Physical wellness
Consortia	Cancer research
Fraternities	Career programs
Sororities	Community outreach

ier, quicker, and more reliable.

The "Honor Roll of Donors" publication is a valuable piece of donor recognition. There is nothing so dear to an individual as his or her own name, and nothing looks so good as the sight of a person's own name in print, carved in stone, or engraved on a plaque. The annual report often includes an honor roll of donors, listing all donors at certain levels and by certain categories. Donors receiving the annual report will always turn first to the honor roll to have a look at their names in print. A name is special. It is unique, and it represents the individual, his or her character, everything about him or her. In the fairy tale, Rumplestiltskin was always careful to guard his name, because "he who knows my name, knows me." What's in a name? Everything. That is why it is so very important to get it right. Seymour said, "Never make a mistake with people's names. John Price Jones, my boss for many years, was never J.P. Jones, or John P. Jones, but John Price Jones— the whole works."[16] People are very particular about how their names appear. Women especially are choosing hyphenated names that include their maiden names. A misspelled name is worse than no name at all, but omission of a name, inadvertently or otherwise, when it should be included is very disappointing to the donor. Little will be said if a name appears by mistake in the President's Club listing when the donor had failed to make a gift, but the development office will hear loud words of displeasure if the $1,000 donor's name is inadvertently omitted.

Putting the donor's name on a walnut plaque, or a brass paperweight, is even better because it can be seen on the wall or desk by friends, relatives, guests, or passersby. In an honor roll it will be read, most likely, by one person, the donor. He or she will scan through the list to find his or her own name, and rarely stop along the way to look for others, but on a plaque or carved in a brick it will be seen by many people for as long as it hangs on the wall or lies in the walkway.

The ultimate donor recognition is to name a university, a school, or a building after the donor. Advancement professionals of the 1990s will not forget that Glassboro State College in New Jersey was renamed Rowan College when Henry M. Rowan made a $100 million gift. He wanted to establish an engineering school and it was done. He earmarked $3 million to establish the Inductotherm Scholarship Program to benefit the children of employees of his company. In March of 1997 the name was changed again to Rowan University.

Recognition is also accomplished through receptions, luncheons, dinners, dedications, and other events and ceremonies. The more recognition occurs before one's peers, the more powerful and memorable it is. Donors have been moved to tears at such occasions, and the spinoff of these occasions is usually a second and third gift. Granted there are some donors who for personal reasons prefer to remain anonymous, but most donors want to stand up and be counted. In the sports world, to be inducted into a Hall of Fame is a lifelong achievement, and the Hall of Fame concept can work in other settings such as an Alumni Hall of Fame, a Musicians Hall of Fame, or a Physicians Hall of Fame. In the world of entertainment, awards like the Oscars, Emmys, and Tonys are fiercely coveted, and millions of people watch the presentations, but awards of all kinds work well for fund raising. There are distinguished service awards, outstanding volunteer awards, and a variety of philanthropy awards. There are certificates, prizes, and medals. Even a simple thing like applause for work well done, or the mere mention of a donor's name is a valued form of donor recognition, and so much the better if it comes spontaneously before one's peers.

Roy Klein, a man for all charities, well known for his philanthropic efforts and volunteer work throughout Delaware, has spontaneously passed out many an accolade to deserving civic and business leaders, including the present and past governors of the state before hundreds of guests at dinners and other occasions. He holds the goodwill and high respect of every CEO in the state. He is not only a master of donor recognition but the recipient of many awards. The entire wall of his corporate office is filled with plaques, certificates, and other awards. He jokingly calls it his "Wall of Fame." He has not sought this recognition. It has come to him because he genuinely cares about others and makes sure they are recognized and honored for whatever achievement they have earned.

There are hundreds like Roy in this wonderful world of philanthropy. Donor acknowledgment and recognition are the keys to second and third gifts, and many more. People like to think their gifts are making a difference, but they also want to know their gifts are appreciated and recognized.

Annual giving takes many forms. Essentially it is the practice of giving something every year. The object of the annual giving program, often called the "Annual Fund," is to get donors into the habit of giving repeatedly, year after year after year. The time-honored methods are direct mail, telephone solicitation, and personal visitation. Materials used in the cultivation and solicitation process vary with the institution, but the centerpiece of any annual giving program is the "Case for Support." The schematic design for the program is the "Master Plan of Action." The program drivers are the members of the development staff and the volunteers. The enabler is the budget.

The annual giving program is the third leg of the development stool. The other legs are the capital campaign and planned giving. All three are equally important to the fund raising efforts of any organization or institution, but the annual giving program is the long-term sustainer of repeated ordinary and current gifts that enhance operating funds. Many things have a bearing on the program, such as timing, materials, scope of awareness, volunteers, and available prospects. Also priorities and needs of the organization pretty much determine how the money will be used. Some programs earmark all annual fund monies as "unrestricted," to be used wherever the need is greatest, but that is an untenable position. Stanley Baumblatt, corporate giving officer of Merrill Lynch & Company, says "It is bizzare to categorize annual fund gifts as unrestricted."[17] Donors want to designate their gifts to programs in which they have an interest. Annual giving in America has a long history and will continue long into the future, because consistent regular giving is the foundation of any fund raising program.

NOTES

1. R.G. Forman, Executive Director of the University of Michigan Alumni Association for more than 20 years, in an oral presentation at a CASE conference in Cincinnati, November 19–21, 1980. Bob, as he likes to be known, is past chair of the CASE Board of Directors.

2. B. Gose and M. Geraghty, "Tuition and Fees Raise Tough Policy Questions," *The Chronicle of Higher Education*, May 30, 1997, A43.

3. J. Mercer, "Private Giving to Colleges Increased 11.8% in 1996," *The Chronicle of Higher Education*, May 30, 1997, A41.

4. Mercer, "Private Giving," A41.

5. H.J. Seymour, *Designs for Giving* (New York: McGraw-Hill, 1947), viii.

6. H. Rosso, *Achieving Excellence in Fund Raising* (San Francisco: Jossey-Bass, 1991), 31.

•

7. E. Pfizenmaier Henderson, "Finding the Fabulous Few: Why Your Program Needs Sophisticated Research," *Prospect Research: A How to Guide* (Washington, DC: CASE, 1986), 38.

8. J. Panas, "A Memo from the Chief," *Contributions*, March/April 1997, 23.

9. G.J. Mongon Jr., *Membership Survey* (Alexandria, VA: NSFRE, 1996), 1–17.

10. J.M. Greenfield, "Eye on Development," *Contributions,* March/April 1997, 17–18.

11. G.A. Evans, "The Annual Fund: The Foundation of the Development Program," *Annual Giving Strategies*, ed. A.D. Gee (Washington, DC: CASE, 1990), 3.

12. A.G. Louden, "The Annual Giving Program," *Educational Fund Raising*, ed. M.J. Worth (Phoenix: Oryx Press, 1993), 73.

13. S.R. McAnally, "Annual Giving," *Handbook of Institutional Advancement*, ed. A. Westley Rowland (San Francisco: Jossey-Bass, 1978), 197.

14. McAnally, "Annual Giving," 187.

15. G. Jindra, "Fund Raising Mistakes To Avoid at All Costs," *Contributions*, March–April 1997, 29–30.

16. Seymour, *Designs for Giving*, 64.

17. Stanley Baumblatt, assistant vice-president for philanthropic programs with Merrill Lynch & Company, in an oral presentation at the *Fund Raising Day in New York*, June 19, 1997.

CHAPTER 3

Major Gifts

Leonard R. Raley and Deborah Ann Weekley Read

Organizations in the late 1990s that are seeking to significantly increase their private giving have come to realize that at the core of their success is the need for a well-honed major gifts program. It is clear that major gifts are the driving force behind a successful campaign or an ongoing successful fund raising effort. Major gifts are defined at many different levels depending upon the type and size of organization. There is one common component, however, organizations all realize. The investment of staff, time, and energy can yield greater results if they are cultivating relationships with donor prospects who have the ability to contribute significant gifts to their cause. Major gifts programs are the backbone of the most successful development programs, and without them most organizations cannot sustain fund raising at the upper levels.

Regardless of the size of the staff, whether it be a one-person shop or a complex organization with a hundred or more development professionals, it is important to remember that this business is all about building relationships with individuals who can and want to be involved with an organization. We have seen numerous examples of this dynamic. We have identified alumni of our institution who were lost in the database for 10 to 20 years. Once we identified them, we made arrangements to meet them and invited them to become involved with the university. Over the course of one to two years of cultivation, we developed a relationship with them, and successfully solicited and closed major gifts. Through consistent and caring cultivation, through increased involvement of the prospect in the life of the institution, through the identification of specific areas of interest for the prospect's support, the seeds are sown to seek a major gift.

There are a number of questions to be asked when developing a major gift program. What are the current trends in the late 1990s? What is a major gift? How do you identify major gift prospects? Where do you find them? Once identified and qualified, what is the best way to involve the prospect? What is the process for cultivation? How and when should you make the ask? How do you bring the gift to closure? What is the role of the volunteer? Why do individuals who make major gifts choose to do so? What is the proper stewardship? What are the qualities of a good development officer?

CURRENT TRENDS

The 1990s have brought the downsizing of state and local governments and shifted the burden to the private sector to support many causes that traditionally received strong public financial support. This has resulted in a number of new trends including the advent of the mega campaigns and mega gifts, and a more visible and increased role with respect to women in philanthropy.

While the largest organizations and universities are raising hundreds of millions and even billions of dollars through campaigning, small colleges, universities, hospitals, and other nonprofit organizations are also mounting campaigns to secure higher levels of giving than ever before. Significant gifts from individuals, which were unheard of 10 years ago, are now becoming more commonplace. For example, Harvard received a $70.5 million planned gift from John L. Loeb and Frances Lehman Loeb in 1995. Michael Bloomberg contributed $55 million to his alma mater, Johns Hopkins University, in 1996. This recent gift was the largest ever received by Johns Hopkins at that time and, according to *Giving USA*, was inspired by his involvement with the university's board of trustees.[1] These mega gifts were truly transformational because of the significant impact each had on the universities.

Further evidence of the private sector's willingness to give financial support to various charities is illustrated in Table 3–1.[2] Over the period 1985 to 1995 there has been significant growth in private giving. In many cases this has helped to offset lost funding from federal, state, and local levels. In the United States, more than any other nation, we are fortunate that philanthropy has become part of the very fabric of our society.

The 1990s have seen the emergence of more women philanthropists who are taking very seriously their role in benefitting many organizations through their support. Brenda Brown Lipitz, a Baltimore philanthropist, supports numerous women's causes and issues at several nonprofits, including community organizations, hospitals, and universities. She said, "Women now recognize that they have unprecedented financial leverage, and they are better positioned than ever before to have an impact on social change. Indeed they are being wooed by many organizations and boards and there is great competition for their talents and their dollars. Recently there has been a surge of interest in the role women play as donors to nonprofits. Amid heightened interest, one reason stands out as the most plau-

Table 3–1 Growth in Private Giving From 1985 to 1995 (dollars in billions)

Recipient	1985	1995	Percent Increase
Religion	38.21	63.45	166
Education	8.17	17.94	220
Health Care	7.72	12.59	163
Human Services	8.50	11.70	138
Arts, Humanities	5.08	9.96	196
Public/Society	2.22	7.10	320
Total	69.9	122.74	176

Source: Reprinted with permission from *Giving USA*, p. 172, © 1996, AAFRC Trust for Philanthropy.

sible; that reason is money. Fund raisers think more and more women will be in control of charitable dollars. Many researchers are looking for reasons why women give. Some suggest individual giving is strongly correlated to three questions: (1) Does the person think she can afford to give? (2) Does the person know the value of the organization? (3) Was the person asked to give?" Ms. Lipitz suggests there is a fourth question: "Does the person feel valuable to and valued by the organization?"

"Clearly by a number of measurements—gains in wage earning status, emerging leadership, increased education—women are positioned to play a dominant role in philanthropic activity." Ms. Lipitz suggests "that it is time for the leaders in philanthropy to investigate, invest in, and recognize that women may hold the critical key to future generations of philanthropy."

She believes she has learned much about philanthropy and women in the last few years, but probably the most valuable is just this:

> If you have a good project,
> And you approach women donors,
> And involve them on your boards,
> And you value them for their wisdom as well as their wealth,
> And you include them in meaningful decisions—
> You will attract some of the best donors you will ever have the
> privilege of working with,
> I DID.[3]

What this points to is that women should be treated as equal players in the field of philanthropy and taken as seriously as men have been for generations. If organizations remember this and include women in a significant way in the life of the organization, these individuals will be the source of significant financial support.

MAJOR GIFTS

Major gifts are integral to all successful development efforts and complement an annual gifts program. Effective development programs typically dedicate separate staff resources to both types of gifts. Annual gifts are important and necessary because they provide a reliable and much-needed source of revenue and form a strong foundation for consistent giving from loyal donors. Often the best major gifts prospects are drawn from the ranks of annual donors. Major gifts often represent a defining gift for both the donor and the organization, in as much as the gift may be the single largest gift ever made by that individual or received by the organization. Major gifts do not need to be made with a gift of cash alone; however, certainly cash gifts are most welcome. Major gifts are often structured over a defined period of time, say for example over a period of three to five years. These gifts can take a variety of forms and a combination of resources, such as an outright gift of cash, appreciated securities, and real property, in combination with a deferred component that can take the form of a trust or bequest. Also, certain types of gifts-in-kind can qualify for major gifts. These typically include important collections and acquisitions of equipment.

Major gifts can be received from individuals, foundations, or corporations. Individuals, however, have the ultimate influence on all decisions if their gifts are corporate- or foundation-related. The primary focus of this chapter will be on individuals, whose gifts may be made through their privately held corporations or family foundations.

MAJOR GIFT PROSPECTS, WHERE TO FIND THEM

In essence one needs to be curious, be willing to dig for information to identify people of influence and affluence. Often it is helpful to have someone of influence introduce you to a major gift prospect with whom there is not an existing relationship. One of the easiest ways to begin the process of identification is to review the list of current donors to your organization, particularly those who have made gifts over a consistent period of time. Often it is not the amount of any single gift that a donor makes, but indeed the consistency in which they make contributions. It is important to remember to review lists of nondonors who have a known interest in the organization, or donors who have made only a single gift to the organization because it is from these ranks that some of the best major gift prospects can be found.

Volunteers who are leadership donors play a key role in identifying other potential donors at the upper levels. It is important to involve these volunteers in reviewing lists of donors and nondonors. Additionally, the volunteers can provide names of potential donors from their contacts—who may not be on your list at all.

The specific information provided by the volunteer about the potential ability of a prospect to give helps to validate the assumptions made by staff of the prospect's ability.

Increasingly, sophisticated development operations are employing staff to conduct research on prospective donors. The competition for major gifts among organizations in the United States has never been greater, therefore the need to have as much reliable information about the prospect pool is critical to the eventual solicitation and closure of major gifts. Much of the information to be learned about an individual's giving potential rests with the development officer or volunteer who visits the prospective donor to learn the pertinent information about the donor's ability to give, interest in the organization, inclination, and potential wealth. In addition to discovery calls with potential donors, it is important to receive input from the prospect's peers. An organization's current supporters will know best who among their contemporaries have the ability and interest to be considered major gift prospects. A series of rating and qualifying sessions with the volunteers and staff need to take place in order to suggest appropriate levels of potential support to be solicited. It is also important to ask who might be the best person to arrange for an initial visit and who should make the eventual solicitation.

Whether an organization has a small or large research staff, there are many common tools to help in identifying potential prospects. With the information superhighway, much of this can be garnered from electronic on-line services. Also, there are a variety of electronic screening services available nationwide that will, for a fee, review an organization's list of constituents to begin to identify those individuals who may have the capability and propensity to give. Purchasing these kinds of services is only a starting point and does not guarantee a qualified list of donor prospects. Qualifying occurs when volunteers review the lists and the development officers visit individually with the prospects.

INVOLVING PROSPECTS IN A SIGNIFICANT WAY

To obtain a major gift from a potential donor, we must first involve them in the life of the organization. Involvement can take many forms and can include serving on various boards, attending cultural or athletic events on campus or other special events hosted by the organization, interaction with students and faculty—if at a university or other teaching institution—and one-on-one meetings with the key leadership. Major donor prospects should be treated as insiders in the organization and contact should be maintained through frequent telephone contact, special letters sharing information from the president or executive director, newsletters, and other mailings.

WRITTEN CULTIVATION PLANS AND STRATEGIES

As managers of a major gifts program, who also work with prospects on major gift cultivation and solicitation, we recognize the value and need to write the specific cultivation plan for each major gift prospect. This is essential to maintaining a successful program.

If a development officer is responsible for managing an overall prospect list of 100 to 200 prospects, there needs to be a written strategy for at least the top 50–75. The best prospects require a specific cultivation plan and strategy, without which it is very difficult for a development officer to successfully manage the prospect pool and close major gifts. The list of 75 prospects with written strategies may change somewhat from month to month, based on who has been solicited, who has made a gift commitment, who has declined to support the organization, and what other names emerge from the list as top prospects.

Each cultivation plan and strategy needs to include the following items:

Staff name: the development officer who is assigned to manage the prospect

Volunteer(s): the volunteers involved in the cultivation process, either other donors, or the president or executive director of the organization

Solicitor: the person(s) to ask for the gift—the development officer, volunteer, or both

Clearance: the project(s) that the prospect is designated to support, i.e., scholarships, endowed chair in a specific college or program area

Target solicitation amount: the specific amount to be solicited, i.e., $100,000, $1 million

Target solicitation date: the suggested date for solicitation

Moves: the steps that will be taken with the prospect, i.e., monthly, quarterly

Cultivation steps: the specific steps to be taken to bring the prospect closer to the institution and for solicitation, i.e., invite to lecture, send follow-up note, schedule luncheon with president, invite to address student group, invite to serve on board, meet to provide update on status of college

Timeline: The specific dates for the cultivation—action steps to be taken

We all recognize that a cultivation plan and process for an eventual solicitation takes careful planning and dedicated attention by the development officer. To be successful, the advancement officer needs to be highly ethical, have a passion for the organization, and care about the individual prospect and his or her interests. For if the staff person does not really care about the project or the organization for which funds are being raised, prospects will sense it, and fund raising efforts will not be successful. This is why, when involving the prospective donors in the life of the organization, it is important to listen to them carefully and take their concerns and questions seriously. It is important to pay attention to their advice and counsel, and to treat them with respect, dignity, and special care. The rewards for careful cultivation and personal attention can be bountiful. Sue Washburn, of the consulting firm of Washburn and McGoldrick, has said on numerous occasions, "before a solicitation can be made, you have to earn the right to ask for a gift."

Earning the right to ask for a gift does not occur immediately. Asking for an immediate gift, without careful cultivation of the prospect over time, frequently results in a gift at a significantly lower level than what the donor is capable of making. One earns the right to ask for a major gift after a more significant period of time passes during which the prospect becomes more deeply involved with your organization. The development officer, the organization's leadership, and volunteers get to know the prospect better over the cultivation period where a sense of trust develops between the prospect and the organization's representatives.

SOLICITATION

How and When Should the Solicitation Be Made?

There is no magic formula to help one determine when someone is ready to be solicited for a major gift. If the proper steps, however, have taken place along the way to cultivate the relationship between the prospect and the organization, its volunteers, staff, and key leadership, the actual solicitation should be anticipated by the prospect. A rule to follow is that it generally takes 18 to 24 months of continuous involvement—from the date of the first discovery call to the major gift solicitation. This time can vary depending upon several factors: (1) how involved the prospect becomes over that period of time, (2) how philanthropically inclined the prospect is, (3) how deeply invested in the life of the organization the prospect is, and (4) whether or not the prospect has ever been solicited for a contribution.

Effective solicitations are completed in several stages. After the development officer has gotten to know a prospect well during the cultivation process, the staff member can decide who is the best person to solicit the donor. Should it be a volunteer, the president or executive director, the vice-president or dean, or some combination of individuals? When that decision is made, the development officer can also determine what form the solicitation should take. First the development officer should discuss with the prospect his or her interest in making a gift, the potential financial range, and the area of interest to support, e.g., scholarships, endowed chair, facilities, or programs. At that juncture the prospect's reaction to the discussion will lead the development officer in the proper direction for the solicitation. Additionally, if there is a key volunteer with whom the development officer works, it is essential that the development officer has a discussion with the volunteer to gain insight into the proper financial amount of the solicitation. Also, the volunteer should accompany the executive director, dean, president, or development officer on the solicitation visit as it may be appropriate and desirable.

Each solicitation strategy is unique to each individual prospect. If the basic steps are followed, namely, proper cultivation of the prospect, involvement in the life of the institution or organization, the decision about who should solicit the gift, and finally the ask appropriately executed, success can usually be ensured. It is helpful to walk through the solicitation strategy, including specific talking points with the cosolicitor or whatever team of people will be making the solicitation visit. It is important to decide who will say what, who will make the case for support, and who will ask for the gift. Equally important is rehearsing the discussion points in advance of the visit.

Development officers should schedule briefings with the key solicitors who will be making the solicitation visit. The briefings provide an opportunity to refine the strategy somewhat with the input of the president, executive director, or volunteer, in advance of the visit.

It is also important to consider when a written formal proposal should be delivered to the prospect. Should the solicitor present the proposal following the verbal solicitation? Should it be presented to the prospect at the end of the solicitation meeting, or should the proposal be mailed to the prospect following the visit with a note from the volunteer or president? When should the follow-up written solicitation occur in a letter format instead of a formal proposal? Again, it is important to consider the dynamics of each situation individually. The development officer should not treat all solicitations the same since each is being made to different individuals with their own interests, needs, personal style, and motivation factors.

Closure

How can the development officer confirm the gift once the solicitation is made? Equally as hard as deciding upon the solicitation strategy is the need to find the right way to bring a gift to closure. Who should place the follow-up call and when should that call be placed? When the call is made, should the solicitor request another appointment, or should the merits of the proposal be discussed over the phone? The object of that call is to determine if the prospect has made a decision to support the proposal. In most cases, it is more effective to have a face-to-face follow-up meeting because it will be easier to deal with any objections and to answer any questions.

In these situations, it is important to set the stage before leaving the meeting where the original solicitation occurs. That means considering and discussing strategy with the solicitors, and if the solicitation does not include the development officer, the discussion with the solicitors should take place in advance of the visit so the actions to be taken are in accordance with a specific plan outlined by you. It is necessary for the development officer to think through how the follow-up should occur. At the end of the solicitation meeting, the solicitor can say he or she will call the prospect in a few weeks to schedule a time for them to meet to discuss the decision. Or, the solicitor can say a formal proposal will be mailed, thus allowing time for the prospect to consider the gift. Should that be the case, the solicitor will follow up in a week to 10 days to schedule another meeting to discuss the prospect's decision.

It is important for the solicitor to take the lead in follow-up. It is a mistake to let the responsibility for follow-up rest solely with the prospect. The solicitor needs to schedule a return visit with the prospect at a certain time, which can be suggested by the prospect, but the follow-up should never be left open ended without a date being set. If a request has been made without any follow-up within three to five weeks, then it is harder to bring the gift to closure. A good rule to remember is, if a request or proposal sits dormant for over three months without any follow through by the volunteer, key institutional leadership or development officer, then you might as well consider that the answer to the solicitation is no.

Overcoming Objectives

One of the hardest tasks that each development officer faces is how to overcome objections to a solicitation, especially when those objections occur during the solicitation meeting itself. It is important to recognize in advance of a solicitation what those objections may be and what the appropriate response should be. In addition to the specific talking points for a request, possible objections and responses should be included in the written solicitation strategy. This will make the solicitors aware of possible objections and prepare them to answer the objections when making the call.

Also, if the development officer does not know the answer to a specific question related to a type of gift, perhaps a planned gift, or to a specific question of how the gift can be used, it is important and necessary to get the answer and get back to the prospect immediately. Remember always to be honest and sincere, upfront as they say, in answering the prospect's concerns. Never promise something that cannot be delivered.

The Role of the Volunteer Solicitor

Volunteers can provide valuable information. Development staff do not always have all the answers or know all of the nuances to every prospect situation. They must always keep an open mind and value the opinions of other staff, key institutional leadership, and volunteer leadership. In particular, it is good to remember why a volunteer was asked to participate in fund raising for your organization in the first place. Volunteers are there to provide guidance, make peer solicitations, and to make their own personal financial commitments. Often the volunteer knows the personal situation of a prospect better than an institutional representative, and it is important to listen to their suggestions and counsel.

RATIONALE: WHY PEOPLE GIVE AND WHY VOLUNTEERS ASK

People give to respected and trusted people who ask. They are motivated to give for a wide variety of reasons. They want to make a difference, to give something back, to create a lasting and meaningful legacy, and to provide opportunities for others that they may not have had themselves. The largest gifts received by an organization are made not necessarily because the donor just decides one day to make a gift, although sometimes this can occur, but more frequently it is because these individuals are involved with the organization for many years. Through the implementation of careful cultivation strategies, they become involved and invested in the life of the organization, and when approached for a significant gift by the president, executive director, or volunteer, are ready, willing, and eager to make a significant contribution. The same is largely true of people who ask. They ask because they believe in the institution or cause and want to help make a difference. They do not become volunteers and advocates because of any monetary compensation. Volunteers are not paid. They will not volunteer if they are uninterested, disappointed, or upset. People agree to ask because they feel a sense of pride and ownership, and because the influence of friends and peers is so strong, institutions and organizations have discovered centuries ago that good volunteers are worth their weight in gold. They are interesting to watch in major gift discussions about who should make the ask. Given the opportunity to choose, they will pick friends and acquaintances to solicit. Volunteers, like any others, are not enthusiastic about soliciting strangers. There are some exceptions, of course. By and large, what makes major donor solicitation work is the established, cordial relationship between the solicitor and the donor.

MAJOR GIFT STEWARDSHIP

Many of the major donor prospects come from the ranks of current donors. People will give again and again if their giving is appreciated by the receiving organization. We have all heard of stories where a donor contributes a gift to several organizations at once, waiting for an acknowledgment and, depending upon the sincere response received or not received, the donor then decides to make another gift, much larger than the first—to the organization that was most grateful for the original contribution. This story has been repeated time and again. The reason the story always hits home is that it may happen more than any of us would want to believe.

Think of it, when we make a gift to an organization that we may or may not care about, when do we give again? When we are asked—yes—but more than likely we give more often and in increasingly larger amounts when we are treated well, and we are no different from the major donor prospects we are cultivating for the mega gift. Professional staff and volunteers must remember to thank the donor, thank the donor, and then thank the donor again. One can never say thank you too many times.

Immediately upon receipt of a major gift, the president, executive director, key volunteer, or development officer, or combination of the above, should place a call to thank the donor. Additionally, a formal thank-you letter should be mailed from the key leadership. Depending upon the size of the gift in relation to what the organization usually received, it is often appropriate to host a dinner party or other special event in recognition of the donor's generosity. The donor should be asked to suggest individuals for the invitation list.

There are several specific items to remember when implementing a stewardship program. It is necessary to report annually on the use of all endowed funds to the donor or the donor's heirs or designees. This is not only the "right thing to do" but is generally required by the agreements that the receiving organization and the donor enter into upon receipt of the gift.

If a gift was made only once and the funds were used for a specific building fund or other operating need, it is still important to report on the use of the funds periodically (i.e., when the project is completed, or quarterly in the building campaign, or twice yearly). If open communication occurs after the gift is given, this certainly increases the likelihood of securing another gift before the project is complete or when the donor is solicited again.

QUALITIES OF A SUCCESSFUL MAJOR GIFTS OFFICER

Certain qualities are important for development officers to possess, and the officers who have more of these qualities than other individuals enjoy greater success and are, in fact, valuable treasures to their organizations.

Development officers, in general, and major gift officers in particular, have the responsibility of raising large gifts for the organization and as such need to possess a true sense of professionalism. They must remain highly committed to ethical standards in all situations. When building relationships between the organization and the prospect, the development professional needs to be honest, to truly care about the organization, to believe in the cause, to care about the person, to respect the prospect's wishes, and to remain focused on the donor. The development officer should be consistent in work, be a self-starter, be highly motivated, have a sense of humor, and not be timid about asking for the gift. Furthermore, the officer should be highly organized, possess strong communications skills, both oral and written, and be recognized as a team player. In a time when we all feel the pressures of being in a campaign, always needing to raise the funds to meet the bottom-line goal, it is ever important to occasionally step back and remember why we are in this business to begin with. We need to be able to say, "I believe in this organization. I support this organization, and I am here to ask you to join me in supporting this organization as well." It sounds so very simple and yet it is true. Before asking for a gift in support of the organization, we need to be a donor ourselves. Before asking someone else to believe in the cause of the organization, we need to believe in it too. Only then can we honestly and sincerely ask another person to join us in supporting the organization. If we cannot do any one of these essential things, then we cannot be an effective advancement officer devoted to raising major gifts.

SUMMARY

Alma Gildenhorn, Washington, D.C., philanthropist and patron of the arts, recently described why it is important to give and how organizations can successfully raise funds, which appropriately brings this chapter to a close:

> Each generation has to be the beacon for the one that follows, so that our children will not become self-absorbed, for children learn from what they are shown to do. Major donors are examples for the rest of the community, for what they do will inspire their heirs and others that come after them. I believe in creating legacies and for inspiring future generations of donors.

> Institutions that will succeed in the late 1990s and beyond are those where the key staff and volunteers develop relationships with those individuals who have a connection with the organization. The staff and volunteers bring a human face to the organization—a personal, hands-on approach in getting to know the individuals who have the ability to give—so that when called upon to make a major gift commitment the individual will be compelled to do so."[4]

To manage a successful major gifts program and to be a successful major gifts officer, the development professional must remember what Alma Gildenhorn, and countless other major donors, already know. The prospect has to be philan-thropically inclined, and the development officer needs to bring the human touch to the process, involving the prospect in the life of the institution, so the prospect becomes invested, and over time, when called upon to make a major gift, will be compelled to support the organization. It sounds so simple, and it is. If the staff and volunteers care about the organization, and the development officer earns the right to ask for the contribution through consistent and careful cultivation over a period of time, the solicitation stands a good chance of being successful. If the process was done well, the prospect will be inclined to be generous and support the institution.

NOTES

1. *Giving USA 1996*, New York: AARFC Trust for Philanthropy, 172.
2. *Giving USA 1996*, 22–23.
3. Author's interview with Brenda Lipitz, February 26, 1996.
4. Author's interview with Alma Gildenhorn, March 1, 1996.

CHAPTER 4

Corporate and Foundation Relations

William W. Tromble

> It seems to me shallow and arrogant for any man in these
> times to claim he is completely self-made, that he owes all
> his success to his own unaided efforts. Many hands and hearts
> and minds generally contribute to anyone's notable achievements.
>
> Walt Disney

We really do need each other. Corporations depend heavily on the academic community, especially in the areas of technology and scientific research, and the nation's colleges and universities depend on companies like DuPont, Eli Lilly, Amoco, and Kraft for financial support. Foundations likewise depend heavily on higher education to carry out their health care, social, cultural, or educational agendas. Colleges and universities look to the foundations for grants to help sustain their research programs and academic activities. Hospitals and social agencies and other nonprofits seek foundation support to enhance and maintain their programs. It is a win-win situation, and to better cultivate and direct this mutual friendship, more and more advancement professionals with expertise in corporate and foundation relations are being recruited.

CORPORATE GIVING

Corporate giving is a fairly recent phenomenon. Rare before the 1920s, it has increased remarkably in the last 50 years. Tax deductions were first allowed for corporate gifts in 1935. During World War II the spirit of giving touched corporations and individuals alike. In 1953 the courts upheld the legality of a corporate gift to Princeton, in effect opening the door for corporate gifts to all institutions of higher learning.[1] In the 1950s and 1960s the civil rights movement began to awaken the social conscience of corporate America. Today corporations, despite

93

their penchant for the bottom line, are increasingly concerned about their roles in the community, and that has helped to increase their giving. In 1996, according to *Giving USA*, corporate entities gave $8.5 billion. Even so, there is room for improvement.

> Enlightened self-interest—such as supporting nonprofit organizations that have the most impact, directly or indirectly, on the corporation—is a prime motivator in corporate support.[2]

The fastest growing companies tend to focus on making money, not on giving it away. Debra Blum and Susan Gray say corporate gifts have not kept pace with their rapid growth. After the American Red Cross in San Francisco spent more than $300,000 to help victims of a devastating fire and nearly depleted their funds, high-tech companies with phenomenal growth such as Lam Research and the Mylex Corporation were approached and asked to give but both declined to do so. Other companies in the Fortune 100 group of fastest growing public companies, like America Online and Starbucks Coffee, are "hot firms" but "cool toward philanthropy."[3] Professional persuasion is the key. Development officers who succeed in taking their case directly to the chief executive officer of the company stand a much better chance of building a cooperative relationship and securing a grant. Vic Murray writes, "Virtually everyone who has studied corporate donations agrees that one of the largest determinants of the size of the donation budget (as well as who receives how much in donations) is the personality of the company's top manager."[4] The chief executive officer's (CEO's) value system, beliefs, personality traits, and background have a significant bearing on how the corporate gift dollar will be spent.

It has become rather common in colleges and universities to include a staff position for corporate and foundation relations. It is not so common in the so-called not-for-profit community, but it is nonetheless important to the long-term development of good relationships with corporate and foundation donors. The function of building good relationships with corporations and foundations goes on in hospitals, social agencies, and other nonprofits as well as in institutions of higher learning, and it is a necessary function. Strengthening positive and supportive relationships is essential to development efforts.

Furthermore, the responsibility for building relationships rests with the institution, not the prospect or the donor. The cultivation of friendships, the overture to partnerships begins with the grant-seeking organization, not the other way around. Corporations are in the business of making money. Foundations are in the business of keeping it and giving some of it away, but they will not come knocking at the door or hand it out easily.

Advancement professionals are continually building good relationships with all publics, constituents, and clients. The corporate world, however, is a special world of its own, and it requires a certain knowledge and understanding of corporate structure, method, and policy to be successful in winning support. Every company has its own unique style, attitude, and operational procedure, and there are certain things advancement professionals have come to know:

- The larger the corporation the more difficult it is to talk directly with the top executives. The first stop is usually with a "contributions officer."
- Corporations are usually bottom-line oriented. They are in the business of making a profit.
- Multiyear pledges are usually not made by corporations or foundations. There are exceptions, of course.
- Corporate philanthropy is less philanthropy and more quid pro quo. Many prefer sponsorships and cause-related marketing to outright gifts.
- Sponsorships are attractive to some companies because of name recognition. With others it is purely a necessary part of doing business.
- Talk with whom you will, but the decision maker is the CEO. Human resources personnel, however, are helpful in opening the door.
- As with all prospects, building relationships is the path to corporate generosity.
- Finding ways to establish partnerships is time well spent in preparation for gift solicitation.

FOUNDATION RELATIONS

Foundations are another story. Foundations, generally speaking, not only discourage building relationships but also often insist that contact be made by letter rather than personal visit. There are exceptions, but by and large foundations prefer to remain impersonal. Unless the president of the university, or the CEO of the nonprofit organization, just happens to know one or more of the major players in a given foundation, the chances of a face-to-face meeting with any of the members of the foundation board, not to mention the principal donors to the foundation, are rather slim, and yet, foundation personnel have to get to know the institution or there will probably never be a grant. Rarely does a cold proposal from an unknown organization get much attention from a foundation director. So it is a Catch-22 situation for the institution. On the one hand, relationship building is not encouraged, but on the other hand, a grant will not be made if something is not done to build a relationship. Out-of-state foundations can be especially frustrating.

One of the best ways to build a relationship with a foundation is to select a project carefully, spend the time necessary to identify one or two foundations best suited to fund the project, and do the necessary research. Follow every guideline.

Submit a letter of inquiry, or call to confirm the procedure. If there is a favorable reply to the letter of inquiry, craft the proposal as clearly and persuasively as possible and deliver it. If the request is denied, try again and again, but be absolutely sure the proposal fits the culture and interests of the foundation. Make telephone calls, try to arrange visits with foundation agents, if that is desirable. If you are persistent, most foundations will allow you to visit. You may not be able to arrange a face-to-face conversation with the foundation director, much less the principal donors, but the chances are you will be able to talk with an agent. Keep it up until they get to know you and begin to see your organization through your personality. Sometimes it takes years, but it pays off. You have to dedicate yourself to building the relationship, whatever it takes. With local foundations, invite the director or secretary to your organization. Show them around. Introduce them to people in your organization. People interacting with people work wonders.

Nothing really happens until people start talking to each other.

Development officers should understand one basic principle. If corporations or foundations do not know the organization, its request will sink to the bottom of the stack of proposals received. Corporate or foundation personnel will be nice and courteous, but that is as far as it goes. You must be creative in finding ways for the foundation to get to know your organization and develop an interest in what you are doing. Sometimes that means being persistent.

Persistence will not work, however, if any of the following prevail:

- the request does not fit the interests and limitations of the foundation
- the foundation guidelines are not followed explicitly
- the draft you submit has too much verbiage and too little substance
- the budget is too general, unrealistic, or ill-conceived
- you attempt to make the request artificially fit the foundation interests, when in truth it does not fit
- site visits are overly staged to impress foundation representatives and perceived to be pseudo

Foundations tend to give more than corporations. At times they can be extremely generous. Grants can be in the millions, which is not frequent in corporate giving. One reason is the difference in the mission and purpose of foundations in contrast to that of corporations. Charitable foundations exist to give money away. Companies exist to make money on the sale of their products and services, and keep as much of it as they can. Foundations are required by their charters to distribute a percentage of their investment returns. Charitable contributions by corporations amount to a very small percentage of their net profits. Corporate sponsorships are often funded out of advertising budgets and can represent a significant piece of change for the college or nonprofit seeking corporate sponsorships.

Another significant difference between corporations and foundations is visibility. Corporations tend to like publicity. Foundations often prefer anonymity. In a recent multimillion-dollar capital campaign for an eastern university, a large corporation in the area made a contribution of $1.5 million and orchestrated the news release. The local newspapers carried feature stories about this outstanding corporate gift. Shortly afterward a leading foundation in the same area made a campaign contribution of $1.2 million but requested anonymity. Somehow the press found out about it and printed the story naming the foundation and the amount. That same day in a telephone conversation with foundation staff, it was made clear foundation board members were unhappy about the visibility of their gift. Although the institution was not at fault, future gifts could be affected. This is not true of all foundations, but taken as a whole it is safe to say they do not seek publicity. Corporations, on the other hand, often encourage it.

Corporate giving declined for a period of years, $7.31 billion in 1987, only $6.44 billion four years later, but since 1991, there has been a steady climb to a high of $8.50 billion in 1996.

Foundation giving has risen from $8.25 billion in 1987 to $11.83 billion in 1996, but neither corporate nor foundation giving can compare with individual giving. For the last 10 years, individual giving has increased from $101.45 billion to $119.92 billion.

Nevertheless, corporate and foundation giving is significant and should be pursued with all vigor. As the years go by, if what company executives are predicting comes true, corporate giving will increase, because most companies have gone through downsizing and right-sizing and are positioning themselves for greater efficiency and bigger profits in the twenty-first century. Unfortunately, the share of those profits that constitute gift dollars will likely continue at less than 5 percent of net profits. On the foundation side, the spend-out rate of investment returns looks to be approximately 5 percent.

UNDERSTANDING CORPORATE AND FOUNDATION CULTURES

One of the best examinations of corporate and foundation cultures in recent years was done by Joseph R. Mixer, recently named outstanding fund raising professional of the year by the National Society of Fund Raising Executives. Among other things, Mixer's research found that these cultures tend to be self-serving, but not self-sufficient. "No organization," he says, "is self-sufficient. All must enter into exchanges with the environment." That environment is characterized by change and turbulence in social, economic, and political conditions. "The overall case for corporate giving lies in the concept of social exchange." He maintains that corporations try to enhance their operational environment by improving some aspect of society, such as education, that benefits both the company and society at large. "Corporations have an interest in effecting change in the views and attitudes of the larger community so these views correspond with corporate values, and this interest affects corporate gifts."[5]

Foundations, for the most part, came into existence to perpetuate the founding donor's values, interests, and preferences. A quick scanning of the 7,549 foundations listed in the 1966 *Foundation Directory* confirms that assertion. Grant seekers who choose to ignore it do so at their own peril. If the interests of the institution seeking grant support happen to parallel that of the foundation, and the foundation directors are aware of the good things the institution is doing, the chances of the proposal being successful are reasonably good, depending also on the discretionary amount available to the foundation.

Foundations do not, as a rule, invade the corpus but fund proposals with a portion of their investment returns. Certain kinds of foundations, for example corporate foundations, are funded by contributions from the company, and the amount available for grants changes. Recently, a number of corporate foundations have seen a decrease in spendable monies, including the Amoco Foundation in Chicago that experienced a reduction of $6 million in available money for grants.

Both corporations and foundations strive to institutionalize their giving. Engineering companies tend to give to institutions and organizations that produce engineers or affect the industry. Health care firms, like SmithKline Beecham, DuPont-Merck, or Eli Lilly, tend to put their grant money into people and programs that in some way, socially or scientifically, are associated with the health care industry. Of recent years they have ceased random giving in favor of focused and institutionally related giving. Increasingly they have structured their grant making to assist in achieving the goals of the existing power brokers in the company or the foundation. Large foundations like Ford, Kellogg, and Pew often stimulate and encourage requests that coincide with foundation interests.

Advancement professionals must do their homework well. They must understand the dynamics of corporate and foundation giving, and use that understanding and wisdom in approaching companies and foundations for grant support.

Professional advancement people are seeing subtle changes in the way corporate gift dollars are being designated. For one thing, very few corporate dollars are unrestricted. Almost all corporate gifts are restricted to particular programs, events, or activities. The same is true more and more for foundations. What is happening in corporate America, however, is a heightened awareness of how gift dollars are being used. There was a time when Sears, for example, would give $50,000 for scholarships and not many questions were asked. Now the giant retailer has pulled back from that approach to philanthropy and is insisting that charitable organizations be national in scope and give high visibility to the company. SmithKline Beecham once contributed heavily to the arts and humanities. Now the company is much more focused toward health care projects, especially those that are model programs for others to follow. Amoco and others have reduced the amount of money their foundations have for grants, and they are taking on no new donor clients, but staying with the organizations they are now funding.

ATTRACTING CORPORATE SUPPORT

Sources of Support

Corporate support comes from interest and involvement with the organization. There are many links to consider. In the A to Z prospect and donor base, the first likely clue to link companies with the institution is whether or not the company has made a previous gift to the institution. This is the first place to look in attracting corporate support, because if the company is a past donor it is safe to assume there is some interest. It could be nothing more than a passing donation that resulted from a special appeal, or it could be the donor is developing a lasting interest in the institution. Eighty percent of the time, if there is one gift, and there is proper acknowledgment and donor recognition, there will be a second gift. No individual or organization makes a gift unless that person or company wants to make it, for whatever reason, and people usually do not want to make a gift unless they have some interest in the cause or organization asking for the gift. So the best place to start is with the past donors.

Another source of gift revenue is vendors. These are the companies that do business with the institution. They have a vested interest because their profits are derived in some part from sales to the institution. They do not give largely, as a rule, but vendors will make contributions. Coca-Cola, for example, contracts for the pouring rights on a university campus or at a hospital and subsequently will contribute several thousands of dollars. ARAMARK catering and food service also makes contributions to the organizations it serves, and there are many others including travel agencies, custodial services, and contractors. Capital campaigns often look to vendors of building supplies for nominal contributions. It should be kept in mind, however, that vendors calculate their profit margin rather carefully and, to some extent, resent being asked to invade their profits to make donations. They do understand, though, that charitable contributions are just a part of doing business.

Another excellent source of funding includes those companies that recruit future employees from the institution. Those that recruit on campus and are successful in getting good managers, accountants, nurses, or engineers are far more apt to give to the institution than those that do not recruit. Many a development officer has heard the phrase, "Sorry, we do not recruit on your campus." Sometimes that recruiting comes in the form of arranging for internships, cooperative agreements, and work/study programs. In fact, internships are often preferred because they allow the companies to get a close look at a prospective employee over a period of time without any obligation to hire. Most students who serve internships hope and pray they will be hired, but it is not a given. Internships are also good for the students because they offer an opportunity to get to know the corporate culture, including the good things and the bad. It helps them to know whether this is the direction they want to take. It is not unusual, after a few months of internship, for a student to decide that "this is not for me," and that is a healthy situation, because neither the company nor the student has made a job commitment, and neither wants to waste time and energy in a situation that is not desirable. Happily, either party can back away gracefully with no regrets.

Another source of corporate support includes those companies that have a presence in the local community. Merchants and businesses other than incorporated companies should be included here as well. They usually know the institution. They have developed an interest in the institution by reading the daily news items and seeing promotional materials. Their CEOs have rubbed shoulders with the president or chancellor and the development staff, in service clubs, civic events, and social programs. Often the local manufacturing plant or store or bank has a favorable working relationship with the institution. This business community is usually receptive to fund raising appeals from a neighborly friend, like the local college or university or YMCA or Red Cross.

Large national corporations, like Kraft, Pillsbury, Texaco, McDonald's, Du Pont, and IBM, though they are not hometown companies, will make substantial contributions if they have a presence in the community, such as an office, a plant, or some other local operation.

Companies that have executives serving on boards of directors or advisory boards will give, even though they do not have a local operation, because they consider it to be, in a sense, having a voice in the affairs of the institution that could benefit the corporation. It is also considered to be their civic duty to allow their executives to serve on local boards and committees.

If companies benefit from services or programs the institution offers, even though they may be located in an adjoining state, they will often make gifts. They recognize the value of the program or service that has the potential to reach into their areas of operation. A large petroleum company, for example, that has a strong interest in engineering may make donations to a preengineering program in some far away location because those students will go on to top engineering schools like Michigan, M.I.T., or Georgia Tech and eventually be found on the company's payroll. These preengineering schools, premedicine, or prelaw schools are considered to be feeder schools bringing students through the pipeline to a larger pool of potential employees.

Alumni sometimes play a large role in attracting corporate support. They serve as advocates for the institution and exert influence on corporations in their home towns to contribute to their alma mater. This is especially true if the alumnus(a) happens to be a leading citizen of the town.

Solicitation Techniques

Techniques for attracting corporate gifts are much like those used in the solicitation of any gift. Companies want to know why they should give and what difference it will make if they give. These questions and many more are answered in the case statement. With companies it is best to focus on economic reasons. Social issues and education are fine, but company executives tend to chase the dollar. A good economic impact study, one that is well researched, clearly articulated, and attractively presented will get attention. A general rule of thumb in figuring economic impact is three times the institutional budget. So if the budget is 40 million, the economic impact is $120 million. To be more accurate, several factors should be taken into account, including payroll, employee purchases, banking services, investments, consumer products, insurance, and real estate, to name a few.

Like any other solicitation, the corporate solicitation should be preceded by ample cultivation, such as personal visits, invitations to special events, and invitations to the agency or college. The development officer should always be on the look out for news items about the company and be quick to compliment and congratulate where desirable. One could even have a special day at the organization or on the university campus in honor of the company. In Delaware, it might be appropriate to have an E.I. du Pont de Nemours Day and invite friends and guests to visit, have lunch, take tours, and celebrate the day. In Indiana, it might be appropriate to have an Eli Lilly Day.

It is always helpful, when asking for a corporate gift, to be able to cite other companies that have made gifts. One needs to be discreet about it, of course, but prospective donors really want to know how they will be positioned when and if they give. Often the institution can leverage the gift with information about what others have done. No one likes to be alone in supporting a project. The haunting question always comes, "If no one else out there is giving, why should I, and if others are not giving there must be something wrong."

Much like individuals, companies are interested in the accountability and reliability of the institution. They want to know how their money is being used. This is one of the biggest factors in annual giving, as well as major gifts. Especially since the United Way scandal of the early 1990s, donors want to know how much, if any, is skimmed off the top to pay for administrative costs. They want to see a strong balance sheet, and companies and foundations in particular want to see an audited financial statement.

Finally, it should be said, with all things considered, the state of the nation's economy affects more decisions for charity than most of the things mentioned above. It is quite logical. If a donor has a pocket full of change, nice clothes to wear, and plenty to eat, he or she is much more inclined to give, simply because he or she is able to give. Being able to give, of course, is only the first consideration. Wanting to give has to be in place also, but as any fund raiser knows, the cardinal rule of closure is the donor needs to be asked. The number one reason prospective donors have not given and do not give is "BECAUSE NO ONE ASKED ME."

In the end what determines the gift comes down to (1) how the company executives perceive the grant-seeking institution, (2) how much discretionary money they have to give, and (3) if, and how much, others are giving. The institution's mission, goals, and objectives; its effectiveness in doing what it purports to do; its fiscal integrity; its value to the company; and the quality of the solicitation all contribute to the equation.

Often in the fund raising battle for dollars, what rules you out is more important than what rules you in. Some of these red flag areas that corporations tend to shy away from are religious issues, political programs, the military, and advocacy groups. The fund raiser may also be told, "You are already funded by the United Way," or "by the State, so you don't need my gift." The answer to that last one is "We're assisted, not funded."

With corporations and foundations, the "ask" is usually in the form of a written letter of request or a formal proposal, and there is a lot more to be said about the art of asking in the chapters on annual giving and capital campaigns. The father of institutional advancement, Harold J. (Si) Seymour, said it best when he wrote:

> Assuming we all aspire to be sought and to be worthwhile members of worthwhile groups, there can hardly be any stronger motivation for supporting a group or cause than simple *pride of association*.[6]

CORPORATE PARTNERS

Private and public partnerships are growing. Corporate America and institutions of higher learning are joining hands to accomplish their goals. In these partnerships it takes big warm hearts to make a difference, to fulfill human need, to stay on course in the midst of tax revision, corporate and institutional restructuring. The value of the partnership is not what organizations get from donor dollars but what they become because of the gift dollars. What really counts in the end is people in all industries working together to make a better world through social contacts, honesty, and integrity.[7]

It is an oversimplification to say, "what universities want from corporations and foundations is financial support," because there is much more to it than that. Higher education needs help with research. Graduates need jobs. Students need internships and cooperative liaisons with industry, but money drives the whole process.

What companies and foundations want most from the organizations they support are measurable results. As one Du Pont executive, Claibourne Smith, puts it, "Show us how our dollars are making a difference." The big question often asked in corporate board rooms is "Does what we give really matter?"

New partnerships with nonprofits increasingly have placed corporations in the role of advocates for social change. SmithKline Beecham, for example, a large pharmaceutical company, challenges higher education to promote human wellness. Kraft has given substantial grant assistance to programs that address children at risk. Pew Charitable Trust and the Annenburg Foundation have contributed millions of dollars to improve public education at the lower levels. Corporate executives are concerned about the way the federal government does business, addressing questions of waste and bureaucratic overkill.

In recent years there has been a move toward greater funding from the private sector for cooperative programs—programs that involve two or more organizations working together to accomplish a single goal. The theory is that big problems cannot be solved with Band-Aid solutions. They may take the combined efforts and resources of several organizations plus the corporate grant to make it happen. Community foundations in particular are moving in that direction. The idea is as old as America. Our national motto is *e pluribus unum*. We are a diverse group of people and organizations, but by working together to solve the problems of health care, economic stability, or welfare we can bring a powerful solution to the table.

Diversity itself has come to the foreground. In its purest meaning, diversity embodies the concept of inclusiveness, bringing together the best thinking and the best efforts of different people and cultures to accomplish a single purpose. The old saying "two heads are better than one" reflects the view that different intellectual approaches are instrumental in solving difficult problems. What the companies, foundations, or other funding sources see in promoting cooperative efforts to complete a project is an opportunity to stretch their dollars a little further, and the idea that they are promoting a sense of community, a convivial, collegial, and diverse approach that has great social value. Stamping out polio on this planet, for example, is a monumental goal of the International Rotary Foundation, and it nearly has been accomplished by hundreds of people and organizations working together in Africa, Europe, and the Far East with the help of foundation dollars.

Institutions that have developed corporate partner programs have found them to be helpful and productive. In earlier years, they were called "cluster" programs, but cluster does not carry the dynamic and relevant meaning institutions desire. "Partners" is much better. It has a "doing this together" feeling that "cluster" does not convey. "Corporate partners" is the best term, because it describes the kind of partnership being sought. One such program, developed at a small university on Maryland's Eastern Shore, is described below.

It began as a concept and a vision to leverage the strengths of the university with those of the corporate community to produce needed research, strengthen academic programs, and assist students in understanding the work force they would soon be a part of. Although some corporate partners programs begin with the objective of increasing corporate gifts to the institution, this one began without even the hint of solicitation for money. The goal was to get as many companies as possible, in the local area, to partner with the university and appoint representatives who would meet with university deans, faculty, and professional staff on a regular basis to explore ways of working together. Much planning and preparation went into it. A statement of organization was drafted. Cultivation and recruiting visits were made, and a formal invitation was given the prospective corporation to join "Corporate Partners." At the end of the first six months there were six companies that said "Yes, this is a worthwhile effort. We would like to participate."

Advancement staff were not interested in recruiting a mass of people in a sort of shotgun effort. Companies to approach were chosen carefully in much the same way prospective donors are chosen. Some had been involved with the university for years. Others had not. The case statement was written and a colorful brochure designed. The concept was presented to the board of visitors for endorsement and assistance. The president, naturally, was an advocate from the very start. Little by little the program grew and soon had taken on a life of its own. Today, there are 25 corporate partners, including the E.I. Du Pont de Nemours Company, Hewlett-Packard, NationsBank, Beneficial Corporation, Xerox Corporation, Sony Music Entertainment, and Honeywell, to name only a few. Meetings are held alternately between the university campus and corporate sites. The group meets monthly to engage in dialogue with students and professors, make presentations, and help solve problems. During the recent spring semester, Corporate Partner meetings dealt with subjects like "Current Trends in Industry," "New Technologies," and "Best Interviewing Practices." Two Corporate Partner committees have been formed, an executive speakers bureau and a communications and publications committee.

Exhibit 4–1 is an example of a Corporate Partners program. It is the model developed by Director of Corporate and Foundation Relations Renee Wright of Delaware State University.

Exhibit 4–1 Corporate Partners

The Concept. Corporate Partners is conceived as an advisory support group consisting of an alliance of corporations recruited by the University personnel, members of the Board of Visitors, and others to participate in mutually beneficial programs and activities.

The Purpose. The purpose of Corporate Partners is to initiate, develop, and expand a mutually cooperative relationship between the business community and the University.

Objectives

- To serve as an informational and advisory group, addressing changes in education necessary to respond to the needs of business and industry
- To improve the University's ability to produce highly qualified graduates who can meet the personnel needs of business and industry
- To increase and improve the number and quality of job and career opportunities, such as part-time work, internships, cooperative arrangements, or exchange programs for university students
- To increase company and university resources to ensure better teaching, research, and service, and improve the quality of life for all constituents

Corporate Benefits

- Access to well educated, highly qualified minority and female graduates, and candidates for internships
- Access to well educated faculty and administrators to facilitate the transfer of academic and industrial information for potential joint research and related partnerships
- Opportunities to get to know prospective employees through workshops, cooperative programs, summer jobs, internships, career days, and youth motivation task force activities
- Reduction in orientation and training costs by hiring University graduates
- An improved community relationship

University Benefits

- Opportunity to receive counsel from the business community in the development and implementation of University programs, projects, and curricula that will strengthen the skills and experiences of University students
- Greater ability to provide students with a practical and relevant education in preparation for entering the job market and making progress in the work force
- Increased professional development opportunities for faculty and administrators through linkages with the corporate community
- Opportunity to keep abreast of developments in business and industry, to better correlate programs of study with the employment needs of the business community

continues

Exhibit 4–1 continued

- Objective evaluation and suggestions for modifying academic programs to ensure their relevance for the business community
- Opportunity for the University to receive technical assistance, equipment, and financial support to enhance existing programs and provide for further development

Student Benefits

- Ability to interface directly with potential employers
- Preparation, through Corporate Partner seminars and workshops, to compete for positions in business and industry, i.e., interviewing techniques, resume writing, and appropriate dress and grooming
- Better opportunities for job placement and career building through internships and cooperative agreements
- Firsthand knowledge of the corporate community through tours, dialogue, and direct involvement with corporation representatives
- Knowledge of what is available in the work place, and what educational preparation is needed to compete

Courtesy of Delaware State University, Dover, Delaware.

According to the plan's guidelines, *qualifications of business participants* include knowledge of management, technology, and material resources, and an understanding of skills needed by college graduates to succeed in business. Corporate Partners are expected to provide insight into curriculum development, to assist in obtaining donations of equipment, to provide opportunities for research and development, lectures, internships, fellowships, scholarships, exchange programs for students and faculty, cooperative positions, and other opportunities.

Depending on their interests, specific corporations may have several individuals participating in Corporate Partners, but working with different schools. For example, because of its diverse interests Du Pont could potentially have someone working with the School of Business, the College of Arts and Sciences, and the School of Professional Studies simultaneously.

Corporate Partners is a subgroup of the Delaware State University Board of Visitors. They meet as necessary to achieve their objectives. They prepare and distribute a report to the Board of Visitors describing their activities for the year. All individuals who represent business and industry, and are currently serving on advisory boards at the university, are invited to participate in Corporate Partners activities, as are representatives of state and federal agencies. Finally, there is a Corporate Partners steering committee, which comprises both company representatives and university personnel, including administrators, deans, and faculty.

In this particular Corporate Partners Program, the cochairs are the university's director of corporate and foundation relations and an individual chosen from the Corporate Partners group. The first cochair from the business side was the human resources manager for Hewlett-Packard. The program has developed over time and become a valued asset to the university and the companies as well, not only in program development and student preparation, but in financial support for the University.

CAUSE-RELATED MARKETING

Another recent twist in corporate charity is the phenomenon of what is being called cause-related marketing. The concept is rather simple but the application is complex. Reduced to its simplest form, cause-related marketing is designating a part of the cost of a sales item for a cause, such as education or health care. John Yankey explains it in some detail in the 1996–97 Winter issue of *Advancing Philanthropy.*[8] Here is how it works. The organization, a university for example, approaches a company that sells pizza and asks that 25 cents on every pizza sold over a certain period of time be contributed to the general scholarship program of that university. An agreement is drawn up and signed by both parties. The pizza company through advertisements and other promotions lets its customers know that every time a pizza is purchased, 25 cents is delivered to the university and used to provide scholarships for deserving students. What is happening is cause-related marketing by the pizza company. The message is clear. Buy a pizza and help put a deserving student through college.

MBNA America, the country's third largest credit card company, does a multi-million-dollar business in cause-related marketing. Universities and other affinity groups sign an agreement with the bank that allows the bank to create a credit card with a picture or logo on the front in the appropriate colors that identify that organization. The card is marketed to the members of that organization with the stipulation that cards will be issued to members only. So, it becomes a very exclusive card. University alumni and members of other affinity groups are proud to carry the card, and every time a purchase is made with the credit card a few cents go to the institution or organization. "When you use this card," the company says, "you support your institution."

One of the reasons the corporate partners program works so well is that companies are a part of the community. Support from the community is essential to their progress, and their support of the community is vital to the prosperity of the good citizens who live in the community.

With that in mind companies are promoting volunteerism. Employees are strongly encouraged to serve as community volunteers. In some cases employees are given time off from work to provide volunteer service. MBNA America, located in Newark and Wilmington, Delaware, is exceptionally successful in getting employees to volunteer. Those who have visited the corporate offices in Newark or downtown Wilmington have seen the pride Chairman Charles Cawley has instilled in his people, a pride to be a part of this outstanding company whose profits increase year after year, and whose service to Delaware is unmatched. Examples of volunteerism are set by upper level corporate executives and imitated by employees down the line to the lowest paid custodian.

Companies are making gifts-in-kind to dispose of inventory no longer needed. These gifts are often welcomed by nonprofits. Granted some gifts-in-kind are refused, and rightly so. No organization wants outdated or unusable equipment or materials, but for the most part these corporate gifts are desired and put to good use. The J.P. Morgan Bank, for example, installed new computer equipment and donated much of the used equipment to nonprofit organizations. It was fully depreciated, so there was no tax benefit to the company, but the personal computers and other equipment found a home with those who needed them.

Like foundations, companies are treating contributions as investments and expecting returns from them. They are increasingly concerned about how their dollars are spent. They expect the organizations they support to be accountable and ethical. There are thousands of institutions and organizations seeking corporate dollars but only a limited number of dollars to go around. In the past some organizations have misused funds that have been contributed. Scandals and scams of recent years have caused donors to be more demanding of ethical behavior, more demanding of accountability, and more concerned about their "investment" in colleges, universities, and other nonprofits.

Companies are embracing the concept of "strategic giving." It is the merging of community needs with corporate interests and seeking ways to make their gifts have the greatest impact. Yankey cites a study of 188 firms that found employee morale to be three times higher in companies with a strong degree of community involvement. In former years just giving to the cause seemed to be enough, but now many companies are seeking other ways to get involved in the issues and activities of the communities they serve, such as helping with volunteer work, sponsoring special events, and making gifts of tangible personal property.[9]

Companies also are helping communities through cause-related marketing discussed above. Proponents say it increases product sales and increases public recognition for the company, while at the same time supporting a cause the company cares about. Cause-related marketing has been around for 20 years or more, but it is getting much more attention now, because corporations and charitable organizations share a common goal to improve the standard of living.

Many companies are making their cash go further by including promotional sponsorships, encouraging employees to volunteer for community service, and offering gifts-in-kind, usually company products. Instead of writing checks and walking away, they are creatively using noncash resources of human energy and finished materials to solve social problems. Corporate sponsorships are frequently preferred by CEOs because they can use advertising money when the supply of gift money runs low. Furthermore, they get value back in the form of name recognition and promotion by sponsoring athletic contests, national events, and local fund raisers, such as charity balls, golf outings, auctions, and dinners. These social events tend to arouse the social conscience and move people to action.

The downside is that many events are too costly and require too many paid or volunteer workers, stretching available resources. It would be easier, in most cases, just to ask for the money and skip the dinner or show, but people love a good show and good food, especially if they think their buying a ticket helps fund a charitable cause.

There is also the challenge from the Internal Revenue Service. Charities are now required to tell the donor how much of the ticket price is a gift and how much went for food and entertainment. Donors are realizing this is a necessity and are not put off by it.

Gifts-in-kind save time and energy for the company, but charities are well advised to go carefully in accepting them. Goods are often out of date or style. Companies have succeeded in lowering their inventory levels of old goods, but charities have acquired items they may not be able to use or maintain.

Service companies, e.g., advertising companies, can give pro bono gifts. IBM, Du Pont, and others encourage employees to do volunteer work on the clock. What they get in return is enhanced public image and improved community relations. The basic elements of employee volunteerism are: (1) that it is employee driven, (2) that volunteers choose their charity, and (3) that volunteers are recognized by management. Often this occurs via newsletters and public recognition. EDiS, a construction firm in Wilmington, Delaware; Kraft in Chicago; and other companies practice employee recognition for volunteerism, and for universities and nonprofits, a good corps of volunteers is invaluable.

CORPORATE SOLICITATION

Stanley Baumblatt of Merrill Lynch, the largest financial service organization in the world, with over 500 branches, offers some tips to those who would solicit corporate gifts. "First of all, keep in mind," he said, "corporations are in the business of making money, not giving it away." At Merrill Lynch, "we see philanthropy as an investment."[10]

Two things are immensely important for the development officer seeking grants from corporations or foundations. He or she should find out what is of current interest to the company or foundation, and second, learn what the company or foundation is all about, its identity, its character. "Current" is the operative word. Interests and priorities change. Unless the fund raiser discovers the "hot buttons," much time and energy will be spent getting nowhere. There are several sources for finding that out. One is simply calling the corporate contributions officer or the foundation director to confirm or to inquire what the current interest may be. It is a big mistake to waste the company's time with requests that will not be funded. That is the wrong way to keep in touch and build proper relationships.

Another source of information is the Foundation Center in New York. Its major publication is *The Foundation Directory*. The 18th edition lists 7,549 active grant-making foundations, but this listing includes only those foundations with assets of $2 million or more, or that make grants of $200,000 or more. Each listing contains name, address, phone number, and contact person, plus a wealth of additional information. For example, one of the listings under the state of Virginia is The Freedom Forum International. The listing includes the name of the principal donor, Frank E. Gannett, financial data including assets, expenditures, total distributions, the range of average grants, the total amount given as matching gifts, and the amount given to support foundation-administered programs. The listing contains narrative about the foundation's purpose, activities, and fields of interest. It gives information about the foundation's international interests. It lists the types of support the foundation gives. It reveals what the foundation's limitations are. It names foundation publications. It gives application information. It gives board meeting dates and lists the names of the officers and trustees, and, finally, it reveals the amounts and recipients of recent grants.[11]

An excellent source of information concerning corporate gifts, however, is *The National Directory of Corporate Giving*, published also by the Foundation Center. The fourth edition lists 2,256 gift-giving company profiles. The majority of them are corporate foundations, but there are a number of companies that give directly.[12] The *Corporate Yellow Book*, published quarterly by Monitor Publishing Company, is a Who's Who directory of leading companies in the United States.[13]

Other than outright gifts, companies and foundations often will assist the institution or organization by purchasing dinner tickets, buying advertising in commemorative booklets, sponsoring special events, offering matching gifts, and encouraging employees to serve as volunteers. Among some foundations, the trend is toward larger gifts to fewer organizations. They want to make an impact. Annenberg's $500 million for the education of school children and Pew's multi-million-dollar initiative to enhance education in selected areas are examples of this largesse. There is also a greater interest in global philanthropy, helping to feed the hungry in Third World countries, alleviating the misery in such places of current turmoil as Europe and Africa. There is a greater focus on business objectives, i.e., business-related gifts, and foundation gifts are more *sui generis*.

UNDERSTANDING THE FOUNDATION MILIEU

Foundations are philanthropic investments established by contributing donors, such as wealthy individuals, families, or corporations, for the purpose of perpetuating the interests of the contributors. One might say foundations are endowments, for the most part, that invest and reinvest the corpus as it continues to grow, giving away a percentage of the investment returns to charity. Elizabeth Boris, vice-president for research with the Council on Foundations, contends "the concept of a freestanding endowed institution that used the income from the donor's gift (and often some of the principal) to benefit humankind through systematic, scientific philanthropy was the product of an era of optimistic belief in the ability of capitalism and science to make the world right."[14] The early foundations had noble ambitions. They sought to cure society's shortcomings and change the standard of living through research and innovative programs, and they gave substantial amounts that made an impact, not small change making a tinkling sound in a tin cup. Modern foundations such as the Pew Charitable Trust, the Ford Foundation, and the Rockefeller Foundations are much the same. Counting all of them, there are probably in excess of 35,000 active foundations in the United States in the late 1990s.

There are five types of foundations: The largest grants are usually given by the independent foundations, like Ford and Kellogg. These foundations were started by philanthropic individuals or a family. (2) Corporate foundations, like the General Electric Foundation and the Amoco Foundation, are extensions of the company and used to further the interests of the company. Their governing boards are often company officials. (3) Community foundations, like the Delaware Community Foundation and the New York Community Trust, are local, community-based, and regionally sponsored foundations. Contributors are local citizens, clubs, and organizations. Grants are usually given to charitable needs unique to the community. (4) The so-called operating foundations, like the J. Paul Getty Trust that funds the Getty Museum and other programs or the Longwood Foundation that funds the Longwood Gardens, exist primarily to fund special programs of interest to the donors. (5) The last type is the institutional foundation, which is really a type of operating foundation, because the mission of the foundation is to support the host institution. Examples are the Ball State University Foundation, The Kent General Hospital Foundation, or the Indiana University Foundation. Over half of the state universities and many hospitals in America have their own foundations. In essence these are stewardship foundations, raising money and investing it wisely for the good of the institution. The foundations are related to the institutions but independent from them, having their own governing boards, directors, by-laws, and guidelines. All of these foundation types are important to the well being of colleges and universities, hospitals, and nonprofits, but many are changing focus.

This is a time of changing priorities. The Duke Endowment that once gave 80 percent of its grant money for health care now gives only 12 percent, according to Elizabeth Locke, executive director of the endowment.[15] "Foundations are fickle," she says, "unpredictable and require frequent, burdensome reports. So why bother with them? For one reason: They fund great projects and stimulate creativity throughout the not-for-profit sector." Other foundations, such as the Pew Charitable Trust and the John D. and Catherine T. MacArthur Foundation, have likewise pulled away from large capital projects in the direction of smaller program grants. The Kaiser Foundation is shifting its dollars toward policy issues that will bring changes in the massive health care industry. The Kellogg Foundation is giving more money to assist young African American males,[16] and new billion-dollar foundations could lead to a boom in philanthropy. Some corporate foundations have had a decline in assets from 1995 to 1996, including General Mills Foundation and AT&T Foundation. Some have trimmed their charitable giving budgets, like Pew (–6 percent), Annenberg (–17 percent), and Heinz (–19 percent).[17]

What development officers sometimes fail to understand is that what is good for their institutions is often not good for the foundations. Speaking for Duke, Locke says "You want and need general support. We seek to support innovation. You wish to establish a long-term relationship. We prefer to fund a project for a year or two and move on. You address social problems that don't lend themselves to quantifiable solutions. We require tangible evidence of impact, progress, return on the dollars invested."[18]

Foundations are not clones of each other. They are widely different in purpose and policy. Small foundations tend to act and respond much like individual donors. They are for the most part local foundations interested in the issues that affect the local community. Large foundations often see themselves through a wider lens. They like to think they are innovators effecting changes on a large scale. They like to focus on research and development. They like to support model programs that can be duplicated in other geographical areas, and they are much more likely to focus on projects that will bring a significant return on their investment.

GRANTSMANSHIP

The good news is foundations are a generous source of grant support. The bad news is pat formulas for submitting proposals will not work like they do with other funding sources. In personal solicitation, the time-honored fund raiser's axiom is: *the right person, asking the right person, at the right time, for the right amount.* In direct mail solicitation, the key to success is the right cover letter and packaging. In telemarketing it is the right dialogue and the persuasive personality of the caller. With foundations, however, there is no tried and proven way. Funds are available but only on the particular foundation's terms. The easiest way to get turned down is to use a one-size-fits-all approach. Every foundation has its own particular demands. Grant writers are courting disaster if they do not do their homework, and that means careful and thorough research.

Research

The first rule of grantsmanship is knowing as much as possible about the foundation. Friends in other organizations that have received grants from the foundation are a good place to start. They will gladly share information that is often helpful in writing the proposal. Another place to begin is with the Foundation Center. The grantwriter's bible is the *Foundation Directory*, but there are other publications that belong in the grantwriter's research library, such as the *Foundation Grants Index, The National Guide to Foundation Funding in Higher Education, Corporate Yellow Book, The National Directory of Corporate Giving,* the *Corporate 500,* and the *Corporate 1000,* plus the tabloids, *The Chronicle of Higher Education,* and *The Chronicle of Philanthropy, The Non-Profit Times, Contributions,* and the various newsletters, including *Charitable Gift Planning News, Foundation/Corporation Grants Alert,* and *Foundation and Corporate Funding Advantage.* Standard reference volumes, such as those of Standard and Poors and Dun and Bradstreet are also necessary sources of information, and on-line electronic selection and screening services, like Dialog, are becoming more popular.

Four steps to foundation research are recommended by Linda Williams of Syracuse University. Grantwriters need to know everything there is to know about a funding source in order to know whom you should ask, what program to seek assistance for, when to ask, deadlines, guidelines, and the right amount to ask for.[19]

The process is simple. Collect all the information possible about the prospect. Organize it and analyze it. Then package it in such a way that it is useful in writing the proposal or letter of request.

> Organizations will receive a grant only when the current priorities of the foundation are addressed and coincide with the interests and priorities of the organization.

This is true even though careful homework is done, and proposals, letters of request, concept statements, and applications are written absolutely correctly. Much like corporations, each of America's 35,000 foundations[20] has its own agenda, which is in fact the agenda of the founding donors and the current directors or trustees. The Ivakota Association, located in Alexandria, Virginia, stands firmly by the wishes of its founder to provide help and assistance to women and children in Northern Virginia. Like many other small foundations, Ivakota is local and has a single purpose. Ivakota's purpose is to make a difference for economically disadvantaged women and children.

The experienced grantwriter knows foundations are as different as the donors who established them, and there are so many of them it would take an army of grantwriters and researchers to keep up with them. Nearly 1,000 of them are corporate foundations, and many are small foundations handled by trust officials in banks, such as the Ruby Vale Foundation. Some foundations prefer to remain anonymous, like the Atlantic Foundation in New York, recently come to light. The donor is Charles F. Feeney, who made his fortune with a string of duty-free airport shops. *The New York Times* said Feeney "covered his tracks so well that business magazines for years have estimated his net worth in the billions, not realizing that he had transferred most of his assets to his two charitable foundations and is actually worth less than $5 million."[21] He has given away $600 million, but he does not own a house or a car. Money does not drive his life, and he started giving it away 15 years ago, but he did it in secrecy. Most recipients, the universities and the medical centers, never knew who their benefactor was.

No one knows for sure how many funding sources there are in America, but they are all important. All play a role in American philanthropy. Those with assets over 100 million are the best known. *The Foundation Directory* (1996, ix) lists over 100. The top 10 foundations are

1. The Ford Foundation, assets over $6 billion, gave over $285 million.
2. The W.K. Kellogg Foundation, assets over $6 billion, gave over $222 million.
3. J. Paul Getty Foundation, assets over $6 billion, gave over $12 million.
4. Robert Wood Johnson Foundation, assets over $3 billion, gave over $135 million.
5. The Pew Charitable Trusts, assets over $3 billion, gave over $157 million.
6. Lilly Endowment, assets over $3 billion, gave over $99 million.
7. John D. and Catherine T. MacArthur Foundation, assets over $2 billion, gave $116 million.
8. The Rockefeller Foundation, assets over $2 billion, gave over $93 million.
9. Andrew W. Mellon Foundation, assets over $2 billion, gave over $105 million.
10. Robert W. Woodruff Foundation, assets over $1 billion, gave over $63 million.

Each foundation has its own mission and purpose, its own special guidelines, governing board, policies, and procedures. The Longwood Foundation, for example, in Wilmington, Delaware, has assets of $475 million and gives approximately $22 million in grants annually. It was established in 1937 by Pierre S. Du Pont for the purpose of supporting and developing the regionally famous Longwood Gardens, a beautiful horticultural exhibition of plants and flowers visited by thousands of people each month of the year. The Longwood Foundation also makes grants to educational institutions, local hospitals, social service and youth agencies, and for cultural programs. Giving is limited to Delaware. The average gift is in the range of $25,000 to $400,000. The Foundation does not require a formal application. Initial approach is by letter of inquiry. Deadlines for requests are April 1 and October 1. Decisions are made by officers and trustees at board meetings in May and November.

Writing Proposals

Assuming all the necessary research has been done, the grantwriter moves to the computer, pulls up WordPerfect, Microsoft Word, or some other word processing program and begins the narrative that constitutes the proposal. Again, the proposal is simply the document that presents the argument for the project and the request for grant support. Typically it has a cover sheet, which is the title page, and no table of contents, but begins the proposal immediately, except to repeat the proposal title on the first page of the narrative. Foundation personnel do not like verbose, erudite material to read. They often will have many proposals to sift through and want to know about the institution, what the problem is and how it will be solved, what the cost is, the budget, who else is contributing, how much has already been raised, who the trustees and administrators are, and why the foundation should be asked to help fund it. Following several pages of narrative, the author always makes it a practice to conclude with a brief summary paragraph with the heading "YOUR GIFT IS IMPORTANT," and at the end, as a matter of information and courtesy a simple closure, "Respectfully submitted," name, title, address, telephone number, and date. Appendixes of relevance and importance should be attached to the proposal.

The above is a general plan for writing a proposal. Some foundations, however, require a specific format and procedure. Kresge, for example, wants to know certain details and provides grantwriters with several pages of instructions and forms to fill out. Others too have application forms to be completed and returned. Some prefer a simple letter of request. Some want multiple copies of the proposal. Some require the contact to be a letter of inquiry. Some encourage invitations for an on-site visit by a foundation officer. Some are highly organized, with a large office staff and specialized personnel to handle education, social service, community projects, or health care. The point to be reiterated is, each foundation has its own preferences in handling requests. Many have specific and detailed guidelines. Rule number one for all grantwriters is: learn the guidelines, limitations, and procedures, and follow them. Number two is: write in a clear informative, but persuasive style. Leave out the bragging. Leave out the cute little jokes and catchy phrases, and by all means leave out the jargon fund raisers like to toss around. Terms like "lybunts" or "suspects" are not appropriate in formal proposal writing. These terms often slip in when several others are asked to review the proposal before submission. A professor will want to insert erudite language. A development officer may want to add some fluff, but it is up to the grantwriter to keep it clean and polished, lean and muscular.

Proposal writing is a learned skill, not an art. Almost any development officer can and should do it. Grantwriters, who do it routinely, are lucky if one proposal in every six will be funded. Thousands of proposals and requests are delivered to foundations across the country. With Ford, Kresge, Kellogg, Pew, and other large independent foundations, the number is overwhelming, and there are only so many millions to give. It all comes down to judging the "excellent against the excellent," as the chairman of Kresge has said. When foundation directors stack them up in three piles, "Excellent, top choice," "Very good, should be considered," and "Sorry, not acceptable," the top group usually represents far more grant money than is available to give. When judging the best against the best, foundation people look for the best "fit" for foundation objectives, and things to rule the proposals out, mistakes, errors, inconsistencies, and the one most commonly used, "failed to follow our guidelines."

There is a feeling among advancement professionals that some foundation grants are made to those well-known to the foundation, those with whom the foundation has developed a strong relationship. That feeling has sound basis in fact. Amoco, Jesse Ball DuPont, Howard Hughes Institute, and many others fund only those institutions with whom they have a working relationship, those institutions "on their list." In that connection, there seems to be a growing number of foundations that accept requests by invitation only.

Happily, there are thousands of foundations that encourage the submission of proposals, and the reward for the grantwriter can be abundantly satisfactory. One single proposal, if approved and funded, can bring in more financial support for the organization than hundreds of direct mail pieces, phonathon solicitations, special fund raising events, or even personal visits. Good grantwriters are well worth the small pay they receive for their efforts. No progressive institution or organization should be without them. Much like planned giving staff, they are on a par with major gifts officers in terms of financial productivity.

In review, writing the proposal begins with foundation research, identifying the right foundation, and compiling all the information possible. The process continues by writing the proposal, following the guidelines, addressing the need and how it can be met, showing the institution to be one of high integrity, productivity, and vision, with administrators competent to complete the task in a timely manner at a realistic cost. Early in the proposal a brief statement to the effect that "this proposal seeks grant support in the amount of $_____" should be made. Foundation personnel do not want to have to go through 16 pages of narrative before discovering what is requested. There must be a tie-in with foundation objectives, answering the question "Why should the foundation be asked to help fund this project?" A cursory look at all the literature available reveals a number of suggested outlines to follow in writing the narrative of the proposal. Cornell's outline, published years ago by CASE, is still a viable model to follow. It begins with an abstract of the project, then addresses the problem to be solved, the strategy in solving it, how that relates to the foundation, the institution's strengths, support from other sources, project budget, and closes with a summary statement and attached appendixes.[22]

Delivery

After the proposal is written and packaged for presentation, complete with cover letter and attachments, the final step is delivering it to the foundation. Obviously, it can be done in a number of different ways. The best way is for the development officer to hand-carry it to the foundation with a big smile, a cordial greeting, and a hearty handshake. It should be delivered well ahead of the foundation deadline. Proposals that arrive at the stroke of midnight are not received enthusiastically. The document can be mailed, but it should be done by Federal Express or priority mail. It should not be sent by facsimile machine or by e-mail, unless the foundation guidelines so permit. Sending the material by fax or e-mail is too impersonal. It does not convey the message of being well planned and executed. Transmissions by fax are quick and easy, but they are also "hot off the press" last minute communications. Even when sending by so-called snail mail, it is best to send it by certified mail. It not only leaves the impression of being something important but also returns to the sender a notice that the mail has been received.

SUMMARY

Corporate and foundation relations are extremely important to the advancement operation. Next to alumni and friends, corporations and foundations represent the largest base of external private support for the institution. Professional staff with experience and understanding of corporate relations and foundation procedures are needed to build relationships and manage the cultivation and solicitation of this significant donor base. Understanding corporate and foundation cultures is key to attracting their interest and support. Working with the business community to bring about partnerships between the institution and the corporate donors and prospects leads to greater financial and political support. Understanding the foundation milieu is an essential prelude to seeking grants. It leads to successful grantsmanship, which includes foundation research, proposal writing, and approved funding. Every institution or organization that has a fund raising unit should have a corporate and foundation relations program. Both constituent groups have major potential for support and should not be taken lightly or considered short-term. Relationships with these donors and prospects should be long-term.

NOTES

1. D.C. Withers, "Generating Corporate Support," *Handbook of Institutional Advancement,* 2nd ed., ed. A.W. Rowland (San Francisco: Jossey-Bass, 1986), 268.
2. Withers, 270.
3. D.E. Blum and Susan Gray, "Hot Firms, Cool Toward Philanthropy," *Chronicle of Philanthropy,* May 15, 1997, 9, 12.
4. V. Murray, *Improving Corporate Donations* (San Francisco: Jossey-Bass, 1991), 45.
5. J.R. Mixer, *Principles of Professional Fund Raising* (San Francisco: Jossey-Bass, 1993), 67, 69, 73, 74.
6. H.J. Seymour, *Designs for Fund Raising* (New York: McGraw-Hill, 1966), 6.
7. P.F. Lewis, president of NSFRE, at the NSFRE International Conference in Dallas, March 10, 1997.
8. J.A. Yankey, "A Marriage of Necessity," *Advancing Philanthropy,* Winter 1996–97, 11–18.
9. Yankey, "A Marriage of Necessity," 15.
10. S. Baumblatt in an oral presentation at Fund Raising Day in New York City, June 19, 1997. Stan is Assistant Vice President for Philanthropic Programs at Merrill Lynch & Company. He is Manager of Corporate Contributions and Assistant Secretary of the Merrill Lynch Foundation.
11. M.M. Feczko, *The Foundation Directory,* 18th ed. (New York: The Foundation Center, 1996).
12. L.V. Hall, ed., *The National Directory of Corporate Giving,* 4th ed. (New York: The Foundation Center, 1995).
13. L. Gibbons, ed., *The Corporate Yellow Book* (New York: The Monitor Publishing Company, 1992).
14. E. Boris, "Foundations as a Part of Overall Fund Raising Programs," *Cultivating Foundations Support,* Mary Kay Murphy (Washington, DC: CASE, 1989), 9.
15. E. Locke, "The Foundations of a Relationship," *Advancing Philanthropy,* Fall 1996, 20.
16. Locke, "The Foundations of a Relationship," 21.
17. D.E. Blum, "Will 1997 Be a Boom Year for Grants?" *The Chronicle of Philanthropy,* February 20, 1997, 12–16.
18. Locke, "The Foundations of a Relationship," 20.
19. L. Williams, "Research as the Keystone for Foundation Fund Raising," *Cultivating Foundation Support,* M.K. Murphy (Washington, DC: CASE, 1989), 57.
20. M.M. Feczko, R. Kovacs, and C. Mills, *National Guide to Foundation Funding in Higher Education,* 3rd ed. (New York: The Foundation Center, 1994).
21. J. Miller, *New York Times,* January 23, 1997, A–1.
22. H.T. Gayley, *How To Write for Development* (Washington, DC: CASE 1981), 14.

CHAPTER 5

Capital Campaigns

William W. Tromble

The intense effort of a capital campaign exposes every flaw within an organization; but it also fosters passion, commitment and esprit—especially among the leadership. That spirit may be the campaign's most significant monument.

(Libby Morse, *Advancing Philanthropy*, p. 11)

GETTING STARTED

Before launching any capital campaign, it is wise to make sure it fits the organization and the people who will be involved. It makes little sense to start a campaign just because the chief executive officer (CEO) wants a new building or a larger endowment. Successful campaigns have their basis in consensus of need. The whole organization must be singing from the same musical manuscript. Professional and support staff must catch the spirit from top administration. Governing boards must feel the need and give their enthusiastic support.

Diversity of opinion should be encouraged. There is no absolute right way to conduct a campaign; although structure and strategy are necessary to bring stability to the campaign, it must remain flexible. Changes will occur during the life of the campaign. Timelines may change. Personnel may change. Any part of the plan is subject to change if something is not working. The trick is for campaign leadership to be alert to the chuckholes in the way as they steer the campaign down the road to completion.

Sometimes capital campaigns begin to falter and grind to a stop because the goal that was set is too high. Often in their moments of euphoria over the prospect of achieving millions of dollars for the organization, campaign leaders will exercise their authority and influence to "think big," and set the goal unrealistically high. One such campaign comes to mind. It was in the Midwest in the 1980s. After the usual preparation and study, and with the encouragement of the president, the goal was set at $75 million. Beautiful campaign literature was printed at considerable expense. Volunteers were recruited, and the professional staff became excited. The campaign began with a good start but soon reached that agonizing midcampaign plateau, as all campaigns do, when nothing seems to happen. Unfortunately, the campaign was never able to move forward and was quietly put to rest far short of the goal. Some time afterward, with regrouping and planning, a new campaign was launched and completed.

Happily, most campaigns succeed, but there are always adjustments in strategy and procedure. Campaign plans have to be flexible. People and situations change. If something is not working, campaign leadership must not hesitate to try something else.

There is a natural sequence of progression, tried and true, that has worked in hundreds of campaigns, especially multimillion dollar capital campaigns. The driving force that gives life to the idea of having a campaign is institutional need or vision. Capital campaigns do not just suddenly appear. They arise after careful thinking about needs assessment and hopes for the future. Once that has happened and a tentative commitment to have a campaign is made, the sequence of campaign events takes a typical form, such as Exhibit 5–1.

A campaign is a campaign, and the basic procedure is pretty much the same whether it is a $5 million campaign for some special project or a $500 million comprehensive campaign. It all begins with an assessment of need, probability of financial support from prospective donors, and an audit of the professional advancement staff. Traditionally, this assessment of need has been done internally, and when the decision is made to launch a campaign, a confidential probe of philanthropic probability is done. This is the feasibility study, and is best accomplished by an outside, independent, objective consultant. Then comes a period of quietly talking to prospects who are capable of making large gifts, getting them excited about the upcoming campaign, and getting their commitment of support. When a large chunk of change is in hand, the campaign is ready to go public, and a kickoff event is arranged when the organization announces to the world that the campaign has begun. The campaign chairperson and cabinet are introduced, an appropriate challenge is given, and the campaign is off and running, using the large amount previously raised in the advance phase to leverage other major gifts. The first order of business after the kickoff is to make everyone aware of the campaign, get prospects interested and excited, solicit all the prospects, and complete the campaign. The hope is to exceed the campaign goal. The strategy is to go after the major gifts first with all the energy and resources available. Then solicit the minor gifts, because in any capital campaign, 80 to 90 percent of the goal is achieved through major gifts. In some campaigns, major gifts make up 95 percent of the goal, and these gifts come from only 20 percent or less of the donors.

The fact is there are a few donors giving most of the money, and many donors giving small amounts that make up a small percentage of the goal, so it just makes good business sense to spend 80 to 90 percent of staff and volunteer time and energy, and of campaign budget, on the major donors. An old saying among advancement professionals is "cultivate the best, and leave the rest." It is said with

Exhibit 5–1 Outline of Capital Campaign Sequence

1. Feasibility Study (or Campaign Assessment)

   Sometimes a broad survey is done by the organization before independent counsel is brought in
   Assess funding probability
   Conduct a staff audit if necessary

2. Preparation for the Campaign

   Institutional need or vision clarified
   Campaign chairperson recruited
   Cabinet or steering committee determined
   National committee recruited if desirable
   Top volunteers recruited
   Case for support written
   Campaign materials printed/assembled
   Plan of action completed, including
       philosophy/mission/goal
       sub-goals for units and divisions
       table of gifts needed to achieve the campaign goal
       personnel, leadership/staff/volunteers
       budget and method of funding the campaign
       prospects, identification, research, profiles
       campaign activities
       time schedule/activity calendar
       gift/pledge processing policy and procedure
       reports
       special events
       expectations/desired outcomes

3. Phase I, The Advance Phase

   Quiet solicitation of lead gifts in preparation for the public announcement
   The Kickoff, i.e., public announcement

4. Phase II, The Awareness and Major Gifts Phase

   Conducting a blitz of awareness activity
   Promoting the campaign
   Openly soliciting major gifts
   Striving to achieve 90 percent of the goal

5. Phase III, The Completion Phase

   Final major gift contacts
   Telephone solicitation

continues

Exhibit 5–1 continued

> Direct mail solicitation
> Victory celebration
>
> 6. Campaign Follow-up
>
> Reminders on outstanding pledges
> Final newsletter, victory edition
> Donor recognition
> Keeping in touch
> Cultivating readiness for the next campaign

tongue-in-cheek, of course, because we never "leave the rest." A good fund raising effort always solicits "the rest" in some way or another, usually by direct mail. The fact remains, however, that most of the money raised comes from the least amount of donors.

Bruce McClintock, chairman of Marts & Lundy, expresses the same sentiment as Ben Franklin and the late Si Seymour when he says, "People give according to their level of interest and involvement. It is not the brilliance of the 'ask,' but an understanding of what concerns and interests the donor." Fund raising professionals often devote far too much time honing their solicitation skills, and far too little time listening to the donor and knowing how the donor feels. This is true no matter what the size of the anticipated gift may be.[1]

Large Versus Small Campaigns

The only difference between large campaigns and small ones is the manner in which the campaigns are approached. Robert Pierpont and Andrea Kihlstedt in the 1997 international conference of the National Society of Fund Raising Executives (NSFRE) in Dallas gave their analysis of the essential differences between large and small campaigns.[2]

In getting ready to start, organizations anticipating a large campaign usually have a fund raising board, a history of receiving major gifts, and an experienced staff. Three years has been the normal campaign time period, but five years is becoming more common. Those anticipating a small campaign are often smaller organizations, driven to begin by a sense of passion, courage, mission, and compelling need. Even the smaller capital campaigns tend to run for three years.

In trying to decide and "testing the water," so to speak, those with large campaigns usually ask "How shall we proceed?" Those with small campaigns usually debate whether or not they should proceed. Large campaigns have been in the works for some time, as a rule. Small campaigns tend to spring up as a result of some immediate pressing need, and with some doubt about the possibility of success.

In using a plan of action, large campaigns tend to let the plan be more of a road map and checklist for management. Small campaigns use the plan more to involve and educate staff and volunteers. Large multimillion dollar campaigns need a definitive chart of action and discipline, rules to live by, as it were, just as large construction projects need a complex architectural plan to specify what materials to use and what procedures to follow. Small campaigns are more inclined to use the plan as a training document to educate the leadership and walk the staff and volunteers through the project.

With regard to the case statement, large campaigns need one that is many faceted. Small campaigns are more likely to use one that is a single-purpose case, simple and direct, an expression of the problem and how to solve it. In major campaigns, it is rather common to see lengthy case statements that lift up opportunities in several areas in what may seem like a series of mini–case statements seeking support for endowed chairs, for student financial aid, for faculty development, and for special projects.

Governing board involvement in large campaigns is expected to be substantial, not only in moral and political support, but also in financial support. Small campaigns tend to stress participation more than giving. Large campaigns are usually conducted by large institutions with affluent and influential boards. The exception might be boards of state institutions, but even with state-appointed board members there is an expectation that they will bring to the table a substantial amount of financial support. Small campaigns are more content to show 100 percent participation irrespective of the amount it represents.

Solicitation in large campaigns is more staff driven than volunteer driven. Big campaigns like the Harvard campaign, the Michigan, Maryland, Ohio State, and University of Miami campaigns, use large numbers of professional major gifts people. Small campaigns rely more on volunteers to be primary fund raisers and bring closure to their solicitations.

The campaign wrap-up in large campaigns is often done by outsourcing direct mail and telephone solicitation. In small campaigns, telephone and direct mail solicitation is done by staff and volunteers. In large campaigns, direct mail is a major item better accommodated by off-campus mail processing vendors. The same could be said of telemarketing. Small campaigns, however, usually do it in-house.

Named gift opportunities in large campaigns are usually pre-set and non-negotiable. In small campaigns, these opportunities arise in the process of running the campaign. In large campaigns, opportunities for gift recognition, such as naming a room, office, or lounge, or the entire facility, is often published in the case statement or campaign brochures. In small campaigns, gift recognition through naming opportunities is somewhat flexible. There is ample room for negotiation and the creation of new opportunities.

The one rather surprising observation is that despite all the motivation and planning, all the cultivation and moving donors up from one gift club to the next, major gifts often come from unexpected sources. According to Bruce McClintock, Chairman of Marts & Lundy, in a recent large campaign for an Ivy League institution, 25 percent of the gifts in excess of $1 million were first-time donors. At the lower end of the scale, 62 percent of the donors who gave less than $1,000 were first-time donors.[3]

Assessment and Feasibility Study

Although there are some who tend to downplay the feasibility study, advancement professionals generally agree on the importance of the traditional feasibility study. Bypassing the pre-campaign feasibility study leaves the institution vulnerable to failure. It is important, even crucial, for several reasons. Independent counsel brings a fresh, unbiased, objective analysis of readiness. Outside counsel is competent and experienced in assessing both the readiness of the institution and the readiness of the patronizing constituencies to float the campaign ship in a sea of uncertainties and change. In the first place, the president needs to be settled in for a year or two after taking office before attempting to launch a campaign, to be past the honeymoon period and to have developed a strong base of trust and support, not only from the external community but also from the clients and employees of the institution.

Professional Staff

There needs to be a competent and enthusiastic professional staff in place to carry out the many administrative responsibilities and conduct the fund raising operation. Outside counsel will do an objective staff audit and advise the CEO. In some instances changes in personnel must be made. Most of the time current staff are adequate and ready for the tasks that await them. If there are problems in staffing, or suggestions for better use of the staff, outside counsel can advise or recommend the appropriate action to be taken in order to successfully complete a capital campaign.

Potential Donors/Independent Counsel

There needs to be a large pool of prospective donors, and counsel can determine whether such a pool exists. The external community must be supportive. This includes city officials, legislators, friends throughout the region that is served by the organization, corporations, foundations, and other organizations. Outside counsel can provide an accurate estimate of internal and external support potential. Many interviews will be held over several weeks by counsel and staff to find out how the bankers, lawyers, parents, friends, social groups, employees, and staff perceive the institution. Confidential reports will be turned over to the institution at the close of the feasibility study, and counsel will meet with the CEO to report frankly and honestly what might be expected in a capital campaign. Counsel will have an informed opinion about how much money can be raised, about possible funding sources, about strategies for implementing the campaign. Ketchum, Grenzebach, Marts & Lundy, and other consultants will contract to provide resident counsel if that is desired. It is expensive, but clearly needed in situations where professional staff is lacking in executive skills.

The true value of independent counsel is the honest, sometimes brutally frank, advice and information the CEO receives from counsel. It is not always what may have been expected, and it is not always followed, but it is usually an accurate road map to campaign success. If subordinates were to say some of this, it would not be received with a smile, but independent counsel's job is not on the line. Counsel will be gone in a few weeks to another assignment. So, counsel is free to tell it like it is. Staff may not be. The feasibility study shows the following:

- how the external community views the institution
- what those on the inside are saying
- what the strengths and weaknesses of the institution are
- what the probable level of support for the campaign will be
- whether or not the organization or institution is ready for a campaign
- whether or not the professional staff is capable of managing a campaign
- what difficulties are likely to be encountered
- when the timing is right to launch the campaign
- what some useful strategies might be
- what the chances are that the anticipated campaign would succeed

Consultants can determine all of the above and more, and they are extremely helpful to the CEO who has a business or academic background but little fund raising expertise. The advice and counsel given can very well determine the success or failure of the hoped-for campaign. There are some things, however, that counsel cannot do, and organizations should understand these limitations. Outside counsel cannot do the following:

- Raise the money! That is the institution's responsibility.
- Predict who will give and who will not.
- Work pro bono! It's their job. They should be paid well.
- Accept kickbacks.

- Relieve certain staff members of their responsibilities.
- Hire development staff or suggest individuals for hire.

CAMPAIGN STRATEGIES

Leadership

Assuming there has been adequate upfront assessment of need and feasibility, the one strategy that pays off big in any campaign, large or small, is to secure good leadership. In most cases, that means an enthusiastic, dedicated, influential campaign chairperson. It also means a strong leadership team, such as a campaign cabinet or steering committee. The volunteers who serve in these roles are the ones who carry the flag into battle. They make their own commitments first. They give direction to the campaign, and they inspire hundreds of others to support the cause. The CEO and his corps of advancement professionals are a part of this leadership group. The governing board also plays a role. In fact, the board is the authority for the campaign. The president or CEO is an agent of the board, and the professional fund raisers are the strategists and executors of the plan. All of these individuals give leadership to the campaign. Without this dynamic force to propel the campaign along, it will surely falter, and the campaign chairperson is the most important and crucial individual of them all. This is true in most campaigns, though there have been successful campaigns whose chairperson was something less than a dynamic leader taking charge of the troops.

Campaign chairpersons are usually recruited for one of two reasons. Either the person is a miracle-working manager or an individual highly recognized and admired for what he or she has been able to accomplish. If the chairperson happens to be a "working chairperson," that is, one who is willing to make telephone calls, write letters, and make personal visits, the road to the goal will be much easier for the professional staff and volunteers. In some campaigns, however, this individual turns out to be the chairperson in name only, leaving most of the work to the CEO and the advancement professionals, and that is not a problem. Advancement people are doing what they do best in visitation, telephone calls, and direct mail. That is what they get paid for, so they better be able to do it well. Unfortunately, the laity regard the president and the advancement staff as "hired guns." A major gift solicitation from the president or the development officer carries little weight compared to that of a top volunteer who is enthusiastic about the campaign and has been trained well in the art of the "ask." The one difference in degree of influence, between the president and the vice president for institutional advancement, is the clout that the top administrator has over anyone else as decision maker for the institution. Big donors want to hear it from the decision maker, to deal with the one who has the power and the authority to make it happen. This is not to say others will not be effective solicitors, but there is something of a sense of high respect and awe on the part of the donor when talking to "the Chief." Perhaps there is also a bit of a desire and hope to be able to exert some influence on the CEO. This is precisely why people go out of their way to curry the favor of the president of the United States. It is partly because they seek to be in the presence of greatness, and partly because they think they can further their own agenda.

So it is of vital importance that much thought be given to recruiting the chairman of the campaign. His or her leadership can make or break the effort. The trick to it is to get someone to be the chairperson who is well-liked, politically correct for the job, and who, in the ideal situation, can give or help the institution get a substantial amount of cash and pledges. He or she should be a person of great influence, or great affluence, or both.

The final person to make up the campaign leadership is the campaign director. This person is usually a staff member, quite often the vice-president for institutional advancement or the director of development. This person is the true executive of the campaign. He or she is an experienced advancement professional with years of hands-on fund raising management, including capital campaigns, major gifts, and planned giving. The director is one who has expertise in recruiting volunteers, constructing a plan of action, conducting prospect research, and managing prospect solicitation. Above all, the director is comfortable and successful in major gift cultivation and solicitation.

Although the real mover and driver of the campaign, the campaign director is not in the spotlight. That honor goes to the campaign chairman. Although the director rarely takes credit for the hard, behind-the-scenes work, don't be deceived. Without the prodding of volunteers, the slavish attention to detail, and the frequent after-hours problem-solving work, the campaign would suffer and the campaign chairperson and cabinet would not look good. Just as in film making, the visionary producer is needed to put the show on stage and the technicians are vital to production, but it is the director who sees the whole picture, weighs all the angles, and tells others what to do to make it work.

Volunteers

Books on advancement, articles on fund raising, and most campaign literature contain abundant material on the importance of volunteers and the use of volunteers in annual giving programs and capital campaigns. The signal message is always the same. They are needed! Even in staff-driven campaigns, volunteers are invaluable. The campaign chairperson is the top volunteer in any campaign, and there are other volunteers in leadership positions, such as those in the campaign cabinet. They serve best in winning support from the external community, though development officers are very much aware of their influence and productivity in the so-called campus campaign. By and large, they are not gophers, running errands, stuffing envelopes, and doing other campaign grunt work, although volunteers are often needed for that. They are advocates for the campaign, and ambassadors of goodwill for the institution. Best of all, many of them are fund raisers, but they do not just drop out of the sky and fall into the production line. They have to be cultivated and courted in much the same way donor prospects are brought into the loop. Anyone who is going to be asked to solicit or assist in soliciting major gifts, for example, should be recruited through a personal visit from a development official, a peer, or a friend. The potential volunteer should have an interest in the cause or institution and become involved in the affairs of the institution. Sooner or later, the volunteer is going to find out that a personal financial commitment is expected in the range of those "asks" he or she is going to make or assist in making later on.

The question is usually not if, but how many volunteers will be needed, because no campaign has been successful without volunteers. They are special people and highly valued. What they can do when they put their minds to it is awesome. One or two talented individuals come to mind, without whose help recent campaigns that the writer directed would have suffered. Barbara Riegel of Wilmington, Delaware, is one such individual. First of all, her personality is strikingly winsome. She listens without butting in. She is willing to call on major donor prospects and place her own reputation on the line for the organization. She is married to a business executive who is an upstanding citizen of the community. She is involved in many social events. She knows many persons of influence or affluence throughout the state. During the Century II campaign for Delaware State University, she organized a large reception at the Wilmington Country Club, inviting VIPs, the governor, heads of corporations and foundations, major donor prospects, and personal friends, like the Honorable Pierre Du Pont. The sole purpose of the reception was to give the president and university advancement people an opportunity to mingle and promote the campaign.

John Land, a member of Delaware State University's Board of Trustees, is another outstanding volunteer. He gladly and willingly took the lead for the trustees in personal solicitation, cultivating friendships with corporate executives he knew and making a number of "asks" for the campaign. As a result of his sincere personality and dedication to the university and the campaign, and because of his strong people skills, he was able to bring in thousands of dollars in gifts and pledges. He was not shy about asking and made most of the calls on his own.

When volunteers begin to take ownership of the campaign, as Riegel and Land did, good things happen. Before that can take place, volunteers need to be trained, especially the newly recruited ones, and the first thing they learn is to make their own gift or pledge up front. That really has to happen before they try to solicit someone else. The prospect to which they have been assigned, most likely, will be a peer, and one of the first questions their colleague will probably ask is "How much did you give?" How embarrassing it is to be asking someone else to give when you have not done so yourself, but that is the negative side. The positive side is that when the volunteer has made a commitment, the ask can be made with pride and confidence, conviction and persuasion.

The number of contacts a volunteer can be expected to make should be limited to five. These wonderful people we call volunteers are giving far more than their gifts and pledges. They are giving the time and energy for the cause we represent. In many cases they are giving time taken away from necessary personal duties, and energy that could have been spent with their families or at the workplace. David Gearhart, vice-president for development and university relations at Pennsylvania State University, offers a word of caution to all who are fortunate enough to have a corps of volunteers.[4]

> Regardless of the size of the institution or of the capital campaign, the use of volunteers demands extensive staff time. Volunteers expect the campaign office to tend to their needs and answer their questions . . . and staff members must treat them with care and respect. The care and feeding of volunteers during a capital campaign is one of the most important staff assignments, and staff should be prepared to spend many hours in this process.

The Case for Support

The most important piece in the capital campaign is the document we call the "Case for Support." It tells who you are, where you've been, and where you are going. It speaks to the character of the institution or organization, its nature, mission, and vision. It gives the prospective donor a brief overview of the institution, and a sense of purpose and destiny. It tells the reader something about the institution's programs and activities, something of its financial condition, and something of its priorities.

Although the case statement is mainly about the campaign, it includes what the campaign is, why it is necessary, what it will do for the institution, what benefits it will bring the community and the surrounding region, who is involved in the campaign, what the financial goal is, what the timeframe is, how the money will be raised, and how the money will be used. It speaks about the progress of the institution and the people associated with it. The document paints a picture of a winner facing the challenge of the future.

It talks about the campaign organization, names the campaign chairman, the campaign cabinet, the men and women who represent the national campaign committee. It outlines the phases of the campaign and the milestones that will be reached. It discusses the several ways of giving and how individuals and organizations can participate in the campaign. It may include a question and answer section in which the CEO addresses questions often raised in campaigns of this sort, but it focuses on the positive outcomes of the campaign, the benefits that accrue to the institution and to the donors. It includes several human interest stories and provides the development office address, telephone number, facsimile number, and e-mail address.

The case statement is the written advocate for the campaign. It tells the story of the campaign in clear and concise words and phrases that "a sixth grader can understand," according to Jerry Panas, widely known fund raising consultant.[5] The case should be reviewed and approved by the governing board of the institution, top administration, and campaign leadership. It should become the compelling rationale for the campaign, because fundamentally the case document is a statement of the institution's mission, vision, and need.

Contents of the statement may include a number of interesting details, but the following items are commonly found in case documents in hundreds of campaigns across the nation. The past 100 years have shown that prospective donors are interested in and want to know the following before they decide to give, and this is especially true with gifts of $10,000 and more:

1. background and current information about the institution, who you are, how you came to be, and what you are about
2. what the campaign is all about, why it is necessary, what it will accomplish, how it will benefit humanity, how it will solve a problem, and why the organization or institution is rising to the challenge
3. the fund raising goal, how the money will be raised, from what sources, over what time period
4. how interested friends and organizations can participate, ways of giving, addresses, phone numbers, and e-mail addresses for further information
5. who is involved—campaign leadership, institutional governing board, top administrative officers—in other words who is responsible for the campaign

The case for support is a reflection of the institution. If the institution is weak, disorganized, and lacks a well-defined mission and vision, no amount of creative writing can mask the problem, because in the end the case statement is a self-revelation.[6] A capital campaign can be no stronger than the case that supports its existence. So, before the campaign, before the case statement, organizations and institutions must deal honestly and seriously with what they are, what they do, and what they hope to become.

Strategic and Action Planning

A master plan of strategy and activity is the road map, or the architectural design, for the capital campaign. It gives order and direction to the campaign. After the case statement, it is the most important piece in the preparation of the campaign. It contains the best thinking of the governing board, the president, and the campaign leadership with respect to campaign philosophy, goal, objectives, structure and organization, strategies, time schedules, materials, special events, prospect research and management, communication and information, personnel, and general policy and procedure.

Appendix 5–A contains a campaign plan written specifically for the Century II Campaign for Delaware State University, a campaign begun in 1991 and completed in 1994 with a victory celebration at the Sheraton Inn in Dover, Delaware. It was a small campaign as capital campaigns go. The goal was $10.1 million, but it was the first of its kind in the 100-year history of the institution. "There were many skeptics, but they soon became believers," President William B. DeLauder said. As it turns out, the campaign exceeded the goal by $400,000, winning national recognition and achieving the Council for Advancement and Support of Education (CASE) Leadership Award at the CASE National Conference in New York City, July 11, 1995, along with five other schools, including Harvard, Rutgers, Pennsylvania State University, the University of Arkansas, and Notre Dame.

The "Master Plan of Action" for Delaware State College (now Delaware State University) is only a single variation on a theme that is played by hundreds of colleges and universities, hospitals, and nonprofits across the nation. No two are the same, but all have the essential parts mentioned above—philosophy, structure and organization, strategies, phases, timelines, materials, events, communications, campaign policies, and procedures.

Strategic planning has its origins in the military and refers to effective moves and battle positions that are favorable to the advancing forces. The term as it is used in institutional advancement means planning to achieve success in fund raising, what moves to make, what people are involved, the timing, and the methods used in accomplishing the goal. Action planning, on the other hand, is planning the techniques and tactics that, for the most part, are realized in activities. Both types of planning are needed in capital campaigns and are usually combined in a master plan for the campaign.

The foundation of this master plan, as shown above, is the philosophy of those who will lead and direct the campaign and includes how they feel about it, what they believe, their ideas, their reservations, and their hopes and dreams for the campaign. Philosophy is tied to institutional heritage, mission, and vision. Stated another way, campaign philosophy is an outgrowth of the history and background of the institution, its purpose, and its direction for the future. This statement of belief begins the planning process and is the opening paragraph of the planning document. Incidentally, the master plan should be in writing, always available as a point of reference, a guide, and a resource. A statement of campaign philosophy might read as follows:

> The Campaign for Excellence is yet another exciting footprint in the 100-year history of The University. Founded on the principle that higher education is the means to better understanding of life and better living, the University has become one of the best undergraduate universities of the Midwest. Our goal is to reach for greater excellence in teaching and learning. This campaign will move us to the next higher level, specifically by creating more opportunities for faculty development, providing additional funding for student scholarships, and improving academic programs.

The following are brief statements from university presidents and a nonprofit CEO reflecting their beliefs about their special campaigns.[7]

> "Wings for the Future" is an ambitious campaign that marks a turning point in the life of Ball State University. On these wings we will support the studies, encourage the inquiry, initiate the programs, and build the facilities that will strengthen the University and in turn contribute to the economic development of the state and improve the quality of life for all the Citizens of Indiana—and the nation.
>
> —John E. Worthen, President
> Ball State University

> The Campaign for Elmira launches a fresh, new phase of development for this fine, old College. It reflects our confidence in the great potential of Elmira College and builds on the strengths that have distinguished Elmira since 1855 . . . . Small and academically distinctive, Elmira develops students' scholastic and leadership potential. The Campaign will assure further enhancement of our students' learning experience.
>
> —Thomas Keith Meier, President
> Elmira College

> The concept for the Food Bank of Delaware grew out of the Food Closet Study Committee, organized by Retha S. Fisher in 1977. It is hard to have hope when your family is hungry. It means children may

find it difficult to do well in school . . . parents may not be able to nurture . . . our whole community suffers.

—Jeremiah P. Shea and Retha S. Fisher, Co-Chairs
Food Bank Capital Campaign

Indiana University was created by the vision of the early pioneers who met in 1816 at the village of Corydon to form a new state and carve a civilization out of the wilderness. Those leaders . . . saw that higher education was essential to the world they wanted to build for their descendants. . . . Their vision is . . . to help create in Indiana a place of economic opportunity, of political democracy, of creativity and enterprise. . . . Today we must build the foundation of excellence for tomorrow.

—John W. Ryan, President
Indiana University

The dollar goal of the campaign must be decided carefully and be in tune with the feasibility study. If the goal is too high, it will likely be unreachable and result in embarrassment for the institution, but it must be one that is challenging. A goal that is too low and too easily attained does not help the institution to stretch its capacity and realize its potential. A situation comes to mind when the board was in a heated debate over what the goal should be, and several around the table voiced concerns about the numbers being considered. "We can never reach that goal," one member said, and another echoed that feeling. One or two others said "Maybe we can go a little higher." Finally, the governor of the state, who was at the meeting, rose to his feet and proposed a figure about $3 million higher than that previously suggested. His challenge was this, "We need a stretch goal, one that will make us work for it, and I believe we can do it." There were a few moments of quiet contemplation in the room, and soon one or two members began nodding their heads in approval. Others joined in, and soon all were in one accord. The goal proposed by the governor was approved. Eventually, the campaign did in fact reach and exceed that goal, but it took the clear voice of a visionary leader to set the course.

The master plan should include a budget. There are campaign expenses to be paid. Printing has to be done. There is the cost of travel and entertainment, and there will be costs for promotion and publicity, and costs for special events. The kickoff dinner will cost around $4,000, depending on how elaborate the decorations are, and the ambiance of the location where the dinner is held. Also there are receptions, cabinet meetings, friendship luncheons, and other events to be factored into the cost of the campaign. Salaries are usually absorbed by the institution and not charged to the campaign, because staff are present before the campaign and will be on payroll after the campaign. The larger campaigns will bring in major gifts people just for the duration of the campaign. That personnel expense is a legitimate campaign expense, but permanent staff salaries go on whether there is a campaign or not. There also may be expense in upgrading the gift processing operation, particularly if new software is required. Normal office overhead for lights, telephone, correspondence, filing, and the like is not charged to the campaign. One of the largest expenditures, however, is that for outside counsel, especially if resident counsel is needed. Some consultants charge a flat fee, others charge by the day, and others charge a percentage of the goal. The latter is easy to figure, but not entirely fair, because actual work done and time spent is not calculated.

A detailed calendar of activity, beginning with day one and continuing through the three major phases of the campaign, in a blow-by-blow, line item, chronology of tasks to be performed, is a desirable part of the plan.

Prospect Search and Research

First you have to find the prospects who will then make the donations and cause the campaign to succeed. One usually starts with a huge list of what the development people call "suspects," that is, people and other funding sources who might contribute. Suspects are those who either could or would make a gift. At least we think so, but we are not sure about it. From that large group of potential donors, after much research, a smaller list is developed. This time the list includes prospective donors who are perceived to be both able to give and also willing to give. If they could, but do not have the "would," they cannot be good prospects. If they are willing, but do not have the financial resources to give, they too cannot be good prospects. All this is determined through prospect research, looking at giving records, talking with friends who know them, even visiting with them personally. Obviously, any conversation with a prospective donor that is initiated for the purpose of discovery must be handled with utmost diplomacy. The author recalls a situation in which a suspect was unknown to everyone on the prospect evaluation committee, except that the donor was an alumnus. Paying an alumni visit to this person, in his lovely home, the author observed an expensive car in the driveway and a boat in one side of the garage, as well as other outward signs of affluence, and after talking with him for a brief while, it became very clear that this person was definitely a prospect. Both the "could" and the "would" were present. More research, however, was necessary.

Prospect research is often lengthy and tedious, but it is vital to the success of the "ask." The goal is to gain as much information about the prospect as possible in order to be able to move the prospect toward closure. It sounds rather crass, but it is not. What is happening is the researcher is putting together a wholistic picture of the prospect, enabling the volunteer or development officer to get to know the prospect, become sensitive to the prospect's interests and desires, and relate those interests to the institution's goals and priorities. All this information results in a profile of the prospect, and there are at least two different profiles the researcher can build for the solicitor, depending on the nature of the ask.

One profile is the short one. It contains basic information about the prospect. Usually, that includes name, address, telephone number, educational background, whether or not the person is a college or university graduate, and what the year of graduation is. It includes information about the person's workplace, employer, business title, business address, and business telephone number.

The long profile contains all of the above but also a biographical sketch, including hobbies, interests, career path, and anything that might tie the individual in any way with the institution. It contains financial information, such as giving history, stock holdings, and business transactions if available. It contains a record of interviews, visits, and other contacts with personnel of the institution. It contains information about the family and any other information that may be relevant to the campaign. It contains information about how the prospect uses his or her wealth. It contains suggested strategies suggesting ways the solicitor can build a relationship. It suggests giving capacity, and what the prospect cares about. It affirms the prospect's interest in the institution, or lack of interest. It names other persons who might have an influence on the prospect's future giving to the institution.

Much of the information in the prospect's file that has been obtained through research is confidential, especially information about the family and about one's giving history or financial status. [If prospects knew all the things we know about them, they would be amazed and perhaps a bit upset.] Some states have laws that require disclosure if the donor requests it, but only to the donor, not the public. It is considered by the profession to be unethical to reveal a donor's giving history to outsiders. Two things are very personal, and charitable institutions should be very careful in the handling of them. One is information about a person's religion or religious association. The other is information about one's financial situation. More and more institutions are being selective about the information they carry in a prospect or donor file.

"Prospect evaluation," or "prospect rating," as it is sometimes called, is important to determine how much to ask for. It is usually done through a screening committee composed of individuals who know the prospects and can shed some light on the financial status and the inclination to support the institution. Often a list of prospects is provided each member of the evaluations committee at the meeting and retrieved at the end of the meeting. It should be made clear to each committee member that the information learned is confidential. It is also important that none of the names of members of the evaluating committee be on the list. It would be unethical and awkward to try to evaluate another committee member sitting at the table. If the list of prospects is large, it will take more than one session, and it will be necessary to conduct sessions in different geographical locations with different committee members. A committee of five or so from the New York metropolitan area would meet, for example, to evaluate a list of 500 prospects from that geographical area, and a similar team of evaluators in the Chicago area would rate the prospects in that area. It will take two or three months to accomplish this evaluation task, but it is most important, because from these evaluations will come the amounts of the "asks."

Prospect Management

Once the prospects are evaluated, the task of management and tracking begins. It is essential to know the current status of each prospect, so that priorities can be set and appropriate moves can be made toward closure. The following questions must be asked. When and for what purpose was the last contact made with the prospect? What is the prospect's current relationship with the institution? What is the tie with the institution? If an alumnus(a), what were his or her major interests or field of concentration as a student? If a former patient, what are the prospect's interests in the hospital or health care? If a former ticket holder to the opera or local symphony, what are the prospect's preferences?

The prospect manager needs to know the prospect's giving history to the institution, total giving for all purposes, the date and amount of the last gift, the aggregate total of all gifts to the institution, any dislikes about the institution, or restrictions on the prospect's giving. What was the prospect's largest gift? How many consecutive years has the prospect given to the institution? How about matching gifts from the prospect's employer?

The prospect manager has to meet with staff to develop strategies and actions to acquire the gift, such as when to ask for the gift, who should make the ask and who should accompany the solicitor on the visit, and, after a second review, what the amount of the ask will be. The key to good prospect management is periodic review of activity. Each meeting with staff should be concerned primarily with what "moves" have been made since the last meeting. Prospects that have reached closure will be moved from active status. New prospects coming on line as a result of research will be evaluated with regard to readiness for cultivation and solicitation. More will be said later about major donor portfolios, but it is sufficient here to say that effective prospect management is also the management of cultivation and solicitation, which in effect is the management of fund raising personnel, both professional staff and volunteers. Each of the major gifts people will have a portfolio of no more than 10 prospects with whom they are currently working. To keep on track, the campaign director or the prospect manager should be aware of, and have input to, every move along the arc of progress that points toward closure.

Prospect research and evaluation provide a pool of potential donors who not only have the financial resources to make a major gift but at least some degree of interest in the organization. Prospects usually do not come forward on their own and offer to contribute. They need to be asked, and the art of asking involves knowledge of who should be asking whom, when the ask should be made, and what amount should be requested. It involves preparation and follow-up, because the solicitation itself is only the top of the curve. This roller-coaster ride does not end there.

The Art of Asking

Asking for the big gift is about 75 percent preparation, about 10 percent solicitation, and about 15 percent follow-up. Preparation, as noted in the chapter on major gifts, is what has to be done to get to the top of the curve, that magic moment when the development officer or volunteer says, "As you consider what your gift may be, I hope you will consider this proposal seeking financial support from you in the amount of $1.2 million." Preparation is an uphill climb. It is never easy to build relationships, earn the donor's trust, respect, and confidence. Sometimes it takes years to accomplish, and the art of doing it requires attention to detail. It is useful to know such things as what the prospect enjoys in leisure are important, or what programs or activities of the organization are of interest. How the prospect conducts business and with what business associates, religious and political preferences, material possessions (e.g., jewelry, cars, houses, aircraft, boats), social events the prospect likes to attend—all of these are important. This information is contained in the confidential profile provided by prospect research, but it is important for the solicitor to observe them first hand as visits are made and positive relationships develop. The art of asking is knowing the prospect's habits, likes, dislikes, hopes, ambitions, interests, hobbies, and value system, knowing all these things and making a connection with the organization. The art of asking is many levels higher than "tin cup" solicitation. You may get some change by standing on the corner looking sad and holding out your tin cup to passersby, but you will never get the paper money, the big checks, the stocks and securities, and the bequests unless you develop and practice the fine art of asking, which is really getting to know people and entrusting them with the opportunity to do something wonderful, something that will make a difference, something satisfying and rewarding because it perpetuates and magnifies the prospect's own personal values.

From the Donor's Perspective

A look at asking from the donor's perspective gives valuable insight. Experienced advancement people are not mind readers, but they have learned that part of the art of asking is understanding what the prospect may be thinking.

Who's buying lunch, and why? Christina Harman of Widner University posed the question to a group of advancement professionals at a NSFRE seminar on fund raising. Her point is that donors are looking at the development person as much as he or she is looking at the donor. If it is a telephone call asking for an appointment, the prospect immediately wants to know who is calling.

For example, the president thinks it would be helpful if she paid a visit to a wealthy friend of the organization and asks her secretary to put the call through. Her intention is to seek an appointment. The telephone rings and the donor picks up the receiver and hears the secretary say, "President Greenworthy is calling to arrange an appointment with you." There is a moment of silence, and then, "President who?" The donor heard it right the first time but wants to make sure who is on the line. Like most of us he is apprehensive of anyone who wants to make an appointment. Intelligent donors are like that. They want to know to whom they are talking before their minds allow them to pick up on the next thought. If they don't know the caller, they are very likely to sign off politely. Educated and intelligent people are usually courteous and polite.

Once they know whom they are dealing with, the second question comes quickly to mind. "What does she want?" You see, even if I know you and I am comfortable with you as a person, I still cannot access my computerlike brain and carry on an intelligent conversation with you until I know what your call is all about. Only then can I be satisfied in my own mind that I want to continue the conversation. Of course the donor could say I'm not going to talk to anyone, but then he would be depriving himself of what might turn out to be a valuable contact. That is why a knock at the door or the ringing of the telephone is so compelling. It is the intrigue, the mystery of it. The donor wants to know as much about you and your organization or institution as you want to know about him. He wants to see your eyes when you visit with him at the office or some other appointed place. He wants to see your reaction when he asks questions. The donor wants to trust you, but he is not quite sure. This is why the cultivation process takes so long.

At first the donor sees the development officer as a salesperson seeking a money solution, and it is not until he sees the university representative or the Young Men's Christian Association (YMCA) fund director as a fund raiser who genuinely cares about his interests and welfare, whose values are similar to his, who is concerned about his special interests, who represents a higher cause, that he begins to take an interest and wants to get involved. The donor wants the development person to focus on him, not his money.

In that connection, every move a person makes affects himself and others years into the future. Every person is different. Every day is different. Every situation is different. Development personnel must learn to step back and view each person as he or she is. The image of the university is reflected every time a letter is sent, a telephone call is made, every time the solicitor is courteous. The important thing is to pay attention to the donor. Listen to what is being said. Be alert to body language, the sigh, the shifting stance, the raised eyebrow. Be prepared. Homework and preparation are indispensable, because every word and every action affects the relationship 5, 10, even 15 years out. Attitude is crucial. It gives you away every time. In fact, attitude, according to Harman, is number one. After all the thoughts and theories are laid to rest, and all the success stories are told, the one thing that stands out is attitude. Unconsciously, it is a part of everything we do or say. The donor picks up on it immediately, especially that donor of wealth and experience whom we would like to cultivate for a major gift to the campaign.

David Dunlop, of Cornell University, has an interesting theory about asking for the gift. He names three approaches to the ask.[8] The first is *speculative fund raising*. It focuses on asking. Very little time is spent in preparation. It is based on the theory that if one asks enough people for gifts, a sufficient number will respond and make the effort worthwhile. This is the theory behind direct mail and telemarketing. The time and resources spent on speculative fund raising is far greater, in proportion to the time, energy, and money spent on developing the donor's sense of commitment, approximately 4 percent preparation and 96 percent asking.

In the second type, *individualized fund raising,* much attention is given to the process of asking. Half of the time and energy is invested in preparing the prospect to receive the ask, and half of the time is spent in solicitation. Preparation involves inviting the prospective donor to special events, or sending the prospect a copy of a newsletter, or having lunch with the prospect. This preparation is referred to as "cultivation" by other authors. The initiatives taken before the ask are equally as important as the solicitation itself. This type is most often found in major gift solicitation.

The third type, according to Dunlop, is *nurturing fund raising*. It takes a long time, sometimes years, to nurture the donor's sense of commitment to the institution, and consequently bonding with the donor until the institution becomes the donor's priority for all types of giving, including annual giving, special projects, or the ultimate planned gift. The proportion of effort put into the nurturing process is approximately 95 percent to 5 percent in making the ask.

An excellent course of study for any development officer is the psychology of adult personality. It gives an understanding of how people react to other people. It teaches how to build relationships and how to recognize and work effectively with different personality types. A course like this is valuable because it helps one understand why certain people should make the ask, and certain people should not. Who it is who shakes the prospect's hand, looks the prospect in the eye, and says "I want you to consider a gift of $10,000" makes a big difference in the way the prospect will respond. If the prospect is able to give and has developed a reasonably strong interest in the organization, and the two who are facing each other respect each other—better yet, like each other—it will be hard for the prospect to turn the solicitor down. Even if there is only a low level of interest, the prospect will probably make the gift if the staff member or volunteer who asks for it is liked and respected. "Like" has a fairly dominant role in the relationship. Amazingly, there is a strong personal bond between people who like each other, even if the one's ethics are questionable. That is why con artists are so successful. They get people to like them and take them for a ride later. Clearly, professional staff and chosen volunteers would not be like that. We live by a strict code of ethics, the full text of which is printed in Chapter 2. The point is, in building a relationship, liking each other is fundamental. It follows then that the people who make the ask should have the potential of being liked by the prospect. If there are suspected personality clashes, if there are perceived conflicting lifestyles, or religious or political views, someone else should make the ask. All things considered, however, most development officers and most volunteers can develop a good relationship with a prospect and make the ask.

Ideally, perhaps, the best person to make the ask is a peer, someone on the same social or business level as the prospect. Heads of companies, for example, like to talk with CEOs of institutions or organizations or with volunteers who are also heads of companies. The right person to make the ask might well be a relative or an old college buddy. Usually some member of the campaign organization, who knows more about the prospect than anyone else, can help identify the connection that will work. The last thing the campaign director wants is a refusal from the prospect, but it happens even in the best of times and with the perfect person to make the ask. Emily Pfizenmaier Henderson, in a chapter for *Prospect Research*, a publication of CASE, noted the following:

> The ideal solicitor could be the business associate who is a major consumer of the prospect's product line, a fellow church member, or a principal donor to the prospect's favorite cause. Good researchers keep track of such connections . . . and, by maintaining our own files on social and business circles, we can determine who moves together and thereby connect old-time friends.[9]

Special Events

The activity calendar of every capital campaign includes a number of special events. These are awareness meetings, a kickoff luncheon or dinner, a victory celebration, and many other indirectly related events that take place during the campaign, such as receptions, dinner/dances, seminars, workshops, ribbon-cutting ceremonies, groundbreaking ceremonies, class reunions, power breakfasts, and campus tours that are all a part of the donor cultivation process.

Some of the events are designed as fund raising events, like concerts, athletic contests, and $200-a-plate dinners, preceded by receptions and followed by dancing or a show. Dinner/theater is also popular. The good news is that these special events are excellent social events. They bring people together to interact with each other in an atmosphere of conviviality and entertainment. They are good mixers and wonderful opportunities for getting acquainted, for sizing each other up over small talk, for seeing others and being seen. The bad news is they are not good fund raisers. Fifty to 80 percent of the cost of admission is for expenses, leaving a small amount for the project or the cause. Fortunately, there are often corporate and individual contributions to the event over and above costs. A company, for example, may pick up the cost of a table for six and assign six of its employees to attend, but in addition to that the company may offer a check for $5,000 as an outright contribution. Even with the corporate contributions, and the contributions of individuals who do not attend, the net profit for the campaign is far less than could be achieved in personal solicitation.

It is fair to say then, special fund raising events are good for building relationships and they are important for social reasons, but they can never hold a candle to plain and simple cultivation and solicitation of gifts. In one "ask" the campaign can realize $150,000, for example, and there is very little cost involved, so it must be concluded that the best way to raise money is not with a dinner but by personal solicitation.

Use of Volunteers

Volunteers are wonderful people. They believe in us. They help us raise money. They support us politically. They lobby for us. They give us good advice and counsel. In some campaigns they are the driving force; in others they merely assist professional staff as needed.

They should be recruited with care. Individuals not fully committed to the organization, who have a negative attitude, or who have to be "talked into it" are not good volunteers, because they will not produce good results. Volunteers who are shy, afraid to talk to people, and apprehensive about asking someone for a gift can be trained and educated, but usually do not make good solicitors.

Men and women, however, who have an interest in the organization, who are willing to make their own commitment upfront, and who are enthusiastic about the cause, are the ones best suited to volunteering. They do not get paid, but they often work as hard as paid staff. They do it for the personal reward and satisfaction they receive, certainly not for any financial gain, but they have the potential for bringing dollars and donors to the institution. They foster respect and confidence in the institution. They generate moral and political support for the organization, and they tend to bring friends and family along with them. Good volunteers are invaluable to any institution or organization.

How they are used is just as important as having them. First, they should be used in situations that make them feel comfortable. They should be asked to help with things they are capable of doing; it should be noted that volunteers also are needed to assist in nonfund raising roles, such as serving punch or making guests feel welcome. They can be used effectively to recruit or train other volunteers, to keep records, to stuff envelopes, or to collate materials.

Volunteer solicitors, though, are a special kind of volunteer. They have to be willing and able to make the ask. They have to be aware of the cultivation process, or at least amenable to learn it. They serve best when they understand campaign policies and procedures. Fund raising volunteers are a valued resource in the campaign. They are truly agents of progress, but one must remember their time and energy are limited. Unfortunately the good ones are worked to death, and the rest are not used enough. Professional staff, as a rule, know this and try to use them wisely. At first many are eager to do something, to get in there and really make a difference, but as time goes on and the cares of life press in, they tend to be less responsive to the call.

The downside of using volunteer help is the lack of commitment many volunteers exhibit. In any campaign, but particularly in a major capital campaign, volunteers are often not very time sensitive and are much less productive than professional staff, but that is to be expected. In a recent capital campaign for excellence at a well-known state university, several problems came to light. First, some of the volunteers were putting off getting started and it delayed the progress of the campaign, but worse than that they were taking forever to bring the prospect to closure. Second, there were several volunteers who were shortcutting the process. They had been told in orientation sessions that they should not leave the pledge card, because as every experienced fund raiser knows, prospects will mislay the card, forget about it, or simply procrastinate about doing anything about it. Even so, volunteers were dropping the card off and telling the prospect "let me know when it's ready and I'll pick it up," or "send it in when you've made your decision." Good fund raisers know that will not work. If you cannot get the commitment made and the card signed at the solicitation visit, hold the card and bring it back another day for the signature. It is all a matter of proper closure, which is the weakest area of much volunteer solicitation. Another sad thing happened. One volunteer, it was discovered, turned in the name of a prospect with a dollar amount he was supposed to have pledged. It turned out the volunteer had nothing more from the prospect than a vague promise to think about it. Wanting to complete his assignment and get on with something else, the volunteer turned it in as a bona fide pledge, forging the donor's name on the card, a violation of professional ethics. These things happen, though not very often.

The upside of using volunteer help is the good they can do for the institution in building goodwill, winning support, and raising funds for the organization. They need to be supervised and managed, however. They need to be trained, and they need to be made aware of the entire campaign operation. The more they know, the more productive they will be. They in effect increase the power of the work force and accomplish far more than the limited development staff can do on their own.

In review, volunteers should make their own commitment first. This pledge to the organization is one of the main motivating factors in soliciting gifts from peers. Volunteers should know the institution well and be comfortable with it and enthusiastic about it. They should be positive. If there are any reservations, choose another volunteer. The volunteer's attitude will affect the attitude of the prospect. The volunteer should be encouraged to use printed campaign materials, because seeing the institution's goals, hopes, and dreams in writing supports the volunteer's verbal request. Finally, volunteers should visit the prospect. A personal heartfelt visit and conversation, one on one with the prospect, has the greatest impact on closure.

Professional Staff Portfolios

To achieve the best results in major gift solicitation, advancement professionals should be assigned prospect portfolios. The portfolio concept is one that is used in business, often by sales people to keep track of clients and activities with those clients. The major gift portfolio is simply a folder containing the names of the several prospects assigned to them for immediate cultivation and solicitation. Each prospect's profile, drawn by the people in donor and prospect research, includes any anecdotal records the staff member may have. This is not to say other prospects may not be contacted, but the ones in his or her portfolio are officially cleared for cultivation, solicitation, and closure. Armed with all this information about the prospects, including who the prospects are, where they live and work, their interests, their financial worth, the persons with greatest influence on them, and what, if any, are their ties with the organization, the staff member or volunteer can move forward in a creative way to initiate a string of contacts through visits, invitations to special events, tickets to athletic events, and concerts to bring the prospect into the loop. Following closure, the staff professional or volunteer thanks the donor in several different ways, a phone call, a letter, even a visit or a luncheon. Nothing pleases a donor more than being recognized before his peers.

After the thank-yous have been said, continuing efforts are made to keep the donor in the loop as a friend of the institution and to prepare for a future solicitation.

The portfolios are merely a means of organizing the solicitation process. It makes each solicitor clear on which prospects attention should focus. Portfolios can be elaborate leather cases with the documents enclosed, or simply manila folders. They are portable, so the solicitor can take them in the car or on the aircraft, giving instant access to the prospect's telephone number, fax number, or e-mail, and giving instant information about the prospect. Typically, a log of contacts and action is also kept in the portfolio.

Periodically, the portfolios are brought to strategy meetings and progress reports are given to the campaign director, who keeps a "moves" chart. "Moves management" is a current buzzword in institutional advancement. It means nothing more than managing the progress of bringing a prospect to closure, beginning with the first move (i.e., the assignment of the prospect to a staff person or a volunteer) and continuing on to the next action point and the one after that, for weeks, even months, until the prospect is brought to closure and the gift or pledge is received. After closure, the prospect profile remains in the portfolio until immediate follow-up is achieved, such as thank-you letters, and a desirable number of post gift/pledge contacts. As this arc of progress is completed, prospects in the portfolio are replaced with new prospects and the process begins all over again. The goal is to move as many prospects through the system as possible without overly pushing and rushing to closure unprepared.

Timelines

Timing is essential to the success of the campaign. There is a time to begin and a time to end. There is a time to prepare and a time to wrap it up. There is a proper time for kickoff, and that time is determined by the number and amount of lead gifts achieved. Generally speaking, when 51 percent of the goal is achieved through large leadership gifts and pledges, the time is right for the public to be brought into the picture with a gala kickoff event of some sort, usually a special kickoff dinner or banquet by invitation only, gathering together the torchbearers, the campaign leadership, key donors and prospects, campaign staff and volunteers, the press, the governing board, top administration, councilmen, and city officials for an evening of celebration and anticipation, jubilation, and entertainment, unveiling a large chart showing the amount already raised to the oohs and aahs of the guests, and the enthusiastic challenge to support the new campaign. This is a time to tell the world all the wonderful things this campaign will accomplish for the organization and the community. This is the time to announce the campaign chairperson, who will rise to the occasion as the head cheerleader. This is the time to recognize the campaign cabinet and volunteers and to acknowledge the members of the governing board and elected officials who may be present. This is also the time to say thanks to the donors present who have already made their commitment to the campaign as they stand and receive a thunderous round of applause.

Then comes the time to buckle up and drive toward the finish line, when staff and volunteers begin working their portfolios. This is the time for personal solicitation across the board. This is the time for making everyone aware of the campaign. This is the time for bringing campaign engines up to speed and rising to a higher altitude of expectation, and that means marketing for all it's worth. This is not the time for holding back and whining about the budget. This is the time to put some money into the campaign.

MARKETING THE CAMPAIGN

The four "Ps" of marketing found in standard textbooks and other writings are PRICE, PLACE, PRODUCT, and PROMOTION. A fifth "P" is "PEOPLE," and rightly so, because individuals relate to others in either positive, neutral, or negative ways just as they do to the product, namely, the campaign. They react to the cost, or goal, of the campaign, to the publicity surrounding the campaign, to the leadership, and to the volunteers. Some have even suggested a sixth "P," for "POSITION," referring to how the organization running this campaign compares with other organizations. Competition among institutions and organizations is strong. Currently there are approximately one million not-for-profit organizations in America; most of them are in campaigns of one sort or another raising dollars to support their causes. There are 3,000 colleges and universities and nearly as many hospitals seeking financial assistance.

Marketing the campaign may take a slightly different turn from the above mentioned "Ps." Instead of price, perhaps COST might be more appropriate, because donors will want to know how much this is going to cost them. Instead of place, TIMING might be more relevant. Product might well be CASE FOR SUPPORT, and promotion equates to what campaign directors like to call AWARENESS.

Issues

Before attempting to market the campaign, several issues need to be on the table for discussion and clarification. First on the agenda is an evaluation of identity and mission. This is fundamental to any campaign. The institution, and more specifically the people who are the institution, must know what the institution is about. "We must know who we are and what we are trying to do," as one administrator phrased it. There must be a clear mission and vision, one that is articulated well and has been bought and accepted by all administrators and staff of the organization. As the campaign progresses, if there is any doubt about the identity or purpose of the organization, donors will back away from it.

Second, the administration must carefully evaluate the product being offered by the campaign. The signal question is, what are the contributions to this campaign supporting? Is it desirable? Is it necessary? Is it worthwhile? How will it make a difference? How will gifts and pledges to the campaign affect the institution, the community, and the region? How will the campaign improve what now exists? "How will my dollars make things better?"

Third, there must be a competent, knowledgeable, enthusiastic management system in place. Campaigns often fail for lack of good management. They fail for other reasons too, but good management of a good plan goes a long way toward reaching the campaign goal. The leadership should be chosen carefully and wisely. The strategic plan should be well thought out and followed systematically through the timelines of the campaign. Good and responsible management keeps everyone on target.

Fourth, there must be adequate provision for financial resources. It takes a bit of capital to run a capital campaign. There are materials to purchase. Supplies are needed. Travel is a factor. Contractual service will be needed. Special events will require funding, and the list goes on. You may have a Rolls Royce of a plan but it will go nowhere without gas in the tank. Likewise, an adequate budget permits the campaign to run smoothly.

The business office may suggest that funding be taken off the top, from the gifts that are made. This is a bad idea unless there is a clear understanding with prospects and donors that a percentage of their gifts will go to defray the expenses of the campaign, and most donors do not like that approach. A better way to handle it is to include an amount in the general operating budget to cover costs of the campaign. Salaries are already in the budget and will be paid whether there is a campaign or not. The same is true of fringe benefits, such as health insurance, pension plan, and vacation and sick days. Campaign costs of supplies, materials, equipment, travel, and telephone are over and above the usual budgetary items, but for the campaign, they need to be included in the budget. Some of the organizations might be heard to say, "If we did that, we couldn't afford to run a campaign." The obvious answer is, "If you need a campaign, you should find a way to fund it just like you do for other necessary items, like electricity, or fuel oil."

Fifth, customer relations must be satisfactory, even admirable. When volunteers, prospects, and donors are dealing with the institution, they must be met with prompt and courteous service. They must never be made to feel they are intruding on staff time. In the campaign, just as in a business, the customer is king. It matters not if administrators are busy and secretaries are overworked, when the civic leader, the parent, the prospective donor, or the person off the street who just wants information asks for assistance, the attitude of the administrator or secretary should be "I'm so delighted you are here, how may I help you?" and that attitude should show in the tone of the voice and the expression on the face.

Marketing Goals

In a marketing plan it is customary to state the primary marketing goals essential to the success of the campaign. The first goal might be to enhance the image of the organization, and the first objective in reaching that goal might be to initiate and complete marketing research, such as a survey of external perceptions and a survey of internal views. The timeframe for that objective might be four months, from April through June. The cost of that objective might be something in the range of $500, and the responsibility for meeting that objective might be placed with the director of public relations. A second objective might be to provide the public with information about the institution, such as paid advertisements, news releases, postcards, and other publications. The timeframe could be 12 months, from April through March of the following year. The cost might run as high as $50,000, and again the responsibility would rest with the public relations director.

A second goal might well be to make all patronizing constituencies aware of the campaign. The first objective might be to provide information about the campaign to the public. The timeframe would be from the date of the kickoff through the duration of the campaign. The cost would be calculated, and the responsibility appropriately placed. A second objective might be to conduct eight "Friendship Luncheons," inviting major donor prospects and civic leaders in the area. Each luncheon would host a different group. The timeframe would be 12 months, from the date of the kickoff and forward. The cost would be calculated, and responsibility assigned. A third objective might be to mail an awareness letter and a mini-campaign brochure to every person or family on the donor/friendship base. Colleges would include alumni. The timeframe could be the second week after kickoff. The cost could be the cost of the postage, printed materials, and handling. The responsibility would be assigned.

A third goal might be to compile a master prospect list for the campaign. Appropriate objectives that could be beneficial are: (1) identify suspects, (2) conduct prospect research, (3) identify viable prospects to be solicited in this campaign, and (4) evaluate prospects and prepare profiles as needed. The intention would be to find as many individuals and organizations as possible that have both the interest and the inclination to make a gift or pledge to the campaign.

A fourth goal might be to cultivate and solicit every prospect, through one means or another. The first objective might be to prioritize the list, and to bring closure to the top prospects, for example, those rated $10,000 and higher, during the 12 months following the campaign kickoff. A second might be to solicit all $1,000+ prospects by telephone during the first month of the second year of the active campaign. Costs and responsibility would be determined. A third objective might be to solicit the remaining prospects by direct mail during the two months following the campaign phonathon, and a fourth to bring the campaign to completion by making final visits, sending reminders, and preparing for the victory banquet.

A fifth goal might be to celebrate the campaign victory with a banquet, inviting donors and their spouses or guests, volunteers, professional staff, administrators, and all members of the campaign leadership group. Objectives might be to bring the campaign to an end with a wonderful celebration, to publically recognize the leadership group and give appropriate awards to special individuals, and to share the good news with all constituencies of the organization.

There are other goals of the campaign, but these could well be the marketing goals. In support of the marketing goals and their objectives, much thought must be given to the several targets the marketing efforts will reach and the means and methods by which those efforts will be carried out. Target audiences would include friends, alumni, former patients, clients, parents, trustees, governing boards, top administration, civic and business leaders, legislators, city councilmen, associations, agencies, corporations, foundations, clubs, religious groups, service organizations, physicians, and vendors.

In conclusion, *marketing is selling*. Simply put, we have something to offer—namely, services, beneficial programs, education, and health care—and we are trying to persuade others to buy. A product is involved. Money is involved, and marketing is the process of packaging the product and enticing the customer to buy it. No matter how good it is, if it does not interest the customer, there is no sale. Consequently, in education, health care, or services there are many variables that influence the buy. Traditional marketing professionals tout the so-called four "Ps" of marketing: Price, Place, Product, and Promotion. For the hospitals, nonprofits, colleges, and universities, *people* must be a part of the equation as well as *position*, because people and their perceptions and attitudes, as well as the niche or position the institutions hold in comparison with competitors, are important to the success or failure of the plan.

Mission and Vision Affect Marketing

The marketing plan must have its genesis in the mission and vision of the institution or organization, and the mission and goals should be placed at the forefront of all planning and implementation. Marketing goals must have a direct connection to institutional goals. To construct the marketing plan, a number of questions will be asked:

- What are we marketing?
- Why will individuals and organizations want to support us?
- What image do others have of us?
- Is this a good time for a capital campaign?
- What will it cost?
- Who will chair the campaign?
- Will we need a cabinet, or steering committee?
- What form will the campaign structure take?
- How long will the campaign run?
- Who will be involved? Staff? Volunteers?
- Is the campaign financial goal too high? Too low?
- Do we have a large enough prospect pool?
- Will there be enough lead gifts?
- What printed materials will we need?
- Would a video be an effective fund raising tool?
- Do we have an adequate gift processing system in place?
- Do we have 100 percent board support? Administrative support?
- How will this campaign make us a better organization?
- What if we cannot reach the campaign goal?
- Is there a "Plan B"?
- When do we hold the kickoff?

These and other questions will arise in the preplanning stages. Much of the anxiety and apprehension will be alleviated, and most of the questions will be answered by the feasibility study. Every capital campaign should conduct a feasibility study, and the study should be done by outside independent counsel. It is tempting for the president or chairman of the board to say "Well, let's just do it. We know who the players are," or "We know how well folks like us. This will be a routine campaign," or "Why do we need to pay big bucks for outside counsel? We've got good people here who can run the show."

More about Independent Counsel

All of that may be true, especially in well established organizations like the YMCA or institutions like the University of Michigan or the University of Pennsylvania, but there is an important and valid reason why independent counsel should be hired. Outside counsel brings objectivity to the table. Professional consultants bring a wealth of knowledge and wisdom based on their years of experience working with other institutions and organizations. Insiders tend to

overlook crucial bits of information that should concern them. They are too intro-
spective. They have become too attached to certain personalities and too preju-
diced against others. They are readily acquainted with the norms, i.e., what the
numbers should be under particular circumstances. They have a great sense of
what the right figures for the campaign goal should be.

One could argue that outside counsel is critical to success. Counsel can give
unbiased objective advice. Council has the aura of experience and professional
expertise that is desired and expected by top decision makers, and because counsel is viewed with confidence and respect, counsel will be heard. If there are
problems with professional staff, counsel can suggest solutions. If strengths and
weaknesses of professional staff are not known, counsel can conduct research on
site and find the answers. In fact counsel is much better at doing a staff audit than
the institution because top administration is often too close to certain individuals
to see a flaw if one exists or, conversely, may have developed a dislike for an individual that is unfounded. Counsel can get to the heart of the matter and give the
president or CEO objective data. Strangely, and yet predictably, CEOs and college
presidents will listen to outside counsel before they will hear what their own vice-
presidents are telling them. This could be good as well as bad. It is good that the
CEO gets sound advice from counsel. It is bad the CEO does not hear what
employees are saying because they are taken for granted.

More than that, however, outside, independent, and objective counsel can tell
the chairman and the president the cold hard truth about community perceptions,
about campaign organization and structure, and about campaign funding and personnel without being intimidated or fearful for their job as might be the case with
insiders and current advancement staff. After doing 50 or more confidential interviews with influential people in the community and across the region, independent counsel can advise the chairman and the president on matters pertaining to
the campaign leadership, the amount of the goal, and what to expect from the
patronizing constituencies. Counsel can "tell it like it is," to use a phrase from the
1970s, because counsel will be paid no matter what the outcomes of the feasibility study are, and counsel will leave. Staff members will still be around, easy to
get to, and subject to reprisal as well as praise.

In the 1990s and beyond, there appear to be many more consultants than in former years. Hundreds of them are listed in resource materials distributed by CASE
and NSFRE. At present they are not widely organized and certified. If one desires
to be a consultant, all one need do is hang out a shingle, as they say, and advertise as a consultant. Generally speaking, consultants are individuals who have
been development officers in some organization and have left the organization to
set up shop for themselves or to join an already established consulting firm.
Ketchum, for example, before its restructuring and change of management, hired
a number of development people to work for them as resident consultants and

part-time consultants. Other large firms like Grenzebach and Marts & Lundy likewise have hired personnel from the health care industry and from higher education and have established offices in major cities across America. Jerry Panas and Associates has hired consultants from the ranks of the nonprofits, such as the YMCA. The trend now is toward smaller local and regional consulting firms who specialize in particular areas of fund raising.

PROGRESS REPORTS

Frequent progress reports to the staff, the donors, the campaign leadership, the public, and most certainly to the prospects and donors are a communications imperative. First you tell them what you are going to do, then you tell them you are doing it, and finally you tell them what you have done. It is the one-two-three punch of campaign awareness. People have to know what you are doing, how the campaign is progressing, and what the plans are for future activity to keep their interest alive. "Out of sight, out of mind" is as descriptive of capital campaigns as it is of romantic relationships.

Prospects and donors need to hear about campaign achievement frequently and regularly, and for different reasons. Prospects need to get as much positive information as possible, because they are being prepared for solicitation. Every time a large gift is achieved, everybody should know about it, especially prospective donors. There is something of the "me too" spirit that invades prospects' thinking when they read about a rival company making a large gift. Good news about the campaign only helps the prospect to make a decision. Donors, on the other hand, have already made commitments but need to be continually reassured that they are not out there alone. Others are following and joining the movement toward the campaign goal. Not unlike the rest of us, donors are pleased to be associated with winners, not losers. Seeing others jump on the bandwagon only helps to reinforce their commitment. It reassures them they made a good decision to make the pledge or give the gift.

Public information is essential. There are many publics, of course, and all of them have a need to know what is happening. These publics include the media, parents, friends, alumni, civic leaders, elected officials, and many more market segments the organization is trying to reach. The more the several publics know about the campaign, the greater will be their support. The campaign public relations director needs to be "in their face" frequently, never letting them forget the good progress the campaign is making. News releases, feature stories, TV spots, cable programs, talk shows, interviews, press conferences, public service announcements, e-mail, and the Internet are the media for the message, and today, the new frontier of public information is the web page on the Internet. Every advancement publication is giving attention to the potential use of the Internet, including CASE's *Currents* (see June 1997 issue); The Public Relations Society of America's *Strategist* (see Summer 1997 issue); the Association of Healthcare Philanthropy's *Journal* (see Spring 1997); and NSFRE's *Advancing Philanthropy*, to name a few. It is predicted that the twenty-first century will see a new wave of campaign solicitation via the Internet.

Staff reports keep "the family" up to speed. Some naive person may say, "Why are staff reports necessary? Institutional personnel already know what is going on." They are necessary because staff tend to be barrel-eyed, as my father used to say. It is like looking down the barrel of a double twelve-gauge shotgun. All you see is a small spot of grass at the end of the gun barrel. The big picture escapes your view. Staff often are too close to a particular part of the operation to see what others are doing or what is happening across the organization, but they need to be informed. Of all people they need to be aware of every aspect of the campaign. Public relations people need to know about the good progress of the development operation, and the development staff need to know what public relations has accomplished, or the chairman, or the administration. A good campaign director knows that to keep the campaign running smoothly, every person connected with the organization needs to be aware of what has been accomplished, what is in the works now, and what the plans are for future activity.

DONOR RECOGNITION

Acknowledgment and recognition are not the same, though some institutions regard them as such. Acknowledgment is merely informing the donor that the gift or pledge has been received. It is a legal obligation of the organization to acknowledge charitable contributions. Often the acknowledgment is made in the form of a thank-you letter, but again, the expression of gratitude and the official acknowledgment of the gift are two separate items.

Thank-you letters, memos, telephone calls, and personal visits are acts of appreciation for the generosity of the donor. They are purely voluntary, but very necessary in the cultivation of good relationships. We have all heard about the donor who made a gift to several institutions and waited to see which one would thank him first, and to that institution he sent a much larger gift. Leonard Raley speaks about the phenomenon in Chapter 3.

Expressions of gratitude are a part of a larger function we call donor recognition. In some institutions, a full-time director of donor relations looks after that function. It is essentially an act of giving back to the donor a high degree of honor and acclaim the institution holds for him or her because of the donor's generosity to the institution. It is a form of praise for the donor's good deeds, and the manner and style in which it is given reflects back on the institution. First of all, donor recognition should never be a flippant, off-the-cuff gesture. It should be well thought out and tailored to the donor's wishes and expectations. An expensive recognition gift and wide publicity would be misunderstood and unwanted by some donors. A simple thank-you letter signed by the president or the CEO is all the donor needs or wants, and occasionally a gift will come from a donor who wishes to remain anonymous, with no publicity and no listing of his or her name in an honor roll of donors. The majority of contributors do appreciate, however, public recognition before their peers.

Donor recognition takes many forms. It can be a nicely engraved plaque presented to the donor at a luncheon, or a silver platter with the donor's name and words of appreciation engraved thereon. It can be the naming of a particular facility after the donor. It can take the form of installing a small brass plate on the door of an office or lounge, or having the name carved in stone on the front of a building.

THE HUMAN ELEMENT OF THE CAMPAIGN

Whatever the size of the campaign, the basic elements remain constant. There are four essential groups of people: the managers, the solicitors, the donors, and those who keep track of it all.

The *campaign leadership,* including the chairman of the campaign cabinet, constitutes the management group.

The staff and volunteers are the solicitors.

The *prospects* are the source from which donors emerge.

The *service personnel* are the ones who process the gifts and keep the records, who run the computers and do the mailings.

In large campaigns, there is often a campaign chairperson as well as a campaign director. The chairperson is a top volunteer. The vice-president for institutional advancement or the director of development is usually the campaign director. In some cases, a special campaign director is hired for the particular campaign. There are a number of professional and support staff, sometimes as many as 100 or more major gifts people hired specifically for the campaign. There are prospect managers, communications staff, planned giving experts, donor relations people, corporate and foundation relations personnel, annual giving professionals, and the major gifts and planned giving officers. There are gifts processing staff, records people, and clerical staff.

In small campaigns, there may be as few as two or three professional staff, a dedicated group of volunteers, and an administrative secretary. The professional staff conduct their own prospect research and evaluation. The secretary handles gift processing and acknowledgment. All of them together handle donor relations and donor recognition.

Reduced to its critical parts, the capital campaign needs (1) those who will organize, strategize, and direct the campaign; (2) those who will ask for gifts; (3) those who will give; and (4) those who will process gifts, keep records, compile reports, acknowledge gifts, and recognize donors.

Campaigns, however, are far greater than the critical elements just mentioned. Rita Bornstein, vice-president for development at the University of Miami, says a capital campaign "celebrates an institution's history and creates a vision of its future. . . . It raises fund raising to a new conceptual and technical level, akin to the difference between making a home movie and a major film classic." A successful capital campaign is one of the greatest legacies a CEO can leave the institution.[10] There is, however, always the possibility that the campaign will not reach the goal. This is not a legacy. This is an embarrassment for the CEO that should never happen. The word of caution is, do not begin a campaign until the institution is ready for it. As pointed out in the beginning of this chapter, a number of things need to be in place prior to kickoff. The timing is important. Strong support from the governing board is an absolute necessity, and that means financial support as well as moral and political support. In effect, the board owns the institution. It holds the assets of the institution in trust and bears the responsibility of the strategic plan for the institution and must play a key role in soliciting financial support for the campaign. A great corps of volunteers, including the top volunteer, the campaign chairperson, is important to the success of the campaign, and a strong, competent, and energetic professional staff are a vital element of success, as is an adequate campaign budget. No campaign is easy! It takes hard work and strong commitment to make it work. Even though the institution has been through previous capital campaigns, the new capital campaign should never be taken for granted. There should always be a fresh new feasibility study and a careful determination of the financial goal. Above all, it must be attainable.

CONCLUSION

By definition, a capital campaign is "an organized and intense effort to secure extraordinary gift commitments during a defined period of time to meet specific needs that are crucial to the mission and goals of the institution."[11] Capital campaigns are intended to raise capital monies for buildings, equipment, endowment, program enhancement, and in some cases, scholarships and fellowships. They are one-time-only fund raising efforts. They are not designed to raise operating funds. Capital campaigns are about goals and objectives, about mission and vision. They are about people, though they are often launched to build buildings and raise endowment. They are about people caring, asking, giving, and being involved, and "the most successful campaigns will be those that involve the most people at all levels and phases."[12]

Campaigns are about relationships, developing and maintaining connections and ties between friends. They are about communication, about listening and learning, about understanding and assimilating information, about knowing to whom we are talking and why.

Capital campaigns in America date back to the mid-1600s at Harvard, and Harvard has been at it ever since, recently launching the largest capital campaign in history, a $2.1 billion campaign in May of 1994 to be completed in five years. Margaret Currie writes about it in NSFRE's *Advancing Philanthropy*.[13] The change in modern campaigns from those of earlier years is the scope of the campaign. Stanford's $1.1 billion campaign in 1987 was the first of these megacampaigns, broad in scope, very large in size. Today, although of lesser size, many institutions, including Florida State University ($200 million) and the Brigham Young University ($250 million) are conducting campuswide comprehensive campaigns. Like the rising tide that floats all boats, these campaigns are designed to benefit all departments. The monumental challenge for the campaign leadership, the prospect managers, and the gift processing units is how to deal with the unprecedented amount of data.

Campaigns are running longer. Three years used to be the norm. Now it often takes five years or more to reach the goal. Alabama's $165 million campaign is 7 years. Michigan's $1 billion campaign is 7 years, and Cornell's $1.2 billion campaign is nearly 8 years. Some institutions and organizations find themselves in a perpetual campaign mode. Campaigns require greater management skills. The mega campaigns involve a complex set of procedures, in multicampus operations. They require hundreds of major gifts officers, and they are expensive. One could say they have almost taken on a life of their own.

The smaller campaigns, much smaller by comparison with Harvard or Stanford, are still very much alive as well. They continue to be conducted in much the same way they have been for the past 50 years. Typically, as discussed above, they begin with a feasibility study done by an outside independent consultant. The goal is set, campaign leadership is recruited, the budget is approved, the case statement is prepared, volunteers are recruited, staff are mobilized, the governing board, the president or CEO and top administration support the campaign, materials are printed, prospects are identified and rated, and the work begins, not necessarily in the above order.

Campaigns have a beginning and an end. Three years is the average time period. After preparation outlined above, there is a so-called quiet phase leading up to kickoff when leadership gifts are cultivated and solicited. The rule of thumb is to get approximately 51 percent of the goal up front before going public. This is Phase I, the "advance phase."

The kickoff begins Phase II, often referred to as the "major gifts phase" when volunteers and staff put their best energies into securing an additional 35 to 40 percent, or more, of the goal. The idea is to go after the best and biggest first. Around 90 percent of the goal will come from major gifts, and those who give that 90 percent are relatively few in number. It is just good business sense to spend the most campaign efforts on securing major gifts. "Cultivate the best, and the rest will make up the difference" is what a mentor once said to the author during an internship at St. Bonaventure University in New York. His name does not come to mind, but the sincere look on his face as he made the remark standing there in his Franciscan robe is as clear as yesterday.

The final phase is Phase III, the "completion phase." This is the wrap-up of the campaign, when everybody gets an opportunity to participate. It lasts about six months and includes campaign telemarketing, direct mail, and final personal solicitation visits. It ends with a gala "Victory Celebration" dinner or banquet where the final figures are announced, and the donors, the staff, and the volunteers join the campaign leadership in praise to the institution and gratitude to the many donors who supported the campaign and brought it to a successful conclusion. As always there is the follow-up period when the loose strings are pulled in, reminders are sent out, and the honor roll of donors is published. Then follows a period of analysis and evaluation, and usually a hint of preparation for the next campaign.

Before leaving this discourse, attention to the question of campaign cost is in order. Presidents and CEOs are asked "How much is this going to cost?" by trustees and directors. It is probably one of the first questions to be asked, so it would be unfair to the reader not to say a final word about it. Campaigns are designed to raise money, not spend it, but if you want to make money, you have to spend money.

Campaign cost depends largely on the amount of materials, special events, time, and energy needed to bring in the smaller gifts. If the top givers contribute 95 percent of the campaign, the cost should not exceed seven cents spent for every dollar raised. This is true because it costs far less to solicit six and seven figure gifts. Sometimes the largest gifts require no more than a visit or two and a typewritten (word processed) manuscript. They are the result of long-term relationships, in most cases, and they are usually achieved in the so-called quiet phase of the campaign before the elaborate materials are printed, and the gala events are planned.

In some campaigns, however, 25 cents on the dollar is not unreasonable. The biggest cost of the campaign will be the printing, publication, and distribution of campaign materials in the promotion of the campaign. They have to look good, because they are a reflection of the institution. Donors tend to perceive the organization in the image they receive from the flyers, the brochures, reports, incentives, and direct mail pieces of the campaign. It would not be unusual to spend $180,000 on the "Case" piece, the pledge cards, the direct mail appeals, and the accompanying brochures and flyers. Publicity is also rather costly. A single-page newspaper ad could run as little as $4,500 and as high as $10,000, and the countless paid advertisements throughout the campaign, both in the print and electronic media, will cost a minimum of $50,000 and could go as high as $300,000 or more, depending on the extent to which television ads are used. Most campaigns, it should be noted, do not use extensive television ads. The bulk of the money is spent on printed matter.

Special events, if done right, are costly. A kickoff dinner, a campaign ball, a victory celebration each will cost the organization approximately $9,000, and there are many friendship luncheons, awareness dinners, receptions, and donor recognition events that cost $300 or $400 or more each. All of this expense is realized, however, after the advance phase of the campaign. So, it is clear that smaller gifts cost more to raise. Leadership gifts cost less.

It is safe to say that a capital campaign will cost between 7 and 25 cents on the dollar. The national average, according to Bruce McClintock, chairman of Marts & Lundy, is 14 cents on the dollar.

Campaigns are financed through a number of creative options, as suggested above in the section on marketing. The easiest, and perhaps the best way to finance a campaign, all things considered, is through a standard budget allocation from the institution's operating funds. With smaller organizations this could be a problem. Often budgets are so tight there is no room for an outlay of campaign expenditures. Another way might be to allocate unrestricted gift dollars to pay for the campaign, but this is considered by some to be unethical and undesirable. It is unethical because it tends to create a conflict of interest. Fund raisers soon get caught in the trap of favoring the unrestricted money and neglecting restricted gifts for program support, scholarships, and other institutional needs. It is especially unethical if donors are led to believe that every penny of their money goes to support the cause, when in fact a large part of it goes toward fund raising.

Some donors will not contribute to operational expense, especially corporate donors, because they feel if an organization is not financially sound enough to pay for its own lights and water, and other operating expenses, it probably should not be in business. In defense of many nonprofits, however, the only revenue received is from charitable donations. That being the case, it is legitimate to take a percentage for administrative costs, but it is most important to let the donors and prospective donors know what that percentage is. Anything more than 30 percent is undesirable with most donors.

With mergers and buyouts in the health care industry, and with increases in cost shifting caused by reductions in Medicare reimbursement, more and more hospitals are starting development programs to raise money for charity care and needed capital construction. The Association for Healthcare Philanthropy (AHP) Think Tank Committee, headed by AHP President and CEO William C. McGinley, is preparing a detailed study of the role of development officers in the restructuring process now going on in many health care institutions. The study results in a new book to be released this summer dealing with the size, scope, and nature of conversions of not-for-profit health care organization to for-profit organizations. It purports to offer guidance to remaining not-for-profit health care organizations as to how they may distinguish themselves as worthy of charitable contributions.[14]

There are other ways to finance a campaign. Soliciting gifts directed to the raising of funds is a possibility. The pitch here is for an up-front investment in the campaign to ensure its success. When campaign gifts are used temporarily to pay for expenses until the campaign gets underway, then the monies diverted to cover early expenses can be repaid. Again, this is somewhat risky. Taking a percentage of all gifts received is another way of financing the campaign, but this practice is also questionable, as discussed above, unless the donors are told about it up front and understand what the percentage will be. Finally, one could borrow from the endowment, or quasi endowment, to cover expenses. This one does make sense, but it would be wise to make some provision to pay it back with interest. It is always easier to borrow from one's self, but it is always much more difficult to pay it back. Clearly, the best way to go is to increase the budget enough to include campaign expenses, and use all the gift dollars for the wonderful cause the campaign is all about.

Capital campaigns have been around for a long, long time, and it is highly unlikely they will disappear in the next century. If the economy continues to be strong as it is currently, with little or no inflation, gift dollars will continue to rise. *Giving USA* reports $150 billion in 1996, which is an increase of 7.3 percent over 1995. Even so, Americans gave only 1.9 percent of their incomes to charity in 1996, slightly more than the 1.8 percent they gave in 1995.[15] So, giving continues to rise, but there are challenges for advancement professionals. More and more government gift dollars are being shifted to the private sector. Radical changes in health care loom on the horizon. An income tax overhaul may impact donors. Most of all, there is increased competition for the gift dollar.

All things considered, however, capital campaigns will continue to be a significant source of revenue for institutions of higher learning, hospitals, and the vast number of nonprofits in the United States.

NOTES

1. B.R. McClintock, Emerging Trends in Capital Campaigns (a presentation at the Fund Raising Day in New York City, June 19, 1997).

2. R. Pierpont and A. Kihlstedt, Lessons from Large and Small Capital Campaigns (a presentation at the National Society of Fund Raising Executives National Conference in Dallas, March 11, 1997).

3. Bruce McClintock, conversation with author.

4. G.D. Gearhart, *The Capital Campaign in Higher Education* (Washington, DC: The National Association of College and University Business Officers, 1995), 60.

5. J. Panas, The No-Nonsense Guide To Help You Prepare a Statement of Your Case, Jerold Panas, Young & Partners, Chicago, n.d., 2.

6. J. Panas, No-Nonsense Guide, 2.

7. Campaign literature of Ball State University, Elmira College, Wichita State University, The Food Bank of Delaware, and Indiana University.

8. D.R. Dunlop, "Major Gifts," in *The President and Fund Raising*, eds. J.L. Fisher and G.H. Quehl (Washington, DC: The American Council on Education, Macmillan, 1989) 175.

9. E.P. Henderson, "Finding the Fabulous Few: Why Your Program Needs Sophisticated Research," in *Prospect Research: A How To Guide*, eds. B. Strand and S. Hunt (Washington, DC: Council for the Advancement and Support of Education, 1986), 38.

10. R. Bornstein, "The Capital Campaign: Benefits and Hazards," in *The President and Fund Raising*, J.L. Fisher and G.H. Quehl (New York: American Council on Education, Macmillan, 1989), 202.

11. W.P. Goldrick, "Campaigning in the Nineties," in *Educational Fund Raising*, ed. M.J. Worth (Washington, DC: American Council on Education, 1993; distributed by Oryx Press, 1993), 144.

12. S.C. Shaw and M.A. Taylor, *Reinventing Fund Raising: Realizing the Potential of Women's Philanthropy* (San Francisco: Jossey-Bass, 1995), 186–197.

13. M. Currie, "Inside the Harvard Campaign," *Advancing Philanthropy* (Alexandria, VA: National Society of Fund Raising Executives, Winter 1995), 41.

14. W.C. McGinly, "1997: The Challenges Ahead for Health Care Philanthropy" (*Association of Healthcare Philanthropy Journal,* Spring 1997), 42.

15. S. Gray, "Gifts Top $150 Billion," *Chronicle of Philanthropy* (June 12, 1997), 39–40.

Appendix 5–A

Master Plan of Action
Century II
Campaign for Delaware State College

(Two years after Kickoff, the institution was renamed Delaware State University by act of the State Legislature, signed into law by Governor Thomas R. Carper.)

I. Philosophy, Goal, and Objectives

Philosophy. The Century II Campaign for Delaware State College is the first multimillion dollar capital campaign in the history of the institution. It has grown out of a vision for a new Delaware State College, reaching for a greater margin of excellence in all areas of the teaching/learning environment. State and federal assistance provide a foundation, but the superstructure of academic excellence requires additional and substantial funding from the private sector.

Goal. To achieve this margin of excellence, the leadership of the college has authorized a $10.1 million capital campaign. Admittedly, it is an ambitious financial goal, but it is attainable by means of the Century II campaign, which is a highly disciplined, systematic, well-organized, three-year capital campaign. It has the full backing and support of the Board of Trustees, the President of the College, the Board of Visitors, the Governor of Delaware, senior administrative officers of the College, and the Alumni Association.

Objectives: The Century II campaign seeks not to build new buildings. Its primary objectives are to provide major funding for faculty, students, and academic programs.

- $4 million for Faculty Development, strengthening teaching and research
- $3 million for Student Financial Assistance, providing educational opportunity for more and more deserving students
- $3.1 million for Program Support, enhancing academic departments

---

Courtesy of Delaware State University, Dover, Delaware.

II. Elements of Success

A Good Public Image. Prospective donors must think well of us, must respect us, and must believe in us. We must build a new Delaware State, reaching for greater excellence in teaching, research, and service.

A Strong Case for Support. Donors want to know who we are, what we are doing, and how the money will be spent. They want to know what good things will happen as a result of their gifts. The first priority of the Case Statement is to convince prospective donors that their gifts are an investment in an outstanding cause.

The Century II Case Statement, endorsed by the President's Administrative Council, April 8, 1991, is the result of writing and rewriting draft after draft. It has been reviewed by civic and business leaders of the Board of Visitors, and ultimately refined to become one of the most powerful case statements ever produced by the College. It serves as the source for all other campaign materials, including the Family Division brochure, the pledge cards, the mini-case brochure for alumni and friends, and the helpful brochures entitled "Ways of Giving," and "Questions and Answers."

Influential Leadership. Delaware State is most fortunate that P. Coleman Townsend has accepted the national chairmanship of the campaign. Under his leadership an outstanding group of top volunteers has been recruited to serve in various positions on the Campaign Cabinet. All of them have made an investment in the campaign, and all of them are committed to achieving the goal and objectives of the campaign.

Large Pool of Prospects. A number of potential donors at the $10,000 level and above have been identified. Each prospect will be evaluated to determine what the asking amount should be, and each prospect will be assigned a volunteer. As of this writing, 273 major gift prospects have been identified. If all of them gave the maximum we asked for, the campaign would easily exceed its goal. We know, however, that many will "buy in" at a lower figure than the "Ask," and many will decline the invitation to contribute. Obviously, top volunteers and staff will be on the lookout for new prospects throughout the duration of the campaign.

An Adequate Number of Volunteers. As has been stated, this campaign is a volunteer-driven campaign, in contradistinction to some of the larger campaigns that are staff driven. Our campaign will recruit approximately 80 volunteers. There are nine top volunteers and 71 regular volunteers, each of whom will make three to five personal solicitation visits.

A Planned and Flexible Time Schedule. There must be a beginning and an end, a time period for soliciting leadership gifts, and a time for personal solicitation of lesser gifts, a time for alumni solicitation, and a well-planned time for soliciting family gifts.

A detailed timetable with specific deadlines will be constructed. Adherence to these timelines is crucial to the achievement of our goal. Experience teaches that when deadlines are ignored, and volunteers do not complete their assignments, the campaign loses its energy and fails to reach its objectives.

Top Down, Inside Out. Successful campaigns are those that begin from *within* the institutional family, and once outside, start from the top of the pyramid of prospects.

We will receive 80% of the money from 20% of the prospects. Professional fund raisers have known for years the best use of volunteer time and energy is in cultivation and solicitation of the biggest and best prospects; and it is logical that it begin with the faculty and staff. If the family, including trustees and top administrators, as well as the rank and file of faculty and staff, sense the urgency of the campaign and make a stretch gift, alumni and friends outside the campus will catch the spirit and do likewise. We must keep in mind that token gifts by the family will result in tokenism from other constituents.

Gifts from the family show our resolve and our commitment. Gifts from the top, such as the Longwood Foundation's $2 million commitment, create an impact, a ripple effect, if you will, on other donors, causing them to lift their sights and make larger contributions than they otherwise would.

III. Structure and Organization

The structure and organization of the campaign is built around three vital components:

- The Executive component
- The Advisory component
- The Volunteer and Staff component

A. The Executive group is composed of the Campaign Chairman, the President of the College, and the Vice-President for Institutional Advancement, who is also Campaign Director. They are assisted by professional and support staff.

B. The Advisory group helps to facilitate the campaign by giving valuable counsel and voluntary assistance. This group is the Board of Visitors, a permanent board formed especially for the Campaign but helpful in other ways long after the Campaign is ended. It consists of 27 outstanding civic and business leaders from Delaware and the surrounding region, including the former living governors of Delaware. Charter members include Charles

Cawley, Chairman of MBNA America; Claibourne Smith, Vice-President of Du Pont; Bernard Taylor, Chairman of Wilmington Trust; Coleman Townsend, Chairman of Townsends, Inc.; Barbara Riegel, Arts Consultant; James Wright, President of Beneficial Bank; Roy Klein, President of Klein Development; Joshua Martin, President, Bell Atlantic; the Honorable Michael N. Castle, Representative, U.S. Congress; and other distinguished personalities.

C. The Volunteer and Staff contingency is vital to the Campaign and consists of top volunteers, such as Cabinet and Board of Visitors members, and a corps of other volunteers from the ranks of alumni and friends assisted by professional and support staff of the Advancement Division. The several categories of volunteers include the following:

> Volunteers for Leadership Gifts ($500,000 and more)
> Volunteers for Key Gifts ($100,000 and more)
> Volunteers for Major Gifts ($10,000 and more)
> Volunteers for Alumni Gifts
> > The Alumni Blue Team
> > The Alumni Red Team
> > Alumni Special Events
> Volunteers for Family Gifts
> > The Trustees
> > The Faculty
> > The Staff
> > The Students

The Campaign Cabinet is a rather special group. These individuals form the Campaign's central management team. They comprise that faithful few who drive the Campaign to its successful completion. They set the policies and the guidelines. They review the prospects and determine the strategies for major gift cultivation and solicitation. The President and the Vice-President for Institutional Advancement are active members of the Cabinet, and other Professional Staff are involved in campaign action plans. Individuals serving in this group for the Century II Capital Campaign deserve credit for the work they accomplished. They include the following:

> ### The Campaign Cabinet
> Campaign Chairman, P. Coleman Townsend, Townsends, Inc.
> Leadership Gifts Division Chairman, Joshua W. Martin III, Bell Atlantic
> Key Gifts Division Chairman, Lawrence I. Zutz, Zutz Insurance
> Major Gifts Division Chairman, Marvin E. Lawrence, Scott Paper
> Alumni Gifts Division Chairman, William Granville, Mobil Oil

Family Gifts Division Chairman, Kenneth W. Bell, Dean, Agriculture
Member at Large, James W. Wright, Beneficial Bank
Member at Large, Barbara C. Riegel, Arts Consultant
Member at Large, Roy Klein, Klein Development

College President, William B. DeLauder
Vice President for Institutional Advancement, William W. Tromble

The second year of the Campaign, advancement professionals Gregory Johnson, Director of Development, and Renee Wright, Director of Corporate and Foundation Relations, joined the team.

IV. Strategy

Best results for major gifts are obtained through personal solicitation, preceded by appropriate and timely cultivation of donor prospects. The game plan is as follows:

A. Through a system of networking, word-of-mouth, personal recommendation and referral, a list of suspects is compiled. "Suspects" is a term often used by professional fund raisers to indicate the potential donor about whom little is known except that someone suspects they might contribute if they are asked.

B. From this list of individuals, corporations, foundations, and other groups, a more definitive list of prospects is compiled. Prospects are those about whom we have gathered considerable information and have reason to believe will make a gift.

C. After the prospects have been identified, they are evaluated. A number of anonymous evaluation sessions are held with members of the Board of Visitors, other top volunteers, past donors, and others in certain geographical areas. The object of the evaluation is to put an "ask" figure on each prospect.

D. When the prospects have been evaluated, strategy sessions are held with the Campaign Cabinet, the professional staff, and other top volunteers to determine who is best to solicit whom. Eventually, beside each prospect's name will be the name of the volunteer or staff member who will solicit the prospect.

E. In the Advance Phase of the campaign leading up to Kickoff, the Professional Staff including the President of the College and the Vice President for Institutional Advancement, together with volunteer when available and desirable, approach and solicit lead gifts from the top prospects. To have these commitments, verbal or otherwise, in hand before the public announcement of the campaign is desirable and necessary.

F. Awareness Meetings, sometimes called cluster meetings, are luncheons, breakfasts, and dinners, to which 6 to 12 people are invited. These are people whom we suspect may have the capacity to make a major gift and may have an interest in Delaware State College. Typically the guest list is made up of names supplied by a volunteer host or hostess, such as names of colleagues, associates, or friends. Names of prospects from the master file are also available.

Invitations are sent from the Development Office with an RSVP to the volunteer host or hostess.

Awareness meetings often produce excellent volunteers as well as donors.

G. Orientation and card selection meetings take place after volunteers have been recruited. They accomplish two things: Training for personal solicitation and the opportunity to choose the contact. Volunteers are brought together for a briefing on how to approach prospects, what to say, what not to say, and how to bring the prospect to closure. Following that, they are invited to the table to choose the prospects they wish to solicit. Where this type of meeting is not possible, because of the small number of volunteers in a given area or city, the orientation and card assignments are done in a private meeting between the volunteer and a professional staff member.

H. When personal solicitation by staff and volunteers is finally begun, the procedure for the cultivation and solicitation must be fully communicated; and if we want to be successful, they must be strictly adhered to. Our strategy is as follows:

1. For individuals, two visits (alumni and friends, and certain corporations).

    a. The first visit is a cultivation visit. The volunteer gets an appointment, makes the visit, and presents the packet of materials containing a personalized cover letter and case for support. He/she suggests an amount for the prospect to think about, and makes an appointment for the next visit.

    b. The second visit is the solicitation visit. The volunteer reviews the materials and the proposal, and asks for the commitment. If the prospect says "yes," the volunteer brings out the pledge card for the prospect's signature. If no, the volunteer does not show the pledge card, but rather thanks the prospect for the visit. If "maybe," the volunteer thanks the prospect for talking and makes an appointment for a third visit later.

General Policy. We never, ever, leave the pledge card for pickup or delivery later. Somehow it just never happens. There are delays. We have to chase it down. The prospect changes his mind, the card gets lost or put aside. All sorts of bad things happen.

Always bring out the card after the prospect has made a verbal commitment in conversation.

If it looks like the prospect is going to give a quick "no," keep talking. Make another visit. Keep cultivating the prospect. Send more material from the College. Give him/her tickets for special events, or whatever it takes to interest the prospect in the campaign.

2. For companies and foundations, a written proposal or letter of request is standard practice in lieu of the presentation packet. A letter of intent is suggested in lieu of the pledge card. As with individual solicitation, there should be a minimum of two visits: (1) the cultivation visit, and (2) the solicitation visit.

In some cases there will need to be more than one cultivation visit before the prospect becomes interested and subsequently involved in the campaign prior to closure.

Foundations in particular require special handling. Each has its own set of guidelines that must be followed carefully. Each has its own time schedule, its own interests, its own traditions, policy, and procedures.

I. Gift Acknowledgment and Donor Recognition

Thank-you letters will be sent to donors immediately, acknowledging gifts and pledges. Major donors will receive a letter from the Vice President for Institutional Advancement. Department Chairs and others involved in procuring the gift are encouraged to express their own personal thanks as they see fit.

J. Fund Raising Strategy

In conclusion, fund raising strategy is based on this formula:

Prospect research, plus cultivation and solicitation, leads to closure, acknowledgment, and follow-up.

First, identify the prospective donor. Make every possible attempt to interest the donor in the College. Try to involve the donor through receptions, luncheons, and visits to the campus. Ask the donor for the gift, follow it up, and by all means say thank you in an appropriate way.

V. Campaign Time Schedule

The active time period for the campaign extends from the date of Kickoff, May 8, 1991, through May of 1994. All gifts and pledges received, however, from July 1, 1990, through December 31, 1994, will be counted.

The usual time allotted for the payment of pledges is three years from the date the pledge was made. If, for example, a pledge is made in 1993, it may extend through 1996.

Phase I–Advance planning, recruitment, and solicitation of lead gifts prior to Kickoff

Dec	1988	Get approval and backing of College leadership
Spring	1989	Conduct a Feasibility Study
Oct '89–Oct '90		Recruit volunteer Board of Visitors; search for and hire a Vice-President for Institutional Advancement
Nov	1990	Preliminary draft, Master Plan of Action
Dec	1990	Prepare prospect list
Jan–Apr	1991	Recruit campaign leadership
Mar	1991	Establish campaign goal and objectives
Nov '90–May '91		Review and rate major gift prospects
Nov '90–May '91		Solicit lead gifts
Apr	1991	Final draft, Master Plan of Action
May	1991	Prepare progress report for Campaign Kickoff
May	1991	Hold Inauguration Dinner to kick off the Campaign

Phase II–Major gift solicitation; Alumni and Family Division Kickoffs; awareness meetings, volunteer recruitment, training and prospect assignment

Jun	1991	Review prospect list
Jun	1991	Prepare and distribute Prospect Notebooks to Chairmen of Leadership, Key, and Major Gifts Divisions
Jul	1991	Review all campaign materials, procedures, and strategies with the Campaign Chairman
Jul	1991	Mail awareness letter to all prospective major donors
Oct	1991	Complete cultivation and solicitation of Leadership Gifts, $500,000+
May	1991	Administrative Council

Jun	1991	Send pledge reminders routinely in month donor has chosen
Jul	1991	Board of Trustees
Sep	1991	Board of Visitors
Jul	1991	Campaign Cabinet
Aug	1991	Top volunteers
Sep	1991	Regular volunteers
Oct	1991	Publish Honor Roll of donors
Dec	1991	Complete cultivation and solicitation of Key Gifts, $100,000+
May	1992	Major Gifts, $10,000+
May	1992	Alumni Gifts Division
May	1992	Family Gifts Division
Jan	1992	Pre-call flyer, prior to telephone solicitation
Jan	1992	Recruit phonathon leadership, night captains, volunteer callers
Feb-Apr	1992	Phonathon
Feb-Apr	1992	Next day Thank-You letters
Jun-Dec	1992	Pledge reminders
Jun	1992	Conduct midcampaign assessment

Phase III–Campaign completion, major gifts follow-up, and direct mail solicitation

May '92–Dec '93	Follow-up
Oct	1992	Publish Honor Roll of donors and deliver appropriate awards
Sep	1992	Direct mail awareness letter
Oct	1992	Direct mail solicitation letter
Dec	1992	Follow-up, year-end letters and reminders
Mar	1993	Second follow-up to nonrespondents
Oct	1993	Publish Honor Roll; give awards
Jan '93–Dec '94	Continue follow-up on previous solicitation
Jan-Dec	1994	Merge Century II solicitation into Annual Fund Campaign
Oct	1994	Publish Honor Roll; give awards
Dec	1994	Hold Victory Celebration Dinner

VI. Campaign Materials

Case Statements
Pledge Cards
"Ways of Giving" brochures
"Question and Answer" brochures
Presentation folders
Faculty/Staff brochures
Faculty/Staff pledge cards

Alumni/Friends mini-case statement
Alumni/Friends response cards
#10 campaign envelopes
#9 return envelopes
Campaign name badges
Campaign memo pads
Campaign letterheads
Invitations to Kickoff event
Invitations to Awareness Luncheons
Invitations to Victory Celebration
Campaign logo
Campaign banners
Mailing labels
Large mailing envelopes
Spring-top cases for members of the Board of Visitors
Pens
Name and address gift booklets
Award plaques
Marble paperweights
Campaign business cards
Pledge Reminder forms
Campaign video

VII. Special Events

Campaign Inaugural Dinner
Alumni Division Kickoff
Family Division Kickoff
Presidential Scholarship Ball
Alumni Golf Tournament
Centennial Ball
Alumni Fund Raising Dinners
Awareness Luncheons and Dinners
Campaign Reception, Wilmington Country Club
Victory Celebration

Board of Visitors meetings will be held once every six months or at the call of the Chair, and will continue indefinitely as needed. Members of the Board of Visitors should rotate on and off at staggered three-year intervals. The Board is a valuable advisory group and should remain in existence as long as the College continues on its present course of advancement and development of external resources.

Campaign Cabinet meetings will be held as frequently as possible during the second phase of the campaign. Meetings will be arranged at the call of the Chair and will continue for the duration of the Campaign.

Awareness meetings will be held in various locations during the second phase of the Campaign. Major donor prospects and influential people will be invited. The purpose of the meetings is to make prospects aware of the exciting things that are happening at the College.

Wilmington, DE
Dover, DE
Selbyville, DE
Philadelphia, PA
Trenton, NJ
Washington, DC
Baltimore, MD and other cities as there is local interest

Orientation and card selection meetings for volunteers will be held as needed in various locations, including Wilmington, Dover, Philadelphia, Trenton, and Washington, D.C.

VIII. Prospect Research and Management

Identification of viable prospects will be made from a macro list of suspects in October of 1990 through May of 1991 and following.

Evaluation of prospects will be made by special review committees comprised of volunteers, interested friends, and alumni for the purpose of placing an "Ask" amount on the prospect's card.

December 1990 Initial general screening
April 1991   Prospect list
April 1991   Alumni major donor prospects
May 1991   Prospect review
June 1991   Revised prospect list

Tracking of prospects will be done by means of a tracking sheet placed in each major prospect's file in the Development Office. As contacts are made, the date and the person making the contact are recorded.

File memoranda are also kept in each prospect's file. After telephone conversations and personal visits are made by the professional staff, a memorandum is written recording the purpose of the contact and the person making the call or visit. Volunteers are expected to report back to the office and similar memoranda will be filed and computerized.

Master Prospect File. For management purposes, a master card file is kept on each prospective major donor. Each card contains only basic information needed for visitation.

Prospect Management Notebooks are compiled and given to each of the major gift chairpersons, including the Chair of Leadership Gifts ($500,000), the Chair of Key Gifts ($100,000), and the Chair of Major Gifts ($10,000). Also a notebook is given the Chair of the Alumni Gifts Division and the Chair of the Family Gifts Division. A master notebook is kept by the Campaign Director, and a duplicate is supplied the Campaign Chairman and updated periodically. Prospect management is delegated to the Campaign Director.

IX. Campaign Communication and Information

Campaign Update is a newsletter distributed to volunteers, management personnel, and selected donors. Publication should begin in the Summer of 1991.

Campaign Reports are generated for the President, the Trustees, and campaign leaders. These reports detail the progress of the campaign, including gifts and pledges received.

Publicity is handled by the Office of Public Relations. Whenever possible, with the donor's permission, press releases will be delivered to the media in a timely manner. No more than one major item will be publicized per week. Following this policy will allow us to stretch the good news out over an extended time and keep the public interest over the life of the campaign.

Authorized Spokesman. During the campaign, a continuous flow of information will be provided the media. We must be careful, however, to speak with one voice. Conflicting information is misleading and confusing. Accordingly, those officially designated to speak for the campaign are the President, the Campaign Chairman, and the Vice President for Institutional Advancement.

X. General Campaign Policies

Several miscellaneous campaign management policies included here are important to the successful operation of this major fund raising effort.

Revised Fund Raising Policy and Procedure regarding gift receiving, gift receipting, gift acknowledgment, and gift reporting has been approved by the President and the Administrative Council. (See Council minutes, "Gift Processing," 12/3/90.) This policy applies to all fund raising in general, but will also apply to the Century II Campaign.

Campaign Authority. In any campaign it is important to be clear about who has authority for the conduct of the campaign. In the Century II Campaign, authority is given the Campaign Chairman, the President, and the Vice President for

Institutional Advancement, who is also the Campaign Director. *Final authority* is vested in the President.

Fund Raising Priority. The campaign will take priority over any other fund raising activity of the College for the duration of the campaign, except for the Annual Fund Campaign that goes on routinely, year after year.

Campaign Accountability. Gifts to be counted in the campaign include routine annual fund gifts as well as capital campaign gifts. All gifts of cash will be counted, and gifts of appreciated securities, gifts in kind that support campaign objectives, gifts of life insurance, charitable annuities, matching gifts, pledges, gifts of real estate, realized bequests, and testamentary commitments. Grant support for programs included in the campaign objectives, such as Saturday Academy, also will be counted.

What will not be counted are gifts made for purposes outside campaign objectives, e.g., to build a building, federal entitlements grants, or grants for sponsored research that require specific returns for the sponsor.

Ways of Giving include outright gifts of cash, pledges, marketable securities, gifts of tangible personal property, gifts of real property, and planned gifts such as wills, bequests, annuities, life insurance, and charitable trusts.

Finally, *Right of Refusal.* Delaware State College will have the final say with respect to accepting or declining gifts. Occasionally a donor will want to make a gift with strings attached that make it awkward for the College to receive it; or someone will want to contribute a piece of outdated equipment or a parcel of land in a remote area not suitable to the College. So it is important the donor realize the College has the right of refusal and may respectfully decline any gift not in the interest of the institution.

XI. Conclusion

The Century II Campaign for Delaware State College will succeed. Feasibility studies and prospect research indicate there is a broad base of support. The case for support is strong. The professional leadership of the campaign is experienced, competent, and highly regarded; and the volunteer leadership is composed of civic leaders and business executives of outstanding ability and strong personal commitment to the College.

The time is right and the opportunity is now, especially during the momentous occasion of the College's Centennial Celebration, marking 100 years of service to the State and the surrounding region. This is the first multimillion dollar campaign in the history of the institution. $10.1 million is a reachable goal over the period of three years.

The President and the Board of Trustees are committed to it, because it is through the enabling power of the Century II Campaign that the "new Delaware State College" will rise to new heights of academic excellence and service.

The people of Delaware and all of us who are touched by the influence of the College will benefit from the economic and academic impact of the Century II Campaign.

CHAPTER 6

Institutional Foundations

William W. Tromble

OVERVIEW

Giving to educational institutions, hospitals, and other nonprofits has increased to billions of dollars over the past few years. With this growth has come a need for greater attention to stewardship and investment. As a result many institutions have established foundations to attend to those functions, as well as to fund raising. What was perhaps the first institutional foundation came into being in 1891 when "12 gentlemen sat down together in the law offices of Gleed and Gleed in Topeka, Kansas, and created the Kansas University Endowment Association."[1] In 1985, Timothy A. Reilley reported that 67 percent of America's four-year state universities had institutional foundations.[2] In 1997, according to Phelan, there are more than 1,000 college and university foundations throughout the United States.[3] Eric Wentworth of the Council for Advancement and Support of Education (CASE) believes that number is high. His research shows around 840 foundations associated with four-year public universities and community colleges, "and they are equally distributed between the two types of schools, approximately 420 in four-year colleges and universities and 420 in community colleges." Several universities do not have foundations, including the University of Michigan, the University of Kentucky, the University of Tennessee, and Pensylvania State University, but 9 out of 10 four-year American public colleges and universities have foundations.[4]

In addition to these, many hospitals and nonprofits have foundations. The Association for Healthcare Philanthropy (AHP) reports there are approximately 5,000 hospitals in the United States. Half of them employ development officers and engage in fund raising activities.

MISSION AND PURPOSE

The mission of the foundation is to serve and support the host institution. It raises money for the hospital or university. It stands as a pillar of political support in the local community for its host and is an independent buffer for the institution. It brings affluent and influential individuals into the loop, and it is a model of stability and consistency in a sometimes shakey and tumultuous world. Above all, it provides third-party stewardship and investment security often perceived by the public to be responsible and dependable.

The case for establishing institutionally related foundations is built around the practical matter of objectivity and professionalism that give donors and institutions a high level of comfort. These are rather special foundations. They are connected to their host institutions, but separate from them. They are incorporated, independent, private entities. They have their own boards of directors and all the flexibility of operation included in their charters. They do not have to go through the bureaucracy of the government in writing grant proposals, taking bids for construction, borrowing money to buy real estate, and brokering appreciated securities. They do not jump as a puppet would when the sponsoring institution pulls the strings, but they fully understand, in most cases, their role is a supportive one. In fact their basic purpose for existence is as a repository for gift monies to be held, administered, and invested according to donors' wishes. Some foundations are indeed the fund raising arm of the institution. Others are mainly keepers, distributors, and investors of the funds. They exist in a unique and convivial atmosphere of cooperation between the institution and its foundation.

Most of the time these two institutions work together in harmony, though there are times when sour notes are heard. Because the foundation is independent and not obliged to follow the dictates of the host institution, university presidents sometimes differ with foundation boards on how the money should be spent. The president may want the foundation to hand over $10 million to assist in the construction of a building, but the foundation board may respectfully decline to do so. There is always the potential for conflict between the foundation board and the institutional governing board, but when members understand the roles the two boards play, there is support and cooperation. Executives of both institutions have one very significant thing in common. They are tied to each other by an umbilical cord of mission and purpose. They have all to gain by supporting each other and much to lose by fighting each other. Foundations are established to assist and advance the host institution. Where there is conflict, it is usually because of ineffective leadership and poor communication. There must be a clear agreement on goals and objectives and an open nonthreatening, nonpower wielding communication between the foundation and the host institution. Many problems are caused by personality conflicts. When they are resolved, both the foundation and the university can move forward smoothly.

There are three reasons for having an institutionally related foundation, according to Michael J. Worth, "The first is to provide a vehicle to keep private gifts separate from public funds and to ensure they are used in the manner intended by the donors. . . . Second, as a private organization, the foundation often has greater flexibility . . . in the investment and expenditure of funds. . . . [Third] it provides a way of recruiting a board of trustees that can focus on fundraising." [5]

Institutional foundations can do things public institutions in many states cannot do. Some states prohibit the use of public funds to pay for fund raising programs and development officers' salaries. Foundations can support the fund raising operation. Public institutions sometimes cannot hold and sell real estate or manage securities. Foundations can perform that function. Foundations can also release monies in short order. State bureaucracies are cumbersome and not very time sensitive. Institutional boards and foundation boards are constituted differently. Institutional boards are recruited or appointed for the political weight they carry, and they have fewer members than foundation boards. Foundation board members are generally selected for their fiscal integrity, their affluence, or their influence. Institutional boards have diverse responsibilities. Foundation boards have a largely fiduciary role.

The foundation is a mirror of the institution. If it becomes too different in style and image from the institution, the relationship suffers and the perception of the institution by the local community suffers. For this reason, presidents and chief executive officers (CEOs) are concerned about the foundations becoming too independent. They would rather exist in a milieu of mutual dependency.

FUNCTION AND PRACTICAL APPLICATION

The prime function of the foundation is stewardship and gift resource management. For some foundations, that function resembles the function a bank performs. Gift funds are deposited in designated accounts. Flawless records are kept, and monies are dispersed according to the donors' wishes. Other foundations include additional functions, such as investment management, insurance, real estate, and brokerage activity, and still others engage in monumental capital campaign efforts, raising millions of dollars for the institution.

Expanded opportunity for civic involvement with, and thus support for, various organizations exists when the foundation is established. Boards of trustees are limited in number to nine or ten individuals. Foundation boards can be much larger, which is good, because the more men and women of stature and prestige the institution can recruit, the better it is for the institution, and this is especially true with foundation boards as well as advisory boards. Few would agree to serve on a foundation board if they were not supportive of the host institution, and their sphere of influence includes family and friends who also have the potential of being supportive. Key alumni who live out of state could serve on a foundation board but would never get the opportunity to serve on a university board.

As has been mentioned, in times of cutbacks and restructuring, when the budget is too tight for comfort and presidents are tempted to make unwise decisions to scale back the development operation, the foundation can help pick up the slack without having to go through the quagmire of legislative wrangling to release needed funds. In fact, some states do not permit tax dollars to be spent on fund raising. Foundations like the Indiana University Foundation, however, can and do provide necessary financial support for carrying out the development function of the university, even to the point of picking up the cost of salaries.

Foundations are the rock of stability for the host institution. Administrators come and go, but institutions and their foundations live on through the years. Faculty and staff may at times create a negative stir with townspeople as they come and go on the stage of life, but foundations, by and large, maintain their above-the-strife posture and keep on exercising good stewardship in the raising of funds and the investment of those funds for the long-term benefit of the host institution. Consistent investment policies and meticulous attention to donor-directed use of the expendable monies quickly earns the respect of the community. Foundations are nonpartisan, very businesslike, dedicated to the stewardship of private funds. It is rare that a foundation director, even a crafty one, can pull the wool over the eyes of a large and diverse foundation board. For some strange reason, the public tends to distrust public institutions and feels more secure in placing trust and money into a private foundation. Also, foundations tend to have more professional resources than their host institutions have, such as attorneys, tax experts, estate planners, insurance people, and trust administrators as well as teachers, clergymen, and brokers, because these influential people are intentionally recruited when vacancies occur on the board.

FOUNDATION FUNDING

Foundations fund their operating budgets in one or two ways common to most of them. Their charters usually determine the manner in which operating funds are derived. First, funding may be derived from gift monies. One option is taking a percentage of all gifts received, 6 percent for example, to pay administrative costs and overhead. This is fairly generous and reasonable, but if gift monies are to be used to fund operating costs, donors must be told of the policy upfront. There is nothing more disappointing to a donor than to find out after the fact that a gift is being discounted to pay salaries and overhead. It needs to be clearly understood by all concerned right from the very beginning. The second option is to use a percentage of the unrestricted dollars. This one is more acceptable to the donor, but it could have ethical implications for foundation staff. When unrestricted monies are used to pay for the fund raising program, there is a tendency to put more time and energy than otherwise might be necessary into raising unrestricted dollars. It is bad news for the host institution when development officers spend more time funding themselves and their programs than they do raising money for the several priorities of the institution. A third option is to use a percentage of investment returns. If the spend-out rate on endowed programs is 5 percent and the investments return 12 percent, it would seem logical to put 4 percent into the operating budget and reinvest the other 3 percent. The 5 percent, of course, is designated for the particular program for which the endowment has been established. This arrangement works out well as long as the investment returns are 12 percent or more, but when they drop to 7 percent, for example, the operating budget could be in real trouble. Finally, there is the possible option, of course, for the host institution to fund the operating budget. The downside to that is some states prohibit tax dollars from being used to fund auxiliary enterprises. Plus, many institutions can barely fund their own gargantuan appetites that swallow huge amounts for instructional purposes and personnel costs. Public institutions in particular tend to have moderate tuition and fees, and thus do not bring in large amounts of cash from their customers, clients, and students. It is a complex situation, and every foundation has to find its own way through the thorny weed patch of budget management.

Foundations are important to American institutions. They have been around for 100 years and will continue to grow and become a part of almost every institution of higher learning, every hospital, and many not-for-profit organizations for one basic reason. They are a source of revenue. More national organizations are becoming foundation advocates, including CASE, National Society of Fund Raising Executives, AHP, and Association of Governing Boards (AGB). CASE has established a National Clearinghouse for institutionally related foundations at its headquarters in Washington, D.C. Presently, as this book is being written, Eric B. Wentworth is shepherding that program.

One of the best books in print to deal with the subject of institutional foundations is *College and University Foundations: Serving America's Public Higher Education.* It was commissioned by AGB and is the most informative definitive writing on the subject currently available. Its publication was made possible in large part by TIAA-CREF, the Indiana University Foundation, and the Common Fund. The work is compiled by Joseph F. Phelan and Associates and published by the Association of Governing Boards in Washington, D.C. Some of the contributors are David W. Bahlmann, president and CEO of Ball State University Foundation; John W. Guy, first vice president, Dean Witter, and Curtis R. Simic, president of the Indiana University Foundation.

Compared to the large volume of material written about fund raising, public relations, and alumni affairs, very little has been written about institutionally related foundations. As they continue to provide ancillary functions so needed by their host institutions, they will continue to be valued by the institutions they represent. One reason for their low profile is they prefer to operate in a quiet way, very businesslike, very efficient, and very effective. Their role is a supporting role to the main event, but they have the financial power to enhance and improve that main event.

NOTES

1. J.F. Phelan, "The Changing Case for Establishing College and University Foundations," *College and University Foundations: Serving America's Public Higher Education* (Washington, D.C.: Association of Governing Boards, 1997), 3. Phelan is citing the by-laws of the Kansas University Endowment Association.
2. T.A. Reilley, "State University Related Foundations," *Raising Money Through an Institutionally-Related Foundation* (Washington D.C.: Council for Advancement and Support of Education, 1985), 9–17.
3. Phelan, "Changing Case," 3.
4. E. Wentworth, in a personal conversation with the author, July 10, 1997.
5. M.J. Worth, "Institutionally-Related Foundations in Public Colleges and Universities," *Fund Raising Leadership*, ed. J.W. Pocock (Washington, D.C.: AGB, 1989), 64.

CHAPTER 7

Planned Giving

Jerry P. Rohrbach and Janine Dlutowski

OVERVIEW

Individuals have practiced what we now call planned giving for well over a century. The Rockefellers, Vanderbilts, and Mellons are well known for their planned benevolence, and more recently the MacArthurs, Kennedys, and Fords. In the 1970s and earlier, it was referred to as deferred giving. Leonard Bucklin, then vice-president for advancement at Purdue University, contributed a chapter on deferred giving to Westley Rowland's *Handbook of Institutional Advancement* in 1978, but that term was misleading, because not all "deferred giving" is deferred. Some of it has present use. The better term is "planned giving," which today is in common use by advancement professionals, estate attorneys, trust officials, and others who deal not only in cash gifts but also those gifts of securities or other property intended for use now or in the future.

The field is growing. There are over a million nonprofits in America and many of them are engaging in planned giving transactions. There are approximately 3,000 colleges and universities in the country, and 5,000 hospitals, all of which in one way or another are involved in planned giving. More and more, development officers are attending seminars and workshops to learn more about this important area of institutional advancement. Robert Sharp, Winton Smith, Conrad Teitell, and a host of other planned giving experts have been informing and enlightening the public for many years. Almost any organization or institution that cares about the future has an interest in planned giving. Properly organized and managed, the planned giving program can make an enormous positive impact on future revenue.

What Is Planned Giving?

Certainly any discussion on this topic should start with a simple and straightforward definition of what we mean by "planned giving." However, in our view, planned giving cannot be effectively defined in a succinct package of a few sentences. This is a term that can be applied to almost any type of contribution; from outright gifts of cash to more complex testamentary trusts or bequests; from gifts of as little as $1,000 to multimillions of dollars. It may be better to attempt to define the term by describing the typical characteristics surrounding planned gifts. We see those characteristics as follows:

1. These are gifts that go beyond the simple check or cash for your annual fund drive. Planned gifts most often come from a person's capital assets, such as certificates of deposit, stocks, bonds, business assets, pension assets, art, antiques, collectibles, personal residences, or other real estate.
2. Usually, a donor making a planned gift is doing some gift planning in the light of actual or potential tax savings.
3. Very often, planned gifts are really "deferred gifts" for a charity. That is, the donor is taking action now to make a gift, but the actual value to the charity will be deferred until some later date—usually at the donor's death. Deferred gifts involve bequests, life insurance, and split interest gifts in exchange for an income such as pooled income funds, gift annuities, and charitable trust arrangements.
4. Planned gifts are often considered in light of the broader issues of retirement and/or estate planning.
5. Commonly, planned gifts are given with the intent of building or leaving a legacy for future generations. Naming endowments or facilities are ways to leave a legacy in perpetuity, and thus sustain the good work of the institution long into the future.

Two other terms that are important to understand in the context of defining planned giving are "revocable" and "irrevocable." When a donor establishes a bequest in a will or trust or designates the charity as the beneficiary of a pension plan or life insurance policy, the donor is essentially making a gift that can be revoked (taken back or changed) at some point in the future. On the other hand, when a donor gives you cash, or comes into a formal agreement, such as a pooled income fund or charitable gift annuity, or establishes a charitable trust, he or she is making an irrevocable gift arrangement. The donor cannot take the money back or decide later that he or she doesn't want your charity to benefit from initial good graces.[1] Irrevocable gift arrangements can be counted (or booked) in your charity's giving records, even though the benefit (actual dollars or assets) that the charity will receive may be deferred to some future date. Revocable gifts should not and cannot be counted or booked.

Why a Planned Giving Program?

Planned giving is the fastest growing segment of philanthropy in America today. It has been that way for some time now and should continue to be so for many years to come. According to *GIVING USA 1996*, $9.77 billion in bequests was given in 1995. This represents an 11.44 percent increase over 1994. Compare this to an 8.39 percent increase in total giving in 1995 over 1994 figures. These figures do not include life insurance and split interest gifts since these have not been effectively measured. However, we believe it is safe to say that more and more individuals are also giving through life insurance, gift annuities, charitable trusts, and pooled income funds because more and more organizations are out there promoting them.

More organizations are becoming sophisticated in marketing planned gifts to their constituents because of two demographic factors. First is the rapid aging of the American population, and second is the occurrence of a huge transfer of wealth from the World War II (WWII) and Korean War generation to the Baby Boomer generation.

According to 1990 census statistics, by the year 2000 some 31 million Americans will be over 65, comprising more than 12 percent of the population. Of this group, the fastest growing portion are individuals age 85 and older. This segment of our population may hold as much as 70 percent of the nation's individual wealth. Mature households contribute to charitable causes 12 percent more than the average household. Men and women in this age group are at the high point of their lives in terms of personal disposable income and assets. The WWII generation in particular has been the fortunate recipient of incredible appreciation in the value of their property over the last 50 years. They are better educated, healthier, and more affluent than their parents were at the same age. Many are in a transition from caring for children and full-time employment to the anticipation of a long retirement and increasing concern about how to dispose of their estates when they finally do pass away.

As America ages and the older generations pass on, the transfer of their wealth to the next generation will be in gargantuan proportions. According to a Cornell University study updated in 1993, over $10.3 trillion dollars will be transferred over the next 40 years. Only those charities that are diligent in cultivating and securing planned gifts will realize a reasonable share of this wealth transfer.

A planned giving program demonstrates a long-term commitment of an organization to its mission and enhances its fiscal health into the future. Individuals who will establish deferred gifts for the mission are making very personal long-term commitments to its future. Split-interest gifts often require a lifetime commitment to donors. Endowments typically are established in perpetuity and will provide for the organization long after current leadership, staff, and donors are gone.

Planned gifts allow for more donor options that go beyond the cyclical character of the annual fund campaign. Gift planning, coupled with an array of optional giving vehicles, helps donors maximize what they can give. Gifts for life income or bequeathed contributions are often the largest gifts donors will make.

Finally, planned gifts optimize the organization's fund raising opportunities in a competitive market. Can you sit on your hands and allow other worthy charities to offer planned gifts to your constituents? Suppose the donor supports you and Charity B and wants to do a charitable gift annuity for $25,000. Charity B has a gift annuity program and yours doesn't. Who gets the gift annuity? Charity B, of course.

Are You Ready for a Planned Giving Program?

Organizing for and marketing planned gifts can involve a considerable undertaking. Not only must you and your organization be well informed about planned giving techniques, your organization must be properly poised to market, accept, and in the case of gifts in exchange for income, be able to manage these giving arrangements effectively. Planned gifts typically demand a greater level of stewardship than other kinds of gifts—stewardship that can last for many years into the future.

The rewards for opening the doors for planned gifts can be substantial. Planned gifts allow for more donor options and often involve larger contributions. Gifts through will planning or in exchange for a lifetime income will enhance donors' partnerships with your mission. Such giving looks to and builds for the future, but first it is necessary to assess the current situation and determine readiness for a planned giving program. Exhibit 7–1 contains two sets of questions and comments for review. The first set will help assess the organization and its readiness; the second should help you evaluate yourself and your readiness.

If you can answer in the affirmative to all of the questions in Exhibit 7–1, then you and your organization are ready. If you answered no to any of the questions, then don't lose heart. You have simply identified areas where you or your organization must begin. Get past these hurdles, and you are ready to launch into the next phase.

A REVIEW OF PLANNED GIFTS

Planned gifts are major gifts that most donors will deduct from their income taxes, although in many instances, gift taxes and estate taxes are affected as well.

Exhibit 7–1 Assessment of Readiness for a Planned Giving Program

---

ASSESSING INSTITUTIONAL READINESS

1. How long has the organization been in existence?

Many states require that an organization be in operational existence for at least 3 years before it can issue gift annuities or establish a pooled income fund. It would be wise to check with your state requirements. Most planned gifts look to the future. There needs to be a strong sense that your organization is well established and will be fulfilling its mission for many years to come before a donor will give his money to endow your work or name a facility or commit to a bequest or some other deferred gift.

2. Will the CEO and board endorse and support a planned giving program?

The CEO and board will need to be informed about the specifics of a planned giving program. This needs to be the institution's planned giving program and not just the development office's program. This will require an educational process and a well-thought-out written plan on how you will market and implement your program. Hiring a consultant to assist you with this process could be most helpful.

3. Can an adequate budget be secured?

It takes money to set up an endowment program, market bequests, or promote other deferred giving arrangements. The commitment of an appropriate budget is critical. It will determine the level of seriousness that your organization has in securing planned gifts up to its potential.

4. Is there ready access to qualified planned giving experts?

You will need legal counsel to assist with various bequests directed to your organization; writing endowment agreements; writing disclosure statements; writing various gift contracts and trust documents. You should have access to a real estate expert to assist you with the acceptance of real estate gifts. A stockbroker can assist you with gifts of various kinds of securities. When and if you are ready to issue gift annuities or a pooled income fund or serve as trustee for charitable trusts, you should have access to a respected investment advisor. For gifts of life insurance, having access to a qualified life insurance agent could be helpful.

5. Is there a critical mass of qualified planned giving prospects?

To justify the spending of money, time, and effort to actively market planned gifts, you will need to identify a group of prospective donors whom you feel have sufficient potential for making these gifts. Such prospects are usually older, at least 50 years of age. The older, the better.

ASSESSING YOUR OWN READINESS AS A DEVELOPMENT OFFICER

1. Do you have sufficient time to give the program?

This is perhaps the most important question to wrestle with and the answer depends largely on what level of marketing or concentration of planned giving you

continues

Exhibit 7–1 continued

feel you can handle. It takes minimal time to promote and handle bequests. It can take a great deal of time to promote and handle a concentrated endowment building campaign and/or split-interest gifts. If you are a generalist and essentially a "one-person" shop, you may need to spend a minimum of 20 percent of your time promoting and handling planned gifts in order to see sufficient results for your effort.

2. What is your level of technical expertise with planned gifts?

You do not have to be a tax expert or a specialist in this area of giving to be successful in promoting a planned giving program. You do, however, have to have at least a solid understanding of charitable tax law and the practical application and administration of the deferred giving vehicles you intend to offer. Are you confident that you can adequately explain these giving instruments to prospective donors? Can you crunch the numbers? If you feel you are not yet technically proficient in planned giving, then become so before you attempt to go any further.

3. Are you personally and thoroughly sold on the program?

Are you convinced that your organization is "missing out" on great opportunities until it gets more into the planned giving arena?

It will probably take a great deal of patience, research, planning, education, trial and error, and personal drive in order to implement a planned giving program. It needs to start with you. Do you have the heart for it? If so, then go for it!

4. Do you feel you have a good balance between the technical and personal aspects of planned giving?

Life insurance, gift annuities, charitable trusts, and pooled income funds can be complicated. There is a good deal of important detail involved in the administration of these gifts. You have to be able to pay attention to these details. On the other hand, you will need to enjoy connecting with people (your prospects) and become proficient in selling them on these giving techniques.

You might want to obtain a copy of Internal Revenue Service (IRS) Publication 526 as a helpful resource. Cash gifts can be deducted in full up to 50 percent of the donor's adjusted gross income for the year. Any excess deduction can be carried forward five additional years. Gifts of appreciated assets, however, are deductible only up to 30 percent of the donor's contribution base (generally, adjusted gross income [AGI] without any net operating loss carryback) in a given year. The 50 percent and 30 percent limitations are not cumulative. Cash gifts (and any carryforwards) are deducted before gifts of appreciated assets. Total deductions cannot exceed 50 percent of AGI.

Planned gifts can be categorized in two ways:

1. By the *type of the assets given*. Our examples include securities, real estate, personal property, retirement plan assets, or life insurance.
2. By the *use of the assets given*. Our examples include funding of charitable bequests, endowments or gift vehicles that produce income, such as gift annuities, pooled income funds, and charitable trusts.

Appreciated Securities

Contributing stocks, bonds, or mutual fund shares that have increased in value may enable your donors to make larger gifts than you expected. A gift of appreciated securities will be tax deductible at the full market value of the stock on the date of the *gift* and your donor will avoid capital gains taxes on any long-term appreciation. The value of the gift is deemed to be the average of the high and low quotes on the date the gift is transferred (or the date the donor irrevocably relinquishes control to your charity).

To avoid capital gains taxes, the donor must have owned the securities for more than one year and must transfer the securities directly to the charity. Two common methods of transfer are through the postal system or electronically. If the donor has possession of the stock certificates, he can mail these certificates to your charity. *It is essential that the donor does not sign the certificates because this makes them negotiable.* Instead, the donor must sign a notarized corresponding stock power form that is available at most banks or brokerage houses. Stock power forms can also be supplied by the charity. The stock certificates and corresponding stock power should be mailed under separate cover for security reasons. When using the postal system, the date of gift can be attributed to the date of the postmark.

If the donor holds securities in a brokerage account, he can arrange for automatic electronic transfer directly to the charity's brokerage account. This is definitely the easiest and safest method for stock transfers.

Gifts of mutual fund shares have all the same advantages of stock gifts. However, transferring mutual fund shares directly to your charity can be a time-consuming and bureaucratic challenge. Many mutual fund companies require the charity to open an account with them before they will transfer your donor's shares. It can take 30 days or longer for you to get the actual cash proceeds if your charity decides to sell any of the shares transferred. Patience and diligence is the key to making gifts of mutual fund shares happen. Exhibit 7–2 illustrates the advantages of giving appreciated securities.

Appreciated securities can be used as outright gifts, to fund endowments, as bequests, or to fund one of the income-producing gift vehicles described below. The donor's tax deduction for a gift of long-term appreciated securities is subject to the 30 percent limitation.

Exhibit 7–2 The Advantages of Giving Appreciated Securities

Mrs. G wants to make a $10,000 gift to ABC Charity. She has a stock that has doubled in value since she bought it 10 years ago. Should Mrs. G sell the stock and give ABC Charity the cash?
    No!

Why not?

Mrs. G will owe a 20 percent federal tax on capital gains (and perhaps state tax as well) when she sells appreciated securities that she has owned at least 18 months.[2] If she transfers the stock directly to the charity, she will pay no capital gains taxes and will receive a charitable income tax deduction for the full market value of the stock.

Options	Gift of Sale Proceeds	Gift of Appreciated Securities
Stock value (1998)	$10,000	$10,000
– Stock purchase price (1994)	– $5,000	– $5,000
= Long-term capital gain	$5,000	$5,000
	x.20	.00
Federal capital gains tax @ 20%	$1,000	No Tax
Gift to ABC University, after taxes	$9,000	$10,000
Charitable income tax deduction	$9,000	$10,000

Real Estate

Gifts of real estate can be risky but highly rewarding. Each opportunity to accept a gift of real estate should be handled on a case-by-case basis. There are four basic ways to receive a real estate gift: as an *outright gift*; as a *retained interest* in a residence or farm; by funding a *charitable trust*; or as a *bargain sale*. The amount of the donor's immediate charitable income tax deduction will vary depending on which gift option is selected. The donor's tax deduction for a gift of appreciated real estate is subject to the 30 percent limitation.

Receiving Gifts of Real Estate

Specific gift acceptance policies for real estate need to be established in advance of gifts being received. For example, prospects should know they will be asked to provide a qualified appraisal, allow you to visit the property, and perhaps permit or provide an environmental survey. At a minimum, you should consider such issues as

- appraisals
- visits to the property
- appropriate decision-making processes and persons with your organization
- debts or liens on the property
- environmental surveys
- marketability of the property
- who bears the cost of the gift/sale costs, maintenance, taxes, renovation
- tax consequences to the donor

Outright Gifts of Real Estate

You may decide to accept an outright gift of any type of real estate property. The organization may then sell the property or use it to further its mission. The donor may deduct the full market value of real estate given to the organization based on an independent, qualified appraisal. For property given outright, the donor will avoid any taxable long-term gain. The donor may carry the unused balance of the deduction forward for up to five years.

Remainder Interest in Farm or Personal Residence

If the property is a farm or personal residence (including a vacation home), the donor may choose *to retain a life interest* while granting a remainder interest to your organization. In this case, the donor or anyone he or she designates may continue to use the property for life. Typically the donor will be responsible for maintenance and property taxes during the retained life interest. The charity, however, may wish to share these responsibilities if it is deemed appropriate. The donor's charitable income tax deduction will be based on the value of your organization's future interest in the property, estimated to be the difference between the appraised value and the value of the retained life interest.

Funding Charitable Trusts

Real estate can be used to fund a charitable remainder trust (CRT) or even a charitable lead trust. There are, however, many more complications to these transactions than can be covered in this chapter. It is essential to have a good attorney at your side to make these giving arrangements work.

Bargain Sale

The donor may also opt for a *bargain sale*, in which he or she sells property to the organization at less than its full market value. This gift structure is useful when there is outstanding debt (a mortgage) on the property, or your donor wants to spread out the gift over time to maximize usable tax deductions. The donor will receive a charitable income tax deduction for the difference between the sale price and the appraised market value. Proceeds from the sale are considered part tax-free return of investment and part capital gain.

Personal Property ("In-Kind" Gifts)

Donors may wish to contribute tangible personal property such as artwork, rare books, equipment, antiques, or collectibles. To preserve the donor's charitable tax deduction, federal tax law requires that the recipient charity's use of contributed personal property be related to its mission. If the "related use" condition can be met, the donor may deduct the full fair market value of personal property, with no capital gains taxes on appreciation. The donor may need a qualified appraisal to substantiate the deduction, depending on the estimated value of the contribution. Deductions for appreciated property are limited to 30 percent of AGI in the year of the gift. The donor may carry the unused balance of the deduction forward for up to five years.

A donor also may give personal property that is unrelated to your organization's mission. In this case, the donor's deduction equals the cost basis in the property or its fair market value, whichever is less, for up to 50 percent of AGI in the year of the gift.

Retirement Plans

Charitable gifts from qualified retirement plans can yield significant tax savings, because assets in these plans can be subject to confiscatory taxation. Qualified retirement plans include 401(k)s, 403(b)s, Keoghs, SEPs, individual retirement accounts (IRAs), and various profit-sharing plans. If qualified plan assets remain after the plan beneficiaries pass away and these assets are rolled into the estate, there may be double or triple taxation. Not only are estate taxes assessed, but income taxes as well, on income in respect of an investment retirement decedent (IRD). If these assets are intended for grandchildren, there may be a generation-skipping tax taken as well. In some cases, heirs may receive as little as 20 to 30 cents on the dollar on these assets. Therefore, a strong case can be made to donors and prospects that if they are considering a bequest to your organization it would be best to utilize any unconsumed qualified pension assets to fund that bequest. Gifts to charity directly from retirement pensions will avoid taxes on IRD and still provide the estate with a charitable tax deduction to reduce estate taxes.

The best way to facilitate such gifts is for your donor to fill out a new designated beneficiary form that can be obtained from the pension plan administrator and to include your charity as a contingent beneficiary if any assets remain in the plan after your donor (and spouse) has passed away.

Another option is to encourage your donor to arrange for a rollover of pension plan assets into a CRT. The trust can name a spouse and even children as lifetime beneficiaries. This option will avoid taxes on IRD and provide some limited estate tax reduction as well. The best method for accomplishing this option is to name the charitable trust as the contingent designated beneficiary of the pension plan. The charitable trust can be created during the donor's life or at death in his or her will. Consulting with a good estate tax attorney is essential in setting up these transactions.

Life Insurance

Donors can make a large gift through life insurance, either by contributing an existing policy or by naming your organization as the beneficiary and/or owner of a new policy. As with any planned gift, you should not accept a gift of life insurance unless you understand how it works. You should familiarize yourself with the nomenclature that describes various types of insurance policies, such as term, variable, universal, whole, and permanent, and their principal characteristics, such as death benefit, exclusions, and cash value. You may wish to consult one or more knowledgeable agents who can educate you on these points.

Key Points

The donor must name your organization as the *owner and beneficiary* of the policy if the donor is to receive income tax benefits. This can be done with a simple form provided by the insurance company. For an existing policy on which future premiums will be due, or a new policy, it is wise to arrange for your organization to take responsibility for paying the policy premiums via annual contributions made by your donor.

In some instances, policies have been marketed on the basis that they will become self-sustaining or "paid off," within some period of time. You should carefully weigh the income and investment assumptions upon which such projections are based. If projections are not met, the donor may have to continue or increase premium payments in order to keep the policy active. It is best if the donor indicates a strong commitment to maintaining the policy through annual premium contributions. A life insurance policy that lapses will result in no gift to your organization unless there is some cash value in the policy that can be collected.

Stewardship

Especially important for gifts of life insurance is having a system for tracking life insurance gifts, soliciting annual gifts to cover premiums, and applying the funds as directed by your donor when the policy eventually is paid. Finally, you will need to decide how to recognize gifts of life insurance. Will recognition include the face value of the policy, or present value of the death benefit, or only the premiums paid by the donor? We recommend that you count the face value for recognition purposes only. Count the present value of the death benefit if it is to fund a named endowment. For auditing purposes, book only the annual gifts that are received for premium payments and any accumulated cash values.

Benefits to the Organization

Life insurance policies can provide the organization with large deferred gifts. In many situations, a gift of life insurance will allow for a larger gift than donors could make from their current or future resources. Life insurance gifts that have accumulated cash values are also available as collateral or for expenditure if it is deemed appropriate.

Benefits to the Donor

A gift of life insurance allows donors to make a large gift at an affordable cost without diminishing their family's inheritance. Depending on the age of the insured and the amount of the insurance, a donor can establish a sizeable legacy for less than half the cost.

Donors can contribute existing policies that are no longer needed for their original intended purposes. Their income tax deduction is equal to the lesser of the cash value of the policy or the total premiums paid. For a new policy, contributions made by your donor to cover the premiums are tax-deductible. Policy proceeds are not subject to estate or gift tax.

EXAMPLE

Ms. A, a 55-year-old female, nonsmoking annual donor, wants to establish an endowment in your organization in memory of her father. Ms. A decides to obtain a permanent life insurance policy with a death benefit of $100,000. The policy premiums will cost her $2,500 per year for the next 12 years for a total outlay of $30,000.[3] Ms. A names your organization as the owner of this policy and names the Mr. A Endowment Fund as the beneficiary. Accordingly, the premiums are tax deductible. Since Ms. A is in the 28 percent tax bracket, her subsequent tax savings reduce the ultimate cost for this policy to $21,600. Ms. A has accomplished a significant future gift in memory of her father, at a low, affordable cost, that will provide support for your organization in perpetuity.

Endowment Gifts

An endowment fund allows the donor to support your charitable organization today *and* tomorrow for future generations. Your organization is responsible for investing the principal of the gift so that the income provides permanent support of your organization. Since only income yield is used, your organization should set a reasonably high minimum amount for gifts to establish individual endowments. A commitment to an endowment gift may take the form of an outright gift, a pledge, or any of the giving arrangements explained in this chapter.

Key Points

Be sure to clearly describe how endowment gifts will be used in your organization. Endowments can be created to support general operating needs, specific projects, or other restricted uses. It is wise to have a well-thought-out organizational policy that directs how endowments can be established in your organization.

We recommend that endowment gifts be formalized with a written agreement between your organization and your donor. Here are some of the key provisions that will need to be included in the endowment agreements.

1. Identify your organization and the donor, the purpose of the endowed fund, how the money will be used, who or what the recipients of the income are, and who has authority or discretion to use the fund.
2. Protect principal from erosion by inflation by returning a percentage of income to principal.
3. Allow for changed circumstances by identifying who has the ability to decide how the endowment will be used if the original purpose cannot be fulfilled or must be altered in some way. For example, many endowments give the charitable organization's board of trustees the ability to determine how funds will be used if the original intention cannot be met.

Benefits to the Organization

Endowment gifts provide a secure, continuous source of funding for your organization and its mission. Endowments are also a rich source of named opportunities and donor recognition.

Benefits to the Donor

Your donors want to know exactly how their gifts will be used and that their contributions will make a difference in the furtherance of your mission. Endowments offer an opportunity for donors to define the use of their contributions and to ensure their lasting effect, as well as to receive special recognition of their gifts or to honor or memorialize someone else.

Bequests

Up to 70 percent of all Americans who die every year leave no valid will. Their estates are distributed by the laws of intestacy—state laws that govern who shall inherit property when the deceased owner leaves no instructions. Laws of intestacy do not provide for gifts to charitable organizations.

It seems rather obvious but bears repeating: gifts by will are the simplest form of planned gift for you to encourage; they are often the simplest form of planned gift for your donors to make; and frequently, they become the largest single gift you will ever receive from a given donor. If your organization cannot support a sophisticated planned giving program, you can at the very least encourage bequests from your known constituents.

Gifts by will or revocable trust can be used for general operating funds; to support a specific purpose or program; to give tangible property such as securities, art, books, antiques, equipment, or real estate; to fund endowments, or to establish testamentary trusts. Charitable gifts by will or trust reduce estate taxes and give your donors the pleasure of knowing that a portion of their accumulated assets will be used to continue their support.

You may wish to provide donors with samples of bequest language. Of course, laws governing wills differ from state to state and periodically change. You have the opportunity to encourage and educate prospects about the need for a valid will, and what they should consider when they meet with an attorney to get the document written or revised. If a donor has a current will, he may add or change a bequest by asking his attorney to use a *codicil,* or amendment, to alter his will. This will avoid the expense of writing an entirely new will.

Residuary Bequest Sample Language

A residuary bequest is used to give your organization all or a portion of an estate *after* all debts, taxes, expenses, and all other bequests have been paid.

> Example: "I give all [or _____% of] the residue of my estate, both real and personal, to [_____ insert the full legal name and location of your organization] to be used for. . . . " (Your donor may fill in a specific designation or whatever purpose he desires. You may wish to suggest language appropriate to your organization.)

Specific Bequest Sample Language

A specific bequest designates your organization to receive a specific piece of property, a certain dollar amount, or a percentage of certain property from an estate.

> Example: "I give to [insert the full legal name and location of your organization] the sum of $ _____ (or % of, or describe a specific piece of property) to be used for. . . . "

Contingent Bequest Sample Language

We all realize that charity begins at home. Most individuals will want to provide first for their families and loved ones. Some donors may choose to structure their bequest so that the charitable organization benefits only if one or more of their beneficiaries do not survive them.

> Example: "If (insert name) predeceases me or disclaims any interest in (describe the property), I give such property to [insert the full legal name and location of your organization] to be used for. . . ."

Testamentary Charitable Trust

A CRT can be established by bequest in a will or revocable trust in order to provide lifetime income for a spouse or someone else, while at the same time ensuring that a charitable gift will go to your organization after the death of the trust beneficiary.

In creating a testamentary charitable trust, the donor must specify the property or amount to be placed in the trust; the type of trust vehicle to be used; the term of the trust (a period of years or the lifetime of the beneficiary); the income payments to be made and their frequency; the beneficiary(ies) of the trust; and the provisions for the eventual transfer of the principal to your organization.

A testamentary charitable trust can be an effective way of saving estate taxes. In the case of assets in qualified pension plans or IRAs, your donors can prevent depletion of their estates by both estate and income taxes. You should recommend that your donors consult their tax advisors or attorneys.

Sample Designation Language for a Bequest to Your Organization

These are only meant as examples and are not an exhaustive list of bequest designations.

> "I give to Your Charitable Organization of Anytown, State [insert specific, remainder, contingent, or testamentary charitable trust bequest] . . .
>
> . . . to be used for its general purposes.
>
> . . . to be used for the Specific Program and its operating needs."
>
> . . . to be used to establish the John Donor Endowment Fund, the yearly income of which is to be used for [identify the objectives of the fund and detail the provisions on how the fund should be operated]."

Gifts That Produce Income

The donor can receive income and make a significant deferred gift at the same time. The donor's contribution will be held in trust and invested. The donor, a spouse, or any individual he or she chooses will receive income for life or a period of years; then your organization will receive the remaining principal of the gift.

As we have already pointed out, a planned giving program of any kind requires a certain investment of time and resources. Income-producing gifts in particular require significant educational and marketing efforts, careful stewardship, and technical, legal, and financial expertise. Documentation, compliance with laws and regulations, calculations of income, and tax benefits are frequently complex. Most planned giving professionals today rely on one or more software packages designed to calculate and manage planned gifts, such as PGCalc or Crescendo.

There are certain donors for whom the ability to retain income from gifted assets is essential. When all is said and done, your organization can reap tremendous rewards from a well-marketed and well-maintained income-producing gift program.

Charitable Gift Annuity

A charitable gift annuity is a simple contract between a donor and your organization, whereby your organization agrees to pay a fixed annuity amount to a donor (or another named beneficiary) for life in exchange for an irrevocable gift. The donor may name a second, successor beneficiary. Your organization keeps the remainder of the gift annuity upon the death of the income beneficiary or beneficiaries.

Key points. As a general rule, the donor's annuity rate and tax deduction will be based upon the ages of the beneficiaries named. Annuity rates are calculated to preserve a remainder interest equal to approximately half of the original gift amount. Gift annuity rates, and therefore annual income, will be higher for older donors. Most charitable organizations refer to the annuity rates suggested by the American Council on Gift Annuities (ACGA), which publishes annuity rates every few years.

Your organization may opt to offer a donor a rate lower or higher than those recommended by the ACGA. Whatever rates your charity decides to use, it will be obligated to pay the agreed annuity income for the lifetime of all beneficiaries even if the original principal of the gift runs dry. A solid investment plan is essential.

Charitable gift annuities are most attractive to older donors because annuity rates are much higher than for younger donors. For example, as of March 1, 1997, the annuity rate for a 50-year-old donor is 6.5 percent, while the rate for a donor age 85 is 10.5 percent. Younger donors may be more interested in a *deferred payment gift annuity*, briefly described below.

Federal law exempts qualified charities from compliance with securities laws when offering charitable gift annuities.[4] Federal law does require your organization, before accepting a gift for a charitable gift annuity, to provide full disclosure to donors as to all financial aspects of the gift annuity, e.g., annuity rate and amount, tax characteristics of annuity income (ordinary income, tax-free income, capital gains income), and estimated gift amount for tax deduction purposes. You will also be responsible for annual tax reporting to annuitants and the IRS on Form 1099. In addition, many states have adopted specific regulations and registration requirements for these gifts. You should comply with the laws in the state where your charity is located and the state of residence of your gift annuity donors.

Benefits to the organization. The organization receives an irrevocable gift for the remainder value of the charitable gift annuity. The promise of a secure lifetime income appeals to many major gift prospects who may be unable to or reluctant to make a large contribution outright. Once established, a gift annuity program can be fairly easy to expand and maintain. Charitable gift annuities offer many opportunities for stewardship and, thereby, cultivation of additional major/planned gifts.

Benefits to the donor. Charitable gift annuities can significantly improve the donor's income from assets that are non–income producing or low yield. The annuity income is guaranteed for life. Your donor receives an immediate charitable income tax deduction for the remainder value of the gift annuity to your organization. If the gift annuity is funded with cash, some of the donor's income will be taxable as ordinary income and some will be tax-free. If the gift annuity is funded with appreciated securities, some of the annuity income will be characterized as capital gains. The principal amount contributed for the annuity is not subject to estate taxes.

EXAMPLE

Mrs. J.C. has $50,000 invested in certificates of deposits at current rates. She wishes to use $25,000 of this money for a gift to Community Service Organization. Her income needs are fixed. Therefore, she opts for a charitable gift annuity that will provide her with a fixed, guaranteed, lifetime income.

Mrs. J.C. is 78 years old. Based on her life expectancy, Community Service Organization agrees to pay her a fixed income equal to 9.0 percent of her gift, or $2,250 annually, of which $1,258 is tax-free. Mrs. J.C. receives an immediate income tax deduction of $11,789[5] for the remainder value of her gift. This tax deduction produces a tax saving of $3,301 based on Mrs. J.C.'s 28 percent tax bracket. The tax deduction coupled with the tax-free income effectively increases Mrs. J.C.'s return to 12.6 percent for her gift.

Deferred Payment Gift Annuity

A deferred payment gift annuity is essentially a charitable gift annuity for which payments to income beneficiaries are deferred until some time in the future, when the annuity rate will be higher and your donor may need supplemental retirement income. This is an ideal gift option for younger donors. A deferred payment gift annuity is especially attractive to high-income professionals whose retirement plans are subject to contribution limitations. There are no contribution limits for a deferred payment gift annuity. A donor may fund a deferred payment gift annuity with one large gift or with periodic contributions, each of which qualifies for a charitable income tax deduction.

EXAMPLE

Bob and Manda, both age 45, decide that it would be to their advantage to consider annual contributions to the Philanthropy Museum's deferred payment gift annuity plan. They decide to contribute $5,000 per year to the plan for 20 years, after which they will begin to receive their lifetime annuity payments. For each annual contribution Bob and Manda will receive an immediate income tax deduction (the average being $2,240), and during their retirement years, they will receive a fixed annuity of $12,505 (or 12.5 percent of their total contribution), of which $2,199 is tax-free.

When Bob and Manda pass away, the remaining principal of their plan (estimated at over $652,809 in 2041) will go to the Philanthropy Museum to support their designated interests.[6]

Pooled Income Fund

A pooled income fund is a deferred gift vehicle in which a donor's gift is placed in a common trust and invested with the contributions of other donors to the fund. A pooled income fund operates much like a mutual fund. Each donor receives a proportionate share of the fund's actual net income each year.

Key points. Unlike a gift annuity, which offers fixed income, a pooled income fund offers donors and their designated beneficiaries income that varies with the fund's earnings. As with a gift annuity, income interests are for life. Donors may name a second, successor beneficiary. Donors may add to their pooled income fund account again in future years. Most charities that offer pooled income funds set a minimum level for the initial gift (e.g., $5,000) as well as a somewhat lower minimum level for subsequent gifts (e.g., $1,000).

Your organization must provide prospective donors with a pooled income fund prospectus disclosing the terms of the fund's trust arrangement, investment results, and certain other specific information. You should consult an experienced attorney to assist you with creating the pooled income fund trust, the prospectus or disclosure statement, and whatever other document forms you may need to receive gifts to the fund.

Benefits to the organization. A pooled income fund distributes only net income each year. Preservation of principal means a significant gift for your organization after the death of the donor and any successor life income beneficiary.

Pooled income funds offer you a good deal of marketing flexibility. Keep in mind that the age of the income beneficiary will not affect the income rate. However, the donor's income tax deduction will be greater where income beneficiaries are older. You may offer more than one pooled income fund, differentiated by investment strategy, rate of return, and perhaps, minimum gift level. You may offer an automatic endowment option for pooled income donors.

If your organization lacks the wherewithal to establish its own pooled income fund, you may be able to benefit from a fund administered by a community foundation in your area. Your donor would contribute to the foundation's pooled income fund and name your organization as the remainder beneficiary of his gift.

Benefits to the donor. Your donors receive a tax deduction in the year of the gift for the remainder value of the gift to your organization. Pooling the gifts allows the opportunity to minimize administrative costs while increasing investment options, so a well-managed fund should offer attractive income returns to donors. Donors who contribute appreciated securities completely avoid capital gains taxes. When rates of return are adjusted to reflect tax savings, pooled income funds can become attractive investments for donors.

EXAMPLE

Dr. and Mrs. B, ages 65 and 63, are interested in establishing an endowed fund. They have a block of stock certificates that they purchased many years ago for $5,000, which are now worth $25,000, paying them a 3 percent annual dividend (or $750 per year). They need additional income during their later years. Dr. and Mrs. B can accomplish both of these objectives by placing these stock certificates in Charity Hospital's Pooled Income Fund. When they do so, Charity Hospital will pay them a variable income for both of their lifetimes. Based on its past performance, the Pooled Income Fund will yield annual income at the rate of 6 percent, so their income from this asset would increase to $1,500. The Bs will also receive an immediate tax deduction for this gift of $ 7,486.[7] This tax deduction, along with their savings in capital gains taxes of $4,000, increases their effective yield to 7.9 percent.[8]

Charitable Remainder Trusts

A CRT allows the donor to make a large contribution, remove assets from his or her estate, bypass capital gains taxes, receive an immediate income tax deduction, and retain income from the assets contributed or provide income for anyone he or she chooses as a beneficiary. The gift is placed in a separate trust and invested. The donor (or any beneficiary named) will receive income for a term of years or the donor's lifetime. The donor may name one or more successor beneficiaries. At the end of the trust term, your organization will use the remaining trust assets for the purpose the donor has designated.

CRTs can be funded with cash, stocks, bonds, mutual fund shares, real estate, pension plan rollovers (at death only), and tangible personal property (such as valuable antiques or art). If the CRT is funded with long-term appreciated assets, the donor will receive an income tax deduction and trust income based on the full fair market value of those assets. There will be no loss to capital gains taxes.

Key points. A charitable remainder trust is a separate legal, tax-exempt entity described in the Federal Income Tax Code. In order for your donor to receive the substantial tax benefits of a CRT, the trust must satisfy the requirements set forth in the Tax Code:

1. The gift to the trust must be irrevocable.
2. The trust must pay income at a minimum annual rate of 5 percent of the original trust principal.[9]
3. The remainder of the trust principal after completion of all income interests must go to a qualified charity or charities.

The two basic types of charitable remainder trusts are the *annuity trust* and the *unitrust*. The amount of annual income from an annuity trust is *fixed* at the time the trust is created, so the beneficiary will receive the same amount of income each year. The income from a unitrust is based on a *percentage* of the trust assets, revalued once each year. Annual income will fluctuate with the value of the trust principal. A variation of the unitrust, the net income unitrust, pays either the stated percentage or the actual income earned by the trust, whichever is less. A net income unitrust may include a "make-up" provision. This allows excess net income to be distributed in high earnings years to the extent that earlier net income distributions fell short of the stated income percentage. Donors may make additional contributions to a unitrust, but may not make additional contributions to an annuity trust.

A donor may fund a CRT during his lifetime (*inter vivos trust*) or upon death (*testamentary trust*). In either case, assets used to fund the CRT are removed from the donor's taxable estate. Assets used to fund a testamentary CRT, however, may still be included in the probate estate.

Income *earned* by the CRT is tax-exempt. However, income *distributed* from a CRT will be taxable to income beneficiaries. The taxable nature of income to beneficiaries is determined by the nature of the income actually earned by the CRT, but the CRT is deemed to distribute income according to a four-tier system, exhausting each tier before moving to the next, in the following order:

1. ordinary income
2. capital gain income
3. tax-free income
4. return of principal

Your organization may choose to act as trustee for CRTs that name your organization as the remainder beneficiary. This requires a significant investment on your part. You will need legal counsel to assist you with the trust documentation and advise you on your organization's fiduciary duties as trustee. Your organization's trustee duties will include managing and investing the trust principal, administering payments to income beneficiaries, obtaining annual trust valuations, and providing appropriate tax reporting documents. However, the rewards can be significant if your organization is ready and willing to undertake these responsibilities.

Benefits to the organization. The unique features of the CRT make this a very marketable gift vehicle to donors of significant means, especially those with taxable estates and/or appreciated assets that do not generate much current income. Because of the legal, administrative, and management costs of a CRT, the gift amount is typically larger than for many other types of planned gifts. Consequently, the remainder value of a well-managed CRT to your organization can be much larger than any other gift a donor will make to your organization. Your organization should establish a minimum CRT gift threshold if your charity is to serve as trustee. Minimums typically range from $50,000 to $100,000.

Acting as trustee is a great service to offer the donors and can be a prime selling point in your CRT program. When your organization acts as trustee, you have the ability to craft each CRT to accomplish the goals of both the donor and the organization. You will have the opportunity to work with your donor on how your organization will eventually use the CRT remainder. You will have many opportunities for stewardship and ongoing contact with your CRT donors.

Benefits to the donor. A CRT allows your donor to continue to receive income, often at a higher rate, from assets that have been removed from a taxable estate.[10] Your donor can also bypass or minimize capital gains taxes if the trust is funded by a gift of appreciated property. In addition, your donor will receive an immediate charitable income tax deduction for the present value of the charitable remainder interest. The remainder value is calculated at the time of the gift based upon the life expectancies of all income beneficiaries and the trust payout rate. Sizeable tax deductions can be carried over five additional calendar years if necessary.

Many donors appreciate the security offered by guaranteed CRT income. Unitrust income will fluctuate with the value of the trust principal, but it is still guaranteed to be at least 5 percent of the principal (revalued annually). The annuity trust is particularly attractive to donors who are very risk-averse, because the amount of their annual income will never change regardless of investment results of the trust principal. The tax savings realized by a donor who funds a CRT with appreciated assets can boost the effective rate of return to a level competitive even with today's stock market, with the bonus of guaranteed income.

EXAMPLE

Mr. and Mrs. K, ages 68 and 65, contribute $100,000 of their stock to a charitable unitrust that will pay them for life a 6 percent return on the trust principal, revalued annually, or $6,000 the first year of the trust. Their cost basis for this stock was $10,000. The gift produces an income tax deduction of $32,818 in the year of the gift that, due to their 28 percent tax bracket, saves the Ks $9,189 in taxes.[11] The Ks also save an additional $18,000 in capital gains taxes. Thus, the Ks' out-of-pocket cost for this gift is $72,816, making their income yield equivalent to an 8.2 percent return.

Charitable Lead Trusts

A charitable lead trust is a unique and powerful giving vehicle that can be used to produce a significant income tax deduction or, when the objective is passing assets on to children or grandchildren, a significant reduction in gift taxes. The charitable lead trust is the reverse of the CRT. In the CRT, the trust income is paid to income beneficiaries and the remainder goes to the charity. In the lead trust, the income is paid to the charity for a term of years or for the period of someone's life, and then the remainder either goes back to the donor (or his estate), or is transferred to the donor's heirs.

Key points. There are two types of charitable lead trusts:

1. *The Grantor Charitable Lead Trust.* In this case, the donor who places assets in the trust is considered the owner of the trust, and trust income being paid to the charity is taxable to the donor, unless the trust is funded with tax-free municipal bonds. However, the donor also receives an income tax deduction for the present value of the future income stream that will be given to the charity.

2. *The Nongrantor Charitable Lead Trust.* The donor who finds this trust gives up irrevocably any future control of the assets and is therefore not considered the owner of the trust assets. Instead, ownership is transferred to heirs. After the trust term, any remaining trust assets are therefore automatically transferred to heirs.

   Either trust above can take the form of a unitrust, paying variable income to the charity or an annuity trust, paying fixed income. It is absolutely essential to have a good attorney experienced with lead trusts to assist you and your donor if you are to be successful with this giving technique.

Benefits to the organization. The organization can realize some very substantial support with a charitable lead trust; for example, if a lead trust were to pay the charity $10,000 per year for 10 years. This is a significant future cash flow that can do many wonderful things to support your mission.

Benefits to the donor. Charitable lead trusts are popular with wealthy individuals who are philanthropic and want to utilize effective tax-saving strategies. For the grantor lead trust, the donor receives an immediate income tax deduction for the present value of the future cash flow to your charity. This can provide a significant accelerated income tax deduction for donors who have very high incomes.

For the nongrantor lead trust, your donor will receive a gift or estate tax deduction for the present value of the remainder interest of the assets that will pass onto his or her heirs.

EXAMPLE: THE GRANTOR LEAD TRUST

Mr. Taxrelief just sells his business and realizes a $1,000,000 gain. He also happens to own a $500,000 portfolio of tax-free municipal bonds. He decides to use these bonds to fund a grantor charitable annuity lead trust that will pay Children's Program a fixed annuity of $30,000 (or 6 percent) for 10 years. In return, Mr. Taxrelief gets an immediate income tax deduction of $210,745 (this is the calculated present value of the $300,000 that Children's Program will get over the 10-year term). At the end of the trust term, the municipal bonds are returned to Mr. Taxrelief.

EXAMPLE: THE NONGRANTOR LEAD TRUST

Among other assets, Mr. and Mrs. Benefactor own a $500,000 stock portfolio with a cost basis of $100,000. They place this portfolio in a nongrantor lead annuity trust that pays 8 percent of its value each year to Animal Shelter for 15 years. Mr. and Mrs. Benefactor will qualify for a federal gift tax deduction of $360,765.[12] Therefore, the taxable portion going to the heirs is only $139,235 (which is the calculated present value of the future remainder interest going to heirs). Animal Shelter will receive a fixed annual income of $40,000 for 15 years or $600,000.

At the end of the 15-year trust term, the Benefactors' grandchildren will receive all of the trust's assets as remainder beneficiaries of this trust. Any new appreciation in value of the trust assets will be distributed to the beneficiaries free of any additional federal gift taxes.

IMPLEMENTING AND MARKETING A PLANNED GIVING PROGRAM

A comprehensive presentation on this topic is not possible in the space allocated to this chapter. However, we can give you some solid starting points from which to proceed and build.

From our point of view, it is essential to make some foundational observations before any discussion on marketing techniques. Besides having an adequate understanding of planned giving techniques, a thorough understanding of your potential planned giving donors is fundamental. You need to have a good sense of who it is you are trying to market to and what it is that *they* may be considering when pondering a planned gift. It is so easy for us to get caught up in what we feel we need to tell our constituents. It is far more challenging to understand what truly gets their attention. It is easy to get lost in explaining the technicalities and tax benefits of planned gifts. It is far more challenging to get at the real motivations of why an individual will establish a legacy for your organization. In this regard we suggest four principles that should be integrated into your thinking and market planning.

1. You are promoting your organization's mission first and foremost. It is the mission of your organization that attracts donors, not the tax benefits of making a gift. Yes, tax benefits are important to the donor, but it is not their first consideration.
2. People want their gifts to make a difference. This principle is related to the first. It gets at the motivations of why people give. In planned giving, the thought of leaving something behind for future generations is a primary motivator. Knowing that a lasting, significant impact can be made through a planned gift; to make a difference in the lives of others; or to improve the lives of others, both now and after we are gone: these are the elements of philanthropy.
3. People relate to people. Use testimonials whenever you can to sell the virtues of planned giving. Static copy or charts with statistics can be useful, but remember, people respond to people. This is a fundamental principle in fund raising and certainly for planned giving.
4. Study the demographic and psychographic characteristics of your planned giving constituents. As we suggested earlier, individuals who are 50 and older are the best planned giving prospects. Individuals in this age group include older Baby Boomers, the Korean War generation, and the WWII generation. Each group has a distinctive world view. Each has a different life experience. Each is at a different stage of life. One should study these distinctive characteristics, and when ready, market appropriate planned giving options to the specific audience in mind.

For all of what follows, it is important to go through a careful process of planning and preparation and then document strategies in writing. The written plan should include the following:

1. an analysis of current planned giving activity
2. an analysis of the potential for planned gifts to the organization, including some description of the prospect pool to be developed
3. a description of the planned giving opportunities you wish to offer and the internal procedures/policies that you will need to steward these gifts

4. establishment or enhancement of an endowment program
5. establishment of a planned giving recognition program
6. a description of the marketing plan including budget and timelines

Identifying Prospects

For some organizations this task will be a considerable challenge if one is trying to identify those prospects who fit the right age categories. For any fund raising program, it is best to start with the prospects closest to the organization and work out to those farthest away. Board members and past donors will be among the best prospects. Next would be those directly impacted by the service you provide, whether they are students, patients, clients, or members. Then come those who are related to those constituents you serve. Finally, there are lists of prospective supporters whom you know or suspect are interested in your cause. It is important to categorize or create lists of prospects specifically for planned giving, whether it is a small list of top prospects to approach through personal contact, or larger lists for mail marketing.

The Planned Giving Survey

At some point it may be useful to conduct a survey of your donors and prospects using a questionnaire. For educational institutions, alumni surveys work quite well for gathering current personal information. A survey could ask respondents to provide birth dates, family information, employment information, and hobby or volunteer service information. Within such a questionnaire it is useful to ask respondents to indicate whether or not they have included a bequest to your organization or would like further information about will planning or some other planned giving vehicle. If you feel it inappropriate to ask for too much personal information from your constituents, a simple survey with five or six questions very specific to planned giving options could be useful in gathering initial leads.

The Planned Giving Committee

There are a variety of approaches to using planned giving committees. Much depends on the particular situation. Two approaches work well. The first is to gather a small group of four or five carefully recruited experts who can offer guidance and technical expertise. A good probate and trust tax attorney, a stockbroker, a chartered life underwriter, credentialed financial planner, a real estate expert—these are the experts that could be of great help in constructing and evaluating prospective planned gifts.

The second approach is to form a group of actual planned giving donors who are willing to assist with the prospect identification, research, and solicitation processes. These volunteers can also help with a program devised specifically to recognize planned giving donors and to evaluate your endowment program. In either case it is essential that one or more board members serve on the committee.

Establish or Enhance an Endowment Program

The organization may already have an endowment of some sort. We define an endowment as a fund or funds whereby the principal of such funds is invested and preserved and only the investment yield of the fund(s) is used for restricted or unrestricted purposes. Many organizations promote various and multiple endowment funding opportunities. In fact, any number of endowment funds can be established by donors to support any number of purposes, such as scholarships, program support, research, facilities maintenance, library purchases, salaries, conservation, or patient care. Almost any program one might think of could be endowed.

It is useful for your organization to identify the specific items within its mission that it would like to endow. These items should range from minimum endowment gifts, such as $5,000, to larger endowment gifts in the millions, depending on the organization's needs. Additionally, it is important to allow donors to name endowed funds, either in their names or in the names of others they want to honor or memorialize. For example, a minimum gift may be $5,000 to name an endowed fund that will support scholarship aid or a specific program. Both outright and deferred gifts can be applied toward the establishment of endowments, but donors will want to know what the organization's endowment needs are and how much it will cost. Literature describing your endowment program is an important marketing tool.

Establish a Recognition Program

Planned gifts can lead to very substantial donations to your organization, even though you may have to wait a while for them. A program designed to recognize individuals that have taken definitive steps to establish an endowment, to include a bequest in their will, or to set up an irrevocable giving arrangement, should be established. Such a program should have a title. The most common in use is The Heritage Club or Society or The Founders Circle—something of that nature. The best names for a planned giving recognition program should have some historical connection to the organization—something that is unique and quickly recognized by donors and friends to have significance to the mission.

The best way to start such a program is to personally recruit the charter members. A brochure that explains the recognition program and its significance to your organization and extends your invitation for the reader to join the Society is an effective tool. A response form accepting the invitation, giving permission to list their names in publications, and indicating the nature of their planned gift is an important part of this piece.

Recognition can be implemented through a variety of means including listing members in publications and on well-placed plaques. An annual event that is reserved just for your planned giving donors is also effective, but public recognition can also occur at events that include other activities as well.

Brochures, Mailings, Ads, Articles, and Newsletters

It may seem obvious that you will need to develop planned giving literature that will describe the giving options you wish to offer. There are a dozen good vendors that can supply you with "canned" literature or customize various pieces to meet your requirements. These vendors can also supply newsletters, articles to be used in newsletters or magazines already in place, and ads. They can also assist with mailing campaigns. If you have the ambition, capacity, and time, you could write and design your own literature. Needless to say, you will need to think through a budget and an implementation plan. We would like to suggest at least the following basic actions.

1. Produce at least one primary brochure that briefly explains all the planned giving options you wish to offer. This brochure could also explain your endowment and recognition programs. Include a response mechanism in this brochure for further information on any of the topics covered.
2. Produce a series of information sheets that go into greater detail on how various planned giving options work, such as steps to a successful will plan, sample testamentary language for charitable bequests, gift annuities, pooled income fund, and charitable trusts, etc. These could be inexpensively produced for handouts and as follow-up pieces. Such literature can be quickly revised if laws and regulations change anything.
3. Use the house newsletter or magazine to carry ads and/or articles on planned giving options. A newsletter designed exclusively for your planned giving program is also very effective, but can be costly.
4. If the organization services the immediate community, ads in local newspapers may be a useful tool.
5. Try to do at least two mailings per year that promote one or more planned giving options. The mailing could include a cover letter and a brochure or flyer. Always devise some response mechanism for further information and then be diligent to personally follow up on any responses.

6. Explaining how planned giving vehicles work can be complicated, statistically oriented, and just plain boring. Try to keep the copy basic and simple for the layperson to understand. Use personalized illustrations and, whenever possible, include testimonials of what donors have actually done.

Seminars

Seminars are an excellent means of educating prospects in the use of various planned giving options. Seminars are effective because they will give you a focused, yet soft-sell opportunity to explain planned gifts in detail. People who come to the seminars are indicating more than a casual interest in the topic. You can also offer a genuine service to attendees who need information on retirement and estate planning.

Seminars should last no longer than two and a half hours. The time of day, location, and whether or not food is offered should be taken into consideration. Use what will work best with your constituency. It is our opinion that you need to recruit a qualified speaker to make the presentation. Consultants who specialize

---

Exhibit 7–3 Suggested Planned Giving Seminar Topics

What You Need To Know When Planning Your Will
Planned giving subjects:
    Various charitable bequesting techniques
    How to write a bequest to establish an endowment
    How to give through your retirement plan
    Giving life insurance
    A charitable gift annuity

Planning for a Prosperous Retirement
Planned giving subjects:
    Charitable gift annuity
    Deferred payment gift annuity
    Giving through your retirement plan

Estate Planning Strategies
Planned giving subjects:
    Charitable gift annuity
    Pooled income fund
    Charitable remainder trust
    Charitable lead trust

in planned giving can help. You might also use a professional financial planner, certified public accountant, or trust and probate attorney to do the presentation, and you may wish to copresent with your expert. Let them cover the general subject matter and you cover specifically the planned giving subjects. In Exhibit 7–3, we suggest some seminar topics and indicate which planned giving vehicles could be presented within the context of the seminar.

NOTES

1. The exception is a charitable trust that includes a provision allowing the donor to change the charitable beneficiary. Once a trust is established, the donor cannot take back the assets. He/she can, however, decide to transfer the benefits established for your charity to some other charity.
2. The Taxpayers Relief Act of 1997 created several new tax rates for capital gains, based on the donor's marginal tax rate and how long the property was held. The new rates range from 8 percent to 28 percent.
3. Based on average policy costs provided by a reputable agent, January 1997.
4. The Philanthropy Protection Act of 1995 (P.L. No. 104-63), the Charitable Gift Annuity Antitrust Relief Act of 1995 (P.L. No. 104-62), and the Charitable Donation Antitrust Immunity Act of 1997 (P.L. No. 105-26).
5. Illustration assumes use of ACGA annuity rates. Based on IRS discount rate of 7.6 percent. IRS discount rates are updated monthly.
6. Illustration assumes use of ACGA annuity rates. Investment assumptions: 2 percent annual income, 6 percent annual capital appreciation. Based on IRS discount rate of 7.6 percent. IRS discount rates are updated monthly.
7. Based on IRS discount rate of 7.6 percent. IRS discount rates are updated monthly.
8. Tax savings are based on an assumed 28 percent tax bracket.
9. You and your donor may agree to a higher payout rate. Remember, however, that higher rates reduce the donor's income tax deduction, reduce the remainder interest to your organization, and increase the risk that income payments will deplete trust principal.
10. Naming income beneficiaries other than the donor and his or her spouse will give rise to a *taxable gift*. Your donor can defer completion of the gift (and its tax consequences) by reserving, in the trust document, the ability to revoke the income interest by will.
11. Based on IRS discount rate of 7.6 percent. IRS discount rates are updated monthly.
12. Based on IRS discount rate of 7.6 percent. IRS discount rates are updated monthly.

PART II

Alumni Affairs

CHAPTER 8

The Alumni Movement: A History of Success

Charles H. Webb

These are the days when birds come back
A very few, a bird or two,
To take a backward look
—Emily Dickinson

Birds come back, as Emily Dickinson wrote, to take a backward look. To take a look at what? They come back to capture an image of themselves a few years earlier, or many years ago. Likewise, we come back to look at the individuals who laid the foundation for today's alumni profession. As we take a backward look, it is gratifying to realize the contributions that alumni relations has had in shaping and advancing higher education for the betterment of society.

It was in the heart of winter, 1913, when representatives from 23 different private and public colleges and universities, representing a wide range of locations, responded to an invitation to meet at the Ohio Union on the campus of Ohio State University. It was a casual and friendly gathering to share information about alumni activities back at their campuses. The minutes recorded that: "The conference opened with an informal smoker . . . no business was transacted." Although no formal constitution was adopted, nor was the organization incorporated during their two days together, the delegates were encouraged by the prospect of forming a new organization to bring together those individuals engaged in alumni work at their campuses. The annual membership fee for each college or university represented was tentatively set at five dollars.

Although February 21–22, 1913, was the beginning of the Association of Alumni Secretaries, it was not the beginning of alumni work at the various campuses. As early as 1792, alumni work at Yale University began when a group of its graduates formed an organization based on the class structure and gathered information that would be published in a newsletter and sent to alumni. These class activities soon became the catalyst for the solicitation of money and the formation of alumni organizations in major cities around the country.

The alumni movement began to gain momentum with the organization of alumni societies at various campuses, including Williams College (1821), Princeton University (1826), University of Virginia (1838), Amherst College (1842), and Michigan Agricultural College (1868). In 1897 the University of Michigan founded its alumni association and was the first to have a full-time alumni secretary.[1] (Source: Reprinted from Handbook for Alumni Administration by Charles H. Webb © 1995 by the American Council on Education and The Oryx Press. Used with permission from the American Council on Education and The Oryx Press, 4041 N. Central Ave., Suite 700, Phoenix, AZ, 85012. (800) 279-6799.)

It is fascinating to read some of these early records of the alumni organizations. For example, in 1868 at Michigan Agricultural College, agitation was abroad concerning a change of vacation for the professors. Some "crazy-heady" people had the strange idea that the proper time for vacations was in the summer. The alumni immediately went on record absolutely opposed to this change.[2]

The men who came together to form the Association of Alumni Secretaries in 1913 decided its affairs were to be managed by five officers and two members chosen at large. The purpose of the Association was to bring together, for conference and mutually helpful discussion, those who were in active charge of the work of college alumni associations across the country. This new association provided an opportunity for an exchange of ideas and served as a clearinghouse of information for those engaged in alumni work.

In the same year, a second conference of the Association of Alumni Secretaries was held November 21 and 22 at the Reynolds Club at the University of Chicago. At the opening session of the conference, H.S. Warwick, alumni secretary from Ohio State University, delivered a speech titled, "The Psychology of the Problem, How To Awaken the Interest of the Alumni." In the speech, Warwick emphasized that alumni can change the history of their alma mater.*

> A university is not what the alumni say it is, but it is what the alumni make it. The alumni are the permanent body about the university; the faculty and the officers are merely transitory. So it falls upon the alumni to back up the school and get behind the movements started for its advancement.
>
> We must impress upon our alumni that they themselves must be representative men. We and they must take care not to be misrepresentative. We must stand for right ideals and right action. What we do as college men reflects upon every college man who goes to any institution of learning. It is not the university campus that makes a university great,

---

*Courtesy of Council for Advancement and Support of Education, Washington, DC.

nor is it its architecture, it is the alumni body. We must show the alumni that they are the men who make the institution. Those men who are secretaries of state universities can go to their alumni and tell them as I tell my alumni that Ohio State University has one of the finest parks that is to be found in the state, that the Ohio State University is the greatest issue in the state except the supreme court; and that the university is the greatest blessing to the people of the state except the public schools—and what I can say about our institution any state secretary can say about his.

I feel that the endowed colleges get more results because their men are willing to put more into them. We can say that the state has invested at least a thousand dollars in each person it graduates and that if he pays 2% interest he would owe $20 a year, and so the small charge of the alumni association lets him off cheap. He ought to be willing to affiliate with an institution that is advancing his interests and those of all other alumni.

It is a mutual obligation that we have all the way through. We ought also to develop an appreciation of the older men, the patriarchs, the men who were there when the institution went through its severest struggles. They are the men who made it possible that we younger men may have the opportunities which are now open to us. Let us tell our undergraduates and young alumni that these men have set a standard and we just maintain that standard.

In these frequent association get-together meetings, we first develop friendship, which in a final analysis results in service; secondly, loyalty which like faith hopes for and cherisheth all things. It is not fickle but clings to the object of its affection with a constancy which death itself cannot destroy. We must not be blind imitators but must develop that individual spirit for the particular school. We are in touch with the undergraduate body; let's get into the whole thing and when in Rome do as Rome does. We must act as the ginger jar as far as possible. We must take with us among the alumni that spirit of enthusiasm which is found at the university. We must create the atmosphere. The men at these come together meetings are from all classes and periods; they will not all get acquainted. We must create an atmosphere of good fellowship. The success of these meetings depends upon us.[3]

Warwick went on to discuss the vital importance of effective alumni relations, particularly through alumni publications:*

---

*Courtesy of Council for Advancement and Support of Education, Washington, DC.

The alumni publication is one of the greatest mediums of keeping up the interest. Show the pictures of older men and women. This is a mighty effective means of creating interest; for the moment one finds his picture was published or he is complimented by a friend over a write-up, he immediately perks up and takes renewed interest in the university. They do not know how you really feel about it; but it is politic. It makes them feel mighty good, and after all that is what you must do. Create a good taste in their mouth and the feeling all over that they are appreciated—and above all that they are the people appreciated back at the university. When an alumnus walks into your office, he feels that he ought to be known—why, he was the man who made the touchdown back there on the championship team of "00"; or he was that prominent debater. It hurts not to be remembered. The younger men are much alike; but the older men stand out more prominently in social and in political life. I have arranged that when some man steps into the alumni building, some one telephones me from below that so and so is coming. When he steps in I say "Hello, Jones." And he is delighted to think somebody about the campus knows him. You must impress upon the alumni that you have the power and push.

Tolstoy has said that no nation will ever become really great or deserve the name of historic unless it feels the value and worth of its institutions and prizes them. So impress on your alumni the good things of their institution and that we are trying to create a distinctive spirit. It is up to us to do it. We must be the men on the job all of the time electrifying the atmosphere.

We cannot all be poets, but we can be men with push and the "go-get-it." We must be the ginger jar; and depend upon it, we are the medium to transfer it from the student to the alumni. We must deal with men who are in a commercial atmosphere. We must create something new and get them out and make them feel that we are working for them and the university. That we appreciate them and yet at the same time, we depend on them to give their assistance to us.[4]

Later that same day at the second session, E.B. Johnson, alumni secretary of the University of Minnesota, presented a long talk on "Alumni Organization and the Secretary," which provides some excellent insights into the philosophy, importance, and work of the alumni organization. This talk is worth quoting at length because of its mature understanding of working with alumni, and Johnson's comments are still relevant and useful today:*

---

*Courtesy of Council for Advancement and Support of Education, Washington, DC.

Last spring, at Columbus, Ohio, there was held a meeting of some two dozen men engaged in a new and peculiar line of business. Not a man who attended that conference had been engaged in work as an alumni-paid officer for a period of ten years. We were and are all pioneers in a new and most promising field of endeavor. Like all pioneer work, our efforts are bound to leave a lasting impression upon the future development of work in this line—tremendously helpful and wholesome, if our work is done with wisdom and discretion, or disappointing if we fail to measure up, in some degree, to our opportunities.

Institutions have had, for many years, paid officers whose duty it was, among a multiplicity of other duties, to look after the alumni. The work of such officers has been directed with a view to making use of the power represented by the alumni body, to carry out definite and settled policies of the institution.

The alumni-paid secretary is a new development, and introduces a new factor into the problem. The alumni are to be no less useful, rather more useful, but they are to be useful in their own way, which makes their service of special value. The rapid development of this work has brought to those engaged in it a feeling that they need all the aid that comes from conferences with others engaged in similar lines of work, hence the first conference and likewise the formation of a permanent association and the goodly attendance at this second conference.

Our association is merely for an exchange of ideas—fundamentally our problem is the same—to substitute organized alumni loyalty for unorganized goodwill and to secure the maximum of efficiency for every ounce of alumni effort invested.

The details of our work will differ but we may profitably adapt ideas that have been found practical elsewhere to our own peculiar needs and conditions. We who attended the first conference found it well worth our while and it is to be hoped that this second conference may be even more so.

THE PHILOSOPHY OF THE WORK

The modern alumni association is a business organization—it is organized for efficiency. Its only reason to be is that it affords the individual alumnus opportunity to greatly increase the efficiency of his individual effort, in behalf of the institution, and enables him to keep in touch with fellow alumni.

The philosophy of organized alumni effort is simply that of the modern business consolidation—for efficiency. It has been brought about through the recognition of the fact, that a very moderate amount of organized loyalty is worth an unlimited amount of organized goodwill. Through a sense of gratitude, or, through a recognition of public duty, as alumni, we are desirous of doing something that is really worth doing for the institution to which we owe allegiance. We are ready to do something if we can be sure that something is really worthwhile. We cannot give the time necessary to go into the problems and determine, for ourselves, just where our individual effort will count. Hence we have employed the paid secretary whose duty it is to keep in touch with the institution and to give us the facts upon which we may predicate our judgment and upon which we may act with intelligence and without loss of effort. The unselfish support of the alumni of any institution, if intelligently directed, represents a tremendous force for the benefit of the institution.

In the case of the smaller institutions whose alumni are not able to support a secretary to give his full time to the work, a permanent secretary is the next best thing. The proper man supplied with a reasonable amount of clerical help, and an allowance for postage and printing, can accomplish wonders.

IMPORTANCE OF THE POSITION

In the case of the larger institutions that employ a secretary to give his whole time to the work, we must recognize the absolute necessity of paying the secretary a salary sufficient to attract and hold for life, men who are on a par with full professors of the institutions which the secretary serves; that is, the secretary's salary must be on the basis of that of a full professor and the secretary should be a man big enough to be recognized as earning his salary. The alumni organization that does not get on such a basis at the earliest possible moment is not living up to its opportunity for service.

The secretary should not look upon his duty as done until the alumni body becomes an indispensable vital force in the life of the institution. Without official recognition from the institution, but with the loyal support of a united alumni body, the alumni secretary may make the alumni a potent and welcome force in the life of any institution. It depends largely upon the man—the possibility is inherent.

THE WORK

Naturally we of different institutions have different problems. You must emphasize one thing, I another. But whatever our problem, there is always one problem involved which we all must face—how to interest and enlist the support of the largest possible number of alumni, and how to direct such interest to ends most effective for the good of the institution.

In such work, the secretary is absolutely essential—he is the eyes, hands, feet, and to considerable extent the mouthpiece of the alumni. He can be and is held responsible for doing things when they need to be done. It is his business to keep in touch with the whole institution and to report intelligently, and advise judiciously, and direct forcefully, the activities of the alumni to any desired end.

OUR BEST SERVICE

The alumni, if they are to be of the highest use to the institution, must represent a new point of view, and a new point of contact with the world, and serve as an interpreter of the institution to the world. Such a possibility cannot be secured unless alumni activity is directed by alumni and not institutional initiative. Our highest service is to furnish a system of checks and balances for the institution. We are in a position to see all sides of questions which affect our institutions, we gladly give such questions our sympathetic and yet judicial consideration, and our conclusions are apt to be safe and sane. Our secretary should be free to speak and act as the representative of the alumni and should not be handicapped by being in the pay of the institution or under its direction.

He should represent the alumni and not the administration's point of view. Only as he can do this with the utmost frankness and directness can he be of the highest service to the institution. To be of the highest service the alumni must represent an independent force working for but independent of the institution.

The secretary, if he is to be really successful, must be broad-minded and open to conviction. He must have the proper perspective; must listen to all sides and be swayed only by what he is convinced is the ultimate good of the institution. When it is necessary, he should not fear to take a stand independent of the administration of the institution, but such stand should only be taken in case he is sure that something vital is at stake and such a stand is absolutely necessary. In all matters, it is vital that he keep his point of view free from prejudice. It is far better, whenever it is possible, to support the administration rather than to run counter to its plan. In any case, he should be sure that his stand is dictated only by considerations of the highest good of the institution and he should never forget that he represents the alumni and not himself.

Naturally the secretary will counsel with his board on all matters that do not demand instant action and his stand on any questions will represent not only his own best judgment but the consensus of the judgment of others who are in a position to know and advise intelligently.

Next to the secretary is the alumni publication; it is the most important factor aside from the secretary, and the only reason that it is not more important than the secretary is that the secretary is necessary to the publication, without him it cannot be a complete success. That the secretary should have an intimate, if not a controlling relation with the alumni publication, goes without saying. Whatever form of management the publication may have, it cannot reach its highest usefulness unless the secretary can speak to the alumni freely through its columns.

In all his dealings with the alumni, the secretary must be absolutely frank and must take them into his confidence. This is the only way in which he can secure and retain their confidence and the limit of his usefulness is measured only by the confidence of the alumni in the absolute integrity of their secretary.

Frequently, it may be necessary for the secretary to take a decided stand for or against something. He must make sure of his ground before he commits himself and be sure that his stand is one that alumni generally would approve if they knew the facts as he knows them. When he has once taken a stand, it is up to the secretary to stand by his guns so long as he is sure that he is right, no matter what a storm of criticism may be aroused, he may rest assured that, if he is right, the alumni will stand by him.

We who are gathered here for this conference, have before us possibilities for service such as comes to few men. Those who constitute the associations back of us are the leaders of the country today. The faithfulness and efficiency with which we do our work will determine, in large degree, the activities of those leaders in their relation to the institutions which we represent.

Our work is unique and its rewards are such as to tempt any man who desires to make his life count for things that are really worthwhile.[5]

These two opening speeches provided the framework for the thoughts and philosophy of alumni associations at the beginning of the twentieth century. At this second conference, substantive discussions centered on such topics as "Raising Money for Special Purposes," "How To Make Alumni Goodwill Effective for the Good of the Institution," "The Local Alumni Association and Its Relation to the Central Organization and the Institution," "The Class Organization and the Class Secretary," "The Alumni Publication," and "Shall the Graduate Publication Be the Official Organ of the University, or Is It Better Policy Not To Have Too Intimate Connection, So That It May Feel Free To Criticize If Necessary."[6]

Of particular interest at this second conference was the discussion of whether the alumni associations should be independent or dependent organizations. Louis Lochner, secretary of the University of Wisconsin, spoke passionately for independence: "This Independence becomes all the more necessary in the case of a state university alumni association when we remember that the alumni themselves represent every shade of political opinion. Consciously or unconsciously, the fact as to whether or not they agree with the political views of the president or majority of the board of regents makes a difference in their attitude toward the university." Later in his remarks, Lochner dared to suggest that even criticism of an institution by alumni can be important to its future: "I am a firm believer in the slogan, 'Turn on the Light.' Criticism, even though temporarily it stings and hurts, cannot but be helpful in the end, provided it be made in the right spirit and followed by constructive ideas to remedy the defects. Now, who is in a better position to make such helpful criticism than the organized body of Alumni?"[7]

Mr. Embree of Yale, chairing one of the closing sessions, challenged his colleagues to consider the ultimate aim of alumni efforts. By raising thought-provoking questions as to what alumni secretaries were trying to accomplish, he challenged the other alumni secretaries to become focused on the ideals that their colleges stood for. He was interested in how alumni could best help their institutions. Embree also felt that the university had a responsibility to its alumni. In the case of Yale that meant establishing a plan of continuous development through education for the individual; facilitating a plan through publications and periodicals or subject matters that were of a serious nature; providing an opportunity for the graduates to return to campus to attend lectures, visit laboratories, meet with professors in their homes, and visit university buildings; and creating the opportunity to be appointed to an advisory board of a department. In these different ways, Embree felt that the Yale Alumni Association was trying to help its graduates so that they would be more favorably disposed toward doing work in behalf of their alma mater.

It is also interesting that various alumni-related organizations during the early part of the twentieth century began with the Association of Alumni Secretaries. In 1918, the editors of magazines who formerly were part of the Association of Alumni Secretaries formed the organization known as the Alumni Magazine Associated. Shortly after 1919, the members of the Alumni Magazine Associated were busy with the challenges of selling advertisements. In 1926, therefore, the Intercollegiate Alumni Extension Service was incorporated for the purpose of selling advertising for the magazines. In 1919, the secretaries of women's colleges formed themselves into the Association of Alumnae Secretaries, which was immediately invited in 1920 to joint conference with the Association of Alumni Secretaries in Ann Arbor, Michigan. Two years later the alumnae secretaries gave up their separate organization and joined the Association of Alumni Secretaries. In 1925, the Association of Alumni Funds (fund raisers) was formed to further the interests of that particular branch of service, which had its genesis with the Association of Alumni Secretaries.

The year of 1927 was pivotal in the history of the alumni movement. The fourteenth annual conference was held at the University of North Carolina, Chapel Hill, on April 28–30, during which the Association of Alumni Secretaries, the Association of Alumni Funds, and the Alumni Magazine Associated consolidated into a new incorporated organization known as the American Alumni Council. The purposes of this new association were the furthering of friendly relations among its members, the interchange of ideas regarding their common problems, and the encouraging of a spirit of professional pride in alumni work. The "stimulating of the individual alumni association" and the promotion of a "universal consciousness among the college-trained citizens that education is man's greatest agency in the fight for freeing human spirit" were added to the constitution as two new thoughts. This was the earliest public document carrying the explanatory note that the word "alumni" should be construed to include both alumni and alumnae. At this conference, the annual dues were increased from $10 to $20; for those institutions that had an alumni office and either an alumni fund or magazine, or both, the dues were set at $25 or $30.[8]

Twenty-five years after the first gathering at Ohio State University, the silver anniversary of the American Alumni Council took place at Columbus, Ohio, from March 30 to April 2, 1938. Subject areas covered at this Silver Anniversary Conference included "Trends in Alumni Funds," "The Philosophy and Psychology of an Annual Giving Plan," " Study of Alumni Magazines," "Bigger and Better Alumni Advertisements," "The Universities and Their Alumni," "Have the Colleges and Universities Met the Problem?" and "A Statistical Study of Alumni Work 1913–1938."

On this silver anniversary, President Rightmire of Ohio State University spoke glowingly of the increased importance of offices of alumni relations to college presidents: "Every College and University President has Alumni Relations at the heart of his program; he deeply desires to know Alumni sentiment and is interested in creating all proper ways the native urge of the Alumni to help in the sound development of the College [sic]. But many Alumni don't know the way; some need cultivating; and here is where the Secretary functions as program inventor and enthusiasm builder. He stands at the elbow of the president and not only informs but stimulates. The president must go all the way in helping with money, in lending encouragement, and in bringing forward substantial planks for the Secretary's Alumni Platform, if he has any!"[9]

At this anniversary, Miss Virginia Van Fossan, representing Oberlin College, reminded all of the central mission of alumni work: "An alumni office gives two kinds of service, to the institution and to the alumni. Although we must not neglect the latter, the former is our real reason for being."[10]

E.K. Hibshman from Pennsylvania State University challenged the delegates with many questions about the mission and purpose of alumni relations, such as, Do you know what your job is as an alumni secretary? Can you sit down and write out a definition of your job? Can you interpret your university to your alumni and to your public in the terms of the contributions your alumni have made to society because of the education and training they have received on your university campus? Can you translate your university to the community in terms of everyday life? Do you have the necessary machinery to present to your university in an orderly businesslike way the true opinion about problems which arise? What Hibshman was trying to accomplish by raising these questions was to show how the graduates, both men and women, have, as a result of their university training, taken useful places in their communities and been equipped to render a real service in our complex society.[11]

The years passed, and each year continued to build upon the success of the previous year. Alumni programs at the campuses were maturing at the same time that the American Alumni Council was becoming stronger. In 1951, after several years of debate and controversy, the time had come for the American Alumni Council to set up a central office in Washington, D.C., and to hire a full-time executive to supplement the remarkable accomplishments of a dedicated force of volunteer officers.[12]

At the thirty-ninth general conference in 1954, nine goals for the American Alumni Council were defined to support its purpose of mobilizing alumni work behind education.[13]

TO THESE ENDS, The Council shall:
1. Insist on high professional standards and practice.
2. Provide media for the sharing of professional experience, methods and ideas.
3. Seek to create an alumni interest where none may exist and make it wholly effective (for the good of the institution) where it does.
4. Promote, through merit and dedication, through outlook and performance, the recognition of organized alumni effort as a vital force in education.

5. Help to develop appreciation of the major role played by the professional alumni worker in that effort.
6. Help the professional alumni worker to increase his effectiveness in serving the enlightened interests of his volunteer leaders.
7. Enlist alumni as continuing participants in education and as informed champions of education.
8. Develop active relationships with other organizations which support and advance the cause of education.
9. Strive to interpret the practical idealism of the alumni with respect to education and in turn to interpret the objectives and needs of education to the alumni and the public, to the end that we may best serve the ultimate beneficiaries of all our efforts—those who teach and those who learn.*

Four years later, in 1958, the American College Public Relations Association and the American Alumni Council received a grant from the Ford Foundation that included funding for 70 participants to attend a three-day meeting in Greenbrier, Virginia, to discuss the challenges of public relations, fund raising, alumni activity and institutional development, and the ways in which they should be coordinated and administered.

One of the outcomes of the Greenbrier conference was the creation of five objectives for an organized program of alumni activity:

1. to encourage the alumni to maintain a continuing relationship with the institution
2. to enlist the alumni in constructive endeavor for the institution
3. to bring to bear on the institution and its policies the judgment and view of the alumni
4. to help the institution find ways for the encouragement of continuing education among its alumni
5. to help create and develop among alumni a sense of responsibility not only to their institution but to higher education in general[14]

Nearly three-quarters of a century after that cold February when alumni representatives first gathered in Columbus, Dan Heinlen, director of alumni affairs at The Ohio State University Alumni Association, convened the Columbus II Colloquium: History's Legacies and Future Strategies. Sixty-three of the nation's alumni executives met to discuss 14 topics in three days. There was a serious attempt during the 38 hours of paper presentations to plow some new ground as well as review some of the fundamentals that have passed the test of time. Topics

---

* Courtesy of Council for Advancement and Support of Education, Washington, DC.

included "An Evaluation of the Relationships of Alumni Cultivation to Donor Patterns," "The Influence of Alumni on the Legislative Process," "Seventy-five Years of Alumni Education," "Philosophical Differences between Associations Driven by University Policy versus Those Driven by Alumni Policy," "Entrepreneurial Activities: Assets and Liabilities," "The Role of Alumni in Institutional Governance," and "Cultural Diversity in America: Its Impact on Higher Education."

In his address on "Power: The Light to Alumni Leadership," James Fisher, president-emeritus for the Council for Advancement and Support of Education, called for alumni work to center on gaining influence for the betterment of higher education:

> Certainly two primary concerns of the university are public and private support: influencing government and fund-raising. Both areas, government relations and development, were once not only preceded by, but born out of, alumni administration. Yet today, many alumni officers minimize the importance of these powerful functions and gladly grant them to others within the university. Assuming the thesis of this paper, every alumni association should have as two of its principal activities, overshadowed only by academic and other substantive programming, development of an impressive program of political influence, and full responsibility for the annual fund (and if this is not feasible, then as much responsibility for fund-raising activities as conditions allow). Yes, friend raising is fine, but when it comes to counting, the friends usually get less, a lot less. If the action (and appreciation) is in influence and money, who better to carry a great measure of the load than the alumni association? The more these things are done, the higher the stock and the greater the legitimacy of the alumni associations.

> In the really important alumni association, its primary dimension of alumni programming must be academic and substantive, not social or athletic. And here I refer to time allocated, disposition of staff and volunteers, and resources allocated more than to bylaws and proclamations. The very legitimacy of the association depends on it. It is ludicrous to argue against the primacy of a substantive mission for an alumni association and in the long run, I believe, profoundly dangerous.

> Today, numerous surveys prove that even our alumni are far more interested in substantive programming than any other. But even if this were not the case, the role of the alumni leader is to demonstrate that a college education does not stop with commencement. And finally regarding programming, in order that it not go without saying, on every

occasion possible, have the university president, trustee chair, and others of high position attend and speak at alumni functions. And get alumni association representation on every important institutional committee possible including, of course, presidential and other key search committees.

And what of alumni programming in the power light? I have suggested that with limitations, rewards are a valuable way of gaining legitimacy which, for all except the perfect, is a crucial way of gaining implied power. Alumni associations should reward what they want to be, not what people may think they are. If you would be more, behave that way. Too often alumni associations confine their awards and resources to programs and activities which convey the wrong messages and imply a more provincial self-serving quality.

Fisher also encouraged associations to think strategically, as we might put it, in making awards:*

Alumni associations and publications are too involved with distinguished alumni awards and athletic halls of fame when, in terms of both service and status, they would be better served by more impressive, well-publicized awards for teaching, research, administrative and trustee leadership, and major donors (even nonalumni). Awards should be in the form of impressive plaques, citations, cash, and grants. And they should be published beyond the alumni magazine. Alumni contributions and awards should be reinforced throughout the campus, the administration buildings, classroom buildings, the student union, and residence halls as well as the alumni offices.[15]

Some three years after the Columbus II Colloquium, another organization came into being. The Council of Alumni Association Executives, with a membership of approximately 100 executive directors of alumni associations representing the major public and private universities, was organized to meet the needs of major alumni associations. At its 1993 conference, papers were presented on "Alumni Leadership in the Next Millennium: What Is Required?" Dr. Steven L. Calvert, assistant vice-president for development and director of alumni relations at Carnegie Mellon University, said alumni directors should stick to the basics and be flexible. He also suggested that they develop "high-tech, high-touch" relationships with their customers, knowing, on the one hand, satellites, e-mail, and cellular telephones and, on the other hand, the intimacy of personal relationships. Dr. Jerry Gill, executive director of the Oklahoma State University Alumni Association, said alumni associations will be challenged to achieve consensus

---

* Courtesy of Council for Advancement and Support of Education, Washington, DC.

among an increasing alumni population living in an era of exploding technology and a rapidly changing society. Dr. Eustace D. Theodore, executive director of the Yale University Alumni Association, challenged his colleagues by calling for reflective leadership during the next millennium.*

> Based on these turbulent times, what kind of individual will make the best employee and leader in the decade ahead? The evidence seems to point to individuals who demonstrate flexibility, adaptability, optimism, and creativity.
>
> Reflective leadership moves toward balance between task and maintenance process concerns. But more than that, reflective leadership focuses not only on outcomes, but on the relationship between outcomes and the future of the organization, its inner voice. The reflective leader tries, no matter what the work content in a specific work group, no matter what the task concerns, to focus on the essence of the organization . . . the reflective leader tries to understand the group and lead it, to capture the direction of the organization and walk behind it . . . reflective leadership puts understanding before action, and depends on shared leadership developed from shared understandings. This is the direction in which we might wish to lead our alumni volunteers; it is a condition to which we as alumni professionals might wish to aspire.[16]

As implied by Emily Dickinson, we too have taken a backward look. The challenge from past to present has been to mobilize the full strength of our alumni in support of our colleges and universities. There are only five things alumni can give back to their alma mater:

1. advocacy
2. advice
3. money
4. students
5. jobs for students

It is the obligation of our colleges and universities to make sure that our greatest resource, our alumni, are listened to rather than ignored, are fully informed rather than kept in the dark, are cultivated rather than coerced, are mobilized rather than left idle, and are appreciated rather than exploited.

---

* Courtesy of Council for Advancement and Support of Education, Washington, DC.

NOTES

1. C.H. Webb, *Handbook for Alumni Administration* (Phoenix: Oryx Press, 1995), 7–8.
2. F. Ayres, "The Michigan State College Report," East Lansing, Michigan, 1925, 5.
3. The Association Office of the Secretary, "Report of the Second Conference," Ann Arbor, Michigan, November 21–22, 1913, 12–14.
4. The Association Office of the Secretary, 12–14.
5. The Association Office of the Secretary, 38–41.
6. The Association Office of the Secretary, 8–9.
7. The Association Office of the Secretary, 88.
8. R.W. Sailor, "The Silver Anniversary of the American Alumni Council," Ithaca, NY: The American Alumni Council, March 30–April 2, 1938, 5–6, 141.
9. R.W. Sailor, "Silver Anniversary," 219.
10. R.W. Sailor, "Silver Anniversary," 40.
11. R.W. Sailor, "Silver Anniversary," 41–47.
12. The American Alumni Council, "Thirty-Ninth General Conference," American Alumni Council *Yearbook*, 1954, Washington, DC: American Alumni Council, 1954, 11.
13. The American Alumni Council *Yearbook*, 1954, 14.
14. The American College Public Relations Association, "The Advancement of Understanding and Support for Higher Education," 1958, 34.
15. The Council for Advancement and Support of Education, "Columbus II Colloquium: History's Legacies and Future Strategies," Washington, DC: Council for the Advancement and Support of Education, 1989, 61–62.
16. E.D. Theodore, "Alumni Leadership in the Millennium: What Is Required?" Council of Alumni Association Executives, August 1, 1993, 11–15.

CHAPTER 9

The Function of the Alumni Office

William W. Tromble

Alumni are the products of schools, colleges, and universities, although the term "alumni" could apply to other institutions as well, like the Young Men's Christian Association (YMCA) or Girl Scouts. The term is derived from the Latin *"alumnus,"* meaning pupil or foster son, and is often used in connection with former members of an organization, former employees, patients, or clients. Most often, however, the term is used in connection with educational institutions, and the office that serves them is the alumni office. This chapter explores the function of that office, whether it be within the structure of an independent alumni association or in the administrative structure of the institution itself. Jerry Gill discusses various models of alumni organization in Chapter 10.

Alumni are the recipients of knowledge and understanding given them by their teachers and classmates, by the administrators and staff, and all they have been associated with in their journey through college on the way to the commencement platform on graduation day. As students they were customers, and as alumni they are customers. Business schools love the word "customer." Academicians hate it, and maybe it is not the best word to describe these wonderful people called alumni, but in these latter years of the 1990s there is a groundswell of sensitivity in American higher education and other segments of the nonprofit community to the way people perceive us and react to us. In the business world it is a matter of buying and selling. That is the bottom line. A company has goods or services for sale. The customer buys, and a profit is made. To get that sale, the company has to create an interest in the product, be competitive with other companies that sell the same product, and treat the customer well. There is much more to it than that, but the point is, these same conditions apply to alumni. To get their support and their loyalty, and to keep them coming back, institutions have to treat them well, and that means three things that make up the function of the Alumni Office: *communication, service,* and *opportunity.*

In a sense, alumni are given birth at graduation. They become offspring of the institution and a part of the family from then on. It is not like they have a choice to be or not to be alumni. They are in fact alumni, the products of their alma mater. Their numbers grow rapidly over time as each new graduating class joins the alumni association. Schools like Michigan or Pennsylvania have nearly 400,000 graduates. The challenge is to keep in touch, treat them well, and provide the service they require. Without current information, alumni soon forget. When they return to the campus, they tend to remember the good things and block out the bad experiences. They are often basking in the remembrance of pleasant and meaningful events, but that goodwill for the institution quickly fades when they encounter apathy, indifference, or even rudeness on the part of some secretary or staff person. Again, communication and service are the keys.

In 1947, Hill Turner, then an executive officer of the Vanderbilt Alumni Association, spoke out strongly against taking alumni for granted. All too common, he felt, was the view that "loyal alumni" did not need to be educated because they already know more about the school than most of the faculty. "Loyal and true" is so flippantly tossed about in school songs and commencement addresses. Turner even remembers a colleague who used the phrase, "pulling the leg of a gullible alumnus." Vanderbilt alumni, in Turner's mind, were not always loyal but never gullible. There are always a few, however, who are truly loyal, and those are the alumni that hold the organization together. They are always supportive, understanding, and helpful, like the alumnus who "assures the coach after an unsuccessful season that a 'moral victory' on the football field" has been won. He is the fellow "who comforts you, stands by and is always ready to pinch hit for you. Many times, in my experience, the loyal alumnus has been my salvation."[1]

Fifty years later, in today's world, there are still a few loyal alumni who form the nucleus of support, but that inner circle has the potential for enormous growth with the proper nurturing and care. There is almost no limit to the good that could be accomplished if this great sleeping giant called alumni ever wakes up and focuses its collective energy and resources. In America, as in no other nation, alumni have been, are, and will be the first line of support for schools, colleges, and universities.

COMMUNICATION

First, alumni must be informed. Granted some may not really care, but to engender interest and understanding, which of course leads to support, alumni have to be kept abreast of the happenings and goings-on at their alma mater. Out of sight, out of mind is the trueism. It is easier to keep alumni "in the loop" when they live close by. News releases, feature articles, special events, and social contacts help to keep the spirit alive, but when graduates live thousands of miles away, other strategies must be used, like newsletters and correspondence. Even invitations to local events let alumni know something is going on, even though they will not be able to attend.

At one institution known to the writer, the alumni operation was really going south in a hurry. Loyal alumni were becoming concerned, and others expressed their feelings by staying away in droves from special events. The problem was a lack of communication. Gradually alumni began to realize they were not getting the alumni magazine, and the loyal few began to complain to the vice-president about it. Truthfully, what had happened was the alumni office had become so involved with keeping records and managing special events that it ceased publishing the magazine. It was not only the magazine, but other informative pieces and announcements became less and less frequent. It was not by design. It happened by default. First came the idea "we will skip this one issue, and then resume publication." Soon another issue was delayed, and another, until publication ceased altogether for a period of almost two years. All the while the alumni director kept reassuring the vice-president this was only temporary. Finally the gravity of the situation became so painful for the institution, the vice-president said, "Enough of this. Alumni want the magazine. They should have it, and we are in default for not producing it." The alumni director's contract was not renewed. A new director was hired immediately and, in the first two months of service, produced a new and improved alumni magazine. It was mailed to all alumni. Subsequent issues followed regularly. Alumni began to respond positively, and soon the complaints turned to compliments. More and more alumni were returning to campus and participating in chapter events.

Alumni need to have this connection with their alma mater. They may not respond. They may not appear to care about it, but they do. They want to know what's going on, and who is doing what, especially as it pertains to classmates or personalities they know. When they pick up an alumni publication, whether it is the magazine or just a simple flyer, they look first at the "Class Notes" section and then for the names and pictures of others they may know. Their interest does not stop there, however. They want to know about programs and activities, because when good things are happening it makes them proud to be associated with the institution. As the organization or institution becomes bigger and better, more noteworthy, more famous, and as the institution becomes stronger academically, or athletically, or in a manner of service, it only makes the alumnus more noteworthy and his degree more valuable.

The argument is often made, "We can't afford to send the magazine to all alumni, only to those who pay their dues, or actively support the institution." The fact is, we should send it to all alumni, because the more alumni are informed, and the more they are brought into the loop, so to speak, the stronger the bonding with the institution. There are many items that are market sensitive, such as class reunion invitations, or notice of chapter meetings. These bits and pieces of information are appropriately targeted to certain market segments, but information of a general nature, especially that which helps alumni to see the big picture of the current institution as it really is, including the challenges as well as the progress—this information must be shared with all alumni.

The operative phrase is "Keep in Touch." Pursue them relentlessly. Do not lose a single one if it can be helped. Communicate. Give alumni something to look at or read every month, and find ways to let them communicate their feelings and interests back to the alumni office, because communication is a two-way street. Unless a way is found to close the circle with a return message, communication does not occur.

Hospitals also have alumni, but they are not called alumni. They are former patients, and they are the single most responsive donors any hospital can have. They give more in fund drives than any other constituent group. Nurses are next highest, and physicians, oddly enough, often give less than nurses. Other organizations, such as the YMCA, Big Brothers, Girls, Inc., and Boy Scouts, have alumni, but again they are not called alumni. They are past recipients of the social service, and they too form a wide base of support for the organization. The symphonies, museums, arts centers, and theater groups have present and past patrons. So, the concept of alumni support, although usually applied to education, is a viable concept for hospitals, health care centers, social service groups, and cultural groups.

These organizations need to establish and maintain communication with their "alumni" constituencies. Information must flow freely. The public relations people working with the development people should together communicate with all their publics on a regular basis.

The alumni clubs or chapters are a means of establishing a connection. They require a large amount of staff time, a corps of willing volunteers, and adequate funding, but they have been a part of alumni programming for many years. The first was founded at Marietta College in 1855.[2] Since then hundreds of alumni clubs have been organized. When active, they are a way of communicating with alumni, a way of keeping the old school spirit alive. The problem is the huge amount of time and money needed to maintain them. They must have off-campus volunteers willing to organize club events and make arrangements for a meeting place and food service. Staff at the main alumni office usually handle the invitations, speakers, planning, and management of these events, which might include dinners, athletic events, theater, or annual meetings. Alumni participating at club events are only a small fraction of the total alumni population for the particular area. Because of the great effort needed to keep clubs alive, some institutions have let them die and put the energy and money into other programs.

To build an alumni program, whatever it might be, it is necessary to organize. One cannot be effective, or efficient, without a well-planned, well-thought-out, alumni organization. In the past, such organization has occurred in one of two ways: (1) as an adjunct of the development operation or a separate department of the institution, or (2) as a stand-aside, independent corporation.[3] The former is preferred in smaller institutions and some larger ones, because it allows the institution greater control and ties alumni more closely to the organization. The latter is preferred by large institutions because it allows a certain level of autonomy for an alumni association, while at the same time encouraging alumni support. In the independent model, programs and activities are paid for by the association. Funding is through the payment of association membership dues. The downside is that alumni pay their dues and still are called upon to make several contributions to the institution. Happily, they receive a charitable deduction on their income tax forms for contributions to either the association or the institution. Both usually have Internal Revenue Service (IRS) 501 (c)(3) status. Dues payments, however, may not be deductible, in accordance with IRS regulations. The contention of some institutions is that alumni loyalty is to their college, not some association. Unless the association is successful in melding with the institution by such means as having offices at the institution and bringing alumni back to the campus frequently, as Michigan has done, for example, alumni will bond with the institution and not the association. After all, it was the institution that gave them a start, not the association. Memories are of the professors, the classrooms, or the stadium, not the association. Having said that, it is well to point out that some of the strongest alumni programs, like summer alumni college, travel programs, and club or chapter organizations, are the products of the large independent alumni associations. This is true in part because they do have the autonomy and the funding to be innovative and creative in alumni programming.

SERVICE

Communication is fine, but without service it is like a left hand without a right. The two work together to build a strong alumni body. First of all, alumni want to be informed, and they are often not shy about talking back. Second, they want service, and there are all sorts of ways in which they expect to receive it. They look to the alumni office to help them get tickets to athletic events or concerts and other happenings. They look to the alumni office when they may be having a problem with getting transcripts, or to help a child of theirs enroll, or to get in touch with a particular professor. They look to the alumni office to supply them with lists of classmates. Young alumni in particular often want to invite the friends they have come to know in college to a wedding or a party. Sometimes they want alumni lists for commercial reasons. Those requests are usually very tactfully declined. Releasing alumni names and addresses for commerce is a violation of alumni trust.

Other limits to service are due to understaffing, lack of budget, or insufficient time to respond and execute the request, but by and large almost anything the alumni office or the association can do to help alumni will be done gladly, and with a smile. Sometimes alumni need help in finding a job, or in moving from one field of employment to another. What the association can do is put individuals in touch with other alumni who have connections and can help. The whole networking potential in alumni affairs is awesome. It is amazing what one big family, like the alumni, can do to assist each other by means of linkages with the institution and the alumni office.

Continuing education is also a real winner with alumni. Lifelong learning is apparent to all who stop and think about it for a moment. Human beings are perpetual students, always learning something new, continually refreshing their minds about things previously learned, and when the college or university offers alumni a chance to return for a few days of continuing education in what is often called an "Alumni College," they are receptive to the idea. Hundreds of alumni return to campus, especially during the summer, or at other times when such programs are offered. It offers them a chance to improve their minds, a chance to relive some memorable times at a place of timeless endurance in an age of continuing change. It offers them a chance to renew acquaintance with old friends and make new friends in a convivial atmosphere where birds of a feather come together, mainly because of one thing. They are alumni and proud of it.

A typical summer alumni college would include one week of classes, usually classes of a general nature: history and political science, the psychology of adult personality, time and your money are popular. Crafts, nature walks, and gems and minerals are also popular. The classes are taught, in so far as possible, by favorite professors. It is understood from the beginning there will be no examinations and no grades but pleasant and interesting opportunities to learn more about "ourselves and the world in which we live." Often the classes are taught in the mornings, leaving afternoons free for leisure activities or field trips, and the evenings for socializing, including dinners, dancing, theater, or singing around a bonfire. Alumni who attend are charged a moderate fee, and they are happy to pay it. The happiness and *joie de vivre* they receive is well worth it, and many will return year after year. Alumni College is similar to the Elderhostel program, which is sponsored in part by a leading foundation.

Alumni Family Camp is another service increasing in popularity. It lasts only a few days, sometimes over the weekend and incorporates some of the ideas of the alumni college, but it involves the entire family, both alumni and future alumni in summer fun-and-togetherness activities, like boating, swimming, fishing, hiking, cookouts, and field trips to learn more about the natural environment. The bond that makes it work, and makes it special, is the tie with the institution.

Travel opportunity is also a service to alumni. Group rates, guided tours, and a common bond of fellowship attract thousands of alumni to the Far East, Europe, Africa, and other interesting places. The writer recalls one memorable tour to the Middle East. It was in the fall of the year. A travel brochure had gone out months in advance advertising the tour and a number of alumni signed on. Air and ground transportation was arranged to JFK Airport where the group assembled for the first leg of the journey, a 14-hour flight to Amman, Jordan. Most of the flight was at night, so alumni were able to get a good night's rest, except for the three or four who laughed and talked most of the way. After arrival in Jordan, the group was fortunate to be able to meet the king, who was just returning from a flight out of the country. It took hours to check the bags through customs, but thanks to the local guide who was assigned to our group, it was not a bad ordeal. People are friendly, but very suspicious in the Middle East. Except for the fact that many alumni had wanted to visit the Holy Land, it might have been wise to have gone to some other part of the world; but this was the tour they all were excited about. After checking into a four-star hotel, which by American standards left a lot to be desired, alumni were free to wander about the city, seeing the sights as they might wish to do, or to stay at the hotel. The following morning a touring bus arrived and the group was taken down the countryside to the famous Red Rocks of Petra, where ancient civilizations had carved temples and houses into the massive rocks. The last mile of the way was by horseback, and it was both interesting and amusing to watch some of the alumni, who had not been used to riding, awkwardly climb on their horses and ride down the trail toward the valley. After that the tour proceeded across the Jordan River, through Jericho, and up the long and dusty road to Jerusalem, where the group was housed for a few days in one of the city's better hotels. Alumni were fascinated by the sights and sounds of Old Jerusalem, appalled by some of the food hanging out in open markets, but excited to be in this famous place, walking on the old city wall, visiting the wailing wall, the Temple Mount, and the stations of the cross. Alumni were quite fortunate in some respects. On the way through Samaria a tour bus just ahead of us was blown up by a terrorist bomb, which caused long delays in traffic and much apprehension on the part of most of the alumni on the tour, including the writer of this book who served as tour guide along with a dear friend, Dr. Carl Schultz, a biblical scholar who had been to the area many times before. After journeying from the top of the country to the bottom, from Dan to Beersheba, as they say, visiting many historical sites, including the Sea of Galilee, where we stopped for lunch and were served St. Peter's Fish, the tour brought alumni across the Mediterranean Sea to Athens, Greece, on the way back home. Favorite places where alumni took many pictures were the ruins of the Parthenon on the Acropolis, the historical arches and gardens of Athens, unforgettable street scenes, and a memorable trip up the coast to Corinth. Shortly afterward, a happy but tired group of alumni boarded a 747 aircraft for the return flight to the United States.

There were only a few negative happenings along the way, but alumni took them in good faith with a positive attitude. Their baggage was searched on several occasions, but coming across the Allenby Bridge from Jordan into Israel, the search was especially thorough and lengthy. One alumnus was even asked to hand over his shoes and watched in disbelief as the soldier ripped off the heels of his shoes looking for contraband. Members of the group were also not altogether happy to be forced to receive shots at the airport when they first arrived in Athens, but you do what you have to do when in strange countries. Throughout the trip, local tour guides warned alumni not to drink tap water. Bottled water and other drinks were fine.

What alumni received from this tour is similar to that received by countless alumni on travel excursions throughout the world, a chance to see and experience historical sites, other cultures, and famous places in the company of old and new friends who share a common bond. They are products of a single institution that gave them a start. They are loyal, for the most part, to that institution. They are proud of that institution. They identify with that institution. They are a part of the extended family of that institution, and they enjoyed this wonderful opportunity as a service provided by that institution.

What the university received from this happening is a closer bonding with a few alumni who will spread the good word to other alumni. The institution received an opportunity to build better relationships with certain alumni and open the door to future conversations about planned giving when the time is right, because as alumni directors know, people who can afford a $2,000 or $3,000 trip are usually capable of making a significant gift to the institution at some appropriate time in their lives. The tour is part of the cultivation process to form lasting and supportive relationships.

Probably the two or three service items alumni seek most are help with finding other alumni, information about upcoming events, and logistic help with reunion planning and reunion gifts. Other requests range all the way from "How can I contact Professor So and So?" to "How can I contribute appreciated securities?" The position of the institution must be to help in any way possible. Alumni are one vast segment of customers. They expect to be treated expediently, with respect and courtesy. They are family, but should be treated as guests. Their requests should never be ignored or delayed, but handled quickly and to their satisfaction. Above all, we want alumni to be satisfied customers.

The writer will concede, "customer service" may not be the best term to use, but it seems to embody the characteristics, behaviors, and attitudes that make alumni feel wanted and needed. It is that kind of service that says "We value you.

We are proud of you. We want you to come back." Alumni have a right to be treated as partners because they are major stakeholders in the corporation. "Presidents and alumni have the same mutual objective: the welfare of the institution."[4] When they see things start to slip, they become concerned. When they see progress being made, they rejoice. They want to be appreciated for their time and talents, their management skills, and their advice and counsel, not just for their financial contributions.

Communication and service—these are the primary functions of alumni affairs. They promote and assist the bonding with the institution. They promote loyalty. They influence support, both financial and political. Communication brings understanding, which opens the door to building relationships. Service is giving. It is reaching out. It is helpful nurturing activity. Both these functions are vital to a successful alumni operation.

OPPORTUNITY

A third function of alumni affairs is to provide opportunity for personal growth and continuing interaction with their alma mater. Some of that opportunity is discussed above in the paragraphs on service, opportunity for travel with a group of friends, opportunity for lifelong learning, and opportunity for family participation. There are other opportunities as well.

Through the class reunions alumni are given the opportunity to renew old friendships and relive memorable times. Reunions are very much alive and well in the 1990s. At Princeton they are one of the main events in alumni relations. They tend to generate the most support in a social setting, compared to other events routinely held. Reunions are also elite in nature, inspiring the view that "ours was the best class ever graduated." They require much time and energy to accomplish. They do not just happen because a few classmates decide to get together. Months of planning and preparation are necessary, sending out invitations, arranging a venue and food service, recruiting volunteers, building a program, and soliciting the usual "Class Gift." Not all reunions feature a class gift, but college presidents are delighted when they do. The writer engineered several class gifts from Ball State University alumni totaling over $100,000 each, usually from the golden or silver anniversary classes of a particular year.

One of the most successful class reunion programs, for which I was personally responsible, involved an annual gathering of the so-called five-year reunion classes at Houghton College in upstate New York. Invitations went out to all alumni of the particular five-year classes being honored. Five hundred or more alumni usually attended the event. It was held every year, but any given class member could participate in this event only once in every five years. In one year, it might be all the classes having graduated in 32 and 37, 42 and 47, 52 and 57,

62 and 67, etc. The gathering was held on a Friday night of alumni weekend. Other events were scheduled for the weekend that involved all alumni and their families, but this special event was the big reunion gathering. It was a gala affair with a reception and dinner program. Tables were creatively marked with standards that announced the year of the class to be seated there. Centerpieces of flowers and artwork adorned each table. The dinner service tablecloths, napkins, and glasses were properly placed. Printed programs were placed at each plate. There was a grand atmosphere of cordiality, as well as competition, but also of coming together as a big happy family. On one occasion, one representative from each table was asked to stand before the microphone and briefly tell of one exciting incident that had happened when he or she was a student. The master of ceremonies kept it moving so that it would not become boring, as can happen when people, especially certain talkative alumni, ramble on and on about this and that. Alumni enjoyed this evening very much and came away from the event with a wonderful spirit of unity and support for the school.

This type of reunion is not suited to all colleges and universities. In the larger ones, the more successful reunions are constituent-based, not class-based. School of business people meeting together or school of journalism graduates holding an event makes much more sense in many universities than any attempt to call together a particular class. The Class of 1978, for example, might well be comprised of 5,000 individuals who have nothing in common, in terms of get-togethers and good times, other than the fact that they graduated from the university. Their sense of pride and loyalty is with their constituent group, and each group has different ideas about socializing. The people from the business school may want a black tie event, whereas the people from the school of agriculture may prefer a buffet and line dance.

However the reunion game is played, it is important to perpetuate the coming together of graduates in whatever configuration, style, or manner that attracts them. Some general events will attract the larger alumni body, but more bridge building and personal bonding will take place in special interest groupings.

Alumni affairs offers other opportunities for participation, as Jerry Gill adequately discusses in the next chapter. There are opportunities for volunteering, opportunities for giving, opportunities for recruiting students, helping students, even mentoring students. There are opportunities for career planning and placement, opportunities for legislative advocacy, and opportunities to be heard by the administration. The more opportunities an institution can offer alumni, the better it is for all concerned.

The three main functions of the alumni association and the office of alumni affairs then are communication, service, and opportunity. Alumni have been, are, and will be the first vanguard of support for the institution. Their goodwill is one of the finest assets an institution can hold. Therefore, giving alumni up-to-date information about the institution and current happenings, and listening to what they have to tell us is the first function of alumni affairs. Providing alumni the service they deserve and request is the second function. Giving them abundant opportunities, such as lifelong learning education, to help themselves and opportunities to help the institution through comments and suggestions, volunteering, and contributions is the third function. These are fundamental to a successful alumni operation.

NOTES

1. H. Turner, *An Adventure in Alumni Relations* (Nashville: The Alumni Association, Vanderbilt University, 1947), 16.
2. R.A. Reichley, "Alumni Clubs and Reunions," *Handbook of Institutional Advancement,* ed. A. Westley Rowland (San Francisco: Jossey-Bass, 1978), 316.
3. R.G. Forman, "The Role of Alumni Relations," *The President and Fund Raising,* eds. J.L. Fisher and G.H. Quehl (New York: American Council on Education, Macmillan, 1989), 110.
4. Forman, "The Role of Alumni Relations," 116.

CHAPTER **10**

Alumni Programs: Principles and Practice

Jerry L. Gill

For more than 200 years, alumni have been actively involved in support of their institutions. Charles Webb, in Chapter 8, pointed out the evolution of organized alumni relations activities, beginning with the organization of Yale University graduates in 1792. Graduates of Williams College held the first recorded alumni meeting in 1821 and built Alumni Hall in 1859. The Morrill Act of 1863 provided for the creation of land-grant state universities, and following the Civil War, many of these new publicly supported institutions joined with private colleges to produce a rapidly growing number of college and university graduates. The second Morrill Act of 1890 provided opportunities for people of color and formed the basis for some of the nation's approximately 117 historically black colleges and universities.

BACKGROUND

These institutions and their graduates, early on, realized the potential for organized alumni activities in support of their schools, and Oklahoma State University, which graduated its first class in 1896 as Oklahoma Agricultural and Mechanical College, is an example of that trend. Members of that first class, even before commencement, were discussing the need for an alumni association. In the summer of that year these graduates formed the Oklahoma Agricultural and Mechanical College Alumni Association and returned to campus on June 8, 1897, the evening before commencement exercises, to induct members of the Class of '97 into the Alumni Association.

Professor Edward F. Clark, a member of the college faculty, delivered a formal address at that meeting entitled, "The Relations That Should Exist Between

Alumni and *Alma Mater.*" The college newspaper reported that the presentation

> was a strong and thoughtful presentation of their mutual dependence
> and helpfulness. He, Professor Clark, showed how the growth and
> development of an educational institution always helps and strengthens
> its Alumni, and how the success and prestige of the Alumni always
> assists the Alma Mater. A blow to one is always a blow to the other; a
> failure by one reacts upon the other, and subtracts something from its
> power for good. No person who heard the address failed to see more
> clearly how inextricably are the interests of an educational institution
> and of the graduates it sends out into the world bound and cemented
> together.[1]

The positive benefits of alumni participation in institutional advancement are
as obvious and important today as they were more than a century ago. Roy
Vaughan, executive director emeritus of the University of Texas Ex-Students
Association, refers to the "convening power" of alumni and their nearly unlimited potential to positively impact their alma mater. Institutional resources are limited, and advancement of the institution will be only incremental at best, if it is
dependent entirely on human and financial resources available on the campus. It
is the collective intellectual capital and financial resources of alumni that provide
the margin of excellence for most institutions of higher education today.

Alumni contribute to their institution in three ways. First, they serve as active
advocates for their school, and in this role, they help develop a positive image for
their institution. Former students are the most enduring and influential stakeholders of the institution. Their lives are inextricably intertwined with their alma
mater, and because they are publicly identified with that institution, they have a
strong vested interest in its success. They share good news and positive accomplishments of their alma mater with others, help interpret the institution to its
many publics, and through exemplary lives and professional accomplishments,
reinforce positive public perception of the quality of their institution and its graduates. They also help influence prospective students to enroll at their institution,
enhancing the quality of the student body and increasing tuition revenue, and they
positively affect state appropriations through participation in legislative networks.

Alumni also contribute significantly to their alma mater by serving as honest
and loving critics. They serve on college and departmental advisory groups,
search committees, and governing boards, sharing their intellect, leadership, and
professional experience. Alumni help the institution to better interpret and understand perceptions and expectations of its alumni and the public, and they help
make the institution aware of social, political, and economic issues that will
impact the institution. In this role, alumni also serve as keepers of the traditions

and values of their school. In an era of continually shorter tenures of faculty, presidents, and other institutional leaders, alumni have the longest corporate institutional memory and tend to have a long-term view of where and how the institution should go. And, finally, alumni support their school with their financial
resources, and they influence other individuals and organizations to make their
resources available, as well. Many alumni participate in annual giving to provide
immediate financial support and in planned giving to provide future support. In
addition to their financial support, alumni serve on fund raising committees and
development foundation boards to help implement annual giving programs and
plan major comprehensive capital campaigns.

The extent to which alumni associations effectively involve large numbers of
alumni in the tasks outlined above and successfully engage their time, talents, and
resources on behalf of the institution is the yardstick by which they should be
measured. Alumni organizations should be inclusive grassroots organizations that
involve, directly and indirectly, as many alumni as possible in their programs and
service to their institutions. Board members and other alumni volunteers, collectively, should reflect the demographics and ethnicity of the student body and
alumni population.

ORGANIZATIONAL STRUCTURE

Through the years, alumni have been organized, governed, and managed in
many different ways, reflecting the varied institutions they represent. The three
basic organizational models are *independent, dependent,* and *interdependent.* An
independent association, typically, is financially self-sufficient, has a self-gov-
erning, policy-making board, is incorporated with 501(c)(3) status, and hires and
determines salary of its staff. A *dependent* alumni association usually is a department of the university. Its budget and staff are provided by the school, and it does
not have a policy-making board. The *interdependent* association is, to varying
degrees, a combination of the first two models. Usually, it is incorporated and has
a policy-making board, but a significant portion of its operations budget is provided by the institution, and some or all of the staff are employees of the institution.

More important than the organizational structure is the relationship between
alumni and their alma mater. Does the association encourage and provide opportunities for alumni to participate actively in the life of the institution? Are alumni informed about the programs and issues of the institution, and do they have a
sense of ownership? Is the alumni organization led by alumni policy rather than
institutional policy? The extent to which alumni feel they can make a difference
is the extent to which they will invest themselves and their resources in the alumni association and the institution.

There is no one best organizational model for all alumni associations. Each
association will reflect the unique history of the institution it serves and will be a

product of the relationship of that institution and its alumni throughout the years. And it will structure itself according to financial resources available and the leadership of its alumni.

MANAGING ALUMNI PROGRAMS

Management of alumni relations programs covers the entire spectrum from the small one-person shop with a budget of just a few thousand dollars to large complex alumni associations with staffs of more than 50 and budgets of several million dollars. Regardless of size or resources, however, there are management principles and concepts common to all.

Recruiting, developing, and retaining a professional staff is the first step toward a successful alumni relations program. The overall composition of the staff should reflect the diversity of the alumni population, including age, gender, and ethnicity. Key qualities to look for in a staff are professional experience and technical competency, strong work ethic, ability to work in teams, experience in working with volunteers, integrity and ethics, and passion for the institution. New employees should be quickly immersed in the philosophy of alumni relations, the traditions and values of the institution and the strategic priorities, and annual objectives and programs of the alumni association. Continuing professional development and networking opportunities for staff members are critical to developing outstanding alumni relations professionals. The budget should include opportunities for staff to attend conferences and workshops for alumni professionals. The Council for Advancement and Support of Education (CASE) is the acknowledged leader in the support of institutional advancement professionals. It provides needed information and offers a professional network. Participation in CASE institutes and conferences is a must for alumni relations professionals.

Warren Bennis says in his book, *On Becoming a Leader,* "the manager does things right; the leader does the right thing." It is imperative that alumni executives lead their organizations by doing the "right things." If they demonstrate passion for their work, integrity in their relationships, and commitment to quality, then their staffs likely will exhibit these qualities. Annual evaluation and appraisal of staff is an effective management tool. Appraisals should include accomplishment of annual objectives assigned to them as well as professional development. It is important to measure personal productivity as well as the individual's effect on the productivity of other staff and volunteers with whom they work.[2]

Another leadership task that at times seems daunting is the involvement and management of hundreds of alumni volunteers. Although developing relationships with alumni leaders and volunteers is perhaps one of the most challenging tasks of alumni professionals, it is also the most rewarding. The extent to which institutions successfully engage alumni in meaningful activities on behalf of the institution will in large measure determine the effectiveness of the institution's alumni relations programs. The number of professional staff members that an association or institution can employ will always be limited, but the number of volunteer staff that can be engaged is nearly limitless, and the intellectual and financial capital they bring is unlimited. The investment in the development of alumni leaders and volunteers will return the greatest yield of any activity of the alumni relations program.

VOLUNTEERS

The term "volunteer" is perhaps a misnomer in the sense that most alumni do not actually volunteer. Dewey Welch simply and profoundly explained this. Former President of the Indiana University Alumni Association and longtime volunteer for the association and his alma mater, Welch received CASE's Ernest T. Stewart Award (1989), an award that is given annually to an outstanding alumni volunteer. During his acceptance remarks at CASE's Annual Assembly, he explained that he had never actually "volunteered" for service on behalf of his alma mater but that he had been "asked" many times to help and to be involved. Competition for the hearts, minds, and time of volunteers is growing keener. Alumni are becoming more selective about their volunteer time, and service to their alma mater is no longer considered obligatory or even necessary. Citizens and alumni are critical in their acceptance and support of higher education. Charitable organizations are making more requests for volunteer involvement, especially in light of declining federal and state revenue for social programs. The baby boomers and generation Xers make decisions about volunteering their time and resources based on what is of value to them and what they expect in return for their service.[3]

These attitudinal shifts and increasing competition from other service organizations are occurring at a time when individuals have less discretionary time. Because of technological change and increasing global competition, employees are required to work longer hours and invest more time and resources in career education and retraining to be productive. Two-career families and single-parent families are having an increasingly difficult time balancing work and family obligations with volunteer expectations.

The recruitment and nurturing of alumni volunteers is more difficult and yet more crucial than ever before. Assignments should be carefully defined and achievable in a reasonable amount of time, and volunteers should receive support sufficient to successfully complete tasks assigned to them and then be appropriately recognized for their efforts. A volunteer never should be allowed to fail because of inadequate support or insufficient information concerning expectations. Successful alumni associations continually identify, recruit, develop, and reward alumni volunteers. They understand that properly prepared, appropriately engaged, and highly motivated volunteers are the lifeblood of alumni relations endeavors.

Board Service

Perhaps no alumni volunteer relationship is more important than that of members of the alumni association board of directors, and their commitment is truly special when board members have a strong sense of ownership. Members invest themselves in boards that set policy for the association, engage in strategic planning, approve annual objectives and budgets, and help develop alumni programs and initiatives. It is obvious, but worth emphasizing, that having an effective board is dependent on continually appointing or nominating outstanding individuals to the board. Factors to consider in selecting new board members include demonstrated leadership ability, influence and visibility with other alumni, commitment of personal resources (time, talent, and finances), and diversity. The board membership should generally reflect its alumni population in terms of age, gender, ethnicity, and geographic distribution. New member orientation should include well-defined job descriptions including specific expectations, a history of the association, philosophy of alumni relations work, and a detailed review of the association's programs, annual objectives, and budget. Knowledge of the strategic priorities and long-range plans of the association also is important.

Strategic Planning

Creating a vision, defining the mission, identifying priorities, and developing a long-range plan are important prerequisites to effectively utilizing available resources and ultimately achieving the goals of the alumni association. Once strategic priorities and long-range goals have been determined, then decisions regarding implementation of programs, annual objectives, and budget allocations should be based on progress toward attainment of these goals. Another important outcome of strategic planning is the buy-in of board members when they are involved in the process. Alumni bring a real-world perspective to strategic planning and ensure a better final product. When they invest themselves in the strategic planning process, they become emotionally involved, sometimes even passionate, about the role and importance of alumni and the alumni programs to the institution. With their passion comes commitment of resources and time.

Outside Perspective, Alumni Feedback

A critical aspect of developing the long-range plan and delivering effective programs is feedback from alumni. At a recent meeting retreat of the Oklahoma State University Alumni Association, board member Larry Watkins stood up and exclaimed, "We are no longer going to assume that we know what alumni want until we have asked them." Alumni need to be surveyed continually, and alumni associations need to initiate focus groups and get program evaluations from participants, alumni volunteers, and staff.[4]

Assessment is hard to quantify. Managing the alumni program requires a high degree of tolerance for ambiguity, and alumni relations activities are sometimes difficult to bottom line, statistically. However, there is a growing trend toward more accountability in alumni relations programs, and many alumni associations are developing internal and external benchmarks to better measure the results of alumni programming and their positive benefit to the institution.

The contributions and potential benefits of alumni participation in the advancement of their institution have been documented, and the challenge for alumni relations professionals is to engage alumni in meaningful programs of service to the institution and to other alumni. The remainder of this chapter will be devoted to a discussion of basic alumni programs offered by alumni associations across the United States and Canada (see Exhibit 10–1). It is not intended to be an exhaustive review but rather an identification and brief discussion of the most common programs offered. There are many other creative and effective programs that are unique to institutions with specialized missions and focus. Of the programs presented, an attempt has been made to succinctly explain the purpose of the program and identify its basic components.

The scope of this study prevents a detailed explanation of each program, but it will help institutional administrators and new practitioners better understand basic alumni programs and how, when woven together, they create an effective alumni relations program. Perhaps it also will stimulate an interest in a more in-depth study of these and other alumni programs. References for further study are included in the back of the book.

ALUMNI PROGRAMS

Reunions

Fundamental to alumni programming are those activities that reconnect alumni with each other and their alma mater. The earliest and most enduring of these have been reunions and homecomings. Class reunions date back to the 1700s, and homecoming activities were initiated in the late 1800s in conjunction with intercollegiate athletic contests. "Coming home" has for alumni both emotional and practical benefits. Returning to "places of the heart" is a fundamental human desire, and one of those special places for alumni is their alma mater. The college years for most alumni were a special time in their lives and a uniquely affirming experience. It was a time of intellectual awakening, when they were exposed to new knowledge and new ideas and to individuals from different cultures and countries. They were nurtured and mentored by faculty and staff who helped prepare them for a professional career and a successful life. Meeting new friends and developing lifelong relationships were important aspects of the college experience for most students.

Exhibit 10–1 Chart of Alumni Relations: Programs and Activities

Homecoming	Alumni Education
Reunions	Community Service
Clubs Chapters Branches	Career Assistance
Alumni Boards	Alumni Tours
Student Advancement	Awards
Campus Constituent Groups	Alumni and Admissions
Alumni Records	Legislative Advocacy
Parents Programs	Technology Applications
Phonathons	Publications
Merchandising	Affinity Cards
Directory	Dues
Other Special Events	Other Fund Raising
Class Agents	Alumni and Athletics

Courtesy of Council for Advancement and Support of Education, Washington, DC.

Former students come back to their roots to renew old friendships, relive special moments in their lives, and meet former and current faculty and staff. They also want to view firsthand how their school is doing. One of the basic defining questions that most graduates are asked is, "Where did you go to college?" Alumni want to be proud of their institution, and they want the prestige and perceived value of their diploma to grow through the years. They seek to strengthen their ties with their alma mater, develop new relationships with institutional leaders and faculty, and ensure that current students have the same opportunities and special experiences that they had.

Reunions and homecomings also provide unique opportunities for institutional leaders and faculty to meet former students, share good-news stories, show off the campus, and cultivate long-lasting relationships that will greatly benefit the institution in future years. These events afford former students an opportunity to look back and remember and also to look to the future and reconnect. Students "enroll for life" if they are given lifelong opportunities such as reunions and homecomings to continue their affiliation with their *alma mater.*

At first, class reunions were held in conjunction with commencement exercises in the spring, and this is still a popular time for reunion meetings. Due to college convocations, however, and other ceremonial activities surrounding commencement, many alumni associations now hold reunion activities in early summer or fall, and some are held even during homecoming week to help boost attendance. Many classes, especially at small private schools, hold reunions every 5 years; other institutions sponsor only 5-year, 10-year, 25-year, and 50-year class reunions. Many alumni associations host special reunions every year for all alumni who graduated more than 50 years ago.

Many smaller institutions have maintained strong class reunion programs, as have some larger institutions. However, as enrollment at many large public universities has grown to more than 30,000 or 40,000, the concept of strong class identity and loyalty has weakened, and many two-year and nontraditional schools as well have never developed a sense of class unity and identity. Many of these institutions have developed reunion programs around other strong student affiliations such as living groups, honorary organizations, academic units, athletic teams, and other highly visible student groups. Some reunions are developed around eras that impacted the campus, such as World War II, the Vietnam War, and the civil rights movement. Institutions that have changed missions (for example, from a private military school to a public educational institution or from a two-year community college to a university) hold reunions recognizing students of different institutional eras. Most alumni were affiliated with organizations or groups that were special to them during their undergraduate experience. Examples would be living groups, student clubs, academic units, leadership organizations, and ethnic groups. There usually is strong interest among these groups in getting together, and reunions of these groups are often referred to as constituent reunions. The purpose of class, constituent, and other reunions is basically the same, to bring back to campus former students who share common experiences and relationships with their institution.

Detailed planning and constant follow-up during implementation are essential to effective reunions. Planning should begin one to two years before the reunion, and prospective reunion attendees should receive reunion dates and general information several months in advance, followed soon after by a detailed schedule of reunion activities and registration information. Having adequate estimates of attendance well in advance of the reunion aids immensely in the scheduling of facilities and careful planning of other reunion needs, including food preparation. A key component of a successful reunion is strong leadership participation by members of the reunion group. Volunteer leaders should be selected who are representative of their reunion group and who will give enthusiastically of their time and talents. These volunteer leaders should be fully engaged in planning and implementing reunion events and have a strong sense of ownership. The mind-set should be that the staff is helping alumni with their reunion. The most important factor to ensure good attendance is telephone calls made by alumni volunteers to members of their reunion group. Personal contact between members of the reunion class or constituent group is the most effective way to increase excitement and enhance attendance. It is important to prospective attendees to know that the reunion will be well attended and that they will be reunited with a large number of their former friends and classmates.

Reunion events and activities vary widely across North America, depending on size of school, institutional mission, and history and traditions. The selection of appropriate activities, integration with campus events and interaction with current students, and faculty and administration are essential to achieving reunion goals. Typical reunion activities include opportunities for alumni to interact with one another, such as receptions and banquets. Scheduling informal, less-structured activities ensures that reunion participants can visit and reminisce. A lounge or other meeting place designated as the memorabilia room helps facilitate this, and yearbooks, historical photographs, and displays, banners, and other memorabilia provide an appropriate atmosphere. Longtime and emeritus faculty and staff interactions with reunion attendees add to the effectiveness of these informal gatherings. Campus tours are usually of great interest to reunion participants and should include buildings that their group will relate to, as well as new facilities. Tours help to evoke powerful memories for reunion members as well as to instill pride in the continuing achievements of their alma mater. Presentations by faculty and administration on current achievements and future directions of the institution help further strengthen the bonds of alumni. Involvement of students in reunion activities and their interaction with alumni are important elements in reunion programming. Former students want to know what current students are like and how they view and value the institution.

Class Gifts

An important component of reunions at many institutions, class gifts may be managed by the alumni association or through the development office in coordination with the alumni office. A growing trend in reunion programming is the inclusion of educational lectures and presentations on topics of interest to reunion participants. These can be presented by faculty, alumni, or guest speakers. Topics include social issues, economic and political trends, the future of higher education, and other subjects of interest to reunion attendees. The reunion organizational committee can help select appropriate and interesting topics. Many alumni associations include planned-giving presentations, especially to older reunion groups. Such programs are usually presented by institutional development officers.

Homecoming

At many institutions in the early 1900s, homecoming began to compete in popularity with class reunions. Interest in homecomings paralleled the rise in popularity of intercollegiate athletics, especially football, on the campuses of colleges and universities. As attendance at football games increased and more alumni began returning to their alma mater on football-game weekends, alumni associations began to host special events and activities for them. Gradually, these activities became more formalized, and associations began to focus their efforts on one football-game weekend, designated "homecoming," and this tradition continues on most college and university campuses that have intercollegiate athletics programs.

Today, many schools that no longer compete in intercollegiate athletics as well as schools that have never had athletics programs have successful homecomings that incorporate the concept and components of traditional homecomings. Also, many homecomings have expanded from a weekend to a full week. Traditional homecoming activities include a parade, decorations on the lawns of fraternity and sorority houses and residence halls, painting of windows of commercial establishments throughout the community, a pep rally in support of the team, and the crowning of homecoming royalty. Many other activities are successfully incorporated into homecoming by institutions across the country. Some schools host reunions in conjunction with homecoming and others organize alumni education seminars, sponsor outstanding speakers, and recognize outstanding alumni at awards ceremonies. The breadth and diversity of homecoming activities is limited only by the creativity of alumni and university officials who develop and implement them.

Successful homecomings will bring large numbers of alumni back to the campus and help reconnect them with the institution and with one another. Ideally, homecoming activities should provide alumni with opportunities to interact with faculty, administrators, and current students and to learn about positive developments at their school—new learning and research facilities, faculty and student achievements, and academic programs. They should help alumni renew old friendships and develop new relationships with other alumni, new faculty, and university administrators. Ultimately, the institution is the benefactor of the positive feelings and closer ties developed by alumni for their alma mater.

Involvement of students is an important factor in a successful homecoming. Students seek opportunities to interact with alumni, and homecoming provides an excellent forum for students to meet former students. Involving students in leadership roles helps them better understand the purpose and importance of homecoming and instills a sense of pride that carries over into their alumni experience. Another practical benefit of involving students is the additional enthusiasm and volunteer manpower that they bring. At many institutions, homecoming events would have to be scaled back if students were not involved in building house decorations, floats, and signs, and if they were not involved in important leadership and decision-making roles.

In addition to reunions and homecoming, special events can include awards programs, founders-day activities, inaugurals, commencements, anniversary celebrations, and fund raising events. The list is nearly limitless. The key to all special events is planning and execution, and as they reflect on the quality of the institution and its alumni, failure is not an option.

Alumni Recognition and Awards

Recognition may include alumni, students, faculty, staff, and friends. Alumni awards most often recognize alumni who have made noteworthy contributions to humanity, have achieved significance in their professional lives, and have rendered valuable service to the institution through a long-term commitment of their time, talents, and personal resources. Common award titles include Alumni Hall of Fame, Distinguished Alumni, Outstanding Alumni, Alumni Service, Distinguished Service, Community Service, and Young Alumni.

Recognition of outstanding alumni is important and valuable to the institution and the alumni association for many reasons. Public recognition of successful and influential alumni demonstrates to the world the quality of individuals who graduate from the school and in turn speaks to the quality of the institution, including its students, faculty, and staff. Award recognition also publicly acknowledges recipients who have given so freely of their talents and resources and serves as an incentive for other alumni who might aspire to dedicated service to their alma mater and society. Award recognition affirms individuals and their need to be appreciated and respected. Lifting up the contributions of alumni to their alma mater helps emphasize to the university community the value and significance of alumni to the long-term success of the institution. Recognition of alumni association volunteers, especially chapter leaders, is important in rewarding, retaining, and attracting effective volunteers, and it is a component of most alumni award programs.

Many alumni relate the quality of their educational experiences to the quality of classroom instruction, academic advising, and faculty relationships that they enjoyed as students, and they want students who follow them to have these same academic experiences. To encourage excellence in teaching and advising, many alumni associations recognize teachers and advisors in their awards program. Awards often include stipends to enhance their perceived value and prestige on campus, and recipients are recognized at public ceremonies and in alumni publications.

Recognition of outstanding students is another important alumni association awards program. Student awards recognize academic and leadership contributions of top students and lift them up as examples of outstanding students who attend the institution, and they encourage other students to strive to achieve these same levels of excellence. Public recognition of outstanding students also helps convince prospective students of the quality of the student body at the institution. Relationships developed with recipients of student awards help bond them to the alumni association and prepare them for an active role in the association following graduation.

There are many different forums for effective alumni awards presentations. Some awards, like hall of fame, are best observed formally with a black-tie-optional dinner in a banquet setting. Others will be presented in conjunction with an athletic event during pre-game or half-time ceremonies, and some may be presented at a board of directors meeting or other university or alumni activity. Award functions are usually held on campus, but off-campus sites can be equally effective, especially in large alumni-populated centers. The more prestigious the award, the more important it is to produce a first-class event. An event that recognizes excellence should reflect excellence in its planning and execution. Integrity in the selection process is essential to an effective, long-term award program, and integrity begins with well-defined criteria and highly respected members of the selection committee. Award recipients should meet and exceed all award criteria and be generally deemed worthy of selection by peers, other nominees, and the university community.

A successful awards program will also include detailed planning of the presentation event; development of the invitation list; communication with recipients, alumni, and university officials; printing of invitations and programs; publicity; and selection and preparation of event facilities. The cliché "bad things just happen, good things are planned" is especially true of awards events. The rewards are worth the effort; quality awards events create a positive and powerful image for the alumni association and the institution.

Resolutions of appreciation by the alumni association board of directors are an effective way to recognize the accomplishments and contributions of individuals and organizations. Retirement of university faculty and staff as well as outstanding accomplishments of alumni leaders, athletic teams, and other groups can effectively be recognized in this manner. Resolutions by the alumni association help point out and publicize excellence of the institution in all forms.

An important goal of all alumni relations programming is to provide networks for alumni to interact with one another and with their alma mater. Alumni chapters (sometimes referred to as clubs or, in Canada, as branches) have for more than a century provided a basic organizational structure for off-campus alumni activities. Traditionally, chapters have been organized in generally well-defined geographic areas such as a community, country, or other specific region. More recently the concept of a chapter has been expanded to include groups clustered around common interests, "virtual" chapters communicating via the Internet, "corporate" chapters of alumni working within a large downtown corporate office building, and even international chapters. Whatever the structure, the purpose has remained the same: chapters provide opportunities for alumni to communicate with one another and their alma mater and a forum to organize activities benefiting alumni and their institution.

Alumni Chapters

Providing visibility and a presence beyond the campus, alumni chapters are important advocacy groups for the institution. They help recruit students, raise money for local student scholarships, support the institution's general fund raising campaign, provide a forum for institutional speakers, disseminate institutional materials, initiate local publicity for the institution through advertising and media coverage, help promote the institution's legislative agenda through interaction with area legislators, engage in community service projects that promote the image of the institution, and generally support the interests of the institution with resources and activities beyond what the school can provide.

Chapters also benefit the alumni association by identifying and developing leaders for other important programs of the association, including future alumni association board members. Alumni, through their chapter activities, help update alumni biographical records, secure new members, provide direct feedback on how the university is perceived, and offer suggestions for effective alumni programming in their areas. Chapters also provide a forum for parents of students, nonalumni athletic boosters, and other friends to participate in activities of the institution. In addition to services provided for the institution and alumni association, chapter activities provide opportunities for social interaction among alumni. Many chapters offer business mixers for young professionals, family-style picnics, athletic watch parties, services for alumni who relocate to the area, career assistance, alumni education programs, newsletters to local alumni, and many more activities.

Organization and management of alumni chapters varies among alumni associations and can be well defined or loosely organized. Chapter leadership should include at a minimum a president, president-elect, secretary-treasurer, and a board of directors to ensure sufficient leadership to conduct the activities of the chapter. Continuity of strong leadership is key to the long-term effectiveness of the chapter. The alumni association staff should be identifying and developing potential leaders for the chapter while ensuring that leadership is diverse and inclusive. Many associations have annual training conferences for chapter officers, especially for incoming presidents. Recognition of "honor chapter" status for chapters that meet established criteria and recognition of outstanding chapter leadership also are important in maintaining a quality chapter program. Many associations have chapter manuals that outline expectations and give directions to officers and board members. Adequate financing is important to the effectiveness of chapters, and funding from the association is critical. Chapters, however, should work to ensure that most local activities, especially social functions, are financed by activity fees or donations.

Constituent Groups

In recent years, programming for groups of alumni who have special relational interests with their alma mater has become more prevalent. Many alumni identify strongly with special aspects of their educational experience and seek relationships with other alumni who shared these same experiences. For many it was the academic curriculum, for some it was common concerns about ethnic issues, and for others it was a living-group experience (residence hall, fraternity, sorority, off-campus) or strong affiliation with a student organization or activity. The list of constituent possibilities is nearly endless: academic departments and colleges or professional schools, ethnic groups, honorary and leadership organizations, club sports and intercollegiate athletics teams, living groups, special friends, parents' organizations, and other groups unique or special to the institution.

Members of alumni constituent groups are bound by strong emotional interests, and they share common educational experiences and perspectives. They are motivated by and can be engaged most effectively in activities that deal with their special interests. They serve as role models and mentors for students of their same background and interests, and they help recruit students, provide scholarships, and in other ways support them. Reunions and other activities that allow constituent groups to interact with one another and with current students and that reinforce common experiences are effective in binding them to their alma mater.

Most constituent groups are loosely affiliated and have no formal organizational structure. Constituent groups that formally organize into associations or societies have relationships with the general alumni association that vary from institution to institution. An effective alumni relations program usually includes a positive, close-working relationship between the institutional alumni association and constituent associations. It is common for a representative of the constituent association to serve on the board of the general alumni association, and sometimes these associations have a joint dues structure. A coordinating council that includes representatives of the constituent associations and the institutional association is helpful in planning and coordinating alumni activities, especially major universitywide events like homecoming.

Alumni Education

Yet another association program of service to alumni for many years, alumni education has been receiving an increased emphasis in recent years. Alumni associations present educational programs for their alumni through short-term noncredit continuing education courses, seminars, lectures, travel programs, and camps. These may be offered in conjunction with reunions, homecoming, and chapter functions. Alumni education is not intended to be a substitute for or to compete with college-credit courses or professional certification courses. Rather it builds on the understanding that education is the essence of all alumni programming and what all alumni hold in common, beginning with their undergraduate experience. Education is lifelong and it is life sustaining, intellectually. The Association of Yale Alumni insists that in keeping with its mission every program offered or contemplated by the association must have an educational component or be offered in an educational context.

Strategic campus alliances are important to alumni education programs. Cooperative relationships and sharing of resources with the college extension unit, study-abroad office, continuing-education office, and other campus units can help jump-start new alumni education programs and sustain existing ones. Working with these groups can help the alumni office find the right niche and develop important allies. Recruiting the right faculty is crucial to the success of alumni education offerings. In addition to academic reputation, faculty should have excellent teaching and interpersonal skills, and they must have the ability to relate to adult learners as intellectual partners.

Alumni education programs generally include seminars and noncredit courses that vary from a day to a week. Some associations, in conjunction with their institutions, have created "alumni colleges" that extend for several weeks through the summer. Faculty lectureships, as well as educational components, are often integrated into travel-abroad programs, alumni camps, homecoming, and reunion activities. The scope and depth of educational programming are bound only by the passion and vision of the organizations offering them. It is important, however, to plan and implement an alumni education program only after thoughtful self-assessment. The interests of alumni, the availability of capable faculty, and alumni association resources should be carefully considered before initiating a program.

Benefits of lifelong learning are numerous for alumni, their institution, and the alumni association. Alumni are offered opportunities for intellectual stimulation and personal development in areas outside their normal professional and educational fields. It is a convenient and cost-effective way to broaden their knowledge and pursue special interests, while they also are enjoying fellowship and interaction with other alumni. The institution benefits from the strengthening of educational bonds with alumni and, in effect, gains a new student body with special interests and abilities. Alumni education programs reconnect many alumni who are not in other ways involved with the institution and who bring unique intellectual capital to the school. The alumni association benefits from enhanced relationships with alumni and especially with faculty who, thereafter, have a different appreciation and respect for the possibilities of alumni relations programs.

Service to alumni is an integral part of the mission of any alumni association, and surveys to alumni confirm that career assistance is a frequently requested priority service. Rapidly changing technology and corporate downsizing due to increasing global competition has changed forever the landscape of the workplace. Graduates entering the work force today face the possibility of a half dozen or more career changes and the prospect of holding a number of different jobs in their professional lives. The need for career assistance is obvious and pressing, and many alumni associations have initiated services to assist their alumni in cooperation with the university placement office.

It is important to understand the limitations and potential liabilities of career assistance programs. Alumni associations are not placement offices and should be careful not to raise unreal expectations of finding jobs for alumni. The association's appropriate role is to help prepare and assist alumni in their search for career opportunities and job placement. Alumni career services most frequently offered include a resource center and a network of alumni across the country who have volunteered to assist other alumni with career information. Career services frequently offered to alumni through the resource center include counseling and assessment, résumé writing skills, and access to job lists. A professional program including the services listed above requires a commitment of significant staff and financial resources on an ongoing basis. However, alumni associations can choose to partner with the placement office and share costs or to offer a limited range of services initially. Technology plays an important role in the delivery of these services. Much of the career information is available via computers, and some schools make this information available on the Internet. Another method for offering career services to a larger number of alumni is to host career fairs, workshops, and seminars in high-alumni-population centers. Many of the services offered in the resource center can be provided at these off-campus events, and career fairs in large metropolitan areas sometimes attract more companies and potential employers than on the campus.

A unique aspect that alumni bring to career services is a grassroots network of alumni located across the country and abroad. Alumni associations through their chapters, publications, Web pages, and promotional material can identify and recruit alumni to help provide job information and assistance to other alumni who are moving into their communities. Alumni are usually asked to provide information about jobs and professional opportunities in their career fields and other general information to assist relocating alumni, such as places to live, schools, cultural opportunities, and alumni activities. Names, business, and biographical information of alumni career network volunteers are maintained in the alumni office, and with the volunteer's permission, this information also can be listed on the Internet. Alumni who are relocating should be able to contact the alumni office or local chapter or to access the Internet to find assistance.

Services rendered to alumni certainly constitute a major thrust of alumni association programming. If communications are successful and if the alumni are made to feel like partners in the association, they return invaluable services to the association and the university.

Advocacy

One of the significant contributions of alumni to their alma mater is their advocacy on behalf of higher education. Today, there is not the same degree of unqualified support for higher education that once existed. While the importance of higher education is still generally understood, citizens and their legislative representatives view investments of public resources in higher education more critically and expect measurable results from increased appropriations. Also, there are strong, competing demands for state revenue, including funding for roads, prisons, and human services. Institutions, more than ever, are looking to their alumni to help champion higher education and positively influence public opinion, and in recent years, alumni associations have become more involved in legislative and governmental relations activities to support their institutions and higher education in general. An example is the Hoosiers for Higher Education program of the Indiana University Alumni Association, which includes a network of several thousand alumni.

Alumni are powerful advocates for several reasons: they extol the importance and benefits of higher education without the appearance of being self-serving, unlike institutional representatives; they help interpret the mood and opinions of citizens and government officials to their respective institutions; and they have access to their local legislators because they are influential constituents of their districts. To maximize the effectiveness of alumni legislative advocacy, alumni associations and their institutions need to consider some fundamental issues. First, alumni advocacy efforts should be closely coordinated with the institution. Alumni associations and their institutions should jointly develop legislative priorities and agree, publicly, on major issues. The governmental relations committee of the alumni association should meet in advance of the legislative session with university officials to identify and discuss legislative priorities. Not all priorities of the institution will be easily understood or readily supported by alumni. It is important that the committee adopt only priorities on which alumni can be expected to reach consensus, and potentially divisive issues should be avoided. It is best to limit legislative priorities to only two or three major issues. Alumni volunteers have limited time, and their efforts should be directed to those issues that will reap the greatest return for the institution. Also, this allows the alumni association staff to focus their limited resources, better educate alumni on important issues, and direct their follow-up as bills move through the legislature.

In proportion to available resources, the alumni association should develop a legislative network that it can effectively manage. The institution has expectations that the legislative relations effort will be carried out in a professional and timely manner; to accomplish this, alumni must be appropriately informed and supported. A modest but effective advocacy program might target only key legislative leaders and require just a few alumni volunteers. Associations with larger staffs and resources might target all members of the legislature and involve hundreds of alumni on a year-round basis. Computer hardware and software to assemble information and generate faxes and letters will be critical if a major effort is planned.

Perhaps, most important to the success of the legislative efforts is the selection of network members, especially those expected to play major leadership roles. Alumni should be recognized leaders in their communities and, more importantly, should be in a position to influence their local senators and representatives. Ideally, they will be financial contributors and serve on the legislators' election campaign committees. A rule of thumb is that if they leave a message for their legislator, the call will be returned the same day. A small number of these individuals can be highly effective and require few financial resources. Additionally, some programs seek the involvement of larger numbers of alumni who are effective but perhaps not quite as influential with their local legislators. There are commercial vendors who provide software services that can identify alumni by legislative districts. It is important to have a clear understanding with alumni that they have the right not to advocate legislation that conflicts with personal or professional interest, but neither should they publicly advocate against alumni legislative issues.

Another component of legislative relations efforts is to have an individual at the capitol every day during the session, following up on critical legislation as it works its way through the legislature. This individual, appropriate university officials, and alumni association staff should communicate regularly, even daily, as key votes come up and other issues emerge. This information must be communicated to legislative network members in a timely manner. To maximize their effectiveness and ensure their credibility with legislators, network members must have up-to-date factual information. It is embarrassing for alumni to contact their legislators, asking support on a vote that has already been taken or to give legislators incorrect information about a bill.

Legislative activities naturally fall into two time frames: when the legislature is in session and when it is not. During the session, efforts are focused on affecting legislation. Regular communication with network members by phone calls, faxes, e-mail, and letters is important, and special action alerts on pending votes are critical. It is important to get alumni to the capitol when possible, and a day can be designated for members to travel to the capitol. For maximum visibility and impact, efforts sometimes can be coordinated with other institutions during a specially designated "higher education day." Also, alumni should be encouraged to contact their legislators, personally, when they are back home in their districts. Planned events at the capitol can include luncheons, receptions, and other meetings with legislative leaders. It is effective to have alumni in attendance along with university administrators, faculty, and students. A special effort should be made to interact, individually or as a group, with legislators who are alumni of the institution. Giving inexpensive gifts of institutional memorabilia to legislators and their staff members and secretaries who have institutional ties is an effective way to develop relationships.

Relationships with individual legislators can best be developed in the "off-season" when the legislature is not in session. The first contact should be to thank legislators who supported higher education legislation in the previous session. Sometimes a legislator's support for higher education conflicts with the interest of other constituents in his or her district and even might have cost that legislator some support. A sincere letter of appreciation is a good start toward future support. Personal contacts with legislators between sessions provide an excellent opportunity to share in-depth information on complex higher education issues and "pre-sell" initiatives that likely will be introduced in the upcoming legislative session. An effective legislative relations program will include contacts with legislators year-round, including one-on-one meetings, regional meetings with key legislators, and personal letters. Also, when the university president makes community visits, it is advisable to include meetings with local legislators.

Relationships developed by members of the legislative network can be used effectively for other governmental relations activities, as well. Alumni can work with appropriate institutional representatives on federal government issues and initiatives, including federal appropriations and grants. Alumni also can play a critical role in helping pass, or defeat, state questions affecting higher education. Appointments of individuals to institutional governing boards and state coordinating boards are critical to the future of the institution and alumni. As major stakeholders of the institution, alumni should have an influential role in recommending and helping determine appointments to these key positions. Alumni also can help fund and participate in public relations campaigns, supporting their institution and higher education.

Alumni and Admissions

Alumni also are invaluable in helping recruit students to the university. New students are the lifeblood of an institution, and perhaps no task is more important than identifying and recruiting prospective students. The quality and diversity of students help to define and sustain the reputation of the institution, and alumni volunteers play an important role in the admissions process. For alumni, helping attract outstanding students is a matter of pride and enlightened self-interest. They want students to matriculate at their alma mater who will excel and bring recognition to the institution through their honors and accomplishments, while in school and after graduation, and thus they are recruiting future alumni who will promote and perpetuate the history and traditions of the institution and help sustain its excellence. From their real-world perspective, alumni have an excellent understanding of the quality and diversity of students that will best serve the goals of the institution and successfully compete in a global society after graduation.

Alumni can be engaged in the admission process in many ways, and they are most effective when their efforts are closely coordinated with the institution. Alumni can be trained as pre-admissions counselors to visit with prospective students and parents. Small, private institutions that recruit nationally often use alumni admissions representatives in this manner. Alumni, especially those in leadership roles, can influence prospective students by sharing "personal testimony" about how their institution influenced their lives and prepared them for successful careers. Campus visits are an important factor in helping students choose a college, and alumni can help provide opportunities to bring prospective students to the campus, early and often in their high school years and even before. And, of course, scholarships are a powerful incentive for financial support and for recognition. Local scholarships funded by individual alumni, chapters, and other alumni groups often provide the additional incentive needed to attract outstanding students.

Activities for engaging alumni in admissions activities are nearly endless. Alumni volunteers help distribute information and answer questions from students and parents at college-night programs. They can work in conjunction with admissions personnel or on their own with proper training and coordination with the admissions office. Alumni are especially important resources at out-of-state student recruitment events that admissions staff often cannot attend. Many alumni associations and chapters host banquets and receptions for high school seniors and juniors and their parents. These events, focused on honor students, leadership students, minority groups, or others, might be simple backyard hamburger cookouts or elaborate banquets. Videos and materials about the institution, students from the institution (preferably hometown students), faculty and administrators who visit with students and parents, and several alumni who can share their special college experiences—these can serve to heighten interest at these events.

Alumni help present scholarships at high school awards assemblies, and they organize awards receptions for recipients of local alumni scholarships to draw attention in the community to the academic excellence of their institution. They also recognize outstanding high school counselors, and they host receptions and luncheons for the counseling staff to express appreciation and to recognize their contributions to college-bound students. These types of activities help build goodwill and develop important local contacts for the institution. And, as mentioned earlier, local alumni bring students to the campus, often in conjunction with special events on the campus. Alumni work with school officials to develop and host local or regional seminars for parents of college-bound students to discuss federal and state financial-aid programs and other options for financing a college education for their children.

Potentially, the most powerful influence that alumni can exert in admissions activities is with their sons and daughters, grandsons and granddaughters, and those of other alumni. Alumni "legacies" have a higher affinity to and knowledge of the institution than any other group of prospective students. Often, they have been on the campus several times and have heard their parents tell about positive experiences at the institution. A key factor in recruiting legacies is, of course, identifying them, and the alumni association plays a key role. Through surveys, alumni publications, and other means, the alumni association can gather information from alumni about their children that can then be loaded on the computerized alumni database. Mailings to legacies, even as early as junior high, are important in letting them and their parents know that the association and the institution have a special interest in them. There are many ways to express this special interest. The Former Students Association even mails bibs with Texas A&M logos on them to babies of former students, and these children receive other A&M

memorabilia and information as they progress through school toward high school graduation. These mailings are especially effective when coordinated with the admissions office. The admissions office can help prepare materials appropriate for the age of the prospective student, and the alumni office can share information with admissions that can be included in their prospective student database for additional follow-up.

Traditionally, alumni associations initiated relationships with students following their graduation, and left student relations during all the college years to the student affairs office and other campus offices. The first contact that most recent graduates had with the alumni office was a letter or phone call asking for money for the annual fund or an alumni association membership. Today, most alumni associations understand the need to connect with future alumni while they are still on campus and subscribe to the philosophy that "students enroll for life" at their institution. Students are viewed as "alumni-in-residence," and alumni associations seek relationships with students that will enhance the quality of their undergraduate experience and create an awareness of their future role as alumni. Alumni associations understand that quality educational experiences and a positive perception of the association will enhance their identification with the institution and their participation in the alumni association as former students. Roy Vaughan, executive director emeritus of the University of Texas Ex Students Association, once noted that an alumni association can send all the junk mail it wants to alumni, but they will not respond if they did not have a good undergraduate experience.[5]

Alumni associations seek to identify with students in a positive manner as soon as possible, sometimes even before classes begin. The Texas A&M Former Students Association provides a three-day "fish camp" experience for incoming freshman as part of their summer enrollment process. While at camp they learn about the history of A&M and its Aggies traditions, and they prepare for their future roles as students and former students. Some alumni associations provide staff and alumni volunteers to help new students and their parents move into their living units, participate in freshman orientation programs, and provide tours for new students. Activities vary, but the key is to identify with students early in their college experience in a manner that will help create and sustain a positive image of the association.

Another phase in developing relationships with future alumni is the transition from students to alumni. Many associations host a "senior send-off" for graduating seniors, featuring food and entertainment, and provide them with information about alumni chapters where they will be locating and other services that the association provides, such as insurance, credit cards, long-distance service, Internet access, and career assistance. The senior send-off offers the association an opportunity to congratulate graduates, welcome them into the association, and acquaint them with services and programs of the association. In addition, some alumni offices host receptions for graduates and their families in conjunction with university commencement activities and college convocations.

Student Advancement

Perhaps the most important initiative in developing student relations is the student advancement program. Organized under the umbrella of the alumni association, these student alumni associations provide students an opportunity to learn more about the history and traditions of the institution, to become involved in alumni relations programming, and to learn more about the purpose and programs of the association. Student alumni leaders become future alumni leaders, who are more likely to invest their time and resources in support of the institution and the association. The two basic organizational models for organizing student advancement associations are the smaller selective organization, in which membership is achieved through selective criteria, and the larger association, which is open to all students. There are advantages to both organizational models, and some associations sponsor both. The smaller association is usually limited to fewer than one hundred students and is composed of the top leadership students on the campus. Association staff can invest more time and resources in developing relationships with key student leaders that will extend beyond their college years. Larger student advancement associations, which sometimes have several hundred members, have the obvious benefit of involving more students in alumni relations programs and preparing them for their future roles as alumni.

Student advancement programs are as diverse as the institutions they represent. A sampling of activities includes conducting campus tours for prospective students, speaking at campus and off-campus university events, and planning and implementing alumni association-sponsored events, such as homecoming and reunions. Students also can help with freshman orientation activities and senior send-off activities, and they can sponsor leadership conferences for high school students.

There are several key components to a successful, ongoing student advancement program. Adequate resources, including staff support, budget, and office space, should be provided and a long-term commitment made to ensure quality and continuity of programming. As the reputation of the program grows, so will the quality of students it attracts. Students seek opportunities to interact and network with successful alumni, and the alumni association can help facilitate this interaction. Students should be invited to participate in socials, board meetings, and other key activities to develop mentoring relationships between alumni leaders and student leaders. When student advancement leaders graduate, the association should maintain close relationships with these individuals and provide leadership opportunities for them in the association.

COMMUNITY SERVICE

An increasing number of alumni associations are becoming involved in community service projects and other programs of service to society. Graduates of institutions of higher education constitute a corps of educated, motivated individuals who can provide leadership for the betterment of society. Participation in programs of service appeals to the altruistic nature of alumni and helps promote pride in their alma mater and fellow alumni. Many alumni who do not participate in other association programs are attracted to community service activities. In addition to benefiting society, these activities, collectively undertaken in the name of the institution, provide positive publicity for local alumni and their school. Most service projects are initiated at the community level and provide excellent opportunities for chapter participation and for alumni to develop stronger relationships with one another and with the greater community in which they reside. Tangible benefits accrue to alumni, the institution they represent, and the community and individuals they serve.

There are many opportunities for service; and alumni engage in a broad spectrum of activities, including literacy programs, academic tutoring, mentoring, work with inner city youth, adopt-a-school programs, Habitat for Humanity, community clean-up campaigns, work with the physically and mentally challenged, crisis intervention for women and families, and counseling and other professional services for the homeless and others living in poverty. The list of opportunities is nearly endless, and perhaps the most appropriate and effective programs are those that include an educational component and utilize the skills and specialized knowledge of university-trained graduates. Service components also can be built into alumni programs conducted on the campus, such as homecoming, reunions, and alumni education. The Notre Dame University Alumni Association and the Duke University Alumni Association are excellent examples of associations that build service components into their regular alumni programming. Alumni community service is a quality program that fits well within an alumni relations program and flows naturally from the interests and skills of alumni. However, community service activities should complement other alumni programs and be appropriately balanced with programs of service to the institution and alumni.

COMMUNICATIONS

Communications as one of the professional areas of institutional advancement is covered in Chapters 9, 13, and 18, but it is appropriate and helpful to discuss the philosophy and practice of alumni communications as a component of the alumni relations program. Timely and effective communication affects every program of the alumni association, and the public image of an association is, in large measure, determined by the quality of its publications and printed materials. Most alumni association mission and goal statements include references to communicating with alumni and to providing networks for alumni to interact with their alma mater and with one another. Communicating with alumni can take many forms including mailers, publications, brochures, phone calls, faxes, media releases, radio spots, electronic mail, Internet information, video and computer presentations, meetings, speakers, and personal conversation.

The primary purposes of alumni communications are to inform alumni about their alma mater, to provide information about programs of their association, and to allow alumni opportunities to communicate with one another and their alma mater. Alumni magazines and tabloids are frequently the primary form of communication with alumni. Alumni publications are often published and funded solely by the association, but many associations publish their magazines and tabloids in cooperation with the institution. Whether alumni publications are published independently or in partnership with the institution, there are important guiding principles to be observed, and it is essential to remember for whom the publications are printed. The readers peering over the editor's shoulder are the alumni. Alumni want to hear good-news stories and learn about the success of the institution and its faculty and students, but publications should not become a mouthpiece for their institution, providing only happy news and predigested information presenting the university's perspective. Alumni readership surveys consistently confirm that class notes are the most widely read section of the publication. Alumni want to read about other alumni and their favorite faculty. Potentially controversial campus issues should be included and covered in a balanced and professional manner. Alumni want to be and should be informed about what is happening on their campus. Alumni publications need to include information about alumni activities and alumni association programs and also information about chapter and constituent group activities, association initiatives, and alumni recognition.

Many membership-based alumni organizations mail their alumni magazine only to dues-paying members, and while it is necessary to offer "for members only" benefits, it is important to connect all alumni to the institution. Many associations send one or more issues of the alumni magazine or a less expensive (but not necessarily less expansive) tabloid to all members, and other associations place their publications on the World Wide Web. Many alumni associations develop an annual comprehensive plan to coordinate all alumni communications and programs. Preplanning helps maximize limited financial resources and helps enhance effectiveness of communications activities.

A recent development in communications is strategic planning for the application of technology in support of alumni programs, and some associations even have developed a "vision statement for technology." Exploding technology is exponentially expanding communications possibilities, and in the future, a major portion of communications with alumni will be electronically driven and delivered. On-line alumni directories and publications, information on alumni programs, chat groups, conferences, "virtual" chapters, and reunions are just a few of the applications currently being used to communicate with alumni.

ALUMNI RECORDS

It all begins with a record! Nearly every program and activity of the alumni association requires access to information maintained in the alumni record system. On-line access to accurate, comprehensive alumni records is essential to carrying out the goals and objectives of an alumni relations program, and it is imperative that the alumni office, independently or in partnership with the institution and development office, develop and manage alumni records. An indication of the growing importance of computer records is the emerging professional specialization in institutional advancement called "advancement services." Individuals in this field are experts in database management, including development of hardware and software systems, maintenance of computer records, and manipulation and retrieval of data to serve advancement professionals. Advancement services professionals may be located in alumni and development offices or in a centralized office that serves all institutional advancement units.

Basic biographical information to be managed for the alumni relations program includes addresses and phone numbers, information about spouse and children, date of graduation, academic information, undergraduate activities, record of alumni leadership and program participation, and other specialized information. It is essential that computer software contain enough fields to allow for the inclusion and retrieval of a large amount of diverse data. Planning needs to provide for unexpected future needs by including unused fields in the software program. For example, how many alumni organizations foresaw a few years ago the need for fax numbers and e-mail addresses? If alumni are not loaded into the system by social security number, it is important to include that information, even though this is an understandably sensitive issue with some individuals. Use of social security numbers is perhaps the most common and effective method for finding lost alumni and updating computer records information. Other important information to include and manage is membership records and gift information, if the association manages an annual fund.

Biographical and gift records of alumni contain personal and sensitive information that must be handled with strict confidentiality. Policies and procedures for handling and releasing biographical and donor information should be established and strictly adhered to. Also, it is important to properly train and limit the number of individuals who will be updating information on the system. It is crucial to the effective management of alumni records to have only one professionally maintained system. Horror stories resulting from out-of-date information on "shadow systems" abound. Irreparable damage results when "Mr. and Mrs. Smith" receive a letter months or years after they are divorced or one of them is deceased.

There is no perfect alumni records system or any one best software program on the market, and computer records systems are as diverse as the alumni offices that use them. Three basic options are available to any alumni office seeking to develop or convert to a new system: write an in-house program, purchase a software program from a vendor and use it as is, or purchase a basic program and customize. The third is perhaps the most common and practical. It is important to coordinate and communicate with the institution and other advancement units when developing a computer records system. When purchasing a system, the alumni office needs to factor in costs in addition to the purchase of hardware and software, including conversion of data to the new system, additional staff or a consultant, ongoing maintenance, software customization, and system upgrades. A planning reminder: it usually takes at least twice as long to convert data as originally projected. Office management needs to schedule accordingly for projected activities that depend on the functionality of the new system. Another crucial planning decision is the implementation of a "distributed system," with functionality at the personal computer (PC) laptop level or a mainframe system. Computer records systems driven by a PC environment are the most likely model for the future. And, finally, no system will be able to serve all the current or future needs of any one alumni office. There are many vendors that provide specialized software to help retrieve and manipulate data from the records system for specific needs. Demographic and psychographic data can be produced to help "qualify" alumni for gift cultivation and solicitation, to provide names of alumni by state or federal legislative districts, and to produce other segmentation of alumni for specific purposes.

Dues

If an alumni association is to function effectively, it must, of course, have significant alumni participation, and it must be adequately funded. For alumni associations that have membership dues, revenue derived from their membership program is often the largest single source of income for their operating budget; but it is important to note that the value of a strong membership program is measured in more than monetary terms. Membership benefits usually include special mailings, including the alumni magazine, that inform members of key events and issues at their alma mater and help keep them connected with the institution and other alumni. A professionally managed membership marketing program complements institutional fund raising. The annual membership payment is often the first gift that alumni make to their institution, and it is the first step in establishing a philanthropic relationship between alumni and their school. Studies have shown that alumni association members are more likely than nonmembers to donate and make larger gifts to the development foundation. Also, alumni association members who are better informed about their school are more likely to be active on behalf of the institution, giving more freely of their time and talents. Another compelling reason for a strong membership program is that an alumni association with a large number of members, sometimes approaching or exceeding one third of the alumni base, can speak more credibly as the voice of alumni and more legitimately act on their behalf.

Annual membership fees generally average $30 to $40, and some associations offer joint or family memberships in addition to single memberships. Joint memberships, offered to married alumni, are higher than a single membership but less than the cost of two memberships. For example, a single membership might be $40 and a joint membership $50, $30 dollars less than if both spouses paid individually for memberships. Reduced revenue to the association is partially offset by being able to market and provide benefits for only one joint membership (one household) instead of two.

Many alumni associations have *societies*, or alumni associations of constituent groups under their umbrella, and some alumni associations rebate a portion of the annual membership to the constituent groups. These constituent societies/associations, discussed earlier in this chapter, are most often college groups, and a common rebate from a $50 membership might be $5 to the college from which that person graduated. A rebate program provides seed money for programs of a constituent organization, and although the rebate is a small percentage of the total membership fee, there are no costs to the constituent groups for membership acquisition or management of alumni computer records. With this kind of arrangement, alumni can join and receive benefits from two alumni organizations for only one membership fee and not have to worry about which alumni membership they may or may not have paid. The alumni association and the university need not account for or explain to alumni such multiple, alumni membership programs.

Memberships

Marketing of memberships is most commonly through direct mail, telemarketing, and chapter membership drives. Marketing efforts are directed to two major groups of alumni: potential new members and renewing annual members. However, many alumni associations provide special membership opportunities for parents of students, faculty and staff, athletic boosters, and other friends of the institution who are not alumni. In some instances, reduced memberships are offered to students, especially seniors. The most powerful incentive for most individuals to pay membership dues is to better the institution and support alumni association programs. Marketing efforts that explain how membership revenue will help accomplish these goals (specific examples are best) generally will be successful, especially with older alumni. However, benefits offered only to dues-paying members are influential in acquiring and retaining many alumni memberships, especially for younger alumni. Many associations, like the University of Kansas Alumni Association, have a "for-members-only" philosophy. They stress the importance of special benefits to dues-paying members and market this concept aggressively and effectively. Important benefits are the opportunities to participate in alumni-sponsored events and to purchase merchandise offerings at a lesser cost than nonmembers. Another key incentive is to offer exclusive services to members only. These offerings might include merchant discounts at business establishments, rate discounts on rental cars and hotels, the use of designated university facilities and services, and special privileges and services offered by the alumni association.

Marketing nonmembers usually is staff intensive and expensive. The day is gone for most associations when they can send out a generic membership mailer and expect a good return. And, what is a good return? According to Dan Heinlen, president of The Ohio State University Alumni Association, any membership mailer that pays for itself is a partial success because of potential membership renewal every year thereafter. A one and one-half to two percent return on a large general mailer is acceptable, but specially designed, targeted mailing can significantly increase the percentage of return. Direct-mail marketing expertise is essential to an effective membership marketing program. An alumni association can hire a marketing director with experience in direct-mail marketing or it can engage an outside consultant. Knowledge of geographic, gender, cultural, ethnic, and generational characteristics is important when targeting alumni populations, and content and design of mailers are also critical.

As important as acquisition of new members is, the key to sustained membership growth is the renewal of a large percentage of annual memberships every year. Renewal rates of 75 percent to 85 percent are good, and rates above 85 percent are excellent; but even with these renewal percentages, alumni associations must add several thousand new members each year just to sustain the membership level of the previous year. Low retention of members makes it very difficult to increase overall membership. Persistence is important, and many associations mail as many as three to five notices to renewing members. Some associations mail renewal notices to all members at one designated time during the year, but most associations mail renewals on the anniversary of each member's initial joining. Advantages of the latter are that mailing costs and manpower requirements are spread over 12 months, and cash flow from membership revenue is more evenly distributed throughout the year. Each renewal notice (first through the last) should have a slightly different appeal, and it is helpful to experiment with the content and design of notices, as well as who makes the appeal. Often a highly visible and admired alumnus or alumna or popular faculty member can help enhance the response. When experimenting with a new approach, it is sometimes best to test it on a small sample of alumni and compare it with results from the usual solicitations.

Membership telemarketing is often effective, especially in conjunction with renewal mailers and with alumni who have dropped their membership in the last one to three years, but telemarketing does have its drawbacks. Many individuals resent being contacted at home, even by well-intentioned calls from their alumni association. Also, mail renewals the following year from memberships that were acquired from telemarketing may drop to 50 percent or less, and of course, the cost of acquiring membership by phone is usually higher than by mail. To minimize cost and personalize phone contacts, many associations use student callers. This approach is often effective, but students must be carefully selected and trained. A telemarketing firm often can achieve better results but at a higher cost. Chapter membership drives can be very effective and have the added benefit of involving alumni in an important alumni association activity that is a source of pride to the participants. Alumni can share, personally, their enthusiasm about the importance and benefits of membership, especially at the local level. It is important for alumni associations to have graduated, long-term membership goals and to understand that some of the most successful alumni membership programs reach only one fourth to one third of their addressable alumni base. But, for reasons mentioned earlier, the benefits are well worth the effort.

Many alumni associations offer life memberships in addition to their annual membership program. The purpose of the life membership program should be to create a permanent endowment that will generate earnings income in perpetuity to help underwrite the alumni relations program. Life membership fees should be high enough to produce sufficient endowment earnings to service the cost of the membership (e.g., for mailings and record maintenance) and provide income for the operations budget, with sufficient remaining revenue to reinvest in the endowment to ensure real growth, with inflation factored in. For these reasons, most life-membership dues are considerably higher than annual dues and range from a few hundred dollars to more than $1,000.

Life memberships are beneficial to alumni because those members do not have to pay dues every year, and yet, their life membership gifts will continue to provide revenue, annually, for the association beyond the giver's lifetime. And members can expect to pay less for a life membership than for annual dues over their lifetime. The association benefits because it does not have to expend revenue and staff resources every year to renew life memberships. Life endowment fund earnings provide a reliable, secure source of annual operating revenue, providing long-term financial stability for the association.

FUND RAISING

Another good benefit of a life-membership program is that it helps identify alumni who feel strongly about their association and are willing to commit financial resources. These special friends can be called on in the future to support special opportunities and needs of the association. Some associations have a "sustaining life membership program" that offers life members an opportunity to contribute annually to the life endowment fund or to specially designated projects identified by the association. Life membership endowments can positively affect the financial viability of the alumni association for the long term, but only if important, immutable principles are observed. The association should never invade the corpus of the endowment, spending only the earnings; a portion of the earnings should be reinvested in the endowment every year; and endowment funds should be professionally managed with an investment strategy that will ensure long-term growth of the fund, in addition to providing earnings. And, finally, the life membership fee should be increased periodically to compensate for inflation and reduced earning power of money over time.

Ross Perot during his campaign for the presidency in 1992 compared some not-too-well-kept government secrets to the crazy aunt in the attic that family members pretend not to know about. Alumni fund raising, in some respects, is like the crazy aunt. In well-intentioned efforts to distinguish between the missions of alumni and development offices, individuals sometimes refer to development officers as "fund raisers" and to alumni relations professionals as "friend raisers." The friend raiser description is certainly true, but only partially so. Alumni officers raise friends, but they also recruit students, influence important legislation, help create a positive public image for the institution, publish periodicals, develop alumni leaders, implement extensive alumni education programs, manage multimillion dollar associations, and raise money. In fact, many alumni associations run the institution's annual fund or the alumni association's annual fund, raise money to fund alumni operations endowments, oversee class reunion gifts programs, raise funds for alumni scholarships, and conduct multiyear campaigns to build alumni centers.

The central issue is to determine how to best coordinate alumni fund raising with the development office's fund raising and to complement those efforts. The institution's annual fund can be managed effectively in either the development office or the alumni office, as clearly demonstrated at colleges and universities throughout the United States and Canada. Today, assignment of annual fund management at individual institutions is more a result of tradition or chance than form and function. The rationale for alumni office oversight is compelling. Alumni professionals have close personal relationships and frequent contacts with large numbers of alumni, and the alumni association has in place a strong volunteer leadership team, many of whom already participate in alumni fund raising activities. The cost of raising annual gifts, on a cost-to-return basis, is much higher than for major gifts, and using alumni professionals and a highly developed organization of alumni volunteers already in place helps minimize the cost of raising annual funds. Relieved of annual fund responsibilities, development officers can concentrate on cultivating and securing major gifts and planned giving and on organizing complex multiyear comprehensive campaigns on behalf of the institution.

A close working relationship between the alumni and development offices is important to the successful fund raising efforts of both groups. Perhaps the strongest catalyst for cooperation is the alumni and development professionals who understand the independent and synergistic relationship of both organizations. In this environment, it is common to find alumni and development volunteers serving on each other's boards and staffs that frequently interact. Many alumni associations have development officers assigned to their staffs who are fully or partially paid by the development office to help lend fund raising expertise and coordinate prospect cultivation and donor solicitation. Many associations at public institutions deposit gift income in development foundation accounts to ensure that gifts are properly receipted and acknowledged. This is easily facilitated when both organizations share and jointly manage a common database.

Management of the annual fund is thoroughly covered in another section of this book, and the principles are similar, whether the annual fund campaign is organized and run out of the development office or the alumni office. Class gift programs, traditionally associated with alumni offices, also have been previously discussed. Two major gift programs of alumni associations should be noted here. Many associations have long-range plans to develop endowments of sufficient size to produce earnings that will provide a large percentage of the annual operations revenue. These associations consider it an obligation to pass on to future generations of alumni a financially viable association that will effectively serve alumni and the institution. Operations endowments can be funded in many ways. A major campaign to jump-start or significantly enhance the endowment is important in generating a large corpus, and ongoing annual solicitations help build the fund. Many associations designate a portion of carry-over money from the previous year's operating budget to the endowment as well as a portion of revenue generated from entrepreneurial activities such as affinity programs and merchandise offerings. A second major gift program and a key to significant long-

term growth of the endowment fund is a deferred gift program. Gifts of life insurance, wills, estates, and trusts are examples of common deferred gifts that over
time can increase the endowment fund significantly.

Careful management of endowment assets is crucial to the long-term growth of
the endowment fund. The first principle is to never invade the corpus—use only
earnings from the assets. The endowment is a gift, a promise to keep to future
generations of alumni. The second principle is to achieve real growth (factoring
in inflation) of endowment funds by returning a portion of the annual earnings to
the fund. And finally, professional management of endowment assets is essential
to achieving the goals listed above. An alumni association may seek to utilize
resources for money management available on the campus or in the development
foundation, but it is probably best to engage an outside money management firm.

Fund raising for an alumni center is a unique and usually once in a lifetime
experience for an alumni association. Building an alumni center necessitates the
planning and implementation of a multiyear major capital campaign, and it is
important to seek professional advice from the development office or an outside
consultant. As in most capital campaigns, it is helpful to have commitments for a
large lead gift and several other significant gifts before publicly announcing the
campaign. A carefully written case statement and a campaign committee that
includes influential and highly visible alumni are important in helping to reach
broad consensus and involvement of alumni. Fund raising plans should include a
provision for an operations endowment fund to ensure that adequate resources are
available to maintain the center without having to reallocate money from the
operations budget.

An important contribution of the alumni office to fund raising is participation
in the institution's comprehensive campaign. Alumni association staff and volunteer leaders can provide valuable insight and support when included in the planning and development of the comprehensive campaign. The alumni association
can help translate the dreams and aspirations of alumni for their alma mater into
priorities for the campaign and help publicize these through their publications and
other communications. Alumni staff help identify prospects and make fund raising calls on individuals with whom they have built strong relationships through
the years. The final phase of a comprehensive campaign includes efforts to get as
many alumni and friends as possible to give to the campaign, regardless of the
size of the gift. Usually the campaign goal will have been reached at this stage,
and it is a time of great celebration. The chapters and network of alumni in the
field provide an excellent organizational structure to implement this final phase,
in coordination with the development foundation's campaign committee. The
comprehensive campaign also provides the alumni association an opportunity to
include major alumni project needs in the funding priorities of the campaign.

A few alumni associations are financially self-sufficient, receiving no operating funds from their institutions, and many more are only partially funded by their institutions. Most alumni relations programs engage in revenue-raising activities to help underwrite their budgets and, especially, to enhance and add new programming. Institutional revenue is often allocated directly to the alumni office, but many separately incorporated alumni associations contract to provide specific services to the university detailed in a contractual agreement. This arrangement has several positive benefits, especially at public institutions. First, it clearly delineates the services to be provided. It also provides accountability for the use of institutional funds, as services must be rendered and documented by the alumni association before it is compensated. School administrators and alumni staff can report, as needed, to alumni, taxpayers, and other stakeholders on specific cost and value of alumni programs. Finally, a contractual agreement helps highlight alumni programs of service and their importance to the institution. In addition to the university funding, many associations receive funding from the development foundation. Sometimes there is a contract, memorandum of agreement, or simply a long-standing understanding of expectations. This financial support is usually an acknowledgment of the importance of alumni association activities in helping to identify and cultivate prospective donors and to manage biographical records.

Most alumni associations have initiated entrepreneurial activities to generate additional revenue to help underwrite expanded programs and services. Merchandise marketing has been a long-time favorite revenue-raising activity of associations. The list of merchandise items offered is lengthy and includes merchandise and services as varied as tennis shoes, clothing, address labels, alumni directories, and personalized automobile license plates. Most associations do not handle orders or carry inventories but instead work with vendors who help develop a marketing piece, handle orders, and ship the product. Many alumni associations have developed policy guidelines for merchandise they market, and these include: uniqueness of the product (not generally available, especially with logos of the institution or association), quality and perceived value of a product that will reflect positively on the association, and competitive pricing. Service to alumni is as important as the revenue raised. Associations should review carefully the products they offer and the frequency of those offerings. Too much marketing can create a "mail order catalog" image of the association in the minds of alumni. Many alumni associations coordinate merchandise marketing with the university bookstore or athletics department.

Credit Cards

Affinity marketing partnerships have been highly profitable to alumni associations, in recent years. Popular affinity programs include credit card programs, long-distance telephone service, and insurance products. Royalty revenue is derived from providing the names and addresses of alumni to companies who market services to them. In addition to receiving revenue, alumni associations benefit from positive relationships with their alumni through ongoing marketing efforts, especially when these services have high perceived value. An example might be a credit card that has no annual fee or a low annual percentage rate and one that affords alumni an opportunity to show their pride with a card that has their institution's name and campus scene on it. Another example might be a major medical insurance program for recent graduates who are not able to purchase affordable medical insurance through other companies and are no longer eligible for coverage under their old student policies or their parents' policies.

Corporate Sponsorships

Some associations offer corporations the opportunity to provide sponsorships for key alumni events such as homecoming, reunions, senior send-offs, athletic event headquarters, and awards ceremonies. Event sponsorships might be priced from $1,000 to more than $10,000. Another important source of revenue is to offer sponsorship opportunities to a limited number of corporate partners, who are recognized at all alumni activities and in association publications and mailers. Selling advertising in alumni publications is another common source of revenue for alumni associations, and it is important in helping underwrite ever-increasing publication costs.

There are some caveats to keep in mind when managing an aggressive revenue-raising program. Revenue needs must be balanced against programming needs. The challenge is to generate sufficient revenue to support effective programming without sacrificing staff resources necessary to implement those programs. Many associations employ a marketing director who works primarily on entrepreneurial activities, sometimes including membership marketing. When estimating entrepreneurial income for the operating budget, it is important to figure net revenue. Salaries, marketing expenses, and possible unrelated business income taxes should be factored into the revenue-raising equation. And finally, a portion of the revenue generated should be set aside in a reserve fund or endowment to help ensure the future financial stability of the association.

In conclusion, the author would like to thank colleagues and mentors who have contributed to his understanding of and appreciation for the alumni relations profession. Special appreciation is due Paul Chewning, vice-president for professional development of CASE, for his invaluable insight and critique of this study.

In this review of the "principles and practices" of alumni relations programs, the author may have allowed some biases from his years of experience with a self-governed alumni association at a large public university to influence the discussion. If this is so, please accept his apology. It is hoped that readers will take concepts presented and modify them to help develop their own unique programs. Alumni relations is more art than science, and it is constantly evolving. It is a challenging and rewarding profession, for there is no nobler endeavor than to participate in the advancement of knowledge and the enlightenment of humankind.

NOTES

1. "The Commencement Exercises," *The College Mirror* (Stillwater, OK), September 15, 1897, 6.
2. W. Bennis, *On Becoming a Leader* (Reading, MA: Addison-Wesley, n.d.), 45.
3. Ernest T. Stewart Award Winners File, Council for Advancement and Support of Education.
4. Minutes of the President's Planning Conference, May 13, 1995, Oklahoma State University Alumni Association Office, Stillwater, Oklahoma.
5. Minutes of the Board of Directors Meeting, April 22, 1994, Oklahoma State University Alumni Association Office, Stillwater, Oklahoma.

PART III

Public Relations

CHAPTER 11

Defining Public Relations: What's in a Name?

M. Fredric Volkmann

What's in a name? That which we call a rose by any other name would smell as sweet.

> William Shakespeare
> *Romeo and Juliet,*
> act II, scene II

Defining public relations is as complicated as the number of names that are used to describe it. Some universities, hospitals, and other nonprofits use the words "public affairs" or "institutional relations," whereas others identify the public relations office by such names as "information services," "communications," "marketing," "external relations," "institutional relations," or any number of other monikers. The reason for so many different ways of identifying public relations is that its role is so varied and complex. In fact, most corporate environments have a number of different offices, each doing a portion of what a typical university public relations office handles:

- relations with the news media and crisis communications
- publications and electronic (World Wide Web) messages intended to recruit students, to raise gift dollars, to encourage other sources of revenue from governmental entities, or to generate fees for services rendered
- advertising on radio and television, and in newspapers and magazines
- internal communications for faculty, students, staff, administration, and governing boards
- marketing and market research to develop better strategies for donor relations, recruitment of traditional and nontraditional students, as well as promoting specialized services at institutions with health care programs and other ancillary revenue-producing programs

- direct-mail programs to recruit students and raise gift dollars
- institutional identity, image, and reputation
- sports information for intercollegiate athletics
- major events and speakers
- communications for community, state, and federal officials and offices
- alumni and parent communications, especially periodicals
- issues management and crisis management
- speech writing for the chief executive
- photography, videos, and CD-ROMS

On small campuses, the above functions may reside in an office of one or two persons, while in other institutions many of these functions may be discrete, relatively independent, and highly sophisticated programs intended to enhance some aspect of institutional identity or reputation. Unlike business and industry, these functions usually report to one administrator, who either reports to the chief advancement officer or to the chief executive of the academic institution.

At a few institutions additional responsibilities of the public relations office may include athletics, university-owned radio and television stations, visitor information and tourist programs, and in rarer cases, such areas as signage, telephone systems, and even advising quasi-independent student newspapers.

This lack of definition for the role of public relations probably has its grounding in the fact that colleges, universities, and independent schools were originally managed either by the faculty or by administrators who rose from within the faculty ranks to become the senior managers. At one time, they handled all of the details of student recruitment, publishing course catalogs, conducting graduation ceremonies, and even coordinating alumni activities. As it became more and more necessary for a clearer division of duties, academic institutions and their governing boards authorized the hiring of persons to take on many of the tasks that are now known as advancement areas, including the varied facets of public relations listed above. This allowed the faculty to return to what they do best, teaching, scholarship, and research, while allowing the institutions to more aggressively pursue agendas that would generate support for the educational process.

In other words, the development of the public relations structure grew out of the increasing sophistication of what have become uniquely North American educational institutions, a model that is now emulated around the world. Other nations are attempting to mimic the success that North American institutions of higher education have enjoyed in developing significant gift support, governmental subsidies and research support, endowment income, and tuition-based revenue. In fact, the growth of public relations parallels the rapid expansion of federal commitment to American higher education and academic research following World War II. Despite the lack of consistently used identifiers, academic public relations today represent a highly complex and unique series of functions.

PUBLIC RELATIONS AND REPUTATION

A common theme among academic institutions is that the school's reputation is never as strong as what really exists on the campus. Somehow, it is the responsibility of the public relations office to bring reality and perception into closer alignment. Achieving this goal is often complicated by the fact that some believe public relations "create" an image for an institution, rather than serving as a mirror that reflects that which already exists, a mirror that focuses on strengths and qualities that can be easily communicated externally and internally. However, the image of an academic institution usually results from a combination of the following:

- the strength of the indicators used to measure student quality, retention, and graduation rates
- general attitudes of faculty and staff, especially those shared with persons outside the institution
- pride and general belief in the quality of the institution by its alumni, parents of current and former students, and friends
- attitudes held by academic leaders of other educational institutions
- research and scholarship of the faculty, as measured in scholarly journals, papers presented, books published, prizes won (Nobel, Pulitzer), and memberships in national academies
- information reported in the news media, including newspapers, radio, television, magazines, and now Internet
- attitudes and perceptions held by the general public, which learns from the above sources and measurements about such areas as teaching, research, and public service
- rankings developed by several major organizations and publications, many of which are not part of the academy

Undoubtedly, there are other ways in which reputations are built, but these generally are accepted as the most important criteria for determining the reputation of an academic institution. No matter how much effort is put into public relations, each of the above-mentioned indicators ultimately will play an important role in any effort. Because so much value is placed on peer review, scholarship, and research, the focus of a public relations program is dependent on accurately and effectively presenting this information to the world outside campuses.

MISSION AND GOALS OF A TYPICAL PUBLIC RELATIONS OFFICE

The mission of a typical public relations office at a college, university, or an independent school is to position and to bring greater recognition to that institution as a local, regional, national, or international leader among institutions with which it wants to be compared. This is accomplished by communicating effectively and regularly with that institution's major constituencies, including: prospective students, parents of prospective students, alumni and other friends, current students and their parents, faculty and staff, print and electronic news media, the general public, other leading academic institutions, and those private and public agencies and governmental entities that provide funding for teaching, research, and public service.

Ideally, emphasis on all communications emanating from a campus public relations office is placed on the high quality of learning and teaching, important scholarship and research, excellence of students and faculty, and upon the services the institution provides its constituencies. Internally, such an office is responsible for keeping faculty, staff, and students informed of events, activities, and administrative actions. Furthermore, the public relations office is responsible for the management and coordination of all institutional communications related to external audiences, particularly with the news media and the general public. This basic premise encompasses much of what the mission statements of most academic public relations offices comprise.

If a mission statement is intended to provide a focused purpose for an academic public relations office, then it must be accompanied with a set of goals that further expand upon what that mission is intended to achieve. The following is a typical set of goals for an academic public relations office:

- to help put the institution's best foot forward, with emphasis on developing significantly greater visibility as a leader among institutions of its type
- to increase the effectiveness of communications, publications, and marketing activities in building understanding of and support for the institution and its work, particularly with prospective students and their parents, alumni and friends, current parents, the general public, and governmental agencies and offices
- to assist student recruitment efforts that increase inquiries, applications, acceptances, deposits, and enrollment of new students
- to support planning and produce communications for major, institutionwide fund raising initiatives
- to handle all relations with news media and with selected constituencies skillfully and professionally

- to focus on issues management with the leaders of the institution and its governing board—particularly on critical issues facing institutions of similar type and character
- to develop, market, and assess news and feature material in a way that ensures that its full media potential is realized and that it reaches as many institutional constituencies as possible
- to ensure that the institution speaks with a clear and consistent voice
- to ensure wise use of institutional resources and to avoid duplicated effort and expense

The responsibility for achieving these goals is generally assigned to a specific manager who may carry the title or equivalent terminology for vice-president or director. It is the role of this individual to embrace the mission statement and its accompanying goals and from them develop a clear set of specific objectives that must be achieved within a specified time frame—usually one year. From that list of objectives then comes specific tasks and responsibilities that are assigned to individual staff and to teams of professionals for action.

The mission statement essentially answers the simple question, "Why does the public relations office exist?" Goals essentially respond to the question, "What does the public relations office do?" Objectives answer yet a third question, "What are the ways that will be employed in achieving the public relations missions and goals?" For example, if a goal is recruiting more undergraduate students, there may be several strategies listed under that goal, such as improved direct-mail efforts, better publications, more hometown news releases to the communities where the students live, better publicizing of academic and sports activities, etc. The tasks that follow the objective of better direct mail might include specific actions, such as mailings to high school guidance counselors, to teachers, and to parents of prospective students.

PRIORITIES

No matter how much effort and support is expended in managing the public relations office through the use of mission statements and objectives, plans of action are often doomed to failure because no umbrella of protection is provided through a clear-cut set of priorities that allows the senior manager to determine which activities are of first, second, or third-level value. But without having an approved set of priorities, it is not unusual for a public relations office to be sidetracked from its basic mission and goals, especially if the staff involved are likely to "oil the squeaking wheel" first. At some institutions, one set of priorities may cover all aspects of public relations, while at large, complex offices with many divisions, the priorities may be different for the news media relations staff than for the publications office. The priorities are worked out within the staff, submitted to senior administrators, and approved as part of an overall strategy for managing the office. When such priorities are not established, public relations offices find themselves focusing more on satisfying the immediate needs of administration, faculty, and students without any consideration for the long-range external communication needs of the institution. Following is a typical set of priorities—all of which follow the needs of the chief executive—for the senior manager for a national research university:

1. national and international image: improvement in the national and international visibility, name recognition, and image of the university and its schools and programs
2. undergraduate student recruitment: support for the recruitment and admission of new undergraduates
3. alumni and development: support for alumni and development programs, including any major campaign initiatives and national advisory councils in each of the schools, international councils, and planning for a campaign
4. internal communications: development of better internal, institutionwide communications that will improve the university's overall self-image, and that will, in turn, support a better external public relations program
5. graduate and professional student recruitment: assist the schools and departments in building the effectiveness of their recruitment programs for graduate, professional, and nontraditional students
6. community relations: Support for local public relations efforts through news media, community leadership groups, campus events, publications, impact statements, etc.
7. vice chancellors and deans: Efforts on behalf of any other external public relations needs of vice chancellors and the deans not covered in the above priorities
8. departments and programs: Furtherance of the other external public relations needs of the departments, institutes, centers, and other academic, service, and research programs of the university not included above

Because these priorities may occasionally prevent the senior manager and the manager's staff from providing full assistance, every effort will be made either to refer the request to another office or to provide consultation on how the office involved can complete the project on its own.

PLANNING THE PUBLIC RELATIONS PROGRAM

Developing goals, objectives, and priorities is a step in the right direction for managing public relations, but setting up a written public relations plan is by far the most essential step.

There is no pat answer to the question of how far ahead one should plan public relations. The answer depends on the type of institution and its management style because some operate in one-, two-, and even five-year increments. Generally, the public relations office should emulate the style of the organization, but realize that plans longer than two years will probably have to be revised annually, and that five-year plans may be ill advised in today's rapidly changing world. Unfortunately, many institutions do not have overall plans. In those instances, public relations planning should operate at the one-year level, with a few long-range objectives included in the plan.

It is essential that the budgeting process be incorporated into any planning activity. Any new initiatives must be costed out, and those projects being phased out must be factored into the financial aspect of the plan.

A typical plan of action includes a list of tasks or services, some of which are ongoing responsibilities that occur year-in and year-out, while others are tasks and services that are specific to a unique timeframe. Regardless, the vast majority of public relations activities are repeated annually with only the dates and names of the participants changing. Examples of ongoing tasks are events such as opening day of school, graduation, and alumni day. Other ongoing tasks would include managing the office and the budget, regular meetings with key administrators and other "beat" responsibilities, coordinating advisory groups, enforcing institutional logotype and identity programs, holding regular meetings with the chief executive, and publishing internal and external periodicals.

Examples of new tasks or services would be unique events that do not repeat year-in and year-out, initiating a special public awareness program on behalf of a specific academic division, or submitting a proposal on a new institutional signage system. Typically, such planning documents include anywhere from 20 to 50 new tasks and between 10 and 20 ongoing responsibilities for a manager in the public relations division.

RECORDING PROGRESS IS ESSENTIAL

Going through the motions of planning in a public relations environment is incomplete unless accompanied by some method of tracking progress. Some managers do this on a monthly basis, while others report activities on a quarter- or half-year basis. The tracking of such progress, whether it's for publications, news media relations, or similar activities, can be aided through the use of computer software packages that employ tracking and spreadsheet options. For those with a low-tech perspective, this also may be done with a production board or a printed planning guide. The end goal is a tightly developed plan of action, saying who is going to be held accountable for the successful completion of all the activities and tasks. Programs may require that each staff person file a report on activities and tasks completed during the month, while others pursue this through regular reporting at staff meetings or during one-on-one meetings with supervisors. The annual plan should note which projects are incomplete from a prior year and should note how the project will be put back on track in the new year. Most important, staff should be tested and graded on ability to meet deadlines and to keep programs on schedule. Without this type of coordination, public relations offices are likely to be seen as chaotic, disorganized, and without ample justification for their existence.

Why Planning Is Important

A commonly related policy in management is known as the "golden rule." In its longer form, it says that "those who possess the gold make the rules." Taken literally, that statement usually refers to budgets and relationships that reach far beyond the business office in a typical campus setting. How many deans have wanted to start up their own public relations and publications operations? How many faculty are there who want to print their own letterheads, designed by one of their students or spouses? How many program directors are there who decide they should have their own logos that would replace the institution's official symbol?

Nothing can more quickly destroy a plan and the morale of the people managing it than a few renegades who decide teamwork, cooperation, and delegation of responsibilities to the professionals involved is unacceptable. Unfortunately, most public relations officers do not have the clout or authority to indulge in top-down management. As a result, the solution has to be negotiated or institutionwide rules must be invoked by others who are perceived to have more authority. Worse yet, many institutions do not have operating manuals, and even if they do, they do not strictly enforce rules. More often than not, faculty and staff are simply advised that public relations services are available and that they should try to use them. Failure to do so, however, rarely results in any wrist-slapping at larger institutions. At smaller ones, these rules are often enforceable where a strong administration is present. Most often, this level of clout is centered in the business office. Engaging that office in enforcing the use of businesslike behaviors can sometimes be an effective alliance for the public relations office.

Evaluation and Accountability

Among the numerous ways to evaluate programs, the simplest and most reliable is asking clients and customers to tell the public relations office how they believe it is doing. By making it a point to meet individually with internal clients to ask for their feedback, public relations officers will learn a great deal about the importance of both reality and perception. Add to that the importance of testing materials and strategies on their target audiences. This includes reporters, editors, prospective students, alumni, parents, patients of health and medical programs, and customers served by other ancillary programs.

Such attention to client and customer concerns also can result in a significantly better public relations program. For example, Washington University in St. Louis tested its video news releases with television editors, its faculty experts director with reporters, its feature service with news writers, and its alumni magazine with readers. What was learned helped to develop better services and better efforts—at less cost. The expense of such testing is only a tiny fraction of the cost expended in sending out those messages.

Another way to determine whether the program is working or not is to establish an institutional advisory group of external experts in public relations and marketing, as described in the next section. Composed of a dozen or so top corporate public relations executives, such a group works directly with the head of public relations and the institution's chief executive to advise, review, and recommend strategies and policies to improve communications. The input of these experts provides helpful information on how the institutional public relations program compares with efforts in other realms.

A common evaluation technique is to initiate an externally managed review of the public relations program. The review can be conducted by an experienced public relations professional from another campus, or a team of professionals who have expertise in communications, publications, and management.

No evaluation, no plan, nor any set of strategies can do anything more than to force an office to focus on its purpose and how it goes about achieving this purpose on behalf of the institution. Ultimately, the more important factor is the quality of the professionals and the working atmosphere in which they must operate. If the atmosphere is negative, productivity will decline. If the feeling is reactionary, then innovation will suffer. Yet, nothing has changed regarding the role of an innovator, the idea person, or the change agent who wants to improve or create a new system. The roles of leadership and individual initiative play an essential part in the successful management of institutional public relations.

CHAPTER 12

Managing Public Relations through Cooperation and Collaboration

M. Fredric Volkmann

Once upon a time there was a parent who was having a hard time getting her offspring to go to school one morning: "Nobody likes me at the school," said the reluctant one. "The professors don't and the students don't. The president wants to transfer me, the department heads hate me, the trustees would rather have me disappear, and the janitors have it in for me." "You've got to go," insisted the parent. "You're healthy. You have a lot to learn. You've got something to offer others. You are a leader. Besides, you are 39 years old. You are the public relations director and you've got to go to school today."[1]

Public relations programs have long been misunderstood and are very difficult to describe—so difficult that one wag noted that understanding what the public relations office does is like trying to "nail Jell-O® to a post." The confusion rests primarily with the emerging differences between academic institutions and the more business-oriented management strategies that have evolved in the last half of the twentieth century. Public relations began its emergence after World War II and today is a clear presence on virtually all of the approximately 3,000 colleges and universities in the United States, as well as on the campuses of many independent schools and public elementary and secondary schools. The persons who head these offices usually are professionals who previously have worked in corporate public relations, with the news media, or in other not-for-profit public relations and marketing environments. As a result, there often is a sense that the public relations office "does not understand" the nature and character of the institution that it represents. It is the purpose of this chapter to recommend ways to remedy this lack of understanding.

By establishing advisory groups for various aspects of the public relations functions at academic institutions, it is possible to develop better internal and external understanding and appreciation for the role of the public relations office, as well as to improve the quality of the effort provided by the professional staff. Externally, a public relations advisory council can be of exceptional value in assisting top management of the institution, as well as the public relations office itself, in understanding issues, strategies, and lessons learned in business and industry about solving public relations problems. Internal organizations, such as communications (or marketing) councils, can bring together the talents of the individuals already employed by the institution, and who otherwise would independently pursue their own agendas—without realizing that a collaborative effort may have profound impact and value on the outcomes the institution is seeking.

A third category of advisors deals primarily with periodicals, such as faculty-staff newspapers and university-alumni magazines. All of these are discussed in this chapter.

PUBLIC RELATIONS COUNCIL

To develop a public relations advisory body, academic institutions should draw upon friends and supporters who are professionals with extensive public relations and marketing experience. For purposes of discussion, we will label it a public relations council. Basically this is an external advisory group that works with the public relations office, with the president or equivalent officer, with the chief advancement officer, and with other key institutional officials. The public relations council usually is composed of chief public relations, marketing, and perhaps news media executives from business, industry, and the fourth estate. Such a group can provide meaningful and significant suggestions for improving planning strategies, communications efforts, and student recruitment activities. At Washington University in St. Louis, a similar advisory group has successfully:

- launched one of the largest market research projects ever attempted by an academic institution
- accomplished complete reviews of admissions materials and strategies that helped lead to a doubling of paid applications in less than four years
- suggested improvements in national and regional news visibility for the institution
- recommended a highly successful institutionwide identity and image program
- reviewed with deans of several colleges strategies to improve the visibility of their programs within the university framework

This council has "adopted" several key schools and colleges for extra promotional efforts on their behalf. Thus far, this has included a communications plan for the School of Medicine, which has now risen to be ranked as one of the five finest in the nation, according to the *U.S. News & World Report* rankings; a plan to make the business school one of the best in the nation (now ranked 17th in *U.S. News & World Report*), and to make the School of Social Work the top national leader in the field (now tied for number one in the nation in *U.S. News & World Report*).

The members are hand-picked and appointed by the chief executive from the ranks of the best in the region, and where appropriate, the nation. Three or four times a year this group convenes, joined by the chief executive, the chief advancement officer, and the head of the PR program, as well as a representative from any area under study and advisement. Also attending are any professional staff who may have to provide reports and information during the course of the meeting. The public relations council is purely advisory in nature and has no decision-making capability at the institution. Top institutional managers learn more about the strategies employed by high-level, recognized professionals, review the activities the staff will be pursuing, learn about the institution's communications and marketing strategies, and gauge their relative value in accomplishing overall institutional goals.

Experience has shown that top professionals from national corporations, public relations and marketing agencies, and friends of the institution will usually jump at the chance to work on such a committee. These volunteers may work without compensation for expenses or expectations for future business from the institution. In fact, most such advisory organizations prohibit their volunteers from providing paid services while serving on the council.

The public relations council will offer a fresh external point of view that can be invaluable in making tough management decisions about marketing strategies, attitudinal research, publications evaluations, new identity programs, news media relations, etc. Such groups can be enormously helpful during major crises when an external point of view is necessary, and an impromptu meeting can be convened via conference calls.

The chair of the public relations council should be a nationally recognized and respected volunteer, preferably someone who works in public relations, as opposed to advertising and marketing. (Advertising and marketing lean more to product and idea promotion than to issues management.) All members must be communications professionals who are perceived as outstanding leaders in their fields. While such volunteers may be naive about academia, they provide invaluable expertise and have extraordinary skills not commonly found in higher education. Membership should rotate on and off the council through renewable terms of no less than two years and no more than three years. Ideally, members of a public relations council would number 9 or 12, with one third of the membership rotating off each year after serving one three-year term. This process allows the retention of particularly good members and the rotation off of those who do not contribute significantly.

INTERNAL COMMUNICATIONS (OR MARKETING) COUNCIL

On many campuses—large and small—there are significant numbers of other employees who engage in some aspect of public relations and marketing activities, yet they do not work in the public relations office. These persons do such tasks as writing and editing publications, producing promotional flyers and announcements, publishing newsletters, developing advertising campaigns, promoting programs, contacting news media, and generally engaging in communications strategies. Many of these persons are self-taught and have no prior public relations experience, but for reasons of necessity, have chosen or have been instructed to engage in public relations activities in such areas as undergraduate admissions, graduate admissions, athletics, alumni relations, continuing education, theater, music, and many other programs that require various levels of public relations support. The persons who do this kind of communications work are usually not senior administration, but range from administrative assistants and secretaries to program directors. While they have a strong interest in the area where they work, they also are willing to learn more about the methods by which they could improve results and services that are not necessarily provided by the central administration's public relations office.

By creating a communications (or marketing) council, an institution can pull together a team that can pool resources at times when extraordinary efforts are needed to solve either an institutional problem, or a problem within one of the subunits of the institution. This council is therefore composed only of those who do the actual communications work, even if they are not necessarily communications professionals. The council regularly and systematically involves staff in promotional, publications, marketing, and other communications activities. This operates by exposing less-experienced staff to more seasoned individuals who can, without using their political power or territorial behaviors, assist and improve the efforts of their colleagues. Membership on a communications council does not involve the chief officers of the various academic or administrative divisions—only those who do the "hands-on" work in public relations, communications, and marketing, with outside publics, and who produce materials for outside distribution.

A communications council would be appointed by the chief executive and should be convened either by the chief advancement officer, or the chief public relations officer. The stated purpose of the group would be to serve as a vehicle to voice institutional prerogatives, to make recommendations to the president, the chief academic officer, and the deans; to share concerns on internal communications management and priorities; to discuss projects like marketing, market and attitudinal research, advertising, publicity, publications, printing and graphic services, photography, community relations, government relations, videos, and telephone management; and to support other functions involved in reaching out to the important internal and external publics of the institution.

At several colleges and universities, communications councils have been successful in bringing about more cohesive efforts by what some might consider to be "competitive" offices performing similar services within the institution. Programs for such groups can include guest speakers on effective writing and editing, ways of doing readership studies and other evaluations, basic design and typography, principles of desktop publishing, planning, and time-management techniques. The group would meet quarterly or monthly.

Top administrators should visibly support the effort by making brief presentations when appropriate, by sharing aspirations and goals with the group, and by suggesting topics for their consideration and recommendation. These administrators also can make sure that their own staffs understand the importance of participating in the group. Because the council should avoid the normal territoriality that goes with campus management, it can communicate across departments and foster staff-level efforts. The range of topics to be covered should not be limited. For example, the communications council can deal with providing resources on videotaping or television production, sharing technical and specialized information, developing an inventory of services available throughout the institution, or alerting colleagues to new marketing and advertising efforts in one school or department that might effect similar efforts of another. The concept of interoffice cooperation must prevail at all times so that sharing becomes a bottom-line goal.

Membership on the communications council should be limited to a manageable size—preferably no more than 20 persons. Since there may be more "unofficial" communications, marketing, and publications persons throughout a large institution, it will be necessary to invite everyone to such events as writing seminars, design presentations, and computer technology updates. However, when major decisions and recommendations are being made to management, these should come only from the core communications council.

EDITORIAL ADVISORY GROUPS FOR INSTITUTIONAL PERIODICALS

Institutional periodicals benefit from editorial advisory groups that have a stake in the content of the publication. For example, a typical college or university magazine should have an editorial advisory group that meets three or four times a year to review the most recent issue of the publication, to determine whether it met expectations, and also to provide suggestions to the editor on future feature content. Editorial advisory groups are excellent sounding boards that can be helpful to editors regarding content, approach, and editorial balance.

Such an advisory group can comprise the chief development officer, the chief alumni officer, a representative of the alumni association, the chief public relations officer, a representative from the student affairs office, the editor, designer, photographer, appropriate individuals from other parts of the institution, and writing or editing professionals from paid circulation magazines. It should be noted that the role of this group is advisory in nature only, and it is critical for the group to meet shortly after the production and delivery of the most recent issue, and before the contents of succeeding issues are finalized. The intent of this process is not to supersede the editor, but to guarantee that key voices on the campus have an opportunity to provide input and feedback on what is probably the most important document the institution produces for its parents and alumni, as well as for major gift prospects.

In addition to an advisory group, any important periodical should have an operating statement that defines the mission of the publication, its purpose, the role of the editor and the advisory group, an outline of a typical issue's content, as well as a detailed production schedule that clearly delineates each and every step of the publication's conceptualization, writing, editing, design, printing, distribution, and delivery.

Internal periodicals also should have editorial advisory groups, generally composed of staff and faculty who are selected because of their roles as opinion leaders among constituencies within the institution. Appointment to this advisory group is usually made by the chief executive's office, and appointments rotate on and off the advisory group. An operating statement should be developed along the same lines as for external periodicals.

Departmental and school newsletters need advisory groups and operating statements. Most often, these periodicals are intended to systematically support the overall advancement program, so it is essential that the advisory group have at least one professional from the central public relations office, as well as representatives from the development and alumni offices of the overall institution—even though the publication may be the purview of a specific office or school.

Yet another collaborative technique is the creation of teams or groups that focus on a specific, one-time project such as an admissions video, revisions to a viewbook, case statement for a development campaign, annual reports, and other projects where a variety of voices are necessary to ensure that the project reflects an institutional perspective.

NOTE

1. Adapted from *Malice in Blunderland* by Thomas L. Martin, Jr., former president of the Illinois Institute of Technology.

CHAPTER 13

High-Touch in a High-Tech World: Putting Public Relations in Its Proper Perspective

M. Fredric Volkmann

When planning communications and public relations strategies that promote educational advancement and institutional identity, managers often assume that the primary goal is to maximize the sum of the program's parts, for example, fund raising and friend raising brochures, publicity, alumni magazines, direct mail, and advertising. Although that is a step in the right direction, there is a much simpler way to produce an effective results-oriented program—making face-to-face, one-to-one personal communications the number one objective.

Most strategists plan an overall advancement program by using news releases, announcements, brochures, pamphlets, and advertising, thereby assuming these will generate the results the client is seeking. In reality, such techniques are not the best way of solving the problem and ignore more effective strategies. People talking to people is how things are accomplished—not by deluging each other with more paper and more electronic messages. High-touch is the byword of the high-tech era.

Unfortunately, in the academic environment, managers—particularly faculty—have learned to equate "publish or perish" with success. For some, the printed word becomes a panacea for all promotional problems. Yet in today's information age, simply "putting it in writing" belies more successful ways of promoting and selling products, ideas, or services. Listed below are the most effective means of communicating an educational institution's message—in order of importance:

1. face-to-face conversation
2. small-group discussion or meeting
3. person speaking before a large group
4. telephone conversation between two persons (voice mail doesn't count)
5. handwritten, personal note

6. "typewritten," truly personal letter that does not appear to be generated by computer
7. computer-generated or word-processing-generated "personal" letter via U.S. mail, office e-mail, Internet, or fax
8. mass-produced, nonpersonal letter ("Dear occupant," "Dear student," "Dear alum")
9. brochures, pamphlets, diskettes, videos, and CD-ROMs sent out as direct-mail pieces or on the World Wide Web
10. article in institutional newsletters, magazines, or tabloids
11. news carried in popular press (newspapers, radio, television, magazines)
12. advertising in newspapers, radio, television, magazines, or on-line services
13. other, less effective communications (i.e., billboards, skywriters, and bus signs)

Given differing conditions, many will argue with the relative positions of some of these items, but few will deny that one-to-one communication is vastly preferable to publicity. If this is true, then why don't educational institutions consistently use the more effective forms of communication? The answer usually is cost. In most situations, the highest per-person-reached costs are incurred by sending out a human being to talk to another human being. The telephone costs less. Mass-produced letters and e-mail are even cheaper, and mailing a news release or putting it on a World Wide Web home page is least expensive, but results can be greatly lessened, too.

A parallel example can be found on campuses: students prefer a classroom lecture over correspondence courses. They are even more interested in a small, exclusive seminar, but their ideal is working on a one-to-one basis with a professor in a tutorial or a laboratory.

Business frequently will announce a new high-end, expensive product with publicity; attempt to raise awareness through a direct-mail campaign and advertising; begin a series of targeted messages such as letters and telephone calls; and finally initiate a sale at a trade show or by a personal visit from a sales representative.

One of the hottest topics in education today—undergraduate student recruitment—uses these same techniques. Publicity is used to raise general name awareness of the institution, while promotional mailings are used to garner prospects. In the case of exceptionally good students, so-called personal letters are used, followed by a telephone call or second personal letter from a key person at the institution, such as a faculty member, a person in the admissions program, or students and alumni volunteers. The next step is bringing the prospect and parents to campus for a weekend visit and a tour, when they'll have a chance to sit through classes, to meet students and faculty, and to experience a typical residence hall situation. The relationship is usually capped off with a one-to-one talk with an admissions officer.

No experienced development officer will say that a news release will raise gifts, or that direct-mail solicitation is consistently more effective than a well-run phonathon, or that a phonathon is more effective than a well-managed program of personal solicitation for medium-sized and major gifts. Instead, the ideal is culti-vation of an individual—often beginning with group events, then narrowing the relationship by urging the person involved to become a volunteer, then a leader, and, simultaneously, to become a committed financial supporter.

Why do many advancement programs neglect these factors and concentrate the greatest part of their efforts on some of the least productive forms of communi-cation? Instead, public relations programs should be assisting and advising the offices it serves to adopt more effective strategies for establishing a one-to-one relationship with a carefully targeted audience—whether it be a donor, a prospec-tive student, a graduate, or a reporter. It is the public relations office's responsi-bility to suggest that there may be better solutions than producing a printed piece; the public relations professional should force communications **up** the ladder of effectiveness, striving constantly to narrow the audience to a manageable size, and to deliver the message on a one-to-one basis.

When the president or a vice-president suggests that the institution should "get out a publication or a news release" to solve a problem or blunt a crisis, think twice about the desired result. Or if a client comes into the public relations office seeking to enroll 10 students for a specialized program, and it turns out that the universe from which these students can be selected is only a few hundred persons, then is it really necessary to do a publication, news release, or any of the other conventional forms of mass communication? Would it not be better to invest time and money in telephones, personal letters, and perhaps one-to-one personal con-tacts? Even if a news release is planned, hand delivering a worthwhile story idea to an editor or reporter is far better than mailing it. Next best is a phone call before the release arrives at his or her desk.

The public relations officer should always stop and ask three questions before proceeding on the solution of a communications problem:

1. What is the desired outcome—more gifts, more students, or just more messages?
2. Is there a more results-oriented but cost-effective way of handling the problem than a brochure, news release, Web-site message, or e-mail?
3. Will one-to-one, high-touch communications solve the problem, sell the product, or fill the need?

By answering these questions, institutional communications and marketing efforts will be more productive—particularly in support of the admissions and development offices. Most important, it will force the program to look beyond conventional, inadequate solutions to complex communications problems at colleges, universities, or independent schools.

CHAPTER 14

Issues Management: Anticipating the Future Before It Happens

M. Fredric Volkmann

Although proactive public relations always has been an essential ingredient in advancement strategy, recent years have shown the value of focusing significant efforts on issues management. In the "good old days" this would have been referred to as damage control, but today's professional sees issues management as part of an overall strategy for every aspect of public relations—news media relations, internal communications, publications, and periodicals.

Discovering the critical issues that affect education is an essential skill required of virtually all public relations professionals, but a skill that also is unevenly applied and practiced. Everyone knows that classes tend to begin in autumn, that semesters usually change in mid-January, and that graduation takes place in the spring. How many know, however, that every August new rankings are issued—sending some campuses into a flurry of activity to explain why the institution has risen or fallen in comparison with its perceived competitors? Who remembers that national tuition data are usually issued in September, giving the relative comparisons between public and private institutions? It is these kinds of announcements that become fodder for the issues management mill. Knowing that important data are routinely issued allows educational public relations professionals to proactively prepare their own institution for these announcements, as well as to prepare statements well in advance of the announcements themselves. This is strategic communications, as opposed to the more traditional role of a public information officer whose job it is to tell all and know all that happens in the day-to-day life of a typical campus.

The need for a proactive approach to public relations is heightened by the fact that the public's image of education has not fared well in the last two decades of the twentieth century. In addition, the media are increasingly sensationalistic in their news coverage. A story on education that would have run only in a few newspapers now has appeal even in small newspaper markets, and television and radio news programs latch onto almost any story that deals with crime, safety, and scandal. Not surprisingly, the stories that are likely to gain the most attention are those that have the most negative value for the institution. Over the past decade, the lists of stories that have consistently received attention expanded significantly—to the point where many publications, newspapers, and electronic news programs no longer have a special section set aside for education but rather group the coverage of this news with crime reports, natural disasters, and all of the other news that vie for front-page coverage.

In a well-managed, proactive public relations environment, the staff reads morning newspapers before regular office hours begin, clips these newspapers and shares the issues-related stories with top managers and those directly affected by the news involved, and then determines whether public relations initiatives are necessary as a follow-up. Also monitored should be morning and afternoon drive-time newscasts, prime-time television news, news magazines, and literature that focuses on educational issues, such as the *Chronicle of Higher Education* and *Education Weekly*.

Some institutions circulate the entire content of news articles and scripts, while others synopsize the stories into daily digests—a more labor-intensive approach that saves trees and avoids copyright infringements by not making multiple copies. In either case, this puts the public relations office in a clearly proactive stance by keeping staff and key managers of the institution readily informed about breaking stories and issues that could affect the institution and the work of their various offices, such as financial aid, admissions, development, or athletics.

Where a news story about another institution has significant potential to affect the institution, it is the responsibility of the public relations office to engage the offices and individuals involved in a series of strategy sessions to prepare for an inevitable call from a reporter seeking a local angle or more specific information on the issue. An example is the publication every fall of tuition data by the College Board. By knowing in advance that this will happen, the institutional public relations office can prepare a statement regarding the justification for the current tuition charged to students, without appearing to be ill-prepared or defensive when the reporter does call to confirm the tuition.

Issues management requires more than monitoring local and national news media, however. Proactive strategies also include regular communication with national associations in Washington, D.C.—groups that routinely track issues, particularly those that arise from the political arena. The associations that routinely track issues include the National Association of State Universities and Land Grant Colleges (NASULGC), the National Association of Independent Colleges and Universities (NAICU), American Council on Education (ACE), the American Association of State Colleges and Universities, the Association of American Universities (AAU), the American Association of Community Colleges, the

Council for Advancement and Support of Education (CASE), and several others. Through a combination of e-mail, newsletters, and mailed-out alerts, these organizations inform their members about the issues that will affect them as well as provide advice on how to prepare for issues that may crop up in a local community or on a campus.

CASE issues a twice-monthly news summary of issues affecting education called "Flash Points." Most helpful is a series of issues papers—26 to date—produced by CASE to assist public relations offices in preparing for concerns and controversies that affect them, such as natural disasters, executive compensation, rape on campus, fraternity and sorority problems, closing academic units, dealing with campus budget cuts, and sexual harassment.

Generally, the advice provided in these issue papers recommends many of the following points:

- Keep up with national issues and keep your colleagues informed about them.
- Maintain files on issues that have particularly high potential for future occurrence.
- Advise the most important persons on your campus as to what actions they should consider taking, if any.
- When a particular problem appears to loom on the horizon, organize a campus group to monitor and make recommendations regarding the issue as it unfolds.
- Never assume that any matter is too small for institutionwide attention. Every campus has ample evidence that little things become big issues when unheeded.
- Don't procrastinate. Act quickly and attempt to defuse situations before they fly out of control.
- Determine what are the core issues and define clearly whether they have primary, secondary, or tertiary importance when developing a proposed resolution.
- Develop background information, including proposed statements, question-and-answer sheets, and basic statements that can be used when answering specific queries from reporters.
- Consult with national associations and other institutions that may be affected by the same issue, and thus may have sage advice on how to deal with the issue or problem.
- Communicate first and foremost with internal audiences, such as faculty, students, staff, and administrators, then with external audiences such as alumni, parents, and the general public. It is always better to find a firsthand way to inform those most affected by an issue than to have them learn about it through a newspaper article or a news broadcast.

- Be direct with the news media and other external audiences, admit fault, apologize, and seek better solutions if it appears as though the institution or a member therein has erred.
- Be preemptive when circumstances permit, so that the institution appears to be taking the initiative, rather than being caught in a defensive posture.
- Encourage news media coverage only after all pieces of the issues puzzle are in place. Occasionally institutions have the luxury of resolving problems before they are played out in the public press. When that happens, decide whether a positive outcome is worthy of a story in the press initiated by the institution, rather than by other parties.

Although no institution is affected by all issues that impact higher education in general, it is best to assume that many issues have the potential to become news stories not only locally, but regionally and nationally. The public affairs office at Washington University assists faculty, deans, and administrators in fielding questions about issues, and annually issues a list of possible stories to its key administrators, asking them to be alert for calls from reporters. When this happens, the institution encourages staff to defer answering questions on the call until after consulting with the public affairs office about what the current status of the issue may be and whether the institution has any reason to participate in a discussion about the issue involved.

The list that follows is developed in collaboration with several colleges and universities, as well as ACE, AAU, NAICU, NASULGC, and CASE. These are issues that were current in spring of 1997. Such lists should be updated at least annually and should accommodate not only news media coverage of existing issues, but predictions from experts in government relations as to what may be appearing on the horizon as issues in months to come:

- tuition, including tuition increases that are higher than the cost of living, cost vs. price issues, escalating tuition at public institutions to make up for declining state aid, and middle-class alienation from private, higher-cost universities and colleges in favor of the "public ivy's" and their lower tuition
- financial aid, including need-aware vs. need-blind admissions, merit-based no-need scholarships, minority-based financial aid, and graduating student indebtedness
- admissions, including affirmative action controversies, early decision admissions, and need-aware admissions
- teaching and learning, including role of computers, virtual universities, control of Internet/World Wide Web content for copyright and pornography, tenure and post-tenure reviews and the national trend away from jobs for life, large classes, research-oriented professors, and unionization of teaching assistants

- accountability, performance, and rankings, such as rankings proliferation—especially *U.S. News*, not-in-profile students, faculty productivity, and accreditation and outcomes measurements
- federal research support, including indirect cost support, earmarked (pork barrel) funds vs. peer-reviewed science, and basic research and technology transfer
- individual and institutional integrity, such as research fraud, conflicts of interest for faculty and trustees, misuse or misdirection of federal funds, and copyright protections
- campus crime and safety, including perceived safety decline on campus, off-campus crimes, and date-rape accusations and prosecutions
- federal regulation/deregulation, such as devolution of federal activities to states; congressional opposition to Departments of Education, Energy, or Commerce, etc.; IRS reviews; and lobbying activities of not-for-profit institutions accepting federal support
- U.S. economy and taxes, including flat tax, line-item veto, federal and state-level focus on K-12, tax-free bond caps, and employer-provided educational assistance
- health care costs and delivery, such as national health care reform, Medicare payments for indirect medical education, fraudulent Medicare claims, and Medicare billing audits at medical schools
- campus-level budgetary problems, including budget cuts, academic downsizing, faculty–staff layoffs, deferred maintenance, low salaries and/or poor benefits for graduate teaching and research assistants, and high salaries, perquisites, and large retirement packages for top academic administrators
- international education, such as declining U.S. enrollments of students from other countries, international students displacing U.S. students, and legal and illegal aliens receiving tax-derived support for education
- animal research, including laboratory animals instead of human subjects and computer modeling, and costs of compliance with federal guidelines for animal care
- campus behaviors, student rights, and expectations, including return of activism to campuses, reduction in student satisfaction, political correctness and free speech/hate speech, diversity and race relations among students, handicapped access, sexual/amorous relationships between faculty and students, and Reserve Officers' Training Corps and other military policies on gays and lesbians
- athletics, including gender equity, poor graduation rates for athletes at NCAA Division I and II institutions, and crimes and misdemeanors committed by athletes

- fund raising, such as loss of charitable deductions if a flat tax is enacted, donor influence on college/university policy, competition between public and private colleges and universities and other charities, and megacampaigns

Issues management relies heavily on the cooperation and collaboration of colleagues throughout the campus. By networking with government relations, business, finance, student affairs, development, alumni, academic affairs, and human resources, the process of developing a proactive issues management program will be more effective.

CHAPTER 15

Understanding Those We Serve: Researching Attitudes, Satisfaction, and Motivation

M. Fredric Volkmann

Plagiarize, plagiarize, plagiarize! Let nothing evade your eyes.

Tom Lehrer, "Lobachevski"

This is the information age, a time when we are beginning to accept the role of customers and clients in building what is euphemistically called total quality management (TQM) systems. Although created by an American academic theorist, the TQM revolution first transformed how business is conducted in Japan, and now the rest of the world. It has not had the same effect on education—yet. In recent years, research on the key audiences of educational institutions and the resulting changes in institutional behavior have moved slightly forward, but not nearly as much as they have in business and industry.

Over the centuries, education has become accustomed to prescribing the solution to problems, rather than seeking the input and assistance of those served. The most dramatic change in this attitude began in the 1960s with the rapid growth of community colleges, which are predicated on meeting perceived needs within their communities. As this movement thrived, industry also began to respond to the successful mastery of world markets by Japanese manufacturers and businesses, finally realizing that a stronger sensitivity to customer satisfaction, expectations, and needs has to be calculated as part of an overall strategy.

By the early 1970s, several traditional institutions of higher education had begun to conduct omnibus attitudinal studies of such key audiences as current students, parents, prospective students and their parents, alumni, friends, community leaders, state and federal leaders, and other audiences that have the ability to affect the overall performance of their institutions. Some institutions evaluated the success or failure of such programs as admissions, alumni, development, and even public relations. Others developed accountability systems that would provide customer-level feedback. The result has been a significant number of approaches, each having a specific purpose in assisting institutional managers to understand the impact of existing programs, as well as the potential for new ones under development. The types of studies that generally are done include the following:

- attitudinal and satisfaction research, also known to some as market research, and including focus groups, mailed-out surveys, telephone surveys, and personal interview surveys
- readership studies that test audiences of magazines, newspapers, newsletters, promotional publications, radio and audiotaped presentations, and television and videotaped presentations
- content analysis that measures the amount of material devoted in any message to specific subjects, topics, interests, or special concerns
- readability studies dealing with how easily the reader is able to scan, process, absorb, and remember information as presented in university messages in print and electronic formats (Readability only reveals how well the material is understood by the reader, not to be confused with legibility studies. One of the most common tests for readability is the Gunning Fog Index.)
- legibility studies that determine how easily the eye scans the letter forms used in presenting material to readers in print or electronic form
- impact studies that generally measure the educational, cultural, and/or economic impact of educational institutions in their neighborhoods, communities, regions, and states
- public relations audits or reviews to discover information either by a self-conducted analysis of publications, news media relations, and other public relations programs, or by inviting external experts to analyze the public relations program, and to provide information as to how it compares to other institutions, as well as how the internal clients within the organization gauge the effectiveness of the public relations program

USE EXISTING RESEARCH BEFORE CONDUCTING NEW EFFORTS

Academic institutions thrive on research even if it is not usually attitudinal or satisfaction research. Vast amounts of information already are available to public relations offices by simply tapping into the resources of admissions, development, alumni, and other offices collecting data that can be used in developing some baseline understanding of key audiences of the institution. These databases include the following:

- Admissions data. Much important information can be collected on applications and on studies done regarding students who inquire but don't apply, apply but don't pay a deposit, pay a deposit but don't attend, and so forth.
- Data on alumni. Most colleges and universities have detailed information on alumni. Although this may not reveal attitudes, it does provide significant amounts of demographic information, which can be useful in future analysis, particularly such items as majors, interests, activities, and annual fund support.
- Parent data. Parents provide significant information to institutions when their children apply. This information can provide useful material for a wide range of applications.
- Admissions testing data. Information provided by test takers applying for college can be the basis for extensive further research on the motivations of prospective students and their families. This is particularly true of students taking the PSAT, SAT, ACT, and other entrance examination tests requiring personal information that later can be provided to the institution about itself, as well as comparing the institution to national norms.
- Fund raising data and profiles. The recent advent of research techniques as tools in fund raising is best demonstrated in the special work now being done to match alumni and parent addresses and other information to the potential of individuals to provide greater gift support to their alma maters. More specific research can be done regarding major donors, also using readily available, public domain information.
- Results-based information. The response rates to annual fund efforts, phonathons, student recruitment direct mail, etc., all provide insights that may be useful in future research. In fact, some college rankings use alumni-giving participation rates to determine alumni satisfaction.
- Studies conducted by educational associations and organizations. Most educational associations are based in Washington, D.C., and do some level of research regarding the needs of their members. These results are often published in aggregate, without the ability to break out data on specific institutions. However, such information can be useful in establishing benchmarks and baselines for future research.
- Focus groups. Many departments and programs within institutions interview groups of clients, customers, or participants in their programs to ask for information that is more anecdotal than statistical—but which can be extraordinarily useful in doing additional attitudinal testing.

These data have uses that extend far beyond attitudinal and satisfaction research, such as preparing information for institutional viewbooks, case statements, fact sheets, proposals to foundations and other donor prospects, reports to bond-rating agencies, responses to rankings and ratings survey requests, and many more uses.

HOW IS ATTITUDINAL RESEARCH CONDUCTED?

When a professor once was asked to define social science in simple terms, the response was "common sense made difficult." Unfortunately, this is the image that social science often conveys to lay persons, as well as to managers and professionals in advancement. When properly managed, conducted, interpreted, and applied, attitudinal research is truly invaluable in managing advancement programs, including public relations.

An example is a small, liberal arts college that saw a dramatic fall-off in annual giving after completing a major capital campaign. No one was able to determine the root of the problem until research was conducted on alumni attitudes and perceptions. The results revealed that the alumni office was continuing to hold campaign-style meetings (even though the campaign was long over) that included "passing the hat" for gifts each and every time alumni chapters met. Word soon passed among alumni that the institution was more interested in their money than in their participation in alumni activities. As a result, both giving and participation tumbled. The college only learned of this situation through conducting a thorough attitudinal research effort with alumni. The institution responded to this information by separating the annual fund from the alumni office, assuring alumni that no more "passing the hat" would be done under any circumstances, and that the institution genuinely cared about alumni involvement more than their money. As a result, alumni club participation climbed and annual fund giving set new records.

Another example of the value of this research is the major public university that discovered that the most powerful source of communication it sent out was not news that appeared on radio, television, or newspapers, nor was it advertising that appeared in those media, nor was it even the direct-mail materials the institution used to communicate with its own external audiences. The institution surveyed a sample from among several thousand movers and shakers who held prominent statewide positions politically, economically, and socially—only to learn that the vast majority of these persons received most of their institutional information directly from students, faculty, and staff. The result was a concerted effort to communicate more directly with internal audiences to inform them about major initiatives, which they in turn could communicate to external leaders. More importantly, programs were developed to raise pride in the institution, especially when it was discovered that students, faculty, and staff did not believe their own institution compared favorably with similar institutions in their athletic league—a fact that was readily conveyed to leaders, and which clearly affected their willingness to support the institution politically and economically.

As more and more academic institutions adopt marketing strategies for delivering messages and services to key audiences, they are using attitudinal research methods to fine-tune programs, to prepare for strategic planning, and to set clear priorities on how problems are going to be solved. Unfortunately, institutions rarely have ongoing attitudinal information from faculty, staff, students, alumni, parents of current students, parents of prospective students, and persons seeking health, medical, agricultural, or social services from the institution, where such ancillary enterprises exist.

Successful programs begin by conducting attitudinal and satisfaction research studies as the basis for strategic planning as well as for marketing institutional programs. It is best to locate firms that specialize in working with educational institutions and therefore have the experience and know-how to proceed in the collection, management, manipulation, and reporting of data and recommendations.

Because of the sensitivity of market research testing, high cost, and sometimes questionable results, the process of finding an appropriate research firm must rely heavily on the use of requests for proposal, binding estimates and bids, careful evaluation of proposals, and recommendations from other institutions, realizing that results of other studies cannot be shared. From the responses, managers should select no more than three finalists to be reviewed by a special committee or task force for final recommendation of a vendor, and followed by extremely tight monitoring of the development of questionnaires and survey instruments, methodology of interpretation, and recommendations on actionable results. The process is not only time-consuming, but it also requires the assistance of knowledgeable professionals who have conducted valid market research previously. At some academic institutions there are faculty who can assist in this process. Also invaluable is the oversight of the public relations council mentioned earlier, simply because communications professionals in business and industry have had more opportunity to work with this kind of research.

Hire an external consultant to assist in the selection of a research firm and to oversee the development of the research effort. In this way, the institution has an independent, experienced voice that does not have a vested interest in either the research or in the institution's point of view or biases. In addition, this individual can advise the institution on which methodologies are most likely to produce reliable results and what reporting methods should be employed in providing useful information that is "actionable." One of the most common mistakes made in conducting market research is asking for information upon which the institution may have difficulty in taking meaningful action.

Among the first tasks for the public relations council, described earlier, could be selecting a long list of attitudinal and satisfaction research firms, and then recommending ways that are both reliable and cost effective for the development and management of the research project. The estimated cost of doing professionally conducted research with an external firm for telephone or personal-interview method research costs anywhere from $10,000 to $250,000, depending upon the size of the sample and the complexity of the research questionnaire.

Institutions planning to do research utilizing mailed-out questionnaires—or by inserting instruments into institutional magazines or other publications—should proceed with caution, since the response rate to these questionnaires tends to be exceedingly low. It is a commonly held view among attitudinal and market research experts that a response rate to a mailed-out survey must be at least 50 percent of the sample and must number greater than 100 individuals to be statistically valid. In all cases, the sample size and the skill and crafting of questions have enormous impact on the reliability of the research. The maximum size audience needed for a statistically valid result is generally thought to be about 1,000 respondents to a questionnaire—as long as this represents at least a 50 percent response rate. Some sample sizes must be larger if accurate data are needed on subsets, such as responses from "female alumnae who graduated in 1963" for an overall study of alumni.

FOCUS GROUPS AS A MANAGEABLE ALTERNATIVE

Because the cost of market research, attitudinal research, and similar types of data collection are so high, the affordable alternative is often the focus group approach, which can be conducted by the institution with small groups of participants, between 10 and 20. Focus groups, however, do not have the validity that is enjoyed by more statistically reliable, large-sample research.

Focus groups are helpful in preparing, testing, and analyzing student recruitment literature, alumni publications, development materials, and marketing materials created to attract clients to programs, services, and events. Focus groups also can be used to pretest advertising and similar strategies. What is revealed are concerns that may be helpful in improving the general quality of the message being produced. Results usually will confirm the wisdom of what is already being done, but small details may have to be changed to accommodate the attitudes of prospective students or other audiences. For example, one such study at a private research university tested three undergraduate viewbook cover designs on high school juniors and seniors. The staffs in the publications and admissions offices had already agreed upon what they thought would be the most popular cover. During focus groups in high school classrooms, the students overwhelmingly rejected the staff's choice and selected the cover believed by the "experts" to be the worst of the possibilities.

All focus group testing of materials, advertising, or other services should be done by persons independent of any special or vested interests—especially firms that produce design, printing, advertising, or other marketing services that are likely to be affected by research results.

Focus group testing often covers a wide range of subjects and materials, including copy, artwork, and even paper stock. Further, when testing a brochure being inserted into a mailing, it is just as important to test the envelope, method of addressing the envelope, cover letter, and reply mechanism as well as the basic brochure or any other materials to be included. If sufficient time is available, focus group testing can include photographs, artwork, typefaces, ink colors, impact, and much more. The most important knowledge to be gleaned is whether the basic message and its theme are effective with the intended audience represented by the focus groups.

READERSHIP STUDIES

Perhaps the most commonly used testing at academic institutions are readership studies of key institutional materials, such as admissions viewbooks, alumni tabloids and magazines, newsletters, faculty/staff newspapers, and now World Wide Web pages. The least expensive method of conducting readership studies is to mail out surveys (done separately from the publication and not tipped into the entire mailing). Although the telephone interview method can provide more statistically reliable information, it not only comes at greater cost but may also have less ability to cover a significant number of questions and concerns. Done properly, readership studies are helpful to marketing and publications professionals in determining the value of story ideas, themes, quality of design, photography, writing style, and other factors important in periodicals and promotional materials. Readership studies are more common in business and industry, where a percentage of the cost of the project is dedicated to focus groups and follow-up readership work. Unfortunately, educational institutions have not yet fully realized the importance of such action, and rarely does a publication's total cost include a percentage dedicated to testing effectiveness.

How valuable are readership studies? A great deal rests on the ability of managers and editors to make sound choices as to how they craft messages for their audiences. In situations where editing decisions have been intuitively and experientially sensitive to audiences, readership studies can show that a vast majority of the readers agree with the editor's decision. Certain predictable institutional messages being tested fail to meet a high standard when readership studies are conducted. Classic examples are alumni magazines that have too few class notes. Virtually all research conducted over the past several decades says that more than 80 to 85 percent of alumni turn to the class notes section of their alumni magazines first. Imagine a graduate's disappointment when there is little or no news about his or her class year because there wasn't sufficient room in that issue to carry enough class notes when compared with "important" institutional messages that often test much more poorly with readers. Readership studies show that the second most commonly read section of alumni periodicals are the news briefs, something that is not always popular with editors; but the section has enormous value for busy readers who have precious little time to devour even a fraction of what is sent to them in the mail every day.

Studies conducted of prospective students show that they prefer viewbooks over Web pages by a resounding percentage—even if they are highly proficient and technologically up-to-speed on their computers. Why? Simply because the graphic quality and the convenience of Web pages have not yet achieved the same level of sophistication enjoyed by high-quality, much more expensive printing techniques. However, it will be only a matter of time before electronic communication replaces many forms of print communication—perhaps within the next 10 or 15 years. One of the most important things to prospective students in reading viewbooks—according to readership studies—is simply a page of facts and figures that synopsizes everything that's in the 32- to 64-page publication, preferably on the inside front cover! While most editors and designers cringe at the thought of "junking up" one of the most important surfaces in the viewbook, readers want to have an efficient way to decide whether or not they will continue reading the document.

RESEARCH RESULTS ARE USEFUL—AND CONFIDENTIAL

One of the reasons that no specific institutions are cited in this article among the market research examples is that all of the studies are proprietary and the results closely held by the institutions that paid for them. In fact, many firms that conduct market research also insist upon protection of the information and have policies that supersede even the institution's control over the information—no matter who paid for it! As a matter of practice, results are only conveyed on a need-to-know basis within the institution.

The results of valid research can have profound and sometimes striking results on administrative decision making within academic institutions. For example, the admissions office of a prominent university had decided to use the school's nickname, rather than the more complicated official name. They insisted that this was the only way to reach prospective students because the staff believed high school students did not like formal names like the one required by the institution's policy. Subsequent testing of names with prospective students, their parents, and alumni showed that a majority of the prospects thought the nickname was inappropriate, lacked sufficient seriousness, and did not convey the level of quality that the institution provides to its undergraduates. Even worse, it was shown that more than two thirds of older alumni abhorred the nickname and found it to be profoundly offensive. Without such research, the admissions office would have plunged ahead and used a moniker that would have brought more negative results than positive.

Another example of why research is invaluable is looking at what can be learned by combining many sources of information into a workable strategy. Research as to why prospective undergraduates do or do not select an institution can be narrowed down to a few general categories: cost, perceived quality and reputation, location, personal and family reasons, potential for career or graduate school preparation, and future success in life. Decisions on what academic institution to attend are made on the basis of facts and perceptions—often with the prospect not distinguishing between the two. While many solutions are actionable, a significant percentage often are not, such as moving the campus to a more desirable region of the country for those who like cool summers, or redesigning the architecture of the signature building on the campus to meet current tastes and preferences.

Even where factors are actionable, the time involved is counted, not in months, but in years and decades. Cost, for example, is sometimes actionable by the institution in such ways as setting tuition and fees at a lower rate of increase than perceived competitors. This can be done in five years or less. At the same time, more appealing financial aid packages of loans, grants, work opportunities, and scholarships can be crafted. On the other hand, such factors as the cost of living in the region surrounding the campus are barely actionable by the institution.

Similar dilemmas occur with other ingredients in college choice for undergraduates—perceived quality and reputation. Marketing research reveals that the overall reputation of the institution has an enormous impact on the type of undergraduate who applies. The institution's ability to change that reputation is in part governed by the amount of time, effort, and resources it is willing to expend. Most academic institutions require decades to build the reputations they have—and an aggressive program predicated on significant change in two or three years is likely to fail. On the other hand, it is possible to focus institutional efforts on a few programs and thereby selectively increase quality significantly in a few years. But these opportunities are rare and often do not have the effect of changing overall institutional perceptions.

CHAPTER 16

Determining Public Relations Potential

M. Fredric Volkmann

An ancient Chinese philosopher was once supposed to have said, "I do not know the road to success, but I do know the road to failure, and that is trying to please everyone." Depending on whom one asks, the institution's success can be measured in numerous ways: the business officer talks about balanced budgets and return on endowment investments; the physical plant director takes great pride in building maintenance and grounds upkeep; the development office proudly announces increased alumni participation in the annual fund and an over-all rise in total giving; and the chair of this year's commencement committee says that the featured speaker is the best ever. Indeed, these are subjects of great interest to those who have labored long and hard to achieve success, but none count strongly as news of interest to the media or to the other audiences of the institution—surprising as this may sound. Trying to please colleagues seeking news media attention can indeed lead to failure if the stories do not merit coverage.

What alumni, parents, students, the public, and the news media want to know about educational institutions is more related to less tangible assets than money, buildings, or alumni loyalty. The outside world wants to know about the important ideas and ideals that emanate from the process of learning, teaching, research, and artistic and literary creativity. Education in the United States is unique and envied among the world's cultures. It is the only nation with such a high concentration of institutions of higher education among its population. Students from virtually every nation in the world attend the more than 3,800 colleges and universities in America because of the strength of the programs and the nation's long-standing tradition of freedom of inquiry and expression. Throughout the second half of the twentieth century, these institutions have built up the level of prominence they enjoy today, including extraordinary incentives provided by support from alumni and friends as well as from federal, state, and local governments. While all of this requires significant administrative oversight and strong management, the real news is what educational institutions produce, not necessarily the process by which they accomplish this end.

This writer has reviewed more than 50 college and university public relations programs first-hand and in minute detail at public and private, small and large, two-year and four-year institutions of higher education from coast to coast. More often than not, institutional public relations programs focus far too heavily on various aspects of management, ignoring the core processes and outcomes developed by the faculty and the students. At a typical university, the news releases, publications, and other promotional materials tend to focus on announcements of upcoming seminars and conferences, speakers visiting the campus, appointments of new faculty and administrators, admissions and enrollment information, gifts and grants, alumni activities, groundbreakings and completions of new buildings, and many other actions that reflect more on the management of institutions. This appears to be true for both internal and external communications.

When institutions systematically conduct the kind of attitudinal and satisfaction research described in a previous section, they find their "customers" prefer reading about a better balance between process-related administrative activity, and the messages that have more news and audience value—those messages that reflect the intellectual capital that is evidenced through learning and research.

Of course, educational institutions must report on the activities that occur in the day-to-day life of their students and faculty, but it should not happen at the expense of why the institution is there in the first place. It is this issue that demands greater parity between process and outcomes. For example, a member of the biology faculty discovers a new genetic marker for Alzheimer's disease; a political scientist reveals that electoral rhetoric is changing in America; a historian reaches a radically new conclusion about the life of Thomas Jefferson; and a student finds in the library archives a heretofore unknown artifact from the jottings of Michelangelo—all of which have significant news potential, but which would not have been reported in the press had it not been for the advocacy of a public relations professional. At most of the institutions studied, these newsworthy outcomes occupy a small fraction of the time spent on projects in the public relations office, and in some cases no such activity exists at all. Instead, news releases, alumni magazines, and faculty/staff newspapers most often carry information about buildings, budgets, admissions successes, fund raising, and all of the important administrative functions that support the core activities of the students and faculty. Unfortunately, this kind of news rarely reveals important aspects of teaching and learning.

Newspapers and magazines began doing readership studies and attitudinal research in the late 1950s and early 1960s to determine how they could best serve the interest of readers, rather than relying entirely on the editors to make these decisions. Television and radio soon followed with Neilsen and Arbitron ratings to see what was of interest to viewers and listeners. Over time, the content and programming of major print and electronic media have been driven in part by the expectations of customers, while struggling with the natural biases of editors and other managers who have strong traditional views of what constitutes news, entertainment, and everything in between. What has emerged is a continuing, across-the-board interest in human tragedy and suffering, wars and warfare, politics and political scandal, and all of the other traditional subjects that have been the bread and butter of the media and the public who read, listen, and watch. These are not areas in which educational institutions fit comfortably—unless faculty are commenting on some aspect of these unseemly topics.

On the other hand, research has led the media to investigate and report on material that relies much more on the expertise provided by educational institutions—health, fitness, medicine, technology, business, performing arts, literature, basic and applied science that can be understood and explained to lay persons, social science as it describes the human condition, and varsity athletics. From these general areas come the greatest proportion of news media attention devoted to academic institutions and the core feature content of institutional periodicals. Surprisingly, what is not thoroughly covered is basic education itself. Although most electronic news media outlets have science and technology reporters, virtually none in the entire nation have reporters and writers who specialize in elementary, secondary, or higher education news. Most sizable newspapers do have education reporters and writers, but these individuals are often stretched so thinly that a significant portion of their time is not spent on issues, but on reporting educational management and other processes not linked to teaching and learning. Sadly, research and learning subjects are not always adequately served by the public relations function of educational institutions.

Instead, many academic institutions believe they are held hostage to the ten-second sound bite and the news media's policy of "if it bleeds, it leads." These are not attributes that academics find comfortable, nor that readers find consistent with educational institutions. Brevity is not a virtue that is evenly understood in academe, and the closest thing to violence usually happens under controlled conditions in a chemistry lab, or in the atom smasher in the physics department. What occurs on campuses has little first-blush appeal to news media, and that is why proactive public relations programs must encourage news media coverage of subjects that are not going to appear on the front page of a newspaper, in the first five minutes of a newscast, or on the cover of a major magazine. In fact, institutions that do find themselves in the headlines are, more often than not, suffering attention for calamities that have little to do with the educational process, but a great deal to do with the tragedy of the human condition.

Educational institutions that enjoy significant positive coverage in the media and that have highly supportive and motivated alumni and parents are often those institutions that communicate best their core processes of teaching, research, and public service. How is it that some institutions are more successful in advocating these areas than others? Here are a few of the overall strategies that successful academic institutions employ in bringing such core messages to all of their audiences:

- *Integrate and coordinate all aspects of internal and external communications.* Pulling together the publications, media relations, community relations, and alumni/parent communications is an ideal more commonly achieved in small colleges and less so in large, complex universities. Regardless of size, speaking with one voice can bring significant results to those institutions that advocate their messages consistently and uniformly.

- *Assess the news value of research and teaching on the campus.* Proactive public relations programs routinely prepare lists of faculty research and scholarship that have significant news potential for the media, as well as for institutional publications and periodicals. But on some campuses, the very thought that the public relations office would dare determine the "value" of a faculty member's work is likely to meet with serious criticism. In these instances, institutions have sought the advice and input of experienced consultants who will routinely interview leading scholars and researchers at the institution as well as those individuals who might have potential as expert commentators. From these analyses are developed strategies for promoting the individual or his or her research externally as well as internally through the faculty/staff newspaper, alumni magazine, and other materials distributed by the institution.

- *Diligently pursue campus beat systems.* Institutions that routinely contact all top administrators, deans, department heads, principal investigators and other faculty, scholars, and scientists are more than halfway toward the goal of achieving greater attention with internal and external audiences. Some scholars may be reluctant to discuss their work until it is published in peer-reviewed journals, but building a trusting relationship with a member of the public relations team can provide ample advance awareness that a major research story is brewing and that careful coordination can maximize its impact on all audiences. Unfortunately, one of the most common criticisms of educational public relations offices is that they do not consistently pursue systematic beat systems on at least a monthly basis.

- *Analyze and adopt successful strategies practiced by your competitors.* Unlike most businesses, academic institutions will generally open their doors and their minds to public relations colleagues who wish to learn more about the successful aspects of public relations practices at institutions with which they believe they are competitive. (The only exception is the reluctance of most institutions to share their media and donor mailing lists with one another.) However, techniques for collecting information and disseminating it are generally shared willingly. Visiting public relations offices at three or four similar institutions can provide eye-opening experiences.

- *Ask the news media and institutional audiences what they most want.* In addition to the market research on alumni and other institutional audiences mentioned elsewhere in this section, it also is important to directly seek the advice and input of reporters, writers, editors, and news directors in the print and the electronic media. Over a two-year period, this writer visited more than 200 such persons in 20 cities nationwide to determine not only what the news media was seeking from academic institutions, but also to provide examples of news stories generated by the institution that might be of interest to the popular press. The most surprising outcome was that more than 85 percent of the media interviewed had never heard of the institution and were amazed when they learned of the important work it was doing in science, medicine, business education, and social work.

- *Invite a team of reviewers to audit your institution's public relations program.* Academic institutions should routinely conduct external reviews of their public relations programs, including all aspects of media relations, publications, periodicals, special events, etc. There are professional consultants who do this kind of work, but most academic institutions find that a team of two or three highly regarded practitioners in academic public relations is much more apt in dealing with both the large issues and many of the subtleties that require attention. Normally, the process includes pulling together examples of a full-year's effort in news media relations, publications, periodicals, and other aspects of public relations management. These materials are submitted prior to the campus visit by the reviewers, and then two or three days of intensive interviews are conducted with key executives of the institution, faculty and clients of the public relations office, news media served by the public relations office, and any other constituencies that are affected by the work of the office, such as alumni, parents, students, etc. Normally, a verbal report is provided at the end of the campus visit portion of the review and is then followed by a detailed, written report complete with recommendations about ways in which the program can be further improved.

All of these techniques will assist the institution in determining its public relations potential, and each of these activities should be shared with the public relations council recommended earlier.

CHAPTER 17

Media Relations: Working Effectively with Print and Electronic Newsmakers

M. Fredric Volkmann

Traditionally, the overall relationship between the news media and educational institutions has been one of cooperation, trust, and general agreement that both communities have much in common. Colleges and universities are in the information business, and so are news media. Both camps are searching for the same goal—truth—albeit they differ in how they report those truths. Academics seek truth in time frames measured by years and centuries, while the media seek the truth in terms of minutes, hours, and days.

The campus office responsible for maintaining relations with the news media is identified in myriad ways on campuses—public information, information services, news bureau, communications, publicity, news and information, press relations, media relations, and many more. For purposes of consistency, these areas will be identified throughout this section under the name of "media relations," which is loosely defined as effective strategies for working with electronic and print news media, including newspapers, magazines, radio, television, wire services, syndicates, and now the World Wide Web. The media determine what constitutes news—not the campus public relations office, nor the faculty, staff, and students.

Before any campus media relations program can operate effectively, it must determine not only what is news, but what is newsworthy. Certain qualities determine what constitutes successful news media initiatives. To be successful, a message must answer as many of the following questions as possible:

- Does the message or material provide new information?
- Is it timely?
- What effect will the message have on the lives or livelihoods of readers, listeners, and viewers?
- How unusual is the information?

- Is the news of interest beyond the campus?
- Is the material useful, educational, or helpful?

If news material meets this test, then it is up to the media to finally decide what constitutes news they will use. This is dependent on the reading or broadcast audience, the circulation or broadcast area covered by the station or newspaper, how well the story competes against other news emerging at the same time, and the individual preferences of the writer, editor, or news director.

NEWS AND NEWS RELEASES ARE NOT THE SAME THING

One of the sad observations of campus media relations is the reliance of many educational institutions on news releases as the primary method of communicating with the media. Despite the fact that experienced professionals in educational public relations began to predict that the news release was dead in the 1980s, the vast majority of educational media relations officers still use this method to send what is generally unimportant information to newspapers, magazines, television, and radio stations. A few years ago, this writer sat in the reception area of a major metropolitan daily newspaper and watched a newsroom assistant sort through one day's pile of news release envelopes, discarding most in the waste basket without even opening them—making the entire judgment based on the name and reputation of the sender in combination with the instructions provided by reporters as to which mail they wanted and did not want. Unfortunately, the same fate often befalls faxes and e-mail. When the volume of material sent to reporters and editors exceeds their ability to manage it, they find workable solutions. This is not to say that news releases do not have a place, but that they are overused and often unreliable unless combined with other communications techniques. In the rest of this section, more effective ways of communicating with the news media will be discussed.

KNOW THYSELF

According to the Roman historian Plutarch, the words "know thyself" were inscribed on the temple of the Oracle of Delphi. Today, 2,600 years later, this admonition has special meaning for campus public relations offices. Gaining an understanding of the institution and the work that goes on in highly independent departments, divisions, and programs requires reportage and investigative skills that equal or excel those employed in the news media. Knowing what is happening on any campus is hard work and requires the diligence to personally visit each and every faculty member, important administrator, and newsworthy student organization to determine whether or not the work they are doing has news potential. However, most institutions have limited personnel, so news gathering must be effected in the following ways:

- *Develop a proactive beat system.* Call all department heads, top administrative officers, deans, principal investigators, and highly productive faculty members on the phone or contact by e-mail at least once a month to see what may have news potential in their areas.
- *Encourage personal contact.* Although telephone and e-mail beat systems are productive, they sometimes fail where personal, face-to-face visits succeed. Making brief visits (less than 10 or 15 minutes) to important faculty and administrators can sometimes reveal significantly greater amounts of newsworthy material.
- *Get on institutional mailing lists and read what is sent.* Have your name put on the circulation lists for all reports, general memoranda, and other information sent out by administrators, deans, department heads, and highly productive faculty. Such materials as faculty research grant reports, lists of faculty articles published in scholarly journals, and reports on travel to present papers at professional meetings prove invaluable in revealing activities that otherwise would not be discussed.
- *Socialize.* Participate in official receptions, alumni reunions, honors presentations, and other activities where people congregate and talk. These activities can reveal significant information not achievable during a phone call or an office visit. Because the atmosphere is unofficial, people are more relaxed and more likely to say what is on their minds.

A personal contact system always works best, no matter the environment or technique employed. Those who send out memoranda to faculty and staff asking for newsworthy ideas rarely obtain significant or meaningful responses.

Once information is in hand, it should be organized in several ways within the public relations office:

- *Keep detailed files.* Each and every faculty member, officer, and newsworthy student should have his or her own file to hold previous news releases, published scholarly work, clippings, notes, résumés, and any other information about the prior and current activities of the individual. While it would be more efficient if this information were wholly stored on computers, most institutions do not have the resources to convert these data to electronic files—yet.
- *Develop a faculty experts database.* Using any number of over-the-counter software packages available, develop databases on faculty and their areas of expertise. Properly managed, these systems allow searches based on subject, name, academic discipline, topics on which prior media interviews were

based, and essential contact information—such as direct-line telephone numbers, e-mail address, Web site address, campus and home addresses, and any other vital information.

- *Maintain a faculty experts directory.* A printed or hard copy faculty experts directory is invaluable within the office to quickly answer news media calls, and a printed version can be distributed to selected editors, reporters, and freelance writers—making certain not to include confidential or protected information, such as unlisted phone numbers, etc. Be certain the format works in electronic web formats, too.

- *Create an on-line experts directory.* While the cost savings of a purely electronic faculty experts directory are inviting, it is important to remember that the vast majority of reporters and editors are still not easily able to access the Internet or the World Wide Web to retrieve such information. In addition, the convenience of having a printed alphabetical listing of topics and names with telephone numbers is still preferable to many and often faster to use than attempting to search databases on the Web. On the other hand, freelance writers and more and more reporters are gaining access to the Web and are developing highly proficient skills in using databases that they know about.

- *Hold regular staff meetings.* One of the most commonly overlooked ways to gain information is to develop a routine of sharing what each news relations staff person has learned in a weekly or an every-other-weekly meeting to review what has been learned through the techniques listed above. Some institutions hold daily "story budget" meetings much as is done in newspapers and televisions news operations. Sharing information on campuses is particularly important where there are large staffs in the news office. However, nothing substitutes for personal contact with the newsmakers themselves.

Is It News?

Before contacting news media, a decision must be made as to whether the information gleaned from campus sources is truly newsworthy. News media editors may make the final decision, but they depend upon the preferences of their reading, viewing, and listening audiences, which differ from area to area. Also impacting what constitutes news are the circulation and broadcast patterns of the media, particularly those that focus more on local than on regional or national news. Here are some other factors that impact news potential:

- *Does it compete?* Campus news must contend with noneducational material that also is newsworthy, timely, of interest to more people, better suited to the news outlet, and better prepared.

- *Does it have a "news peg"?* Journalists like stories that have a hook or peg on which to hang the message. It is the role of the news media relations professional to establish that the message is compelling, can be explained easily, and relates to broader topics of high appeal to readers, viewers, and listeners.
- *Does the story idea have relevance in a local market?* While many institutions would like to think that their news has national and international value, the reality is that most campus-based news has greatest appeal in a local market. Whether local or national, a story idea must convince reporters and editors that they should be doing a story on the subject or activity in question.
- *Is your message prepared in an acceptable format?* A news release is not necessarily a news story, but regardless of the form in which a story idea is conveyed (e.g., news release, letter, backgrounder, or tip sheet), it must answer the journalist's basic questions of who, what, when, where, why, and sometimes how. Furthermore, the message should contain this key information within the first paragraph, then be supported by important details, and then followed up with miscellaneous information that may be helpful to the editor or news director in making a decision. The approach should be
  - *Direct.* The 10-second sound bite applies to writing, too.
  - *Singular.* Don't mix several stories together.
  - *Specific.*
  - *Well written.* Use journalistic style.
  - *Formatted conveniently.* Use news release hard copy, script, backgrounder.
  - *Suitably conveyed.* Consider a personal letter or individually crafted news release, fax, or e-mail.
  - *Localized.* Use a hometown story on a student or faculty member, or research that parallels other similar activities in the news medium's circulation or audience area.
  - *Sent sparingly.* Inundating the news media with too many messages means that important news is overlooked and lumped in with the materials routinely discarded.

Emulating and practicing journalistically sound approaches will prove significantly more successful than simply sending out messages that are not prioritized and not carefully targeted.

Working with News Media

Communications consultant Keith Moore says there are five basic steps to building news coverage of academic institutions:

1. **Educate** yourself to the needs and tendencies of the media gatekeepers.
2. **Communicate** personally.
3. **Cultivate** a reputation for good service.
4. **Investigate** a variety of approaches, perspectives, or angles.
5. **Anticipate** opportunities for coverage.

Contacting news media begins with the identification of resources that provide the addresses, telephone and fax numbers, and e-mail addresses of reporters, editors, and news directors at

- daily and weekly newspapers
- television stations and networks
- AM and FM radio stations and networks
- campus radio and television stations
- cable news networks
- wire services and syndicates
- Internet and Web news services
- regional and national magazines
- suburban and shopper newspapers
- internal publications for employees and customers of businesses and industries
- professional journals and magazines
- high school and college newspapers
- education press and association newsletters and magazines
- scientific and scholarly journals

Information about these news sources can be obtained from a wide variety of providers, including directories published by Gale, Bacon, and Hudson's—for example, *Editor & Publisher* and *Broadcast Yearbook*. Most academic institutions develop mailing lists based on locality (local community, region, and national and international media) as well as subject matter—science, art and entertainment, religion, ethnicity, sports, obituaries, etc.

Mailing lists are most effective when they not only are computerized, but also contain individual names and titles for each recipient of a message sent via mail, fax, e-mail, or any other method. Detailed, differentiated lists are particularly important at large, complex universities with significant numbers of academic disciplines and sources of expertise. The best systems for generating letters, advisories, and news releases imprint directly on the envelope rather than using labels, and print upper and lowercase letters that look as close to old-fashioned typewriting as possible. All direct mail research shows that this technique is more likely to guarantee that the message will be opened. Computer lists also should allow for broadcast faxes, e-mail, and the use of telephone numbers for later calls to reinforce awareness that the message sent has been received.

Personal visits to the news media are an excellent way to learn the organization of local newspapers, magazines, radio, and television stations. The visits should be brief, effective, and allow for the exchange of important information that will be helpful to the institution in future contacts, but should also provide information to editors and reporters that is worthy of a personal call or visit. Be sure to note the names of specific editors and reporters that may have future interest in what the institution can provide. These would include those who cover education, business, science and medicine, arts and entertainment, and general news. Also of importance can be book reviewers and reporters of consumer news, environment, fashion, food, gardening, decorating, special events, travel, and lifestyles. All of these names must then be integrated into the office's list systems.

Institutions that seek attention outside their locality, such as national universities and colleges, may want to target key cities in which alumni reside and from which students are recruited. Here, too, the technique of making personal visits to cultivate relationships is essential, and the development of mailing lists specific to each market is vital. In all cases—local or national—nothing works better than consistent, personal contact with reporters, broadcasters, and editors. Just as running a beat system on campus is critical, so is the time necessary to make repeat, effective calls on journalists in their own offices. All media cultivation activities require excellent interpersonal skills, strong journalistic background, and a sense of what is appropriate and newsworthy for each individual reporter.

Participation in national journalism organizations also can be productive if the institution has significant expertise in selected disciplines of interest to reporters, such as the Society of Environmental Journalists, the Education Writers Association, Council for the Advancement of Science Writing, and the National Association of Science Writers. When key faculty make presentations at national or international meetings of scholars, media frequently will flock to these events, such as the American Association for the Advancement of Science, the Modern Language Association, and many more.

A third category of journalism contacts consists of freelance writers and television producers who sell their story ideas to print and electronic media. Freelancers can be highly successful in working with national media outlets and should be cultivated as a potential conduit for news and story ideas. Virtually all popular magazines, as well as news magazines, now rely on a stable of these writers to provide them with both news and feature material. Addresses and telephone numbers may be obtained by contacting the publication in which their work appears, as long as the author has agreed to let them give out that information. Another source of freelancers is the directory of the American Society of Journalists and Authors.

Whether contacts are made with regular news media staff or with freelancers, it is important to remember the following admonitions:

- Always submit the material in the proper format, free of errors and consistent with accepted style, including news releases, scripts, backgrounders, and news features.
- Allow sufficient time for deadlines, which for newspapers may be days, for electronic media hours and minutes, and for magazines weeks and months.
- Once you have submitted material, you cannot ask to review the final article or script and you must not ask for special consideration or favors.
- After the story is submitted, be judicious in contacting the media if it does not appear in a timely fashion, and never appear to question an editor's decision not to use a submission.
- Do not be surprised if additional questions arise from the submitted material, which in some cases may be embarrassing, controversial, or contradictory to the intended effort.
- On stories with wide appeal, avoid offering exclusives to one medium over another. This practice can backfire and leave a bad taste in the mouths of journalists who are cut out of the process.
- Always tell the truth, no matter how painful, but remember how you say something can be just as important as what is being reported.
- Read, watch, and listen to news media with whom contact will be made. Nothing is more insulting to a journalist than contact with a public relations professional who is not current on what that reporter or broadcaster has written or produced in the past few days and weeks. This requires reading several newspapers daily, monitoring radio and TV news programs, and tracking news material via Internet and the World Wide Web search services.

Finally, a new category of news media contact services has emerged with the development of the Internet and the World Wide Web, for example, ProfNet and QuadNet. These services share information via electronic mail with reporters, scholars, and educational public relations professionals. Charges are made for these services, and significant daily attention is required if they are to be effective and utilized in ways that are productive both for reporters and for faculty experts. Institutions that routinely monitor these services often find they are valuable new assets in the mix of contact methods with journalists.

ORGANIZING THE NEWS MEDIA RELATIONS OFFICE

At most large academic institutions, the operation of the news media relations office relies on a team of professionals, each a specialist in an area of writing, editing, or editorial management. Generally this area is managed by an individual with the title (or its equivalent) of director, who has extensive experience in public relations, journalism, and staff management. Much of this individual's time will be taken up with institutional matters, budgets, committees, and coaching the staff on news issues and opportunities. Reporting to this individual are reporters and writers who specialize in coverage of selected academic disciplines that coincide with the expectations of print and electronic media. Examples are science writers who cover engineering, natural sciences, and mathematics; social science writers who cover political science, history, sociology, social work, law, and other areas that impact the human and socioeconomic aspects of society; business writers who cover business schools, economics, political economy, and any other subjects that are of interest to the business editors in the news media; and sports writers who cover primarily varsity athletics. While these are the more common areas of specialization, research institutions also may have specialists in the arts, the humanities, continuing education, health and medicine, hometown news about student achievements, agriculture, and so forth.

Typically, an elementary or secondary school will have one individual who virtually does all news, as well as publications work, for the entire institution. A small liberal arts college will typically have one full-time person covering academic subjects and institutional news, with either a half-time or full-time individual covering varsity athletics.

Mid-size universities and colleges with 3,000 to 7,500 students will often have 2 or 3 persons covering news about academic subjects and a full-time sports information director. Large urban and research universities with enrollments ranging from 7,500 to more than 50,000 students can typically have staffs ranging in size from 4 or 5 persons in the news operation to more than 20 individuals. Sports information will range in size from two to four professionals. In the very largest universities, it is common for the news operations to be distributed throughout the institution, rarely reporting to a specific, single manager. These separate news operations could include business, medicine, agriculture, sports, and central administration. While distributed, decentralized news operations are not always as effective, many institutions with multiple news offices voluntarily collaborate to share information and to avoid unnecessary and embarrassing duplication with editors and reporters in the print and electronic media.

Because academic institutions—large and small—have internal newsletters and tabloid newspapers for employees, it is not uncommon for an individual to produce this material on either a part-time or a full-time basis, gleaning material prepared by the news staff. At larger, more complex institutions, these internal publications can have a complement of editors and writers, totaling as many as four or five individuals, for a large, 8- to 12-page institutional tabloid.

Regardless of staff size, all institutions require the use of systematic office procedures, annual planning, and strategies that focus only on the most important activities. This is just as true for a one-person shop as it is for a team of 10 or 20 professionals.

BEYOND NEWS RELEASES: GETTING THE STORY OUT

While news releases will probably remain the primary tool of most educational public relations offices, institutions are finding more effective ways of communicating important messages and story ideas to journalists in both print and electronic news. Each of these techniques relies heavily on the strength of a good "news peg" or expert resource, a well-organized message, and strong sense of timing and timeliness.

Here are just some of the techniques developed in recent years on a number of campuses:

- *Feature service.* On a weekly or monthly basis, the institution sends out two- and three-page-long background stories on cutting-edge research and scholarship of high news value in such fields as medicine, science, social science, and applied technology. These are sent either individually or more often as packages of 3 or 4 stories with a cover sheet synopsizing the contents in 50-word or shorter statements. Generally, feature services are not as timely as breaking or embargoed news stories that are better handled through traditional news releases and perhaps press conferences.

- *Tip sheets.* Issued daily, weekly, or monthly, these brief sheets contain a number of story ideas (described in 25 words or less) that rely totally on the reporter or broadcaster to develop the story subjects. Tip sheets are particularly valuable for prime-time news and for breaking stories where journalists are looking for a quick solution to fill time or space. The preferred way to distribute tip sheets is via fax and electronic mail.

- *Calendars.* Weekly and monthly event calendars produced expressly for the news media can often replace wasted effort on news releases announcing activities of low news value, such as student music recitals, dance programs and art exhibits, etc., that only will appear on the calendar published by the local paper, city magazine, or radio or TV stations. Be sure the calendar entries cover *all* potentially newsworthy events—even those for which separate news releases are warranted. Remember that monthly publications need calendar announcements as much as eight weeks beforehand, weekly publications need two weeks, and daily papers and programs may need copy a week in advance. Send the calendar to all reporters and editors who may have an interest in covering the events listed.

- *Expert commentary.* By hourly and daily monitoring of broadcast and electronic news, educational institutions can quickly respond to breaking news stories and natural disasters by providing articulate experts knowledgeable in the subject under consideration, especially those faculty who are candid, poignant, and concise. The result is inclusion in a national or international story following a telephone call or other personal contact with the reporters working on the breaking story. Major discoveries and natural disasters provide particularly high potential for expert commentary.

- *Op-Eds.* For nearly three decades, newspapers have been accepting opinion pieces of generally no more than 750 words from experts on a wide array of timely topics relative to current news and to social and political trends. Op-eds have become a favorite vehicle for scholars in humanities, the arts, and the social sciences. Because the expert writes his or her own copy, it is essential that editing advice and assistance be provided, so that the newspapers will consider the submission for use in the page that is often opposite the editorial page (hence the term, "Op-Ed").

- *Hometown news.* Significant accomplishments by students and faculty may not warrant coverage in the general media, but will receive excellent play in hometown weekly newspapers and some local electronic media if properly presented. Educational institutions routinely write hometown stories of no more than one page in length about academic honors, election to honorary club memberships, graduation honors, athletic achievements, and a wide array of other items that appeal to small media markets. Institutions will frequently send a copy of the hometown release to the parents of students, noting that copies were sent to local media and that the parent should inquire if the story does not appear within a few days. Hometown stories also are done on faculty with not only hometown media, but also with the alumni magazines of their alma maters. *Note: Do not expect major metropolitan newspapers or large electronic news outlets to use hometown stories. They have appeal primarily in smaller markets.*

- *Radio news services.* Just as a news release is a very traditional source of information for print media, a radio actuality (live recording) can be helpful in radio news and radio programming if the material is journalistically sound and of high broadcast quality. Through the use of a relatively inexpensive broadcast-quality tape recorder, news media relations offices can record and edit comments for significant stories and press conferences and then convey this information via delivered tape or by telephone transmission to stations looking for more depth on a routine news report. In addition, some larger institutions produce weekly or monthly radio news services, often focused on such specific topics as medicine, science, and the environment. These are sent as tapes with the accompanying scripts to stations, syndicates, and networks for use either in the form submitted, or as edited comments to be included with other programming materials and news reports. Another popular technique is an 800-number that the station can call to "download" a broadcast-quality recording from your campus. (Not all radio outlets can use these materials, but they may use the tape as a guideline for a later interview to be conducted directly with the subject involved.)

- *Television news services.* Because most television news staffs are overextended and unable to travel more than 40 or 50 miles to cover education and research stories, academic institutions have discovered that by submitting broadcast-quality, edited video news materials to television stations, they will receive significant usage from science and medicine, business, and lifestyle reporters. Stations and particularly networks may be more likely to use these materials if copies of the field tapes are submitted as well—so that the station can check to be certain that the interviews are journalistically sound and that editing was appropriate. Some networks will review these video news releases and will then replicate them in their own coverage of the very same story! Before proceeding with a television news service, institutions should determine whether stations in the region have union restrictions on the use of videotape not provided directly by station personnel. Generally, these restrictions only apply to a radius of 50 miles or less from the station itself.
- *Media events.* Not to be confused with press conferences, media events are opportunities for the print and electronic news media to visit the campus and to cover some important activity or event, such as speeches by prominent politicians and social leaders, demonstrations of a new science or technology, major seasonal events, such as alumni reunions and commencements, etc. These "opportunities" are organized and orchestrated to accommodate the deadlines of the print and electronic media whenever possible.
- *Press conferences.* Judicious care should be taken in calling press conferences. News media are interested only if a truly major, earth-shaking announcement is forthcoming, such as an appointment of a new chief executive, naming of a faculty member as a Nobel laureate, or a catastrophic tragedy, such as an earthquake, fire, or tornado. Press conferences should never be called for anything but the most important breaking news, which does not include gifts that are less than mega size (under $25 million), appointments of deans and chaired professors, or a new higher ranking by *U.S. News.*
- *Press kits.* Whenever a press conference or a media event is held, it is important to prepare a press kit that contains such related materials as news releases, background information, fact sheets, photographs, speeches, clippings, and anything else that would be of interest and use to reporters.
- *Photographs and videotapes.* Newspapers and television stations generally take their own images and rarely accept them from local sources—unless they are head-and-shoulders portraits. However, when a press conference or a media event is staged, it is sometimes impossible for them to obtain copies of such images as architectural renderings, aerial views of the area in question, or video clips of historic importance or conceptualizations of buildings,

research images, etc. These situations require that the institution provide images as part of the announcement. If outside assistance is needed, it is best to secure the services of experienced news photographers and news videographers, rather than persons who do other kinds of images, such as photographers who specialize in advertising or documentaries. By using a seasoned professional, the institution will not only receive the appropriate images, but it also may benefit from the contacts that the photographer has with news media in disseminating the images he or she has supplied. All photographs must have a caption attached to the back, whether it is a head-and-shoulders portrait or a complex image of a research activity.

- *Sponsored mega events.* Events that have significant interest to the news media, such as the presidential debates, Olympic festivals, or international summit meetings, provide a venue that combines the qualities of a campus setting with the news potential of events that draw hundreds and sometimes thousands of representatives of the news media. Events of this magnitude require either highly trained and specialized campus staff, or the services of outsourced providers who can advise the institution in staging and hosting the activity, as well as managing the services needed for print and electronic media—including electrical power, satellite hookups, telephone systems, computer links, food service, and security.

- *Meet with editorial boards.* Most newspapers and some electronic media have regular editorial board meetings to which experts and leaders are invited to present a point of view and to be questioned by staff from the editorial page, the newsroom, and by columnists and special investigative reporters employed by the newspaper or station. Editorial boards are particularly useful in trying to explain complex issues, such as financial aid, federal research funding, community relations issues, etc. In some cases, the meeting is requested by the editorial board, but most often it is the result of a query from the institution, primarily from the public relations office. These can be particularly helpful for the chief executive in sharing vital information with the media, and these types of meetings should be routinely scheduled at least annually with local news media. Also important are editorial board meetings with visiting dignitaries and prominent leaders attracted to campus for commencements and special events.

- *Consider media placement counsel.* Institutions seeking attention in large, metropolitan areas, particularly New York and Washington, D.C., may find the use of news media placement advisory firms helpful. These services are available from public relations firms that primarily serve business and industry, but the retaining fees are so high and the cultures so different that these relationships rarely last more than a few months. Most educational institutions work better with firms that specialize in academic media relations.

Firms such as Gehrung Associates, Dobisky Associates, Dick Jones, or College Connections generally do good work, but their ongoing effectiveness is directly related to the amount of pressure brought to bear by the institution in answer to the question, "What are you doing for us now?"

- *Embargoed stories.* Whenever possible, media appreciate advance warning that a major story or event is coming. A commonly used (and misused) technique is to embargo the story for a specific time and date before sharing it with editors and reporters. This should only be done with stories that are exceptionally newsworthy and for which a clear reason exists as to why the story cannot be released sooner. The most common reasons are scholarly journal research stories that have a specific publication date and efforts to ensure that the parties affected by the event or action can be notified directly by the institution before they see it on the newspaper or on television or radio. It is common for embargoed releases to be shared only with a few select media whose prior behavior indicates that they can be trusted to honor the request for holding the story. (*A note of warning: There is no law or rule that says the embargo must be honored if the news media feel that it is unwarranted to wait until the appointed time and date to release the information.*)

- *Try talk and interview shows.* The hottest area in electronic media is the talk show format, which literally is the sole format of some radio stations and occupies a significant portion of daytime and late-night television. These programs are always seeking new material, and they are not offended when approached with ideas about individuals who are willing to put themselves before questioners, whether they are call-in listeners and viewers or talk show hosts. Radio shows will often arrange for a special telephone hook-up, avoiding the need to go directly to the station or city from which the program is aired. On the other hand, television almost always requires the presence of the administrator, student, or faculty member on the television stage set. Be sure to research the subject matter of the program involved so that the match between the institution's expert and the general approach of the program is compatible. Avoid putting students, faculty, and administrators on programs that have a history of outrageous behavior or inappropriate questioning.

- *Public relations wire services.* For a fee, institutions can contract with public relations wire services that have arrangements with the newsrooms of print and electronic media to share news releases either as hard-copy output from teleprinters, as specially formatted electronic information for newspaper computers, or as e-mail sent via the Internet. These services are expensive and have met with mixed reviews by the campuses that use them. On the other hand, some services offer electronically distributed text capabilities that are not available to academic institutions and often at a cost that is competitive with postal rates. Institutions electing to attempt these services should track costs and impact carefully.

- *Pitch letters.* The use of highly focused, targeted letters with selected editors and reporters can be particularly effective when seeking coverage of a newsworthy special event or an unusual process that may be taking place on the campus, such as highly interesting research or a seminar on issues of importance to news media. By crafting a letter intended to promote the specific event, results can be significant, although personal telephone calls and visits generally are more effective when time and money allow these more personal approaches to be used. However, pitch letters are generally much more effective than news releases, tip sheets, or other generalized forms of contact with the news media.

- *Cable television.* Some institutions have attempted to develop programming for use on public access channels and higher education channels on local and regional cable systems, only to discover viewership is generally very low and has difficulty competing with commercial and public television programming. Those institutions that invest in these commitments should assess cost-effectiveness whenever possible.

- *Educational television programming.* A few universities and colleges actually own and operate their own television and radio stations, which usually are independent of the public relations division. Most of these stations are categorized as public, but a few commercial stations also are owned by academic institutions. When funds and talented producers are available, some of these institutions produce educational programming that can be aired not only on the local station, but also can be syndicated and sold on a national and international basis. In these situations, institutions benefit from an agreement that the programming will be clearly identified with the institution, including favorable treatment toward faculty experts—without challenging the need for expert sources external to the institution. Some stations are required to identify the parent institution at least hourly throughout the broadcast day. (*Note: Access to campus television satellite uplink and downlink systems can assist the public relations office in sending out important messages, particularly during a crisis.*)

- *Sports events and broadcasts.* Athletics are an essential ingredient in the life of academic institutions, whether or not they offer athletic scholarships for students. The coverage of these events can range from campus radio stations for NCAA Division III institutions all the way up to international broadcasts on networks and sports cable systems for NCAA Division I competitors. Savvy institutions require that the contracts for these programs include opportunities to communicate information about the institution at some point during the broadcast. For bowl games, some universities receive at least one minute of free television air time. The production of these messages can help build a better appreciation for the activities in the classroom and other nonathletic academic activities. Some Division I institutions require that at least three or four pages of the printed program at home games include specific academic information about the host institution, its mission, and its strengths.

None of the techniques listed above is a panacea. Each can be employed effectively under the right circumstances and conditions. Seasoned public relations officials often will review such a list before deciding how to tackle a specific project or problem. The techniques described in this section will work best if the public relations office is equipped with state-of-the-art equipment, such as Web and Internet-capable computers networked to all other staff, not only in public relations, but throughout the institution via e-mail and other ethernet connections. In addition, the staff needs fax machines, high-speed copiers, high-resolution laser printers for computers, beepers, hand-held cellular phones, and telephone systems that are capable of establishing at least a three-way telephone conference call and supporting call-in "hot lines." These are the basics. A few institutions are equipped with sophisticated radio and television studios, complete with broadcast-quality equipment. On-line video editing capability also can be a significant asset where the institution can afford such investment and upkeep.

With the advent of high-quality digital images now approaching, photography is quickly going toward a filmless environment in which all images will be taken on magnetic or optical recording devices and used to create electronic images on the Web, printed publications, and wire-service-quality photographs that can be sent nearly instantaneously to news media. And virtually all radio and television editing is now done with digital technology. Keeping pace with the rapid development of new technology is a costly but necessary component of successful public relations, especially media relations.

CHAPTER 18

Public Relations Begin at Home: Why Good Internal Communications Are Vital

M. Fredric Volkmann

When a Midwestern, publicly assisted university surveyed the opinion leaders in its state, it discovered to its great surprise that the academic quality of the institution was perceived to be significantly less than that of its primary out-of-state competitor. Even more shocking was the fact that more than half of these opinion leaders were graduates of the university in question. Because the institution had embarked earlier on a program to improve its academic reputation with alumni and the general public, no one could understand why the institution was held in lower-than-expected regard. The answer revealed itself when subsequent research showed that the primary source of the opinion leaders' information about the institution was not the material sent out by the alumni office nor was it information gleaned from the news media (which were being supplied with ample quantities of positive news by the institution). The primary source of information was direct, personal contact with faculty, staff, and students of the university, no matter how far these opinion leaders lived and worked from the campus and the city in which it was located.

Surveys of employee opinion showed that a significantly negative perception existed on the campus about its academic quality and about the efforts to improve the institution's reputation. The out-of-state competitor was perceived by employees to be a vastly stronger academic entity.

The lesson is that good public relations must begin at home. Employees come first in any communications effort to alter perception, build reputation, or increase pride. In this instance, the university embarked upon an aggressive program of improved communications with employees, beginning with a vastly better faculty-staff newspaper. It launched a number of other efforts intended to build a sense of pride and trust and to establish a factual foundation about the real improvements the institution had made in its curriculum and overall reputation.

INTERNAL AUDIENCES VARY WIDELY

The internal audiences of a typical educational institution are complex combinations of widely disparate socioeconomic groups of varying educational achievement. These audiences range from governing boards to faculty, graduate and professional students, graduate teaching and research assistants, staff, administration, undergraduates who either commute or live in residence halls, continuing education students who attend classes evenings and weekends, and contract employees who work at the institution but are employed by outsourced providers. Additionally, other internal audiences are neighbors living close to campus, visiting prospective students and their families, parents, and returning alumni. Insiders can be vendors, volunteers who serve on various councils, and guests attending cultural activities that take place on the campus. Each of these internal audiences has special needs, expectations, and biases regarding the institution. For reasons of economy, many institutions mistakenly divide these audiences into three groups—faculty, staff, and students. These oversimplifications do not account for the significant subgroups in each of these categories. For example, faculty clearly divide themselves between those who are tenure track and those who are not—up to and including the right of nontenured faculty to vote in faculty senate actions. Graduate and professional students represent not only a wide array of disciplines, but also such subgroups as medical school interns and residents attached to affiliated teaching hospitals; they do not appreciate being categorized with undergraduates.

Educational differences between internal audiences also are profound: Faculty usually have the Ph.D. or other highest terminal degree, while many support staff may range from high school dropouts to college undergraduate degree holders. Salaries are highly inconsistent within many faculties—particularly at universities with medical schools where faculty can earn several times more than the administrators who run the institutions.

Complicating all of this is the sense of territoriality that grows around each division of the institution. The scientists have their buildings, the humanists theirs, the medical and other health educators are often on a separate campus, and the athletics department is usually tucked away on a far corner of the campus. Bridging the psychological, intellectual, and physical gaps between all of these various categories makes campus internal relations a daunting prospect.

Among the most profound societal changes to affect the American workplace has been the rapid and radical downsizing of business and industry and conversion toward management structures commonly referred to as Total Quality Management. Streamlining and cost pressures have profoundly altered the way in which employees look at their work—away from jobs for life toward transportable skills for life. To varying degrees, campus employees are being affected by similar changes. Because of tenure, faculty have been impacted less by such changes, but the overall effect is clearly being felt and requires much more efficient internal communications between management, staff, faculty, and students, as well as communication within various subcategories.

Paralleling these changes is the advent of computers and related technologies that are changing how staff work and how productivity is measured. The result is not fewer messages, but in some cases, a doubling and tripling of information sharing through e-mail, electronic file transfer, Web site utilization, voice mail for telephone systems, and new software and hardware still entering the workplace. The outcome is a complex hodgepodge of vastly greater numbers of messages competing for attention and clearly affecting how work is carried out and evaluated.

To some, these are threats to the traditional "Ivory Tower" that affect how campus communities are now evolving. For generations the typical academic institution limited itself to being a place where students lived and learned, faculty taught and researched, and administrators did their best to preserve and protect this thriving enterprise from interference from the outside world. Now campuses are being forced into global perspectives, whereby virtually all who live and work there can instantaneously communicate with colleagues, parents, business, and any other internal and external audiences via the World Wide Web, Internet, digital telephone, and even television and radio satellite uplinks and downlinks.

HOW CAMPUSES COMMUNICATE WITHIN THEMSELVES

Left to their own devices, all employees of academic institutions will do what comes naturally in sharing news and information. They talk to each other. Unfortunately, word of mouth is not a reliable way of communicating, because it is usually fueled with a mixture of facts, rumor, fantasy, fear, and outright falsehoods. Institutions that do not earnestly attempt to communicate regularly and candidly with employees are failing to pursue the very reason for their existence—the academy's continual search for truth and knowledge. Instead, the rumor mill is the most trusted source of information, whether rumors are true or not. Although rumor and gossip will never be eliminated, a proactive, employee-sensitive communications program can do a great amount toward improving internal relations, which will subsequently impact the external relations of the institution.

Institutions with the best internal relations programs realize that good news and bad news must be shared first with faculty, students, staff, and all the ensuing subgroups they represent. Not telling the campus community that it will be the subject of an Internal Revenue Service (IRS) institutional audit is just as bad as failing to quickly announce the selection of a faculty member as a Nobel laureate—and maybe even worse. Why? Because the facts surrounding the audit or similar bad news are often clouded with innuendo, half truths, and false assumptions as to why the IRS is coming to campus. The truth may be that this is truly a routine audit to which any 501(c)3 institution may be subjected. To be effective, a proactive internal relations program must also be perceived as trustworthy and timely. Otherwise, the rumor mill will always rule. For these reasons, successfully managed academic institutions work hard to be sure that all employees and students hear good news and bad news before it becomes general knowledge off the campus. This says that the institution cares about its internal constituencies before it worries about reactions from the press, politicians, and the general public.

Any strategies for effective internal relations must capitalize on the wide and varied channels of communication that exist on a typical campus. These include various types of traditional mail, telephone systems, computer and other electronic communications, bulletin boards and kiosks, organized meetings, and the employee newsletter or tabloid newspaper. In the following information are the most common aspects of campus communications, explained in the context of getting important news out quickly to affected parties on and off the campus:

- *Speeches and presentations.* Nothing is more effective than a first-hand, face-to-face, earnest effort on the part of institutional leaders to convey a message through the various constituencies on a campus. This can be done by speeches and presentations at institutionwide assemblies, special meetings for select, targeted groups of employees and students, and any other number of combinations. Most often these efforts address institutional policies that affect the lives of those who learn and work on the campus—policies ranging from parking (the most volatile issue on virtually any campus) to such difficult situations as layoffs, salary freezes, and reductions in operating expenses. If the message has broad appeal both on and off the campus, it also is possible to invite the news media to attend the presentation, followed by a press conference or interview session. Generally, this is done only when the news is positive and not where the announcement will adversely affect students and staff.

- *Videotapes, CD-ROM disks, computer presentations, slides, and audio tapes.* The explosion of electronic technologies to support communications has been particularly strong for visual presentations, particularly as support for speeches and events. Since many of these technologies are used for instructional purposes, they are readily available on campus to support internal activities that involve students, faculty, or staff. Each has its advantages and disadvantages: videotapes are expensive to produce, and most institutions therefore cannot afford to make videos with high production values. CD-ROM is an emerging technology that still is limited in its quality and convenience. The use of slides remains a relatively inexpensive presentation technique and compares favorably in cost with overhead transparencies and other older technologies, simply because most of these materials can now be produced on desktop computer systems with relatively inexpensive software. Computer-projected presentations are emerging as one of the primary techniques for internal communication, simply because of the improvement in technology and the reduction in cost of computers and the requisite software. However, the better presentation packages require extensive training and experience to fully utilize all of the bells and whistles that come with them. For simple computer presentations that emulate more traditional overhead presentations, many institutions use PowerPoint or similar software. Of lesser interest today is the use of audiotapes to augment presentations, unless the material is intended for background purposes, such as music.

- *Traditional mail.* Once considered the primary means of campus communications, traditional mail has become less reliable because it is not as fast or as responsive as many newer forms of electronic communication. However, many institutions find that major announcements sent with an accompanying short memorandum attached to a news release or a similar document are greatly appreciated by employees and students if it is clear that the announcements are sent to them at least 24 hours before similar announcements are made outside the institution. While this is not always possible, it is a generally accepted practice to make an attempt to use "snail mail" when absolute urgency is not necessary. The sender of the covering memorandum or letter can be as important as the message itself. A message signed by the chief executive will be perceived as carrying much more value than something sent by the human resources office, the public relations office, or the business office.

- *Telephone voice mail and hotlines.* Highly sophisticated telephone systems, which are becoming much more commonplace on campuses, include the ability to provide voice messaging services to every student and employee. Many such systems also have the ability to put a common message in the voice mail boxes of all people on the system simultaneously. This means that an important—but very short—announcement can be simultaneously shared with virtually every telephone user at the institution. Such messages often refer the listener to the institutional Web homepage, to traditional mail, or to a telephone hotline containing longer messages. At some institutions hotlines are maintained year round as information sources, so that anyone can call a prepublished number for a daily or weekly update on institutional news. Other institutions use hotlines only during emergencies and for important announcements. Campuses are discovering that maintaining routinely updated information lines has lost effectiveness, and Web pages and other forms of electronic communication are preferable.

- *E-mail.* Electronic mail has revolutionized how employees communicate not only with each other, but also with the institution's leadership. Campuses with uniform e-mail systems can instantaneously place important announcements in the e-mail boxes of all constituents quickly and with minimal disruption. Unfortunately, academic institutions have dozens of different e-mail systems that are difficult to connect when an emergency announcement has to be sent quickly and simultaneously to hundreds or thousands of staff members and students. In fact, some institutions can crash their computers by attempting to force a long e-mail message into an already overburdened server. For these reasons, some institutions limit institutional e-mail messages to very short announcements that refer the reader to voice mail, hotlines, traditional mail, and to institutional Web sites. Regardless, individualized e-mail is probably the most popular form of communication on most campuses, because it is efficient, cheap, and highly reliable when dealing with modest numbers of people at the same time.

- *Web sites.* The World Wide Web is a phenomenon that is yet to be fully understood and appreciated. In most environments the use of Web pages and other information is passive—awaiting the interest of a reader to search out information about the institution or its programs, students, and faculty. On the other hand, Web pages have become personalized bulletin boards that allow virtually every member of a campus community to post his or her own messages as well as to seek and read those of virtually everyone else. While most of these systems do not permit rifle-shot prompts encouraging someone to read a message on a homepage, the use of voice mail and e-mail can combine to make Web pages extremely effective communications tools when rapid, high-volume messages need to be made available to all constituencies in relatively short order. For example, information about a particularly serious crime can be quickly typed up and posted on the institutional homepage, and then rapidly followed by e-mail and voice mail prompts telling the campus community that full details on the incident can be accessed via the institutional homepage. Additional advantages include the ability to quickly scan pictures and diagrams for inclusion on a Web site message as well as the possibility on some campuses of voice and video enhancements. The one great disadvantage is the fact that virtually all campus computer systems are hardwired and leave those who are attending class and working in nonoffice environments or off campus unable to read the message until they can access a network-capable computer. A few campuses are now experimenting with wireless computer communications that will make it possible for someone to use a computer notebook or even smaller portable computer that receives and sends information via high-frequency, high-capacity radio waves similar to cellular phones.

- *House organs.* This category of campus communication, discussed at greater length later in this section, includes tabloid newspapers, newsletters, flyers, magazines, annual reports, periodic letters from the chief executive, and department-level messages. These can be daily, weekly, or monthly communications, now often supported by a nearly simultaneous posting of printed messages on the institutional Web site.

- *Student newspapers.* While student newspapers generally are either wholly or semi-independent from institutional control, they can be effective institutional communications vehicles through the use of paid advertisement or inserts. Large, complex institutions with frequently published student newspapers (at least twice a week) have found that purchasing advertising space as a place to publish its own message can be effective when routine information needs to be communicated, such as proceedings of a trustee meeting, faculty meeting, or any announcement where the precision of the language is critical, such as judicial procedures, drug-use sanctions, etc.

- *Bulletin boards.* Although the advent of the Web has diminished the use of employee bulletin boards in lunchrooms and hallways, other versions of these traditional message holders have continued to blossom. Kiosks in student residence hall areas, banners strung between trees across sidewalks, and sidewalk "chalking" have become popular alternatives to electronic communication and offer the opportunity for large-scale, aggressive messages. Particularly popular are vertical event-related banners attached to street light poles along the boundaries of campuses. Although these require the permission of the power company or municipality to install, they do provide a significant opportunity to promote and advertise arts events and a number of other internally important activities to the campus community. On campuses where athletics have a particularly high profile, some institutions also use the electronic scoreboards at football and basketball games to provide institutional messages.

- *Campus radio, television, and cable stations.* As the cost of installing and managing student-run radio and television stations has dropped, even small institutions have instituted campuswide services not unlike the expansion in the 1950s and 1960s of low-power radio stations or closed-circuit stations that use existing power lines as radiators for their signals. Campus television stations use coaxial cable or fiber-optic cable to deliver commercial cable television signals to residence hall rooms and classrooms, with a channel reserved for institutional use. Some institutions can employ these cable or computer fiber-optic systems with enough flexibility that a special channel can be set aside for use when making major announcements, holding press conferences, or televising significant campus events or activities of interest to students, faculty, and staff. This allows any person on campus with a cable-connected television or video-capable computer to tune in a university transmission. These are relatively inexpensive to produce, as long as a television camera and conversion unit can be easily connected to the cable or fiber-optic system itself.

- *Public address systems.* More commonly used in elementary and secondary institutions, public address systems can be used for brief messages that must be conveyed in a timely fashion to a large number of students and faculty. The systems can be especially useful in announcing upcoming events, recognizing individual student achievement, and dealing with institutional policy issues that are not complex or that will be dealt with in more detail in a separate, upcoming mailing to those affected by it. (These systems were attempted on college campuses in the late 1960s and early 1970s, but the "big-brother-is-watching" image soon discouraged the use of this technique for internal communication.)

- *Posters, tent cards, and door hangers.* Communications that promote events often are lost in the background noise of the thousands of messages that are rained upon the average person each day. Some campuses have discovered that the use of special printed posters on doorways, bulletin boards, windows, and other places where they can be easily removed are effective ways to provide short-term awareness of major events. Another technique commonly used on campuses is to place table tent cards in the faculty, staff, and student dining areas with a short announcement of an upcoming activity. A third technique commonly used in residence halls is to print door hangers that slip over the door handles and often are used to announce theater, athletic, or student social events. Each of these techniques only works as long as it is used sparingly and does not become part of the overall background noise.

- *Paycheck envelopes and stubs.* Despite the advent of electronic payroll deposits, most institutions still provide a paper receipt to employees to indicate that the electronic deposit has taken place. The receipts have space to add limited-length messages directly onto the paycheck stub or onto the electronic deposit receipt. These are becoming less frequently conveyed in envelopes where additional information can be inserted.

- *Performance evaluations and exit interviews.* A commonly overlooked but important aspect of internal relations is the value of exit interviews with departing employees, not only to determine the quality of management and work relationships, but also to acquire candid appraisals of how well the institution communicates with its employees. It is rare that these interviews are seen as part of an internal relations communications program. The same can be said for performance evaluations, which are employed in varying degrees at academic institutions. While still uncommon in assessing faculty performance, these documents are more likely to be used with staff and administration. If the evaluation is a two-way effort, the criticisms of employees about the work environment can be helpful in developing a better internal communications program, as long as the human resources office has a method for evaluating this feedback.

The most common techniques for reaching students, faculty, staff, and other constituencies are effective only when employed in a strategic, coordinated fashion that maximizes the impact of important messages. In the past these messages were communicated only via house organs. Today, a major announcement of a significant event, such as hosting a presidential debate, can be announced via a press conference aired on the closed circuit campus television system with simultaneous messages sent via voice mail and e-mail inviting the campus community to either tune in the broadcast, or to check the institutional Web site for more details, and then followed by articles in the house organ, clippings posted on bulletin boards, and smaller meetings throughout the institution with programs and groups most affected by the announcement. There is no formula that says which form of communication must come first: every situation demands a unique and carefully strategized solution that leaves employees and students believing that they are being given special consideration and that every effort has been made to inform them first.

INTERNAL PERIODICALS AND PUBLICATIONS WILL RETAIN THEIR IMPORTANCE

Some have suggested that the advent of electronic communications—Web sites, e-mail, and voice mail—will rapidly replace the more traditional use of periodicals and publications to communicate within campus communities. Unfortunately, since computers are not easily transportable, new e-mail and Web pages must be read wherever a computer is physically located, rather than at a lunch table, on a commuter train, while walking across campus, or (heaven forbid!) during meetings and lectures. Further, most computer screens are extremely difficult to read under adverse, brightly lit conditions. Computer monitors lack the precise resolution of quality printing, and the screens do not readily expand in size to tabloid or newspaper formats. Until computer technology allows greater flexibility in receiving and reading electronic information, there will be a need for traditional printed matter, especially newsletters, tabloid newspapers, magazines, annual reports, flyers, promotional brochures, posters, and any number of other "low-tech" messages. Don't count out these old fashioned techniques until computers are readily usable in bedrooms and bathrooms, at beaches and ballgames, or in any other places where hookups, ambient light, or portability are not critical issues. Most believe that such improvements will not be fully integrated into personal and campus lifestyles for another decade or two.

Experienced advocates for internal periodicals and other publications know that it is not only the messages that the institution sends that are important, but what the reader accepts, absorbs, remembers, and acts upon. Before embarking on any new or revised efforts with house organs, the institution needs to know whether or not the various internal constituencies read and heed what already is being sent.

- Has the institution conducted readership studies to test the writing, design, and photography? Has the value of the content and its meaningfulness to readers been tested?
- Have focus groups been conducted to start dialogues on what may or may not be key issues that such readership studies should address?
- Have advisory committees been created to represent the interests and needs of various readers, in such categories as faculty, staff, and students?

Internal periodicals benefit from the results of focus group analysis and readership studies—and particularly from content analysis (all of which are described in a previous section). The use of advisory committees can be particularly helpful in balancing the personal and professional biases of the editors and writers with the needs of readers. Without testing and external validation from advisory groups, house organs may fall victim to becoming either a publishing medium for administrative dicta or a sounding board for the biases and interests of the editors.

A critical step in the development of an internal tabloid newspaper or newsletter is the operating statement, which usually contains the following: a statement of purpose or mission, a description of content, a definition of length and special sections, a listing of the editorial staff, a set of procedures and production steps, a typical production timetable, a description of the audience and the strategy for distributing the publication to that audience, and guidelines for the preparation and writing of special sections, such as features, tenure and promotion announcements, obituaries, and campus crime reports.

A typical statement of purpose for an employee newspaper would read something like the following:

> Open and thorough communication is key to creating and maintaining a sense of community on the campus. It is important that employees feel that they belong to and contribute to the success of a single community. It is the purpose of this vehicle to keep employees informed in a timely, accurate, and consistent manner, particularly of significant

issues and decisions that affect the entire community. The publication focuses on institutional goals and overall mission, as well as reporting on the activities of important faculty, committees, and task forces. This publication is a medium for recognizing the activities, research, and achievements of individuals and units. Keeping people informed about what others are working on and about accomplishments encourages participation and increases motivation. Additionally, readers are better able to discuss institutional issues and activities accurately when communicating with persons outside the campus community. Thus, readers can serve as a positive force in keeping the public informed about institutional achievements, goals, and challenges.

Therefore, the purpose of this publication is to:

1. Communicate the current academic (teaching and research) activities of the faculty, students, staff, and administrators.
2. Publicize the events on campus, such as lectures, art exhibits, and concerts.
3. Communicate news events that affect the entire community, such as new academic or administrative appointments or the construction of new buildings.
4. Provide information on human resource matters, institutional policies, and decisions by the trustees, faculty senate, academic, and administrative committees.*

The content ratios of a typical internal periodical will vary from issue to issue, but certain consistent information generally is carried in every issue: a calendar of campus events; reports on campus crime; announcements of research grants and awards, prizes, and honors recognizing faculty achievement; special events and presentations of campuswide interest that require more than a calendar mention; reports of books and journal articles published; recognition of presentations and professional meetings attended by faculty; alerts about deadlines for research and grant applications; announcements of important meetings of faculty governance and key committees; want ads for and by employees; and what is generally the best-read section of the publication—job postings prepared by the human resources office.

All of this is basic maintenance copy, but without the necessary "sizzle" that attracts readers and provides them with a framework of information that goes

---

*This statement of purpose is adapted from the operating statement of the Record, the official faculty/staff publication of Washington University. Courtesy of Washington University, St. Louis, Missouri.

beyond the routine. The critical differences are stories about outstanding people who study, research, teach, or serve the institution; feature stories and photographs on important programs that are receiving strong recognition; new units and programs; and stories about admissions progress, financial status, gift campaigns, athletic results, and even the proceedings of trustee meetings. Also carried in many of these publications are updates on human resource policies, official notices on benefits and application deadlines, vital statistics of the institution, and obituaries. The most important single purpose of the publication, however, is to reflect the core mission of the institution and to recognize the particular accomplishments that support teaching, research, and service.

Commonly overlooked in educational institutions is the importance of distributing internal periodicals not only to employees but also directly to homes where the entire family can read and enjoy the publication as well as take advantage of the activities and events it reports. Business and industry have long seen the value of engaging employees' families in the life of the company, but schools, colleges, and universities have not allocated the resources necessary to do this. Unfortunately, the cost of mailing a typical eight-page tabloid to the homes of employees adds—depending upon the address—between 12 cents and 20 cents per reader per issue. This small investment per employee is worth the cost, because virtually all readership research shows that employees rarely take these publications home to share with families. It is up to the institution to decide whether to invest in engaging entire families in the institution through these kinds of messages.

CHAPTER 19

Crisis Communication: Make the Best of a Bad Situation

M. Fredric Volkmann

One cannot necessarily be communicated out of what one has behaved oneself into.

> Richard W. Conklin, Associate Vice-President
> University of Notre Dame

A significant number of campus emergencies are avoidable, or at least predictable, making oxymorons out of terms like "crisis communication" or "crisis management." By the time events have deteriorated to the point where such language is necessary, it already may be too late to salvage the situation. Perhaps it is better to think about such matters as crisis avoidance or crisis preparation, so that coping with bad news can be seen as a matter of advance planning that is no different from the proactive promotion of the good news about institutions.

For the campus communicator there are three components to a crisis:

- *The event or problem.* A crisis is often an event over which the institution has little or no control, let alone advance warning. An earthquake, tornado, building fire, or a dishonest employee is something that you pray never happens, but planning to deal with the reaction to these events is essential.
- *Institutional action to deal with the effects of the event or problem.* Despite the unpredictable crisis, institutions do have strong control over how they react to a specific problem, up to and including detailed plans that are intended to cope with natural disasters and human-made problems. Wise is the institution that maps out such strategies well in advance of any possible occurrence.
- *Communication about the event or problem.* Here, too, the institution does have a modicum of control, and planning can be done well in advance of the crisis, especially where the institution already has disaster plans that address basic needs of those affected by the event. Depending upon the openness and

access provided by the institution to external news media, the coverage of catastrophic events can be coordinated with cooperation of the news media, as long as everyone understands the ground rules that have been prepared in advance.

Assuming institutions have crisis and disaster plans to deal with adverse events, this section will review managing the communications aspects of these events. For those institutions without such proactive efforts, this advice herein may require a significantly greater amount of communications expertise, as well as divine intervention. Planning for natural disasters is a fairly routine process at many institutions, but anticipating human-made problems is less common. For example, it is rare to see academic institutions with in-place, ready-to-activate plans for such things as arson, bombings, criminal actions (such as rape, murder, and robbery), ethnic or racial strife, or animal rights protests.

Regardless, the key agencies that generally deal with emergencies begin with the campus security or police force, physical facilities personnel, residential life professionals living in dormitories with students, and on some campuses, medical emergency response personnel. In collaboration with these offices, proactive institutions can draft guidelines for preparedness, reactions to disasters, and response to other emergencies. These include everything from instructions on whom to call to what deployment of resources and personnel is required for each situation. Assuming that these protocols are in place, the institution can then move forward to communicate information about the event and about steps being taken to deal with it.

PREDICTING DISASTER: THINGS THAT CAN BE DONE BEFORE A CRISIS STRIKES

Every campus communications program should have a special cache of materials that anticipates the worst-case scenario in a bad disaster where it is possible that there is no electricity, no running water, no food, or any other services. This is particularly likely to happen during hurricanes, tornadoes, floods, earthquakes, or other natural disasters that strike the entire campus. Most important, find a secure, safe area that is above normal flood levels, is earthquake proof, and that is accessible to the communications staff under the worst-case circumstances. Equip this area with manually operated typewriters, hand-operated mimeograph machines, battery-operated flashlights, cellular telephones (most cell phone towers and systems are much better protected during emergencies than conventional telephones), and survival and medical equipment that can be used by the staff in the process of communicating the crisis. Don't forget adequate supplies of paper, mimeograph ink, and other low-technology solutions. Unfortunately, the conventional ways of communicating—computers, fax machines, copiers, and land-line telephones—may not be available for hours and days following catastrophic events.

Here are a few suggestions for planning ahead, before a crisis occurs.

- *Establish a command center* well in advance where essential services can either be utilized or instituted from your cache of emergency equipment. Additional equipment that may be necessary includes battery-operated radios and television sets, emergency band radios, and battery-operated computers. If possible, a small gas-powered generator can be helpful in recharging batteries.
- *Plan on going to the news media before they come to you.* Creating an atmosphere of openness and accessibility goes a long way with the press. Plan to be accessible 24 hours a day for the duration of the problem. Once coverage begins, establish regular times to update news media, especially for events that have a news life of longer than two days. Be sure to plan on dating and putting the exact time on all statements and news releases so that they are not confused with one another and so that old information is not mistaken for new.
- *Establish in advance rules of media conduct.* For example, should reporters go into student residence halls without administrative permission; should photographers take pictures of individuals without their permission; and should TV cameras and lights be used or not used? These and other questions must be answered.
- *Decide who should and should not have access to confidential information.* It is better for a spokesperson addressing a sensitive subject to say, "I do not know the answer to that question, but I will try to find out for you as soon as possible." Such statements must be said truthfully.
- *Train spokespersons to be straight up with the press without appearing to be evasive, noncommittal, speculative, blaming, or Pollyannish.* Train them to use sensitivity when making statements affecting those who may be suffering or who may be connected in some way to these individuals. Choose spokespersons and contacts for major types of crises ahead of time, taking into account personal abilities, enthusiasm, and stamina to withstand the ongoing pressure. Identify experts and resource people for such catastrophes as tornadoes, hurricanes, lightning strikes, fires, etc.
- *Avoid "no comment" at all costs.* Train spokespersons to use generic answers, such as "the institution is deeply concerned about this tragedy, and our concerns and sympathies go out to all of those affected by this event," or "we do not have information on that at this time, but we are working hard and will have a statement for you shortly." Just remember that all statements

must satisfy more than the news media, particularly where students, staff, alumni, and parents are involved and affected.

- *Teach staff to understand that reacting to disasters, crises, and stressful events is an emotional and not a rational activity.* Learning to appreciate this difference helps in preparing statements and questions that show compassion and concern.

- *Learn from the mistakes made and the successes accomplished in previous crises.* Review and compile results of postmortems conducted after crises have passed, revising communications planning documents accordingly.

WHEN TROUBLE DOES HAPPEN: IMPORTANT STEPS IN CRISIS COMMUNICATIONS

Judith M. Jasper, associate vice chancellor at Washington University in St. Louis, defines seven key steps for coping with an unfolding crisis. As the university's chief communications professional, Jasper recommends the following media strategies:

- *Define the situation clearly.* Then create a short overview statement about what has happened, making sure that everyone is on the same page at the same time. Be certain that the facts are presented clearly, that the message is written in a form acceptable to reporters, and that questions from journalists are fully anticipated. Responses must be continually assessed and revised.

- *Determine the chain of command for this crisis and the key players.* No situation has the same solution or set of actors. It is best to make a list of all internal and external audiences, who is responsible for them, and what those audiences need to know and the order in which they need to learn about it.

- *Decide which details can be disclosed and which ones cannot.* Working closely with campus police and legal staff, the communications office must decide quickly the information that can be released—both pro and con—particularly where a preemptive statement may reduce later damage from what could be perceived by the media as equivocation or suppression of the facts.

- *Establish a spokesperson.* Decide who is going to be the spokesperson and who will not. Deciding early on a few, competent individuals to talk with reporters is essential. Always prepare statements in writing before presentation to the media.

- *Assign a media manager.* Decide who is responsible for day-to-day news media relations—who will take the calls, write the statements, compile the backgrounders, and organize the press conferences. If the team is large enough, have one person do the organizing and another pull the information together.

- *Establish a press staging area.* Choose appropriate locations for the press that allow both for ample space and services to accommodate television, lighting, and camera equipment, seating, tables, and easy access for satellite trucks. Be certain, however, that the location allows for control over unauthorized access to areas off-limits to persons outside the institution.
- *Control institutional telephone and e-mail systems.* Crises result in immense numbers of phone calls that flood switchboards, as well as e-mail that can overpower systems quickly. Support from professionals in the telephone and computer divisions of the institution is essential to avoid overloads, crashes, and dissemination of false or misleading information. Statements should be provided for all who answer telephones and respond to e-mail.

Jasper also recommends some important tips during media interviews:

- *Be in control.* Do not be defensive. Stay calm in the face of tough questions, and ask about deadlines.
- *Note the reporter's name,* telephone number, and request, then seek advice before responding.
- *Schedule the press event* or interview at a time or place convenient to the institution.
- *Know what is public information* and what is not.
- *Know when an answer is required* no matter who is asking the question. If the answer is not known, say so and then indicate that efforts will be made to assist in finding the information.
- *Double-check all facts.* Never "wing it" and never lie.
- *Determine only a few points* to make to reporters and the public about the situation, and then be certain to make those points, whether or not the questions are raised by the media.
- *Keep responses and language simple,* short, jargon free, and straightforward.
- *Never speak "off the record"* and remember anything said to a reporter, either directly or indirectly, is fair game.
- *Correct the error before answering* the question if reporters ask questions that contain erroneous information.
- *Where you cannot answer,* say so and repeat the points you wish used.
- *Do not speculate* or give opinions and do not answer hypothetical questions that ask "what if. . . ."
- *Encourage call backs from reporters* for clarification if they are unclear about your statements.
- *If you made a mistake* during the interview and didn't realize it until later, call the reporter to correct the error.
- *Announce who will be available* for follow-up questions or additional stories.

Once the interview process is complete, do not expect to review the reporter's story. However, complicated concepts that are difficult to express in writing may require additional time with the reporter, and it is appropriate to ask the reporter to read the interview notes to be certain that the facts were correctly copied down. If there is a resulting error in the printed story, reacting in anger is far less effective than calling to indicate that an error has occurred and providing evidence to that effect. However, if the statement is a matter of interpretation or opinion, do not complain.

Most importantly, Jasper recommends, debrief after the situation has ended. Meet with key campus officials who were involved and learn from mistakes and build upon accomplishments.

Richard W. Conklin, associate vice-president for university relations at the University of Notre Dame, has some additional advice for interacting with the news media. As he correctly notes, "There is no correlation between intelligence and behavior." In other words, campuses are just as likely to experience stupidity and inexplicable human behavior as any other segment of society. Here are 10 tips from Conklin:*

1. If there is not one voice, there will be babble. (It is necessary to select a single spokesperson.)
2. The quick hemorrhage is better than the slow bleed. (Get bad news out as quickly and as completely as possible.)
3. Don't shoot your parents and expect sympathy as an orphan. (Anticipate when institutional actions will create negative reactions and prepare to handle them.)
4. Race to get the facts, but do not outrun them. (Don't speculate when you don't know the facts.)
5. Be as composed in the hurricane as in the zephyr. (Treat the news media the same, whether the news is good or bad.)
6. Bad news is like rain—inevitable and passing. (Don't panic. Everyone has a negative day and the interest of the news media is transitory.)
7. Think of the worse thing you can do, and then don't do it. (Reflect before reacting. Sometimes the best action is no action.)
8. Lawyers deal with facts, public relations people with perceptions. (There will be tension between the two.)
9. Treat others' mistakes as you would have them treat yours. (When complaining about coverage, think carefully about motives and institutional benefits.)
10. Even Quasimodo can teach something about posture. (Look for the silver lining in bad news.)

---

*Courtesy of Richard Conklin, Notre Dame, Indiana.

Chapter 20

Publications: Producing Messages That Promote and Market Institutions

M. Fredric Volkmann

Man needed a way to store communication with unchanging fidelity and to transport it across small or vast chasms of time and space. Written language was the only solution to these problems, and man began writing in many ways.

Edmund C. Arnold,
Ink on Paper 2

When Güttenberg created movable-type printing technology in the middle 1400s, he sought to produce books inexpensively, but Güttenberg could not have imagined the impact his invention would have upon academic institutions, which first saw the value of lower cost books in the teaching and learning process, and then extended the urge to publish into virtually all aspects of institutional life. Now academic institutions publish not dozens, but thousands of publications every year—most of which are intended to communicate, promote, and market some aspect of the institution's effort to expand knowledge and to encourage learning. Güttenberg might be shocked to learn that virtually none of the materials produced by the publications offices of schools, colleges, and universities are books, or any other form of truly academic, scholarly, or scientific research literature. Instead, the modern public relations office produces a wide array of promotional materials, including brochures, pamphlets, posters, periodicals, advertisements, and electronic messages intended to recruit students, raise gift dollars, engage the hearts and minds of alumni and parents, and engender greater public support.

Indeed, the days of the editor with a green eye shade and sharp red pencil have expanded to a much more complex and sophisticated array of services that assist departments and programs on the campus to implement marketing strategies as well as to provide professional consultation, program development, creative problem solving, publications and Web page production, audience testing, and many other services.

Ultimately, the role of a publications office is to assist institutional clients in producing messages and materials that advance the institution, primarily with external audiences. The process begins with consultation. The initial meeting with a client addresses certain key issues and questions that must be answered before any solutions are considered. Unfortunately, many clients will approach this process believing they already know exactly what is needed to solve the communications problem. A systematic analysis, however, will benefit the process by answering crucial questions.

- *What is the communications problem or issue that the client is trying to address?* Determine what constitutes the project and its overall goals, so that the communications proposal will be consistent with the character and nature of the project.
- *Who is the audience?* Identify the persons or groups with which the client wishes to communicate, making sure to indicate information about age, gender, socioeconomic characteristics, education, geographic location, ethnicity, etc. Most importantly, ascertain what it is the client wishes the audience to do.
- *What is the key message (or messages) that need to be communicated to the audience?* Be certain that they are simple, easy to understand, and previously agreed upon by the client's committee, office, program, or division.
- *Is a printed message the best way to go, or should the client consider a letter, series of telephone calls, personal visits, etc.?*
- *Does the client have a specific design or look that he or she believes will help convey the message effectively?* Ask for samples of what competitive programs are currently using, as well as any prior publications or ideas that may have already been considered by the client's colleagues—even if these may not be deemed practical or workable. Sensitivity to the client's expectations and prior efforts is essential to building trust, especially if the final product may be significantly different from what the client originally envisioned or previously produced. Determine whether the project needs to complement or coordinate with any existing materials.
- *What is the method of distribution for the message?* Often clients have not thought through the many ways in which a message can be delivered to a prospective customer, ranging from hand delivery to electronic mail. Further, there are many ways in which traditional mail can be delivered, including the U.S. Postal Service (which offers several classes of delivery) to commercial competitors such as UPS, FedEx, and DHL. Determine what mailing lists are available and whether the client already has centered on a specific medium such as letters, brochures, posters, booklets, catalogs, or Web pages.

- *When does the project need to be delivered to the customer?* Deadlines are among the most troublesome aspects of working with publications and electronic communications projects. Rarely does the customer know the intricate processes and steps through which a professionally managed and effective project must go. These must be described in detail, perhaps aided by a short, easy-to-read publications guidelines booklet or typescript produced for clients.
- *What is the quantity needed?*
- *What is the budget the customer has to spend on the project, and is it realistic?*
- *Who will be involved in the approval process?* Does the customer know that the greater the number of approvals, the longer the process will take?
- *Were all basic procedures described and detailed to the client,* including realistic time frame needed for production, requirements for purchase orders and other expense authorizations, format for manuscripts, sources for photography and art, approval protocols, and any other aspects of printing or electronic production?

STEPS TOWARD SOLVING THE PROBLEM

After the initial consultation with the client, the publications office provides a series of vital steps in developing a solution strategy:

- *Communications and marketing strategy.* So often the initial consultation with a client determines a serious lack of the helpful information that would guarantee maximum effectiveness for the project or effort. In some cases this requires conducting focus groups or audience research with the prospective recipients of the messages, and in other cases it requires significant analysis of the strengths, weaknesses, threats, and opportunities that the sender of the message must consider. Without the development of a clear strategy, the value of the communications effort may at best be ineffectual and, worse yet, wasteful. Strategy must include market analysis, institutional analysis, strategy development and implementation, methods for mobilizing resources, and a clearly defined marketing program that identifies goals, objectives, and bench marking/satisfaction mechanisms. In solving many promotional problems, the more advance effort expended on developing communications strategies, the more effective the overall effort will be.
- *Creative concept.* Once the pertinent market and promotional information is in hand, then the development of a concept can begin, usually in a meeting between the client representative, a production coordinator, an editor, a designer, and sometimes a writer and a photographer. Among the issues that must be determined are the types of solutions, such as letters, brochures,

posters, electronic messages, etc., as well as the dimension and format for the message, and the methods for distribution. (Editors and designers must have a thorough knowledge of current postal regulations to ensure that a finished piece will be mailable at the postal rate determined.) At this time, editors and designers must clarify with the client what expectations they have for coated or uncoated papers, colors of ink and paper, whether four-color process will be employed (and is within the budget), and in what form the product will be delivered to the reader, such as a self-mailer, an envelope, and shrink-wrap.

- *Writing and editing.* At the time the concept is being created, determination must be made on who will write and edit the text for the publication. In most academic settings, the written word is ultimately of greater importance than graphic materials, simply because of the traditional value placed on language and writing. If the client has produced a weakly written piece, this must be discussed and a decision made as to whether an outside professional should be employed to rewrite the copy. At the same time, the client must be informed of the editing style preferred by the institution and be given adequate opportunity to review the official style for punctuation, spelling, and sentence/paragraph structure, including style manuals and guidebooks utilized by the publications office.

- *Design and art direction.* As writing and editing are clarified for the client, so must the graphic representation be determined in what can sometimes be a much more open-ended, less structured portion of the process. Creating a look for a publication can be highly subjective and requires careful management of the process so that the staff designers and illustrators, while aware of the parameters the client will accept, may try to encourage the client to consider solutions that may not have been considered originally. By the same token, the design must enhance and promote the message and support the marketing strategy without presenting unnecessary complication or confusion. This is a delicate balance that requires experience and skill on the part of the designer, as well as a willingness to try new ideas on the part of the customer. It is during this process that key issues of artwork, photography, paper selection, final format, and type specifications need to be worked out in collaboration with the client.

- *Electronic formats.* As the design is agreed upon, a simultaneous decision needs to be made as to whether the message will be converted to electronic form for posting on a Web page or for utilization on diskettes, CD-ROM, or other formats that can be easily transmitted to readers with compatible computer technology. The cost and the additional time necessary for these steps are often mystifying to the client, as well as frustrating. When a printed version of the publication has a strong vertical page orientation, it can be difficult to explain why the Web version has to operate within the more restrained horizontal format determined by computer screens. Although new software is constantly being developed to simplify the conversion of print format materials into electronic form, the historically different formats can make the effort difficult and can cause significant disappointment when they do not appear to be sufficiently similar.

- *Production schedules and printing supervision.* Once the final text, design, and format have been determined, it is then necessary to solicit estimates of the cost of producing the project in the quantity and form agreed upon. These estimates for electronic production, typesetting, printing, and conversion to electronic formats require competitive bids as mandated by most state institutions and now required at private institutions that receive federal grants. As will be discussed later, competitive bidding and estimating are essential aspects of the production process. Equally critical is explaining the process of proofs, corrections, and resulting costs and delays to the client. A detailed production schedule is an essential contract that must be developed between the client and the publications office, no matter how small the project. At this stage the final determination of distribution, labeling, and packaging must be confirmed.

- *Test and retest.* The investment academic institutions make in publications and Web sites to recruit students, raise gift dollars, and to communicate with key constituencies is staggering. Add to this the cost of postage and handling, as well as expenses for advertising, and the total can easily exceed one percent and sometimes two percent of the gross annual expense of some institutions. It is not uncommon for a small institution to produce more than 150 different promotional publications each year, while some major universities produce literally thousands of different printing jobs annually. Yet virtually all of these institutions—large or small—fail to test their materials for effectiveness! As described in the section on research and testing, it is imperative that the most important publications (i.e., viewbook, annual reports, magazines, etc.) be routinely tested with their intended audiences to determine whether or not these institutional investments are worthwhile as well as what improvements can be made to increase reader interest and results. Marketing is not just telling an audience what the sender wishes them to hear; it also requires careful and thorough feedback to determine what the audience expects from the institution.

STAFFING THE PUBLICATIONS OFFICE

Because the publications office requires skills in editing, writing, design, production, marketing, and analysis, a small publications office must have an extraordinarily versatile individual, while larger publications shops will have highly specialized professionals in each of these areas.

In elementary and secondary school environments, it frequently is the case that one person manages all news media relations and publications—a difficult challenge under any circumstance. In small liberal arts colleges there is normally one full-time professional, and sometimes two handling anywhere from 100 to 300 publications annually—often outsourcing design and photography to freelance providers. In these situations, the staff usually are experienced in writing and editing, electronic layout, as well as publications production, and often photography.

In mid-size universities of up to 7,500 students, the publications staff normally have a director, who manages much of the day-to-day matters regarding personnel, budgets, committee meetings, client meetings, and usually larger, high-profile publications such as viewbooks, annual reports, catalogs, etc. In these situations, there is usually a staff of three to six or seven editors and designers, as well as a production coordinator who handles all relationships with printers and other vendors, and who tracks all jobs as they enter, are processed, and leave the publications office. Within this team there also may be an expert in marketing, as well as a staff person who is skilled in advertising, particularly for commuter-based, urban institutions.

At institutions ranging from 7,500 to more than 50,000 students, it is not unusual for a publications office to have as many as a dozen or more professionals, with three or four editors or account representatives who serve as the office's primary contact with clients, an equal number of designers who work collaboratively with the editors, the clients, and sometimes with vendors to be sure that complex graphic techniques are properly printed. A production coordinator is essential for larger offices, as is the emerging role of Web page designers who specialize in Hypertext Markup Language (HTML) and other software formats used in creating Web home pages and Web sites. Some offices also have full-time computer experts who focus on maintaining hardware, training staff and updating software, and coordinating transmission of digital information between the publications office, vendors, and clients.

Regardless of staff size, the need for careful management and tracking of all projects is one of the most important aspects of managing staff and the publishing process. The great majority of publications are repeated year in and year out, within a relatively predictable time frame. For example, course catalogs and viewbooks are usually published during the spring and summer. Annual reports are normally published in late fall or early winter. Because these patterns exist, it is possible to initiate the kind of proactive, prioritized planning described elsewhere in the section on public relations.

One ongoing issue unique to publications offices is the method by which the salaries of staff and the costs of maintaining operations are appropriated. While most small colleges see the publications office as a so-called free service to all clients, they tend to focus the publications staff almost entirely on materials intended to recruit students and to raise gift dollars. However, at larger, more complex institutions, it is more likely the publications office operates on a cost-recovery basis by which all clients are charged for not only the cost of the publications that are produced, but also for the time and materials expended in the production of projects. In these situations revenue becomes an extremely important motivator, and offices tend to operate less often on the basis of institutional priorities, i.e., student recruitment, fund raising, and government subsidies, and more on finding paying customers who can keep the staff busy, especially since staff jobs depend upon generating enough revenue to pay for the cost of running the program.

At larger institutions, there also can be a close connection as well between the publications office and institutional printing plants that operate on a cost-recovery basis. In fact, it is not uncommon for a central administration publications office to compete for business with other publications offices and graphic design production services offered by the institutional printing operation.

Institutions of all sizes routinely utilize outsourced experts to produce highly specialized student recruitment materials as part of an overall marketing and direct-mail effort to attract more prospects to the applicant pool. Such situations offer challenging complications to a well-managed, proactive publications program that seeks to serve all aspects of the institution—especially those divisions that generate revenues, including student tuition, gifts, government grants and contracts, and research agreements with industry and business.

PUBLICATIONS AND ADVERTISING AUDITS ARE NECESSITIES

Because publications, advertising, and related promotional and marketing activities are significant cost centers for academic institutions, it is essential that periodic reviews of these areas be conducted, either by internal committees or preferably by external teams of publications and marketing professionals from institutions that have successfully contained costs and overhead in promoting themselves through printed matter and electronic communications.

Regardless of how the audit is conducted, it should be done at least once every five years and requires the collection of all materials produced within a 12-month period, regardless of who paid for the materials, what offices the materials were done for, and what external or internal audiences are the intended recipients of such messages. At smaller institutions of fewer than 2,500 students, the review will normally include less than 200 publications, including official letterhead, envelopes and business cards, as well as student recruitment materials, fund raising publications and direct-mail materials, continuing education promotion, sports media guides and athletic recruitment guidebooks, course catalogs, alumni magazines and newsletters, internal tabloids and newsletters for employees, institutional Web sites that require routine maintenance and updating, and any other printed materials that are distributed internally or externally to promote the institution.

Excluded from such audits should be any academic and scholarly materials, such as literary magazines, peer-reviewed journals, books, and other efforts that are part of the teaching and research process, and which, therefore, should not be audited under institutional criteria that might be misperceived as abridging freedom of inquiry and expression.

Not only should samples of each item be collected, but each also should include the name of the office producing the document, the contact person responsible for its production, the total cost of the project, the total quality printed, unit cost, and the intended audience and the means of distribution to that audience. If any readership research were done on a specific item, that should be attached.

The persons reviewing the materials during an internally managed audit should include a representative from the publications office, but also persons representing key management and academic divisions of the institution, including the business office, academic affairs, student affairs, alumni, development, admissions, and a faculty person who is particularly adept at or interested in institutional communications.

The volume of materials also will help determine the size of an audit review committee or external review team, which normally is composed of one or more professionals from institutions that have recognized, successful publications and promotional programs. Reviewing printed materials and Web pages can be an enormously daunting task—covering thousands of pages of printed material—which requires that the review process be divided among the participants. Reviewers report on the overall quality of the printed materials, such as writing, editing, organization, photography, design, printing quality, cost-effectiveness, and most importantly, whether the publication should be produced at all. This author once reviewed a year's production of printed matter at a large research university, and ended up with 10,000 different items, including individually designed letterhead and envelopes for more than 1,000 different offices!

What is often learned during these audits is that the institution is wasting vast sums of money on printed matter that is either needless or that should be combined with other materials to create more effective, useful messages for the audiences to which they are distributed. For example, complex universities may have individual catalogs for each of the undergraduate schools, rather than a single, unified catalog that can be produced at a significantly lower cost per copy. Another example is the academic department that believes it is better to send a glossy, four-color, expensive brochure about its undergraduate program, rather than include itself in a compendium of similar departments organized by academic area, such as natural sciences, social sciences, humanities, or the arts. On the other hand, experience shows that graduate and professional student recruitment requires highly differentiated and separate publications to be effective, but also that these publications do not have to be expensive and ostentatious; many graduate students are highly suspicious of hype and are looking for information, not promotion.

The results of an audit should be shared with the offices that spend the greatest amounts of money and time on promotional materials in the hope that they will see the wisdom in reducing expense and consolidating materials, rather than continuing to proliferate messages every time a new idea or program appears on the horizon. Unfortunately, it is rare for academic institutions to mandate reductions in these areas. It is more likely that self-initiated cost containment and control will determine whether or not the institution reduces expense. At smaller institutions it is more feasible for control of these expenses to be managed through the office of the chief executive or the chief academic officer.

MANAGING THE PRODUCTION OF PUBLICATIONS AND PROMOTIONAL MATERIALS

The single most common criticism leveled at publications offices is failure to meet deadlines. "Better late than never" is a cliché that has no place in the lexicon of publications professionals. Recruiting prospective students, fund raising, and alumni relations require promotional tools that are timely and available, and that dovetail into the overall plans and strategies of the offices managing these areas. Unfortunately, avoidable circumstances can deny the client the needed product on time and in the form requested. Sometimes these delays result from the publications office's failure to deliver, but more often than not they are the result of inadequate or incomplete communication between the client and the publications office, which is responsible for educating the customer as to how timely delivery is accomplished. For this reason, this section will focus on managing the publications process to achieve not only an effective product, but on-time delivery.

Producing publications and other communications materials used to be relatively routine and mechanical, but today's emphasis on marketing and promotional strategies requires a significant focus at the front end of the process. Before specifications, printing estimates, and final bids can be processed, the project officer must obtain data from three major sources—client, audience, and suppliers. Exhibit 20–1 contains a sample planning guide that can be used during an initial contact with a client—a guide that asks the basic questions of quantity, budget, content, audience, means of distribution, and deadlines. Using a form such as

Exhibit 20–1 Publication/Project Planning Guide

Use only during initial contact with client, making sure that the publication/project officer and the client have discussed all of the questions and points that follow. This is not a specifications form, which should be completed after editor and/or designer have reviewed the manuscript and have decided upon a direction the publication should take, based upon strategies developed from the information below.

Department Seeking Assistance: Date

Person Contacted   Title

Phone   E-mail   Fax

Title or description of publication/project

Audience(s): Be specific. Indicate age(s), sex, socioeconomic characteristics, etc.

What data or research exists about audience?

What does client want audience to do?

Determine key message(s) to audience.

Distribution: ❑ by hand _____ ❑ how many by hand?
Who will be handling distribution by hand?
❑ by mail ❑ first class ❑ periodicals class ❑ standard class (bulk rate)
❑ e-mail ❑ Web page(s) ❑ other
❑ envelope ❑ self-mailer ❑ other
mailing and/or e-mail lists required (describe)

Format (proposed): ❑ dimension ____ ❑ quantity ____ ❑ number of pages ____
Type of publication ❑ letter ❑ brochure ❑ poster ❑ booklet ❑ catalog
❑ other

Message: Describe publication's or project's written contents

Design: What is client's expectation/interest in design?

Illustrations will include ❑ photographs – how many?
❑ illustrations – describe
❑ sizes – describe
❑ University Publications must arrange photographs or illustrations
Does client expect to use ❑ cheap white paper ❑ colored offset paper
❑ white textured stock ❑ colored textured stock ❑ book white ❑ cover white
❑ one-color ink ❑ two-color ink ❑ four-color process

continues

Exhibit 20–1 continued

> **Budget and Expense:** Client's maximum budget $_____ If this is insufficient, can client obtain more funds? ❏ yes ❏ no
>
> **Samples:** Did client supply samples of previous publications or samples from other schools? ❏ Yes ❏ No
>
> **Protocols:** Were basic office procedures described to client? ❏ yes ❏ no
> ❏ time frame needed for production of this type of publication (including tentative delivery date of _____)
> ❏ requirements as to submitting purchase order authorizations for expenditures of their funds
> ❏ understanding of delays in production schedule that will result in delays of delivery
> ❏ manuscript must be submitted in final form, in the following computer software _____
> ❏ that all photographs and art should be supplied, unless otherwise noted
> ❏ all approval slips must be signed before next stage in process will be begun
> ❏ that contact is to be maintained through one person in client's office
> ❏ that only the publications office contacts printer and other suppliers, other than purchasing
> ❏ that client should contact only (name) _____ when wishing information regarding status of job at publications office
> ❏ that changes made in job at any stage following submission of manuscript will require additional expenditures on the part of the client, increasing in cost with each succeeding step of production
>
> Any other comments regarding client: _____
> _____
> _____
> _____
> _____
> _____
> _____
>
> Name of persons completing this interview form: _____
>
> Courtesy of Washington University, St. Louis, Missouri.

this is essential in collecting information required by persons engaged in marketing strategies, writing, editing, design, and printing production so that decisions are based on adequate front-end information. Note that the primary purpose of this initial contact is to determine whether or not the client fully appreciates the importance of understanding the audience and attempting to communicate on a level and in such a manner that will be effective. For example, the client may come with a preconceived notion that all he or she needs is a Web page to promote the service or product, without realizing that Web pages currently operate in a highly passive environment. The Web requires the prospective customer to go through the sometimes torturous steps of accessing the Web page, a process unlike receiving a proactive, rifle-shot message that is sent directly to the prospective customer via standard mail or e-mail. As any experienced marketer knows, waiting for a prospective client or customer to take the initiative in establishing a relationship may be Pollyannish at best. That is why business has not yet fully embraced the Web as a sales tool; it is usually seen as an informational aid.

In addition to learning as much as possible about the intended audience, it also is essential to gain significant information about the client's ability to distribute the message, after determining what the message content should be! Learn what format the client is considering, what expectations or biases he or she may have about design, what budget is available for the project, and whether or not any samples have been collected from competitors or similar programs that appeal to the client.

Of greatest importance during the initial contact with the client is explaining office protocols. How the process of producing an effective message proceeds is critical and must be clearly understood by the parties involved. Although this procedure may appear to be extraneous paperwork, it is essential for any size of publications operation, especially where several persons will be handling the same job. Using a planning guide also discourages "convenient memories" of what was said during the publications planning session with the client. Some institutions prepare these forms in multiple sets so that the client and each participating staff person has a copy, thereby avoiding the necessity of several persons talking to the client again. This form becomes the nucleus of all future activities dealing with the project. From this initial contact several basic processes must be initiated immediately:

- *Create a specific file for each and every project.* Because publications and promotional projects require significant amounts of paperwork, traditional file folders are frequently used to store information, even though an electronic file may be created at the same time. Everything ranging from market research to samples of similar publications goes into this file, along with manuscripts, photos, all notes, printing specifications, estimates, bids, purchase orders, approval slips, and production schedules.
- *Production schedules must be issued immediately.* Perhaps the greatest mistake made in establishing relationships with clients is the failure to produce a precise, complete production schedule as early in the process as possible. This document (see Exhibit 20–2) serves as a contract between the office and the client and establishes accountability for meeting deadlines on the part of all those involved. The sample production schedule has three important

Exhibit 20–2 Washington University Publications Office Production Schedule

Job name	Job #		00/00/00
Editor:			
Designer:			
Client: Deadline			
		# of working days	Date(s)

Planning and Concept Development

	# of working days	Date(s)
Meeting to plan project and discuss concept	————	00/00/00
Photos assigned	————	00/00/00
Photos received	————	00/00/00

Development

	# of working days	Date(s)
Preliminary copy received	————	00/00/00
Editing begun	————	00/00/00
Editing completed	————	00/00/00
Editing approved	————	00/00/00
Design begun	————	00/00/00
Design completed	————	00/00/00
Design approved	————	00/00/00

Production

	# of working days	Date(s)
Layout begun	————	00/00/00
Layout completed	————	00/00/00
Final numbers (tuition, etc.) received	————	00/00/00
First corrections to copy/layout received	————	00/00/00
First corrections to copy/layout made	————	00/00/00
Second corrections to copy/layout received	————	00/00/00
Second corrections to copy/layout made	————	00/00/00
Third corrections to copy/layout received	————	00/00/00
Third corrections to copy/layout made	————	00/00/00
Fourth corrections (if needed)	————	00/00/00
Fourth corrections made	————	00/00/00
Client approval of laser printout (may include outside proofreader)	————	00/00/00
Prepare final art for printer	————	00/00/00
Final art completed	————	00/00/00
Final art approved	————	00/00/00

Printing and Delivery

Color images:

	# of working days	Date(s)
Release all new images to printer	————	00/00/00
Random Chromalin (matchprints) for review	————	00/00/00

continues

Exhibit 20–2 continued

Randoms approved or returned	————	00/00/00
Second round of randoms	————	00/00/00

Prepress:
Final art/disk to printer	————	00/00/00
Review assembled Chromalins	————	00/00/00
Final signoff of Chromalin proof	————	00/00/00
Printer corrects & provides final proof	————	00/00/00

Presswork
Printer plates	————	00/00/00
Printing	————	00/00/00
Bindery	————	00/00/00
Delivery	————	00/00/00

Note: Delays in any of the above deadlines will result in similar (or even longer) delays in delivery date. Your cooperation is appreciated.

Courtesy of Washington University, St. Louis, Missouri.

ingredients—a listing describing all stages in the production process, a column reflecting the number of working days required for each key step, and a precise set of deadlines by which the client and the publications office are required to complete each step. If any step in the process is delayed by the publications office, it must make up the difference without failing to meet the final delivery date. If the client fails to meet a deadline, this will result in a recalculation of the delivery date, especially if the delay caused the publication to miss the printer's "window of opportunity" to actually print the project on time. Note that every aspect of the job is involved, including photography, editing, design and illustration, production, printing, and binding. From the outset, the production schedule must be based on achievable deadlines that are appropriate and realistic.

• *Know vendors and the reliability and quality of their services.* Before any projects are launched, a system of collecting information on various suppliers and vendors must be carefully developed and maintained. This includes information on printers, freelance graphic and Web-page designers, freelance writers and editors, external image-setting services, paper merchants, market and audience research firms, fulfillment houses (companies that label, sort, insert, and mail materials), and freelance photographers. Two basic rules apply when dealing with outsourced providers—seek candid references from other customers and obtain samples of what they have produced previously.

A filing system with this information is particularly useful, especially when using designers and photographers, and where the matching of a client to a specific designer is critical. Paper merchants often can provide libraries of samples, as can printers that maintain their own inventories of paper.

- *Follow trade customs and copyright law.* In addition to a working knowledge of suppliers, the publications professional must have a constant awareness of trade customs in the printing industry and copyright law as it applies to all aspects of publishing—writing, editing, illustration, photography, design, and especially electronic communication and Web pages. The printing trade issues standardized guidelines on how printing jobs will proceed in such matters as quotations for bid; alterations costs; proofs; press proofs; ownership of electronic, photographic, or plated information; when and where title passes to the customer; etc. Failure to heed these guidelines and to accommodate exceptions in the bidding process can prove embarrassing and costly for those who do not write into the bid any exceptions to trade customs. Perhaps the most common example is the fact that trade customs allow printers to have overruns or underruns of 10 percent without customer authorization—unless the customer specifies exactly what is and what is not acceptable on the bid request. Consider adding the following statement to printing specifications and to bid requests: Underruns not accepted, and maximum of five percent overrun will be permitted. Equally difficult is the emerging debate on what is (and what is not) protected by copyright on the World Wide Web. Negotiations with the printer about getting a copy of final electronic files—especially if changes are made by the printer—needs to be done before files are completed to avoid added cost of retrieving files.

When creating a job file similar to the example from Mary Ellen Benson, executive director of publications at Washington University in St. Louis (see Exhibit 20–3), some institutions put the pertinent information on a form printed on the file itself, which allows important data to be recorded as the job moves from stage to stage in production. Although the file folder may repeat some of the information included with the original planning guide, it provides a more specific and technical record of production, including every single item connected with the job. Only oversized artwork and photographs that must be refiled are kept separately from this file folder.

SPECIFYING PRINTING FOR FINAL BIDS

Of critical importance is the development of precise specifications that can be used in (1) determining the design, (2) obtaining rough estimates, and (3) creating the final binding bid:

Exhibit 20–3 Example of Job File

Washington University   PUBLICATIONS OFFICE   Campus Box 1086   199—
in St. Louis   One Brookings Drive
                                               St. Louis, MO 63130-4899
                                               (314) 935-5233
                                               FAX: (314) 935-8533

Job _____

Editor _____ Designer _____ P.O.# _____

Client_____ Campus Box # _____ Dept. # _____

Phone # _____ FAX # _____ E-Mail _____

OF PIECES IN PACKAGE _____

| QUANTITY |
| SIZE |

Cover: flat ____ x ____ finished ____ x ____

Cover: flat ____ x ____ finished ____ x ____

# of pages ____ ❏ self cover ❏ plus cover

PAPER Accept equivalent ❏ yes ❏ no

Cover: _____
       Brand   Weight   Color

Text: _____
       Brand   Weight   Color

INK

Cover: outside _____ ❏ 4-color process

inside _____ ❏ 4-color process

Text: _____ ❏ 4-color process

❏ Bleeds _____ ❏ Varnish _____

❏ Reverses _____ ❏ Trap reverses _____

❏ Screens _____ ❏ Large areas of heavy
                         coverage

PHOTOS   Regular   Silhouette

❏ Halftones   _____   _____

❏ Duotones   _____   _____

❏ 4-color process _____   _____

BINDERY

❏ Fold _____

❏ Score_____ ❏ punch

❏ Stitch: ❏ saddle ❏ side _____ ❏ corner

❏ Perfect ❏ Plastic_____ _____

❏ Perforate _____ _____ _____

❏ Pad: in sets of ____ chipboard _____

❏ _____ ❏ glue _____ ❏ die-cut

PROOFS

❏ blueline/dylux ❏ color key

❏ random Chromalins ❏ composite Chromalin

❏ b/w randoms ❏ digital ❏ laser

ADDITIONAL SPECS _____

ELECTRONIC SPECS

Program(s) used _____

Printer responsible for:

❏ color breaks ❏ 4-color tint mix formulas

❏ traps ❏ bleeds ❏ screens ❏ gradations

Special effects to be created in pre-press _____

DELIVER TO _____

Building_____ room # _____

❏ Box ❏ Shrink _____ per package

_____ samples to Publication Office

PRODUCTION SCHEDULE	Due Dates	Completed
Initial contact		
Final copy received		
Design assigned		
Photos needed by		
Copy to production		
First layout returned		
Corrections to production		
Layout complete		
Laser copy routed		
Final corrections		
Final art approved		
Color to printer		
To printer		
Proofs received		
Proofs returned to printer		
DELIVERY		

continues

Exhibit 20–3 continued

ENVELOPES	ADMINISTRATIVE INFO
Quantity_____	Previous job number: _____ ❑ Reprint
Size _____	_____ Bid requested
Paper _____	_____ Estimate sheet to client
Ink _____ Flap _____	_____ P.O. requested _____
Proof _____	

Activity	Vendors		Cost Estimate
WRITING SERVICES	1. _____	$ _____	
	2. _____	$ _____	
	3. _____	$ _____	
DESIGN SERVICES	1. _____	$ _____	
	2. _____	$ _____	
	3. _____	$ _____	
PRODUCTION SERVICES	1. _____	$ _____	
	2. _____	$ _____	
	3. _____	$ _____	
PRINTING	1. _____	$ _____	
	2. _____	$ _____	
	3. _____	$ _____	
	4. _____	$ _____	
MISC.	1. _____	$ _____	
_____	2. _____	$ _____	
	3. _____	$ _____	

ACTUAL COST

Date	Vendor	Activity	Estimate	Cost
			$	$
			$	$
			$	$
			$	$
			$	$
			$	$
			$	$
			$	$
			$	$
		Total	$	$

Courtesy of Washington University, St. Louis, Missouri.

Exhibit 20–4   Printing Specifications

Description of job: _____

❑ Request for cost estimate   ❑ final printing specifications

Printer job no. _____ User job no. _____

Quantity _____ Folded size _____ Flat size _____ ❑ Special items ____

No. of pages _____ ❑ Self cover ❑ Separate cover ❑ Other _____

Paper stock

❑ Inside, or ❑ Self cover: Brand _____ Weight _____ Color _____ Finish _____

❑ Cover, or ❑ Cards: Brand _____ Weight _____ Color _____ Finish _____

Other: (Describe) _____

Ink ❑ Inside pages, or ❑ self cover, or ❑ ____	Ink ❑ Separate cover or ❑ cards, or ❑ _____
1st color ink__ Prints on: ❑ Two sides ❑ One side	1st color ink__ Prints on: ❑ Two sides ❑ One side
2nd color ink__ Prints on: ❑ Two sides ❑ One side	2nd color ink__ Prints on: ❑ Two sides ❑ One side
3rd color ink__ Prints on: ❑ Two sides ❑ One side	3rd color ink__ Prints on: ❑ Two sides ❑ One side
4-color ink__ Prints on: ❑ Two sides ❑ One side	4-color ink__ Prints on: ❑ Two sides ❑ One side
❑ Varnish on: ❑ Two sides ❑ One side ❑ Spot	❑ Varnish on: ❑ Two sides ❑ One side ❑ Spot
❑ Bleeds (explain)_____	❑ Bleeds (explain)_____

Typesetting/Imagesetting

Preferred typeface(s): Body _____ Headlines _____ Body type size(s) _____

Headline size(s) — Column Width(s) ____ Estimated total column inches ____ Page proofs, no. __

Photos and other art work

No. of photos (halftones) _____ Original size(s) _____ Printed size(s) _____

No. of line art pieces _____ Original size(s) _____ Printed size(s) _____

No. of color separation(s) __ from: ❑ 35mm slides ❑ Photo or art ❑ Other __ Printed size(s) __

Special effects: ❑ Reverses ❑ Solids ❑ Screen tints ❑ Duotones ❑ Other (explain) _____

Layout preparation

❑ Electronic file in: ❑ QuarkXpress ❑ Pagemaker ❑ Other _____

❑ Prepress services needed: ❑ Color breaks ❑ Drop shadows ❑ Image editing ❑ Other ____

❑ Camera ready from customer, or furnished by: ❑ Printer ❑ Other _____

Special printing items

❑ Die cutting ❑ Scoring ❑ Perforating ❑ Numbering ❑ Flysheet

❑ Blind embossing ❑ Other _____

Folding (job does not bind)

Describe fold _____

Binding

❑ None ❑ Saddle stitch ❑ Side stitch ❑ Perfect ❑ Plastic ❑ Drill ❑ Pad ❑ Other _____

Proofs

❑ Blueline, or ❑ Color key, or ❑ Chromalin, or ❑ Press proof, or Other

continues

Exhibit 20–4 continued

Deliver to _____ Date wanted by _____

Packaging: ❏ Box ❏ Shrink wrap _____ per package ❏ Other _____

Finished samples to _____ Number of samples wanted _____

Estimated Cost $_____ Costs for additional or fewer ❏ 100's $_____ ❏ 1,000's $ _____

Costs for additional or fewer pages in multiples of _____ are $_____

These specifications prepared by _____ Phone _____ Date _____

For _____

Courtesy of Washington University, St. Louis, Missouri

- *Printing specifications must be precise and thorough.* As the project moves forward, it is necessary to structure a set of specifications that define what the client is seeking, and in such a way that it can be used to obtain reliable estimates and formal bids. Exhibit 20–4 is a typical set of printing specifications, which includes pre-press information, a description of the job, size, number of pages, paper that is to be used, ink colors, typography, photographs and artwork, prepress method of layout preparation and software used, special expense-adding printing items, binding and folding, proofs, and detailed delivery information. It is from this information that final estimates and bids will be developed.

- *Use estimate sheets with clients.* Once the printing specifications are agreed upon, it is possible to use the information sheet to obtain rough estimates from a vendor to determine whether or not the final bids will be within acceptable cost and delivery parameters. By sending the information on the specification sheet to a vendor, costs for production, prepress, printing, binding, and delivery can be developed and submitted to the publications office by a local supplier. In-house estimates can be generated by employing any number of over-the-counter software packages used to approximate costs. A word of caution: using in-house software to estimate costs requires that the information be localized to accommodate such market conditions as paper costs, prepress operations, printing labor, and outsourced services, etc. It may not take into account peak period local market factors, such as heavy customer loads and overtime.

FINAL, BINDING BIDS ARE ESSENTIAL

Institutions that print small and large jobs without obtaining final, binding bids from vendors are surprised when the bill arrives and reflects costs that were not previously discussed. Binding bids force the institution and the vendor to be fastidious in revealing minute details that could impact final costs, especially if the vendor is required to honor the estimate. No bid, however, will cover cost-adding changes made by the customer during the production process. It only applies to the costs incurred by the printer. The final request for bid will look very much like the printing specifications sheet included with this section, but is often best accompanied by a rough layout of exactly what the publication will look like. The rough layout is a mock-up of the publication to its exact size and shows the text, photographs, illustrations, and other visual materials in place, plus any unusual treatments such as bleeds, tip-ins, die cuts, special binding, and unusual folds. This can be done with virtually all layout software currently on the market, up to and including color output on the paper stock being considered (given the limitations of many computer printing devices). Paper merchants sometimes will assist in the preparation of bound page layouts or "dummies" if they have a significant potential profit from the sale of the paper to be used. (Or the printer can ask the paper merchant for dummies.)

The process of preparing a publication or other project for bidding can be overwhelmingly complex and time-consuming, so the benefit must be cost-effective. Where the price tag previously was too high, the benefits will be immediate and noticeable. Yet for small jobs costing less than $1,000, bidding the items singly may be counterproductive because it is sometimes uneconomical and inefficient to request bids on small jobs as well as overly time-consuming for the publications staff. It should be noted, however, that an institution accepting federal funds is now subject to governmental guidelines on obtaining at least three estimates on any job costing more than $25,000, as a general rule. If a small job is not competitively bid, it still is essential that detailed specifications be prepared and submitted to the printer with the job. This paper trail is the only way that the customer can seek and obtain corrective action for the printer's mistakes. As in all aspects of project management, the basic rule should remain: "Put it in writing—always."

Some institutions that do significant numbers of small jobs have discovered that it is possible to "gang bid" standardized formats up to a year at a time, thereby selecting a specific printer to which all such work would be sent. This technique is particularly effective for such standard items as letterhead, envelopes, business cards, 4-x-9-inch brochures, $8^{1}/_{2}$-x-11-inch and 11-x-17-inch one- or two-color flyers and posters, and any other commonly used format. The technique often limits the client to a predetermined array of paper stocks, sizes, and formats.

The bidding process does require strategy on the part of the customer, including the use of standardized signatures and page formats. For example, 8-, 16-, and 32-page signatures are not always standard. Certain papers and press formats can economically run in multiples of 12, 24, 36, and so on. Caution should be exercised when requesting special treatments such as unusual varnishes, press proofs, large ink solids, folding against the grain of the paper, and folds that may require

a hand operation. Unusual treatments must be noted and described on the specification sheet and accompanied by the rough layout when requesting final bids.

Last, but not least, watch out for the free lunches and other so-called innocent
favors that vendors provide. Sales efforts are based on gaining trust and friendship, and not always on competitive costs and high quality. As a practice, it is
always best to go Dutch treat on lunches and never to accept any favors or gifts
from printing representatives or other vendors. Never discuss one printer's quota-
tion with another printer until the bids are opened and become public information.

Because virtually all printing is conceived first on computers, the need for special services from outsourced providers has mushroomed and often requires that
estimates be provided for keyboarding information, unusual scans and manipulation of artwork and photographs, electronic page layout, and correcting electronic files just before the job goes to the printer for high-resolution formats. Some
printers pull digital proofs at this stage (varying from low-resolution "rainbow"
proofs to higher resolution "scatter" proofs)—thereby saving the cost of going to
film. Some institutions have separate forms for the following:

- *Requests for image-setting/typesetting.* Another specialized service provided
  by outsourced vendors is image-setting that not only provides the final computer file and camera-ready art, but also includes artwork, photographs,
  color separations, and any other special treatments. Because so many publications are done now directly from computer to film, and with direct imaging—directly to printing plate, image-setting has become less common,
  except where customers need a high-resolution output for a less sophisticated printing operation, or for advertisements and other graphic applications
  that require reflective camera-ready artwork.
- *Requests for photos.* Institutions that either have staff photographers or that
  purchase freelance photography have discovered that written instructions before
  the assignment can be extremely helpful in clarifying exactly what is needed.
  Exhibit 20–5 shows a photo request form. Photographers appreciate not only
  knowing who will be in the photograph, but also what the preferred location and
  background is, how the pictures will be used, whether the photos will be needed
  for printed matter, slide projection, video, CD-ROM, or any other number of
  applications that often rely heavily on the correct photographic materials and
  techniques being used. Furthermore, the photographer needs to know what kind
  of prints or digital output will be required by the designer and printer. (See
  Exhibit 20–4.)
- *Approval slips.* To be certain that the client is fully apprised of and accountable for the final version of the proofs on any project, it is critical to include
  an approval slip with each and every step in the process. (See Exhibit 20–6.)

Exhibit 20–5 Washingon University Photographic Services Photographic Assignment Request Form

---

Please complete the following information and submit completed form to Photographic Services for <u>Director's approval</u>. If request form is faxed (935-4259) or sent via campus mail (Box 1070) to our office, please notify our department at 935-5244 of its forthcoming arrival. If you have any questions, please call Elaine Pittaluga at 935-5244.

Today's Date: _____

Photographic Assignment Information

Person making request: _____ Phone #:_____

Office or Person for which request is being made (if different from above):

_____ Phone #: _____

In which publication(s) will photo(s) be used: _____

Publication's editor: _____ Phone #: _____

Date of assignment: _____ Time: _____

Location/address of assignment: _____

_____

Name of event, class, scene, or person(s) to be photographed:

_____

_____

Give specific details of photograph assignment—(who, what, type of setting, pose, atmosphere/background, set-up, etc. Use back side of form if necessary)

_____

_____

_____

_____

_____

Which type of film: _____ black and white (only with Director's approval)
                       _____ 35mm color negative (this can be printed in color or b/w)
                       _____ 2 1/4 transparency
                       _____ 35mm slide

For Office Use Only:

Director's approval: Yes ___ No ___ Photographer assigned: _____

continues

Exhibit 20–5 continued

Photographic Print Request Form

Today's date: _____

Person ordering prints: _____ Phone #: _____

Prints for which publication: _____

Charge images to department: _____

Department contact person: _____

IDENTIFICATION NUMBERS OF PICTURES/SLIDES ORDERED (include file number and frame number):

ID NUMBER	QUANTITY/SIZE	COLOR OR B/W

Any additional instructions: _____

_____

_____

DATE YOU NEED JOB COMPLETED: _____

(Normal delivery time is 10 working days)

Courtesy of Washington University, St. Louis, Missouri.

Exhibit 20–6 Approvals Checklist

please initial and date	
Client _____	❏ Design Comp
Editor _____	❏ Rough Layout
Designer _____	❏ Laser Copy for Output
Art Director_____	❏ Final Art
Director _____ or Assoc. Dir.	❏ Proof
Courtesy of Washington University, St. Louis, Missouri.	

The form should be signed and dated by those who are required to approve it. Of utmost importance is written, signed authorization to proceed with printing after review of final proofs. If something is wrong with the final product, a signed proof means that the client and the publications office are more likely to work together in a shared solution to the problem. This final sign-off is in addition to the printer's final approval slip.

• *Request for computer services.* This document contains information about the job, the designer and editor working on it, the client for whom it's being produced, the name of the computer supplier, software and type fonts to be used, and then all of the various procedures that must be performed to deliver the service requested.

There are many other forms that can be employed in managing a publications office, but these represent the most commonly used documents, whether the office is a one-person shop or a large, complex operation with highly differentiated roles and expertise.

ENCOURAGE GOOD EDITING AND WRITING

Editing and writing are among the most difficult and most important tasks in an academic environment. In a world where "publish or perish" are bywords of faculty, editors and writers face particularly complicated challenges—simply because so many within the academic community consider themselves expert communicators. Unfortunately, a great number of these self-styled editors and writers are indeed proficient when speaking the language of their own academic disciplines, but often are unprepared to translate professional jargon and technical language into a form easily understood by prospective students, alumni, or the general public. To shed their ivory-tower reputations, academic institutions must disseminate information that is user-friendly and easily understood.

Publications offices at academic institutions most commonly receive material that already is written, but that requires significant editing or rewriting before it is suitable for publication. Indeed, publications offices rarely have full-time writers to prepare original materials, simply because this has not proven to be practical or cost-effective over time. Where clients are not prepared to draft their own text, it is important that the publications office have a stable of freelance writers whom they can call for assistance, making certain to differentiate the writing styles necessary for each and every task. For example, the writing required for student recruitment literature is wholly unlike that needed to write a feature article for an alumni magazine. The skills required for writing formal annual reports, case statements, and descriptions of academic programs for catalogs are other areas of writing expertise. Knowing persons who can provide these services is an essential ingredient in the business of managing publications.

Because writing is often completed by the time contact is made with the publications office, hiring staff with flawless editing ability and some rewriting skills is important for a successful program. In an academic community there is no latitude for errors in spelling, usage, syntax, or punctuation. The editor's role is to protect the client from publishing errors that can cause enormous embarrassment and significant cost for reprinting—especially course catalogs, student handbooks, annual reports, donor honor roll lists, alumni magazines, or undergraduate student recruitment viewbooks. All of these are long, sometimes dense documents that must be read and understood by persons with no prior experience in academe. Far too often, the clients preparing this information believe it to be accurate, final, and without error—when the opposite is most likely the case.

The editor's job is to review all materials that will be published, to determine that the organization of the material is logical and effective, to decide if the basic goal of the project will be met with the existing text, to judge whether the material is readable to the average recipient of the message, to determine whether or not it conforms to the institutional style for externally distributed materials, and to decide if the length of the text will fit within the agreed-upon format for the proposed publication. Quite often this requires rewriting the material to conform to an institutional editing standard and to reduce the length of the material.

While it is not the purpose of this chapter to provide specific advice on editing style, it is important that editors be familiar with the expectations and capabilities of the readers to whom each publication is directed. For example, a viewbook intended for high school juniors and seniors is best written in a style that says "we" and "you," rather than in a more formal third-person style. Just the opposite is most commonly used in producing annual reports and case statements where a more journalistic, expository style works best with readers. These decisions are based, not on the personal preferences of the editors, but upon readership and focus group studies, described elsewhere in this book—studies that have revealed what is most effective with each audience. The time required to make these editing changes in copy is enormous and can often take additional weeks and months for which the client was unprepared and which can cause significant delays in delivery. That is why proactive, annual publications planning is so critical. It is common for work to begin a full year ahead of the publication date for a viewbook and six months before an annual report is to be delivered.

The process of establishing an institutional style is best accomplished by adopting existing style manuals, such as the *Chicago Manual of Style* or the *Associated Press Style Book and Libel Manual*. To these universally used documents, the institution can add its own style manual for titles, degrees, class years, institutional nicknames, and other idiosyncrasies specific to the institution itself. When used together, the institutional style manual and the commercially produced stylebook can be highly effective in covering virtually all questions of style and usage. It should be remembered that no rule is written that cannot be broken. For example, most dictionaries spell the word "theater," yet many academic performing arts departments prefer the spelling "theatre." An institutional style manual will allow flexibility in these situations, as long as the usage is consistent throughout all materials produced by the institution! It is not the role of the editor to have supreme authority in these matters, but to negotiate a workable, acceptable accommodation between the expectations of faculty and the less flexible rules imposed by stylebooks and by dictionaries.

GRAPHIC DESIGN: ART AS A COMMUNICATIONS TOOL

Art and artistic expression long have been protected by the academic community. While this is as it should be, it does not guarantee the effective use of art and design in the business of graphic communication. Here, the skills and creativity that enhance written messages must be a compromise between the creator's idea and the ability of a reader or viewer to comprehend artistic and graphic enhancements of marketing and promotional communications. In other words, good graphic design makes the message stronger and more effective. Through the use of legible typography, easily comprehended page layout, and excellent photography or illustrations, the successful graphic designer utilizes proven techniques to help ensure that the written word is appealing, informative, and appropriate.

Because graphic design is a much younger profession than writing, there are fewer guidelines and rules, as well as precious little significant research into what defines effectiveness. Graphic design is not painting, sculpture, or drawing—

although it may use them to solve design problems. Graphic design is not individualistic expression, even though it may strongly express a personal point of view. Properly practiced, graphic design is not art for its own sake, but rather art for the sake of good communication.

The subjectivity of artistic license is a perpetual dilemma, simply because educated, sophisticated people respect the right of artists to freedom of expression. Nearly 200 years ago, the composer Ludwig van Beethoven wrote to a friend: "Art! Who comprehends her? With whom can one consult concerning the great goddess?" The answer in graphic design lies with the intended recipient of the message and whether or not the message works.

All that said, good graphic design is essential in any publications and marketing program. Experienced designers are problem solvers who can take the basic message, the client's expectations, and the customer's capabilities all into account to produce a graphic solution in the format of promotional and informational publications, Web pages, advertising, or periodicals. Good designers know the importance of consistent institutional image in developing a message. They strategically select paper, ink, illustration, photography, layout, printing, binding, and means of distribution—while staying within the prescribed budget.

Whether hiring staff designers or selecting freelance help, remember that résumés are not nearly as important as portfolios. One designer may be particularly good at small two-color brochures, while another may specialize in four-color magazines, and yet another may do best in large-scale newspaper formats. Picking the right person for each job is critical, just as finding the correct writer is vital to the written message. Do call references.

Design is a way of packaging information so that it has more appeal to the user of the message—but it is not decoration. Beware of portfolios that are over designed, too trendy for conservative institutional tastes, insensitive to legibility and clarity of written messages, incompetent blending of written themes with visual messages, and impractical sizes, folds, and formats. As will be noted elsewhere in this section, good design means good legibility to enhance reading and to encourage more effective written communication. Be aware that poor design or no design is more common than good design.

The other side of the coin is the inability of staff and clients to recognize good design and to know when not to interfere with a workable solution that will get the job done successfully. Individuals and committees that tamper with color combinations, reconfigure the layout, substitute typefaces, and select different paper stocks that are not suitable for the graphic material are likely to suffer a poor outcome. A good rule of thumb is to judge the overall design as acceptable or not acceptable, and not attempt to let those with significantly less experience attempt to redesign the publication themselves. Clients and customers should ask questions about design, but it is essential they have professional advice while reviewing design concepts. Democracy may be a good thing, but one must remember that committees not only invented the camel, they also rarely reach consensus on graphic design.

As yet, there are no rules as to what constitutes good or bad design, but there are practices that do help make effective design decisions. Two of the most important principles are "keep it simple" and "less is more." Good design integrates, simplifies, and sometimes magnifies aspects of the message that have the most importance or value. An example in writing is the importance of a good headline that invites the reader to investigate further. Good design can serve the same purpose by encouraging the reader or viewer to explore or to experience the message because of the effective use of a poignant photograph positioned strategically with a compelling headline. The masterful use of typography, ink colors, layout, and other visual treatments requires that each piece of the message supports the rest, does not compete in ways that complicate the visual design, and does not confuse the reader. Following these basic principles will generally result in a more satisfactory communication.

When the right designer is selected, set specific budgets that cap what will be spent on the design effort. Then engage the designer with the writer, editor, and especially the client. Few would ask a reporter to craft a story without interviewing the primary subject, yet it is not uncommon for designers not to have the same opportunity to learn firsthand about the customer, his or her needs, and the problem that the publications effort must solve.

Be certain to share with designers the publication's operating statement, statement of purpose, the written content, samples of competitor's work, and any prior publications that since have been discarded. Share problems that may emerge in the process of producing the material, especially if there are strong biases on the part of clients and amateur meddlers who believe they are naturally gifted designers (often these are relatives, frustrated secretaries, and committee members). Be sure that the designer knows what the precise job specifications are—particularly if this determination already has been made and cannot be significantly altered. Most importantly, set specific deadlines and make arrangements to track progress toward meeting each stage in the production process.

Ultimately, the success or failure of design lies in the hands of the viewers, readers, and other customers who receive the final message and who therefore become the ultimate arbiters of taste—whether or not the design is good or bad in the eye of the creator. One must always remember the lesson learned by NBC television in the 1970s when it hired a major design firm that abandoned the traditional peacock symbol and replaced it with a stylized letter N. Not only did the public object to the removal of the traditional corporate symbol but they didn't see any advantage to the new symbol either. Worse yet, the new symbol was not properly investigated, and an identical symbol had been in use for many years at

Nebraska Public Television! The end result was that NBC eventually returned to its original peacock and had to write off millions of dollars in costs for the abortive attempt at a new symbol. More careful testing of viewer tastes and expectations would have avoided this problem from the very outset, as would have careful research of existing symbols. Apparently, NBC did neither to the extent it should have been done. The lesson to be learned is that all design must be tested, preferably before a new concept is launched and definitely after the publication, product, or promotion is in use.

PHOTOGRAPHY THAT WORKS

An old adage says that a great photograph is worth 1,000 words. Why? Because a photograph freezes a moment in time forever. Finding the right photography for a publication requires a professional who recognizes a powerful image, frames it in the viewfinder, and then captures that fleeting event for perpetuity. Finding the right photograph means finding the right photographer.

Successful editors and designers know not only a great photograph when they see one, but how to find the right person to take those pictures and to illustrate a written message with more emphasis, poignancy, and excitement. The majority of publications offices do not have staff photographers, so that maintaining a stable of talented and affordable freelance photographers becomes an important asset.

Photographers are specialists: Some focus on people in candid situations, while others are highly skilled at posing people to look completely candid. Sports photography, architectural photography, portrait photography, and studio photography all require highly differentiated skills and aptitudes. Knowing whom to hire for what assignment takes experience and good management skills.

Photographers do not operate in a vacuum, and they require special treatment as the publications process moves forward. Engage the photographer in discussions with the writers and designers, as well as the client. Some of the finest photographs are not candids, but the result of a carefully thought out visual strategy that requires a "shooter" with the directorial skills of a designer, visual artist, and psychologist. By involving a photographer at the beginning of a project, a proactive effort can be developed to be certain that everyone understands how the subject matter will be portrayed, and whether or not there are any special effects necessary, including props, special lighting, framing, camera angle, or even the focal length of the lens involved.

Since institutional publications are more and more likely to utilize four-color printing, color photography is essential. This requires additional skills in understanding lighting and color balance, especially in classrooms and laboratories where fluorescent lighting leads to bizarre skin tones on human subjects, as well as unappealing colors on what otherwise would be white or off-white walls.

Knowing which film to use is important. High-speed film can sometimes be grainy and may lack sufficient contrast and color reproduction, while high-resolution, slower films can make it difficult to stop any motion in the picture. Understanding these factors can assist in the collaborative relationship among editors, designers, and photographers.

Experienced publications officers keep detailed files on freelance photographers, noting examples of their best work and the areas in which the photographer specializes. Some photographers work entirely on their own, while others are more productive when a designer or art director accompanies them to help set up the photograph. Knowing when to apply these principles is difficult but necessary if the end result is to be a powerful visual message that meets the client's expectations. Expect to pay anywhere from $500 to $2,000 per day for a photographer, plus transportation, film, processing, and prints.

Because photographers have different visual "signatures," it may be best to use the same photographer throughout a specific publication when it comes to candid photographs. The same can be true of architectural photography, portraits, and studio photography as well. Otherwise, the different techniques employed may create a glaring visual problem in the final printed product.

When negotiating for photographic services, find photographers who are willing to sell unlimited rights to the use of a photograph, with the negatives remaining in the photographer's possession. Some institutions will hire only photographers that sell their time and who turn over their raw film to the institution for processing, proofing, and filing. In these cases the institution retains full rights to the images, but the photographer will likely charge a higher shooting fee, simply because of the loss of future revenue from making photographic prints. Regardless, all relationships with photographers must determine who owns not only the photographs themselves, but the rights to use the negatives. Even where photographers retain the negative, it is not unreasonable to demand that the pictures be limited to institutional use only, and that they cannot be sold to other customers without the permission of the publications office.

An ongoing debate is whether the institution should require model releases from students, faculty, and other institutional family members for any photograph used in the publication. Experience and legal precedent have shown that—as long as the photograph does not in any way denigrate or embarrass the subject—pictures taken within the institution and intended for institutional publications generally do not require a formal model release if it represents a routine activity, such as lecturing, studying, research, etc. On the other hand, any photograph that might cause embarrassment or anguish to the subject or to family members requires a model release, as do specialized photographs of patients taken by medical and other health-related departments as well as psychology, social work, etc. Be certain that the model release has been approved by the institution's legal counsel.

Skimping on photographs is counterproductive. Photographers will commonly shoot several rolls of film to obtain one good image—a practice that is not as wasteful as it may seem. Taking four or five rolls of 35-mm, 36-exposure film to obtain a powerful image of a lecturer teaching, students listening raptly, or a quarterback making a key play is not unusual. After the photographs are processed, the editor and designer should insist on seeing all proofs so that they can participate in the selection of the final image or images. Some institutions do this electronically with special video units that convert negatives or transparencies into a television image that can quickly determine whether the photograph is suitable—even before proofs or a final print is made. Copies of proofs should be kept by the institution, regardless of who owns and maintains the negatives or transparencies.

The advent of computerized layout and digital photography is rapidly changing the profession. Already, news photographers are using modestly portable digital cameras to take pictures that can then be instantaneously transmitted throughout the world via satellite for reproduction in newspapers and magazines—just as television images are instantly available on a global scale. At the time this is being written, no portable digital cameras compete as yet with the quality of silver-image technology, but that will change soon. Since virtually all photographs are now scanned digitally and placed electronically in page layouts, the advantages of a purely digital, portable camera are evident. Furthermore, the control over color and contrast is greatly improved with digital technology and new computer software.

Regardless of how the proofs are edited, always demand full-frame prints from the original negative or transparency. This provides the designer maximum flexibility in fitting the photograph into the layout and avoids any artificial cropping to fit standard photographic papers, which do not match the formats of 35-mm and $2^1/_4$-inch square images. Tell the photographer how the pictures will be used, in case special considerations have to be made about contrast, density, and color balance in the printing process. For example, black-and-white photographs reproduced in a newspaper will often require a totally different set of contrast values from photographs printed in a high-quality glossy magazine.

Final selection of photographs must first be based on the impact of the picture's content. Pictures that tell stories are always more valuable than those that require significant explanation. Images that work best evoke strong emotions, look candid and spontaneous, appear to be naturally (not artificially) lighted and draw the viewer's eye directly to the center of the action or scene portrayed. Nothing is worse than photographs that are inappropriately soft or out of focus, poorly cropped with extraneous and confusing information, or obviously posed.

Like art, the selection of photographs also can be highly subjective. This requires that a more strategic approach be used where several choices are possible, including the use of informal testing with colleagues or more formal use of focus groups to review photographs with the intended receivers of the printed message. Testing photographs with prospective students and current students can be particularly revealing of the differences in perception between middle-aged editors and designers and 17-year-olds.

Computer technology also makes it possible to retouch, crop, and modify photographs extensively. The removal of dust specs and scratches or the toning down of a disturbing item in the background are generally acceptable, but ethical dilemmas arise when images are added to photographs, subjects are moved significantly from one place in the photograph to another, or reality is altered in some significant way from the original image—unless these alterations are noted in the cutline that goes with the photograph.

Graphic design relies strongly on photographs, but too much of a good thing has deleterious effects. If a great photograph on a two-page spread is indeed worth 1,000 words, then two great photographs on that surface are worth 500 words, three are worth 250 words, four are worth 125 words, and so forth. Publications and Web pages are not scrapbooks with lots of pictures, rather they are carefully crafted surfaces that carry a blend of visual and written images to ensure a maximum result with the intended audience. Too many photographs can be just as ineffective as none at all.

A bad photograph never gets better. Attempts to "dress up" a poorly taken picture through the use of four-color printing, duotones, posterization, and so on only make the outcome worse.

No matter how good the story told by any photograph may be, all images require explanation in some form. Just as a newspaper would not think of publishing a photograph without a cutline, so should all brochures, viewbooks, annual reports, and catalogs contain descriptions of who or what is in the picture itself. Testing shows that readers want to know the names and titles of professors, identification of buildings, and information about the laboratory or studio being pictured. Despite the irrefutable research supporting this approach, the great majority of academic promotional publications do not use cutlines with photographs. After photographs are used in the publication, a file system should be developed for easy future retrieval, whether it uses low-tech folders or the new CD-ROM imaging equipment. Computers can be particularly helpful in the indexing of photographs on the basis of general subject matter, names of persons in the photographs, departments or building involved, and a number of other criteria.

LEGIBLE TYPOGRAPHY: SOME DOS AND SOME DON'TS

The integration of written messages with illustrations requires design and editing skills that effectively marry messages and images that maximize audience attention. An area often overlooked in this process is the research conducted over the past half century on legibility of typography. Few editors and designers have received significant training in what works and what does not with readers of varying ages.

Selecting a typeface to be used in a publication is not something that should be left to the untrained professional. The selection of a typeface that can be read effectively and conveys information pleasingly should be based on legibility first and artistic taste second. Here are some simple rules about typography:

- *Less is still more.* Lots of different typefaces, ornate type designs, and wide variations in line length all contribute to a feeling that a publication is amateurish. Most newspapers, magazines, and promotional publications limit themselves to one or two text faces and a judicious number of headline styles as well.
- *Select text type sizes for the audience.* Young readers generally can read smaller type sizes, while those approaching middle age find that larger faces are more appealing. The x-height (the height of the lower-case x in a specific type face) determines whether a 9-, 10-, 11-, or 12-point type has optimum legibility. Smaller sizes are hard to read as text, although they may be used effectively for lists and directories, while 14-point or larger typefaces can slow reading speed significantly.
- *Readers generally prefer serif-style type.* Popular typefaces with readers are Times Roman, Garamond, Bodoni, Century Schoolbook, Baskerville, and Goudy, to name only a few. Unlike sans serif typefaces, the letter forms in serif faces have an unexplained appeal, whereas sans serif is more legible for headlines, signage, and low-resolution computer screens.
- *Avoid extremely light or bold text faces.* All readers find them hard to scan.
- *Avoid at all costs highly illegible typefaces,* such as calligraphic styles, hand-lettered styles, and "cutesy" faces—all of which are unwise for text and should be sparingly used for headlines.
- *Avoid italic and bold face for text.* A great shortcoming of campus-produced publications is the overabundant use of italic and bold typefaces for regular text. Both of these letter forms are strongly disliked by readers according to all testing ever done, whereas Roman is preferred. On the other hand, bold and italic both can be effective in headlines when used appropriately, and a sans serif bold face like Helvetica works well on signage.
- *Specify medium line lengths.* A good rule of thumb is to specify line lengths that average between 35 and 55 characters and spaces per line. This translates into about five to ten words per line. Shorter line widths for text are disliked by readers because they're difficult to read and have been discarded by most newspapers and news magazines that test reader preferences. Very long lines are extremely difficult to scan unless significant spacing is put between each

line to assist the eye as it returns from the end of one line to the beginning of the next. The rapid advent of Web and HTML formats has generally ignored the optimum legibility for line length, with some home pages using lines of more than 100 words in length, thereby greatly slowing reading speed.

- *The space between lines of text is important.* Setting type solid (no spacing between lines) is completely acceptable for telephone directories, donor lists, or class schedules where the reader does not have to track complex thoughts and sentences. News and editorial texts, however, are best read when they are slightly leaded with 1, 2, or 3 points of spacing between lines, if the type size ranges between 9 and 12 points. The longer the line, the greater the leading needed, which also is a good rule of thumb for heavier weight typefaces.
- *Flush left, ragged right is preferred.* A never-ending debate is whether typography should be justified (even on the left and right sides) or flush left, ragged right (even on the left side only). Research shows that slower readers prefer flush left, simply because the spacing between the words and letters is uniform, whereas justified type requires the addition of space between words and letters to accomplish an even margin at the right side. Children also read flush left, ragged right better. Readers do not like flush right, ragged left layouts, nor do they prefer centered, line-for-line type.
- *Use lowercase for text.* Uppercase type (all capital letters) is sometimes viewed as emphasizing a message, hence the reason it is sometimes overused in academic publishing. Not only are words set in all capital letters harder to read, but they also take at least 25 percent more lateral space on the printed page.
- *Dark type on light surfaces is better for printed text.* For printed material, testing shows that readers prefer dark type on a light-colored surface. Just the opposite is true for signage, where drivers tend to prefer light type on a dark surface. Not yet clearly understood is the most effective combination on computer screens, partly due to the differing technologies now on the market. A significant number of computer users seem to prefer light-colored type on a dark field, which is just the opposite of readers of conventional printed material.
- *Select text colors and background for maximum contrast.* The difference in density between the letter forms and the background on which they are printed needs to be significant—at least 65 percent—for ideal legibility. That is why readers of printed matter prefer black ink on white paper, which represents a difference of more than 95 percent in contrast. Printing light text, such as a washed-out gray, blue, or brown, is not preferred by most readers, and presents hardships for elderly readers with diminished visual acuity. For mailed pieces, the U.S. Postal Service specifies a minimum reflectance between background and type for their optical scanning equipment.

- *Insist on high-quality letter spacing.* Text that is set in poorly designed computer typefaces that have inconsistent letter spacing and uneven baselines can be subliminally disturbing to the reader and probably affects reading speed significantly. Be certain that the software and the fonts selected meet the same high standard expected of traditional typefaces that were once prepared in handset or linotype forms.

Decisions about selection of typefaces should be based upon artistic taste, but only after the type answers a much more basic question—can the message be easily read by the specific audience for which it is intended? Elderly readers of planned giving brochures and annual reports are going to be much more satisfied with 11- and 12-point text, while young readers of admissions literature will probably tolerate types as small as 9 point. Starting from this premise, the editor and designer can make intelligent, strategic type selection decisions.

PRINTING THE JOB: REMEMBER WHO THE CUSTOMER IS

Printing is a business, and the institution is the customer. The printing trade is one of the oldest, longstanding crafts left relatively unchanged from the Middle Ages in its philosophy and practice of delivering quality products. Unfortunately, the customer must take certain steps to guarantee that those standards are met and that the final outcome is both a credit to the printing trade as well as satisfactory to the client the publications office represents.

All of the best writing, editing, photography, design, and layout are wholly dependent on a first-rate printing job. Earlier in this section the processing of bids was discussed, an essential step in developing a relationship with the printer. It is also important to be aware of the printer's reputation for customer satisfaction, to see how the shop is managed, and to have a mutual understanding that the printer will follow acceptable norms of performance. Editors, designers, production coordinators, and publications directors all need to know about the printing industry and what the strengths and weaknesses of each vendor may be. This begins with knowing the printing and binding equipment in each shop, the method by which paper is stored, and the types of computer imaging and plating technology used by the vendor. Further, learn which printers are good at suggesting solutions to problems regarding ink, paper, formats, sizes, binding, and conformity to postal regulations. Consult with trusted printers on suggestions for cost savings and ways in which formats can be altered to avoid wasting paper and press time.

Remember a low bid is not always the best solution to a printing problem, despite the fact some publicly assisted institutions are required by law to use the lowest bidder. A printer with a poor track record can only add ultimately to time and cost, not to mention frustration. Institutions that allow selection of bidders that are close in price generally are more satisfied with their printing relationships than those who always insist on low bidder only.

Printers respect customers that make any needed changes before final proofs. Making changes on bluelines, color keys, chromalins, match prints, etc., can be extremely frustrating and, if the customer's fault, very expensive.

Checking on-press proofs is essential for highly important publications, such as annual reports, viewbooks, and other documents that may be the first contact prospective students and other key audiences will have with the institution. Do not confuse true press proofs (which are done on press to get only one or two copies of what the product will actually look like) with on-press proofs, which is the process of checking a product while it is actually being printed. The latter is generally preferable and less expensive, as long as no customer changes are anticipated. The most important things to check for on press are density of ink, broken or lost type on printing plates, registration of ink colors on four-color work, consistency of color, and alignment of the folios and signatures that will ultimately make up the finished, bound product. Be sure to keep copies of all signed, authorized press sheets until the final job is delivered and approved.

CUTTING PUBLICATION COSTS

The most effective cost-cutting technique is to manage the publications process well, ensuring that all aspects of production stay within the parameters agreed on between the client and the publications office. However, clients frequently do not have sufficient budgets to do what is recommended, and they require assistance in finding less costly (and perhaps less effective) methods of producing the final product. Following are a few cost-cutting recommendations:

- *Don't print.* There is no rule that says printing is required in the academic environment: It is only a myth perpetuated by the "publish or perish" burden shared by the community. One way to avoid printing is to combine the message with an existing publication going to the same audience or using vastly less expensive techniques for communicating, such as the use of Web pages or the Internet. Unfortunately, although these technologies may be less expensive for distributing messages, they also are not easily received by a majority of the population.
- *Edit. Edit. Edit.* The length of a printed message usually affects the cost of printing it. By judicious editing, it is possible to significantly reduce the length of the message to fit on a smaller piece of paper, on fewer pages, or in a different format that will significantly reduce the cost of the message. Ways in which tight editing can be achieved are cutting the course descrip-

tions in catalogs, removing duplicated information, streamlining language, and dropping information that has no defensible value.

- *Prepare the job in-house.* The advent of computer-based layout, typography, and prepress preparation has driven the cost of printing services down significantly, but this has transferred the burden of these operations onto the publications office. Outsourcing often costs anywhere from $50 to $150 per hour, whereas in-house staff can cost as little as $20 per hour, including benefits, overhead, and depreciation of equipment. The shortcomings of in-house production are long-term commitments to staffing, front-end costs for equipping a computerized workstation, and the frustrations of managing the staff.
- *Select less-expensive paper stocks.* Paper prices have been volatile in recent years, and differences in prices between high-end and low-end papers have become less evident as newsprint skyrocketed in cost. That said, the difference in price between a magazine and a tabloid newspaper printed on newsprint can be dramatic, not to mention that mailing costs can be lower due to the lighter weight of certain paper stocks. Newsprint is usually limited to printing on web presses, which makes it less economical or impractical for sheet-fed printing. Other techniques include using thinner stock, as long as opacity is not significantly altered, and slightly reducing the outer dimensions of a printed product.
- *Use nonrag stationery.* A major cost-saver is the elimination of all rag-content letterhead, envelopes, and business cards. Substitute a number-one sulfite bond, which can be significantly less expensive without altering shelf life and laser-output characteristics.
- *Ask your printer for help.* Printers know cost-cutting better than anyone. Ask for ways to reduce cost in conjunction with the designer. Avoid expense-adding techniques such as bleeds, large areas requiring solid ink coverage, difficult ink and paper combinations (such as a light ink on a dark surface), or anything that requires a hand operation for folding, binding, or mailing.
- *Do your own color separations.* Color separations are best done on expensive, high technology equipment. But where the printed product does not require a high-quality result, in-house scanners can be used to produce color images for tabloid newspapers on newsprint or other low-end printed products.
- *Reduce frequency.* Periodicals such as alumni magazines and employee newspapers are more effective the more frequently they are published—if sufficient funds are available. A common technique today is the reduction in frequency of these periodicals to save costs. The only risk is the diminished number of messages going to key audiences and the possible impact this will have on fund raising, or employee relations. The two-year course catalog has

become more common in a cost-conscious environment, and some rely heavily on on-line catalogs.

- *Cut distribution costs.* Various classifications of nonprofit mail have escalated in cost over the past decade to eliminate the privileges accorded educational institutions by the U.S. Postal Service. In some instances this has brought about a five-fold or larger increase in postage for the very same publication. The best way to avoid these costs is to find alternate methods of distribution. For example, does the course schedule have to be mailed to all students, or can it be distributed through campus mails or to special locations for easy pickup? Does the city in which the institution wishes to distribute a message door-to-door have an alternate service for this purpose? Can the mailing list be significantly reduced without affecting results? Can the fulfillment house use computerized information more effectively to reduce labeling and sorting costs, as well as to achieve a lower postal rate?

These are only a very few suggestions to cut costs. The best methods of cutting costs are known to vendors and to professional publications colleagues on other campuses. Consulting these sources will provide literally dozens of additional ways in which small, incremental savings can be made. The experience of learning from the success and the mistakes of others in a world of rapidly changing technologies and printing techniques is still the best teacher.

CHAPTER 21

Essential Publications: Making Them More Effective

M. Fredric Volkmann

The great majority of publications on a typical campus fall into three categories, student recruitment, development, and alumni/parent relations. Not only do these constitute three of the primary sources of revenue for typical colleges and schools, but they also represent a significant portion of administrative expense for printing and postage. Without including the cost of writing, editing, and design, the cost of printing and mailing a typical course catalog ranges anywhere from $1 to $5 per recipient. Undergraduate viewbooks usually range from $2 to $4, while alumni magazines may cost as much as $1 each to print and mail. Donor honor rolls and institutional annual reports typically run between $2 and $3 per copy. Total institutional expenditures on these publications and others like them add up rapidly when one realizes that even a small college or independent school may have a mailing list of more than 30,000 alumni, parents, past parents, and other friends. Add to this the cost of recruiting students where mailing lists easily can exceed an additional 50,000 names, and one can see why total institutional expenditures on promotional publications and periodicals can exceed $500,000 per year at a small institution, and several million dollars annually at large research universities.

Making the most effective use of these investments requires publications and periodicals that achieve results that will more than repay the initial investment in printing and postage.

Unfortunately, there are no guaranteed formulas or magic bullets that will ensure effective printed materials—unless the institution routinely tests and audits the impact and response rates generated by search mailings, viewbooks, course catalogs, alumni/parent magazines, newsletters, annual reports, annual fund mailings, and development campaign literature. However, testing has shown that certain basic expectations are universally shared by prospective students, by alumni and parents, and by prospective donors. This section will deal with some of the archetypes that seem to apply in most cases. Caution should be exercised not to embrace every solution, simply because institutional audiences do differ and not even common archetypes will necessarily fit every situation.

STUDENT RECRUITMENT MATERIALS

What once was called admissions has shifted from a passive process of evaluating applicants to a much more aggressive marketing strategy that seeks out prospects and engages their attention and interest. Hopefully, this results in an application, followed by acceptance or rejection of the applicant, and culminating in the decision of the accepted applicant to enroll—or not to enroll. The days of simply mailing out a viewbook, and then perhaps a course catalog, have long been superseded by a much more sophisticated series of direct-mail strategies. Repeated experience has shown that such strategies tend to follow the ladder of communications described at the outset of the section on public relations.

Whether parents of prospective private, elementary, and secondary students; prospective freshmen for a typical college or university; or future graduate and professional students—all these audiences seem to have commonly held preferences for the printed materials they receive:

- *Personal letters outperform publications.* There is a reason why highly successful membership organizations rarely use publications for their initial contacts with prospects. Instead, they send a personally addressed letter asking for a membership, donation, or involvement. Examples include the Republican and Democratic national parties, American Civil Liberties Union, National Organization of Women, National Rifle Association, and hundreds more. The reason no publications are used in these initial mailings is simple: most people will trust a personalized letter that appears to be sent and signed by a real human being much more than they trust a slick, printed brochure. Sending a brochure without an envelope usually gets the lowest response rate, followed by a brochure in an envelope, and then by a brochure with a cover letter. Many colleges experience the greatest response rate when a brochure is not included and the mailing consists of a letter, along with a postage-paid response card or envelope. The more personalized the letter appears to be, the better the response rate. Schools, colleges, and universities that employ this technique soon learn what commercial users and politicians learned long ago. Make people believe you care about them as individuals by treating them that way.
- *Target messages to each market segment.* When the specific interests of a prospective student are known, the use of generic letters and publications is far outdistanced by highly focused messages that deal with individual inter-

ests. Because of sophisticated software, it is a relatively easy matter to craft a letter targeted specifically at engineers, accompanied by a brochure on engineering as well as a reply envelope that goes directly to an admissions officer who is a specialist in engineering admissions.

- *Well-written letters and publications are necessary.* Far too often the letters and brochures used to recruit students are unimaginatively written, poorly organized, and inconsistent. If they read as if they were written by a committee, they probably were. Nothing can substitute for a talented writer to craft all parts of the material going into a typical mailing, such as the cover letter, brochure, and even the reply card. Well-stated, compelling messages are still more important than photographs, artwork, design, paper, or ink colors. Simple, concise, and serious language is essential. Be careful when using humor, since many prospective students and their families view the admissions process with a great deal of seriousness.

- *Involve and test the intended audience at the earliest stage.* Begin any student recruitment mailing and publications effort by consulting the intended audience first. For private grade schools and high schools this means parents of students and perhaps the prospective students themselves; for undergraduate programs this means high school sophomores, juniors, and seniors; and for graduate students, seek input from graduating college seniors. For continuing education students, often one can safely test those already enrolled in the program, but this is not true for traditional, full-time students because of the significant transformation that takes place once they are enrolled. Second, engage the services of an expert in student recruitment publications and direct-mail strategies. Third, pull together a team from the campus involving professionals in admissions, financial aid, development, alumni, media relations, publications, and faculty in such programs as marketing, communications, and advertising.

- *Keep it simple.* The "keep it simple" principle applies particularly in the direct-mail field. First-contact efforts with persons who may not have any prior knowledge of the institution require a straightforward simplicity that focuses the reader on one or two key messages. Sending a viewbook of 32 or more pages, or worse yet, a course catalog of several hundred pages, will have a much lower impact than a simple, 6- to 12-panel publication folded to fit in a business envelope. Besides describing the special qualities of the institution or program, be certain to communicate important information about your location.

- *Stress location.* One of the key factors used by prospective students in deciding whether or not to inquire further at the beginning of a relationship is location. For example, an urban school should talk about the advantages of the city around it, but a rural college should talk about the positive aspects of a natural environment, safety, and other advantages often perceived to be part of rural life. Remember, though, location soon takes a back seat to much more important factors as students come closer to making a final choice of a college, so it is important to also include information on financial aid and cost, curriculum, and evidence of perceived quality of the institution.

- *Print all publications in full color.* Two-color brochures have gone the way of black-and-white television. Even the nation's best-known single-color publication, the *New York Times*, has begun to add color to many of its sections. Why? People expect to see color television, full-color magazines and catalogs, and even color photographs throughout the pages of their daily newspapers. The mailings sent by academic institutions must compete in this same marketplace. Additionally, the paper stock should be good for color reproduction, photographs must be superb, and the design and printing should reflect highest professional standards.

- *Personalize computer-generated messages.* The more technology we use to generate messages, the more important it is that they look personalized. While we use computers to create more efficient, personalized messages, remember that computers are not friendly. People are. The cover letter addressed to each prospect must look, read, and even feel like a personal message crafted specifically for the recipient by the signer. Readers know what a letter produced by dot matrix, ink jet, laser jet, or strike-on technology looks like—especially if it is set on paper that still has the serrations from the pin feed along the edges. Use the technique that most feels like old-fashioned typewritten messages, and be sure to sign every letter with an ink pen. There are now computer systems that actually use either blown-on ink or ink pens to simulate a fountain-pen signature. Most importantly, make sure that an envelope is used without a label. Envelopes with directly imprinted addresses that look as though they were applied by a typewriter are much more likely to be opened and believed. Bulk-rate indicia or postage meter imprints are dead giveaways for junk mail. Using postage stamps, whether bulk-rate or first-class, can be applied in ways that can fool even experts into believing they have been sent a personal letter.

- *Mail early and mail often.* A former Chicago major reportedly once urged his constituency to "vote early and vote often." While that is illegal in politics, it is good advice in the direct-mail industry. Prospective students and their families are inundated with mail, and the earlier a message is received, the less likely it is to be lost in the flood of materials that goes into the homes of prospects. And the better the student, the more mail he or she will receive.

- *Always pay for reply postage and return phone calls.* Longstanding evidence shows postage-paid reply cards and envelopes are more likely to engender a response, as is the use of "800" telephone numbers. Now that young people are becoming more universally acquainted with the Internet and the Web, they are even less accustomed to paying the costs of replying to any communication. Unfortunately, many academic institutions are still penny-wise and pound-foolish when it comes to reply postage. Try to imagine the number of young people you know who have postage stamps on their persons or in their homes to affix to a response to a mailing! On the other hand, institutions have almost universally adopted the use of toll-free 800 numbers. Remember, getting the prospect to increase the level of personal contact with the institution is more likely to result in further interest—especially if the telephone system is well managed. Always try to have a real human respond to 800 calls, rather than voice mail messages that tend to delay the response from the institution.

- *Track responses and test results.* Knowing who replied when to which mailing is information that will go a long way toward determining the strategies that are cost effective and that are most likely to encourage prospects to begin a dialogue with the admissions office. By the same note, testing the materials on the audience is a never-ending process and should continue throughout each cycle, even after the publication is printed and in use.

While these pointers focus on a few strategies that seem to work with virtually all types of prospective students, subtle techniques specific to each audience need to be incorporated in a direct-mail program. For example, parents are much more likely to have a major hand in the selection of a specific private grade school or high school than they are in assisting a son or daughter pick an undergraduate college. Parents are almost never involved in a graduate student's selection of a college or a university. In fact, just being too promotional in a "pitch letter" to a graduate student can backfire—simply because they have learned to resent aggressive, pushy messages while they were undergraduates. That is why testing must be conducted on any communications strategy with each specific audience.

VIEWBOOKS AND CATALOGS

Although the initial contact with students requires highly sophisticated direct-mail programs, the follow-up messages involve a complex matrix of publications and correspondence, often beginning with a viewbook or prospectus that utilizes a combination of photographs and text about the institution and its programs. The viewbook or prospectus often is at least 32 and sometimes more than 64 pages in length and generally is $8^1/_2$ by 11 inches in size. Even though the publication covers many aspects of the institution, it does require support materials that go into more detail. For this reason, the admissions publications arsenal also will include brochures on financial aid, housing, careers, special programs for freshman students, flyers or brochures about departments and majors, and at larger universities, special viewbooks for such schools as business, engineering, and art. Often the course catalog is not sent to prospective students until they submit an application.

Today's viewbook or prospectus is a glossy, colorful, and often expensive compendium of the best attributes and qualities of a typical school, college, or university. While viewbooks are almost universally used to recruit school children, college undergraduates, and professional students, they are less commonly employed in admission strategies for traditional graduate students and for continuing education students.

For more than two decades, I have annually collected more than 100 randomly selected undergraduate viewbooks and prospectuses from among the 3,800 colleges and universities in the United States. Through analyzing these publications and then testing a select number of them on high school students, certain expectations and patterns emerge as to what constitutes an ideal viewbook or prospectus for a typical college or university. This testing did not include viewbooks from private elementary and secondary high schools, but many of the principles involved will likely apply to those audiences as well. Here are a few of the lessons learned from this analysis:

- *Viewbooks must assume the reader knows nothing about the institution.* Leave nothing to chance. Institutions recruit students from such a wide range of backgrounds, interests, levels of achievement, and regions. Assuming the prospect has any clear picture of the college or university would be a serious mistake. The transition from high school to college is often dramatic: what students learn about survival in a typical high school is wholly unlike the experience of going to college. Rarely do prospects have any inkling of what it's like to be in college, and they usually have not had any experiences that prepare them for the culture they are about to enter. Therefore, it cannot be assumed that the reader can translate jargon, complex concepts, or unique experiences into his or her own frame of reference. That is why viewbooks are more explanatory and have become longer and longer over the past quarter century.

- *Viewbook covers matter greatly.* The old adage that says "one cannot tell a book by its cover" simply does not apply to viewbooks. The cover must be a clear, inviting indication of what is to follow. Virtually all testing shows that the publication needs to have full-color photographs and artwork, and that the printing quality must be of high caliber. Covers that work best either are excellent photographs of the campus' signature building, or an informal, natural-feeling photograph of a group of no more than four students in the foreground, perhaps with a campus building in the distant background. Other cover techniques such as montages, collages, sketches and paintings, display typography, or studio photographs of book bags filled with computers, pennants, notebooks, pens and pencils, etc., rarely test as well. Special caution should be taken when using expensive-looking techniques such as blind embossing, foil stamping, die-cutting, or special translucent fly sheets. Prospective students and their families may see these techniques as evidence that the institution is overpriced and a little too fancy for them. Testing has shown time and again that straightforward, simple photographs of buildings or people work best.

Also included on a viewbook cover should be the complete name of the institution and the year or years for which the viewbook is in effect. Adding additional text can sometimes dilute the impact of the photograph or artwork. The back cover always should include not only the name of the institution again, but also the complete mailing address, as well as the toll-free 800 telephone number that students may call and possibly an e-mail address and World Wide Web site. The back cover is an opportunity for another display photograph of the campus, as long as enough space remains for address labels required by postal services if envelopes are not used.

- *Put a one-page institutional profile on the inside front cover or page one.* Don't think of a viewbook as a coffee table magazine or as a bound volume of glamorous photographs. It is a sales tool, and as it becomes longer and longer to accommodate the expectations of readers, it requires a synoptic message at the very beginning to give the reader reasons to continue to wade through page after page of pictures and information. The simplest way to achieve this end is to put together a fact sheet that profiles the institution in an easily understood format. Of utmost importance is listing the undergraduate majors, preferably in alphabetical order (not alphapolitical order). This fact sheet often contains such information as academic programs, enrollment, size of freshman class, class rank, Scholastic Aptitude Test or American College Test average scores, distribution of students by state and country, ethnic make-up, fees for tuition, room or board, financial aid programs, enrollment by school and department, and typical class size. Also important on the opening spread is a concise table of contents.
- *Say what distinguishes the institution from its competition.* Despite the fact that many institutions open their viewbooks with a letter from the chief executive or the head of admissions, these invariably test very poorly and have little value in the publication. Much more important is a well-written, carefully illustrated brief introductory message about what makes the institution special or unique. The language should be open, welcoming, and unpretentious. The approach should be matter of fact without the appearance of bragging or boasting. It should answer the question: "Why would I, as a prospec-

tive student, want to consider this institution as a place where I will spend the next few years of my life?"

- *Talk next about learning and teaching.* Most students come to college to get an education, and they give that highest priority in their screening of institutions. After an institutional introduction, a page or pages should be devoted to describing the teaching and learning process that distinguishes the institution from the rest of the pack. This is not a place for academic philosophy or institutional sermonizing. The language should simply describe the process and the expectations of which the academic experience is comprised and what those mean to the recipient. Some viewbooks delve heavily into explaining the complexities of liberal arts education, while others deal more with down-to-earth, practical classroom experiences with featured professors. Subject matter covered can include majors, opportunities for independent research and scholarship, study abroad, teaching incentive programs, learning programs geared toward new freshmen, and any other qualities that best describe what is unique or special in the learning experience. In some viewbooks this section can be as long as eight or nine pages and may also include extensive information about libraries, computing facilities, advanced studies, non-traditional learning experiences, and preparation for careers and/or graduate school. In this section, some viewbooks include brief profiles of outstanding faculty, or statements by faculty that reveal some special quality about their teaching and research activities.
- *Focus on academic divisions and disciplines.* The viewbook must delve more deeply into the divisions, departments, disciplines, or other academic specialties that offer a more focused view of the academic experience on campus. For liberal arts colleges this often is a description of each department and its majors, whereas a larger university would divide this section by schools and colleges. In either form, this section describes what makes the academic area unique when compared to similar programs at other institutions around the country. Normally, these sections work best when they focus on the curriculum and the faculty, particularly in the freshman year. The previous section describes what makes the institution unique, but this section differentiates each discipline from its counterpart elsewhere. If possible, it is best to give also some indication as to the enrollment of each academic unit, the number of faculty, the majors and minors that can be earned, student academic organizations affiliated with the school, department, or program, and career information specific to the discipline involved.
- *Feature life outside of the classroom.* Surprisingly to some, students at even the most rigorous academic institutions usually spend half or less of their waking hours in classes or studying. The balance of the waking day is spent recreating, eating, commuting, and socializing. This is the first opportunity

many students have had to take charge of their own lives. That process is an important ingredient in the college experience and deserves thoughtful exploration in the viewbook. These sections normally cover student volunteer and social organizations that pursue dozens and hundreds of interests. Also included in a campus life section are opportunities for participation in music, dance, theater and literary organizations, politics, social responsibility, religion, student government, fraternities and sororities, community service, student newspapers and radio stations, preprofessional organizations, military service, and activities that are unique or special to the institution. For many institutions, varsity and club athletics, as well as intramurals, play a key role in the out-of-classroom activities of students. But perhaps of greatest importance are the opportunities to socialize through dating, dances, and dorm life. This section also must deal with food and meal plans on the campus, activities in surrounding neighborhoods, safety and security, counseling, services for those with disabilities, health services, and special tutoring programs for those who seek them.

- *Build on the institution's location and surroundings.* Because prospective students often begin their college search by considering location first and foremost, it is imperative that a viewbook devote at least two or more pages to describing the community or area surrounding the campus or campuses. If the institution is in an urban setting, describe attractions that include professional sports, entertainment, museums and libraries, parks and recreation, natural attractions (including nearby mountains, lakes, rivers, or oceans), leading businesses, neighborhoods, transportation, and any number of other attributes that are perceived to be positive qualities. For campuses located in smaller communities and rural settings, focus on quality of life, personal safety, access to urban areas, relationships with other nearby academic institutions, etc. Again, remember that location is an important factor early in the process, but at the time of final decision, it often takes a back seat to cost and financial aid, academic quality, and career opportunities after graduation. Be sure to include factual information about population of the region, any rankings of quality of life, time and distance to other important cities or regions, cost of living, or any other attribute that could add an advantage.

- *Consider a section on famous alumni, careers, and graduate study opportunities.* For those prospective students who see college as simply a step toward a lifetime career, a section devoted to previous success stories and to opportunities for internships and employment after graduation can be extraordinarily helpful, especially where the institution is perceived not to be one that prepares college students for the workplace—namely a liberal arts college. Some institutions list famous alumni, while others offer testimonials from these individuals, and yet others describe students who are already beginning their careers while in college. For those institutions that measure success in the number of graduates who go on to additional academic study, listing the institutions that are most commonly attended for graduate and professional study can be a good market-positioning strategy. Include any available data on placement rates and admission to graduate program rates.

- *Include the application for admissions, along with instructions regarding admissions and financial aid.* Because viewbooks are intended to move students as quickly and inexpensively as possible to become applicants, most include either a postage-paid reply form, a preliminary application for admission, or a complete application. Accompanying this section should be detailed information about applying for admission, including important dates for early decision and regular student applicants, as well as information for transfer and international students on how they may need to apply separately from graduates of U.S. high schools. Also included should be information on how to apply for financial aid, noting that this usually is not done until the application for admission process has been initiated. Repeated here should be complete information about tuition, fees, room and board, and typical charges that students may incur for books, transportation, and other incidentals necessary to their education.

- *Encourage campus visits.* Experience has shown time and again that those prospects who visit campuses are much more likely to apply for admission than those who do not, and admitted students who visit are much more likely to enroll. For that reason, most viewbooks contain instructions on how to visit the campus, to take campus tours, to arrange for an overnight stay, and to have interviews with an admissions officer, faculty, and current students. Frequently included with this section is a map of the campus and transportation information on how to reach the campus by road, rail, or air. Institutions that attract students more than a day's round-trip drive from campus also may want to include basic information about hotels nearby. Also included in this section are telephone numbers of important campus offices that prospective or admitted students and their families may have to contact in addition to the admissions office.

- *Consider using student testimonials throughout.* Some institutions find that testimonials by currently enrolled students are very helpful in establishing peer-level understanding of what it is like to go to college. These must be candid and should include a photograph of the individual, as well as information about hometown, high school, and academic interests. For some prospective students, testimonials are important persuaders and information sources, so include information that has value and avoid insincere language that sounds too much like glowing praise.

- *Some tips about text.* Testing shows that viewbook copy is most effective when it addresses the reader as "you" and the message sender as "we." Formal, third-person language does not sit well with prospective students and their families when they know they are investing in something that will be a life-transforming experience. They need to feel involved from the very outset. Also be careful not to make exaggerated claims or to suggest that something is truly unique. Unique-o-mania is an unfortunate behavior that often lacks believability. All text should be read by current students, as well as by several prospective students to gauge their reactions. Hire proofreaders to double-check spelling, grammar, and to test readability. Be sure to use easily understood words and sentences that do not require dictionaries. Organize information in ways that people think, and be careful with humor. "Punny" is not necessarily funny. Students and their families are deadly serious about college and sometimes are mystified by the use of cute language, puns, and satire.
- *Integrate photographs with text.* Virtually all testing of viewbooks shows that photographs do not operate independently from the text and the headlines. Additionally, all photographs require identification—cutlines that describe who or what is in the photograph. Don't select photographs on the basis of artistic merit alone; test them with 16- and 17-year-olds. For example, a campus night-time scene may look gorgeous when properly framed and photographed, but to some it may suggest serious personal risk because of a natural, subliminal fear of the dark. Most important, count noses. Make certain that the identifiable faces in the viewbook accurately reflect what exists on the campus in terms of gender, ethnicity, academic interest, extracurricular activities, and so on. Both photographs and text must tell the truth.

Course catalogs once were thought to be equally important to the viewbook but have lost significant ground in the past few years. Testing has shown that course catalogs have very little value or meaning to prospective students—until they actually apply or have been admitted to the institution and have to begin thinking seriously about what courses to take and what requirements to meet for majors. Because most high school students have virtually no experience understanding how institutions of higher education operate, the content of the catalog can be not only confusing, but downright off-putting. Because the publication is generally written by the faculty for the faculty, course names often do not reveal the nature or content of the subject matter, and course descriptions that are loaded with jargon or too general and oblique may actually mislead the reader as to what will be studied in the classroom or laboratory.

Where significant misunderstandings have occurred, litigation has arisen that holds institutions accountable for what is said in the catalog, indicating that it is actually perceived to be a contract between the institution and the student. The result has revolutionized how institutions see catalogs and how they are edited for publication. Until recent decades, course catalogs were printed as though they were library books intended for long-term shelving. In truth, they usually have a useful lifetime of one or two years, and then they are superseded by new editions that change and update what was published previously. For most students, this means that the information included in the catalog used as an entering freshman may actually change during the course of the undergraduate educational experience.

Trained professionals are important in the editing and preparation of these documents, and this has led to a better understanding of audiences, reduction in length of wordy course descriptions, clarification of course names to more closely match what is taught, and reduction in expenditures for printing and distribution. Graduate and professional students, however, have spent several years learning how to decipher and interpret course catalogs and often use them very effectively in planning their graduate educational experiences. For this reason, catalogs can be of highest importance to students pursuing advanced studies, even though they may not have much value for a prospective freshman.

Most undergraduate course catalogs contain the following basic information:

- Table of contents
- Academic calendar
- Important university addresses, phone numbers, Web sites, and e-mail addresses
- Statement of institutional mission and/or philosophy
- List of majors, minors, and degrees
- Information about class size
- Instructions on applying for admission and financial aid
- List of scholarships
- Details about housing, meals, parking, etc.
- Student support services, such as academic advising, tutoring, career counseling, and personal counseling
- Campus resources, including libraries, computing labs, museums, athletic facilities, health services, and campus security
- Information on proficiency and placement examinations
- University academic policies and academic integrity
- Tuition and fees
- Institutional affiliations and accreditation
- Descriptions of each school, department, degree, and all requirements for majors and minors

- Academic regulations on course loads, grading, absences, credit/no credit, withdrawals, incompletes, and probation
- Academic honors including organizations, graduation recognition, and special awards
- Listing of courses with course descriptions, course prerequisites, course abbreviations and computer codes, and the number of credits that can be earned
- A listing of officers of the institution, as well as all faculty with titles, degrees, and dates of appointment
- A list of graduating students in the prior year (less and less common)
- An index

The result is generally a book of several hundred pages that is literally out of date the moment it comes off the printing press. As a result, more and more academic institutions are putting the course catalog on-line as part of a Web site arrangement. This way, the information can be updated regularly and accessed at any time by persons with appropriate equipment and software. Fewer and fewer catalogs are printed with photographs and most now use fairly thin, inexpensive papers—including newsprint and glued bindings that have a shelf life of only a few years. Because catalogs can have significant importance in reviewing a student's prior academic work, a few copies must be kept as archival records. As paper quality and bindings have shorter and shorter lifetimes, institutions are preparing a few separate office and library copies of catalogs with special plastic or spiral bindings to give them more permanence and to extend shelf life.

Skyrocketing postal rates for educational materials over the past two decades have forced institutions to distribute catalogs either as periodicals or to avoid the mails altogether through the use of hand distribution within the campus only. Another cost saver is the two-year catalog. Some public universities charge for them, although testing shows strong dislike of this practice by prospects.

The offices and persons responsible for organizing course catalogs usually include a staff member attached to the chief academic officer, registrar, undergraduate admissions, or the publications office. Because the publication is cyclical, some institutions hire part-time editors to work for only a few months on preparing each year's new edition. As catalogs have moved to on-line availability, the editing responsibilities have shifted toward the registrar and chief academic officer's areas. From these data, the production of the book becomes a more mechanical effort that translates digital information into printed form. This has relegated the involvement of the publications office to the mechanics of converting computer text into typographic formats that are both legible and practical for inexpensive printing production. Because course catalogs are not read continuously like textbooks or novels, they can employ smaller sizes of type, sans serif faces, and more efficient, narrow columns that also help keep costs down by reducing the number of pages.

Although this section has dealt only with viewbooks and course catalogs, the value of other admission publications cannot be underestimated. Additionally, visual presentations such as videos and slide shows, photographs, displays at college fairs, Web pages, on-line publications, and even campus signage must be considered in the mix of materials that cultivate and build a relationship between the prospective student and the institution.

FUND RAISING PUBLICATIONS AND CAMPAIGN MATERIALS

One of the major benefactors of this writer's alma mater was able to attend the college for only a short time before he ran out of money. He moved to the Pacific Northwest, but he never forgot the college, and the college never forgot him. During the ensuing years, he received the college magazine, annual reports, and an occasional annual fund request. Nothing much happened for several decades when the long-absent alumnus appeared in the president's college office without an appointment, asking if he could make a gift to the institution. He remembered his short stay as a student, and now he wanted to do something for an institution that had faithfully been sending him publications and other mailings. Having made his fortune, now he wanted to put it to good use. The rest is history, including two buildings named in his honor on the campus.

Virtually every campus has a story like this one. Keeping in touch with alumni and with parents of current and former students is a cornerstone of the cultivation process. As every experienced development professional knows, everything sent to prospective donors has the ability to in some way touch their lives and to motivate them to provide support that allows future generations access to quality education.

Some printed materials used in fund raising are direct-mail similar to that used in student recruitment search mailings. Generally known as annual fund mailings, these efforts strive to raise unrestricted gift dollars, build membership in giving clubs, and elevate those donors of highest potential to the major gift society. Another category of direct mail used in fund raising is a bit more subtle—urging persons to volunteer for various institutional activities, to participate in alumni clubs, and to return to the campus for reunions, homecoming, and sporting events. Some institutions actually run alumni colleges, while others sponsor group travel opportunities to destinations around the world.

Informing donors about the institution and the ways in which gifts are utilized is a significant publications category and includes annual reports, donor honor rolls, and newsletters that describe various giving opportunities ranging from annual gifts for scholarships to trusts, wills, and other planned giving opportunities.

"Friend raising" publications make up the third and most important category of development materials. What motivates a donor to support an institution rarely is generated by direct-mail fund raising efforts alone. Cultivation of prospects takes place over years and decades of explaining the work and success of educational institutions, often in the form of institutional magazines, alumni magazines, periodic letters from the chief executive outlining the status of various initiatives, and any other general information publications that reinforce and build the beliefs and allegiances of key institutional audiences. For example, the prodigal donor described above was motivated by the repeated stories of outstanding students, extraordinary teachers, and grateful alumni.

ANNUAL FUND PUBLICATIONS

Since annual fund mailings operate much like an admissions search mailing, the most successful mailings are those that contain:

- a compelling letter explaining why unrestricted gifts are so important
- examples describing the good that these donations do in attracting the best students and retaining the best faculty
- a postage-paid reply envelope that boosts response rates as well
- brochures used sparingly, explaining the annual fund and how it impacts aid to deserving students, renovations of laboratories and classrooms, special learning opportunities for students and faculty, or just explaining how each annual fund dollar is spent throughout the year

In other words, the core message is the letter, and the printed matter simply serves as an informational device that should be used only when necessary.

Annual giving publications should not appear to be expensive or extravagant, but simple, clearly written messages that support the central theme of the overall mailing. Because people expect it, full-color often is more appealing, although there is no proof that it actually increases response rates or level of giving. Depending on how the annual fund mailing is processed, the size and weight of the enclosed publication should not put the postage at a higher cost than the letter itself. The reply envelope can be used as a publication, since many use long flaps on which inspirational or motivational messages are printed, along with listings of various opportunities and options for gifts. When additional space is available on these long-flap envelopes, consider putting a place for the respondent to include a classnote or other personal information that later can be published in the alumni magazine.

Despite the intrusion of voice mail, answering machines, and other deterrents to phonathons, solicitation of annual gifts over the telephone still remains an important part of many institutional giving programs. Here, too, a simple letter is often the most effective communication, including an alert that a volunteer will be calling soon, as well as a follow-up letter confirming that a commitment has been made. It is common, however, for these efforts to have special letterhead, envelopes, confirmation and reply forms, as well as brochures carrying much the same information as used in the direct-mail effort. Phonathons also require printed place mats for callers to use, sample scripts to be used in making calls, and volunteer handbooks that explain how each step of the phonathon and follow-up process works.

If a publication is planned for an annual fund mailing, here are some pointers to consider:

- *Pick one, easy-to-explain theme.* Don't try to squeeze multiple messages into a small brochure.
- *Illustrate the message with photographs* that appeal to persons who may not have been on the college campus for many years.
- *Use typography that is easily read by all ages*, ranging from recent graduates to octogenarians.
- *Be certain that the letter and the brochure work in tandem.* Sometimes it is best to have the same writer prepare both documents.
- *Avoid humor and gimmicks.* Education is a serious matter to most people and the use of humor or visual gimmicks rarely works in printed matter. (One Midwestern institution sent out a greeting card that said "Please don't send cash" on the cover, and then on the inside instructed the sender to "Send us a check instead!" The mailing did not even pay the cost of its own bulk-rate postage.)
- *Design the format to control costs.* Because a brochure or a flyer does not deliver the key message in an annual fund mailing, be certain it does not appear to be costly, that it is easily machine-insertable in the envelope, and that its weight does not add appreciably to the postage.
- *Test, test, test.* As in the case with any direct-mail effort, no publication, reply envelope, or cover letter should be sent without informal or formal testing on a small sample of alumni similar to the intended audience. Volunteers love to be asked for their advice.

For most institutions the annual fund is the first step to engage a donor in a lifetime of commitment. Each contact is intended not only to renew the previous year's effort, but to increase it and to encourage ever higher levels of support that involve the giving clubs and major donor societies mentioned earlier. As no experienced admissions officer would believe that a publication is the deciding factor in a prospective student's selection of one institution over another, so would an experienced development professional note that major gifts are often the result of personal contact and face-to-face cultivation of gift prospects.

ANNUAL REPORTS AND DONOR HONOR ROLLS

Annual reports may be the most enigmatic of publications published by educational institutions. Unlike corporations with publicly traded stock regulated by the federal Securities and Exchange Commission, not-for-profit institutions have no laws that require them to prepare a detailed annual report on the previous year's management of the company as well as a detailed fiscal history. In fact, recently instituted accounting guidelines have not made the financial reporting of educational institutions any more meaningful to the lay person than was the case under previous guidelines.

There is no one type of annual report universally employed. Publicly assisted colleges and universities, as well as many public elementary and secondary schools, are required by state or local law to publish an annual report that must be distributed to a very limited audience of legislators, state governmental agencies, governor's staff, and the institution's own governing board. No state requires that this publication be a slick, glossy, promotional public relations document, only that it contain certain vital financial, educational, and public service data. The design, packaging, and wider distribution of such an annual report is up to the institution. Some publicly assisted institutions actually publish unedited annual reports from all departments and bind these in a volume that is sent only to a very limited number of campus offices and governmental agencies.

A second category of annual report is published both by public and private institutions under the title of "President's Annual Report," or whatever title may be appropriate. Whereas these may resemble the first category, they tend to feature not only the president, but also highlights of the year and reports on various academic and institutional initiatives. This version may include some financial information, but is likely to relay information that sounds more like bragging than reporting. The packaging is usually slick, expensive, and very self-serving. Even the financial section tends to emphasize only positive information.

The third category of annual report incorporates much of the first two, but with the addition of a donor honor roll to recognize all the contributors in the just-ended fiscal year. Less practical at large institutions with tens of thousands of donors, the honor roll approach is highly successful with small to mid-sized academic institutions because it engages readers in discovering information about friends and classmates and recognizes their own largesse. To produce this type of annual report, consider the following:

- *Appoint an advisory committee and prepare an operating statement.* Complex and costly publications require input from a wide array of affected individuals, including the institution's chief executive, and the chief officers for development, finance, public relations, academic administration, alumni, and student affairs. The only purpose of this group is to provide feedback on the previous year's efforts, and then to recommend a general outline for the new edition. Since the group's role is purely advisory, the final approval of the publication generally lies in the hands of the chief executive and the chief advancement officer, although the sections affecting the various divisions of the university should be reviewed for accuracy by the leadership of those areas. The operating statement should clearly delineate these facts and define a specific production schedule and delivery date.

- *Put one person in charge.* Even in the best of circumstances, annual reports are horrendously difficult to write, edit, and print. Appointing a specific person, preferably an editor, to take ownership of the publication from start to finish will expedite matters and will more likely ensure on-time delivery of a satisfactory product. This requires an individual who can rewrite, negotiate delicate changes with persons of significant ego, argue for clarity in financial and academic reporting, and negotiate with development recordkeepers for clean, reliable donor lists.

- *Pick one major audience and make all others secondary.* Annual reports frequently fail because they cover the waterfront, and therefore fail to hone in on a specific message for a targeted audience. Generally, the type of annual report described herein is written first and foremost for major donors. It is valuable to legislators, administrators, and governing board members, but not as critical as it is for donors.

- *Be aware that institutional annual reports are not perceived as valuable by external audiences.* Of vital importance is knowing that virtually all audiences of educational institution annual reports find them to be much less valuable than corporate annual reports from publicly traded companies. Reader research on a college's or university's annual reports shows that they receive low ratings for interest, content, value, and useful information. The addition of donor honor rolls appears to increase the likelihood that the report will be read and kept as a coffee-table piece. This writer stopped publishing the annual report at one of the nation's largest public universities without telling anyone! Three years later no one had even noticed, until the president was asked by another president to send a copy. Then he began to ask questions of what had happened to the annual report.

- *Strategically time annual report delivery.* The typical academic institution frequently works on a July 1 to June 30 fiscal year, while the rest of society operates on a January 1 to December 31 calendar—including corporations. Difficult as it may be, it is for this reason that educational annual reports should be delivered as soon after July 1 as possible and certainly before mid-November. Otherwise, donors are not certain to which year their reported gift relates, and persons familiar with financial matters are thoroughly confused as to whether the financial information applies to a fiscal year or to a calendar year.

- *Avoid extravagance and hyperbole.* Imagine the shock of the Big Ten University president who was attacked by the legislative appropriations committee for the institution's "extravagant medical school annual report" during the final, delicate stages of budget negotiations! Unbeknownst to him, the dean of the medical school had commissioned a report that cost nearly $10 a copy, and then distributed it to legislators without even sharing a copy with his chief executive. An even greater gaffe was made because the editor failed to include this important phrase, "No part of the cost of this annual report was paid for by state funds. All costs were paid for by gifts." A businesslike, standard, 8½-by-11-inch annual report with full-color covers and moderate use of color photography throughout is generally acceptable. Avoid die cuts, foil stamping, blind embossing, unusual gatefolds, translucent fly sheets, tipped-in special sections, or anything else that would lead the reader to believe that the report was unnecessarily expensive. Keep the cost between $1 and $2 per copy; state institutions should be prepared to reveal the precise cost per unit.
- *Pick a theme that points to the future.* While annual reports generally talk about past accomplishments, they often are intended to prepare the reader for even greater future accomplishments. Selecting a theme that looks ahead is more likely to invite reader interest, even though much of the content will be historical.
- *Organize the report to attract reader interest.* Imagine how unexciting it must be for virtually any reader to open an annual report to a letter from the chief executive, rather than to the recounting of a major accomplishment, or to the recapping of a significant event. Personal letters sent in envelopes are more important than most publications, but "Dear Reader" letters printed in publications tend to have very low value and are not seen as worth reading by many. If a letter from the chief executive and chair of the governing board is required, either prepare it as a separate letter to be attached to the outside of the annual report, or as a message on the outside back cover. Readers enjoy scanning highlights that recognize new discoveries, important faculty honors, student accomplishments, and activities that impact society, public service, and so on. The highlights should reinforce the theme of the report, but the central section should focus several pages of text and photographs in feature format, rather than on the clipped, telegraphic style in which highlights are often written. Include a complete report on financial status, including a revenue and expense sheet; assets information; report on endowment performance; local, state, and federal support; and a review of total giving, including types of gifts and amounts. Be sure to list the names of the governing board and the chief administrative officers of the institution at the back.

- *Make donors lists interesting.* Donors lists read like the pages of a telephone book, except they are often much more confusing and disorganized because they are divided by artificial categories not necessarily understood by readers. An alphabetical listing of donors is preferred, although most institutions prefer to list annual fund donors by class year, major donors by giving club, and so forth. A few institutions list names both ways to be sure that the donor can find his or her name mentioned within. While the text does not have to be as legible as editorial material, it should be as easily read as a telephone book. For years, telephone directories have conducted legibility research and, therefore, are a good model to follow for lists that will be scanned rather than editorial copy that will be read in detail. To increase interest, sprinkle the donor's list with little factoids, anecdotal information, or photographs of activities and events held on campus during the previous year.
- *Use the annual report strategically.* Sending an annual report to all constituencies is not necessarily wise or effective. Because readers do not usually perceive annual reports to be as valuable as magazines or newsletters, send it only to those who are mentioned, as well as to the key constituencies that are most likely to use the information to advance the institution. This includes volunteers whose names are listed, donors, governing boards, advisory groups, and selected faculty and administrators. If the report is intended to serve community purposes, send it to the persons in charge of waiting rooms and offices for corporations, businesses, doctors, dentists, and selected leaders throughout the community. It also can be helpful to use this publication with the news media, with other college and university presidents, and for permanent filing in libraries.

Despite the fact that readers do not favor annual reports highly, they can be highly effective tools in cultivating relationships with future donors. Arrange with your development office to have copies available for volunteers and for gift officers to use when making personal calls on prospects, foundations, and alumni clubs.

DEVELOPMENT CAMPAIGN PUBLICATIONS

Nothing energizes an institution more than the preparation for and announcement of a capital campaign. The academic leadership and the faculty see their priorities and needs—identified through a strategic planning process—at a level far in excess of achievable goals. Students, administrators, trustees, alumni—and virtually everyone else with a stake in the institution—will soon surface with a previously unvoiced priority deserving of the major effort to raise funds at a level never previously achieved by the institution. The average effort is eight years in the making: two or three years in a quiet phase, followed by a grand announcement and then five or six years of frenzied effort to exceed the goal.

Even though, most experts say, at least 90 percent of the funds raised in a capital campaign will come through personal solicitations of less than 10 percent of the donors, publications and public relations take on a much higher profile than they do for normal development efforts. Dozens of specialized publications, specialized letterhead, slide shows, videos, programs for special events, banners, posters, and a wealth of other graphic materials are needed—usually all at once. When well planned and carefully coordinated, a capital campaign requires this significantly larger amount of printed material to be planned not months, but years in advance. Following are the key ingredients in organizing publications for a capital campaign:

- *Develop a unifying theme and logotype.* Deliberation and arriving at consensus about a capital campaign theme can take enormous amounts of talent, time, and even money. Because the naming of the campaign will be the unifying message around which all other messages are created, it is imperative that the theme carry the right tone and that it serve to rally all participants to the cause. In some cases, this is simply a campaign name. In others, it is a slogan. Once the precise words are agreed on, then a unified graphic theme must be built around these words—a logotype that will appear when the campaign is announced on letterhead, envelopes, business cards, all publications, videos, banners and signage, all printed materials, Web sites, and even on existing publications, such as annual reports, facts brochures, newsletters, magazines, etc. The logotype will have to stay in use for at least five years, which means that it must be designed by an experienced professional, which means an institution should consider outsourcing this to specialists in developing graphic symbols.
- *Create a case statement that contains all agreed-upon themes and core messages.* As the logotype is the unifying graphic symbol of a campaign, the case statement is the foundation on which all other campaign messages are eventually built. This publication is usually at least 32 pages in length, measures at least $8\frac{1}{2}$ by 11 inches, and contains an inspiring message from the campaign leader, a historical perspective on the institution's progress to the present, and an announcement of what the future will bring, including the amount of the goal. Critical to this message is developing arguments that say why it is essential for the campaign go forward successfully. For private institutions this often says why gifts to independent institutions have made such a disproportionate impact on the education of America's leadership and the success of its enterprises. For publicly assisted institutions the theme often focuses on the critical difference between the support provided by tax dollars

and the extraordinary advantage that additional gift income will make in building an even better institution. The rest of the publication describes needs, goals, and the campaign leadership. Essentially, a typical case statement includes the following:

- a full-color cover giving the name of the institution and the logotype/theme of campaign
- an inspirational statement either by the campaign leader or by a past chief executive of the institution
- a historical perspective on why the institution has achieved its current status and what will be possible in the future if the campaign goal is met
- a statement positioning the institution with its perceived competition, describing why it is important that it achieve even greater levels of success and recognition
- examples of the outstanding national leadership and accomplishments of alumni throughout the history of the institution (optional—the risk is not including someone who believes he or she should have been included)
- facts and figures that inspire readers with the accomplishments and quality of current students as well as a suggestion as to the type of students who will come in the future
- poignant examples of the cutting-edge research and leading scholarship conducted by faculty as part of the instructional program and learning experience of students
- examples of bridge building to the community, business, industry, and other academic institutions with whom the institution would like to be compared
- examples of public service by which the institution contributes to the betterment of the region and to society at large, including examples of not only students and faculty but also of alumni and parents of current students
- a description of the organizational and planning process that logically led to the announcement of a campaign, giving particular emphasis to how the process helped establish the goal and the need for it
- the financial objectives of the campaign, broken down by categories such as endowed professorships, endowed scholarships, research and teaching funds, departmental support, library improvement, new facilities for teaching and research, facilities to improve the out-of-classroom experiences of students (athletics, student life, residence halls, and gifts intended to support the unrestricted purposes of the annual fund)
- a section announcing the "lead" gifts already in hand (i.e., gifts that already have been given or pledged but previously have not been announced, often totaling as much as half the campaign goal)

- a detailed description of each specific goal, delineating exactly how the gift funds will be used for the categories mentioned above
- a listing of the campaign leadership and perhaps an inspiring message of why they chose to get involved
- a pocket on the inside back cover to hold specially prepared messages for specific donors

Case statements are not generally mailed out to large numbers of people, but more often are used as part of a solicitation with a major gift prospect. Some institutions will draft the case statement as much as two years ahead of the campaign announcement, and then will discreetly circulate it in manuscript form to a select group of major volunteers and gift prospects to seek their "advice" on whether the written message is effective. Of course, the real purpose behind this strategy is to be sure that the persons most able to assist in the campaign will read every word. Asking people to comment on and edit copy will achieve that goal.

If you do not plan a pocket on the inside back cover of the case statement, consider a folder with pockets to include the case statement, as well as any other materials that might be useful in making presentations to prospects.

Special versions of case statements are sometimes prepared to accommodate unusual needs, such as universities with multiple schools and campuses that all need their own version, case statements that address local concerns rather than national ones, and so forth.

As with annual reports, extravagance in producing case statements can backfire with donors who want to think that the institution is using their gifts in ways that help students and faculty, not the pocketbooks of printers and designers. Avoid blind embossing, foil stamping, die cutting, and other expensive-appearing techniques. However, the publication must be elegant and unlike anything the institution has ever done before. This delicate balance is difficult to achieve. Case statements have been produced for as little as $1 per copy and as much as $10 per copy.

- *Consider a mini case statement.* Because of the generally high cost of case statements, the rank-and-file alumni, parents, and other donor prospects should receive a less elaborate, stripped-down version. Often, this is a document that is about half as long as the basic case statement and that is mailed to all audiences—even those who receive the more expensive version used in personal contacts. The contents of the versions of the case statement are basically similar, but the mini version will have less photographic content, smaller type sizes, less expensive paper stocks, and a more economical method of distribution.

- *Create brochures for campaign subgoals.* Because most capital campaigns raise money for a variety of purposes, it may be necessary to create brochures to cover each important subcategory. These may include endowed scholarships, endowed professorships, new buildings, and special funds necessary for such things as building restorations and renovations, annual fund, improvement of departments, and implementation of new academic programs. These brochures can be used in tandem with the full case statement in presentations to gift prospects, as well as for attachments to grant proposals sent to foundations and other funding agencies. These more targeted versions should fit the unifying graphic look and theme established by the campaign logo and embodied in the layout of the case statement itself. Although reasonably brief, these brochures generally follow the same strategy and rationale used to develop the institution's case statement.
- *Order basic office supplies that support personal messages in the solicitation process.* Letterhead, envelopes, business cards, gift reply envelopes, large envelopes for case statements, and above all, pledge cards and envelopes, all need to be ordered before the campaign is announced publicly. Some institutions provide these materials during the quiet phase of the campaign without the logo, and then order a new array of similar materials that display the campaign logo to be put into play immediately following the grand announcement. As above, the graphic design must be consistent with all other materials in order to adequately support the campaign theme.
- *Create campaign volunteers handbook.* Training volunteers for a campaign begins well before the public announcement and requires not only detailed information on the arguments for the campaign, but also helpful advice on gifts in kind, ways to approach potential donors, a method of reporting the results of donor contacts, schedules for future volunteer meetings, and literally dozens of other important messages. Often these are contained in ring binders with room for at least 2 inches of material. The ring binder will have the campaign logo printed prominently on its cover and, for special volunteers, may have the individual's name foil-stamped on it.
- *Provide a methods-of-giving brochure.* Nothing is more confusing to a prospective donor or volunteer than trying to decipher tax law or comprehend a unitrust. For this reason, most campaigns provide basic brochures including elementary information on how gifts in kind, cash, properties, stocks, and other assets can be conveyed to an educational institution. Also prominent in these publications are the names and phone numbers of experts who can be contacted to deal with such not-so-simple gifts.
- *Create a named-giving opportunities brochure.* Despite the specialized brochures listed above, some donors are much more concerned about memorializing a loved one, a former professor, or even themselves, by providing a

gift with a name attached to it, such as a faculty chair, a scholarship fund, or a building. Particularly useful in situations where it is clear that the gift prospect wishes to memorialize his own or a loved one's name in perpetuity, these publications contain lists of possibilities, noting the absolute minimum by which named gifts are allowed.

- *Publish a campaign newsletter.* Using the existing university periodical to communicate information about a campaign is a serious oversight, simply because existing periodicals are usually published infrequently and take a significant amount of time to prepare. Campaign newsletters are often brief (4 pages or more) and produced to allow fast turnaround with readily available printers. A flexible publication schedule is key to a campaign newsletter so that an unexpected gift or challenge grant or an important milestone in the campaign can be quickly announced. However, campaign newsletters are most commonly published three or four times a year throughout the campaign.

- *Major gift honor roll.* In addition to the regularly published honor roll and annual report done by many institutions, some campaigns also produce special recognition for major donors (such as all gifts larger than $25,000). This publication is circulated only to those who have made such gifts and to prospects who are believed to have the potential to do so. The honor roll operates similarly to the traditional institutional recognition effort, but is focused entirely on campaign contributions. Included are stories and photographs reviewing the activities of the prior year in the campaign.

The above listing is by no means a complete compendium of what is required during a campaign. This list touches upon the most important tools used in fund raising efforts and includes essential materials such as: invitations to special events, event programs, videos, special phonathon materials, or publications used to raise money internally from faculty and staff. In just the planned giving area alone there may be several dozen additional publications that deal with special giving opportunities. Each should be crafted to resemble campaign materials where possible—acknowledging the fact that some may be produced by independent providers who copyright both the text and graphics.

INSTITUTIONAL AND ALUMNI PERIODICALS

The best has been saved until last—institutional magazines and newsletters that communicate with alumni, parents, other institutions of higher education, internal audiences, and a wealth of others. More commonly referred to as "alumni magazines," these vehicles actually can be a complex array of newsletters, tabloids, magapapers, and traditional glossy magazines. Originally, many of them were developed by alumni relations staff to stay in touch with other alumni as part of their membership in the alumni association. As time passed and as institutional communications became more sophisticated, alumni periodicals have emerged as some of the most valuable tools for sending institutional messages to important constituencies, as well as a way for alumni to continue to share information with and about one another.

Make no mistake about it, alumni publications are successful not because they are necessarily sent out by institutions that do exciting things, but because of the heightened self-interest of alumni in hearing more about themselves and their classmates. Readership studies of typical alumni periodicals show that between 80 and 90 percent readers turn first to alumni classnotes before they begin to read virtually any of the rest of the publication. Although some university periodicals do not include classnotes, any that have conducted readership studies with alumni will quickly discover that they most prefer a classnotes section above any other news or information the institution can provide them. Alumni periodicals require advisory groups and operating statements to assist the editor in dealing systematically with important issues such as audiences, content, point of view, and the protocols and procedures for checking stories, managing printing production, and achieving successful delivery to readers.

Whether the alumni periodical is produced by an independent alumni association, by an institutional alumni association, by the alumni office staff, by the development office, by a specialized group within institutional advancement, or by the public relations office, it must have a mission statement to clearly delineate its purpose and define its content. Here is an example of a mission statement:

> The first priority of the [periodical] is to reflect [university's] teaching, learning, and research, as well as to capture the heart of the university—the wide-eyed wonder of ideas and questioning and dialogue. It must nurture the lifelong friendships that begin here. The content of the magazine reflects a balanced coverage of research, teaching, service to society, news, student life, and universitywide issues that include profiles of exceptional work by faculty, staff, and students. Each academic division must be considered in the planning and will be covered in the magazine as appropriate over time. [University] strongly depends on alumni for its support: More specifically, the university's future is linked directly to alumni in leadership positions and to groups that have a particular interest in the institution. The time and resources alumni and friends contribute are invaluable. Therefore, the purpose of the alumni section of the magazine is to showcase the accomplishments of our alumni and to reflect the university's teaching, research, and service in a way that promotes understanding of and builds alumni support for the institution. The magazine seeks to engender among alumni readers

a sense of pride in the institution and in themselves, as well as an appreciation for the university's quality, accomplishments, and contributions to [city], the nation, and the world. Specifically, the alumni pages best reflect these qualities by highlighting alumni activities, achievements, and feature stories; brief profiles, classnotes, and synopses of alumni association activities and programs.

This mission statement embodies what is typically said on most campuses about institutional periodicals. A slightly different statement is likely when the periodical is produced by an independent alumni association. What is not noted is the unfortunate struggle that sometimes goes on between the institution and its various constituencies for greater coverage in this publication. That is why an editorial advisory committee representing all of the key constituencies is a vital tool for the editor—not to control content, but to serve as a sounding board for concerns and issues before they become problematic.

The point of view of the publication is most often the center of concern and discussion. Following is an example of a point-of-view statement that defines the editor's role in the selection of content and the institution's responsibility in supporting the cost of production:

[Periodical] is an advocate of the university specifically and higher education generally. In order to be credible, however, it must always deal with subjects in an honest, effective, and straightforward fashion. Selected stories should accurately reflect the scope and vigor of the university's intellectual and cultural life. Alumni stories should make graduates feel they are an important part of the ongoing life of the institution. To the extent that such stories are printed credibly, interestingly, and according to high editorial and graphic standards, the magazine will succeed in building support and understanding for the university. By its very nature in reporting academic and scholarly research, the magazine is a primary friend raising tool. Through its balanced reporting, [periodical] especially encourages [university] graduates and others to take pride in and provide support of the institution.

Some magazines insist on covering institutional problems in the name of journalistic objectivity and the reader's right to know the bad—as well as the good—news. Selecting the format of an institutional periodical can engender a great debate, particularly between a magazine format and the often less expensive tabloid. Research never has shown a significant reader preference for these formats, as long as the content maintains a high standard and inveigles the interest of the readers. A compromise between the two formats is the magapaper, which is often printed on better quality stock than newsprint, but has a format similar to that of a tabloid newspaper and includes a feature section similar to that in a magazine. Here, too, there may be economies in cost, although recent improvements in web printing and cost increases for less expensive paper stocks have wiped out some of the advantages previously enjoyed by magapapers. The larger size of tabloid and magapapers can affect postal rates, too.

Newsletters are not intended to resemble magazines, since they most often contain newsy information rather than feature stories or in-depth examinations of programs and people. Rarely do newsletters contain extensive classnotes. Generally, newsletters tend to be shorter, 8 pages or less, while magazines generally have at least 24 and as many as 100 pages.

The following criteria are for a typical institutional magazine, magapaper, or tabloid newspaper sent to alumni, parents, other donors, employees, and community leaders:

- *Full-color covers are obligatory.* Competing against popular magazines, institutional periodicals must recognize the fact that they are struggling to achieve the attention of busy readers in a highly message-laden world. Not only should the cover be full color, but the publication will fare better if the contents are also printed in process color. It goes without saying that the quality of photographs, artwork, and the overall graphic design must compete successfully in today's highly charged marketplace.
- *Readers prefer simplicity.* Cover designs that show a montage of photographs, wild use of typographic treatments, or a long listing of contents ignore the lessons learned by news magazines. These publications always focus on one simple message both graphically and editorially, even though the publication is loaded with dozens of different stories. Alumni reflect the mainstream tastes of America, which translates into "less is more." One outstanding image on the cover supported by a meaningful headline is more likely to encourage a reader to open the publication.
- *Use all four covers effectively.* The front cover may be the first surface the reader sees, but the outside back cover and the two inside covers are also important in magazine publishing—either as a place for important images and messages, or where advertising can be sold at a premium by those institutions that use it as a revenue source. Anything from varsity sports championships to major breaking news stories receives maximum attention when placed on the inside front or outside back cover. Don't waste these surfaces on soft news or subject matter.
- *The contents page is a promotional tool, so use it that way.* Other than the front cover, the editor's greatest opportunity to encourage readership is the contents page. Although it is important to list the editors, advisors, and pertinent postal information, the focus should be on the feature stories and spe-

cial sections. A judicious combination of illustrations, photographs, and teaser headlines should help the reader decide where to start reading. Do not assume that periodicals are read from front to back. Unless detoured by compelling information, alumni readers will turn first to the classnotes invariably located in the back of the publication. Always include a correspondence address, fax number, and an e-mail address on the contents page.

• *Establish and organize editorial content to meet readers' needs, as well as institutional priorities.* Editors struggle with the balance that must be maintained between the expectations of readers and the demands of institutional programs and politics. The fact that readers almost always turn to classnotes first suggests that their heightened self-interest needs to be tempered with compelling, inviting information about the institution and its future potential. Readership research shows that—other than classnotes—readers most prefer magazine and tabloid content about the following subjects:

– short news items, which are often published at the front of a magazine or tabloid
– history of the institution, its people, and its buildings
– articles or profiles about faculty and their activities inside and outside the classroom, laboratory, or studio
– stories about research that impact health, medicine, fitness, and clinical research
– scholarship and creative efforts in the humanities and the arts
– feature articles about successful alumni, particularly classmates
– activities on campus that alumni and other readers can attend
– photographs that show the campus as it currently looks, students, and faculty
– letters to the editor

Readers say there are certain subjects that do not appeal to them:

– stories about administrative activities and routine appointments
– "from the desk of" columns and letters by the chief executive, dean of a school, head of the alumni association, the editor, or the chief advancement officer; people always prefer receiving letters in envelopes, not printed as part of a publication
– donor features based primarily on gift size and development stories; however, donors do like to read about interesting people who love their alma mater and who—in the process—may provide gift support
– gift solicitations and gift reply envelopes
– inserted annual reports; always try to mail these separately
– advertising

Reader reactions vary greatly, depending on how well written the subject matter is. For example, if a donor makes a $10 million gift for scholarships, don't write about the gift, write about the people who receive the scholarships and how their educations would not be possible without the support. When doing profiles on faculty, select the individuals to be featured based on their accomplishments in teaching and research, not on their personal popularity or other factors that would damage the publication's editorial credibility. Always base story subjects on the merit, content, and news value of the subject matter.

- *Seek editorial balance over time.* Because most institutional periodicals are published quarterly, it is virtually impossible to show editorial balance among the various academic disciplines, external audiences, and institutional priorities in each issue. Instead, think in terms of one- to five-year increments. Through content analysis track which subjects receive the most attention and then determine how better balance can be achieved in future issues among various competing subjects. Remember that in a five-year period, a quarterly is only published 20 times. If the institution has 20 or 30 academic departments, a dozen varsity sports, nearly 100 student organizations and tens of thousands of alumni, it is very difficult to be editorially fair to all within a five-year time frame! The editor never can please everyone, but a fair-minded, earnest effort to show concern and balance will be appreciated by the campus community as well as by readers. As in the case of student recruitment literature, editors should try to reflect the gender, ethnic, and socioeconomic makeup of the institution. For example, if the graduates are 50 percent women, shouldn't the alumni features and classnotes reflect this? Editors can receive lots of letters from alumnae complaining about a preponderance of balding, white males or about the lack of an adequate ethnic presence.

- *Organize classnotes to achieve the highest possible volume.* Because readers most want to learn about classmates, the alumni classnotes will continue to be the runaway favorite of readers and should be treated as such. Typical shortcomings of classnotes include the following:
  - Too little coverage of graduates over the age of 60. (More mature people move less, change jobs infrequently, and then retire so insufficient information is no excuse. Include a classnote reply form in each issue; put classnote forms on gift reply envelopes; and collect all of the letters and memory books at each reunion. These are outstanding resources for classnotes.)
  - The classnote took almost a year to publish. (Since quarterly magazines require up to six months' preparation for each issue, be sure to date and cycle classnotes to appear within that time frame. Otherwise notify the classnote sender of delays.)

- *Think and plan at least one year in advance.* The successful institutional magazine or tabloid is planned as much as two or three years before it is actually published. This allows the editors and writers ample time to collect and review information, add items that were overlooked, and to chart a new course where story ideas were unproductive. Maintaining a working list of story ideas, subjects, and individuals worthy of coverage is essential. Stories should be assigned as much as a year in advance and final story budgeting for each issue of a quarterly periodical should occur at least six months before delivery. Following is a typical production timetable for such a publication:
  - 24th to 26th week: Contents of issue finalized. Assignments made to writers, illustrators, and photographers. The editor, art director, designer, photographer, and vice-president receive the issue outline.
  - 16th week: Stories received, reviewed by editor, and returned to writers for revisions. Stories are sent to subjects interviewed to check for accuracy and to obtain approval where appropriate.
  - 10th to 20th week: Final photo and illustration assignments made.
  - 10th week: Rough layout begun.
  - 5th week: Rough layout and storyboards completed and approved by editor. Storyboard presented to vice-president, if appropriate.
  - 4th week: Laser output copy inspected by editor before final image setting. Color instructions shipped to printer.
  - 4th week: Corrections to all electronic files completed.
  - 4th week: Random color separation proofs checked.
  - 3rd week: Final proofs received from printer and approved by editor, art director, and, where appropriate, vice-president.
  - 3rd week: Printing and binding completed and addressing begun.
  - 2nd week: Periodical mailed to readers by fulfillment house or printer.
  - Delivery date: Publication received in homes and offices of readers.
- *Seek critiques from readers and the editorial advisory committee.* Editors become isolated from their readers far too often. Letters to the editor are insufficient indicators of reader attitudes, often dealing with the ends of the normal bell curve. Encourage feedback on every issue by asking the editorial advisory committee to critique it as part of its regular meeting. Readership studies should be conducted at least once every five years to find out what the rank-and-file alumni and parents think about the publication. The survey should be conducted with assistance from experienced research professionals. Maintain a continuing content analysis to measure editorial balance. Review and, if necessary, update the periodical's operating statement annually.

- *Make certain the format matches content.* Publishing a magazine requires that it have feature stories and significant content that explores issues in greater depth. Far too often some institutions publish magazine formats that read like newsletters—filling the pages with short news items and an occasional full-page story of dubious reader interest. Remember, the most successful magazines read like a combination of *Life Magazine, Atlantic Monthly, Newsweek,* and the classified ads (classnotes) in the local newspapers. Maintaining an equitable balance between these various types of content requires diligence and vigilance. Because people read less in depth nowadays, limit features to three or four pages.

- *Use designers who understand periodicals.* Just as there are experts who design only advertising, there are gifted, creative voices in the periodicals world, too. Before attempting to create a "look" using in-house staff, try seeking the advice of a recognized regional or national expert to create the grid or motif for the periodical. Once a concept has been finalized, then it can be improved and maintained by the regular design staff. Seeking the advice of a guru will help make the words and images work together as well as provide excellent pointers on how to deal with photographers, illustrators, graphic artists, and other designers.

- *Seek expert assistance with budgeting, advertising, mailing, and subscriptions.* Magazines and tabloids represent some of the largest expenditures made by academic institutions, and therefore must be fiscally managed to achieve highest levels of effectiveness at affordable costs. Rapid increases in postal rates and paper costs have threatened institutional ability to continue to publish many periodicals, forcing either a significant reduction in quality or frequency. To resolve these issues, some institutions have tried advertising, only to discover that it may not be a panacea and may not pay for even its own cost. Seeking professional advice and assistance is essential when considering selling advertising, or joining an advertising consortium. The complexity of postal regulations and the unrelenting increase in postal costs require advice from direct-mail experts who can advise on everything from labeling to printing dimensions. Unless the periodical competes with popular magazines for content, subscriptions will be an unlikely source of revenue. Some institutions have attempted to solicit freewill gifts, but this could affect the annual fund in the eyes of many development officers.

SUGGESTED READING

Arden, K., and W. Whalen. 1991. *Your Guide to Effective Publications, A Handbook for Campus Publications Professionals.* Washington, DC: Council for Advancement and Support of Education.

Arnold, E. 1972. *Ink on Paper 2*. New York: Harper & Row.

Cutlip, S. 1994. *The Unseen Power: Public Relations, A History*. Hillsdale, NJ: Lawrence Erlbaum Associates, Publishers.

Cutlip, S., et al. 1994. *Effective Public Relations,* 7th ed. Upper Saddle River, NJ: Prentice Hall.

Dilenschneider, R., and D. Forrestal. 1987. *Public Relations Handbook*. Chicago: The Dartnell Corporation.

Martin, Jr., T. 1973. *Malice in Blunderland*. New York: McGraw-Hill Book Company.

Rehe, R. 1974. *Typography: How To Make It Most Legible*. Carmel, IN: Design Research International.

Rowland, A., ed. 1986. *Handbook of Institutional Advancement,* 2nd ed. San Francisco, CA: Jossey-Bass, Publishers.

Smith, V., and P. Alberger. 1984. *How To Cut Publications Costs*. Washington, DC: Council for Advancement and Support of Education.

Tinker, M. 1969. *Legibility of Print*. Ames, IA: Iowa State University Press

Topor, R. 1988. *Your Personal Guide to Marketing a Nonprofit Organization*. Washington, DC: Council for Advancement and Support of Education.

Topor, R. 1993. *Media & Marketing: A Powerful New Alliance for Higher Education*. Mountain View, CA: Topor and Associates.

Wilcox, D., et al. 1986. *Public Relations Strategies and Tactics*. New York: Harper & Row, Publishers.

Epilogue

In the millennium just before us
knowledge will be the new key,
the priority for existence.

Knowledge is infinite, knows no boundaries,
is not a natural resource, and is
common only to the prepared mind.

Frank H.T. Rhodes
President Emeritus, Cornell University

Institutional advancement is now, and in the coming years will be, information based. Information is power. Intelligent men and women have always known that, but never before has there been such a passion for knowing. At times when e-mail on our ubiquitous computers piles up with page after page of reports and attachments, we find ourselves suffering from information overload. C. Peter Magrath, president of the National Association of State Universities and Land Grant Colleges (NASULGC), says the enormous impact of information technologies on our universities and the ever-increasing need for lifelong learning affect all of us. Emerging new technology is clearly a dominant part of our lives "in a world where knowledge and information multiply, change, and develop so rapidly that even the most sophisticated among us are often bewildered." Jokingly, Magrath refers to himself as being "electronically impaired."[1] New and faster hardware to accommodate newer and faster software emerges as the cerebral geniuses keep improving information delivery systems with upgrades and add-ons, and it is not all for the love of knowledge. Continual advances in technology fill the entrepreneur's pockets with cash, make the stock market soar, and cost the user a bundle. Bill Gates, the creator of MicroSoft, is a multibillionaire. Intel announced a stock split in 1997, and other high tech stocks have pushed the market to record heights. Users are paying less as the market for computers and software becomes more competitive, but they are paying a significant amount each year on software and hardware upgrades as faster modems and processors are needed, and on Internet services such as America Online, CompuServe, Netscape, and others.

The number of virtual universities and "cyberschools" is increasing on the Internet and through distance learning. In the June 16, 1997, issue of *Forbes* magazine, Lisa Gubernick and Ashlea Ebeling reported that in the last several years, the number of students earning collge degrees by means of distance learning, whether by interactive television or the Internet, has jumped significantly "despite attempts by traditional educators to smash cyberschools."[2] Since 1993, the count has gone from 93 to 762. "More than one million students now take courses from those colleges, compared with 13 million who attend bricks-and-mortar colleges." Cybercolleges make it possible for students of all ages, including working adults around the world, to earn degrees from faraway institutions without paying residence fees. Conventional schools in the twenty-first century may have to rethink the way they do business.

Advancement programs are heavily dependent on artificial intelligence. Annual giving campaigns and capital fund drives are dependent on the computer to generate those everlasting lists of prospects, prepare donor profiles, and provide information for strategic planning. The fact is, the more the advancement officer knows about a donor or a prospect, the better the chance for making contact and building a relationship. Frank Rhodes, president emeritus of Cornell University, is right on target when he says "knowledge will be the new key" that will unlock the secrets of the next few decades. The human brain has marvelous potential yet to be discovered. Knowledge is our quest, and our new means of attaining it is by such means as the Internet and other electronic media. Knowing, however, in and of itself is not enough. Understanding and wisdom, value systems, virtues—these are the effective uses of knowledge in the present and future years. Our challenge then, according to Rhodes, is to assist the institutions we serve in the making of

- leaders with understanding
- leaders with candor
- leaders with a talent for encouragement
- leaders with skills of advocacy
- leaders with the will to support

As advancement professionals, in public relations, alumni affairs, or development, our priorities should be the advancement of learning, for "scholarship is a public trust, not a personal indulgence," and the advancement of service, for "service is a social obligation."[3]

In all the fund raising, the prospect research, the drive for increased annual and capital giving, and the push to increase the endowment, advancement people cannot lose sight of the human endowment that is a reservoir of energy and talent supporting the work of advancement. This human endowment is that vast corps of volunteers we depend on to accomplish those larger-than-life goals we set for ourselves. The term was used at the presentation of the Ernest Stewart Award for volunteer work to Harold and Estelle Tanner for Harold's outstanding volunteer support of Cornell University and Estelle's effective and enthusiastic volunteer support of Wellesley College. The award was made at the Council for

Advancement and Support of Education (CASE) 1997 Annual Assembly in Washington, D.C.

The gratitude for volunteer support is so strong in CASE that a special honor roll of more than 2,000 volunteers was published and distributed. Even now as we approach the twenty-first century, those professionals who volunteer their time, skills, and talents in the nonprofit world of education, social service, health care, and the arts are the real wealth of advancement. They come from all backgrounds with willing hearts and active minds. They join hands with development officers and help to make it happen. The beneficiary of this enormous "human endowment" is the "commonwealth of learning," represented by the peoples of the world who seek to engage their minds in a quest for continuing education.[4]

THE COST OF ADVANCEMENT

With restructuring, innovative programming, and creative planning, advancement offices are facing skintight budgets. The question is, what does it take to run an advancement operation, and will that cost escalate in the years to come? The answer to the second part of the question is yes. It takes about $100,000 per year for the small shop with one professional and somewhere in the range of $600,000 for a medium-sized shop with three to six professionals. For the large operations, the numbers can reach $1.2 million and more. The Association of Governing Boards (AGB) asked Barbara Taylor to do a national survey of fund raising practices and expenses. Her findings were published in 1989. Since then the numbers have increased, but here are the data from her study. Questionnaires were mailed to 1,042 institutions, both private and public, including four-year multicampus institutions, four-year single campus institutions, two-year schools, and specialized schools. Forty-five percent, 470, responded.[5] (See Table E–1.)

In an article for *Fund Raising Management*, the writer suggested a development office start-up budget of $283,000, based on the need for personnel, equipment, travel, contractual services, supplies, and overhead.[6] (See Exhibit E–1.) These are 1996 costs, and they are conservative. Personnel costs vary with different geographic locations and the scope of responsibility. A development director for the University of California at Berkeley would receive more compensation than a development director for a smaller university or college in the Midwest.

One of the challenges advancement people continually face is budget. To recognize the fiscal reality of promotion, marketing, fund raising, alumni relations, communications, and public relations is to recognize the need for adequate funding. The chief executive officer (CEO) and the governing board have to provide an adequate budget to achieve the desired return. Fortunately, the return on the dollar spent for fund raising is usually 85 percent or more, and for business-minded, bottom-line administrators that should speak loudly. What business executive

Table E–1 Advancement Expenditures

	Four-year Multicampus	Two-year	Four-year Single campus
Fund Raising	104,500	75,436	480,713
Public Relations	55,000	187,000	126,815
Alumni Affairs	14,000	20,514	147,353
Gov't Relations	0	189	20,048
Publications	9,000	21,321	90,834
Total	182,500	304,460	865,763

in the corporate world would not heartily rejoice to have an investment return of 85 percent? The development office of the division of institutional advancement is worth the weight of its professional staff in gold. Strangely, however, there seems to be some nit-picking about increasing budgets for the development office. Millions are spent on other divisions, student affairs, academic affairs, business and finance, but quite often budget support for fund raising, alumni relations, and public relations is less than desirable. In a certain small eastern university, the athletic program is funded by the university in the amount of $2.5 million each year, largely because of the football program, but the return is less than $250,000. Those institutions and organizations that are serious about increased funding, both annual and capital, will have to upgrade their support, both financial and political, for the advancement operation, meaning fund raising, alumni or client relations, and external affairs.

College presidents and hospital CEOs are tempted to cut advancement operations in tough times. They approach their respective boards in times of budget freezes and uncertainty about future revenue with disquieting news about rising costs and fewer dollars to pay them. As Edward G. Coll, president of Alfred University, wrote in *Trustee Portfolios*, March/April 1993, "Bad times are no time to allow fund raising, alumni relations, and public relations efforts to falter."[7] Institutional advancement is an administrative division often perceived by presidents and boards as having negligible impact on students and faculty, patients and nursing, but advancement is truly the front line of support because it touches the heart strings and purse strings of the external community. Coll said he learned that from his 20 years in advancement at Miami University. "In my front line experience in advancing the university's mission, and thereby increasing support for it, I learned how important this work is to a campus's long-term health, invisible though the work may be to faculty, students, and sometimes even trustees."[8] Before taking an ax to the advancement budget and trimming staff, presidents and their boards should review the study done by CASE in cooperation with the

Exhibit E–1 Midsized Development Office Suggested Start-up Costs for First Year Operation

(Assuming space, furniture, and overhead are a part of the institution's operating budget)	
Personnel	$188,500
Director of Development	
Annual Fund Director	
Major Gifts/Planned Giving Officer	
Corporate/Foundation Relations Officer	
Senior Secretary	
Financial Secretary	
Receptionist	
Equipment	29,000
Computer hardware and software	
Facsimile machine	
Copier (leased @ $170 per month)	
Travel	15,500
Conference fees	
Fund raising trips	
Lodging and meals	
Entertainment	
Telephone (3 lines)	2,500
Postage	3,500
Printing	15,000
Brochures, flyers, stationery	
Case documents, folders, etc.	
Contractual Services	20,000
Video production	
Marketing	
Food service	
Incentives, awards	
Supplies and Materials	9,000
Professional resource books	
Subscriptions	
Office supplies	
Total	$283,000

National Association of College and University Business Officers. Funding for the study was given by the Lilly Endowment. Appropriately, it was called the Lilly Study. Coll summed up the findings.[9]

> *In a well-run advancement program, fund raising doesn't cost. It pays.*

The study found it costs the institution an average of 16 cents to raise a dollar. The median cost was 11 cents. These costs included all direct fund raising staff and programs. It did not cover presidents' or deans' salaries, or overhead costs such as space, heat, water, and lights.

Annual and capital monies do contribute to the operating budget, the so-called E & G budget. Total income varies widely, from 6 percent to more than 37 percent of the E & G budget. The average was 23 percent. The amount raised for current operations was 10 percent. This was the average over a three-year period. The amount of the total E & G budget spent by the institution on fund raising is 2 percent, an average over a three-year period.

The most pertinent question is, what return does an institution realize on each dollar it spends on fund raising? The Lilly Study found the three-year average to be a very significant return, 425 percent. This means that for every $100 institutions spent on fund raising, it got $525 back. On average, the Lilly Study showed, advancement offices spent 8 percent of the total E & G budget on fund raising, and brought in 23 percent of that budget. The 425 percent return on investment would be considered spectacular by any Wall Street analyst. Yet, institutions often take it for granted.

INTERNAL GOVERNANCE

Part of the challenge has to do with internal governance, which is another issue of current value, open for discussion, deserving of attention. A variety of issues, such as tenure, enrollment management, quantitative assessment of outcomes, student/customer relations, and intrusion by federal and state agencies all have a bearing on the quality and desirability of the product, and on the effectiveness of the division of institutional advancement. The AGB has dealt with these issues, as well as NASULGC and the American Council on Education, but the final word has not been said. Perhaps the greatest forces affecting our institutions are political forces, one of which is the institution's governing board. All too often, these boards of directors have individual members who delight in micromanaging the institution at large, and the development office in particular. It is not uncommon for board members to suggest management options, even to the point of hiring staff or choosing the color of carpeting. All too often they see the advancement staff as hired guns, not partners, in institutional advancement. On one occasion the writer calls to mind a board member, who was asked to assist in making contact with a major donor. His reply was, "That's what we hired you for. I don't have time." While the responsibility of the board is to hold the assets of the institution in trust, set policy, and give oversight, AGB recognizes also the role of the board in fund raising. In fact, with private organizations and institutions, board members are recruited on the basis of their affluence or their influence. The unwritten expectation with some boards is "give, get, or get out." Board members of public institutions often serve by political appointment and are much less inclined to become involved in fund raising.

Committees, task forces, and focus groups are another bane or blessing to internal governance, however one might view them. For the most part they serve a good purpose and are helpful, but they are time-consuming, slow to act, and generally not very efficient. They are, as Peter McGrath puts it, "participatory bureaucracy."[10] The quickest way to get an idea or a proposal sidetracked is to appoint a committee to deal with it. Advancement professionals are just as guilty as faculty members. We love our strategic planning sessions, our development committees, and our meetings in preparation for special events. The truth is, individual initiative and management is the best way to accomplish a task. The downside, of course, is the risk of individuals doing their own things without reference to policy and guidelines approved by the team, or not keeping others informed, which could be embarrassing and counterproductive if two people were planning an approach to the same major donor prospect.

Likewise, it is just as important for different administrative areas in colleges and universities to communicate. If it is important for advancement officers to work together, sharing plans and ideas, it is just as important for the several schools and departments of the institution as a whole to share ideas, concerns, and work in progress. President M. Peter McPherson of Michigan State University made the comment in testimony before Congress that "Running Michigan State University is more complex than running the foreign aid program in the 1980s, and that is saying something."[11] McPherson was talking about rising college costs, limited resources, and critical decisions, but his reference to the complexity of university administration helps make the point that internal governance is a many splendored thing and deserves a second look. It is an issue that will affect future progress.

In the close out years of the wonderful twentieth century as advancement personnel work even harder to position the institutions they serve for their continuing and changing roles in the next few decades, it is interesting, even fun, and sometimes frightening to speculate on what the future will bring. *CASE Currents*, in its June 1997 issue, offers a rational and plausible peek inside the twenty-first century. For advancement services, there will be better data collection, storage, and retrieval allowing prospect research, gift processing, and records management to be more a central part of the development office. "More of us will know the big picture," says Patricia Kovalcheck of Vanderbilt University.[12] Terrence Handler of Bentz Whaley Flessner believes development people will become more dependent on complex software and hardware for reports and profiles and data management. Gay Donohoo of Texas Christian University thinks fund raising will become more and more specialized, and advancement services will take on a larger responsibility in phonathons and mass mailings. Lynne Becker of the University of the South believes "we'll be more team oriented."[13]

With regard to staffing, there will be more turnover. The number of senior executives is increasing, and it is quite possible there will be a number of personnel changes just after the turn of the next century. There is no question but that the advancement office will require more people to manage new technologies. With the World Wide Web a new day of opportunity is dawning for experts in Web page layout, design, and maintenance. There will be increased traffic on the Internet, more inquiries, more uploads and downloads, and certainly more e-mail. There will be more competition. The same old business as usual will not "compute" as they say. Jack Miller of the University of Denver predicts an increase in prospect diversity. "We now have college graduates ages 21 to 101. Some are millionaires, some are not. . . . Also, more colleges and universities are reaching out to their international constituencies."[14] We will choose more carefully what data we collect and what data we keep. Systems are vulnerable to viruses and hackers, but of greater concern to all is the glut of information coming in. We have more information now than we can handle. Internet data may become somewhat suspect, not totally reliable, because there is not the secure checks and balances for accuracy and authenticity. Literally anyone can put anything on the Internet and tout it as the gospel truth, when in truth it could be a boldface lie. Inter- and intraoffice communication by means of facsimile machine and e-mail will become more common, and regrettably, personal contact less common. The society of tomorrow may well be more aloof, more detached, and less sociable than that of today. The closest thing possible to the dynamic of interpersonal communication is a face-to-face visit. Looking someone in the eye and asking "What is on your mind?" is a powerful means of communication. The next would be teleconferencing by interactive television. Less effective, but still potent is the old-fashioned telephone conversation. Next comes the quick communication of voice mail and the facsimile machine, the personal letter, and last, though instantaneous, is e-mail. E-mail is perfect for the individual who wants to get the message through but still remain somewhat detached from it.

The writer sees little change in the reasons why people make charitable contributions. Donors are and will still be motivated by their interests and the degree of involvement they have with the institution or the cause. Individuals will continue to be motivated by purely philanthropic motives, love of humanity, social welfare, and goodwill. Advancement professionals will continue to build relationships. Fund raising, alumni affairs, and public relations is always a matter of people interacting with people. Technofiles are advocating a paperless society and virtual applications for education, but as long as humans are physically and psychologically composed as they are, with all the sensations of life that motivate and drive our words and deeds, there will be a place for that which is tangible and real. This is not to suggest in any way that men and women will not continue to pursue technological advances and use them to their advantage. It is simply to affirm our human qualities and suggest that until such time as people no longer get sick there will be a need for health care, including the healing touch of the surgeon, physician, and nurse. As long as the basic needs of humankind exist, for security, for belonging, for food and shelter, there will be real intelligence, real emotions, and a desire for learning more about the world and its multifaceted challenges, as well as about its diversified people with their varied needs and wants. Education and philanthropy will always be linked. Both are deeply concerned with human welfare.

The future is as bright as the past is memorable. Institutional advancement will continue to play a major role in the affairs of colleges, universities, hospitals, and other nonprofits.

NOTES

1. C. Magrath, President of the National Association of State Universities and Land Grant Colleges, letter to the author, dated May 20, 1997, 4.
2. L. Gubernick and A. Ebeling, "I Got My Degree through E-Mail," *Forbes*, June 16, 1997, 84.
3. F. Rhodes, address to CASE.
4. Rhodes, address to CASE.
5. B. Taylor, "Results of a National Survey of College and University Fund Raising Practices," *Fund Raising Leadership*, ed. J. Pocock (Washington, DC: Association of Governing Boards, 1989), 103.
6. W. Tromble, "Building for Success," *Fund Raising Management*, September 1995, 18.
7. E. Coll, Jr., "Avoid Cutting Advancement in Tough Times," *Trustee Portfolios* (Washington, DC: Association of Governing Boards, March–April 1993), 15.
8. Coll, "Avoid Cutting Advancement," 15.
9. Coll, "Avoid Cutting Advancement," 17.
10. Magrath, letter to author, 4.
11. M. McPherson, quoted in C. Peter Magrath's letter to the author, May 20, 1997, 6.
12. P. Kovalcheck et al., *CASE Currents*, June 1997, 13.
13. Kovalcheck, *CASE Currents*, 13
14. Kovalcheck, *CASE Currents*, 14.

The Role of
Institutional Advancement

The role of institutional advancement is primarily the building of good external relations. As a functional part of the mission of an institution or organization, institutional advancement provides meaningful and relevant education and information while it builds political and moral support for the institution. Advancement programs provide both human and financial resources necessary to fulfill the mission and achieve the vision. Advancement staff assist the president or chief operating officer (CEO) in raising funds and building cordial and supportive relationships with alumni and friends in the community, throughout the patronizing region, and around the world. Advancement staff serve the public as well as the institution by providing information, programs, and activities in a timely manner. Advancement personnel strengthen ties with alumni, encourage outside participation, and establish partnerships with corporations and foundations.

ADVANCEMENT STRUCTURE

There are several structural models for institutional advancement, but the one most commonly used is the model that includes three external relations components, namely, development, alumni affairs, and public relations, each with its own director, professional staff, and support staff to carry out the several tasks of the division (see Figure A–1). Whatever the structure, the advancement function should be given high priority, authority, and visibility under the direction of a vice-president, vice-chancellor, or some other executive-level staff person.

Development is largely fund raising management, but it is more than fund raising. It is also building relationships, cultivating friendships, and helping to realize the mission and vision of the institution. The development function includes major gifts, annual fund gifts, planned giving, matching gifts, memorial gifts, class gifts, prospect research and prospect management, gift processing, donor acknowledgment and recognition, corporate and foundation relations, capital campaigns, and special events. It involves strategic planning, assessment, and evaluation. It includes cooperative arrangements with other departments and staff.

Alumni affairs serves the needs of alumni and endeavors to build and strengthen a bond of friendship and loyalty to the alma mater. Alumni staff are engaged in class reunions, alumni publications, programs, and activities. The annual phonathon (or telefund) is best achieved through a cooperative effort with the development staff. For many years since the beginning of the so-called alumni movement in the nineteenth century, institutions have put much time and energy into service-oriented programs like travel, merchandising, receptions, and other special events. Recently, however, with shrinking budgets and restructuring, CEOs and college presidents have placed greater emphasis on tying alumni benefits to contributions.

Public relations is concerned with public information, publications, promotion, marketing, image building, media relations, and communications in general. Public relations staff are service oriented, providing accurate and timely information to the several publics of the institution, as well as overseeing publications, assisting the CEO in crisis management, cultivating the print and electronic media, and building the image of the institution.

OUTLINE OF STAFF RESPONSIBILITIES

The chief advancement officer, usually a vice-president, vice-chancellor, or executive director of development, is an administrator, supervisor, and manager who frequently exercises hands-on involvement in fund raising, especially during major gift or campaign activity. The chief advancement officer will do the following:

- work with the CEO in developing and managing short-term and long-term plans for each of the advancement departments
- work with the CEO to develop strategic plans for the institution at large, including campus facilities, enrollment management, student financial aid, patient care, customer relations, marketing, assessment, and evaluation
- build a strong professional staff
- assess, evaluate, and build cost-effective and productive advancement programs to help achieve institutional goals
- maintain a cordial and professional relationship with colleagues at home and away, as well as with staff, faculty, physicians, patients, administrators, clients, employees, and civic and business leaders in the external community

- give attention to continued development and improvement of data management, i.e., computerized records, data input, and data retrieval
- help recruit, train, and supervise top volunteers, especially members of the board and high level advisory groups
- supervise the building of corporate partnerships
- cultivate the interest and goodwill of foundations
- supervise the planning and management of departmental budgets
- supervise and manage advancement personnel
- direct capital campaigns

The *director of development* is a senior officer whose primary role is fund raising, but also creating, planning, and working with others to make good things happen for the institution. The director of development will do the following:

- develop an effective short-term and long-term master plan for annual and capital cultivation and solicitation of gifts and pledges
- conduct prospect identification and research, utilizing demographic studies and electronic screening
- cultivate donors and prospective donors through personal visits, special events (receptions, dinners, groundbreakings, ribbon-cutting ceremonies), publications (updates, newsletters, brochures, flyers), Honor Roll of Donors, advisory groups, and gift clubs (President's Club, Founders Club)
- solicit charitable gifts and give attention to gift receiving and processing, acknowledgment and thanks, donor recognition, and follow-up
- work closely with the chief advancement officer and other professional staff to develop and carry out fund raising policies and procedures
- manage budget and staff
- plan, implement, and manage fund raising programs and activities such as annual fund, major gifts, deferred and planned gifts, corporate and foundation relations, special campaigns, and grant writing
- utilize all the techniques of professional fund raising management, including direct mail, telemarketing, and personal solicitation
- reach all known sources of charitable gifts, including alumni, friends, faculty/staff, patients, clients, trustees, parents, agencies, corporations, foundations, clubs, consortia, and other groups
- write grant proposals, reports, letters, case statements, and action plans
- create and design, when necessary, or work with graphics people to publish flyers, brochures, reports, and other documents
- build and strengthen corporate and foundation relations
- encourage aggressive and responsible planned giving activity
- assist in capital campaigns

The *director of alumni affairs* maintains good relations between the institution and its alumni. This has top priority and is often accomplished through alumni associations or alumni departments within the organization. Good relationships often occur as a result of publications, special events, fund raising activities, travel programs, job referral, and regional chapter activity. The director of alumni affairs will also do the following:

- offer alumni various merchandising programs
- bring alumni together for times of reunion and fellowship at Homecoming, Alumni Weekend, Parents Day, chapter events, receptions, athletic contests, perhaps a week-long Summer Alumni College, and travel
- provide information regarding alumni activities and programs, help alumni locate friends, and offer help with finding jobs
- solicit gifts for the institution through direct mail, telemarketing, and personal solicitation in cooperation with the development office
- manage staff and budget
- carry out strategic planning

Two essential ingredients of a successful alumni affairs program are SERVICE and COMMUNICATION. Budget and staff limitations may define the extent of service or communication, but both must be present in any successful operation.

The director of public relations oversees public information, publications, and communications, both internal and external. The director will do the following:

- maintain good relations with the print and electronic media, with faculty and staff, administrative staff, and with alumni, patients, clients, and friends
- continually strive to provide the public with information about the institution and its many programs and activities
- run advertisements, as budget permits, utilizing highway billboards, journals, newspapers, and television, calling attention to special and ongoing programs and activities
- act continually to build and maintain a good image for the institution
- continually assess and strive to improve the quality and content of all institutional publications
- take an aggressive role in marketing the institution to its several publics
- manage staff and budget
- assist the president in crisis management, being continually sensitive to the needs and wishes of the several publics served, but always guided by mission, goals, and policies of the institution
- work with athletics staff in the marketing and promotion of sports programs, and in maintaining good media relations

SUMMARY

The division of institutional advancement has a responsibility to promote the various departments of the institution and raise funds for them, but in a much larger way institutional advancement must look after the interests, goals, and dreams of the macro institution.

The chief advancement officer and the entire advancement staff must catch the feeling of purpose and destination that makes every professional officer, every administrator, and every support staff member a familial part of the institution.

Finally, it is incumbent upon the chief advancement officer to assist in every way possible, as assignments are made and procedures are established, to carry out the mission and goals of the institution and to give support to the staff and administration across the board in the overall advancement of the institution. Necessarily, the vice-president/chancellor is involved in admissions; in career planning and placement; in personnel; in long-range strategic planning; in plant and facilities planning and management; in student, customer, client, or patient aid; in program excellence; in marketing the institution; in finance and investment; and in major fund raising activity. It is a big order, but vital to institutional progress.

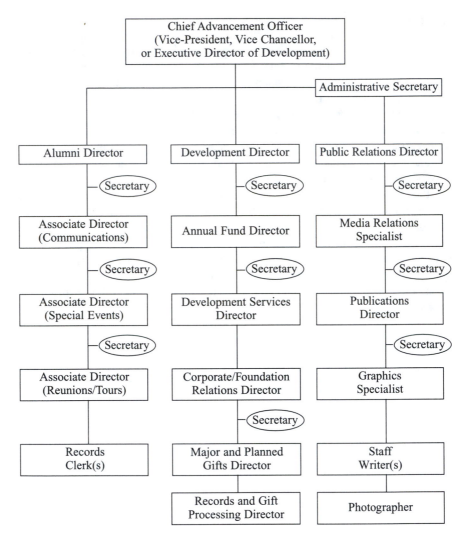

Figure A–1 Staff Organization

APPENDIX B

Recommended References

ALUMNI AFFAIRS

Homecomings and Reunions

Barbalich, A., D. Shoemaker, and A. Harris. Great show: Experts share 30 spicy ideas for top-performing special events. *Currents*, July–August 1992, 44–50, 52–53.

Benninghoff, D. Learning by tradition: A post-graduate version of a popular general studies course brings Colorado College alumni back to campus. *Currents*, May 1991, 32–34.

Bonney, M. All fired up: When the heat of the reunion season hits campus, solid planning principles can keep you cool and calm. *Currents*, October 1991, 26–30, 32.

Council for Advancement and Support of Education, 1986. *CASE answer file: Reunions and homecomings: How to stage a great comeback.* Washington, DC: CASE.

Desoff, A. A dream deferred: If your visions of strong class cohesiveness aren't materializing, don't despair: Use these ideas to turn fantasy into fantastic support. *Currents*, July–August 1993, 13–18.

DeWees, D. Traditions for nontraditional campuses: Homecomings can also benefit community colleges. *Currents*, September 1993, 18–19.

Fisher, M. Say cheese: Photographers offer their tips on taking picture-perfect homecoming shots. *Currents*, September 1993, 30–32.

Jackson, L. Come one, come all: As more alumni flock to reunions with their families, campuses are finding ways to provide child care and deal with liability. *Currents*, September 1995, 30.

Larson, W. 50 ways to stretch your dollar: Alumni administrators beat the budget blues with a combination of common and clever sense. *Currents*, September 1991, 36–42.

Rochlin, J., and S. Ruhl. Taking a hard look at homecoming: Has this major celebration become an unnecessary habit on your campus? Use these research techniques to determine whether your program is meeting a real need. *Currents*, September 1993, 11–15.

Sabo, S. Tinkering with tradition: A few adjustments can keep the crowds cheering year after year. *Currents*, September 1993, 17–22.

Swift III, J. Cooperate to celebrate: A great reunion means working with—not dictating to—alumni volunteers. *Currents*, November–December 1987, 32–34, 36.

Wallach, V. Ingredients for success: Spice up your class reunions by finding ways to add more fun. *Currents*, September 1995, 26–29, 31.

Webb, C., and P. Chewning. 1993. *Resource book in alumni administration: Managing alumni programs*. Washington, DC: CASE.

Clubs, Chapters, and Branches

Adams, R. Lifestyles of the young and driven: Even a well-established association can get behind the times. Here's how one college grapples with today's alumni. *Currents*, September 1992, 28–32, 34.

Blansfield, K. High-tech connections: Still relying on phone and mail to communicate with alumni clubs? The World Wide Web, e-mail, and even video and satellites can help you reach regional audiences faster. *Currents*, March 1996, 34–38.

Burdette, M. Grand-slam strategies: Winning tips for cutting chapter costs. *Currents*, September 1992, 36–38, 40.

Delizia, J. 1993. *The national-chapter partnership: A guide for the chapter relations professional*. Washington, DC: American Society of Association Executives.

Feudo, J. Sound investments: Clubs don't have to be costly. Five tactics can save money and make your volunteers more self-sufficient. *Currents*, March 1996, 40–44.

Kraft, B. New rules for the road: A survey shows alumni want programming with more social significance. *Currents*, September 1992, 30–31.

Rankin, L. Alumni chapters: Burden or benefit. Informal alumni groups can accomplish the same goals for less money. *Currents*, September 1992, 23–25.

Todd, J. Something for everyone: Young alumni can also benefit from continuing education—If you use creative ways to catch their interest. *Currents*, February 1994, 28–32.

Alumni Boards

Brinckerhoff, P. A user's guide to effective board retreats: An interruption-free environment that supports creative thinking will help directors focus on association issues. *Association Management*, July 1996, 45–46.

Lillestol, J. Blue-chip board: Take stock of your alumni board—and then increase its value with these insider tips. *Currents*, February 1992, 22–26.

Stone, W. Alumni aboard: How to get maximum mileage from your alumni governors. *Currents*, May 1984, 42–45.

Thiers, N. Speaking volumes: A comprehensive handbook can keep your alumni board on target and on schedule. *Currents*, February 1992, 28–31.

Student Alumni Programs

Fisher, M. Shining examples: 15 inspiring ideas for Student Alumni Programs. *Currents*, May 1992, 20–23.

Jackson, L. On the road to alumni: If you want involved graduates tomorrow, steer your students in the right direction today. This year-by-year road map can help. *Currents*, October 1994, 20–24.

Olson, B. SAAs: The student's view. *Currents*, May 1992, 8–11.

Patouillet, L. Our goodwill ambassadors: What a student-alumni association can do for your institution. *Currents*, January 1986, 40–42.

Todd, B. SAAs: The adviser's view; for the alumni association student programs are investments with unbeatable returns. *Currents*, May 1992, 12–16, 18.

Todd, B. 1993. *Student advancement programs: Shaping tomorrow's alumni leaders today*. Washington, DC: CASE.

Campus Constituent Groups

Amos, R. Going the distance: How to give your special-interest groups the tools for long-term success. *Currents*, March 1995, 8–12.

Bailey, A. Welcome back: A volunteer tells how to get minority alumni interested, inspired, and involved. *Currents*, March 1995, 56.

Boyers, K. Thinking about diversity: Five association executives discuss the value of difference. *Association Management*, June 1995, 42–47, 68.

Burr, D. Improving with age: How a Canadian university developed a successful special program just for older alumni. *Currents*, April 1990, 42–43.

Carter, L. Minority interest: Brown University meets the needs of minority alumni with a program they can call their own. *Currents*, April 1988, 46–48.

Forman, R. Diverse goals, common problems: How America's changing population affects higher education—and offers new opportunities to alumni professionals. *Currents*, July–August 1988, 8–11.

Hay, T. Common ground: Catering to alumni who share similar interests can strengthen your association as a whole. *Currents*, April 1990, 26–32.

Nicklin, J. Wooing minority alumni: Colleges report mixed success in programs for Black, Asian, and Hispanic graduates. *Chronicle of Higher Education*, February 23, 1994, A29–A30.

Norris, D., and J. Lofton. 1995. *Winning with diversity: A practical handbook for creating inclusive meetings, events, and organizations*. Washington, DC: American Society of Association Executives.

Alumni Records

Barre, N. What's lost can be found: Alumni associations tell about the many ways they use to trace missing alumni. *Currents*, May 1989, 48–50, 52.

Joyce, P. For the record: The alumni information you need—and six good ways to get it. *Currents*, January 1985, 36–37.

Pendil, M. Beyond Gallup: Alumni surveys give you people, not just numbers. *Currents*, September 1985, 40–42.

Pollick, A. Survey sense: Want to know more about your alumni body? Smart research by mail can give you the personal data you need. *Currents*, July–August 1995, 50–54.

Parents Programs

Detmold, J. Dear Mom and Dad: Please send money: Practical ideas to help your institution start and sustain a parents' fund. *Currents*, June 1985, 14–15.

Goldman, R. Grandparents are softies: So says the volunteer of the year. He raised $1 million for Renbrook School from easy marks like himself. *Currents*, June 1985, 6–9.

Halsey, M. What parents want: Princeton's survey gave the university plenty of parental guidance. *Currents*, June 1985, 10–13.

Lindemuth, T. A relative success: Casting parents in leading roles can bring box-office hits to your campus. *Currents*, April 1991, 12–13, 15–17.

McNamee, T. Ask and ye shall receive: A survey helps Hartwick College find new ways to involve parents in everything from internship programs to fund raising. *Currents*, June 1985, 16–18.

Alumni Education

Calvert, S. 1987. Alumni continuing education. Phoenix: ACE/Oryx Press.

Calvert, S. Fame and (mis)fortune: Alumni officers recall their best and worst experience with traveling faculty. *Currents*, February 1994, 34–39.

High, M., and A. Dessoff. Measure of success: Continuing education programs can be self-supporting, but they can't thrive unless your campus appreciates their intrinsic value. *Currents*, February 1994, 24–27.

McHugh, G. More than a sentimental journey: Give your alumni something to think about with a reunion mini-college. *Currents*, February 1984, 26–27.

Oliver, W. Education after graduation: Columbia University alumni know that learning continues long after commencement. *Currents*, May 1991, 35–37.

Sullivan, K. Education via satellite: Telecommunications technology helps the University of Notre Dame deliver continuing education on the air. *Currents*, May 1991, 24–26.

Todd, J. Considering minority interests: Remember your diverse constituencies when you plan continuing education programs. *Currents*, February 1994, 31.

Alumni Community Service

Kobara, J. Helping others, helping ourselves: Community service programs don't just benefit society. They bring alumni offices greater participation and increased campus value. *Currents*, March 1994, 50–51, 53–55.

Lennon, C. Service with a smile: Helping alumni reach out and make a difference in their communities. *Currents*, June 1991, 56.

Levine, S. "Won't you be my neighbor?" Eleven award-winning ways to get in touch with the community. *Currents*, October 1989, 36–37.

McDaniel, S. Joint ventures in volunteering: Community service projects can bring current and former students closer to campus—and each other. *Currents*, March 1994, 52.

Scalzo, T. The proof is in the program: The best way to be of service is to get results. Here's how to create and evaluate effective alumni activities. *Currents*, January 1993, 30–34.

Alumni Career Assistance

Barre, N. Natural resources: Your alumni can become one of your most valuable tools for recruiting students. *Currents*, July–August 1988, 34–36, 38, 40.

Carter, L. Job descriptions: Alumni directors tell how they share career network responsibilities with the career office. *Currents*, February 1989, 36–39.

Dessoff, A. Computer classified: Electronic career services link alumni with employers. *Currents*, July–August 1992, 10–14, 15.

Myers, J. Two part harmony: Alumni and admissions offices learn how to play the same tune when they run alumni student recruitment programs together. *Currents*, August 1988, 28–32.

Zagoren, A. 1982. *Involving Alumni in Career Assistance Programs*. Washington, DC: CASE.

Alumni Awards

Carter, L. Rewarding experiences: When you're presenting alumni awards, passion and creativity take the prize. *Currents*, July–August 1991, 22–24, 26.

Gupta, H. May I have the envelope, please? Ideas for alumni awards programs that just can't lose. *Currents*, March 1985, 20–23.

Hunter, B. Eyes on the prizes: Looking for ways to improve your alumni awards? Set your sights on solutions to 10 common problems. *Currents*, April 1996, 10–14.

Alumni Legislative Advocacy

Duncan, P., and C. Lawrence. 1996. Politics in America, *Congressional Quarterly*, Washington, DC.

Gaby, P., and Gaby D. 1982. *Nonprofit organization handbook.* Englewood Cliffs, NJ: Prentice Hall.

Garnett, J. 1992. *Communicating for results in government.* San Francisco: Jossey-Bass, Publishers.

Hooper, M. The alumni lobby: How alumni clout can strengthen a government relations program. *Currents*, July–August 1984, 36–39.

National Council of State Legislatures. 1991. *Inside the legislative process.* Denver: NCSL.

Roane, S. 1988. *How to work a room.* New York: Shapolsky Publishing.

Rosenthal, A. 1993. *The Third House.* Washington, DC: Congressional Quarterly Press.

Scalzo, T. The power of politics: How to turn supportive alumni into political capital for alma mater. *Currents*, March 1992, 20–24.

Technology Applications

Pallone, R. Bringing alumni online: A whole new world of computer technology is available today. Here's how association directors can use it to reach out to former students. *Currents*, October 1993, 42–45.

Sabo, S. Joint ventures on-line: Teaming up with a commercial service may help your alumni communicate with alma mater electronically. But is this partnership right for you? *Currents*, February 1995, 18–23.

Shaindlin, A. Alumni learning online: Brown's electronic continuing education course makes the grade with former students. *Currents*, January 1995, 72.

Woodbeck, D. Computer connections: How four alumni offices are using electronic communications to stay in touch with former students. *Currents*, November–December 1994, 11–16.

DEVELOPMENT AND PUBLIC RELATIONS

Altizer, A. *Seeking major gifts: How 57 institutions do it.* Washington, DC: CASE, 1992.

American Association of Fund Raising Counsel. *Giving USA: The annual report on philanthropy* (New York: AAFRC [published each year]).

American Prospect Research Association. 1991. *The American prospector: Contemporary issues in prospect research.* Rockville, MD: Fund Raising Institute.

Aston, D. 1991. *The complete guide to planned giving.* 2nd ed. Cambridge, MA: Jeffrey Lant Associates.

Bailey, A., and B. Millar. United Way: The fallout after the fall. *Chronicle of Philanthropy*, March 10, 1992, 1.

Barrett, R., and M. Ware. 1995. *Planned giving essentials.* Gaithersburg, MD: Aspen Publishers.

Bayley, T. 1988. *The fund raiser's guide to successful campaigns.* New York: McGraw-Hill.

Bennis, W., and B. Nanus. 1985. *Leaders: The strategies for taking charge.* New York: Harper-Collins.

Bergan, H. 1992. *Where the money is: A fund raiser's guide to the rich.* Alexandria, VA: BioGuide Press.

Bergman, J. et al. 1995. *Managing change in the nonprofit sector.* San Francisco: Jossey-Bass, Publishers.

Bryson, J. 1995. *Strategic planning for public and nonprofit organizations.* 2nd ed. San Francisco: Jossey-Bass, Publishers.

Burlingame, D., and L. Hulse. 1991. *Taking fund raising seriously: Advancing the profession and practice of raising money.* San Francisco: Jossey-Bass, Publishers.

Burlingame, D. 1993. *Philanthropic studies index.* Indianapolis: Center on Philanthropy.

Carlson, M. 1995. *Winning grants step by step.* San Francisco: Jossey-Bass, Publishers.

Ciconte, B. 1995. *Fund raising basics.* Gaithersburg, MD: Aspen Publishers.

Council for Aid to Education. *Voluntary support of education.* New York: CAE [published each year].

Craig, D. The tango of solicitation: If you know the steps to dance to when asking for the big gift, prospects will follow your lead. *Currents*, November–December 1996, 24–28.

Cumerford, W. 1993. *Start to finish fund raising: How a professional organizes and conducts a successful campaign.* Chicago: Precept Press.

Cunningham, R. *Asking and giving: A report on hospital philanthropy.* Chicago: American Hospital Association.

Detweiler, G. Credit card Q & A: Do alumni affinity cards require a lot of staff time? How do they affect the annual fund? Here's advice on these and 10 other common concerns. *Currents,* September 1996, 36–42.

Dove, K. 1988. *Conducting a successful capital campaign.* San Francisco: Jossey-Bass, Publishers.

Drucker, P. 1990. *Managing the nonprofit organization: Practices and principles.* New York: Harper-Collins.

Flannigan, J. 1982. *The grassroots fundraising book.* Chicago: Contemporary Books.

Gearhart, G. 1995. *The capital campaign in higher education.* Washington, DC: NACUBO.

Gee, A. 1990. *Annual giving strategies.* Washington, DC: CASE.

Geever, J. Spin control: Move your grant request to the top of the pile by learning grantmakers' preferences and pet peeves. *Currents,* July–August 1997, 38–44.

Gooch, J. 1987. *Writing winning proposals.* Washington, DC: CASE.

Gurin, M. 1981. *What volunteers should know for successful fund raising.* New York: Stein and Day.

Heeman, W., ed. 1985. *Criteria for evaluating advancement programs.* Washington, DC: CASE.

Heinrichs, J. Publish without perishing: Advice for editors on handling conflicts between what administrators want and readers demand. *Currents,* September 1996, 50–54.

Hesselbein, M., and R. Beckhard, eds. 1996. *The leader of the future.* San Francisco: Jossey-Bass, Publishers.

Hopkins, B. 1991. *The law of fund raising.* Somerset, NJ: John Wiley and Sons.

Hopkins, K. 1997. *Successful fundraising for arts and cultural organizations.* Phoenix: Oryx Press.

Huntsinger, J. 1982. *Fund raising letters: A comprehensive study guide to raising money by direct response marketing.* Richmond, VA: Emerson.

Jenkins, J., and M. Lucas. 1986. *Fund raising research.* Ambler, PA: Fund Raising Institute.

Joyaux, S. 1997. *Strategic fund development.* Gaithersburg, MD: Aspen Publishers.

Kelley, K. 1991. *Fund raising and public relations.* Hillsdale, NJ: Erlbaum.

Kihlstedt, A. 1997. *Capital campaigns: Strategies that work.* Gaithersburg, MD: Aspen Publishers.

Kinney, M., and E. Goerlich. University builds successful phonathon. *Fund Raising Management,* March 1996, 29–33.

Kotler, P., and A. Andreason. 1991. *Strategic marketing for nonprofit organizations.* 4th ed. Englewood Cliffs, NJ: Prentice Hall.

Kotler, P., and K. Fox. 1985. *Strategic marketing for educational institutions.* Englewood Cliffs, NJ: Prentice Hall.

Lawson, D. 1991. *Give to live: How giving can change your life.* La Jolla, CA: ALTI Publishing.

Lindahl, W. 199-. *Strategic planning for fund raising.* San Francisco: Jossey-Bass, Publishers.

Lord, J. 1983. *The raising of money.* Cleveland: Third Sector Press.

Matros, M. Getting coverage that counts: Reaching your audience in this electronic age requires a plan—and the willingness to experiment. *Currents*, March 1997, 8–12.

May, W. 1990. *Ethics and higher education.* New York: American Council on Education, Macmillan.

McLaughlin, C. 1986. *The management of nonprofit organizations.* New York: John Wiley & Sons.

Metz, A. Welcome to Camp Phonathon: Here's how to transform your callers from raw recruits into polished campus ambassadors. *Currents*, May 1997, 10–14.

Mixer, J. 1993. *Principles of professional fund raising.* San Francisco: Jossey-Bass, Publishers.

Murphy, M. 1989. *Cultivating foundation support for education.* Washington, DC: CASE.

Murray, D. 1985. *How to evaluate your fund raising program: A performance audit system.* Boston: American Institute of Management.

Nelson, D., and P. Schneiter. 1991. *Gifts-in-kind: The fund raiser's guide to acquiring, managing, and selling charitable contributions other than cash and securities.* Rockville, MD: Fund Raising Institute.

Nichols, J. 1990. *Changing demographics: Fund raising in the 1990's.* Chicago: Bonus Books.

Odendahl, T. 1990. *Charity begins at home: Generosity and self-interest among the philanthropic elite.* New York: Basic Books.

Panas, J. 1988. *Born to Raise.* Chicago: Pluribus Press.

Panas, J. 1984. *Mega gifts.* Chicago, Pluribus Press.

Panas, J. 1989. *Official fundraising almanac.* Chicago: Pluribus Press.

Payton, R. 1988. *Philanthropy: Voluntary action for the public good.* New York: American Council on Education/Macmillan.

Phelan, J. et al. 1997. *College & university foundations: Serving America's public higher education.* Washington, DC: Association of Governing Boards.

Pocock, J. 1989. *Fund-raising leadership: A guide for college and university boards.* Washington, DC: AGB.

Powell, W. ed. 1987. *The nonprofit sector: A research handbook.* New Haven: Yale.

Prince, R. 199-. *The seven faces of philanthropy: A new approach to cultivating major donors*. San Francisco: Jossey-Bass, Publishers.

Reilly, T. ed. *Raising money through an institutionally related foundation*. Washington, DC: CASE.

Rosso, H. and Associates. *Achieving excellence in fund raising*. San Francisco: Jossey-Bass, Publishers.

Rowland, A. ed. 1986. *Handbook of institutional advancement*. 2nd ed. San Francisco: Jossey-Bass, Publishers.

Ryan, E. Annual fund answers: Experts in direct mail, phonathons, and in-person asks tackle some of the annual fund's perennial problems. *Currents*, May 1996, 30–37.

Seltzer, M. 1987. *Securing your organization's future: A complete guide to fundraising strategies*. New York: The Foundation Center.

Seymour, H. 1988. *Designs for fund raising*. 2nd ed. Rockville, MD: Fund Raising Institute.

Sharron, Jr., W. ed. 1982. *The community college foundation*. Washington, DC: National Council for Resource Development.

Shaw, S., and M. Taylor. 1995. *Reinventing fundraising: Realizing the potential of women's philanthropy*. San Francisco: Jossey-Bass, Publishers.

Strand, B. et al. 1986. *Prospect research: A how-to guide*. Washington, DC: CASE.

Thomas, E. Turnover trends: A new study says turnover among advancement professionals is lower than it was a decade ago—and less the employer's choice. *Currents*, September 1996, 28–34.

Warwick, M. 1990. *Revolution in the mail box: How direct mail fund raising is changing the face of American society—and how your organization can benefit*. Berkeley, CA: Strathmoor Press.

Weiss, L. ed. *Parents programs: How to create lasting ties*. Washington, DC: CASE.

Williams, M. *The FRI annual giving book*. Ambler, PA: Fund Raising Institute [published annually since 1972]).

Williams, R. Presidential partners: Veteran PR officers tell how to build a strong relationship with the campus CEO. *Currents*, January 1997, 28–32.

Wood, M. 1995. *Nonprofit boards and leadership*. San Francisco: Jossey-Bass, Publishers.

Worth, M. ed. 1985. *Public college and university development*. Washington, DC: CASE.

Additional Advancement Reference Sources

GENERAL

Advancement Services
9431 Westport Road
Louisville, KY 40241

Alexander O'Neill Haas & Martin
181 Fourteenth Street, Suite 500
Atlanta, GA 30309

Alford Group
7660 Gross Point Road
Skokie, IL 60077

American Association of Fund Raising Counsel (AAFRC)
25 West 43rd Street
New York, NY 10036

American Management Association (AMA)
135 W. 50th Street
New York, NY 10020

American Society of Association Executives (ASAE)
1517 Eye Street, N.W.
Washington, DC 20005m

Association for Healthcare Philanthropy (AHP)
112-B East Broad Street
Falls Church, VA 22046

Bentz Whaley Flessner
Suite 2150 Northwest Financial Center
7900 Xerxes Avenue South
Minneapolis, MN 55431

Carlton & Company
101 Federal Street, Suite 1900
Boston, MA 02110

Center on Philanthropy
550 W. North Street
Indianapolis, IN 46204

Chronicle of Philanthropy
1255 23rd Street, N.W.
Washington, DC 20037

Contributions
P.O. Box 336
Medfield, MA 02052

Council on Foundations
1828 L Street, N.W.
Washington, DC 20036

Council for Advancement and Support of Education
Suite 400, 11 Dupont Circle
Washington, DC 20036

Dialogue Information Services
3460 Hillview Avenue
Palo Alto, CA 94304

Dini Partners
2727 Allen Parkway, Suite 700
Houston, TX 77019

Dun & Bradstreet
99 Church Street
New York, NY 10007

Edwards Group
P.O. Box 2176
Terre Haute, IN 47802

The Foundation Center
79 Fifth Avenue
New York, NY 10003

The Fund Raising Institute (FRI)
Box 365
Ambler, PA 19002

Grantsmanship Center
P.O. Box 6210
650 S. Spring Street
Los Angeles, CA 90014

Grenzebach Glier & Associates
55 West Wacker Drive
Chicago, IL 60601

Hoke Communications, Inc.
224 7th Street
Garden City, NY 11530

Hospital Development, Inc.
67 West Kagy Blvd., Suite 8
Bozeman, MT 59715

Independent Sector
1828 L Street, N.W.
Washington, DC 20036

Jackson & Associates
P.O. Box 2827
Evergreen, CO 80437

Ketchum, Inc.
Three Gateway Center, Suite 1726
Pittsburgh, PA 15222

Marquis Who's Who, Inc.
200 E. Ohio Street
Chicago, IL 60611

National Center for Nonprofit Boards
2000 L Street, N.W., Suite 411
Washington, DC 20036

National Society of Fund Raising Executives (NSFRE)
1101 King Street, Suite 3000
Alexandria, VA 22314

Non Profit Times
P.O. Box 408
Hopewell, NJ 08525

Schofield Associates
304 W. Franklin Street, Suite 200
Syracuse, NY 13202

Staley/Robeson, Inc.
3010 Westchester Avenue
Purchase, NY 10577

Standard & Poors
Registry of Directors & Executives
25 Broadway
New York, NY 10004

Taft Group
12300 Twinbrook Parkway, Suite 450
Rockville, MD 20852

Thornwood Group
101 Federal Street, Suite 1900
Boston, MA 02110

Woodburn Kyle & Company
400 East First Street
Madison, IN 47250

TECHNOLOGICAL ASSISTANCE

American Fundware
1385 S. Colorado Blvd., Suite 400
Denver, CO 80222

Blackbaud
4401 Belle Oaks Drive
Charleston, SC 29405

Campaigne Associates
491 Amherst Street
Nashua, NH 03063

Crescendo Planned Gifts Software
1601 Carmen Drive, Suite 103
Camarillo, CA 93010

JSI Fund Raising Systems, Inc.
4732 Longhill Road, Suite 2201
Williamsburg, VA 23188

KMS Software, Inc.
790 Coit Central Tower
12001 North Central Expressway
Dallas, TX 75243

Master Software Corporation
5975 Castle Creek Parkway, N. Drive, Suite 300
Indianapolis, IN 46250

Micro Information Products
505 East Huntland Drive, Suite 340
Austin, TX 78752

P G CALC Planned Giving Software
129 Mount Auburn Street
Cambridge, MA 02138

RGS, Real Good Software
5200-A Philadelphia Way
Lanham, MD 20706

Technology Resource Assistance Center
610 Cowper Street
Palo Alto, CA 94301

Glossary of Terms Used in Institutional Advancement

As with any profession, there are terms used in institutional advancement that have special meaning for advancement professionals but not for the general public. Accordingly, a list of these terms and their definitions has been compiled with the hope that knowledge and understanding of them may be helpful to those who read this book.

AAFRC—American Association of Fund Raising Counsel.

Accounting policy—Policy that specifies which types of gifts will be counted toward a campaign goal and which types will be excluded.

ACFRE—Advanced certified fund raising executive.

Acknowledgment—A printed form, usually a receipt, legally confirming the gift, but also an expression of gratitude for a gift, most often in the form of a letter.

Add-on gift—a gift in addition to the main gift, usually relatively small by comparison. For example, a $20,000 endowed scholarship gift is made but it will not generate enough interest income to make an award for several months, so an add-on gift in the amount of $5,000 is made to underwrite the scholarship award for the present year.

Advance division—That part of the campaign that is executed prior to public announcement of the campaign.

Advance gifts—Gifts or pledges in advance of the public announcement of a capital fund drive. Often the success of a campaign depends on the size of the advance gifts, also called "lead gifts."

Advancement—The entire area of external relations, including development, alumni affairs, public relations, communications, and in some cases government relations.

AHP—Association for Healthcare Philanthropy.

Annual fund—An organized fund raising effort to obtain gifts for the institution on a yearly basis.

Annual giving program—Same as annual fund.

Annual report—A report of fund raising activities and results during the previous year.

Annuitant—A person who receives or is scheduled to receive annuity payments.

Annuity—A series of equal payments at fixed intervals. See also *Gift annuity*.

Anonymous gift—A gift, which by the donor's wish is not publicly attributed.

Appreciated securities gift—A gift of securities with market value greater than the donor's cost or basis.

APR—Accredited in public relations.

Area campaign—A concentrated fund raising effort in a particular geographical area.

Ask—"The ask" refers to soliciting the gift.

Assignment—The designation of a volunteer or staff member for the solicitation of one or more prospective donors.

Audit—An objective professional evaluation of internal development operations, usually conducted by outside professional counsel.

Bang-tail envelope—An envelope with a large flap that can be used as a check off for desired information and for gift designation. A similar term is "wallet flap."

Bargain sale—Sale of property at less than the market value.

Benchmarks—A specific achievement essential to success.

Benefactor—A contributor, usually at one of the highest levels.

Bequest—A transfer, by will, of personal property or real estate.

Book value—The amount of an asset stated on the books, not necessarily the market value.

Bricks and mortar campaign—Refers generally to building projects, not intangibles such as endowments and operating funds.

Brochure—Printed document used to provide information or to promote a program or project.

CAE—Council for Aid to Education.

Campaign—A well-planned, organized, systematic, fund raising or marketing effort.

Campaign cabinet—The executive committee of the campaign.

Campaign chairman—The top volunteer who leads the campaign.

Campaign director—The professional staff member who directs and manages the campaign.

Campaign newsletter—A publication updating campaign activities and results, sent periodically to volunteers, donors, selected prospects, and other interested parties.

Campus community campaign—That part of the fund raising effort directed to faculty, staff, retired and emeriti faculty and staff, and other employees.

Capital—Pertains to that which has a useful life over a long time, usually more than one year.

Capital campaign—A large fund raising campaign, extending over several years, designed to obtain gifts for capital purposes such as buildings, endowments, enhanced program support, and other major projects, rather than for current and annual expenditures.

CASE—Council for Advancement and Support of Education. Most college and university advancement professionals belong to CASE.

Case statement—A document that justifies the reasons for the campaign and discusses needs the campaign will address. It builds a "case for support."

Cause-related marketing—A type of marketing in which a percentage of the profit from the sale of company products is donated to the charity, the idea being that the logo and name of the institution or cause appears on the company product. Thus the cause is brought to the public's attention through the product and each item sold generates a certain amount for the cause.

CFRE—Certified fund raising executive.

Challenge gift—A special kind of gift that is promised on the condition that the institution will raise other gifts according to a prescribed formula, e.g., a donor will agree to contribute $50,000 on the condition that the organization will raise another $50,000 for the project. Challenge gifts are used as a device to stimulate gifts from other donors.

Challenge grant—The same as *Challenge gift* above, except grants are usually made by corporations or foundations. Kresge is the best known national foundation that gives challenge grants.

Class agent—An alumnus who has agreed to be point person for members of his/her class, usually in the context of planning a reunion or fund raising. Class agents serve as representatives for the class.

Corporate giving—Contributions from companies.

Corporate foundation—A foundation established by a company to handle its philanthropic interests as distinguished from other foundations, such as private foundations.

Corpus—The principal or capital of a fund or estate, in contradistinction to interest or revenue.

Counsel—Professional advice and opinion relative to fund raising, public relations, or alumni affairs, usually from an outside source. See also *Resident counsel.*

Cultivation—The act of motivating an individual or group to want to give, developing an interest in the institution by involving the prospect in special events, activities, and programs, making friends aware of needs as well as progress being made.

Current expenditures—Expenditures that are made for short-term obligations, usually less than 12 months, e.g., for supplies, travel, or service.

Current giving—Generally synonymous with annual giving. Gifts may be restricted or unrestricted as the donor wishes but will apply to current operations of the organization.

Decentralized development—A development system in which responsibilities for fund raising are given to the several schools or colleges of a university, as opposed to keeping them in the central office.

Decoy—A bogus name and address placed in the institution's donor, prospect, or alumni lists for the purpose of monitoring use of the lists.

Deferred gift—A gift to be received in the future from a transaction occur-

ring at present, which includes such things as pooled income funds, annuity trusts, charitable remainder trusts, gift annuities, life insurance gifts, and testamentary commitments.

Demographics—The study and application of social and economic data, e.g., a study of people, with certain variables such as sex, age, geographic domicile, and education.

Designated gift—A gift that has been made to benefit a particular department, program, activity, or project. See also *Restricted gift.*

Development—The total program of institutional fund raising, sometimes includes public relations and alumni affairs, though the all-inclusive term more commonly used is *institutional advancement.* Most often, however, the term *development* is a euphemism for fund raising, though ideally it would include all aspects of building and developing the institution.

Direct mail—More properly called *direct response mail,* it is usually associated with solicitation by mail, but also applies to marketing.

Donation—A contribution or gift.

Donee—The recipient of the donation, i.e., the organization.

Donor—The individual or organization that makes a gift.

Drive—An effort to accomplish something, usually a fund raising effort.

Earmarked—Restricted or designated.

Endowment—A fund that generates interest to be used for a designated purpose. The corpus is never invaded, only invested and reinvested. The investment returns may be used at the discretion of the institution according to investment policies and approved spend out rates, and according to the wishes of the donor. Investment returns from an endowed scholarship fund, for example, are used, in part (usually at a 5 percent spend out rate) to fund scholarship awards.

Expendable gift—A gift that may be spent, as distinguished from an endowment gift that is invested and gives back investment returns.

FASB—Financial Accounting Standards Board.

Feasibility study—An objective study of the institution's fund raising potential, assessing the strength of its case, the availability of leaders and competency of staff, and the probable inclination of donors to support the campaign. Some prefer to call it an *assessment*. It is usually done by outside professional counsel for a fee. Objectivity and confidentiality are the primary reasons for going outside.

Fiduciary—A person or agency charged with the duty of a trust on behalf of the beneficiary.

501(c)(3)—The section of the Internal Revenue Code that defines nonprofit, charitable, educational, tax exempt organizations. Gifts to 501 (c) (3) institutions and organizations are tax deductible.

Flagging—Identifying data for special attention.

Flyer—Generally a single sheet promotional piece.

Follow-up—Continued activity after solicitation to make sure the gift comes in and to further cultivate the goodwill of the prospective donor: return visits, additional phone calls, letters, memos, all those activities that are crucial to bringing closure and building relationships.

Foundation—A philanthropic organization established to look after the investment, stewardship, and distribution of funds. Several types of foundations exist, including corporate foundations, independent foundations, private foundations, operating foundations, and institutional foundations.

Friends—A generic term meaning individuals having some positive interest in the institution, often seen in the context of "alumni and friends," meaning individuals who are not alumni, or "friends and family," meaning those who are not employees. Sometimes the term is used in the group sense, e.g., "Friends of the Library," or "Friends of the Museum."

Fund raising—The act of seeking gifts from various sources.

FY—Fiscal year.

FYI—For your information.

GAAP—Generally accepted accounting principles.

Gift—A voluntary, irrevocable transfer of something of value without consideration. If the donor has any thoughts of calling it back at some time in the future, it is not a gift but a loan. If it is intended to pay a debt, e.g., a son's tuition, it is merely payment for value received. If part of it is to pay for a meal or entertainment, as is the case with fund raising dinners, and part of it is a charitable contribution, then only that part that is a charitable contribution is a gift.

Gift annuity—A contract between the donor and the institution or its foundation wherein the donor agrees to transfer property to the institution or foundation in exchange for the institution's or foundation's promise to pay the donor a fixed amount annually.

Gift crediting—A policy regarding what gifts will be received and credited to the donor for purposes of the campaign. Gifts from a third party, for example, may be credited to the donor's gift account on request of the third party, such as a son making a gift of $500 and requesting that his father receive credit for the gift.

Gifts-in-kind—Gifts of tangible personal property such as equipment, works of art, or other items; as well as gifts of real property, such as land or real estate.

Giving clubs—Honorary clubs recognizing gifts, e.g., Century Club ($100+) or President's Club ($1,000+).

Goodwill—That intangible quality of feeling good about the institution that is continually cultivated by advancement personnel, administration, and staff. Without it, efforts at fund raising, public relations, and alumni relations have less than a ghost of a chance of succeeding.

Grant—A transfer from a corporation, foundation, individual, or group of individuals, generally in response to a written request for funds. Grants may be gifts, or they may be allocations in support of programs or project for which something is expected in return, e.g., a report or research finding. The latter are called *sponsored programs.*

Grant proposal—A formal written document seeking financial support.

Grantee—The recipient of the funds granted.

Grantor—The person, company, or foundation granting the funds.

Hard copy—Letters, memos, reports, pledge cards, and other printed, written, or published materials usually kept in files as backup data for the information entered into computer files.

Hardware—Computers, modems, printers, copier machines, facsimile machines, and other equipment used in the course of doing business.

Holographic will—A handwritten will.

Honorary chairman—A person who agrees to lend his/her name to the campaign, committee, or task force with the understanding that he/she will not assume an active role, usually a person of some prominence, a president emeritus, a past governor.

Identification—As in prospect identification, meaning the process of investigation, research, and analysis used to determine who the most promising prospective donors are.

Independent sector—A term used to describe not-for-profit institutions and organizations, not to be confused with *Private sector*. See below.

Indicia—The mailing permit that appears in the upper right corner of an envelope and identifies the sender by permit number.

Information retrieval—The act of recovering information stored in computer files or hard copy files.

In-house—Internal constituency, e.g., in-house directory, to be used only by employees, not intended for outside use.

In-kind contribution—A gift of equipment, supplies, or other property in lieu of money.

Initial gifts—Contributions usually from trustees and other leaders that demonstrate a commitment to the campaign and give life to the fund drive before it is publicly announced and outside solicitation is undertaken. See also *Advance gifts*.

Input—Transferring information from an external source to the internal memory of the computer.

Institutional advancement—The entire external relations area, including development, alumni affairs, public relations, communications, advancement services, and sometimes government relations, athletic promotion and marketing, and the campus radio and TV station. See also *Advancement*.

Intensive phase—The peak period of campaign solicitation.

Inter vivos transfers—Transfers of money, stocks, etc., made during one's lifetime, not to be confused with testamentary disposition made under a person's will.

Irrevocable trust—A trust that cannot be changed or terminated by the person who established it.

Itemizers—Taxpayers who list deductible contributions on their income tax returns.

Kickoff—Formal announcement and start of a fund raising drive, usually a special event to which certain key individuals have been invited.

Laissez-faire—A style of leadership with minimal involvement, the french meaning is "to let happen."

Laser letter—A letter printed by means of a laser printer.

Layout—A hand-drawn arrangement of copy, art, and pictures that shows how the finished product will look.

Leadership gifts—Often the top tier of gifts, $500,000, $1 million, and more. These are the gifts in a capital campaign that come during the so-called quiet phase of the campaign from top donors. They are called leadership gifts because of their tendency to inspire generous gifts from other donors.

Letter of intent—A letter that states a prospective donor's intention to make a specified gift, often used by corporations and some major donors in lieu of pledge cards.

Lettershop—Same as mailing house, a company that specializes in addressing, inserting fund raising materials, and delivering the mailing to the post office. Lettershops often have printing capabilities, whereas mailing houses often do not.

Leverage—The concept of giving a certain amount for the purpose of influencing other donors, e.g., the idea of giving a challenge gift with the condition that others will give an equal or greater amount. Also used in the context of using certain gifts to get other gifts, e.g., using the fact of company A's gift to get company B to give the same or more. In Delaware, for example, if DuPont gives generously, others will too. In fact, some donors will not give a dime until they know that DuPont has made a commitment.

Life income gift—An irrevocable gift that will generate income for the donor for a specified time period through an annuity or trust arrangement.

Life insurance gift—The assignment of a life insurance policy to the institution or its foundation. Requirements are that the institution both own the policy and be the beneficiary of the policy.

Lists—A general term used by fund raising professionals to denote files and records pertaining to donors and prospects, sometimes called rosters or printouts.

Live sample—A sample direct-mail piece, with all the inserts, sealed, stamped, and ready to go.

Live stamp—A postage stamp ready to be affixed by hand or machine, as opposed to a postal imprint from a postage meter.

Logo—Two or more letters forming a short word or acronym, an identifying symbol or mark for the institution, program, or campaign.

Lybunt—A category of donors who gave "last year but unfortunately not this year."

Mail campaign—A fund raising effort conducted entirely by mail. See also *Direct mail*.

Mail drop—Delivery of sorted and bundled mail to the post office.

Mailing house—A company that specializes in sorting, stuffing, sealing, stamping, and mailing. A mailing house is often used for large mailings that would be difficult for in-house operations.

Major gift clubs—Clubs that recognize and honor contributors whose giving has attained a certain level, e.g.,

Fellows, $10,000+ or Benefactors, $100,000 and more.

Major gifts—Gifts of substantial amounts, usually $10,000 and more.

Market value—The current value of an asset if sold on the open market.

Mass appeal—An appeal to a large number of donors, often quite general in nature, tends to be least effective because it lacks the specificity of other targeted appeals.

Matching gift—A gift that matches another gift. The term is used frequently in connection with companies or foundations that match individual gifts of employees. Some companies match two for one, others one for one, and some three for one. Usually there is a floor or minimum amount that can be matched and a ceiling or maximum amount above which the company will not match. Different companies have different criteria for matching gifts. Published guidelines must be followed.

Memorial gift—A gift in loving memory of a loved one.

Microcomputer—A small complete computer system that consists of both hardware and software. Most personal computers are "micros."

Mini case statement—An abbreviated version of the full case statement, usually in brochure form, suitable for inclusion with a cover letter in a number 10 envelope.

Mini proposal—A condensed proposal leaving out some detail and calling attention immediately to the need, the amount sought, and the importance of the gift, often used with corporate and other donors where a full proposal is not required, but something more than a letter is needed.

NACUBO—National Association of College and University Business Officers.

Named gift opportunity—An opportunity for the donor to receive recognition for the gift by having a name attached to the building or facility, program, endowment, scholarship, fellowship, or professorship. Generally to receive such an opportunity, the donor would need to contribute 51 percent of the cost of the building, or 100 percent of the cost of a facility, such as a classroom, or 100 percent of the cost of a scholarship.

National campaign committee—The advisory body of a capital campaign, usually including as many as 50 or more members chosen for their interest, involvement, and investment in the institution and its campaign.

Needs—The necessary items, programs, facilities, personnel required, but not yet attained, by the institution. Needs are the basis for fund raising efforts, as opposed to a shopping list of wishes and wants. They include both short-term and long-term necessities.

Needs assessment—An analysis of the institution's table of needs, which becomes the basis for developing a

"Case for Support," a rationale for solicitation.

Never-evers—A category of prospective donors who have never given to the institution.

Newsletter—See *Campaign newsletter* above.

Nixie—An undeliverable piece of mail returned to sender by the post office.

Nonprofit organization—An organization that provides services or benefits to mankind without financial incentive, e.g., colleges, universities, some hospitals, social welfare groups, arts groups, youth groups, museums, health care causes.

NSFRE—National Society of Fund Raising Executives.

Nucleus fund—The amount raised for the campaign prior to public announcement, usually 50 percent of the total campaign goal.

Objectives—Specific aims of a program or campaign.

Organizational chart—A chart of the structure of the campaign, showing top leadership and all operational committees. The term applies to many other institutional structures as well.

Outright gift—The transfer of a gift to the institution without condition.

Overprinted—Material that has been pre-printed with certain information and then is reprinted with additional information or graphics.

Overrun—Additional envelopes, letters, or other printed matter beyond the quantity requested. A 10 percent overrun is common and desirable in fund raising operations.

Pacesetters—A category of donors making larger gifts that encourage others to follow, usually at the lower end of the range of gifts, e.g., $250 donors to encourage $100 donors to move up. The term is often used in annual giving campaigns.

Paid staff—Professional staff employed by the institution to direct and manage advancement programs.

Patrons—Individuals who lend their names to promote a cause or campaign.

Patterns of giving—The tendency of donors to make gifts to particular programs or projects, usually in previously established areas of interest. Analysis of giving will yield patterns in both interests and amounts.

Payroll deduction—A program whereby employees can have their gifts taken out of their paychecks.

Phase—A specific stage of a campaign.

Philanthropy—The philosophy and practice of giving voluntarily, derived from the Greek and roughly translated "for the love of mankind."

Phonathon—A program of solicitation by telephone, sometimes called telefund.

Pilot mailing—A first-time mailing to determine whether an appeal will be successful.

Plan of action—The blueprint for the campaign or program, showing activities and time schedule for carrying out the operation. The emphasis is on implementation rather than feasibility.

Planned giving—The act of giving according to a sound personal financial plan that addresses the present and looks toward the future by making charitable provisions through life insurance, trusts, and testamentary commitments. See also *Deferred gift*.

Pledge—Technically a signed, dated commitment to make a gift in a particular amount over a specified period of time payable according to the wishes of the donor. Most institutions and organizations do not regard the pledge as legally binding.

Pooled income fund—Separate contributions from a number of donors that are pooled for investment and management purposes, similar to a mutual fund, which provide life income to named beneficiaries.

Precall flyer—Information sent to the potential donor that alerts him or her to expect a call from the organization in a few days for the purpose of soliciting a gift.

Premium—An incentive to give, usually offered for gifts in a particular range, e.g., donors sending $500 or more might receive a plaque.

Premiums are not as widely used as in prior years because of recent IRS regulations discounting contributions by the amount of the premium.

Printout—A printed copy of information stored in a computer.

Private foundation—Generally speaking, a foundation that is originally funded from one source, often a family source, that derives revenue from its investments and makes grants to other charitable organizations. Not to be confused with corporate foundations, which are essentially the philanthropic agencies of the corporations that established them.

Private sector—Sources of support other than the government and other public sources.

Proposal—A formal written document asking for grant support. It states the need, builds a rationale for the request, identifies those individuals who will be responsible for the program or project, and gives a breakdown of the cost.

Prospect—Any logical source of potential support.

Prospect card—A profile of the prospect compiled by the research staff to enable the solicitor to know more about the prospect and ultimately be more successful in bringing the solicitation to closure.

Prospect rating—A procedure for evaluating prospects, usually done by members of the professional staff in cooperation with top campaign volunteers. Rating is highly confidential.

Prospect research—The act of seeking information regarding potential donors and current donors.

PRSA—Public Relations Society of America.

Public relations—The act of cultivating goodwill and better understanding on the part of external constituencies.

Publicity—Attracting attention to an activity, program, or event through the established media or other networks.

Pyramid of giving—A reference to the distribution of gifts by size and donor source. Generally speaking, the pyramid shows that 80 percent of the money comes from the top 20 percent of the donor base. That is why leadership gifts are vital to the success of the campaign.

Q & A Sheet—A sheet composed of questions and answers about a particular project or program. It is another means of helping prospects understand what the campaign is all about.

Quasi-endowment—An endowed fund with provision that under certain circumstances the principal may be invaded.

Quid pro quo—Something for something, e.g., securing an advantage in exchange for a similar favor.

Ranking—Usually in reference to donors, meaning listing of prospects in order of their ability to contribute.

Real property—A legal term meaning land and all physical substances above, below, or attached to the land, i.e., the land, trees, houses, fences, oil, minerals, and air space above the land. All else is classified as personal property.

Records—As in "donor records," meaning all files, lists, and other data pertaining to donors and prospects.

Remainder—Generally an interest, usually in a trust, meaning the right to receive the trust property that remains when the trust terminates.

Resident counsel—Professional assistance on a full-time basis, provided to help direct the campaign, usually for two years. Periodic counsel is part-time.

Restricted gift—A gift specified by the donor for a particular purpose.

Revocable trust—A trust that can be changed or cancelled by the person granting the trust.

Rifle-shot approach—Solicitation narrowed to include only a very select group of prospects, as opposed to "shotgun" approach that solicits broadly without selection.

Risk capital—Funds set aside for a project that may or may not succeed.

Role playing—A training technique

to prepare volunteers for solicitation. They are asked to assume different parts in a dramatization of personal solicitation where one will pretend to be the solicitor and the other will be the prospective donor.

Rule of thirds—Si Seymour's rule for fund raising, simply stated is that

(1) the first third of the funds raised in a capital campaign comes from approximately 10 donors.

(2) the second third of the money comes from 100 donors, and

(3) the final third of the money comes from the thousands of donors that remain.

What might not materialize in the first third often can be made up in the second third, but experienced fund raisers know that what is not achieved at the top level can never be made up by the masses at the bottom level. Modern fund raisers question the value of the rule.

Sacrificial gift—A gift that causes some hardship and discomfort for the donor because it is larger than the giver has budgeted for charitable giving to the organization. Such a gift requires that something be sacrificed in another area of the budget.

Salting lists—The practice of inserting "control" names in mailing lists for the purpose of monitoring their use.

Screening—As in "screening pros-

pects," the practice of assigning prospects to certain broad ranges of giving. Also, it is often used to indicate prospects with no potential.

Seed money—A substantial gift intended to attract other donors and help the project grow to full stature.

Self-mailer—A direct mail package that requires no separate envelope to carry it and no inserted return envelope. Typically, it is a flyer folded over, stapled, and mailed as is by the attachment of a gummed label and a stamp.

Shotgun approach—Broad general indiscriminate solicitation. See also *Rifle-shot approach.*

Sight-raising—Getting donors to increase their contributions to a higher level of support.

Sleeper—An unexpected prospect who emerges as a major donor.

Software—The programs that make a computer function.

Solicitation—The act of asking for the gift.

Special gifts—Gifts that require special attention by the institution in order to attract donor participation.

SPH—A code to indicate special handling, used by some organizations in computer records indicating that a particular donor requires special attention by a professional development officer. Records with SPH, or other codes like DNS (do not solicit), are routinely dropped from annual fund solicitation.

Sponsored research—Research done by faculty or staff, but paid for by the donor, who usually expects to benefit from the research.

Stretch gift—A gift that is larger than the donor might usually make.

Suspect—A potential donor whose interest is very weak. The donor is not a good prospect but is suspected to have some spark of interest that might be coaxed into a flame through cultivation.

Sybunts—A category of donors who gave "sometime in the past but unfortunately not this year." They may have given two or three years ago, or perhaps 10 years ago, but have not made a contribution this year.

Syndicated gift—A collection of gifts, usually from a single family, group, consortium, or agency, e.g., a gift from a particular family, representing smaller gifts from several different family members.

Tangible personal property gift—A gift of equipment, art, jewelry, or other personal property in lieu of cash. These are commonly called gifts-in-kind.

Target—Any specific fund raising objective. It could be a certain market group, such as parents, or a particular public served by the institution, such as local merchants.

Telemarketing—Raising funds (or selling products) by telephone. See also *Phonathon*.

Telethon—Raising funds by means of television.

Testamentary gift—A gift by means of a will, such as a bequest, effective upon the death of the donor.

Token gift—A gift well below the capacity of the donor to give, often given to get "off" the hook, and sometimes given to make a statement of displeasure with the organization, like a woman in Delaware who returned the direct mail solicitation with a terse note and a penny taped to the page. Sometimes it is given by a competitor or colleague in a neighboring organization to get on the mailing list.

Training session—A meeting of professional staff and volunteers with instruction and guidance to prepare for solicitation.

Transmittal sheet—A form that accompanies the transfer of a gift to the proper accounting authority.

Trust—A fiduciary relationship with respect to property, i.e., placing confidence in another person or legal entity by giving over property to keep, manage, invest, or administer for another's benefit.

Trustee—A person or agent of a trust, such as a bank, holding legal title to property to administer it for a beneficiary. Also, a member of the institution's governing board is referred to as a *trustee*.

Turnaround time—The time it takes to complete a project, mailing, or solicitation.

Ultimate gift—The largest gift a donor is capable of giving, usually through a trust or estate plan.

Unitrust—A separately invested trust that treats the whole fund, both the principal and interest as a unit. It pays the beneficiary a designated percentage of the market value of the trust's assets as valued each year by the manager of the trust.

Unrestricted gift—A gift that is designated to be used wherever the need is greatest. An unrestricted gift is a gift with no conditions attached.

Upgrading—The practice of moving a donor up to a higher level of giving, similar to the sight-raising concept described above.

Value—The worth of property, goods, or services.

Vendor—A seller of goods or services. Vendors are one category of prospects often overlooked.

Verbal pledge—Not legally binding, valuable only as an indication of intention.

Vest—To confer ownership.

Victory dinner—A special dinner event at which volunteers are recognized and awards given for goals achieved, usually held at the conclusion of a campaign.

Volunteer—Any person who works without compensation.

Will—A legally executed instrument by which a person makes disposition of his or her property to take effect after death.

Window between mailings—The period of time between mailings.

Window envelope—A mailing envelope having a window through which a name and address typed onto the enclosure can be read.

Window dressing—Statements that appear to be more substantive than they really are.

Word processing—Computerized programs for the writing and editing of text.

Year-end giving—The practice of making gifts in the last few days of the calendar year in order to take advantage of tax benefits.

Zero-based budget—A fiscal management technique that begins the new year on the new budget without benefit of carryover from the preceding year, i.e., starting from a new point of beginning (zero) without built-in factors for inflation, without unspent amounts from the prior year.

INDEX

(Page numbers in *italic* indicate figures. Page numbers followed by "t" indicate tables.)

CONTRIBUTING AUTHORS

The men and women who contributed to the book are from various parts of the country with particular areas of interest and expertise. Their writing represents current thinking in the three areas of institutional advancement, development, alumni affairs, and public relations. Their ideas and intellectual positions are applicable to educational institutions, health care facilities, social service organizations, cultural groups, and other nonprofit agencies. They have had years of experience and are recognized by their peers as successful practitioners of institutional advancement.

The editor and author, William W. Tromble, is vice chancellor for External Affairs at Indiana University Southeast in New Albany, Indiana. Prior to this appointment, he was vice president for institutional advancement at Delaware State University in Dover, Delaware, where he recently completed a multimillion dollar capital campaign, winning national recognition and achieving the Council for Advancement and Support of Education (CASE) Leadership Award. He was the chief external relations officer of the university and was responsible for five departments, including the three major areas of advancement—development, alumni affairs, and public relations. In prior years, he served as development director and special campaigns director at Ball State University in Muncie, Indiana; as development director at Spartanburg Methodist College in Spartanburg, South Carolina; as alumni director at Houghton College in upstate New York; and as associate professor at Olivet Nazarene University in Kankakee, Illinois. He is a graduate of Michigan State University (MMus) and the University of Michigan (PhD) and has postdoctoral work in financial accounting and business law from Ball State University. He is active in CASE and a board member of the National Society of Fund Raising Executives (NSFRE), Brandywine Chapter in Wilmington, Delaware. At Delaware State University, he was a member of the President's Administrative Council, Liaison to the University's Board of Visitors, and a member of the Trustees Committee on Finance. He chaired a task force on marketing and was a member of the university's Strategic Planning Committee. He was recently named Honorary Commander of the U.S. Air Force CRS, Dover Air Force Base, Dover, Delaware.

Ronald J. Stephany is vice president for university relations at the University of Redlands, Redlands, California, where he guided the university's $45 million comprehensive capital campaign to a successful conclusion. He supervises the departments of development, alumni relations, public relations and publications, and alumni information services. He is a member of the president's senior staff and represents the president and the university at a variety of university and community functions.

Judith Tuch is executive director of information management at the University of California—Los Angeles (UCLA). She has more than 18 years' experience in management of information systems. At UCLA she coordinates and integrates comprehensive client support services for all levels of computing. She has the responsibility for implementation and administration of several enterprisewide databases to support alumni and development professionals in their efforts to cultivate and solicit donors and prospective donors. She was conference program chair for the 1997 District VII Conference of CASE.

Leonard R. Raley is vice president for alumni relations and development at Ohio University and executive director of the Ohio University Foundation, Inc., Athens, Ohio. Prior to this position, he was assistant vice president for institutional advancement at the University of Maryland, College Park, Maryland. He also served as acting vice president for institutional advancement at the University of Maryland, executive director of the alumni association, and director of alumni programs. He was also associate director of admissions at Towson State University in Towson, Maryland. He is a member of the Commission on Philanthropy, established by CASE, and is immediate past district chair of CASE Middle Atlantic District II.

Deborah Ann Weekley Read is vice president for advancement at Lebanon Valley College, Annville, Pennsylvania. Prior to this position, she was director of university development at the University of Maryland, College Park, Maryland. She also has served at Maryland as acting assistant vice president, director of planned giving and special assistant to the vice president, and director of development for the College of Arts and Humanities. Prior to that, she was director of finance in the congressional campaign of Stewart Bainum; senior consultant with the American Association of University Consultants in Landover, Maryland; and associate director of development, director of annual giving, and assistant director of alumni affairs at the Central Administration Office of the University of Maryland in Adelphi. She has also served as a paralegal with the United States Department of Justice in Washington, DC. She is a graduate of the University of

Maryland, a member of the CASE II Board of Directors, and a member of the American Association of University Women.

Jerry P. Rohrbach is director of planned giving at Temple University in Philadelphia, Pennsylvania. With over 20 years' experience as a professional fund raiser, he has worked for a variety of nonprofits in the Delaware Valley. He has been with Temple University for eight years and over the course of his career has become an expert in charitable and estate tax law. He has extensive experience in assisting individuals with the establishment of testamentary gifts, charitable trusts, gift annuities, life insurance gifts, and named endowments.

Rohrbach earned his BS degree from Philadelphia College of the Bible and his MA degree from Wheaton College in Illinois. He is a Certified Fund Raising Executive of the NSFRE and is a member of the board of the Greater Philadelphia Chapter. He is also a member of the Delaware Valley Planned Giving Council, and the American Society of CLU & ChFC.

Janine Dlutowski is planned giving officer at the Pennsylvania State University, University Park, Pennsylvania. Prior to that position, she was major gifts officer/planned giving at Temple University. After more than five years in the private practice of law, she joined the Temple University Office of Development and Alumni/ae Affairs in 1994 to launch fund raising effforts for the Apollo of Temple, a 10,000-seat basketball arena and convocation center on Temple's main campus. Since 1996, Dlutowski has focused exclusively on marketing, cultivating, soliciting, and stewarding planned gifts and endowments.

Charles H. Webb is vice president for university development and president of the MSU Foundation at Michigan State University, East Lansing, Michigan. He has served in university advancement for over 24 years. Prior to his present position, Webb was executive director of the MSU Alumni Association from 1982 to 1995. Before that, he was assistant vice chancellor for development and alumni relations for the 64-campus State University of New York system. Webb received his doctorate in higher education administration from MSU in 1982 after earning a bachelor's degree in social science from Spring Arbor College and a master's degree in counseling and student personnel from Western Michigan University.

Jerry L. Gill is executive director of the Oklahoma State University (OSU) Alumni Association, Stillwater, Oklahoma. Prior to that, he was interim director of high school and college relations at OSU, director of Athletic Gift Programs, OSU, and adjunct professor in the Department of History at OSU.

M. Fredric Volkmann is vice chancellor for public affairs at Washington University in St. Louis, St. Louis, Missouri. At Ohio State University, he was director of university relations. At Albion College he was director of information services. At Iowa Wesleyan College he was director of information services. He has been affiliated with CASE for many years as a faculty member for summer institutes, as chair of the governance committee, committees on periodicals and publications, the computerization committee, and as national chair of the CASE Board of Trustees. He is a prolific writer and recipient of many awards, including the Frank L. Ashmore Award for service to the educational advancement profession and the Steuben Apple Award for excellence in teaching. He has a bachelor's degree from Iowa Wesleyan College and has done graduate work at MSU School of Communications.